Lecture Notes in Computer Science 779
Edited by G. Goos and J. Hartmanis

Matthias Jarke Janis Bubenko
Keith Jeffery (Eds.)

Advances in Database Technology — EDBT '94

4th International Conference
on Extending Database Technology
Cambridge, United Kingdom, March 28-31, 1994
Proceedings

Springer-Verlag
Berlin Heidelberg New York
London Paris Tokyo
Hong Kong Barcelona
Budapest

Series Editors

Gerhard Goos
Universität Karlsruhe
Postfach 69 80
Vincenz-Priessnitz-Straße 1
D-76131 Karlsruhe, Germany

Juris Hartmanis
Cornell University
Department of Computer Science
4130 Upson Hall
Ithaca, NY 14853, USA

Volume Editors

Matthias Jarke
RWTH Aachen
Ahornstrasse 55, D-52056 Aachen, Germany

Janis Bubenko
SISU-ISE
Isafjordsgatan 26, S-1250 Kista, Sweden

Keith Jeffery
SERC Rutherford Appleton Laboratory
Chilton, Didcot, Oxfordshire OX11 0QX, United Kingdom

CR Subject Classification (1991): H.2, E.2, D.3.3, F.4.1, H.5.1, I.2.1, I.2.4

ISBN 3-540-57818-8 Springer-Verlag Berlin Heidelberg New York
ISBN 0-387-57818-8 Springer-Verlag New York Berlin Heidelberg

CIP data applied for

Printed in Germany

Typesetting: Camera-ready by author
SPIN: 10131950 45/3140-543210 - Printed on acid-free paper

Foreword

The fourth international conference on Extending Data Base Technology (EDBT 94) was held in St. John's College (Cambridge, UK), March 28-31, 1994. After successful events in Venice (1988 and 1990) and Vienna (1992), the bi-annual EDBT has established itself as the premier European database conference. The conference provides an international forum for the presentation of new extensions to database technology through research, development, and application.

This proceedings volume contains the scientific papers of the conference. The programme committee faced the difficult task of selecting 31 papers among more than 180 submissions from 28 different countries. A major theme seemed to be the integration of database technology as a core technology in the larger context of large-scale and distributed computing systems. This problem was addressed from many different angles, ranging from novel view concepts to data access in mobile computing.

EDBT is the flagship conference of a broader initiative which strives to maintain the traditionally strong role of Europe in database research, and to improve the transition from research to practice. Related activities include summer schools organized by the EDBT Foundation, the European Network of Excellence in Databases and Information Retrieval (IDOMENEUS), and ongoing collaboration with the database journal *Information Systems*.

For the first time, EDBT 94 was held jointly with an industrial conference, the annual meeting of the British Data Management Specialist Group. The relationship between database research and practice was also the topic of a keynote address by Chris Stone, president of the Object Management Group, and of a panel introduced by Andrew Herbert, a pioneer in distributed computing environments. The conference programme was augmented by tutorials on interoperability, multimedia, object data models, and object-oriented databases by Michael Brodie, Stavros Christodoulakis, Moira Norrie and Hans Schek, and Roberto Zicari, respectively.

Many people deserve special thanks for their efforts to make EDBT 94 a success. Thanks are in particular due to the "British team" which admirably covered all aspects of conference organization, especially to the conference secretary Anna Duckworth, and to the members of the international programme committee, technically supported by Christoph Quix and Martin Staudt. Last not least, we are grateful to the sponsors for their enthusiasm despite difficult economic times.

Cambridge, March 1994

Matthias Jarke, Janis Bubenko, Keith Jeffery

Sponsorship

Promoted by EDBT Foundation, UK Database Foundation,
IDOMENEUS Network of Excellence

Sponsored by British Computer Society
In cooperation with IEEE, CEPIS

Organization

Conference Chairman: Janis Bubenko (SISU, Sweden)
Program Committee Chairman: Matthias Jarke (RWTH Aachen, Germany)

Organising Committee

K. G. Jeffery (SERC Rutherford Appleton Laboratory, Chairman)

A. Duckworth (BCS)
M. S. Jackson (Wolverhampton)
R. G. Johnson (Birkbeck)
J. Mabon (DMSG)
B. J. Read (SERC)
R. Williams (DMSG)
W. A. Gray (Cardiff)
A. J. Jenkins (DMSG)
J. Kennedy (Napier)
K. Moody (Cambridge)
G. Sharman (IBM)
R. F. Winterson (DMSG)

Regional Co-ordinators

R. Andersen (Norway)
J. Fong (Hong Kong)
M. Kersten (Netherlands)
M. Leonard (Switzerland)
S. Nishio (Japan)
A. Pirotte (Belgium)
S. Sa (China)
G. Schlageter (Germany)
C. K. Tan (Singapore)
Y. Vassiliou (Greece)
R. Carapuca (Portugal)
J. B. Grimson (Ireland)
K.-C. Lee (Taiwan)
B. G. Lundberg (Sweden)
M. E. Orlowska (Australia)
F. Plasil (Czechoslovakia)
F. Saltor (Spain)
D. Shasha (USA)
L. Tucherman (Brazil)

EDBT Foundation Consultants

S. Ceri (Milan)
J. Schmidt (Hamburg)
M. Missikoff (Rome)

Program Committee

M. Jarke (Germany - chairman)
M. Agosti (Italy)
E. Bertino (Italy)
A. Borgida (USA)
M. Brodie (USA)
J. Clifford (USA)
H. P. Frei (Switzerland)
G. Gottlob (Austria)
V. Jagadish (USA)
L. Kalininchenko (Russia)
M. Lenzerini (Italy)
P. Loucopoulos (United Kingdom)
F. Matthes (USA)
J. Mylopoulos (Canada)
A. Olive (Spain)
M. Papazoglou (Australia)
A. Reuter (Germany)
T. Risch (Sweden)
T. Rose (Canada)
M. Scholl (Germany)
D. Shasha (USA)
A. Solvberg (Norway)
M. Stonebraker (USA)
B. Thalheim (Germany)
J. Widom (USA)
S. Abiteboul (France)
R. Bayer (Germany)
J. Bocca (Chile/United Kingdom)
J. Bubenko (Sweden)
M. Carey (USA)
M. Freeston (Germany)
H. Garcia-Molina (USA)
P. Gray (United Kingdom)
K. G. Jeffery (United Kingdom)
H. Kangassalo (Finland)
F. Lochovsky (Hong Kong)
L. Mark (Denmark/USA)
G. Moerkotte (Germany)
S. Nishio (Japan)
M. E. Orlowska (Australia)
A. Pirotte (Belgium)
R. van de Riet (Netherlands)
C. Rolland (France)
H. Schek (Switzerland)
T. Sellis (Greece)
E. Simon (France)
A. Stogny (Ukraine)
K. Subieta (Poland)
Y. Vassiliou (Greece)
J. Zlatuska (Czech Republic)

Additional Referees

S. Al-Naemi
S. A. Ananevsky
S. Azarov
M. Baaz
P. Bayer
W. Becker
J. Besancenot
C. Bettini
S. Blott
A. Bouguettaya
S. E. Bratsberg
Y. Breitbart
J. Brunet
F. Bry
C. Cauvet
V. K. Chaudhri
R. Colomb
G. Costa
P. Creasy
A. Croker
A. Deacon
A. Delis
V. Dhar
P. Drew
T. Eiter
M. Eitler
G. Fahl
N. Frakash
B. Freitag
K. Froeschl
D. Georgakopoulos
U. Geuder
F. Gire
H. Grabner
J. A. Gulla
M. Haerdtner
T. Haplin
K. Harumoto
C. Hasse
L. Hermosilla
M. Hornick
R. Hull
G. Höfling
M. Iwamuro
M. Jeusfeld
I. Jurisica
G. Kappel
K. Karlapalem
H. Kaufmann
J. Kempe
A. Kemper
H. Knolle
M. Kogalovsky
V. Kolinko
M. Koubarakis
W. Kowarschick
R. Kramorenko
J. Krogstie
W. Kuhn
G. Kuper
S. Kuznetsov
C. Laasch
R. A. Lehn
Q. Li
L. Lin
A. Listl
G. Lohman
P. J. Lupton
J. Maier
G. Mamier
R. Marti
I. McLaren
M. Melucci
Z. Mikal
A. Montesi
K. Moody
I. S. Mumick
V. Murthy
I. Narang
B. Nebel
W. Nejdl
M. C. Norrie
B. Novikov
J. K. Obermaier
E. Omodeo
M. W. Orlowski
J. Overbeck
M. Pawlowski
I. Petrounias
P. Pistor
D. Plexousakis
R. Pollak
B. Polyachenko
N. Prakash
E. Rahm
A. Reiser
C. Rich
J.-P. Richter
S. Rizzo
M. A. Sakchnuk
S. Salza
G. Santucci
U. Schmidt
F. Schwenkreis
S. Schwer
A. P. Sexton
E. Shekita
S. Shimojo
A. Shrufi
C. O. Shum
M. Sköld
R. Smith
W. W. Song
C. Souveyet
G. Specht
P. A. Spruit
S. Sripada
M. Stumptner
A. Swami
Z. Tari
B. Thedoulidis
T. Topaloglou
R. Torlone
M. Tresch
A. Tuzhilin
R. Unland
V. Vianu
P. Vogel
H. Waechter
X. Y. Wang
B. Wangler
M. Werner
A. Wickler
S. Wiesener
J. P. Wilks
G. Willumsen
B. Woerner
M. F. Wyne
B. Wüthrich
V. Yaremenko
M. Yoshikawa
P. Zabback
V. Zadorozhny
Y. Zhang
R. Zink

Contents

Invited Papers

Object Views

Intelligent User Interfaces

Distributed Information Servers

Transaction Management

Information Systems Design and Evolution

Semantics of Extended Data Models

Accessing New Media

Join Algorithms

Query Optimization

Multimedia Databases

Accessing New Media

Data Mining

Query Optimization

Advanced Databases

The Object Management Group Standardization of Object Technology

Christopher M. Stone
President & CEO
Object Management Group, Inc.
Framingham, Massachusetts, USA

Abstract

Object technology (OT) which has been described by some as a remarkable paradigm shift in computing is in reality a technology that allows people to think, literally, in terms of nouns and verbs as they assemble software programs. Too often, contemporary software development is characterized as an artform with mystical heritage.

The Object Management Group, with over 330 members, has become the industry focal point for the development of interface standards in distributed computing. The OMG focuses its attention on creating specifications for distributed applications using object technology. The group's first specification, the *Object Request Broker*, has already been endorsed and committed to by over one hundred (100) companies. OMG is funded by the top computer, software, networking, and end user organizations in the information processing business.

Mr. Stone will discuss the rule of OT, the OMG, and the impact on the future of client server computing and distributed applications.

Databases in Distributed Systems: The New Frontier

– Extended Abstract –

Andrew Herbert

Architecture Projects Management Ltd., Poseidon House, Castle Park, Cambridge CB3 ORD, United Kingdom

1 Introduction

Database technology is rooted in the 1960s mainframe culture. It has been very successful at enabling complex applications to share and manage enormous bodies of data. However, for many users the future resides with distributed computing as previously separate applications are linked together to provide new services in support of new business goals.

Within a distributed system there is still a role for databases per se, but not as the focus of the system. Processing will be shared with small personal computers providing the user interface and departmental machines providing integration services and local data caching. This is too complex a system to model as a single "database".

Research on distributed databases, multi-databases and federated databases will enable integration of databases to a greater or lesser extent, but does not contribute towards problems such as applications interoperability and distributed system management. For these functions "distributed objects" (see for example the work of the Object Management Group) show greatest promise.

Objects provide both modularity and abstraction; they encourage genericity thereby reducing special cases and complexity. In a distributed sysem object management can include functions such as object migration to balance loads and reduce latency, object replication for fault tolerance and enhanced availability.

Distributed objects have to be modelled, objects providing specific functions have to be located, objects have to deliver consistent results. These are all echos of database concepts (schema, query, transaction), but applied to a sea of distributed objects acting as a logical repository rather than a single physical one. The priority for database research must be to discover how to unbundle the ingredients of a successful database and make them work effectively in the distributed context. In a nutshell: data management - a successful past and a glorious future, but not in dumb old databases.

2 Distributed Systems

In the near future, most industrial computing will be based on a distributed computing architecture. A key notion is that of services. A service is some collection of software and data that delivers a business function, for example billing for a telecommunication operator, customer account management for a bank or utility. To its clients, a service has a well defined interface which provides operations to inform the service of changes in the real world (the crediting of an account) and to obtain information from the service (e.g. a client's current balance). To the client the service is just an object which embodies a set of business functions. How those functions are implemented in terms of data and applications is a matter for the service provider.

The interface concept is crucial - it enables the service implementation to evolve without disrupting clients, even to be replaced totally by an alternative technology. It gives a view of an information technology system in terms of how it supports the operations of the enterprise that owns it.

Services can be large, as illustrated in the preceding examples, or very small: each window on a screen can be a service, each element within a window can be a service. From a service point of view granularity is of no issue. From an implementation point of view it is important to choose an appropriate infrastructure (i.e. Object Request Broker) to the kind of object being used. However the programming interfaces to each infrastructure for managing objects and invoking operations can be the same, and infrastructures at different granularities can be made to interwork with one another providing a uniform sea of distributed, remotely accessible objects.

3 Objects Need Management

Databases arose when programmers recognized that ad hoc schemes for data management were out of control and that carefully designed mechanisms and programming abstractions were called for. Distributed objects are running into a comparable problem.

3.1 Trading for Services

How do you find a service? Perhaps you know its type - i.e. the operations you want to invoke. Then you'd like to be able to query the distributed system to find objects that provide an interface of the right type (or a suitable subtype). To exercise some control over selecting from the available objects we should assign attributes to them such as location, owner, cost of use. Immediately we have asked for a schema function (so that types can be described and compared), and a query function. If you are new to a system you might want to find out what operations are available in terms of more abstract descriptions of the kind of behaviour required of a service. This implies that schemas should include behavioural specifications as well as structural informaion such as operation signatures.

3.2 Schemas for Distributed Objects

The schema function is complicated by the fact that whilst we may be able to superimpose the same conceptual object model on our services there are many implementations to choose from (e.g various flavours of OMG CORBA, OSF DCE RPC, ISO GDMO notation, various OODBMS notations) and as part of deciding if a client can interact with a candidate server we have to decide if appropriate adaptors can be put in the path to make all necessary conversions. At the simplest level our types can be just names and we rely on administrators to define type relationships. We can automate comparison of operation signatures (i.e. function prototypes) using type checkers. Maybe we can automate some aspects of checking semantics (e.g. by comparing pre and post-conditions as part of operation specifications). One of the challenges of interface schema design is to capture as much information as possible about a service, how to use it and its infrastructure requirements. The schema representation should be part of the operational system and universally accessible (i.e. schemas are also "services").

3.3 Traders and Distributed Query

Giving objects attributes and querying those attributes suggests some sort of repository of attributes and object references will suffice (called a "trader" in ANSA). As systems grow we will want to combine traders to build up a composite trading space. Therefore we want a notion of querying that expresses not only what to look for in a particular trader, but also how to include information from other traders in the resolution of the query. This capability is likely to be the responsibility of the traders rather than their clients so that programmers see a single interface to a local trader as their window on the system, and that local trader maps the information available to it into a form suitable for its users. Different users might have quite different views of the same system.

3.4 Generalized Query

Since objects provide services, they can be asked questions. Therefore it would seem useful to extend the simple trading concept to include a wider notion of not only including attributed held in one or more repositories, but also data dynamically obtained from the object. This raises interesting questions about consistency and caching - whilst an object might satisfy a query now, it might not tomorrow. How do we represent (protect) the temporal validity of the result of a query?

3.5 Concurrency Control for Objects

Significant applications will invoke many services as they perform their function. They must be able to recover from failures of individual objects en route or to back out of activities that turn out to be redundant or impossible to complete. All this has to be managed in a concurrent world. A transaction function would provide the application programmer with a tool for managing concurrency. However this is a transaction function that works on any object in a distributed system, not just those that choose to live in a database. It must therefore be capable of fine grained locking: it must support some form of nesting so that services can call other services within a transaction. Since objects can be very small it must be transaction function that can protect longer pieces of activity as well as individual operations, bringing in notions of workflow. Not all objects can be rolled back - once a message has been sent it cannot be recalled, instead a compensation must be issued. Therefore forward as well as backward recovery must be provided. It is an interesting question to debate how much application semantics (as captured in a interface specification) can be used to generate locking disciplines.

3.6 Persistence

Finally not all of the objects in a system need be active at once, and can migrate out from main memory to secondary storage - this is the persistence function. Here the challenge is transparency. Ideally the client of a persistent object should not be aware of it movement to and from disc. The object's manager however will probably want to exercise a great deal of control over its placement. Persistence might include replication (for fault tolerance). Persistence and transactions must interact correctly in the sense that only consistent versions of objects should be made stable.

4 Wither Databases

The DBMS community has made many contributions to computing. In fact, they are so good that they are of greater value outside DBMSs than inside them. Just one of the examples above is transactions.

Transactions should be a general purpose service available to all programs (database applications or not) to update any computing resource (database or not). This is all already happening. There are a number of research systems providing distributed transactions for objects (e.g. Argus at MIT, Arjuna at Newcastle University), in products like Transarc's ENCINA and in standards (e.g. the Transaction Service RFP process underway in the OMG).

Just about all of the capabilities associated hitherto with databases have significance to distributed systems, but ripped apart into a number of independently usable parts rather than as a monolithic whole

- general purpose queries over all computing resources
- query optimization
- workload optimizations (data and application migration)
- run time accessible schemas (for trading, on the fly "adaptor generation") - schema and systems evolution - transactions - persistence.

DBMSs qua DBMSs will continue to provide useful functionality, but lurking, together with their intimate applications, behind a service interface.

The challenge facing the DBMS community is that databases, as we know and love them, simply do not address all of the needs of a general purpose, distributed computing environment. They need to be generalized and broken down into smaller functions. This is what is being done under the name of distributed object management. If the DBMS folks don't do this work, others will, and are (e.g. the vendors and ISVs supporting the OMG).

The message is: don't be parochial. Topics such as query optimization, query language design, object modelling, concurrency control are all interesting in the database world, but not of wider significance. Consider the greater challenge of: distributed computing query optimization, distributed processing language design, distributed object modelling, distributed concurrency control. More challenging but vastly more profitable when the solution is reached since it then applies to all of computing.

Acknowledgements
The author has had valuable discussions with Mike Brodie of GTE, Gomer Thomas of Bellcore and Rob van der Linden of ANSA in preparing this paper.

Type Derivation Using the Projection Operation
(Extended Abstract)

Rakesh Agrawal Linda G. DeMichiel

IBM Almaden Research Center
650 Harry Road, San Jose, CA 95120

Abstract. We present techniques for deriving types from existing object-oriented types using the relational algebraic projection operation and for inferring the methods that are applicable to these types. Such type derivation occurs, for example, as a result of defining algebraic views over object types. We refactor the type hierarchy and place the derived types in the type hierarchy in such a way that the state and behavior of existing types remain exactly as before. Our results have applicability to relational databases extended with object-oriented type systems and to object-oriented systems that support algebraic operations.

1 Introduction

In relational database systems, it is often useful to define *views* over sets of related data items for purposes of abstraction or encapsulation. Views are specified by using the standard algebraic query operations. Views are defined over relations, and the "type" of a view, like that of a relation, is implicitly given by the types of its attributes. The instantiation, or materialization, of a view is determined by the contents of those relations over which the view is defined.

Because of their usefulness in relational databases, views have also attracted considerable attention in object-oriented database systems. However, unlike in relational systems, types and type extents are often decoupled in object-oriented type systems. Thus it becomes important to separate two aspects of view operations: (1) the derivation of new types as a result of the view operation; (2) the manipulation of instances of the source types of the view to obtain the instances of the type derived by the view operation. It is the first of these that we shall address in this paper.

In object-oriented type systems, there are two aspects to such type derivation that must be considered: (1) The behavior of the derived type must be inferred—that is, it must be determined which of the methods that are applicable to the source types of the derived type are applicable to the new type itself. (2) The new type must be correctly inserted into the existing type hierarchy in such a way that existing types have both the same state and the same behavior as before the creation of the derived type.

We consider type derivation using the relational algebraic operations, focussing here only on the projection operation. Of the relational operations, projection poses the greatest problems for type derivation because of the implicit refactorization of the type hierarchy that it entails.

Several proposals on views in object-oriented systems have suggested the derivation of a virtual type for a view [1] [6] [10] [11]. As pointed out in [9], many of the current proposals do not discuss the integration of the derived type into the existing type hierarchy. In some proposals the derived type is treated as a separate entity (e.g., [6]), in some the derived type is made a direct subtype of the root of the type hierarchy (e.g., [7]), and in some only the local relationship of the derived type with respect to the source type is established (e.g., [11]).

Previous work in the area of inserting derived types into the type hierarchy include [8] [9] [10] [12]. This problem has also been addressed in the knowledge representation literature (e.g., [3] [5]). However, none of this work has addressed the problem of determining the behavior of the new type. It was proposed in [1] [4] that the type definer specify which existing methods are applicable to the new type. Determining which methods apply to a new type is a complex problem, and leaving it to the type definer is error-prone. Furthermore, it must be determined that the methods selected are indeed type-correct and mutually consistent.

2 Model

We assume a type system in which a data type consists both of state and of a set of operations that can be applied to instances of the type. The state consists of a set of named ***attributes***. Types are organized in a hierarchy and a ***subtype relation*** is defined over them: A is a subtype of B exactly when every instance of A is also an instance of B. The type hierarchy is a directed acyclic graph—that is, we allow multiple inheritance. The semantics of this inheritance is as follows: (1) If A is a supertype of B, then every attribute of A is also an attribute of B. (2) If D has supertypes B and C, and B and C have a common supertype A, then attributes of A are inherited only once by instances of D. We assume there is a precedence relationship among the direct supertypes of a type. (For a discussion of the role of this precedence relationship in method selection, see [2].) To simplify our presentation, we also assume that attribute names are unique.

Operations on the instances of types are defined by ***generic functions***, where a generic function corresponds to a set of ***methods***. A method is defined for a set of arguments of particular types and can be executed for any arguments that are instances of those types or their subtypes. The selection of the method to be executed depends on the types of the actual arguments with which the generic function is called at run time. A method can be an ***accessor*** method, which directly accesses the state associated with a single attribute of the type, or a method can be a general method, which may invoke other methods, including accessors. The only access to the attributes of a type is through such methods.

We consider the general case in which methods are multi-methods. That is, when a generic function is called, the method dispatched at run time is selected on the basis of the types of all of the actual arguments to the call.

We represent the subtype relation by $\preceq$. If $A \preceq B \wedge A \neq B$, we say that A

is a ***proper subtype*** of B and represent this relation by $\prec$. If $A \preceq B$, we also say that B is a ***supertype*** of A. The supertype relation is correspondingly denoted by $\succeq$. We will denote a particular method m_k of an n-ary generic function m as $m_k(T_k^1, T_k^2, \ldots, T_k^n)$, where T_k^i is the type of the ith formal argument. The call to the generic function will be denoted without a subscript on m.

3 Projection over Types

The algebraic projection operation over a type T selects a subset of the attributes of T, specified in terms of a ***projection list***, and derives a new type $\tilde{T}$. Intuitively, it seems natural that any methods associated with type T that are "appropriate" for $\tilde{T}$ should be applicable to instances of the new derived type $\tilde{T}$, and, correspondingly, that $\tilde{T}$ should be related to the source type T as its supertype, since $\tilde{T}$ contains a subset of the attributes of T.

For example, consider a simple type hierarchy consisting of two types, *Person* and *Employee*, where *Employee* is a subtype of *Person*. The type *Person* has attributes *SSN*, *name*, and *date-of-birth*. *Employee* inherits these attributes, and additionally defines the attributes *pay-rate* and *hrs-worked*. We assume that there are accessor methods corresponding to each of these attributes: e.g. *get_SSN*, *get_name*, etc. Consider the three methods *age*, *income*, and *promote*:

age(*Person*) = {...*get_date-of-birth*(*Person*)...}
income(*Employee*) = {...*get_pay-rate*(*Employee*); *get_hrs-worked*(*Employee*)...}
promote(*Employee*) = {...*get_date-of-birth*(*Employee*); *get_pay-rate*(*Employee*)...}

The attributes used by each of these methods are indicated implicitly by calls to the corresponding accessor methods.

We now apply the projection operation to *Employee*, selecting only the *SSN*, *date-of-birth*, and *pay-rate* fields, thus deriving a new type, say, $\widetilde{Employee}$. We would like automatically to infer the methods that are applicable to $\widetilde{Employee}$ and to insert $\widetilde{Employee}$ into the type hierarchy such that it inherits the correct state and behavior. Note that the *income* method clearly does not apply to this new type, since it depends on the *hrs-worked* attribute, not present in $\widetilde{Employee}$. The *age* and *promote* methods, however, should be applicable.

In the refactored type hierarchy, *Employee* must be a subtype not only of *Person*, but also of $\widetilde{Employee}$. Note, however, that $\widetilde{Employee}$ cannot inherit from *Person* because of the absence of the *name* attribute in $\widetilde{Employee}$. The type *Person* is therefore refactored into two types: $\widetilde{Person}$, consisting of attributes *SSN* and *date-of-birth*, and *Person*, from which these attributes have been removed. Both *Person* and $\widetilde{Employee}$ are thus made subtypes of the new type $\widetilde{Person}$. The methods are modified to reflect this factorization:

age($\widetilde{Person}$) = {...*get_date-of-birth*($\widetilde{Person}$)...}
income(*Employee*) = {...*get_pay-rate*(*Employee*); *get_hrs-worked*(*Employee*)...}
promote($\widetilde{Employee}$) = {...*get_date-of-birth*($\widetilde{Employee}$); *get_pay-rate*($\widetilde{Employee}$)...}

It can be checked that all types have the correct state and behavior, and that *Person* and *Employee* have the same cumulative state and behavior as before.

4 Computing Method Applicability

We say that a method $m_k(T_k^1, T_k^2, \ldots, T_k^n)$ is *applicable to a type* T if there is some T_k^i, $1 \leq i \leq n$ such that $T \preceq T_k^i$. Any method m_k that is applicable to a type T is *applicable to a derived type* $\tilde{T}$, $\tilde{T} = \Pi_{a_1,\ldots,a_n} T$ unless m_k accesses an attribute of T not included in the projection list of $\tilde{T}$ or m_k invokes a generic function n on the argument T and there is no method of n applicable to $\tilde{T}$.

We say that a method $m_k(T_k^1, \ldots, T_k^n)$ is *applicable to a generic function call* $m(T^1, \ldots, T^n)$ if $\forall i$, $1 \leq i \leq n$, $T^i \preceq T_k^i$. In general, because of subtype polymorphism, there can be more than one such method.

The applicability of a method to a type can be determined by considering the call graph of the method. In the absence of recursion, the call graph must bottom out on accessor methods. If those accessor methods only access state that is present in the derived type, then the method being tested is applicable to that type. The actual algorithm is considerably more complex because it takes into account cycles in the method call graph, multiple applicable methods, and multiple arguments of the same source type.

The function *IsApplicable* comprises the heart of this algorithm. *IsApplicable* tests a given method $m_k(T_k^1, T_k^2, \ldots, T_k^n)$ by analyzing its call graph, examining all generic function calls in the method body that are applicable to those method arguments that are supertypes of the source type T. In order for $m_k(T_k^1, T_k^2, \ldots, T_k^n)$ to be applicable, there must in turn be at least one applicable method for each such generic function call $n(T^1, \ldots, T^j, \ldots, T^m)$ in the body of m_k. We assume that the set of generic function calls in the body of m_k that need to be checked in this way is determined by data flow analysis.

Consider a generic function call $n(T^1, \ldots T^j, \ldots, T^m)$ in the body of m_k. We distinguish two cases:

(1) If only one of the arguments of the function call $n(T^1, \ldots T^j, \ldots, T^m)$—say T^j—is of type T or a supertype of T and corresponds to an argument of m_k, then the set of methods of n from which an applicable method must be found consists of those methods that are applicable to the call $n(T^1, \ldots T, \ldots, T^m)$. To see why, assume that $A \preceq B$ and that we are determining applicability of methods for the projection type $\tilde{A}$ derived from A. Assume that we have a method $m_k(B)$ whose body consists solely of the generic function call $n(B)$. We need to determine only if there is some method of n that is applicable to the call $n(A)$ that is also applicable to $\tilde{A}$. If such a method exists, then $m_k(B)$ should also be applicable to $\tilde{A}$, regardless of whether there is any method of n that is applicable to the call $n(B)$ that is also applicable to $\tilde{A}$.

(2) If multiple arguments of the function call $n(T^1, \ldots T^j, \ldots, T^m)$ are of type T or supertypes of T and correspond to arguments of m_k, then we consider a method of n to be applicable to the call only if it is applicable to all combinations of non-null substitutions of $\tilde{T}$ for those supertypes. To obtain this, we require that the set of methods of n from which an applicable method is to be found consist of those methods that are applicable to the call $n(T^1, \ldots T^j, \ldots, T^m)$. To see why, assume that $A \preceq B$, $A \preceq C$ and that we are determining applicability of methods for the projection type $\tilde{A}$ derived from A. Consider a method $m_k(B, C)$

whose body consists solely of the generic function call $n(B, C)$. The existence of a method of n that is applicable to the call $n(\tilde{A}, \tilde{A})$ does *not* imply that there are applicable methods for the calls $n(B, \tilde{A})$ and $n(\tilde{A}, C)$.

We maintain three global data structures: *MethodStack*, *Applicable*, and *NotApplicable*. Initially, all are empty.

MethodStack is a stack of methods, corresponding to the call stack of *IsApplicable*. Each entry is a pair <*method*, *dependencyList*>, where *dependencyList* keeps track of those methods whose applicability is contingent on the applicability of *method*. At the end of each top-level call to *IsApplicable*, *MethodStack* is empty.

Applicable is a list of those methods that have been determined to apply to the derived type $\tilde{T}$. *Applicable* is computed optimistically in the following sense: Suppose a method m_i calls a generic function n which requires determination of the applicability of n_j. If the applicability of n_j is already in the process of being determined (i.e., n_j is a method inside *MethodStack*), then we assume that n_j is applicable, and conditionally determine the applicability of m_i. If n_j is later determined to be not applicable, then m_i is removed from *Applicable*.

NotApplicable is a list of those methods that have been determined to not apply to the derived type $\tilde{T}$.

```
function IsApplicable(m:method, T: type, p: projectionlist)
    returns {applicable, notapplicable}
  if m ∈ Applicable then
    return applicable
  else if m ∈ NotApplicable then
    return notapplicable
  if m is an accessor method then
    if m accesses a field in p then
      Applicable ← Applicable ∪ m
      return applicable
    else
      NotApplicable ← NotApplicable ∪ m
      return notapplicable
  if m is anywhere in MethodStack then
    dependencyList(m) ← dependencyList(m) ∪ all methods above m
      in MethodStack
    return applicable
  else
    push m onto top of MethodStack /* for recursive calls to IsApplicable */
    for all relevant functions calls n(x_1, ...x_n) in the body of m do
      for all methods n_k of generic function n that are applicable do
        if IsApplicable(n_k, T, p) then
        /* if any method checks out, the call to n succeeds */
          continue to next generic function call in body of m
      od
      /* there is no applicable method for some function call n */
```

```
    for all methods d in dependencyList(m) do
        Applicable ← Applicable − d
    od
    NotApplicable ← NotApplicable ∪ m
    pop MethodStack /* remove m from top of stack */
    return notapplicable
  od
  /* there are applicable methods for all calls in m */
  Applicable ← Applicable ∪ m
  pop MethodStack /* clean up the stack */
  return applicable
```

5 Factoring State

The creation of a derived type $\tilde{T}$ as a result of a projection operation induces a *refactorization* of the original type hierarchy in order to accommodate the inclusion of $\tilde{T}$. The original type hierarchy is factored into a derived type hierarchy by introducing what we shall call ***surrogate types***. A ***surrogate type*** is a type that assumes a part of the state or behavior of the source type from which it is spun off. The surrogate type plus the modified source type, when combined by means of inheritance, have exactly the state and behavior of the original source type. The state of the surrogate is determined by that portion of the projection list that applies to its source type: it consists precisely of those attributes that are contained both in the projection list and in the local attributes of the source type. The behavior of the surrogate type is determined according to which methods are applicable in the sense defined in Section 4.

The factorization into surrogate types is necessary to capture that portion of the state or behavior of the source type that is applicable to the derived type while not including attributes and behavior from the source type and its supertypes that are not. The factorization is recursive in the sense that each type Q through which the new derived type inherits attributes or methods is factored into two types: a surrogate type $\tilde{Q}$, which contains only those attributes that are inherited by the derived type $\tilde{T}$; and the modified source type Q, from which those attributes are removed. Q is then further modified to be a direct subtype of its surrogate $\tilde{Q}$. Type $\tilde{Q}$ is given the highest precedence of any of the supertypes of Q in order that this factorization be transparent from the standpoint of the state and behavior of the combined Q–$\tilde{Q}$ types.

We present below the algorithm for state factorization.

procedure *FactorState(A:attributeList, T:type, $\tilde{R}$:type, P:precedence)*
  if the surrogate type $\tilde{T}$ for T and A does not already exist **then**
    create a new type $\tilde{T}$
  make $\tilde{T}$ a supertype of T such that $\tilde{T}$ has highest precedence
    among the supertypes of T
  if $\tilde{R} \neq NULL$, make $\tilde{R}$ a subtype of $\tilde{T}$ with precedence P
  if type $\tilde{T}$ was created in this call **then**

```
∀ a ∈ A such that a is a local attribute of T do
  move a to T̃
od
let S be the list of the direct supertypes of T, excluding T̃
  ∀ s ∈ S in order of inheritance precedence do
    let p be the precedence of s among the supertypes of T
      let L be the list of attributes in A that are available at s
        if L ≠ ∅ then
          call FactorState(L, s, T̃, p)
  od
```

The initial call is *FactorState*(*projection-list*, T, $NULL$, 0).

6 Factoring Methods

Because the surrogate type is the direct supertype of its source type and because it is the supertype of highest precedence, any method $m_i(T_i^1, \ldots T_i^j, \ldots, T_i^m)$ that is applicable to a type $\tilde{T}_i^j$, $\tilde{T}_i^j \succ T_i^j$, can be treated as if it were a method on $m_i(T_i^1, \ldots \tilde{T}_i^j, \ldots, T_i^m)$. The following algorithm associates the applicable methods for a type $\tilde{T}$ with those types from which $\tilde{T}$ inherits according to the refactored type hierarchy.

```
procedure FactorMethods(T:type)
  ∀ methods m_k ∈ Applicable(T̃) as determined by IsApplicable do
    let the signature of m_k be m_k(T_k^1, T_k^2, ..., T_k^n)
      create a new signature for m_k in which T_k^i is replaced by T̃_k^i (1 ≤ i ≤ n)
        for all T_k^i for which a surrogate type T̃_k^i was created by FactorState
  od
```

Because of assignment and variable binding, however, modification of the method signature alone may not be sufficient. In particular, if done naively, such modifications may cause type errors in the method body. Consider the method $z_1(c : C) = \{g : G;\ g \leftarrow c;\ \ldots\ u(c);\ \ldots\ return(g); \}$. If we change the method signature of z_1 to $z_1(c : \tilde{C})$, we introduce a type error in the assignment $g \leftarrow c$ if $\tilde{C}$ is not a subtype of G.

It is necessary to analyze in the method body the reachability set for the use of all parameters that are to be converted to surrogate types. The type declarations for any variables in this set need to be changed to declarations in terms of the corresponding surrogate types. In some cases, these surrogate types may not yet exist. The following algorithm shows how they are added to the type hierarchy. The result type of the method is processed in the same way.

```
let X = set of types for which a surrogate was created by FactorState
let F = set of methods determined applicable by IsApplicable
let Y = set of types that are are assigned transitively a value of one of
        the types in X by one of the methods in F (this set is determined
        by the standard definition-use flow analysis)
let Z = Y − X
```

```
procedure Augment(T: type, Z: set of types)
  if T has a supertype that is a subtype of one of the types in Z then
    for all direct supertypes of T except T̃ in order of precedence do
      let S be the direct supertype with precedence p
        if S̃ does not exist then
          create S̃
          make S a subtype of S̃ with highest precedence
          if T̃ is not already a subtype of S̃ then
            make T̃ a subtype of S̃ with precedence p
        Augment(S, Z)
    od
```

The initial call is *Augment*(A,Z).

7 Future Work

The work presented in this paper opens up several interesting areas for future work. It needs to be investigated how—if at all—the number of surrogate types with empty states can be reduced, particularly when views are defined over views. The mechanisms presented here are complex because we have considered the general case involving multiple inheritance and multi-methods. It will be interesting to specialize the solutions presented for specific cases of object-oriented type systems that do not require this generality. Finally, the methodology presented needs to be applied to the remaining algebraic operations.

References

1. Serge Abiteboul and Anthony Bonner. "Objects and Views." *SIGMOD*, 1991.
2. Rakesh Agrawal, Linda G. DeMichiel, and Bruce G. Lindsay. "Static Type Checking of Multi-Methods." *OOPSLA*, 1991.
3. S. Bergamaschi and C. Sartori. "On Taxonomic Reasoning in Conceptual Design", *TODS*, 17(3), Sept. 1992.
4. Elisa Bertino. "A View Mechanism for Object-Oriented Databases." *EDBT*, 1992.
5. R.J. Brachman, A. Borgida, D.L. McGuinnes, and L.A. Resnick. "The Classic Knowledge Representation System, or, KL-ONE: The Next Generation." *Workshop on Formal Aspects of Semantic Networks*, February 1989.
6. Sandra Heiler and Stanley Zdonik. "Object Views: Extending the Vision." *Data Engineering*, 1990.
7. Won Kim. "A Model of Queries in Object-Oriended Databases", *VLDB*, 1989.
8. M. Missikoff and M. Scholl. "An Algorithm for Insertion into a Lattice: Application to Type Classification." *FODO*, 1989.
9. Elke A. Rundensteiner. "MultiView: A Methodology for Supporting Multiple Views in Object-Oriented Databases." *VLDB*, 1992.
10. Marc H. Scholl, Christian Laasch, Markus Tresch. "Updatable Views in Object-Oriented Databases." Technical Report, ETH Zürich, 1990.
11. Michael Schrefl and Erich J. Neuhold. "Object Class Definition by Generalization Using Upward Inheritance." *Data Engineering*, 1988.
12. Katsumi Tanaka, Masatoshi Yoshikawa, and Kozo Ishihara. "Schema Virtualization in Object-Oriented Databases." *Data Engineering*, 1988.

Subsumption between Queries to Object-Oriented Databases*

- Extended Abstract -

Martin Buchheit[1], Manfred A. Jeusfeld[2], Werner Nutt[1], Martin Staudt[2]

[1] DFKI, Stuhlsatzenhausweg 3, D-66123 Saarbrücken, Germany
[2] RWTH, Informatik V, Ahornstr. 55, D-52056 Aachen, Germany

Abstract. Subsumption between queries is a valuable information, *e.g.*, for semantic query optimization. We approach the subsumption problem in the setting of object-oriented databases, and find that reasoning techniques from Artificial Intelligence can be applied and yield efficient algorithms.

1 Introduction

In object-oriented databases (OODB's), objects are organized as elements of *classes*, and they are constrained by some type expression. Similar expressions for describing classes of objects, called *concepts*, have been investigated for knowledge representation languages of the KL-ONE family [WS92]. The research in these languages, which express fragments of first-order logic, has come up with techniques to determine satisfiability and subsumption of concepts and has assessed the complexity of such inferences for a variety of languages (see *e.g.*, [DLNN91]). This paper transfers and adapts these techniques to the following problem in OODB's:

> *Given the schema of an OODB and two queries, decide whether in every possible state the answer set of the first query is contained in the answer set of the second.*

Since there is no standardized data model and query language for OODB's, we present a language that features just the properties which are common to most object-oriented systems: *Classes* group a finite set of objects (their instances). Instances of a class are also instances of its *superclasses*. Domain and range of an *attribute* are restricted by classes. Attributes are *set-valued* in general, but can be specified to be *single-valued* (at most one value) or *necessary* (at least one value). *Queries* are formulated as classes.

The expressiveness of query and schema languages in OODB's makes a general solution of our problem impossible. Thus we identify portions of the schema and queries which can be mapped to a concept language where subsumption can be decided efficiently. This simplification is sound if the more general query can be captured entirely by a concept.

* This work was supported by the Commission of the EC under ESPRIT BRA 6810 (Compulog 2), by the German Ministry of Research and Technology under grant ITW 92-01, and by the Ministry of Science and Research of Nordrhein-Westfalen.

2 Object-Oriented Databases and Queries

We introduce a simple frame-like database language $\mathcal{DL}$ which provides a generic data model for OODB's and has a simple first-order semantics. Queries can naturally be represented in this framework as special classes. A $\mathcal{DL}$ schema

```
Class Patient isA Person with     Class Person with                   Attribute skilled_in with
  attribute                         attribute, necessary, single        domain: Person
    takes: Drug                       name: String                      range: Topic
    consults: Doctor              end Person                            inverse: specialist
  attribute, necessary                                                end skilled_in
    suffers: Disease              Class Doctor with
  constraint:                       attribute
    not (this in Doctor)              skilled_in: Disease
end Patient                       end Doctor
```

Fig. 1. A part of the schema of a medical database

consists of a set of attribute and class declarations. An example is presented in Figure 1.

Attributes are binary relations with specific classes as domains and ranges. It is allowed to define synonyms for the inverse of an attribute. Thus skilled_in is a relation between persons and general topics whose inverse is called specialist. Synonyms for attributes are not allowed to occur in other declarations of a schema, but are useful for formulating queries. *Classes* group objects, which are restricted by specific conditions. These conditions are necessary, but not sufficient for class membership, *i.e.*, an object is not automatically recognized as a member if it satisfies the restrictions of a class. There is a top class Object, of which every object is an element.

A class declaration may restrict the admissible values of an attribute to a subclass of the attribute's range (*e.g.*, the skilled_in attribute of Doctor). Beside this typing condition, attributes of a class may be declared as mandatory (necessary) or functional (single). General integrity constraints for class members can be stated as first order formulas in the constraint clause. The only atoms allowed are (x in C), denoting membership of x in class C, and (x a y), assigning y as value for attribute a to object x. The variable this ranges over the members of the declared class. The subclass and attribute part of a class declaration is called the *structural* and the constraint part the *non-structural* part.

By analogy to relational databases where queries specify answer relations we specify queries in OODB's as classes. The answers to such *query classes* are the existing objects satisfying their membership conditions. In contrast to the schema classes the membership conditions of query classes are necessary *and* sufficient. It should be noted that in some object-oriented data models new objects can be created as answers to queries (see *e.g.*, [AK89]).

An example for a query class is given in Figure 2. Just as schema classes, query classes may be specializations of other classes, especially query classes, and answer objects must be common instances of all superclasses. In order

```
QueryClass QueryPatient isA
     Male, Patient with
  derived
    fem: (consults: Female)
    doc: (suffers: Object)
           .(specialist: Doctor)
  where
    fem = doc
  constraint:
    forall d/Drug not (this takes d)
    or (d = Aspirin)
end QueryPatient
```

```
QueryClass ViewPatient isA
     Patient with
  derived
    nam: (name: String)
    dis1: (consults: Doctor)
            .(skilled_in: Disease)
    dis2: (suffers: Disease)
  where
    dis1 = dis2
end ViewPatient
```

Fig. 2. A query and a view definition

to express more specific conditions on answer objects, so-called *derived* objects can be specified in the derived clause through labeled paths. A *labeled path* is a labeled chain of attributes with value restrictions and has the form l: (a_1: C_1).(a_2: C_2)....(a_n: C_n), where l is the label, the a_i's are attributes, and each C_i is a class D or a singleton set {i}. Labels stand for derived objects. A restricted attribute (a: D) ((a: {i})) relates all objects x, y in the database such that y is an instance of D (y = i) and an a-value of x. The chain of attributes in a labeled path can be conceived as a new attribute obtained by composing the components of the chain. For a given object, a chain denotes the set of objects that can be reached following it. The label of a path serves as a variable ranging over this set, and for an object to be an instance of the query class this variable has to be bound to some element of the set. Labeled paths generalize common notions of paths (*e.g.*, [KKS92]) in that they filter intermediate objects in the path by classes or singletons. The where clause contains equalities l = l′ between path expressions to be satisfied by the derived objects. The constraint clause of query classes (again called *non-structural part*) specifies additional membership conditions. The variable this refers to the answer object itself. We use the notion of (intensional) *view* for those query classes that don't have a non-structural part. The view extension or materialization is the set of all answer objects. The class ViewPatient in Figure 2 is an intensional view on patients.

The relationship between QueryPatient and ViewPatient is not obvious. However, taking into account schema information, one can show that ViewPatient subsumes QueryPatient.

3 Deciding Subsumption of Queries

In this section we introduce two languages $\mathcal{SL}$ and $\mathcal{QL}$ for describing schemas and queries, respectively, as abstractions of $\mathcal{DL}$. They are inspired by KL-ONE-like concept languages. We will show how to represent with these languages the structural parts of class and attribute declarations by a set of *schema axioms* and query classes as *concepts*. The elementary building blocks of the languages are primitive concepts (ranged over by the letters A, B) and primitive attributes (ranged over by P). Intuitively, concepts describe sets and thus correspond to unary predicates while attributes describe relations and thus correspond to binary predicates. We assume also that an alphabet of *constants* (ranged over by a, b, c) is given. Different constants denote distinct objects.

In the *schema language* $\mathcal{SL}$ attributes must be primitive. Concepts (ranged over by C, D) in $\mathcal{SL}$ are formed according to the following syntax rule:

$$
\begin{array}{lll}
C, D \longrightarrow & A \mid & \text{(primitive concept)} \\
& \forall P.A \mid & \text{(typing of attribute)} \\
& \exists P \mid & \text{(necessary attribute)} \\
& (\leq 1\, P) & \text{(single-valued attribute).}
\end{array}
$$

Schema axioms come in the two forms $A \sqsubseteq D$ and $P \sqsubseteq A \times B$. The first axiom states that all instances of A are instances of D. The second axiom states that the attribute P has domain A and range B. An $\mathcal{SL}$ *schema* Σ consists of a set of schema axioms.

In the *query language* $\mathcal{QL}$, attributes (ranged over by R) can be primitive attributes P or inverses P^{-1} of primitive attributes. Furthermore, there are *attribute restrictions*, written $(R{:}\,C)$, where R is an attribute and C is a $\mathcal{QL}$ concept. Intuitively, $(R{:}\,C)$ restricts the pairs related by R to those whose second component satisfies C. *Paths* (ranged over by p, q) are chains $(R_1{:}\,C_1)\cdots(R_n{:}\,C_n)$ of attribute restrictions and stand for the composition of the restricted attributes. The empty path is denoted as ϵ. In $\mathcal{QL}$, concepts are formed according to the rule:

$$
\begin{array}{lll}
C, D \longrightarrow & A \mid & \text{(primitive concept)} \\
& \top \mid & \text{(universal concept)} \\
& \{a\} \mid & \text{(singleton set)} \\
& C \sqcap D \mid & \text{(intersection)} \\
& \exists p \mid & \text{(existential quantification over path)} \\
& \exists p \doteq q & \text{(existential agreement of paths).}
\end{array}
$$

The intersection of concepts denotes the intersection of sets, the existential quantification over a path denotes those objects from which some object can be reached along the path, and the existential agreement of paths denotes those objects that have a common filler for the two paths. Observe that concepts and paths can be arbitrarily nested through attribute restrictions.

We give a semantics for these languages by mapping concepts C, attribute restrictions Q and paths p to first order formulas $F_C(\gamma)$, $F_Q(\alpha,\beta)$, and $F_p(\alpha,\beta)$

Construct	FOL Semantics	Construct	FOL Semantics
$\forall P.\, A$	$\forall x.\, P(\gamma, x) \Rightarrow A(x)$	$\exists P$	$\exists x.\, P(\gamma, x)$
$C \sqcap D$	$F_C(\gamma) \wedge F_D(\gamma)$	P^{-1}	$P(\beta, \alpha)$
$(R{:}\, C)$	$F_R(\alpha, \beta) \wedge F_C(\beta)$	Qp	$\exists z.\, F_Q(\alpha, z) \wedge F_p(z, \beta)$
$\exists p$	$\exists x.\, F_p(\gamma, x)$	$\exists p \doteq q$	$\exists x.\, F_p(\gamma, x) \wedge F_q(\gamma, x)$

Table 1. Semantics of $\mathcal{SL}$ and $\mathcal{QL}$ (examples)

that have one or two free variables, respectively. Primitive concepts A and primitive roles P are mapped to atoms $A(\gamma)$ and $P(\alpha, \beta)$. Complex syntactic entities are transformed as shown by way of example in Table 1. Thus, in every interpretation $\mathcal{I}$ a concept C denotes a set $C^{\mathcal{I}}$ and every attribute P denotes a binary relation $P^{\mathcal{I}}$. We say that an interpretation $\mathcal{I}$ *satisfies* the axiom $A \sqsubseteq D$ if $A^{\mathcal{I}} \subseteq D^{\mathcal{I}}$ and the axiom $P \sqsubseteq A \times B$ if $P^{\mathcal{I}} \subseteq A^{\mathcal{I}} \times B^{\mathcal{I}}$. If Σ is an $\mathcal{SL}$ schema, an interpretation $\mathcal{I}$ that satisfies all axioms in Σ is called a *Σ-interpretation*. A concept C is *Σ-satisfiable* if there is a Σ-interpretation $\mathcal{I}$ such that $C^{\mathcal{I}} \neq \emptyset$. We say that C is *Σ-subsumed* by D if $C^{\mathcal{I}} \subseteq D^{\mathcal{I}}$ for every Σ-interpretation $\mathcal{I}$.

Table 1 shows that $\mathcal{QL}$ concepts are equivalent to formulas whose prefix has only existential quantifiers and whose matrix is a conjunction of positive function free atoms. Such formulas are known as *conjunctive queries* in the context of relational and deductive databases [Ull89]. So $\mathcal{QL}$ queries are conjunctive queries with a particular hierarchical structure.

Next, we show how to represent the structural part of a $\mathcal{DL}$ schema by a set of schema axioms and the structural part of a query class by a $\mathcal{QL}$ concept. Figure 3 gives the translation of our medical database schema from Figure 1 into schema axioms. We demonstrate the transformation of query classes into

Patient	$\sqsubseteq$	Person
Patient	$\sqsubseteq$	$\forall$takes. Drug
Patient	$\sqsubseteq$	$\forall$consults. Doctor
Patient	$\sqsubseteq$	$\forall$suffers. Disease
Patient	$\sqsubseteq$	$\exists$suffers
Person	$\sqsubseteq$	$\forall$name. String
Person	$\sqsubseteq$	$\exists$name
Person	$\sqsubseteq$	($\leq$ 1 name)
skilled_in	$\sqsubseteq$	Person $\times$ Topic
Doctor	$\sqsubseteq$	$\forall$skilled_in. Disease

Fig. 3. Schema axioms of the medical database

$\mathcal{QL}$ concepts by translating as an example the query classes QueryPatient and ViewPatient from Figure 2 into concepts C_Q and D_V. The inverses of attributes have to be made explicit.

$$C_Q = \mathsf{Male} \sqcap \mathsf{Patient} \sqcap$$
$$\exists(\mathsf{consults}\colon \mathsf{Female}) \doteq (\mathsf{suffers}\colon \top)(\mathsf{skilled\_in}^{-1}\colon \mathsf{Doctor})$$
$$D_V = \mathsf{Patient} \sqcap \exists(\mathsf{name}\colon \mathsf{String}) \sqcap$$
$$\exists(\mathsf{consults}\colon \mathsf{Doctor})(\mathsf{skilled\_in}\colon \mathsf{Disease}) \doteq (\mathsf{suffers}\colon \mathsf{Disease}).$$

Let Σ denote the translation of a $\mathcal{DL}$-schema $\mathcal{S}$, C that of a query Q and D that of a view V. Since we neglect the non-structural parts of $\mathcal{S}$, the restrictions for Σ-interpretations are weaker than those for database states. Therefore a database state always corresponds to a Σ-interpretation in a natural way. Since we forget about the non-structural parts of Q, the answer set of Q is a subset of the denotation of C. So the instances of Q are surely contained in V if C is Σ-subsumed by D (recall that a view has no non-structural part and thus is entirely captured by the concept).

We have devised an algorithm (see [BJNS94]) for deciding subsumption between concepts C and D that is based on the following idea. We take an arbitrary object o and generate a canonical Σ-interpretation such that o is an instance of C. Then we evaluate D in this interpretation. If o belongs to the denotation of D we can conclude, since o is arbitrarily chosen and the interpretation is canonical, that C is subsumed by D. If o is not an instance of D, we have an interpretation where an object is in C but not in D and therefore C is not subsumed by D.

In so far, our approach is similar to the technique for deciding containment of conjunctive queries (see [Ull89]). This problem is more complicated than ours in the sense that arbitrary conjunctive queries are considered whereas we consider only concepts *i.e.*, conjunctive queries with a particular structure and it is less complicated in the sense that schema information is not taken into account. Deciding inclusion of arbitrary conjunctive queries is NP-hard, even without considering schemas. However, our algorithm runs in polynomial time because it exploits the hierarchical structure of concepts. In addition we have to take the schema axioms into consideration. In particular, axioms of the form $A \sqsubseteq \exists P$ lead to complications, since they can enforce the generation of new objects when building up the canonical interpretation. To guarantee that the interpretation is of polynomial size and that D can be evaluated in polynomial time, D is used to provide guidance for the construction of the interpretation. The details of the algorithm and the proof of the following theorem can be found in [BJNS94].

Theorem 1. *Σ-subsumption between $\mathcal{QL}$ concepts can be decided in time polynomial in the size of C, D and Σ.*

Our languages are designed so as to gain maximal expressiveness without losing tractability. For instance, polynomiality is lost if we allow inverses of attributes in the schema language or if we add constructs to $\mathcal{SL}$ that allow one to specify schemas with unsatisfiable primitive concepts. In both cases deciding Σ-subsumption becomes NP-hard. Extending $\mathcal{QL}$ by difference of primitive concepts makes subsumption co-NP-hard (see [BJNS94]).

4 Related Work and Conclusions

The problem of recognizing that one query is more general than a second has already been addressed in the context of relational databases. Finkelstein [Fin92] presented an algorithm that detects common subexpressions of relational algebra queries. He proposed to compute answers to such subqueries only once and then to reuse them. His approach is too general to permit a polynomial algorithm. In contrast to our work, he did not make use of schema information.

The subsumption problem for $\mathcal{QL}$ queries is a special case of the containment problem for conjunctive queries, which has been studied extensively (see [Ull89]). However, the objective of this work was not reusing queries, but computing for a given query an equivalent one by removing unnecessary conjuncts. It is known that deciding containment of conjunctive queries is NP-hard. Several subclasses have been found for which polynomial algorithms exist (see [Ull89]). Neither of these classes comprises the language $\mathcal{QL}$ so that $\mathcal{QL}$ concepts can be considered as a naturally occurring class of conjunctive queries with polynomial containment problem. Recently, Chan [Cha92] has adapted optimization techniques for conjunctive queries to an object-oriented setting but did not address complexity issues.

Semantic query optimization exploits integrity constraints for constructing query evaluation plans. Originally, only simple types of constraints in relational databases could be handled [Kin81]. Later, techniques for more general integrity constraints in deductive databases were developed [CGM90]. Within this framework, our method belongs to the category of approaches that exploit constraints of specific kinds, namely those expressible in the abstract schema language $\mathcal{SL}$. It is tailored to the typical needs of an object-oriented data model.

In [KKS92] an object-oriented query language called XSQL has been defined. Similar to $\mathcal{QL}$, in XSQL intermediate nodes in path expressions can be constrained by classes. XSQL exceeds our language in expressivity. For instance, it provides generation of object identifiers, which we have not considered.

Specific OODB views called materialized functions have been investigated in [KMWZ91]. Cost models and benchmark results for using such views in query answering are in [KKM91]. In the COCOON system views are seen as special classes defined by queries. When integrating them into the schema they are checked for subsumption by ad-hoc techniques [SLT91].

Summarizing we used the following ideas: class declarations and queries of OODB's are separated into a *structural* part and a *non-structural* part. The structural parts are mapped to abstract concept languages. We devised a polynomial time algorithm for deciding subsumption between concepts. We apply the algorithm to determine whether an arbitrary query is subsumed by another query whose non-structural part is empty. Our algorithm incorporates schema level knowledge for finding subsumptions which are not derivable from the query definitions alone.

Acknowledgements. We would like to thank Maurizio Lenzerini and Matthias Jarke for fruitful discussions that contributed much to the contents of this paper. We also thank Alex Borgida and Peter Patel-Schneider for commenting on earlier drafts.

References

[AK89] S. Abiteboul and P. Kanellakis. Object identity as a query language primitive. In *Proc. of ACM-SIGMOD Int. Conf. on Management of Data*, pages 159–173, Portland, Oregon, 1989.

[BJNS94] M. Buchheit, M.A. Jeusfeld, W. Nutt, and M. Staudt. Subsumption between queries to object-oriented databases. *Information Systems*, 1994. To appear.

[CGM90] U.S. Chakravarthy, J. Grant, and J. Minker. Logic based approach to semantic query optimization. *ACM Trans. on Database Systems*, 5(2):162–207, June 1990.

[Cha92] E. P. F. Chan. Containment and minimization of positive conjunctive queries in OODB's. In *Proc. of the 11th ACM Symposium on Principles of Database Systems*, pages 202–211, San Diego, CA, 1992.

[DLNN91] F. M. Donini, M. Lenzerini, D. Nardi, and W. Nutt. The complexity of concept languages. In *Proc. of KR-91*, pages 151–162. Morgan Kaufmann, 1991.

[Fin92] S. Finkelstein. Common expression analysis in database applications. In *Proc. of ACM SIGMOD Int. Conf. on Management of Data*, pages 235–245, Orlando, Florida, 1982.

[Kin81] J.J. King. QUIST: A system for semantic query optimization in relational databases. In *Proc. of the 7th VLDB Conf.*, pages 510–517, 1981.

[KKM91] A. Kemper, C. Kilger, and G. Moerkotte. Function materialization in object bases. In *Proc. of ACM SIGMOD Int. Conf. on Management of Data*, pages 258–267, Denver, Colorado, 1991.

[KKS92] M. Kifer, W. Kim, and Y. Sagiv. Querying object-oriented databases. In *Proc. of ACM SIGMOD Int. Conf. on Management of Data*, pages 393–402, San Diego, CA, 1992.

[KMWZ91] A. Kemper, G. Moerkotte, H.D. Walter, and A. Zachmann. GOM: a strongly typed, persistent object model with polymorphism. In *Proc. of BTW*, pages 198–217, Kaiserlautern, Germany, 1991. Springer.

[SLT91] M.H. Scholl, C. Laasch, and M. Tresch. Updatable views in object oriented databases. In *Proc. 2nd Int. Conf. on Deductive and Object-Oriented Databases*, pages 189–207, Munich, Germany, 1991. Springer LNCS 566.

[Ull89] J. D. Ullman. *Principles of Database and Knowledge-Base Systems, Volume 2: The New Technologies*. Computer Science Press, 1989.

[WS92] W. A. Woods and J. G. Schmolze. The KL-ONE family. In F.W. Lehmann, editor, *Semantic Networks in Artificial Intelligence*, pages 133–178. Pergamon Press, 1992.

Composite-Object Views in Relational DBMS: An Implementation Perspective

(Extended Abstract[1])

H. Pirahesh, B. Mitschang[2], N. Südkamp[3], B. Lindsay
IBM Almaden Research Center
San Jose, CA 95120, USA
e-mail:{pirahesh, bruce}@almaden.ibm.com

Abstract. We present a novel approach for supporting Composite Objects (CO) as an abstraction over the relational data. This approach brings the advanced CO model to existing relational databases and applications, without requiring an expensive migration to other DBMSs which support CO. The concept of views in relational DBMSs (RDBMS) gives the basis for providing the CO abstraction. This model is strictly an extension to the relational model, and it is fully upward compatible with it. We present an overview of the data model. We put emphasis in this paper on showing how we have made the extensions to the architecture and implementation of an RDBMS (Starburst) to support this model. We show that such a major extension to the data model is in fact quite attractive both in terms of implementation cost and query performance. We introduce a CO cache for efficient navigation through components of a CO. Our work on CO enables existing RDBMSs to incorporate efficient CO facilities at a low cost and at a high degree of application reusability and database sharability.

1 Motivation

It is widely agreed now that complex applications, such as design applications, multi-media and AI applications, and even advanced business applications can benefit significantly from database interfaces that support *composite (or complex) objects* (shortly, CO). A generally accepted characterization defines a CO consisting of several components (possibly from different types) with relationships in between [2,3,17,11]. Interestingly, object oriented DBMSs (OODBMSs) have adopted a very similar model [1,21,9,13]. This is particularly true for OODBMSs used in practice. Especially OO programming environments have made advances in handling of COs. Such environments facilitate the growth of complex applications. As a result, there is considerable pressure on RDBMSs for better support of COs. To respond to this demand, several systems today are bridging OO environments with relational. An example of such a system is the Persistence DBMS [12], which builds a layer on top of RDBMSs, providing better support for COs. These systems essentially extract data from a relational database and load it into OO environments.

In summary, relational systems to be viable must be able to understand COs (a language extension issue), and must be able to handle them well (optimization issue). Given the prevalence of SQL as a database interface language both for application and database interoperability, we have proposed an extension to SQL to handle COs. In our approach, called SQL Extended Normal Form (for short XNF) and introduced in [18], we derive COs from relational data. That paper covers the language part giving details on syntax and semantics. One major achievement is that such a powerful extension was made with full upward compatibility with SQL, hence opening up a path for the current DBMSs in research

1. The EDBT committee decided to present the full version of the paper in Information Systems, special issue: 'extended database technology', Spring 1994.

2. University of Kaiserslautern, Dept. of Computer Science, P.O.Box 3049, 67653 Kaiserslautern, Federal Republic of Germany, e-mail: mitsch@informatik.uni-kl.de

3. IBM Heidelberg Scientific Center, Vangerowstr. 18, 69115 Heidelberg, Federal Republic of Germany, e-mail: suedkamp@dhdibm1.bitnet

and industry to move forward toward handling of COs. In this paper, we attack the implementation issues, showing how to evolve a relational DBMS to handle this problem. Again, we show a growth path for RDBMSs. As mentioned before, good optimization is essential. Given the extensive optimization techniques implemented in RDBMSs, we have paid attention to reusing these capabilities. From a practical viewpoint, this is very attractive since the optimization component is not cheap.

2 XNF Language Overview: Basic Concepts, Syntax, and Semantics

XNF's notion of CO is based on the view paradigm. Instead of a single normalized table, as in standard relational systems an XNF query derives an ER-like structure [4,21,11,13] from an underlying relational database. Those *CO views* (also called object views [16,22] or structured views) are defined using a powerful *CO constructor* and consist of component tables and explicit relationships between components.

An XNF query is identified by the keywords OUT OF and consists of the following parts:

- definitions for the component tables, in general identified by the keyword SELECT,
- definitions for the relationships, identified by the keyword RELATE, and
- specifications for the output, identified by the keyword TAKE.

Table and relationship definitions are mainly expressed using existing SQL language constructs. They make out XNF's CO constructor which can be seen as a proper extension to SQL by a compound query statement. With this, an XNF query simply reads like this:

'**OUT OF** ... *the CO* (that is constructed by the CO constructor
TAKE ... *the parts projected* (that define the resulting CO)'

As an introduction to XNF syntax and semantics, let us discuss the example CO abstraction called *dep_ARC* given in Fig.1. The upper part of Fig.1 shows on the left the schema and on the right the instance level showing the COs derived, whereas the lower part of Fig.1 gives the corresponding CO query that defines this abstraction.

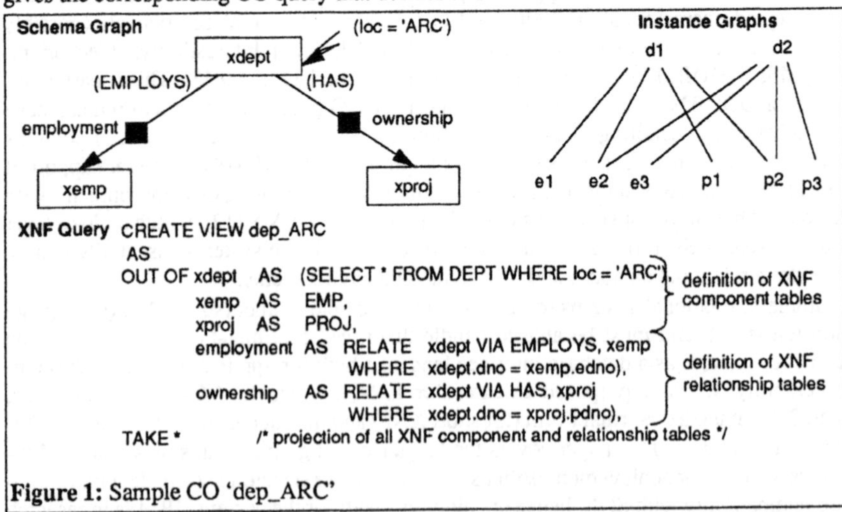

Figure 1: Sample CO 'dep_ARC'

This XNF query retrieves the departments located at 'ARC', and to each one the corresponding employees as well as the projects are connected. As shown by this sample XNF query, the nodes, i.e. the component tables, are derived through standard SQL queries. Syntactic short-cuts (see definition of *xemp* and *xproj* component tables) are provided for sake of brevity. In our example the base tables departments (*DEPT*), employees (*EMP*) and projects (*PROJ*) of the underlying relational database are used for derivation. The relationship tables that make up the edges of the query's schema graph show a different syntax, but basically also adopt SQL query facilities. The RELATE clause gives the parent table first and then the child table, and the WHERE clause holds the (standard SQL join) *predicate* that specifies the criteria for relating the partner tuples via *connections*. In order to read the relationship-defining query expressions in a convenient way, we have given role names (VIA clause) to the parent partners of the relationships. Based upon their predicates, the relationships establish for any given department connections to the employees it *EMPLOYS* and to the projects it *HAS*.

Retrieval of such an XNF CO results in retrieval of all the tuples of the component tables and provision for the relationship information, i.e. connections defined by the XNF relationships. So far, an XNF CO specifies a heterogeneous set of records with different record formats. If a component tuple is used multiple times within a view, then it exists, of course, only once in the view, but it participates in multiple connections (possibly from different relationships). Therefore the important notion of *object sharing* (illustrated by the instance graphs in Fig.1 showing the employees *e2* and *e3* as shared objects) is a fundamental part of the XNF CO concept. An XNF query may also specify a *recursive CO* being identified by a cycle in the query's schema graph. This cycle basically defines a 'derivation rule' that iterates along the cycle's relationships to collect the tuples until a fixed point is reached and no more tuples qualify.

XNF COs may be combined, projected, and restricted. Combination is done by simply defining a relationship between any node of one CO and any node of another one. Projection is defined by listing all the nodes and relationships to be retained. The star '*' is used as a special syntactic construct for projection of all the components with their attributes and all the relationships defined. Restriction can be done through additional predicates on the node tables and the relationships. There is also a set of CO update operators, enhancing the interface to handle insert, read, update, and delete operations. In addition, the interface supports connect and disconnect operations on relationships.

All retrieval and manipulation operations of the XNF language work at the XNF level, taking into account the given graph structure and the heterogeneous tuple set. Since the result of an XNF query consists of a set of component tables and relationships, an XNF query (or XNF view) can be used as input for a subsequent XNF query or view definition. This is also true for all other XNF operations. Therefore the model is closed under its language operations. More information on the XNF language, the multi-lingual API, and (update) semantics can be found in [18].

3 Composite Object Processing

Since both the XNF language as well as the XNF API are built on SQL ideas, we decided to develop the XNF system as an *extension* to an existing RDBMS rather than building a new DBMS. Hence we advocate for an integrated DBMS, which handles both the tabular as well as the CO data. In doing so, we are able to reuse important system features that have taken years to build and are vital for e.g. system robustness, failure tolerance, and system performance. Especially, since the specification of XNF views mostly reuses the relational query language (SQL in our case), almost all of the optimization techniques developed in the context of RDBMSs remain applicable. From a technical viewpoint (and also from an economic one) we chose Starburst DBMS [10] as the starting point. Starburst was particularly attractive due to its extensibility features as we will see shortly.

3.1 Query Processing Architecture

The query processing architecture of Starburst incorporates the *query language processor* CORONA [10] and the *data manager* CORE [14]. CORONA compiles queries (written in extended SQL) into calls to the underlying CORE services to fetch and modify data. As depicted in Fig. 2, there are five distinct stages of query processing in CORONA; each stage is represented by a corresponding system component. For the moment, we consider only the unshaded parts of Fig.2; the shaded areas mark XNF extensions and will be discussed in the next subsection.

An incoming SQL query is first broken into tokens and then parsed into an internal query representation called *query graph model* (shortly QGM). Only valid queries are accepted, because *semantic analysis* is also done in this first stage. During *query rewrite*, the QGM representation of the query is transformed (rewritten by transformation rules) into an equivalent one that (hopefully) leads to a better performing execution strategy when processed by the subsequent stage of plan optimization. *Plan optimization* chooses a possible execution strategy based on estimated execution costs, and writes the resulting *query execution plan* (QEP) as the output of the compilation phase. This evaluation plan is then repackaged during the *plan refinement* stage for more efficient execution by the *query evaluation system* (QES). At runtime QES executes the QEP against the database.

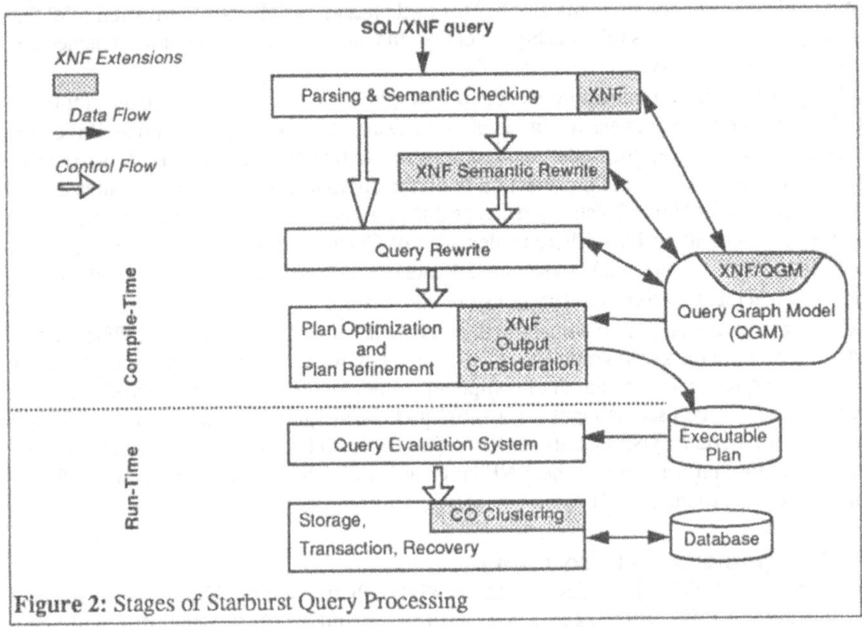

Figure 2: Stages of Starburst Query Processing

3.2 CO Processing Steps

The distinguished stages of XNF's CO query processing are shown in Fig.2. Those features that are different to the ones used in the traditional Starburst are shaded. Fig.2 already exposes that the XNF language processor is truly an extension to the SQL processor. XNF queries are translated to a form very close to standard SQL, allowing reuse of the extensive optimization and evaluation machinery of the RDBMS with little change. This translation is performed at compile time, and is optimized, eliminating any runtime overhead.

3.3 XNF Semantic Checking

The crucial extension to the relational case was the CO constructor. Since this extension affected the language grammar, both the language parser and the semantic checking had to be extended correspondingly. In the same way as the standard SQL processor created during this phase the internal query representation, i.e., a normal form QGM graph (for short NF QGM), the XNF processor had to create the so-called XNF QGM graph that has to incorporate the XNF query semantics. In order to do this, a new operator had to be installed for QGM. The purpose of this *XNF operator* is to reflect the semantics of the language's CO constructor. Therefore, the XNF operator had to be able to incorporate n>=1 incoming tables and to produce m>=1 output tables being the resulting node tables and relationship tables of the CO constructed. In addition to this, regular output processing had to be modified to allow generation of a heterogeneous set of tuples in the answer set (generation of tuples belonging to different nodes and relationships). This is done by the so-called 'top' operator, which deals with the interface between the query processor and the application program. Each QGM graph has a single top operator.

In the first stage of XNF query compilation the internal query representation is built by means of the XNF semantic routines. As already mentioned, XNF QGM uses the XNF operator in order to incorporate XNF query semantics.

Since an XNF query consists of three building blocks, there are also three semantic routines that together construct the final XNF query graph:

(0) QGM initialization

(1) Derivation of XNF component tables

(2) Consideration of component restrictions and XNF predicates

(3) Handling projection.

3.3.1 XNF Semantic Rewrite

In this step the translation from XNF QGM (and XNF semantics) to NF QGM (and NF semantics) has to be accomplished, thereby transforming an XNF query graph into a semantically equivalent NF query graph. Speaking in other words, this component has to replace the XNF operator and the XNF predicates by corresponding NF operators organized in an NF QGM graph. In this step we exploit that the components (i.e., the building blocks) of COs are tables, whose derivation is already specified via NF query graphs within an XNF operator (see Sect. 4.1). XNF semantic rewrite proceeds in two major steps:

(1) Removal of the XNF operator box

(2) Consideration of XNF predicates, e.g. reachability.

Finally, there is only one NF QGM graph constructed for such a multi-table XNF query, i.e. common subexpressions are immediately installed such as the derivation of a component is also used for the derivation of its child(ren) component(s), and both are used for the relationship derivation. Comparing this multi-table derivation as applied by XNF with the single component derivation in SQL clearly shows the impact of XNF's inherent treatment of common subexpressions and that the XNF rewrite approach is optimal w.r.t. processing common subexpression. A formal proof of this is beyond the scope of this paper.

3.3.2 Rewrite and Plan Optimization

Since the previous step already produced a clean NF QGM (that reflects the CO query semantics), the remaining compilation work can be done by the components of the original SQL language processor. That is, the NF QGM graph built by XNF semantic rewrite is transformed by the NF query rewrite component to a semantically equivalent one that, in general, allows more efficient evaluation strategies to be chosen for the QEP when being processed by the plan optimization and query refinement components. For example, existential subqueries can be converted into joins. Remember, all these components are shared between the XNF language processor and the SQL language processor. A detailed description of these components can be found in [10,19].

4 Data Extraction, XNF Cache, and API

In addition to standard SQL cursor support, we allow the retrieval of *all tuples* contributing to the result of an XNF query and the materialization of the *complete* COs. The XNF processing model has been designed for a workstation/server environment, where the database server can deliver complete COs on request.

In Fig.3 we show the overall structure of our prototype implementation. An application sends a data request, i.e. an XNF query to the DBMS. Query translation and optimization takes place as described in the previous Section (these compile-time activities are marked by the shaded area in Fig.3). At runtime the generated query plan is executed and the complete result is delivered by the database system, converted into an internal main-memory representation and made accessible to the application program via the cursor interface. For long transactions, XNF allows the cache to be stored on disk and retrieved later, thereby protecting the cache from client machine's failure.

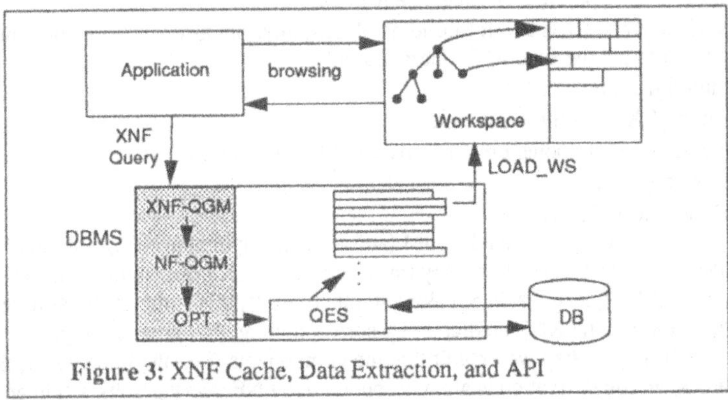

Figure 3: XNF Cache, Data Extraction, and API

The workspace is constructed from the output tuples of the XNF query by converting connections into pointers which allow traversing the structure in any direction. In addition we generate pointers to allow browsing all elements of a component and all elements of a node which are connected to a given component by a specified relationship. These pointers provide primitive access support for the cursors to be defined upon the component tables.

In our prototype we have implemented a subset of XNF API and the XNF cache manager. We have used this prototype to measure the performance of XNF. One significant result is that the performance of XNF cache is quite comparable with fast OODBMSs reported in Cattell's benchmark [8]. Using the traversal operation from that benchmark, we could access in a pre-loaded XNF cache more than 100,000 tuples per second which matches the requirements for CAD applications.

5 Conclusions

The novel approach of supporting COs as an abstraction over relational data is quite attractive. This approach brings the advanced CO model to existing relational databases and applications, without requiring an expensive migration to other DBMSs which support COs. The salient features of the approach are:

- a data model and query language that unifies CO and relational constructs by means of CO views,
- an elegant implementation approach that guarantees efficient data extraction, and
- a multi-lingual API with efficient navigation and manipulation facilities, and a seamless C++ interface to the cached data.

XNF defines an evolution path from RDBMSs to Composite Object DBMSs. It is interesting that we needed to make very little changes in order to make RDBMSs capable of efficiently handling COs. This is a tremendous advantage, and is very significant in practice. Therefore we called XNF an *enabling technology*. It enables RDBMSs to be extended to deal with CO and CO processing patterns. The technology is inexpensive because it heavily reuses already existing query processing components (with only comparatively small changes), and other system components as for example transaction, recovery, and storage management are totally kept unchanged. Although XNF technology largely builds upon basic relational technology, further extensions (e.g. parallelism and clustering facilities) introduced to the relational part of the system become automatically available to XNF.

XNF technology has been successfully integrated into and is now operational in the Starburst extensible database system developed at IBM Almaden Research Center. Although the extensibility feature provided by Starburst helped a lot in integrating the XNF technology, there is at least conceptually no problem in getting it also into other (non-extensible) DBMS. This is due to the fact that XNF clearly extends SQL, and XNF technology rewrites a CO query into a semantically equivalent NF query. Therefore, only the rewrite component as well as the language extensions have to be incorporated into the query processing component of a DBMS. Extensibility just simplifies that attempt.

Another major conclusion drawn from the discussion so far, should perceive XNF as a high performance approach - as an enabling technology - that provides a path for incorporating relational data into any CO application similar to the Persistence DBMS [12] already mentioned. For example, we can use an XNF DBMS (e.g., the Starburst DBMS presented here) to provide server services to an object-oriented programming system running on the application site. This idea was realized in the prototype system called 'Object/SQL Gateway' [15] that provides object-oriented access to data residing in a relational DBMS. This gateway connects the object-oriented DBMS ObjectStore [13] to the Starburst relational DBMS exploiting XNF technology. It is a first step in providing an integrated access to both types of DBMS using a uniform object-oriented interface. Here, XNF's multi-query optimization helps in considerably reducing the cost of data extraction from relational repository into an object cache. Another important issue is improving XNF query processing with special emphasis on CO cluster facilities, as well as on parallelism technology [6,7,20]. Further, in trying to assess XNF technology, there is already considerable confidence that the query processing concepts for COs presented (especially the multi-query framework as well as its inherent exploitation of common subexpressions) plays an integral part also in query processing for object-oriented languages as well as for deductive database languages [5].

Acknowledgments

The cooperation of the whole Starburst staff is gratefully acknowledged. Special thanks are due to Peter Pistor, who helped in our joint effort of getting the good stuff into XNF, whilst streamlining the syntax and semantics. Guy Lohman improved the optimizer to handle our complex queries, and George Wilson provided valuable implementation experiences in his work on an earlier prototype. We would like to acknowledge V. Srinivasan and T. Lee of DBTI for their work on XNF cache manager and C++ application interface. We would also like to thank J. Thomas for his comments on an earlier version of this paper.

References

1. Atkinson, M., Bancilhon, F., DeWitt, D., Dittrich, K., Maier, D., Zdonik, S.: The Object-Oriented Database System Manifesto, in: Proc. of the 1st Int. Conf. on Deductive and Object-oriented Databases, Kyoto-Japan, Dec. 1989, pp. 40-57
2. Albano, A., Ghelli, G., Orsini, R.: A Relationship Mechanism for a Strongly Typed Object-Oriented Database Programming Language, in: Proc. 17th VLDB Conf., Barcelona, 1991, pp. 565-575
3. Batory, D.S., Buchmann, A.P.: Molecular Objects, Abstract Data Types, and Data Models, in: Proc. 10th VLDB Conf., Singapore, 1984, pp. 172-184
4. Chen, PP: The Entity Relationship Model: Toward a Unified View of Data, in: ACM Trans. on Database Syst., Vol.1, No.1, 1976, pp. 9-36
5. Cheiney, J., Lanzelotte, R.: A Model for Optimizing Deductive and Object-Oriented DB Requests, in: Proc. of Data Engineering Conf., Phoenix, February, 1992
6. DeWitt, D., Gray, J.: Parallel Database Systems: The Future of High Performance Database Systems, in: CACM, Vol. 35, No. 6, 1992, pp. 85-98
7. Graefe, G.: Volcano, an Extensible and Parallel Query Evaluation System, Research Report University of Colorado at Boulder, CU-CS-481-90, 1990
8. Gray, J. (ed.): The Benchmark Handbook for Database and Transaction Processing Systems, Morgan Kaufman Publ. Inc. (1991)
9. Guzenda, L, Wade: ANS OODBTG Workshop position paper, Objectivity, Inc., in Proc of the First OODB Standardization Workshop, May 22, 1990
10. Haas, L., Freytag, J.C., Lohman, G., Pirahesh. H.: Extensible Query Processing in Starburst, in: Proc. of the ACM SIGMOD Conf., Portland, 1989, pp. 377 - 388
11. Kim, W.: Introduction to Object-Oriented Databases, MIT Press, (1991)
12. Keller, A., Jensen R., Agrawal, S.: Persistence Software: Bridging Object-Oriented Programming and Relational Database, in: ACM SIGMOD Conf., 1993, pp. 523-528
13. Lamb, C., Landis, G., Orenstein, J., Weinreb, D.: The Objectstore Database System, in: Communications of the ACM, Vol. 34, No. 10, 1991, pp. 50-63
14. Lindsay, B., McPherson, J., Pirahesh, H.: A Data Management Extension Architecture, in: Proc. of the ACM SIGMOD Conf., San Francisco, 1987, pp. 220-226
15. Lee, T., Srinivasan, V., Cheng, J., Pirahesh, H.: Object/SQL Gateway, presented at OOPSLA workshop, 1993
16. Lee, B.S., Wiederhold, G.: Outer Joins and Filters for Instantiating Objects from Relational Databases through Views CIFE Technical Report, Stanford Univ., May 1990
17. Mitschang, B.: Extending the Relational Algebra to Capture Complex Objects, in: Proc. 15th VLDB Conf., Amsterdam, 1989, pp. 297-305
18. Mitschang, B., Pirahesh, H., Pistor, P., Lindsay, B., Südkamp, N.: SQL/XNF - Processing Composite Objects as Abstractions over Relational Data, in: Proc. of Ninth Int. Conf. on Data Engineering, April 1993, Vienna, pp. 272-282
19. Pirahesh, H., Hellerstein, J., Hasan, W.: Extensible/Rule Based Query Rewrite Optimization in Starburst, in: Proc. of the ACM SIGMOD Conf, San Diego,1992, pp.39-48
20. Pirahesh, H., Mohan, C., Cheng, J., Liu, TS, Selinger, P.: Parallelism in Relational Data Base Systems: Architectural Issues and Design Approaches, in: Proc. of the Int. Symposium on Databases in Parallel and Distributed Systems, Dublin, 1990
21. Zdonik, S., Maier, D: Fundamentals of Object Oriented Databases. Readings in Object-Oriented Database Systems, ISBN 1-55860-000-0, ISSN 1046-1698, Morgan Kaufmann Publishers, Inc., (1990)
22. Zdonik, S.: Incremental Database Systems, in: Proc. of the ACM SIGMOD Conf., Washington, 1993, pp. 408-417

Matrix Relation for Statistical Database Management

Rosine CICCHETTI
Aix-en-Provence IUT

Lotfi LAKHAL
Clermont-Ferrand University II

IUT d'Aix-en-Provence, Département Informatique
Av. Gaston Berger, 13625 Aix-en-Provence Cedex 1 - FRANCE
E-mail : rosine@mimosa.unice.fr - Tel : 42 27 92 17 - Fax : 42 26 68 73

Abstract - One of the important issues of statistical database management is to define a data model and language for modeling and manipulating complex statistical summaries in the database. This paper proposes a matrix relation model and language for statistical database management. The matrix relational data structure combines relation and matrix organizations. It offers a natural and densly built-up representation of complex statistical summaries. It proposes new objects and constructors for statistical database organization. The matrix relational language is an algebraic query language, using an extended relational algebra.

1 Introduction

Since the first LBL international workshop on statistical and scientific database management (Menlo Park, California, 1981), research efforts have started examining the basic problems associated with statistical database management systems [3, 12, 25, 26, 29]. Statistical DataBases -SDB- contain collected or raw data, also called micro-data, describing a population to study. Some common examples are census, mortality and environment data for socio-economic applications. The two main characteristics of SDB are: data stability (indeed they may be perceived as a snapshot of the examined population, hence updates are not involved in this context) and voluminous size. Because of this last feature, aggregated data sets, called statistical summaries or macro-data sets [29], are preserved in the database once they have been computed from raw data. It is established that the derivation of relevant summaries may avoid the handling of detailled data and some authors refer to SDB as databases that only contain statistical summaries [6].

The model that we propose for SDB makes use of relational structure in order to represent raw data and introduces a matrix relational data structure, for summaries. The associated language, MARELA (MAtrix RElation LAnguage) allows the user to manipulate statistical data whether raw or summarized. It operates on a twofold structure: relation and Matrix Relation -MR. Its basic idea is to take advantage of all the capabilities of relational algebra while extending it (by a set of suitable operators) in order to take new needs into account.

Later on, we describe the different aspects of our proposals. We present our structural approach for statistical summaries (section 4). Then we detail the manipulation capabilities of our algebraic language and pay particular attention to its most original possibilities for both raw and summarized data (section 5). But first of all, we present the SDB concepts (section 2) and summarize the previous works dealing with SDB. We focus more particularly on relational and nested relational models and pay particular attention to their inadequacies for statistical data management (section 3).

2 Statistical database concepts

The statistical data are described in terms of two types of attributes: category and summary attributes. The latter are numerical since they correspond to quantitative data being measured or summarized. The category attributes are descriptive fields that characterize summary attributes.

The statistical summaries are initially derived through a twofold operation over raw data. Actually, micro-data are classified according to category attribute values. Then statistical aggregations (e.g. Count, Sum) or statistical analysis functions are applied. They compute for each class of individuals a summary value, which is uniquely identified by a combination of category attribute values. From these summaries, other ones may be derived by using aggregations or calculus ... and so on (this is called summary proliferation).

The criterium classification of a statistical summary matches a multidimensional space. Furthermore, since macro-data are dense, this space matches the Cartesian-product of sub-sets of category attribute domains. A null value may be assigned, instead of a summary value, to missing combinations.
In statistical databases, two kinds of summaries may be distinguished:

- Elementary statistical summaries which have a unique summary attribute and one multi-dimensional space;
- Complex statistical summaries grouping elementary summaries according to their common category attributes. Of course they have several summary attributes and are characterized by a set of multidimensional spaces.

The semantics of summary attributes is fundamental. It accounts for the fact that their values translate counts, averages, standard deviations, ... What we then call the "summary attribute nature" is essential in data interpretation. Furthermore it adds fundamental information on the possible summarizability of macro-data. Actually, the summaries may be derived or not, according to the statistical function used to compute them. The derivable summaries are, in fact, limited to the ones achieved by applying an additive function (Count or Sum). But it is established that most of classical functions may be expressed in terms of additive ones [6]. When such an expression can be stated, then they are called calculable functions and their results are equivalent to those of an arithmetic calculation on summaries achieved by using their additive parameter functions. For instance, the average may be achieved from "count" and "sum". Covariance parameter are "count", "sum of products" and "sum of squares". Regression analysis is calculable according to "count", "sum", "sum of products" and "sum of squares". The statistical functions "min" and "max" extract some particular values of summary attributes. They may be considered as selection operations.

A SBD describing student census is used, throughout this article, to illustrate our presentation. The individuals of the examined population are students characterized in particular by: their sex (SEX), socio-professional class (CLASS), study year (YEAR), discipline studied (DISCIP), the fact they are or not grant-holders (GRANT_H) and the possible amount of their grant (GRANT). The four elementary statistical summaries A, B, C and D are supposed to be derived from an individual sub-set. A and C respectively permit to count students (summary attributes ANB and CNB):

- By sex, socio-professional class, study year and the fact that they are grant-holders or not;
- By sex, discipline, study year and the fact that they are grant-holders or not;

The summary attributes BTT_GRANT and DTT_GRANT of the summaries B and D correspond to the total amount of student grants. They are achieved by summing up the values of the attribut GRANT, for the considered individuals. They respectively give this amount:

- By sex, socio-professional class and study year;
- By sex, discipline and study year.

Let's consider, for example, the multidimensional space of A. It matches the Cartesian-product of attributes SEX, CLASS, YEAR and GRANT_H. The grouping of the two elementary statistical summaries B and D, according to their common category attributes SEX and YEAR, creates a complex summary, having two summary attributes and two multidimensional spaces that share these category attributes.

3 Related work

Some statistical data models and query languages have been proposed in litterature. They may be classed in:

- Semantic data models and languages such as in [4, 5, 18, 28]. They provide new concepts relevant to issues of SDB design.
- Extended relational models and languages, like STBE [22], QBSRT [14], STAQUEL [23], Category-Summary-Statistical Function Model [6], Category-Numerical Relation Algebra [10, 11, 13, 15]. They deal with summary modeling and use relations as a SDB management support.

MARELA shares with the second class approaches the motivations to extend the relational model. We indicate these reasons and briefly present the mentioned research works.
The relational model provides neither explicit concepts for statistical data representation nor efficient processing capabilities. Its first drawback is that a clear distinction between category and

summary attributes cannot be stated [10]. Nevertheless, such a distinction is fundamental for statistical data interpretation and also for manipulations. Actually, the operations on category attributes are very different from summary attribute handling.
Another constraint of relational modeling concerns the representation of the summary attribute nature. It cannot be entirely explicit even through the concept of semantic domain. Nevertheless, it determines the summarizability of macro-data sets. Therefore, it is not possible to check the exacteness of derived summary values, specially when cascades of aggregations are performed.
The only complex summaries to be represented through relation must have a unique multi-dimensional space, i.e. their summary attributes must be described by the same category attributes. Therefore, in most common cases, several relations are required to represent statistical summaries. This is very embarrassing specially when considering the problem of summary proliferation in SDB [26].
Example 1. The statistical database "student census" needs the four following 3NF relations:
R1(SEX, YEAR, GRANT_H, DISCIP, ANB) R3(SEX, YEAR, GRANT_H, CLASS, CNB)
R2(SEX, YEAR, CLASS, BTT_GRANT) R4(SEX, YEAR, DISCIP, DTT_GRANT)

Finally, the relational algebra cannot answer the statistician's requests. No restructuring data capabilities are supplied for relation data structure. The relation derivations are not controled and the interrogation primitives ought to be used in a more restrictive frame.

Nested relations [1, 2, 24] have claimed that they are suitable for modeling and handling statistical data. This is true but nevertheless they are partly inefficient [12], because they inherit some inadequacies of the relational data structure (no distinction between attributes, no possibility to take into account summarizability, ...) They also complicate the identification of elementary statistical summaries within a complex one.
Example 2. To illustrate our purpose, we have chosen the nested relational model Verso of S. Abiteboul and al. [2], since it integrates transposition abilities.
A clear representation of our example needs two nested relations in the Verso model. Actually this model does not allow the attributes to be repeated.
VR1(SEX, YEAR, GRANT_H, (DISCIP, ANB)* (CLASS, CNB)*)
VR2(SEX, YEAR, (DISCIP, DTT_GRANT)* (CLASS, BTT_GRANT)*)

All the proposals concerning summary modeling have, at least, a common point: the distinction between the two kinds of attributes.
Statistical query languages [20], such as ABE, STBE, QBSRT, extend relational algebra by integrating a few new Filter and Composition operations, like aggregation (in all the mentionned languages), aggregation-by-template, i.e. aggregation on relations with multivalued attributes [21] (in STBE), bi-directional outer join (in STBE), restrictions and statistical procedures (in QBSRT, and Category-Summary Statistical Function Model). The two major attempts to define an algebra for SDB management have been proposed by S. Ghosh [8, 11, 13], and by E. Fortunato and al. [10]. They encompass a large number of suitable category numerical operators, with varying complexity. Nevetheless, the underlying data structures can only represent summaries with one multidimensional space and do not capture the summary attribute nature. So the user is supposed to be forewarned of operator functioning. None of these works include structure reorganizations as query language primitives. Although these manipulations are considered (with aggregation) as some of the most common operations in SDB [19, 26].

4 Matrix Relation data structure

To represent summaries we propose a new data structure: Matrix Relation -MR- (also called Complex Statistical Table in [17]). It combines relational and matrix organization. Actually, it is inspired by concepts such as those of attribute, semantical domain and relation, which are adapted in order to represent category attributes and multidimensional spaces. It also makes use of a matrix organization for summary attribute values.
The aim of MR structure is to make explicit all the specific concepts of SDB. The MR structure may be seen as a modular one since the elementary summary representation, through Atomic Matrix Relation -AMR-, is a particular case of complex summary structuration. Futhermore any AMR may be identified within MRs. In the same way as AMRs may be grouped to achieve MRs, the latter may also be gathered within a more complex MR.

In the organization choices, we try to avoid the gap between the formal definition of the structure and its perception by the user and propose a tabular presentation for MRs (workable for a user-friendly interface).
In this section, we detail the objects and constructors of the model. Then we present AMR and MR in an intuitive and formal way. We also have a glance at their compatibility.

4.1 Objects and constructors

The two basic objects in MARELA are those of category attribute and summary attribute. They can be perceived as atomic information of different types. To represent complex summaries, the attribute organization requires the constructors: Cartesian-product and List. The category attributes are organized according to a category attribute schema, i.e. a list of attributes. Its instances permit to represent a multidimensional space by using the Cartesian-product constructor. Such schemas take place in the row and column dimension that structure an AMR. AMR allows the representation of elementary summary. The values of its unique summary attribute are organized in a matrix form, achieved by the List constructor. Any AMR is characterized by the statistical function used to compute its summary values.
AMRs are grouped to achieve MR representing complex summaries. Observed on the component elements of MR, such an organization process uses the List constructor. This permits to define category attribute multi-schema, in an intensive and extensive way, from category attribute schemas of the AMRs components of the MR, and from their instances. Through two multi-schemas, the row and column ones, achieved by the List constructor, it is possible to represent heterogeneous and potentially shared multi-dimensional spaces. The summary attributes of the components AMRs are organized as a matrix in the MR. The summary-value structuring is based on List constructor. MRs are characterized by the statistical functions (organized in a matrix way) that permit to derive their summary attributes.

4.2 Atomic Matrix Relation

The AMR schema may be perceived as an array in which the category attribute names appear in the row and column headings and the unique summary attribute matches the cell. The statistical function used to compute its values is associated to the AMR. Row and column dimensions of the AMR are organized according to category attribute schemas, defined as a list of category attribute names. The category attribute schemas may be perceived as "all-key" relation schemas.

SCHEMA(AMR) = (Xr, Xc, V, f) where:

- Xr = [$xr_1, \ldots, xr_m$] is the row category attribute schema;
- Xc = [$xc_1, \ldots, xc_n$] is the column category attribute schema;
- V is the summary attribute of the AMR and
- f is the function used to compute V.

Futhermore, we have: $Xr \cap Xc \cap \{V\} = \emptyset$.

Example 3. The representation of the statistical summaries A, B, C and D through AMRs are given below and their tabular presentations are illustrated in the figure 1.

A = ([SEX, CLASS], [YEAR, GRANT_H], ANB, Count)
B = ([SEX, CLASS], [YEAR], B_TT_GRANT, Sum)
C = ([SEX, DISCIP], [YEAR, GRANT_H], CNB, Count)
D = ([SEX, DISCIP], [YEAR], D_TT_GRANT, Sum)

A : Count		YEAR GRANT_H
SEX	CLASS	ANB

B : Sum		YEAR
SEX	CLASS	BTT_GRANT

C : Count		YEAR GRANT_H
SEX	DISCIP	CNB

D : Sum		YEAR
SEX	DISCIP	DTT_GRANT

Fig. 1. A, B, C and D schemas

The AMR instance may be seen as an array, filled up with category attribute values and those of the summary attribute. The latter are structured according to the instances of row and column category attribute schemas, defined by the Cartesian-product of value sub-sets of their attribute domains.
AMR extension is defined as follows:
EXTENSION(AMR) = (VAL(Xr), VAL(Xc), M(V)) where:

- $VAL(Xr) = [tr \,/\, tr \in \bigotimes_{i=1}^{m} DOM(xr_i)\,]$

- $VAL(Xc) = [tc \,/\, tc \in \bigotimes_{j=1}^{n} DOM(xc_j)\,]$

- $M(V) = [^{V}|VAL(Xr)|,|VAL(Xc)|] \,/\, ^{V}P(tr),P(tc) \in DOM(V)$

 with DOM(V) = REAL ∪ NULL | INTEGER ∪ NULL ; tr ∈ VAL(Xr) and tc ∈ VAL(Xc).
 P : VAL(Xr|Xc) → |VAL(Xr|Xc)| and ⊗ stands for the Cartesian-product.

Example 4. The instances of AMRs A, B, C, and D are shown in figure 2.
Let's consider the AMR B and more specially female students in the class "farmers". The total amount of their grants for the first and second study years are respectively 23.625 and 11.700.

A : Count		1 Yes	1 No	2 Yes	2 No
F	Farmers	15	14	9	12
F	Workers	30	25	23	29
F	Managers	2	5	1	5
M	Farmers	10	9	3	5
M	Workers	43	40	35	42
M	Managers	7	8	5	8

B : Sum		1	2
F	Farmers	23.625	11.700
F	Workers	45.000	34.500
F	Managers	1.600	1.000
M	Farmers	13.220	4.560
M	Workers	60.200	50.750
M	Managers	7.700	5.500

C : Count		1 Yes	1 No	2 Yes	2 No
F	Computer science	25	39	24	33
F	Mathematics	18	21	15	20
F	Physics	27	14	20	18
M	Computer science	38	37	29	42
M	Mathematics	17	29	19	28
M	Physics	25	23	25	25

D : Sum		1	2
F	Computer science	26.250	28.800
F	Mathematics	27.000	17.900
F	Physics	37.125	28.200
M	Computer science	46.740	41.730
M	Mathematics	23.630	28.880
M	Physics	27.250	29.250

Fig. 2. A, B, C and D extensions

4.3 Matrix Relation

MR is a grouping of AMRs. It allows the representation of complex statistical summaries. It is achieved by a twofold concatenation, according to rows and columns, of different AMRs. The row and column dimensions of MR are said to be structured according to row and column multi-schemas of category attributes (List of category attribute schemas).
MR instances may be perceived as an array of category and summary attribute values, achieved by concatenation, according to rows and columns, of instances of its AMR components.
MR is defined as follows:

MR = [AMRm,n] / ∀ i ∈ [1...m]

Let AMRij(Xr) be the row category schema Xr in the AMRij and AMRij(Xc) the column category schema Xc in the AMRij.

AMRi1(Xr) = AMRi2(Xr) = ... = AMRin(Xr).

AMRi1 (VAL(Xr)) = ... = AMRin (VAL(Xr)).

and ∀ j ∈ [1...n],

AMR1j(Xc) = AMR2j(Xc) = ... = AMRmj(Xc).

AMR1j(VAL(Xc)) = ... = AMRmj(VAL(Xc)).

Example 5. If the user whishes to work on the summaries A, B, C and D, he may gather the corresponding AMRs, within MR Z1 whose schema and instances are given in the figure 3.

Z1		YEAR	YEAR
A : Count	B : Sum	GRANT_H	
C : Count	D : Sum		
SEX	CLASS	ANB	BTT_GRANT
SEX	DISCIP	CNB	DTT_GRANT

Z1		1	1	2	2	1	2
A : Count	B : Sum	Yes	No	Yes	No		
C : Count	D : Sum						
F	Framers	15	14	9	12	23.625	11.700
F	Workers	30	25	23	29	45.000	34.500
F	Managers	2	5	1	5	1.600	1.000
M	Framers	10	9	3	5	13.220	4.560
M	Workers	43	40	35	42	60.200	50.750
M	Managers	7	8	5	8	7.700	5.500
F	Computer science	25	39	24	33	26.250	28.800
F	Mathematics	18	21	15	20	27.000	17.900
F	Physics	27	14	20	18	37.125	28.200
M	Computer science	38	37	29	42	46.740	41.730
M	Mathematics	17	29	19	28	23.630	28.880
M	Physics	25	23	25	25	27.250	29.250

Fig. 3. Z1 schema and extension:
Matrix relational representation of statistical database "Student Census"

The tabular presentation, used in previous figures, shows the MR schema in form of an array encompassing four areas:

- Title area displays the MR name and, in a matrix way, component AMR identifiers with the associated statistical functions;
- Row heading area (in grey) allows the presentation of the row multi-schema of category attributes, in such a manner that any row i describes, from left to right, the ith schema of category attribute multi-schema;
- Column heading area (in grey) presents in the same way the column multi-schema;
- Cell area groups summary attribute names as a matrix.

In the chosen presentation for AMR and MR instances, the four described areas are preserved. Any row (or column) of the row heading area describes, from left to right, one instance of row multi-schema of category attributes. The summary values appear in cells.

4.4 Compatibility of MR

Any two MRs are compatible according to rows (or columns) if their row (or column) multi-schemas encompass compatible category attributes (i.e. with the same domain). Moreover if their multi-schema instances are identical, they are said to be completely compatible. These two kinds of MR compatibility supply the semantic rules necessary to build up more complex MRs. Later on, these kinds of operations will be refered as compositions.

Example 6. The AMRs A et B (respectively B and D) are completely compatible according to the row (respectively column) dimension.
MR Z4, whose schema and instances are shown in figure 4, represents the population of students on one hand by sex and class (matching with AMR E), and on the other hand by sex and discipline (matching with AMR F). The MRs Z1 and Z4 are compatible according to rows but not completely, for the category attribute CLASS has not the same values in these MRs.

Z4		
E : Count		Ø
F : Count		
SEX	CLASS	ENB
SEX	DISCIP	FNB

Z4		
E : Count		Ø
F : Count		
F	Farmers	150
F	Workers	320
F	Tradesmen	405
M	Farmers	102
M	Workers	370
M	Tradesmen	390
F	Computer sciences	294
F	Mathematics	212
F	Physics	120
M	Computer sciences	350
M	Mathematics	195
M	Physics	164

Fig. 4. Z4 schema and extension

5 Matrix relation language - MARELA

In this section, we describe MARELA but, first of all, in order to emphasize its interests, we give the functions that a manipulation language for SDB must offer according to us.

5.1 Operation classes on SDB

To properly achieve workable SDB, it is necessary to propose suitable summary manipulation capabilities. For this reason, an identification of specific needs of statisticians is essential. Some of them have been suggested in [18, 25, 29]. We keep and complete them through the following generic classification: Composition, Filter and Transposition operations.

Composition. In research works whose major objective deals with complex summary modeling, composition facilities are strongly required. They concern the building up of more complex summaries. We think that statisticians cannot satisfy their needs with elementary summary manipulation. A significant example, illustrating this need, is to consider an elementary summary and the totals derived from the aggregation of several (or all) category attributes. Associating these totals with the macro-data from which they are computed (in order to manipulate them as a whole), imperatively requires capabilities of complex summary modeling. A data structure allowing complex summary representation may be, if required compositions are supplied, an interesting tool for grouping elementary statistical summaries. Such groupings may be operated to make comparisons but also to optimize storage (by sharing common data). They also may be perceived as an organization tool for SDB. Actually gathering coherent summaries can facilitate the retrieval of relevant ones. This last objective is particularly interesting when considering summary proliferation.

Filter. To allow users to select relevant data within a summary, filter operations must be supplied. They work on attribute value sets, by refining or enlarging them. They also permit to extract a summary belonging to a more complex one. The first purpose of these manipulations is macro-data retrieval but they also play a part in the joining of statistical summaries with homogeneous, but nevertheless different, multidimensional spaces. However the main operations in this class refer to summary aggregation. It consists in removing one or several category attributes whilst operating an aggregation of the corresponding summary values, in order to achieve a summary with a coarser level of detail than the initial one. This class must also propose calculus operators.

Transposition. One of the identified needs for summary manipulation is to introduce a dynamic aspect in the summary structure [19]. Actually the data structure must be able to change, i.e. to be restructured according to user requests. These reorganizations, that we call transpositions, have a presentation goal, since they allow users to examine data exactly the way they want to. They also take an important part in the joining of statistical summaries that are organized in a different way but with homogeneous multidimensional spaces. Transpositions are also essential when combined with summary aggregation and composition.

5.2 Principle of MARELA language

Based on relational primitives, MARELA makes also use of the relational aggregation operator, defined by Klug [15], and of the outer joins [9]. The former permits to create aggregated relations and the latter play a part in MR compositions.
MARELA proposes an arithmetical aggregation to complete A. Klug's one and two operators RELATION and MATRIX, that perform the translation between the two data structures being used. To prepare the conversion between relation and AMR, the DPJOIN operator is proposed.
RELATION and MATRIX seem, at least in their principle, like the Nest and Unnest operators, being proposed in N1NF relational models [1]. But the latter proceed to the creation of a hierarchical and then a "flat" structure even through the operators that we introduce create a matrix and then a "flat" structure.
Every time it is possible MARELA makes use of relational algebra to manipulate summaries and when this algebra cannot answer the needs, it proposes specific operators. Consequently we can offer the user possibilities to make aggregations which are controled and really adapted to summaries. We also come up to users' expectations in matter of summary reorganization. The different operators defined for this goal, have few equivalents in the other approaches of summary management. Nevertheless, they answer a need considered as essential by the specialists. MARELA also propose calculus operators that achieve the same results as calculable functions used over raw data. For lack of space, they are not presented in this paper [16].
MARELA encompasses possibilities of creation, transposition, composition and aggregation with additive functions of complex statistical summaries. The principle of MARELA is illustrated in the figure 5.

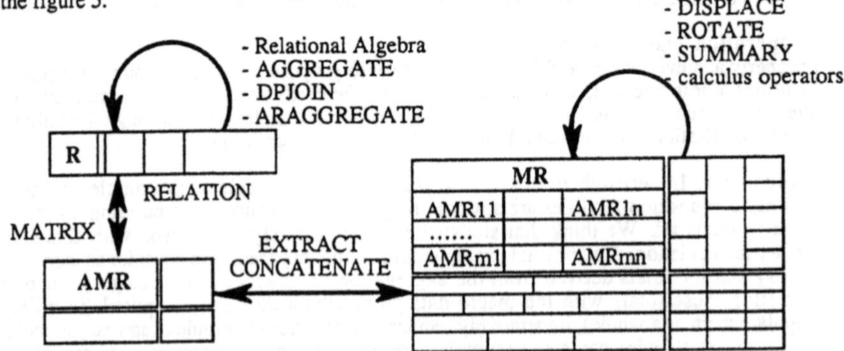

Fig. 5. MARELA principle

5.3 Algebraic operators

This sub-section gives a survey on the three components of MARELA language, i.e. an extended relational algebra, primitives consecrated to the structure translation and specific operators to manipulate MRs. For each component, we pinpoint the more interesting operators.

manipulate MRs. For each component, we pinpoint the more interesting operators.

Extended relational algebra:
Relational algebra is really suitable to manipulate raw data since they are not very different from classical data in management applications. However, the summary creation possibilities are too restrictive. Actually, in a statistical context, the aggregations and arithmetical calculations must be combined to produce the required parameters of calculable functions (for example sum of products, sum of square, ...). MARELA language offers this possibility through the ARAGGREGATE operator. It is defined as follows:
Let R(U) be a relation, X a subset of U attributes, t[X] the projected tuple t on X, f a statistical additive function, A and B two numerical attributes of U that are not necessarily distinct.

ARAGGREGATE(R(X), f(op(A,B) = Y) = R'(X,Y)
$= \{t[X] \circ y \,/\, t \in R \text{ and } y = f(op(t'[A], t'[B]))/\, t' \in R \text{ and } t'[X] = t[X]\}$

where op is one of the basic arithmetical operators and o stands for concatenation.
Such an operator, after a preliminary grouping of tuples, makes for each tuple an arithmetical calculation from the values of two numerical attributes and adds up the achieved results for each stated classe of tuples.

To translate a relation R(X, Y, Z), with |Z| = 1, and $X \cup Y \rightarrow Z$, into an AMR(Xr, Xc, V, f), the join dependency $\oplus$(X, Y) must be hold in $\Pi_{X,Y}(R)$, (Π is the project operator symbol), since there is a summary value $v_{P(tr), P(tc)}$ for each couple (tr, tc). If a relation does not satisfy this dependency, DPJOIN must be applied. It is is defined as follows:
let R(U) be a relation, X and Y two subsets of U such that the join dependency $\oplus$(X, Y) is not hold in $\Pi_{X,Y}(R)$.

$$\text{DPJOIN}(R(X, Y)) = \underset{X \cup Y = X \cup Y}{\circledR} (R, \otimes(\Pi_X(R), \Pi_Y(R)))$$

where ® is the symbol of the right outer join and ⊗ stands for the Cartesian-product.

The join dependency $\oplus$(X, Y) is hold in R'.

Example 7. The DPJOIN operator is illustrated in the following figure, where:
R' = DPJOIN(R({x, y}, {z})

R

x	y	z	w
x1	y1	z1	1
x1	y1	z2	2
x1	y2	z1	3
x1	y2	z2	4
x2	y1	z1	5

R'

x	y	z	w
x1	y1	z1	1
x1	y1	z2	2
x1	y2	z1	3
x1	y2	z2	4
x2	y1	z1	5
x2	y1	z2	NULL

Fig. 6. DPJOIN illustration

Translation operators:
To allow the AMR creation from relation and conversely, we introduce the primitives MATRIX and RELATION. They make up a bridge between relation and MR structures.
Aggregated relations, achieved by AGGREGATE or ARAGGREGATE, may be converted into AMRs using the MATRIX operator. To perform such a translation, the aggregated relation must represent an elementary summary and have to satisfy the two following constraints :
- it exists a functional dependency between all the category attributes and the summary one;
- a join dependency is hold in the projection of the relation on category attributes.

The MATRIX operator is defined as follows :
AMR = MATRIX(R(X, Y, Z), f) with :
SCHEMA(AMR) = (Xr, Xc, V, f) and, Xr = X, Xc = Y, V = Z.

EXTENSION(AMR)
= (VAL(Xr), VAL(Xc), M(V)) where :
VAL(Xr) = ΠX(R), VAL(Xc) = ΠY(R) and,
M(V) = [$v_{P(tr),P(tc)}$] / ∀ t ∈ R, $v_{P(tr),P(tc)}$ = t[Z], where tr = t[X], tc = t[Y].

Example 8. The AMR represented in the following figure is built up, from the relation R' of the previous example, as follows: AMR = MATRIX(R', {x, y}, {z}, w, 'Count')

AMR': Count		z
x	y	w

AMR': Count		z1	z2
x1	y1	1	2
x1	y2	3	4
x2	y1	5	NULL

Fig. 7. AMR schema and extension

When the DPJOIN result is converted into an AMR, by MATRIX, the introduced null values have the following semantics. They are considered like 0 if the function used to aggregated the relation is Sum or Count. They are similar to $-\infty$ or $+\infty$ if the statistical function is Max or Min.

The RELATION operator performs the reverse translation. It creates an aggregated relation from an AMR. It is defined as follows :
RELATION(AMR(Xr , Xc, V, f)) = R(X, Y, Z)
= {t / t[X] = tl, t[Y] = tc, t[Z] = vP(tr),P(tc)} with X ∪ Y → Z.

Example 9. This operator, applied on the AMR illustrated in the figure 7, gives as result the relation R' of the figure 6.

Specific operators on MRs :
To manipulate summaries, MARELA makes use of relational algebra. But it cannot be sufficient to answer statisticians' needs. This is why we propose some additional operators, working on one or two MRs and achieving a new one.
In the composition class, we define the CONCATENATE operator. It allows to gather completely compatible MRs, in order to achieve a more complex one. It is defined as follows :
Let MR1 and MR2 be the two following MRs :
MR1 = [AMRm1,n1] and MR2 = [AMRm2,n2]

CONCATENATE(d, MR1, MR2)

= [AMRm1+m2, n1]

if d = 'c', i.e. MR1 and MR2 are completely compatible according to columns.

or

= [AMRm1, n1+n2]

if d = 'r', i.e. MR1 and MR2 are completely compatible according to rows.

Example 10. To build up the MR Z1 (figure 3) from A, B, C and D (figures 1 and 2), the following operations are used: Z2 = CONCATENATE('r', A, B)
Z3 = CONCATENATE('r', C, D) Z1 = CONCATENATE('c', Z2, Z3)

Two filter operators in MARELA are EXTRACT and SUMMARY. The first one extracts a MR from a more complex one. We consider the MR = [$AMR_{m,n}$]
EXTRACT(MR, [$AMR_{m1,n1}$]) = [$AMR_{m1,n1}$] with m1 ≤ m and n1 ≤ n.
Example 11. Z3 = EXTRACT(Z1, [C, D])

The SUMMARY operators provide MR aggregations, by removing one or several category attribute and summing up the associated summary values. Before this calculation, SUMMARY makes sure that additive functions characterized the MR to be aggregated.

The SUMMARY formal definition is given in [17].
Example 12 : AMR'' = SUMMARY(AMR', y).

AMR'': Count	z
x	w

AMR'': Count	z1	z2
x1	4	6
x2	5	NULL

Fig. 8 . AMR' schema and extension

The transposition class is made up of two basic operators : DISPLACE, ROTATE. The first one modifies the order of category attributes within a schema. The second one changes the dimension to which a category attribute belongs.
Let's note that CONCATENATE and EXTRACT may play a transposition part by offering possibilities of dynamic modifications of the schema order within a multi-schema.
We do not present here the formal definitions of the transposition primitives. They are given in [17]. But we emphasize their importance, particularly in a grouping process of MRs, with an example.
Example 13. Let C' be an AMR (the AMR C (figures 1 and 2) is supposed to be derived from C', and is informationnaly equivalent to it, i.e. RELATION(C') = RELATION(C)). Its schema and instances are given in figure 9.

C': Count			GRANT_H
SEX	DISCIP	YEAR	C'NB

C': Count			Yes	No
F	Computer sciences	1	25	39
F	Computer sciences	2	24	33
F	Mathematics	1	18	21
F	Mathematics	2	15	20
F	Physics	1	27	14
M	Physics	2	20	18
M	Computer sciences	1	38	37
M	Computer sciences	2	20	42
M	Mathematics	1	17	29
M	Mathematics	2	19	20
M	Physics	1	25	23
M	Physics	2	25	25

Fig. 9. C' Schema and extension

Transposition possibilities allow to group together A and C' (by using CONCATENATE operator), after having transformed C' into C, by using ROTATE operator, in order to have the column category attribute schema: [YEAR].

Finally complementary filter operations are provided through relational primitives. For instance, outer joins may be used to produce aggregated relations which are completely compatible. This possibility is important particularly when considering the complete compatibility constraint of CONCATENATE operator.

6 Conclusion

The great difference between raw and summary data has convinced us that a twofold structure is necessary to represent them in a suitable way. Furthermore they must be manipulated through adapted (and consequently different) operators. With MARELA, we propose a formal framework for SDB management. The MR data structure is really suitable for summary representation. To make sure that its advantages are convincing, let's have a short comparison with the models examined in the third section.

From a structural point of view, MR is beyond relation and nested relation, for at least two reasons. The first one concerns the distinction between category and summary attributes. The second refers to its ability to represent summaries without restrictions on their multidimensional space sets. This last argument may also be used in the comparison with summary modeling approaches. Furthermore, the latter do not offer a rigourous frame for summary representation. Nevertheless, we think that such a frame is strongly required, at least to be a solid base to define manipulation operators.
Another interesting point is that elementary summaries are explicit within MRs. This is important to make the structure easy to comprehend for the user and to facilitate his interpretation of data. Finally, MR proposes to capture summary attribute semantics, by integrating the functions used to calculate the macro-data sets.

From a functional point of view, MARELA encompasses operators for each class of SBD manipulations. We note that no satisfying answer is made in other approaches for transpositions and aggregations. Since these operations are the most common ones in SDB, particular efforts have been made to integrate related primitives in MARELA. In our model, MR structure may be reorganized through the two transposition operators in order to satisfy statisticians' needs. Summary aggregations are intentionally limited to the correct ones, i.e. they cannot create wrong summary values. Another strength of MARELA is the formal description of the combined use of relations and MRs. We propose conversion primitives and enrich the relational algebra to properly achieve workable translations.
A final pratical advantage of our approach must be noted. MARELA may be implemented using a relational DBMS as support. A prototype has been developped on ORACLE with a dictionary approach.

Without reopening the whole question, we note a constraint inherent to MARELA approach : the resorting to relational algebra for summary handling is not an ideal solution. Actually, the user must pay particular attention to relational primitives as they may create macro-data sets which are semantically wrong. Furthermore they imply multiple conversions between the two structures. To avoid this difficulty, it is necessary to propose some new operators on MRs (and to eliminate the RELATION operator). They would perform on summaries the operations made through relational algebra, i.e. filter operations as selections, additional composition facilities like outer joins or calculus operators. There is no particular difficulty to define and integrate them in MARELA [16]. So, it is quite easy to avoid the mentionned constraint whilst preserving all the advantages previously detailed.

7 References

[1] Abiteboul S., Fischer P. C., Schek H. J. (Eds), "Nested Relations and Complex Objects in Databases", Lecture Notes in Computer Science, Vol. 361, Springer Verlag, 1989.

[2] Abiteboul S., Bidoit N., "Non first normal form relation - An algebra allowing data restructuring", Journal of computer and system sciences, Vol. 33, 1986, pp. 361-393.

[3] Adam N. R., Wortmann J. C., "Security-Control Methods for Statistical Databases : A Comparative Study", ACM Computing Survey, Vol. 21, 1989, pp. 514-556.

[4] Batini C., Di Battista G. " Design of Statistical Databases : A Methodology for the Conceptual Step", Information Systems Vol. 13, N° 4, 1988.

[5] Catarci T., D'angiolini G., Lenzerini M., "Conceptual Definition Language for Statistical Data Modelling", Proceedings of the International Conference on Very Large Databases, Brisbane, Australia 1990.

[6] Chen M.C., McNamee L., "On the Data Model and Access Method of Summary Data Management", IEEE Transaction on Knowledge and Data Engineering, Vol. 1, 1989, pp. 519-529.

[7] Cicchetti R., Lakhal L., Miranda S., " Matrix Relational Model For Statistical Database Management", Database Systems For Next-Generation Applications : Principales and Practice. Word Scientific Publishing, 1992, pp. 156-169. W. Kim, Y. Kambayashi, In Sup Paik (Eds.).

[8] Cicchetti R., "Contribution à la modélisation des résumés dans les bases de données statistiques", Thèse de Doctorat, Université de Nice, Juin 1990.

[9] Codd E. F., "The relational model for database management. Version 2", Ed. Addison-Wesley , 1990.

[10] Fortunato E., Rafanelli M., Ricci F. L., Sebastio A., "An Algebra for Statistical Data" , in Proceedings of the International Conference on Statistical and Scientific Database Management, 1986, pp. 122-134.

[11] Ghosh S. P., "Statistical Relational Databases : Normal Forms", IEEE Transaction on Knowledge and Data Engineering, Vol.3, 1991, pp. 55-64.

[12] Ghosh S. P., "Statisticians and Statistical Database Management", IBM Research Report N° RJ 6975, San Jose, 1989.

[13] Ghosh S. P., "Numerical Operations On Relational Database", IEEE Transaction on Software Engineering, Vol. 15, 1989, pp. 600-610.

[14] Ghosh S. P., "Statistical Relational Tables for Statistical Database Management", IEEE Transaction on Software Engineering, Vol. 12, 1986, pp. 1106-1116.

[15] Klug A, "Equivalence of Relational Algebra and Relational Calculus Query Languages Having Aggregate Functions", ACM Transaction On Database Systems, Vol. 29, 1982, pp. 699-717.

[16] Lakhal L., Cicchetti R., "STAR+, un langage de manipulation de résumés statistiques structurés", Revue AFCET-DUNOD RAIRO-Recherche opérationnelle, Vol. 24 N°4, pp. 365-432, 1990.

[17] Lakhal L., Cicchetti R. , Miranda S., "Complex-Statistical-Table Structure and Operators for Macro Statistical Databases", Foundations of Data Organization and Algorithms. Lecture Notes in Computer Science, Vol. 367, Springer Verlag, 1989, pp. 421-438.

[18] Olken F., Rotem D., Shoshani A., Wong H. K. T., "Scientific and Statistical Data Management Research at LBL", Proceedings of the International Conference on Statistical and Scientific Database Management, 1986, pp. 1-20.

[19] Olken F., "Physical Database Support for Scientific and Statistical Database Management", Proceedings of the International Conference on Statistical and Scientific Database Management, 1986, pp. 44-60.

[20] Özsoyoglu G., Özsoyoglu Z. M. , "Statistical Database Query Languages", IEEE Transaction on Software Engineering, Vol. 11, 1985, pp. 1071-1081.

[21] Özsoyoglu G., Matos V., Özsoyoglu Z. M., "Extending Relational Algebra and Relational Calculus With Set-Valued Attributes and Aggregate Functions", ACM Transaction On Database Systems, Vol. 12, 1987, pp.566-592.

[22] Özsoyoglu G., Matos V., Özsoyoglu Z. M., "Query Processing Techniques in the Summary-Table-By-Example Database Query Language", ACM Transaction On Database Systems, Vol. 14, 1989, pp.526-573.

[23] Rafanelli M., Ricci F. L., "STAQUEL : A Query Language for Satistical Macro Database Management Systems", in Proceedings of Convention Informatique Latine, 1985, pp. 16-19.

[24] Sheck H. J., Sholl M. H., "An Algebra for Relational Model With Relation-Valued Attributes", Information Systems, Vol. 11, 1986, pp.137-147.

[25] Shoshani A., Wong H.K.T., "Statistical and Scientific Database Issues", IEEE Transaction on Software Engineering, Vol. 11, 1985, pp. 1071-1081.

[26] Shoshani A., "Statistical Databases : Characteristics, Problems and some Solutions", in Proceedings of the International Conference on Very Large Databases, 1982, pp. 147-160.

[27] Stonebraker M. (Ed.), "Special Issue on Database Prototype Systems". IEEE Transactions on Knowledge and Data Engineering, Vol.2, N°1, 1990.

[28] Su S. Y. W., "SAM* : A Semantic Association Model for Corporate and Scientific-Statistical Databases", Information Science, Vol. 29, 1983, pp. 151-199.

[29] Wong H. K.T., "Micro and Macro Statistical / Scientific Database Management", in Proceedings of the IEEE International Conference on Data Engineering, 1984, pp. 104-110.

Deductive Database Support for Data Visualization

Mariano P. Consens, Alberto O. Mendelzon and Dimitra Vista

{consens,mendel,vista}@db.toronto.edu
Department of Computer Science
University of Toronto
Toronto, Canada M5S 1A4

Abstract. We describe how deductive database technology can support data visualization. In particular we show how we have used the deductive languages LDL and CORAL for the implementation of the visual query language GraphLog. We discuss in detail the translation function from GraphLog to each of LDL and CORAL, considering aggregation as well. We also present an example of using GraphLog and its environment Hy$^+$ in order to support software design understanding.

1 Introduction

The data used in new applications of database technology, such as CAD/CAM, hypertext, software development support, and network management, often have graph-like structures that can be exploited to provide visual presentations of the data and visual query mechanisms. Many of the operations that arise naturally in such visual environments involve pattern matching and finding and traversing paths of various kinds. Such operations are beyond the power of first-order query languages such as relational algebra and SQL; they require additional expressive power, as provided by deductive databases such as LDL [12] or CORAL [13].

In this paper we show how deductive databases can help support the growing demand for visible and visualizable data and for queries and operations on such data. We do so in the context of the Hy$^+$ visualization system [7] and the database query language GraphLog [1, 6]. As a graphical formalism for visual manipulation of database visualizations, GraphLog is especially suitable for application areas where the data exhibit certain graphical structures, such as system design and software development [9], network monitoring [3], and hypertext [5]. The current version of the Hy$^+$ system, under development at the University of Toronto, implements GraphLog by mapping visual GraphLog queries to Horn clauses which are compiled and executed by one of several deductive back-ends, including Prolog, LDL, and CORAL.

The rest of the paper is organized as follows. In Section 2, we show, using an example from the software design field, how Hy$^+$ and GraphLog are used to manipulate visual data in a visual way. Section 3 briefly introduces GraphLog. Section 4 describes the translation from GraphLog to LDL and CORAL. Emphasis is placed on the implementation of aggregate functions. We conclude in Section 5.

2 Data Visualization Example

In this section we present an example of using GraphLog and its environment Hy$^+$ for visualizing the structure of an OOT program. OOT is an object-oriented programming language and its programming environment [11] contains a variety of tools. One of them, the Software Landscape, is a tool that displays a complete and concise graphical description (the Landscape) of the architecture of a system at various levels of granularity.

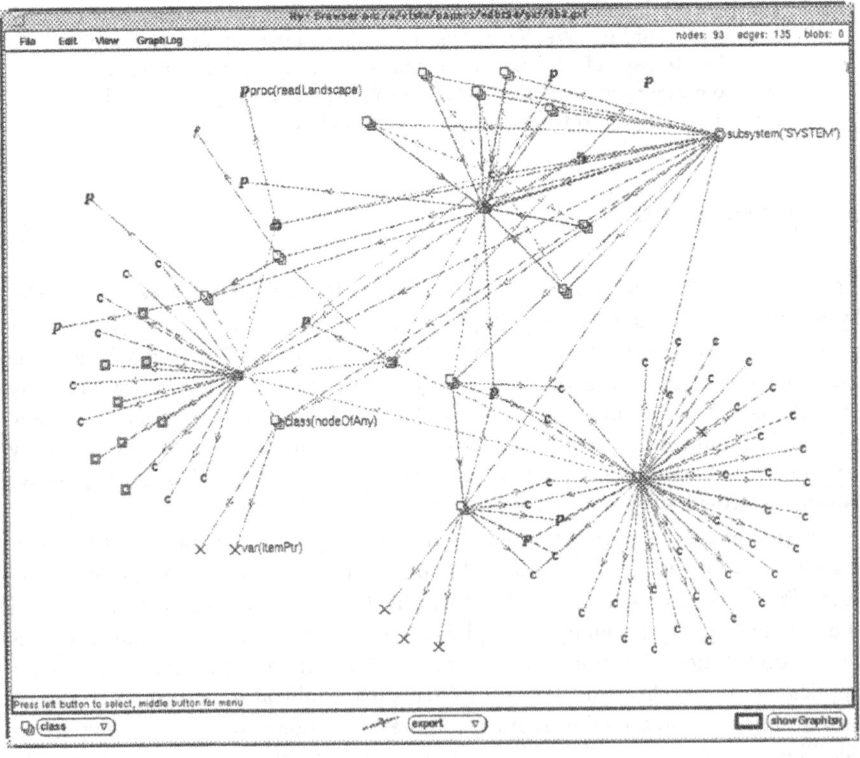

Fig. 1. The database describing the software Landscape

The Software Landscape provides a static visualization of the architecture of a system. GraphLog queries permit a more flexible approach to the visualization process where the user can obtain different visualizations of the same component through different queries.

Landscapes have a set of entities including classes, modules, subsystems, libraries, etc., which are interrelated through relations. Among them are:

- the relation `contain(X,Y)` that states that entity `X` contains sub-entity `Y`,
- the relation `export(X,Y)` that states that entity `X` allows access to its contained entity `Y`,
- the relation `import(X,Y)` that states that an entity `X` accesses external entity `Y`.

The database of Figure 1 depicts the organization of these relations for the specific Landscape of the OOT program that we imported into Hy$^+$. The edges are color-coded according to the predicate name labelling them. Different icons are displayed according to the functor labelling the the nodes, e.g., **P** refers to procedures, **C** refers to constants (i.e., the tokens of the code), **X** to variables, **f** to functions, the icon with the three overlapping pages is for classes, and so on. To avoid clutter, only a few textual labels that were interactively selected have been turned on.

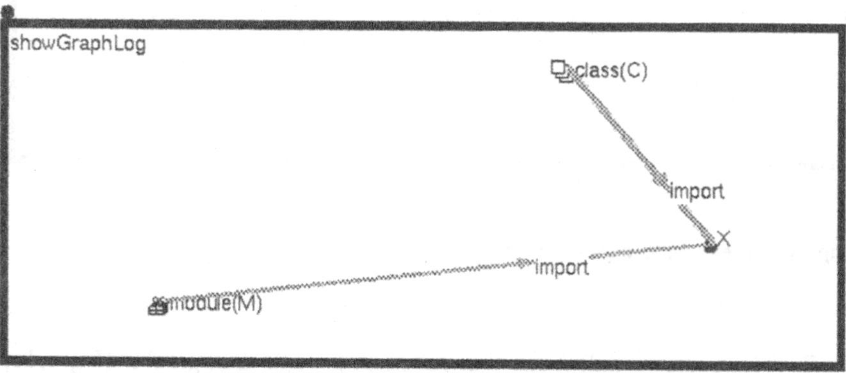

Fig. 2. An example *filter* query

Any visualization within Hy$^+$ can be queried. Figure 2 contains a GraphLog expression inside a box labelled **showGraphLog**, known as a *filter query*. Filter queries (introduced in [2]) are at the core of Hy$^+$'s capabilities for manipulating database visualizations, as opposed to just querying databases. Informally, when executing a query in *filter* mode the pattern does not define any new relation, but it filters out information from the input visualization to produce an output visualization that contains the union of all the sub-hygraphs in the input that match the query pattern. As one can see in the figure, one of the edges in the pattern is thicker. This is a visual way of distinguishing edges that the user actually wants to see after the match is found. This particular filter query searches the database for all pairs of classes `C` and modules `M` that both import the same entity `X`, and for each such pair it displays only the `import` relation for the classes that are found.

The GraphLog expression inside the **`defineGraphLog`** in Figure 3 describes a *define query.* A thick edge here has a different meaning. It represents a relation that is defined every time the pattern consisting of all the other edges in the query is found in the database. The *define* query in Figure 3 searches for the same pairs of classes `C` and modules `M` and defines the new relation `common_import` between them.

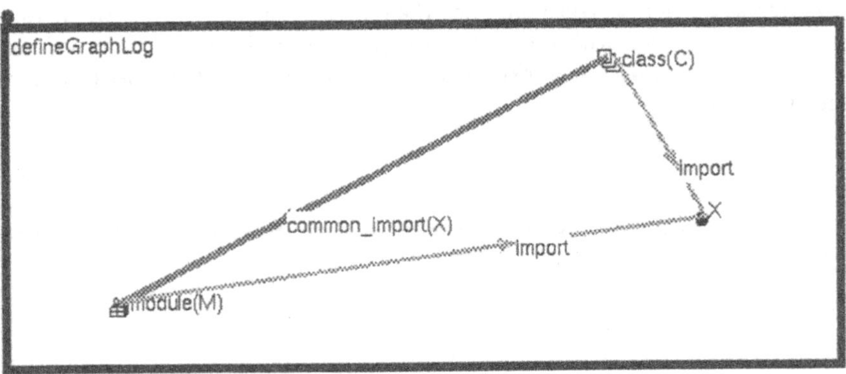

Fig. 3. An example *define* query

Hy$^+$ supports visualizations that are more general than graphs. Hygraphs, defined in [2], are a hybrid between Harel's higraphs [10] and directed hypergraphs. Hygraphs use *blobs* in addition to edges to represent relationships among nodes. A blob in a hygraph represents a relation between a node (called the container node) and a set of nodes (called the contained nodes). Blobs are hence generalizations of edges and can be used to cluster related nodes together. Visually they are represented as a rectangular area associated with the container node. The define query of Figure 4 demonstrates how we can change the representation of a relationship from edges to blobs. The blob `contents` clusters together the sub-entities contained in some entity: an entity labeled `E` is enclosed in the blob whose container node is labeled `C`, whenever `contain(C, E)` holds. The filter query in Figure 4 (defined by the three `showGraphLog` boxes) produces a hygraph with `contents` blobs and `import` and `inherit` edges.

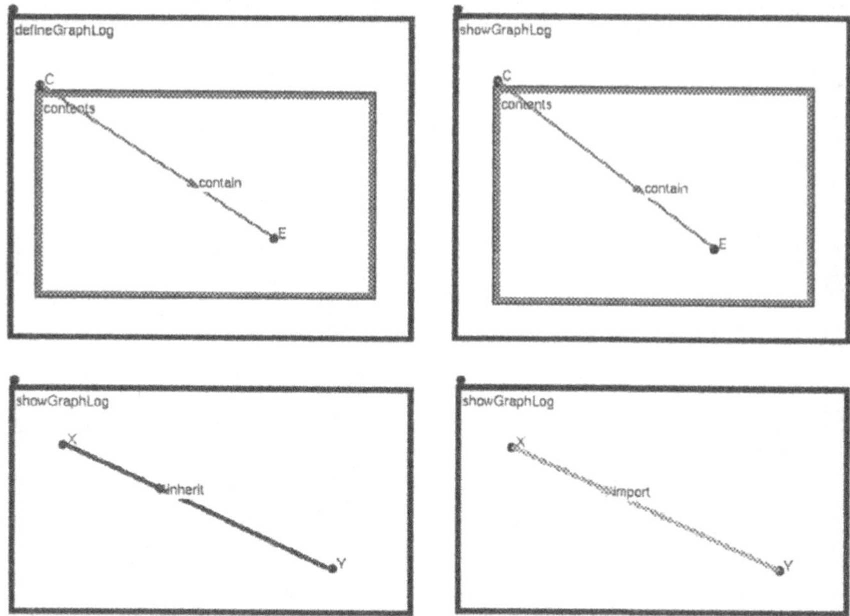

Fig. 4. Define and show queries to produce a hygraph

When Hy$^+$ executes the queries in Figure 4 against the database of Figure 1, the result is the hygraph visualized in Figure 5.

3 GraphLog in Hy$^+$

In this section we give a more precise definition of GraphLog, and we describe how it is used in the Hy$^+$ system. GraphLog database visualizations and query expressions are based on the notion of hygraphs.

In GraphLog, a *term* is a one of a constant, a variable, an anonymous variable (as in Prolog), an aggregate function $f \in$ { MAX, MIN, COUNT, SUM, AVG} applied to a variable, or a functor f applied to a number of terms. An *edge (blob) label* is a *path regular expression* generated by the following grammar, where $\bar{T}$ is a sequence of terms and p is a predicate:

$$E \leftarrow E|E; E.E; -E; \neg E; (E); E+; E*; p(\bar{T})$$

Database instances are hygraphs whose nodes are labelled with ground terms and whose edges and blobs are labelled with predicates. Database instances of the object-oriented or relational model can easily be visualized as hygraphs.

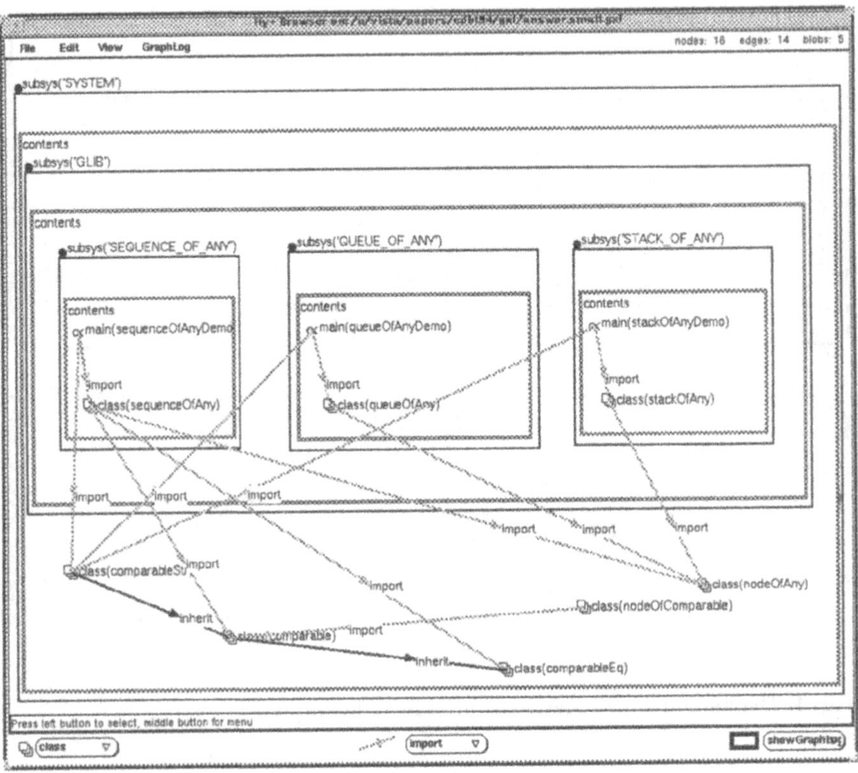

Fig. 5. The result of filtering **contents**

For example, an edge (blob) labelled $p(\bar{X})$ from a node labelled T_1 to a node (containing a node) labelled T_2 corresponds to tuple $(T_1, T_2, \bar{X})$ of relation p in the relational model.

Queries are sets of hygraphs whose nodes are labelled by terms and each edge (blob) is labelled by an edge (blob) label. There are two types of queries: *define* and *filter*. In both types, the query hygraph represents a pattern; the query evaluator searches the database hygraph for all occurrences of that pattern. The difference between the two types of queries stems from their interpretation of *distinguished elements*, explained below.

A hygraph pattern in a **defineGraphLog** blob must have one *distinguished* edge or blob, labeled by a positive literal. The meaning of the *define* query hygraph is to define the predicate in this distinguished literal in terms of the rest of the pattern. The semantics of *define* queries is given by a translation to stratified Datalog. Each *define* hygraph G translates to a rule with the label of the distinguished edge or blob in the head, and as many literals in the body as there are non-distinguished edges and blobs in G. For example, the meaning of the query of Figure 3 is the following: `common_import(class(C), module(M))` ← `import(class(C), X), import(module(M), X).`

It has been shown elsewhere [1, 6] that the expressive power of GraphLog is the same as stratified linear Datalog, the same as first-order logic with transitive closure, and the same as non-deterministic logarithmic space, when an ordering in the domain is assumed.

A hygraph pattern in a **showGraphLog** blob may have several *distinguished* nodes, edges and blobs. The meaning of a *filter* query hygraph is: for each instance of the pattern found in the database, retain the database objects that match the distinguished objects in the query. As an example, consider again the hygraph of Figure 2. The pattern requested consists of all pairs of classes `C` and modules `M` that import the same entity `X`. From the portions of the database that match this pattern only the `import` relation is displayed to the user. From a logic programming point of view, a define query corresponds to a conventional set of Horn clauses defining a certain predicate, while a filter query can be viewed as a set of Horn clause *bodies* in which certain literals are retained after each match and the rest are discarded. In a way, define queries generate *theorems* while filter queries generate *proofs*.

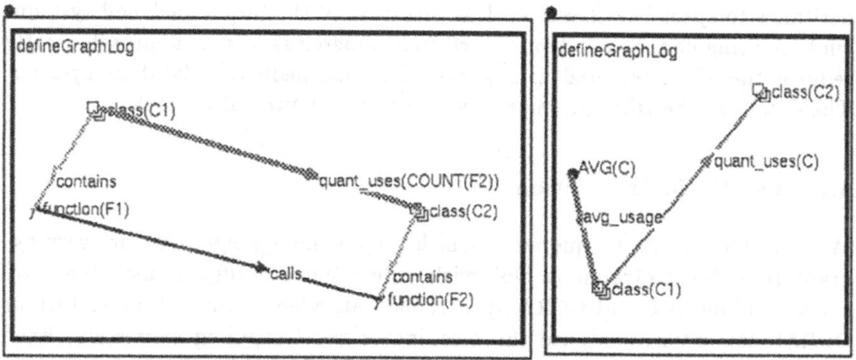

Fig. 6. An example with aggregate functions

GraphLog has the ability to collect multisets of tuples and to compute aggregate functions on them. These functions allow the specification of a large class of queries not expressible in relational algebra or relational calculus. The aggregate functions supported in GraphLog are the unary operators MAX, MIN, COUNT, SUM, and AVG. They are allowed to appear in the arguments of the distinguished relation of a *define* query as well as in its incident nodes. As an example of the use of aggregation in GraphLog, consider the two **defineGraphLog** blobs of Figure 6. The first one defines the relation `quant_uses` as follows: the relation `quant_uses(C1, C2, C)` is defined between two classes `C1` and `C2`, whenever `C1` contains a function `F1` such that `F1` calls `C` functions `F2` that are contained in class `C2`. The second pattern defines the relation **avg_usage** as follows: the relation **avg_usage** is defined between a class `C1` and a number `C`, if `C` is the average of all numbers `C` that count the number of calls from functions of class `C1` to functions of some other class `C2`. Note there is no explicit `GROUP BY` list (as in SQL). Instead, grouping is done implicitly over all variables appearing in the distinguished edge and its endpoints.

In this paper we are only concerned with non-recursive aggregation. For a review of recursive aggregation in GraphLog see [8].

4 Translating GraphLog

This section describes the translation from GraphLog to LDL [12] and CORAL [13]. The translation of a program resembles the logical function used to define the semantics of GraphLog in terms of Datalog programs [1, 6]. An alternative optimized translation is described in [14].

Since Hy$^+$ is implemented in the Smalltalk object oriented programming language, we were able to encapsulate within classes the functionality that deals with parsing and translating **defineGraphLog** blobs. In addition, we used inheritance to specialize classes to deal with each of the target back-end systems, while re-using common code inherited from superclasses. This approach greatly reduces the effort required to support additional deductive database systems. The details of the translation are given in the next two subsections.

4.1 The Basic Translation

We consider first *define* queries in which there is no aggregation. For every hygraph in a **defineGraphLog** blob with a distinguished edge or blob there are corresponding LDL and CORAL programs that, when evaluated under LDL or CORAL semantics, compute the meaning of the GraphLog expression. Each **defineGraphLog** blob corresponds to a set of logical rules that expresses the relation labelling the distinguished edge or blob in terms of the literals that correspond to the non-distinguished edges and blobs in the hygraph. Additional rules may be necessary to define these literals. For example, a transitive closure relation requires two rules to be defined.

We describe the translation to LDL below and provide a sample of the output code produced by Hy$^+$. The basic translation (no aggregation) to CORAL [13] is almost identical, except for some trivial syntactic differences between the two languages. The main difference is that CORAL requires the information to be organized into modules. Every GraphLog *define* query is translated into a module that defines the predicates indicated by the distinguished edges of the query. This module exports the query form that is generated by the query.

Let $P(\bar{T})$ be the label of the distinguished edge (blob) e in the *define* hygraph with non-distinguished edges e_i. Also suppose that the nodes incident to e (the container node and a containing node) have labels T_1 and T_2. Program P produced by the translation contains the rule

$$p_e(T_1, T_2, \bar{T}) \leftarrow p_{e_1}(\bar{X}_1), \ldots, p_{e_n}(\bar{X}_n).$$

where p_{e_i} is the predicate of the relation of e_i. In particular, if edge e_i is incident to nodes with labels X_1 and X_2 and $\bar{X} \equiv X_1, X_2, \bar{X}_3$, then

1. if e_i is $p(\bar{X}_3)$, then $p_{e_i}(\bar{X}_i)$ is $p(X_1, X_2, \bar{X}_3)$,
2. if e_i is $\neg p(\bar{X}_3)$, then $p_{e_i}(\bar{X})$ is $\neg p(X_1, X_2, \bar{X}_3)$,
3. otherwise $p_{e_i}(\bar{X})$ is defined by the following rules (also in P):
   - $p_{e_i}(X_1, X_2, \bar{X}_3) \leftarrow p_{e_1}(X_1, X_2, \bar{X}_3)$, if $e_i \equiv (e_1)$,
   - $p_{e_i}(X_2, X_1, \bar{X}_3) \leftarrow p_{e_1}(X_1, X_2, \bar{X}_3)$, if $e_i \equiv -e_1$,
   - $p_{e_i}(X_1, X_2, \bar{X}_3) \leftarrow p_{e_1}(X_1, X_2, \bar{X}_3)$, and
     $p_{e_i}(X_1, X_2, \bar{X}_3) \leftarrow p_{e_1}(X_1, Y, \bar{X}_3), p_{e_i}(Y, X_2, \bar{X}_3)$, if $e_i \equiv e_1+$,
   - $p_{e_i}(X_1, X_1, \bar{X}_3) \leftarrow p_{e_1}(X_1, X_2, \bar{X}_3)$, and
     $p_{e_i}(X_2, X_2, \bar{X}_3) \leftarrow p_{e_1}(X_1, X_2, \bar{X}_3)$, and
     $p_{e_i}(X_1, X_2, \bar{X}_3) \leftarrow p_{e_1}(X_1, Y, \bar{X}_3), p_{e_i}(Y, X_2, \bar{X}_3)$, if $e_i \equiv e_1*$.
   - $p_{e_i}(X_1, X_2, \bar{X}_3) \leftarrow p_{e_1}(X_1, X_2, \bar{X}_3)$, and
     $p_{e_i}(X_1, X_2, \bar{X}_3) \leftarrow p_{e_2}(X_1, X_2, \bar{X}_3)$, if $e_i \equiv e_1 \mid e_2$,
   - $p_{e_i}(X_1, X_2, \bar{X}_3) \leftarrow p_{e_1}(X_1, Y, \bar{X}_3), p_{e_2}(Y, X_2, \bar{X}_3)$, if $e_i \equiv e_1 \, . \, e_2$.

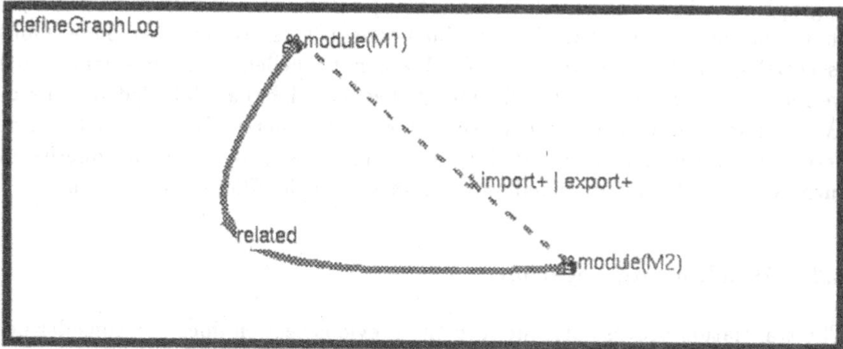

Fig. 7. The relation `related`

The query hygraph in Figure 7 defines the relation `related`: a module `M1` is related to module `M2`, if `M1` either imports or exports `M2`, directly or indirectly. The translation produced by Hy$^+$ is:

```
related(module(M1), module(M2)) ← alter(module(M1), module(M2)).

alter(module(M1), module(M2)) ← tc_import(module(M1), module(M2)).
alter(module(M1), module(M2)) ← tc_export(module(M1), module(M2)).

tc_import(Xtemp1, Ytemp1) ← import(Xtemp1, Ytemp1).
tc_import(Xtemp1, Ytemp1) ← import(Xtemp1, Ztemp1),
                            tc_import(Ztemp1, Ytemp1).

tc_export(Xtemp1, Ytemp1) ← export(Xtemp1, Ytemp1).
tc_export(Xtemp1, Ytemp1) ← export(Xtemp1, Ztemp1),
                            tc_export(Ztemp1, Ytemp1).
```

We now turn our attention to describing the translation of *filter* queries. Originally, hygraphs in **showGraphLog** blobs were implemented by translating them to sets of define queries (in a process outlined below). The motivation for this approach was to speed up development by directly reusing existing code. We later modified the translation to generate a single CORAL module per filter query.

Given a hygraph G in a **showGraphLog** blob, for each distinguished edge (blob) e, we generate a set of *define* queries that *match* e, i.e., when evaluated they determine all e that exist in the portions of the database that match the pattern of G. These *define* queries are constructed as follows. We consider the hygraph which is identical to G but where all edges and blobs are non-distinguished. If distinguished e of G is labelled with a predicate, then in this hygraph we add a distinguished edge (blob) between the two nodes e connects (between the container and the contained nodes). This distinguished edge (blob) essentially matches the predicate of e. If e is not labelled with a predicate, then we recursively expand e until all generated edges (blobs) are labelled with predicates. Then, we create the corresponding *define* queries for each of them as described above. The query evaluator evaluates each of the *define* queries in turn. The results are combined and the answer to the *filter* query is found.

4.2 Handling Aggregation

The translation process presented in the previous section does not consider aggregate functions. If aggregation is present in a GraphLog expression, additional rules to compute the aggregate functions are necessary. On top of this, since LDL does not directly support multisets (over which GraphLog defines aggregate functions), the translation must add rules to simulate multisets using lists. To illustrate this, Figure 8 shows the output of the Hy$^+$ translation for the rightmost **defineGraphLog** blob of Figure 6.

The translation provides a rule that groups together all variables that appear in the rule body (cf. line 1). Values that are bound to these variables form a tuple.

```
1:  body_avg_usage(class(C1), <(C1, C2, C)>) ←
        quant_uses(class(C1), class(C2), C).
2:  avg_usage(class(C1), Result_C) ←
3:      body_avg_usage(class(C1), TheSet),
4:      aggr(setToList, TheSet, TheList),
5:      laggr(sum, 3, TheList, Sum),
6:      laggr(count, 3, TheList, Count),
7:      Result_C = Count / Sum.
8:  empty(setToList, []).
9:  single(setToList, L, [L]).
10:  multi(setToList, L1, L2, L) ← append(L1, L2, L).
11: laggr(Op, Pos, [], V) ← lempty(Op, V).
12: laggr(Op, Pos, [T], V) ← component(T, Pos, Comp),
                             lsingle(Op, Comp, V).
13: laggr(Op, Pos, [H|T], V) ← component(H, Pos, V1),
                             laggr(Op, Pos, T, V2),
                             lmulti(Op, V1, V2, V).
14: lempty(sum, 0).
15: lsingle(sum, X, X).
16: lmulti(sum, N1, N2, N1+N2).
17: lempty(count, 0).
18: lsingle(count, _, 1).
19: lmulti(count, _, N2, 1+N2).
```

Fig. 8. The LDL program for a GraphLog query with aggregation.

The set **TheSet** in line 3 contains all such tuples. The LDL built-in predicate **aggr** is used to generate the list **TheList** from all elements in **TheSet** (cf. line 4).

In LDL the built-in **aggr** predicate is used to define relationships involving the manipulation of sets. It is defined by the following:

```
aggr(Op, S, V) ← if empty(Op, V) then true
            else if S = {X} then single(Op, X, V)
            else (partition_once(S1, S2, S),
                  aggr(Op, S1, V1),
                  aggr(Op, S2, V2),
                  multi(Op, V1, V2, V)).
```

The rule uses variable Op that should be thought of as the parameter that describes the aggregate function to be computed using the rule. If Op is bound to **max**, for example, the instantiation of the rule will be a description of how the function **max** is performed on sets. The body of the rule uses three built-in predicates: **empty**, which describes how the function is performed on the empty set; **single**, which says how to perform the function on a singleton; and **multi**, which says how to perform the function on a set of cardinality greater than one.

To provide the definition of some aggregation function, all one must do is to specify the values for the predicates `empty`, `single`, and `multi`. The translation uses this technique to specify how we can transform a set to a list. The operation is called `setToList` (cf. lines 8–10).

Imitating the definition LDL provides for sets we can obtain a definition of how to perform aggregation on positions of list elements. Note that every position of an element of the list corresponds to a distinct variable in the rule body. If we consider, for example, the position `Pos` of list elements, all values that appear in the position `Pos` form a multiset because the same value may appear several times. Aggregation is performed on positions of list elements or positions of the list for short. Performing aggregation over position `Pos` is semantically equivalent to performing aggregation over the multiset that contains all different values of the variable that corresponds to position `Pos`.

The next program describes how an aggregate operation `Op` can be computed on the position `Pos` of a list. It is a general definition in the sense that only the parameter predicates `lempty`, `lsingle`, and `lmulti` need to be specified in order for `Op` to be performed on position `Pos` resulting `V`. The definition assumes a predicate `component(T, Pos, Comp)` specifying the component `Comp` in the position `Pos` in a list element `T`.

```
laggr(Op, Pos,[], V) ← lempty(Op, V).
laggr(Op, Pos, [T], V) ← component(T, Pos, Comp),
                         lsingle(Op, Comp, V).
laggr(Op, Pos, [H|T], V) ← component(H, Pos, V1),
                           laggr(Op, Pos, T, V2),
                           lmulti(Op, V1, V2, V).
```

The set of rules that describe the parameter predicates for the definitions of the aggregate functions `count` and `sum` appear in lines 14–19 of Figure 8..

In contrast with LDL, CORAL provides grouping by multiset construction. Furthermore, in CORAL certain common aggregation functions, such as `count`, and `max`, are built into the language. These functions are computed on the fly, thus avoiding the generation of multisets that was necessary for LDL. CORAL does not support user-defined aggregate functions but the functions that it already supplies include the set of aggregate functions currently supported by GraphLog. Due to some implementation problems of the CORAL release currently used by the system (and not restrictions of the CORAL language per se) only one aggregate function may be specified in each rule head.

Since aggregate functions are part of the CORAL language the translation of GraphLog constructs containing aggregate functions into CORAL code is much simpler, as can be seen from comparing the program below with its equivalent LDL program in Figure 8.

```
module bodyModule.
export avg_usage(ff).

avg_usage(class(C1), avg(<C>)) :-
        quant_uses(class(C1), class(C2), C).

quant_uses(class(C1), class(C2), count(<F2>)) :-
        contains(class(C1), function(F1)),
        calls(function(F1), function(F2)),
        contains(class(C2), function(F2)).

end_module.
```

5 Conclusions

We described how deductive database engines can be used as back-ends for a data visualization and visual query system. We discussed the technical details of the translation from visual GraphLog queries to LDL and CORAL rules.

We have showed how the GraphLog visual language can provide an intuitive and consistent user interface for deductive database systems with different underlying semantics (in particular, concerning aggregation). In addition, we mentioned how the use of an object oriented programming language in the implementation of Hy^+ reduced the effort required to support multiple deductive databases.

We have applied the Hy+/GraphLog prototype to several domains, including software design [9], network management [3], and debugging of parallel programs [4]; preliminary experience indicates that the combination of a visual interface with the power of deductive database technology provides unique advantages over more conventional tools.

References

1. M. P. Consens. Graphlog: "Real Life" Recursive Queries Using Graphs. Master's thesis, Department of Computer Science, University of Toronto, 1989.
2. M. P. Consens. Visual Manipulation of Database Visualizations. PhD Thesis Research Proposal, 1992.
3. M. P. Consens and M. Hasan. Supporting Network Management through Declaratively Specified Data Visualizations. In *Proceedings of the IFIP/IEEE 3rd International Symposium on Integrated Network Management, III*, pages 725–738. Elsevier North Holland, 1993.
4. M. P. Consens, M. Hasan, and A. O. Mendelzon. Debugging Distributed Programs by Visualizing and Querying Event Traces. In *Declarative Database Visualization: Recent Papers from the Hy^+/GraphLog Project, University of Toronto Technical Report CSRI-285*, pages 11–34, 1993. Available by ftp to db.toronto.edu, in pub/papers.

5. M. P. Consens and A. O. Mendelzon. Expressing Structural Hypertext Queries in GraphLog. In *Proceedings of 2nd ACM Hypertext Conference*, pages 269–292, 1989.
6. M. P. Consens and A. O. Mendelzon. GraphLog: A Visual Formalism for Real Life Recursion. In *Proceedings of 9th ACM SIGACT-SIGMOD Symposium on Principles of Database Systems*, pages 404–416, 1990.
7. M. P. Consens and A. O. Mendelzon. Hy$^+$: A Hygraph-based Query and Visualization System. In *Proceedings of the ACM SIGMOD Conference on Management of Data*, pages 511–516, 1993. Video Presentation Summary.
8. M. P. Consens and A. O. Mendelzon. Low Complexity Aggregation in GraphLog and Datalog. *Theoretical Computer Science*, 116(1):379–394, 1993.
9. M. P. Consens, A. O. Mendelzon, and A. Ryman. Visualizing and Querying Software Structures. In *14th. Intl. Conference on Software Engineering*, pages 138–156, 1992.
10. D. Harel. On Visual Formalisms. *Communication of ACM*, 31(5):514–530, 1988.
11. S. Mancoridis, R. C. Holt, and D. A. Penny. A Conceptual Framework for Software Development. In *Proceedings of the Twenty-First ACM Computer Science Conference*, 1993.
12. S. A. Naqvi and S. Tsur. *A Logic Language for Data and Knowledge Bases*. Computer Science Press, 1988.
13. R. Ramakrishnan, D. Srivastava, and S. Sudarshan. CORAL: Control, Relations and Logic. In *Proceedings of International Conference on Very Large Databases*, 1992.
14. D. Vista and P. Wood. Efficient Visual Queries for Deductive Databases. In *Proceedings of the Workshop on Programming with Logic Databases*, 1993.

Subsumption-Free Bottom-up Evaluation of Logic Programs with Partially Instantiated Data Structures

Zoltan Somogyi, David Kemp,
James Harland and Kotagiri Ramamohanarao
{zs,kemp,jah,rao}@cs.mu.OZ.AU
Department of Computer Science, University of Melbourne
Parkville, 3052 Victoria, Australia

Abstract

Most deductive databases impose restrictions on the terms that can be used in them: they require that generated tuples be fully ground, i.e. contain no variables. Without this restriction, query evaluation of general programs needs subsumption tests in order to terminate correctly, and subsumption tests are expensive.

We study a class of programs that can handle terms with both variables and function symbols but for which subsumption tests are not necessary. This class is based on the notion of *modes*, which generalise adornments by not requiring that "bound" be synonymous with "ground". We show how programs in this class may be recognized and how they should be transformed into an executable form, and then prove that bottom-up evaluation of the resulting programs does not require subsumption tests.

1 Introduction

Deductive databases are logic programming systems designed for applications that handle large amounts of data. Since logic programs can be viewed as an extension of relational databases and since relational databases handle large amounts of data, deductive database researchers usually try to use techniques developed for relational systems whenever possible. One consequence of this tendency is that unlike implementations of general-purpose logic programming systems, most deductive database systems use bottom-up evaluation methods.

Bottom-up evaluation methods work in two phases. The first phase rewrites the program and the query into a more efficient form using algorithms such as the magic set transformation [1] and the context transformation [3]. The second phase starts with the facts in the rewritten program, and uses the rules of the rewritten program to derive new facts until it can generate no more new facts, and then returns the facts that the query asked for. The task of the first phase is to reduce to the minimum the number of facts the second phase must consider.

Most deductive databases that use bottom-up methods compute only with ground terms (e.g. Aditi [10]). Some (e.g. CORAL [6]) can handle non-ground terms, but only by using subsumption as a frequent operation. Consider the following program:

```
p(X).
p(f(X)) :- p(X).
```

A bottom-up evaluation of this query produces first p(X), then p(f(X)), then p(f(f(X))), and so on. The evaluation will therefore not terminate unless newly derived tuples are tested for subsumption by existing tuples.

Subsumption is especially difficult to implement when the relation being computed is large. When the evaluation algorithm produces a tuple, we must be able to check whether this tuple is subsumed by a previously generated tuple and whether this tuple subsumes any previously generated tuples. This can be done quickly only if we can limit the number of places in which we have to look for potentially interfering tuples. Unfortunately, in general this is not possible.

```
p(a1,b1,c1).
p(X, B, C) :- p(A, B, C).
p(A, Y, C) :- p(A, B, C).
p(A, B, Z) :- p(A, B, C).
```

The first iteration computes p(a1,b1,c1). The second iteration computes the tuples p(X,b1,c1), p(a1,Y,c1) and p(a1,b1,Z). Since p(X,b1,c1) subsumes p(a1,b1,c1), p(X,b1,c1) will replace p(a1,b1,c1) in the temporary relation storing the extension of p; the rest of the iteration will then add p(a1,Y,c1) and p(a1,b1,Z) to this temporary relation. These three tuples will all be replaced in the next iteration with three tuples that each have two variables: p(X,Y,c1), p(X,b1,Z) and p(a1,Y,Z). The final iteration will replace all these with the tuple p(X,Y,Z).

This example illustrates the difficulty of implementing subsumption efficiently. There are eight tuples that subsume p(a1,b1,c1): p(a1,b1,c1) itself, p(X,b1,c1), p(a1,Y,c1), p(a1,b1,Z), p(X,Y,c1), p(X,b1,Z), p(a1,Y,Z) and p(X,Y,Z). When we generate p(a1,b1,c1), we must look in the temporary relation for each of these before we can say that p(a1,b1,c1) is in fact a new tuple. If the temporary relation were bigger, this could mean up to eight disk accesses. This is not all: one can increase the number of probes required exponentially by adding more arguments to p.

Since subsumption can be so expensive, it is natural to ask whether there are any useful classes of programs for which it is not necessary. The problem in this example is that some clauses of p define all three arguments while some other clauses don't. Most systems based on adornments prevent this by requiring that the programmer state for each argument whether it will be free or ground in the query.

This approach works, but it prevents us from computing with partially instantiated data structures, i.e. terms which may contain function symbols and variables. We would like to be able to execute queries such as ?- path(X, Y, [S1,S2]) with answers such as path(melbourne, new_york, [honolulu,los_angeles]). In this case, the third argument is partially input and partially output to path, so it cannot be adorned either free or bound. One can handle this by loosening the meaning of adornments, allowing queries to bind only some parts of an argument declared bound, as in CORAL [6], but this still requires subsumption.

Our solution is to make use of the type of the third argument, which is a list of placenames, and require that the query define the list skeleton (which our *modes* declare to be input to path) but not the placenames in the list (which they declare to be output from path). This clear division of responsibilities lets us avoid subsumption tests.

The structure of the paper is as follows. In Section 2 we introduce our notions of selectors and types as necessary background for the description of our mode system, which follows in Section 3. In section 4, we show how to transform mode correct programs for bottom-up evaluation, which, as we prove in section 5, does not need subsumption. The proofs of our theorems are available in [8].

2 Selectors and types

2.1 Selectors

Definition 2.1 A *term* is defined as follows: a variable X is a term, and if f is a function symbol of n arguments (n $\geq$ 0), and $t_1, \ldots, t_n$ are terms, then $f(t_1, \ldots, t_n)$ is a term. A function symbol of arity 0 is a *constant*. A term that is not a variable or a constant is also called a *structured* or *complex* term. A term that contains no variables is called a *ground* term. We follow deductive database convention in denoting variables by identifiers starting in upper case and function and predicate symbols by identifiers starting in lower case.

Definition 2.2 We denote the set of function symbols in the program and query by $\mathcal{F}$. We denote the arity of a function symbol f by arity(f); we assume that the arity is uniquely determined by the function symbol itself.

We define two new notions, position selectors and function selectors, to be more precise about the components of terms. Both require viewing terms as trees in the usual way, i.e. with the main function symbol as the root of the tree and an arc from the main function symbol to the roots of the subtrees of the arguments, whose trees are defined similarly.

Definition 2.3 A *position selector* is a finite sequence of pairs describing a position in a term. The root of the term is labelled with the empty sequence, denoted by ϵ. If the label of a node is ps, and the tree contains the function symbol f at that node, then the i'th child of that node is labelled ps:[f,i]. A *function selector* is a position selector followed by the function symbol at that position.

Example 2.1 In the term f(g(a), h(X, b)), the set of all position selectors is: ϵ, [f,1], [f,1]:[g,1], [f,2], [f,2]:[h,1], and [f,2]:[h,2], and the set of all function selectors is: f, [f,1]:g, [f,1]:[g,1]:a, [f,2]:h, and [f,2]:[h,2]:b. The term at the position [f,2] is h(X, b). Note that there is no function selector for the first argument of the h, since the term contains a variable there.

Position selectors and function selectors are intimately related. A position selector can be extended to a function selector by naming the function symbol at the designated position, while a function selector can be extended to a position selector by naming one of the argument positions of the last function symbol, *provided* that the last function symbol is not a constant. On the other hand, one can *always* derive a position selector from a function selector by removing the final function symbol. We will write ps(fs) to denote the position selector derived from the function selector fs in this way; we will write PS(FS) for the set of position selectors derived from the set of function selectors FS.

One can derive a set of function selectors from any ground term t; we will call this set fs(t). This set will have one element for each function symbol in t.

2.2 Types

Definition 2.4 A *type* is a (possibly infinite) set of function selectors FS.

Example 2.2 The infinite set of function symbols in the type "list of booleans" contains

nil	cons	[cons,1]:true	[cons,1]:false
[cons,2]:nil	[cons,2]:cons	[cons,2]:[cons,1]:true	[cons,2]:[cons,1]:false

and many others; all can be generated by the scheme

[cons,2]^n:nil [cons,2]^n:cons [cons,2]^n:[cons,1]:true [cons,2]^n:[cons,1]:false

where n can be any non-negative integer. The term cons(true, cons(false, nil)) belongs to the type. The term cons(nil, false) does not, because neither [cons,1]:nil nor [cons,2]:false is in the scheme above.

Schemes like the one just above are necessary if we want to represent types in finite storage space. For this example, the scheme says that there are two kinds of positions in lists of booleans. Variables appearing in positions of the form [cons,2]^n are of the type "list of booleans" and must therefore be bound to either nil or cons; variables appearing in positions of the form [cons,2]^n:[cons,1] are of the type "boolean" and must therefore be bound to either true or false. Using the syntax of one of the NU-Prolog [9] type checkers, this can be expressed by declarations such as

```
?- type listbool ---> nil ; cons(bool, listbool).
?- type bool ---> true ; false.
```

In some parts of the paper, we denote the function symbol cons by the infix operator ".".

Types such as integers can in principle be declared just like booleans, although in practice they must be built-in. Our examples in later sections will use a type called listint, which contains a list of integers.

The information in such declarations can be expressed in a graph with two kinds of nodes: one for sets of position selectors and one for function symbols, with the links between them given by the natural relation between position selectors and function selectors. Such graphs not only represent a type, they also state that some position selectors are in some sense *equivalent*. One sense is that two position selectors represent the same type; another sense is introduced in the next section. For example, the declarations and the scheme above state that variables appearing in positions of the form $[cons,2]^n$ are of the same type. We can formalize this idea through the notion of a type graph.

Definition 2.5 A *type graph* is a pair (FS, ≡) where FS is a (possibly infinite) set of function selectors and ≡ is a relation on PS(FS) obeying the property that if ps1 ≡ ps2, then

choice equivalence	$\forall$ f $\in \mathcal{F}$, ps1:f $\in$ FS $\Leftrightarrow$ ps2:f $\in$ FS
subnode equivalence	$\forall$ f $\in \mathcal{F}$, $\forall$ i $\in$ {1..arity(f)}, ps1:f $\in$ FS $\Rightarrow$ ps1:[f,i] $\equiv$ ps2:[f,i]
nonconvergence	ps1 = p1:[f,i] $\wedge$ ps2 = p2:[g,j] $\Rightarrow$ p1 $\equiv$ p2.

The first two properties together imply that ps1:ext ≡ ps2:ext if ps1 ≡ ps2. The third makes sure that ps1:ext ≡ ps2:ext *only* if ps1 ≡ ps2.

Lemma 2.1 *A relation on two sets of position selectors that obeys the properties of choice equivalence and subnode equivalence is reflexive, symmetric and transitive, and hence an equivalence relation.*

Definition 2.6 A *position node* in a type graph ⟨FS, ≡⟩ is an equivalence class induced by ≡ on PS(FS). We denote the position node that a position selector ps belongs to by pnode(FS, ≡, ps). We denote the set of position nodes in a type graph by pnode_set(FS, ≡). A node n_1 in a type graph is a descendant of another node n_2 if $n_1 \neq n_2$, ps $\in n_1$ and ps:ext $\in n_2$.

We can label the position nodes by a scheme that yields the position selectors in that equivalence class, or if the set of equivalence classes is known, by a single position selector in the class (preferably the shortest). In this paper, we will use the label *skel* to refer to position nodes of the form $[cons,2]^n$, the label *elt* (short for element) to refer to position nodes of the form $[cons,2]^n$:[cons,1], and the label *root* to refer to position nodes of the form ϵ.

Two type graphs (FS_1,$\equiv_1$) and (FS_2,$\equiv_2$) represent the same type if $FS_1 = FS_2$.

Definition 2.7 A *signature* is a function from a sequence of argument types to a result type.

We require every function symbol to have a unique signature: each argument of the function symbol must have the type given by the corresponding sequence element, and the type of the term created by applying the function symbol to the arguments is the result type of the signature. This allows us to unambiguously deduce the type of every ground term, and the type of every non-ground term as well if we know the types of the variables occurring in each term.

Since we need a strong type system as a foundation for our strong mode system, we assume that the program contains a type declaration for every predicate, giving the type of the arguments of that predicate.

Definition 2.8 A program and query are *type correct* if there is an assignment of types to the variables occurring in the program and the query such that the type of every argument of every atom in the program and the query (including those in clause heads) is identical to the declared type of the corresponding formal argument.

In the rest of the paper, we assume that the program and the query are type correct, and that the type checker that establishes type correctness gives us the type of every variable in the program and the query in the form of a finite type graph.

Our type system is very similar to the Mycroft-O'Keefe type system [5], which has its roots in the type systems of functional languages such as ML [4], and which has been adopted for new logic programming languages such as Gödel [2]. The main differences are that for simplicity of presentation, in this paper we assume that each function symbol has one signature, and that all types appearing in the program are monomorphic, i.e. we do not deal with polymorphic types. Since both differences make type checking easier, we omit a description of the type checking algorithm and refer the reader to papers describing type checking algorithms for related type systems (see e.g. [5]).

3 A strong mode system

Definition 3.1 A *substitution* is a set of mappings from variables to terms, denoted by $\{v_1/t_1, \ldots, v_n/t_n\}$.

Definition 3.2 An *instantiation state* of a variable of type (FS,$\equiv$) is a mapping from the set PS(FS) to the set {bound,notbound}. A variable is in a given instantiation state with respect to a substitution if the substitution maps the variable to a term such that for all the position selectors in that term

- if that position is mapped to bound, then there is a function symbol at that position
- and if that position is mapped to notbound, then there is a variable at that position.

Example 3.1 Consider the instantiation state for lists of booleans that maps position selectors of the form $[\text{cons},2]^n$ to bound and those of the form $[\text{cons},2]^n$:[cons,1] to notbound. The term cons(A, cons(B, nil)) is in this instantiation state. The term cons(A, L) is not, because [cons,2] is mapped to bound yet the subterm in that position (L) is a variable, not a function symbol.

During the evaluation of a query, a variable may go through several instantiation states. For describing mappings between instantiation states, we use the concept of *modes* that we introduced in [7].

Definition 3.3 A *mode* is a mapping from the nodes of a set of type graphs, one type graph for each argument of a predicate, onto the set {inbound,infree,outbound,outfree} (elements of which are also called modes). We refer to the modes inbound and infree as *input modes*, and the modes outbound and outfree as *output modes*.

The intention of each of these four modes are as follows:

- Positions mapped to inbound represent information that must be provided by the caller of the predicate. Initial and final instantiation states are both bound.
- Positions mapped to outbound represent information that is provided by the predicate to its caller. Initial instantiation state is notbound while final instantiation state is bound.
- Positions mapped to infree mark parts of data structures that are ignored by the predicate. Initial and final instantiation states are both notbound.
- Positions mapped to outfree represent distinct free variables created by the predicate. Initial and final instantiation states are both notbound.

In a conventional deductive database such as Aditi [10], an argument all of whose pieces are mapped to inbound would be given the "b" (bound) adornment, while an argument all of whose pieces are mapped to outbound would be given the adornment "f" (free). Our modes thus subsume the notion of adornments, and extend that notion with the ability to talk with precision about partially instantiated terms.

The semantics of modes impose the following constraints on mode declarations:

- If ps is mapped to inbound, then any ps:[f,i] must not be mapped to outfree.
- If ps is mapped to infree, then any ps:[f,i] must be mapped to infree.
- If ps is mapped to outbound, then any ps:[f,i] must not be mapped to infree.
- If ps is mapped to outfree, then any ps:[f,i] must be mapped to outfree.

A mode declaration obeying these constraints is *valid*.

A mode declaration associates one or more modes with a predicate: it lists the inbound nodes, infree nodes, outbound nodes and outfree nodes (in that order) of the type graphs of the arguments. We assume that the program contains a valid mode declaration for every predicate.

Example 3.2 Consider the predicate len:

```
?- pred len(L: listint, N: int).
?- mode len([L:skel], [L:elt], [N:root], []).
?- mode len([N:root], [], [L:skel], [L:elt]).
len(L, N) :- L = nil, N = 0.
len(L, N) :- L = cons(H, T), len(T, N1), plus(N1, 1, N).
```

It has two principal modes:

mode 1 (forward):
L:[cons,2]^n → inbound
L:[cons,2]^n:[cons,1] → infree
N:ϵ → outbound

mode 2 (backward):
L:[cons,2]^n → outbound
L:[cons,2]^n:[cons,1] → outfree
N:ϵ → inbound

The queries len(cons(A, cons(B, nil)), N) and len(cons(1, cons(2, nil)), N) are legal invocations of len in its first mode, and len(A, 3) is a legal invocation of len in its second mode.

Definition 3.4 A *mode assignment* is an assignment to every atom in the body of a clause (including the head) of one of the modes of the corresponding predicate. An *assigned clause* is a clause together with a mode assignment on that clause. An *assigned program* consists of *assigned clauses.*

If a predicate p has n mode declarations in the original program, then the assigned program has n predicates derived from p, one for each mode, that are treated as completely separate predicates. Systems that use adornments do the same thing (see e.g. [1]).

Definition 3.5 The head of an assigned clause is the *producer* of a position if the mode of the head maps that position to inbound; a body atom is the producer of a position if the mode of that atom maps that position to outbound. The head of an assigned clause is a *consumer* of a position if the mode of the head maps that position to outbound; a body atom is a consumer of a position if the mode of that atom maps that position to inbound.

Example 3.3 In the first mode of len, the head is the producer of L:skel in both clauses; the unification L = nil is its consumer in the first clause and the unification L = cons(H, T) is its consumer in the second clause.

Definition 3.6 An assigned clause is *mode correct* if every position that has at least one consumer also has at least one producer in the clause, and if every position that is mapped to infree or outfree either in the head or in a unification in the body has no producer in the clause.

Definition 3.7 A mode-correct assigned clause is *non-circular* if the atoms in the body can be ordered so that each atom consumes only positions whose producer is either an atom on its left or the head.

The algorithm for finding a correct mode assignment for a clause keeps track of the instantiation state of each node of each variable of the clause. Initially, each node is unknown except the ones mapped to inbound in the head. The algorithm then considers the atoms in the body: if an atom takes as inbound only nodes whose instantiation state is bound, then we mark the atom and set the instantiation state of its outbound nodes to bound. We continue until all atoms are marked (in which case the clause has a non-circular assignment) or until we cannot mark any more atoms (in which case the clause either has a circular assignment or has no correct assignment at all). For the details of the algorithm, including how to find circular mode assignments, see [7].

4 Transformations

Constraints on modes may be imposed by the implementation as well as by their semantics. For example, a mode that makes an inbound node a descendant of an outbound node requires a top-down implementation that supports coroutining; other implementations have to prohibit such "upside-down" modes.

Definition 4.1 An assigned program P is a *sequential program* if in all arguments of all predicates, if a node is mapped to an output mode, then all descendants of that node are also mapped to an output mode.

Implementations that are unable to take a partially instantiated term and further instantiate it (by binding some of its variables) will outlaw predicate arguments that contain both input and output positions. We call a program in which all arguments of all predicates contain either only input modes or only output modes a *separated program* (referring to the separation of inputs from outputs in different arguments).

Definition 4.2 An assigned program P is a *separated program* if for every argument of every atom in the program, either the mode assignment maps all nodes in that argument to input modes or it maps all nodes in that argument to output modes.

Bottom-up implementations are even more strict. Because naive bottom-up computation cannot use any bindings given in the query, all the producers have to be in the body.

Definition 4.3 An assigned program P is an *output program* if in the head of every clause, every node of every argument is mapped to an output mode.

We will prove in section 5 that bottom-up evaluation of non-circular output programs does not require subsumption tests. To make this result useful, we need to be able to transform a wide class of programs to this form.

We do this transformation in two stages. First, we apply a new transformation called the *argument-splitting transformation* that takes possibly circular sequential programs and produces non-circular separated programs. Second, we apply the magic set algorithm to transform these programs further into non-circular output programs.

To make the presentation of the transformations and the theorems simpler, we will assume that the programs we handle are in *superhomogeneous* form. In this form as in homogeneous form, clause heads must contain distinct variables as arguments. However, in superhomogeneous form atoms in clause bodies must also contain distinct variables as arguments, and all unifications must be of the form X = Y or of the form X = f(Y1, ..., Yn). It is clear that all clauses can be rewritten into this form.

4.1 The argument splitting transformation

In the next example program, the **pred** declaration specifies the types of the arguments, and the **mode** declaration gives a valid mode. This mode says that iota1 should be called with a query such as ?- iota1(A.B.C.nil, 1), which will compute an answer such as iota1(1.2.3.nil, 1).

```
?- pred iota1(L: listint, N: int).
?- mode iota1([L:skel,N:root], [], [L:elt], []).
iota1(L, N) :- L = nil.
iota1(L, N) :- L = cons(N, T), plus(N, 1, M), iota1(T, M).
```

This program is circular because in the second clause, the unification L = cons(N, T) instantiates the skeleton of T before the recursive call to iota1 but transmits the values of the elements of T to L after that call.

The idea behind the transformation is to split the argument(s) that are used for both input and output (in this case, L), into two separate arguments, one for input and one for output. The result of applying the transformation to iota1 is iota2, whose first argument is all input while the second is all output:

```
?- pred iota2(L0: listint, L2: listint, N: int).
?- mode iota2([L0:skel,N:root], [L0:elt], [L2:skel,L2:elt], []).
iota2(L0, L2, N) :- L0 = nil, L2 = nil.
iota2(L0, L2, N) :- L0 = cons(_, T0), plus(N, 1, M),
                    iota2(T0, T1, M), L2 = cons(N, T1).
```

The query is transformed into ?- iota2(A.B.C.nil, L, 1), and its answer is iota2(A.B.C.nil, 1.2.3.nil, 1): the original list skeleton is untouched while iota2 creates another list of the same shape and fills it in. The circularity is gone too: the first unification instantiates T0, the recursive call creates T1 from T0 (and M), and the second unification creates L2 without touching L0. Therefore iota2 is non-circular and separated.

The mode of the argument replacing L in its input role (L0) is derived from the instantiation state of L in the query: whatever was bound (the skeleton) becomes inbound and whatever was notbound (the elements) becomes infree. The mode of the argument replacing L in its output role (L2) is derived from the instantiation state of L in the answer: whatever was bound (the skeleton and the elements) becomes outbound and whatever was notbound (in this case nothing) becomes outfree.

The transformation of a clause starts from the mode assignment of the clause. For each variable that has more than one instantiation state (apart from all notbound, which is the state variables are in before their first appearance), we create several replacement variables, one for each such instantiation state. Occurrences of the original variable in an atom, either in the head or in the body, fall into two classes. In an atom whose mode says that it *does not* cause the variable to become more instantiated, we substitute the replacement variable corresponding to the instantiation state the mode requires. In an atom whose mode says that it *does* cause the variable to become more instantiated, we substitute two replacement variables, corresponding to the initial and final instantiation states. (We count transitions from "all notbound" as falling into the first class.)

Unifications in which data flows one way present no problem. Unifications in which data flows two ways have to be split into two or more unifications in which data flows one way, one for each instantiation state to be achieved. The first unification in the second clause of iota2 binds T0 while the second binds L2. The details of the algorithm can be found in [8].

4.2 The magic set transformation

Naive bottom-up evaluation of logic programs does not make use of data provided in the query and is therefore very inefficient. The magic set transformation is the standard technique for restricting the set of tuples generated to the ones actually relevant to the query. It does this by building and using a "magic set", which is essentially a representation of the queries and subqueries on a predicate. It replaces each clause H :- $L_1, \ldots, L_n$ with another clause H :- magic_H, $L_1, \ldots, L_n$, and for each call to a derived predicate in (say) L_m it adds the clause magic_L_m :- $L_1, \ldots, L_m$. It also adds a clause for the query itself. The magic relations magic_L_m have one attribute for each *input* attribute of the predicate being called.

For the query ?- iota2(A.B.C.nil, L, 1), the magic set transformation gives:

```
?- pred magic_iota3(L0: listint, N: int).
?- mode magic_iota3([], [], [L0:skel,N:root], [L0:elt]).
magic_iota3(L0, N) :- L0 = cons(A, cons(B, cons(C, nil))), N = 1.
magic_iota3(T0, M) :- magic_iota3(L0, N), L0 = cons(_, T0),
                      plus(N, 1, M).

?- pred iota3(L0: listint, L2: listint, N: int).
?- mode iota3([], [], [L0:skel,L2:skel,L2:elt,N:root], [L0:elt]).
iota3(L0, L2, N) :- magic_iota3(L0, N), L0 = nil, L2 = nil.
iota3(L0, L2, N) :- magic_iota3(L0, N), L0 = cons(_, T0),
                    plus(N, 1, M), iota3(T0, T1, M),
                    L2 = cons(N, T1).
```

This program still handles partially instantiated data structures, but it is an output program and as such can be evaluated bottom-up. Neither iota1 nor iota2 could be evaluated bottom-up in finite time.

Proposition 4.1 *The result of applying the magic set transformation to a non-circular separated program and a query is a non-circular output program.*

The proof of this result appears in [8]. Previous results imply that with a well-founded SIPS (sideways information passing strategy) the well-founded models of the original and the transformed programs agree on the query.

The magic set transformation is not the only transformation that can turn non-output programs into output programs. Similar results ought to be possible for other such transformations, e.g. the context transformation [3]. This is important because such more specialized transformations can produce more efficient code.

5 Subsumption freedom for output programs

Each predicate in an assigned program has a single mode. This means that if an answer to query has a variable at a particular position selector, then *all* answers to that query must have a variable at that position selector, and that if an answer has a function symbol at a particular position selector, then *all* answers to that query must have a function symbol at that position selector. Therefore every answer will have the same basic "shape".

Definition 5.1 A set of terms $\mathcal{T}$ is ***independent*** if $\forall t_1, t_2 \in \mathcal{T}$, either t_1 is identical to t_2 up to renaming or t_1 does not unify with t_2.

Example 5.1 {a, f(X)} is independent, and so is {f(X), f(Y)}. However {f(a), f(X)} is not independent, and neither is {g(a, Y), g(Y, b)}.

Definition 5.2 We denote the set of all ground atoms as $\mathcal{H}$ and the set of all atoms as $\mathcal{H}'$. An ***interpretation*** is a subset of $\mathcal{H}'$.

Definition 5.3 Let I be a set of atoms. We refer to the set of all instances of all elements of I as $\mathit{inst}(I)$. Note that $I \subseteq \mathit{inst}(I)$. We define the relation $\sqsubseteq$ by $I_1 \sqsubseteq I_2$ iff $\mathrm{inst}(I_1) \subseteq \mathrm{inst}(I_2)$.

Note that interpretations form a complete lattice under the partial order $\sqsubseteq$. Note also that if $I_1 \sqsubseteq I_2$ and $I_2 \sqsubseteq I_1$, then I_1 and I_2 only differ by the names of variables.

In order to show that subsumption is not necessary for output programs, we use the fixpoint semantics for logic programs; in particular, we will show that each application of the T_P operator produces an *independent* set of atoms. Since the standard T_P operator can only generate ground atoms, we must introduce a non-ground version of the T_P operator that is careful about preserving the independence of the interpretations it manipulates. However, we first have to make sure that the first iteration of T_P generates some interpretations.

Definition 5.4 Given a superhomogeneous program P, we can derive a corresponding program $|P|$ that contains no explicit calls to =. Where P contains $X = \mathit{term}$, in $|P|$ we apply the substitution $\{X/\mathit{term}\}$ to the clause containing that unification.

Definition 5.5 Let P be a program and I be an interpretation. Then we define

$$T_P(I) = \{A\theta \mid A \in |P| \text{ and } \theta = \{\},$$
$$\text{or A :- G} \in |P| \text{ such that } G\theta \subseteq I$$
$$\text{and } \theta \text{ binds only variables that occur in } G\}$$

$$T_P^\omega(I) = \bigcup_{i=1}^{\infty} T_P^i(I)$$

We have the following results, the proofs of which appear in [8]:

Proposition 5.1 *The least fixed point of T_P is $T_P^\omega(\emptyset)$.*

Theorem 5.1 *Let P be a non-circular output program. Then for any $k \leq \omega$, $T_P^k(\emptyset)$ is independent.*

The only way that two answers can have any instances in common is for them to have all instances in common, and thus to be identical. Therefore when we generate an answer during bottom-up evaluation, which essentially implements the T_P operator, we know exactly the place in the answer set we should look at to see if we have generated a variant of this answer before. And since no variable occurs twice in the answer set, we can replace all variables by the same new constant and use equality tests instead of subsumption.

Furthermore, since the modes specify exactly where in the structure variables will be found, this theorem lets us avoid storing them altogether, since one knows how to put them back in later. This is needed only if they occur in the final answer.

This approach requires us to omit certain argument positions, both from type declarations and from the code, as in this version of iota:

```
?- type listint1 ---> nil1 ; cons1(listint1).

?- pred magic_iota4(L0: listint1, N: int).
?- mode magic_iota4([], [], [L0:skel,N:root], []).
magic_iota4(L0, N) :- L0 = cons1(cons1(cons1(nil1))), N = 1.
magic_iota4(T0, M) :- magic_iota4(L0, N), L0 = cons1(T0),
                      plus(N, 1, M).

?- pred iota4(L0: listint1, L2: listint, N: int).
?- mode iota4([], [], [L0:skel,L2:skel,L2:elt,N:root], []).
iota4(L0, L2, N) :- magic_iota4(L0, N), L0 = nil1, L2 = nil.
iota4(L0, L2, N) :- magic_iota4(L0, N), L0 = cons1(T0),
                    plus(N, 1, M), iota4(T0, T1, M),
                    L2 = cons(N, T1).
```

This version manipulates only ground data structures, and as such can be executed on any current deductive database.

6 Conclusion

Mode declarations give us precise and reliable information about which parts of its arguments a predicate expects to be bound in queries to it and which parts it will itself instantiate. We can use this information to separate the input and output parts via the argument splitting transformation, and then make *all* arguments output via the magic set transformation. The resulting program can then be evaluated bottom-up without subsumption tests.

We would like to thank Will Winsborough for conversations that clarified some of the concepts in section 2, the referees for their comments, and the Australian Research Council and Centre for Intelligent Decision Systems for their support.

References

[1] F. Bancilhon, D. Maier, Y. Sagiv, and R. Ramakrishnan. Magic sets and other strange ways to implement logic programs. *Proceedings of the Symposium on Principles of Database Systems*, pages 1–15, 1986.

[2] P. M. Hill and J. W. Lloyd. The Gödel report. Technical Report 91-02, Department of Computer Science, University of Bristol, England, 1991.

[3] D. Kemp, K. Ramamohanarao, and Z. Somogyi. Right-, left- and multi-linear rule transformations that maintain context information. In *Proceedings of the Sixteenth International Conference on Very Large Data Bases*, pages 380–391, Brisbane, Australia, 1990.

[4] R. Milner. A proposal for standard ML. *Conference Record of the ACM Symposium on LISP and Functional Programming*, pages 184–197, 1984.

[5] A. Mycroft and R. A. O'Keefe. A polymorphic type system for Prolog. *Artificial Intelligence*, 23:295–307, 1984.

[6] R. Ramakrishnan, P. Bothner, D. Srivastava, and S. Sudarshan. CORAL - a database programming language. In *Proceedings of the NACLP '90 Workshop on Deductive Databases*, pages 2.1–2.9, Austin, Texas, 1990.

[7] Z. Somogyi. A system of precise modes for logic programs. In *Proceedings of the Fourth International Conference on Logic Programming*, pages 769–787, Melbourne, Australia, 1987.

[8] Z. Somogyi, D. Kemp, J. Harland, and K. Ramamohanarao. Subsumption-free bottom-up evaluation of logic programs with partially instantiated data structures. Technical Report 93/26, Department of Computer Science, University of Melbourne, Melbourne, Australia, 1993.

[9] J. Thom and J. Zobel. NU-Prolog reference manual, version 1.0. Technical Report 86/10, Department of Computer Science, University of Melbourne, Melbourne, Australia, 1986.

[10] J. Vaghani, K. Ramamohanarao, D. Kemp, Z. Somogyi, and P. Stuckey. Design overview of the Aditi deductive database system. In *Proceedings of the Seventh International Conference on Data Engineering*, pages 240–247, Kobe, Japan, 1991.

Schema Equivalence in Heterogeneous Systems: Bridging Theory and Practice (Extended Abstract)

R. J. Miller* Y. E. Ioannidis** R. Ramakrishnan***

Department of Computer Sciences, University of Wisconsin-Madison
{rmiller, yannis, raghu}@cs.wisc.edu

1 Introduction

Current theoretical work offers measures of schema equivalence based on the information capacity of schemas. This work is based on the existence of abstract functions satisfying various restrictions between the sets of all instances of two schemas. In considering schemas that arise in practice, however, it is not clear how to reason about the existence of such abstract functions. Further, these notions of equivalence tend to be too liberal in that schemas are often considered equivalent when a practitioner would consider them to be different. As a result, practical integration methodologies have not utilized this theoretical foundation and most of them have relied on ad-hoc approaches.

We present results that seek to bridge this gap. First, we consider the problem of deciding information capacity equivalence and dominance of schemas that occur in practice, i.e., those that can express inheritance and simple integrity constraints. We show that this problem is undecidable. This undecidability suggests that in addition to the overly liberal nature of information capacity equivalence, we should look for alternative, more restrictive notions of equivalence that can be effectively tested. To this end, we develop several tests that each serve as sufficient conditions for information capacity equivalence or dominance. Each test is characterized by a set of schema transformations in the following sense: a test declares that Schema S1 is dominated by Schema S2 if and only if there is a sequence of transformations that converts S1 to S2. Thus, each test can be understood essentially by understanding the individual transformations used to characterize it. Each of the transformations we consider is a local, structural schema change with a clear underlying intuition. These tests permit reasoning about the equivalence and dominance of quite complex schemas. Because our work is based on structural transformations, the same characterizations that underly our tests can be used to guide designers in modifying a schema to meet their equivalence or dominance goals.

* R. J. Miller has been partially supported by NSF Grant IRI-9157368.

** Y. Ioannidis has been partially supported by NSF Grants IRI-9113736 and IRI-9157368 (PYI Award) and by grants from DEC, IBM, HP, and AT&T.

*** R. Ramakrishnan has been partially supported by a David and Lucile Packard Foundation Fellowship in Science and Engineering, by an NSF PYI Award and NSF grant IRI-9011563, and by grants from DEC, Tandem, and Xerox.

2 Motivation

Schema equivalence plays a central role in many schema integration tasks. For example, algorithms for detecting equivalent schemas can be used to automate the detection and resolution of structural schema mismatches (or type conflicts). Schema equivalence also plays an important and less recognized role in many other problems encountered in heterogeneous systems. Below, we describe one such problem, that of providing automated support for ad hoc changes to a schema that is being used as a view onto data stored under another schema.

Consider a schema translation tool in which a schema is translated into a schema in a different data model. Many tools produce a translated schema that can be used as a view to pose queries on data stored under the original schema. Within such tools, the translation process produces not only the translated schema, but a set of correspondences between the schemas that defines how an instance of the former corresponds to an instance of the latter. We call these correspondences *instance mappings*. For example, the Pegasus import tool [2] translates relational schemas to Iris schemas (Iris is a functional object model). For each Iris type, the result of translation includes a rule over a collection of relations in the original schema that defines the instances of the type.

Such translation tools fully automate the production of instance mappings. A designer need only be concerned with the resulting schema; all details of establishing schema correspondences are hidden. We now want to permit the designer to change the translated schema. Again, we want the tool to automatically infer and record any changes necessary to the instance mapping.

For example, suppose Schema R1 of Figure 1 is produced by a translation tool from an underlying schema in another data model. A designer may wish to change the default translation and represent `Grant` as an attribute of *Workstation* not *Project* as in Schema R2. If the tool can test for equivalence (or dominance) and automatically produce an instance mapping between schemas, then the designer does not need to manually update the instance mapping as a result of this change. Currently, translation tools, such as Pegasus, do not give such support for ad hoc view changes. Rather, they provide some form of data definition language in which default mappings are expressed and which may be used by a designer to manually change a mapping.

Schema R1	Schema R2
Project [**ProjectNo**, Leader, Grant]	*Project* [**ProjectNo**, Leader]
Workstation [**SerialNo**, Name]	*Workstation* [**SerialNo**, Name,Grant]

Fig. 1. Parts of two relational schemas. Keys are depicted in bold.

This problem is clearly not restricted to translation and applies to a number of applications in heterogeneous databases in which one schema is maintained as a view over other schemas. Our study of schema equivalence has been motivated by the needs of such applications. For these applications, the notion of equivalence must be based on the capacity of schemas to store information. In addition to algorithms for producing equivalent schemas (this is the translation or transformation problem), these applications also require algorithms for both deciding if two schemas are equivalent and for producing the correspondence between the schemas (that is, an instance mapping).

3 Schema Intension Graphs

In this section, we briefly sketch the basic constructs of the *Schema Intension Graph* (SIG) data model, which will be used to present our results. A discussion of the motivation for using SIGs and a full definition are given elsewhere [8].

The basic building blocks of the model are sets of data values (represented by the nodes of a graph). These sets may be combined by nested applications of union and product constructors to form new sets. The model also permits the expression of binary relations between pairs of sets (represented by graph edges) and simple constraints on them, i.e., totality, surjectivity, functionality and injectivity (represented by annotations on the edges).

Let $\mathcal{T}$ be a finite set of mutually exclusive abstract types, where each $\tau \in \mathcal{T}$ is an infinite set of symbols. The universe U is the union of symbols in all types. Let $\mathcal{T}^*$ be the closure of $\mathcal{T}$ under finite products and sums. A SIG is a graph, $G = (N, E)$, defined by two finite sets N and E. The set N contains *simple nodes* and *constructed nodes*, which are the products and sums of other nodes. Each simple node $A \in N$, is assigned a type, $\tau(A) \in \mathcal{T}^*$. The type of a constructed node is the product or union of the types of its constituent nodes. The set E contains labeled *edges* between nodes in N. Each $e \in E$ is denoted $e : A - B$, for $A, B \in N$. For each edge $e \in E$, its inverse, denoted e°, is in E. If $\tau(A) = \tau(B)$ then $e : A - B$ may optionally be designated as a selection edge. We use the term constraint to refer to any annotation or selection constraint on an edge.

An *instance* $\Im$ of G is a function whose domain is the sets N of nodes and E of edges. For each simple node, $A \in N$, $\Im[A]$ is a finite subset of $\tau(A)$. For each product node, $A \times B \in N$, $\Im[A \times B]$ is the full cross product of the sets $\Im[A]$ and $\Im[B]$. For each sum node, $A + B \in N$, $\Im[A + B]$ is the union of the sets $\Im[A]$ and $\Im[B]$. For each edge, $e : A - B \in E$, $\Im[e]$ is any subset of the product of $\Im[A]$ and $\Im[B]$. For each selection edge, $\sigma : A - B$, $\Im[\sigma]$ is a subset of the identity relation on $\Im[A]$. The set of all instances of G is denoted $I(G)$.

An annotation of a SIG $G = (N, E)$ is a function $\mathcal{A}$ whose domain is the set of edges E. For all $e \in E$, $\mathcal{A}(e) \subseteq \{f, i, s, t\}$. A *SIG schema* S is a pair $S = (G, \mathcal{A})$. An instance $\Im$ of G is a *valid instance* of $\mathcal{A}$ if for all $e \in E$, whenever $f \in \mathcal{A}(e)$ (respectively i, s or $t \in \mathcal{A}(e)$), $\Im[e]$ is a functional (respectively injective, surjective or total) binary relation. The set of all valid instances of S is denoted $I(S)$. The set of symbols of an instance, denoted $Sym(\Im)$, is the set of elements of U that appear in the range of $\Im$. For a subset of the universe, $Y \subseteq U$, $I_Y(S)$ denotes the set of instances of S that contain only symbols in Y.

4 Information Capacity

We consider formal notions of correctness for schema transformations that are based on the preservation of the information content of schemas[3, 4, 7, 9]. For a schema S, the latter is the set of valid instances, $I(S)$. Intuitively, a schema $S2$ has more information capacity than a schema $S1$ if every instance of $S1$ can be mapped to an instance of $S2$ without loss of information. Specifically, it must be possible to recover the original instance from its image under the mapping.

Absolute equivalence characterizes the minimum that is required to achieve information capacity equivalence and provides a foundation on which more specialized definitions of equivalence may be built. It is based on the existence of invertible (i.e., injective) maps between the sets of instances of schemas.

Definition 1. An *information (capacity) preserving mapping* between the instances of two schemas $S1$ and $S2$ is a total, injective function $f : I_Y(S1) \rightarrow I_Y(S2)$, for some $Y \subseteq U$. An *equivalence preserving mapping* is a bijection $f : I_Y(S1) \rightarrow I_Y(S2)$.

Definition 2. The schema $S2$ *dominates* $S1$ *absolutely*, denoted $S1 \preceq_{abs} S2$, if there is a finite $Z \subseteq U$ such that for each $Y \supseteq Z$ there exists an information preserving mapping $f : I_Y(S1) \rightarrow I_Y(S2)$. Also, $S1$ and $S2$ are *absolutely equivalent*, denoted $S1 \sim_{abs} S2$, if for each $Y \supseteq Z$ there exists an equivalence preserving mapping $f : I_Y(S1) \rightarrow I_Y(S2)$.

Decidable characterization of absolute equivalence are known for relational schemas with (primary) key dependencies and for types formed by the recursive application of product, set or union constructors on finite and infinite base types [1, 4, 5]. SIGs permit the representation of sets formed from nested product and union constructors, as well as simple constraints between these sets. These additions make testing for equivalence (and therefore dominance undecidable.

Theorem 3. Testing for absolute equivalence of SIGs is undecidable.

In principle, arbitrary mappings f may be used to satisfy the definitions of absolute dominance and equivalence. In fact, the definitions do not even require that the mappings can be finitely specified; they can simply be an infinite list of pairs of schema instances. Clearly, such mappings are of little use in a practical system. Furthermore, there exist very simple schemas with no "natural" correspondence between them that satisfy the definition of absolute dominance through a very complex instance level mapping [4]. This result, coupled with our undecidability result, show that absolute equivalence and dominance do not provide a sufficient foundation for analyzing practical integration problems.

To overcome the limitations of absolute equivalence, various abstract properties have been proposed that restrict the class of allowable instance mappings [4]. For example, *internal equivalence* states that two instances can be associated by an instance mapping only if they contain (almost) the same set of symbols. However, testing for both internal equivalence and dominance of SIG schemas is also undecidable [8].

5 Structural Transformations

Given Theorem 3 and other similar results, the question remains as to how practitioners can develop rigorous methodologies. Our response is to propose sets of schema transformations on SIGs that preserve or augment information capacity and are similar to transformations in existing integration and translation methodologies [3, 6, 7, 9]. For each set of transformations, we characterize precisely when a schema can be created from another through any arbitrary sequence of transformations. Our characterizations are couched in terms of definitions of dominance and equivalence having the following properties: 1-each is a sufficient condition for internal dominance or equivalence, respectively; 2-each is complete for a given set of transformations; and 3-each leads to a decidable procedure for testing if one schema can be transformed into another and for producing an information preserving (respectively, equivalence preserving) instance mapping between the schemas.

In the following definitions, $S1$ and $S2$ denote SIG schemas. A transformation T on $S1$ that produces $S2$ is denoted by $S1 \xrightarrow{T} S2$. An arbitrary (possibly empty) sequence of transformations $\xrightarrow{T}$ is denoted $\xrightarrow{T}^*$. For each class of transformations, an intuitive description is presented first, followed by a formal definition.

5.1 Definition of the Transformations

An *annotation transformation* (or α-transformation) removes constraints from an edge of a SIG schema. An example is shown in Figure 2.

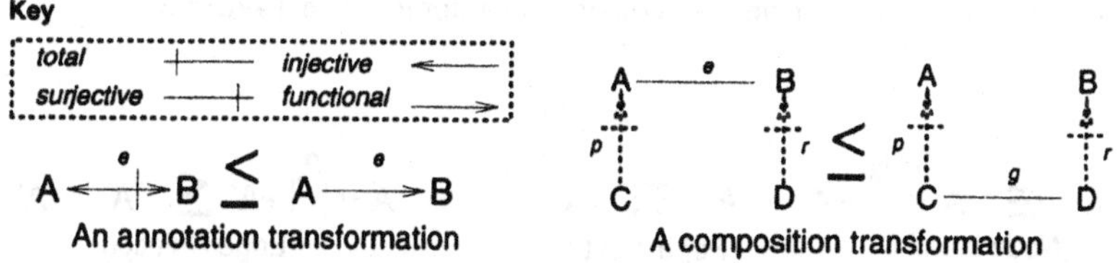

Fig. 2. An α-transformation and a o-transformation.

Definition 4. Let $S1$ contain an edge e. Let $S2$ be identical to $S1$ except that the constraints on e in $S2$ may be any subset of the constraints on e in $S1$. Then $S1 \xrightarrow{\alpha_e} S2$ and α_e is called an *annotation transformation (α-transformation).*

Theorem 5. *If $S1 \xrightarrow{\alpha} S2$ then $S1 \preceq_{int} S2$.*[4]

[4] Subscripts or superscripts indicating specific edges or nodes involved in the transformations may be omitted in denoting a transformation.

A *composition transformation* (or $\circ$-transformation) replaces an edge $e : A - B$ with another edge $g : C - D$. An example is shown in Figure 2. Such transformations permit attributes and entities to be moved in a schema. The instance mapping populates an instance of the edge g with an instance of the path $r^\circ \circ e \circ p$.

Definition 6. Let $e : A - B$ be an edge of $S1$ and let $p : C - A$ and $r : D - B$ be (possibly trivial) surjective functional paths in $S1$ not containing e. Let $G2 = G1$ except e is replaced by $g : C - D$ and the constraints on g in $S2$ are exactly the constraints on the path $r^\circ \circ e \circ p$ in $S1$. Then $S1 \xrightarrow{\circ^e_g} S2$ is called a *simple composition transformation* (a *simple $\circ$-transformation*).

Theorem 7. Let $\circ^e_g$ be a simple $\circ$-transformation that uses the surjective functional paths p and r. If $S1 \xrightarrow{\circ^e_g} S2$ then $S1 \preceq_{int} S2$. If $\mathcal{A}1(p) = \mathcal{A}1(r) = \{f, i, s, t\}$ and constraints of g are equal to the constraints of e then $S1 \sim_{int} S2$.

We can also construct information preserving mappings for simple $\circ$-transformations applied in parallel and $\circ$-transformations that move an edge to multiple edges. We therefore define a larger class of transformations.

Definition 8. A *$\circ$-transformation* is a set of one or more simple $\circ$-transformations. A $\circ$-transformation is denoted $S1 \xrightarrow{\{\circ^{e1}_{g1}, \ldots \circ^{en}_{gn}\}} S2$ where the $\circ^{ei}_{gi}$ are simple $\circ$-transformations and all g_i are distinct.

Theorem 9. If $S1 \xrightarrow{\{\circ^{e1}_{g1}, \ldots \circ^{en}_{gn}\}} S2$ then $S1 \preceq_{int} S2$. If each component simple $\circ$-transformation is equivalence preserving and all e_i are distinct then $S1 \sim_{int} S2$.

A *selection transformation* (or ς-transformation) creates or deletes nodes and edges. The ς-transformations we consider are depicted in Figure 3.

A ≡ A ↔ A' ($\sigma_{A'}$) — Node creation; A ≡ A (σ_A) — Edge creation; A ↔ A' ($\sigma_{A'}$) ≤ A A' — Edge Deletion

Fig. 3. Selection transformations.

A *node creation ς-transformation* creates a new node that is isomorphic to an existing node. A bijective selection edge between the two nodes enforces the constraint that the nodes be assigned identical sets in any valid instance.

Definition 10. Let A be a node of $S1$. Let A' be a new node not in $S1$ and $\sigma_{A'} : A \leftrightarrow A'$ a new bijective selection edge. Let $S2$ be $S1$ with the addition of A' and $\sigma_{A'}$. Then, $S1 \xrightarrow{\varsigma_A} S2$ is called a *node creation ς-transformation*, and $S2 \xrightarrow{\varsigma_A} S1$ is called a *node deletion ς-transformation*.

An *edge creation* ς*-transformation* creates a new edge. To preserve information capacity, the new edge is a bijective selection edge on a node.

An *edge deletion* ς*-transformation* removes an edge. If information capacity is to be preserved, arbitrary edges cannot be removed from a SIG. However, instances of bijective selection edges are fully defined by the instances of the incident nodes. Such edges may therefore be removed.

Definition 11. Let $\sigma_A : A \leftrightarrow\!\!\leftrightarrow A'$ be a new bijective selection edge between nodes A and A' of $S1$ and let $S2$ be $S1$ with the addition of σ_A. Then, $S2 \xrightarrow{\varsigma_{\sigma_A}} S1$ is an *edge deletion* ς-transformation and if $A = A'$ then $S1 \xrightarrow{\varsigma_{\sigma_A}} S2$ is an *edge creation* ς-transformation.

Theorem 12. *Let* $S1 \xrightarrow{\varsigma} S2$. *If* ς *is a node creation, node deletion or edge creation* ς*-transformation, then* $S1 \sim_{int} S2$. *If* ς *is an edge deletion* ς*-transformation that removes an edge from a node to itself, then* $S1 \sim_{int} S2$, *otherwise,* $S1 \preceq_{int} S2$.

When ς-transformations, o-transformations and α-transformations are combined, they permit complex additions and modifications to be made to a schema. Also, the information preserving mappings created by ς-transformations, o-transformations and α-transformations can be composed.

Corollary 13. *If* $S1 \xrightarrow{\alpha o \varsigma}{}^{*} S2$ *then* $S1 \preceq_{int} S2$.

5.2 Characterization of Dominance and Equivalence

We develop a characterization of dominance and equivalence that is complete with respect to all three types of transformations considered.

Definition 14. $S2$ $\alpha o \varsigma$-dominates $S1$, denoted $S1 \preceq_{\alpha o \varsigma} S2$, if there exist a surjective, injective node map $\psi : N1 - N2$ and a surjective, injective edge map $\theta : (E1 \cup N1) - E2$ satisfying the following.

1. If $A \in N1$ and ψ is not defined on A, then there exists a bijective selection path in $S1$ from A to a node B where ψ is defined on B.
2. If $A \in N1$ then for all $g' \in \theta(A)$ (where $g' \in E2$ and $g' : C' - D'$, $\psi^{-1}(C') = C$ and $\psi^{-1}(D') = D$), there exist surjective functional paths $p : C - A$ and $r : D - A$ in $S1$ and the constraints on g' in $S2$ are a subset of the constraints on the path $r^{\circ} \circ p$ in $S1$.
3. If $e \in E1$ and θ is not defined on e, then e is a bijective selection edge in $S1$.
4. If $e : A - B \in E1$ then for all $g' \in \theta(e)$ (where $g' \in E2$ and $g' : C' - D'$, $\psi^{-1}(C') = C$ and $\psi^{-1}(D') = D$), there exist surjective functional paths $p : C - A$ and $r : D - B$ in $S1$ (not containing e) and the constraints on g' in $S2$ are a subset of the constraints on the path $r^{\circ} \circ e \circ p$ in $S1$.

$S1$ is $\alpha o \varsigma$-*equivalent* to $S2$, denoted $S1 \sim_{\alpha o \varsigma} S2$, if $S1 \preceq_{\alpha o \varsigma} S2$ and $S2 \preceq_{\alpha o \varsigma} S1$.

One can show that $\alpha o \varsigma$-dominance is complete with respect to ς-transformations, o-transformations and α-transformations. This result and Corollary 13 imply that $\alpha o \varsigma$-dominance is a sufficient condition for internal dominance.

Theorem 15. *Let* $S1$ *and* $S2$ *be two SIG schemas. Then,* $S1 \overset{\alpha o \varsigma}{\longrightarrow}^{*} S2$ *iff* $S1 \preceq_{\alpha o \varsigma} S2'$ *where* $S2' \cong S2$.

5.3 Testing for Dominance

Definition 14 essentially gives an algorithm to test if two SIG schemas are in an $\alpha o \varsigma$-dominance relation, which by Theorem 15, also determines if a schema may be obtained from another through a sequence of transformations. Furthermore, our proof is constructive so we have the following result.

Corollary 16. *If* $S1 \preceq_{\alpha o \varsigma} S2$ *then we can construct a sequence of* α*-transformations,* o*-transformations and* ς*-transformations such that* $S1 \overset{\alpha o \varsigma}{\longrightarrow}^{*} S2$ *via this sequence and an information preserving mapping* $f : I(S1) \rightarrow I(S2)$.

The complexity of algorithms for testing $\alpha o \varsigma$-equivalence and $\alpha o \varsigma$-dominance and producing instance mappings is examined elsewhere [8].

References

1. S. Abiteboul and R. Hull. Restructuring Hierarchical Database Objects. *Theoretical Computer Science*, 62:3–38, 1988.
2. J. Albert, R. Ahmed, M. A. Ketabchi, W. Kent, and M. C. Shan. Automatic Importation of Relational Schemas in Pegasus. In *Proc. of the 3rd Int'l Workshop on Research Issues in Data Eng.: Interoperability in Multidatabase Systems*, pages 105–113, Vienna, Austria, Apr. 1993.
3. C. F. Eick. A Methodology for the Design and Transformation of Conceptual Schemas. In *Proc. of the Int'l Conf. on Very Large Data Bases*, pages 25–34, Barcelona, Spain, Sept. 1991.
4. R. Hull. Relative Information Capacity of Simple Relational Database Schemata. *SIAM Journal of Computing*, 15(3):856–886, Aug. 1986.
5. R. Hull and C. K. Yap. The Format Model: A Theory of Database Organization. *Journal of the ACM*, 31(3):518–537, 1984.
6. L. A. Kalinichenko. Methods and Tools for Equivalent Data Model Mapping Construction. In *Proc. of the Int'l Conf. on Extending Database Technology*, pages 92–119, Venice, Italy, Mar. 1990.
7. V. M. Markowitz and A. Shoshani. Representing Extended Entity-Relationship Structures in Relational Databases: A Modular Approach. *ACM Transactions on Database Systems*, 17(3):423–464, Sept. 1992.
8. R. J. Miller, Y. E. Ioannidis, and R. Ramakrishnan. Schema Equivalence in Heterogeneous Systems: Bridging Theory and Practice. To appear in: *Information Systems*, 19, 1994.
9. A. Rosenthal and D. Reiner. Theoretically Sound Transformations for Practical Database Design. In *Proc. of the Int'l Conf. on Entity-Relationship Approach*, pages 115–131, New York, NY, Nov. 1987.

Virtual Schemas and Bases*

Cássio Souza dos Santos**, Serge Abiteboul and Claude Delobel

INRIA, BP 105, 78153 Le Chesnay CEDEX, France
email: {souza,abitebou,delobel}@cosmos.inria.fr

1 Introduction

Views are intended to increase the flexibility of database systems and their definition in the object-oriented database (OODB) context comes as a natural extension of the original paradigm. The yet relatively young research on this topic has introduced a large variety of indispensable new features. However, the organizational aspects have been overlooked and a coherent way of integrating theses features is still missing. To solve this problem, we propose the notion of *virtual schema*. This concept is far from revolutionary: together with virtual bases, such schemas are intended to model the external level of the database exactly in the spirit of the architecture proposed by the Ansi/X3/Sparc Study Group [12]. We show how the flexibility they provide can be used to cope with various dynamic features of database systems.

A number of extensions to the object oriented paradigm have been proposed, e.g. [4, 13, 20, 10, 9, 20], which try to increase the flexibility of the paradigm and overcome some of its drawbacks. Many proposals have been recently made for the introduction of a view mechanism in object-oriented databases [1, 3, 7, 15, 16, 18, 19]. An important aspect of object-oriented views is that unlike relational views they are not only intended to restructure data. Operations on data play an essential role and combining classes is far more complicated than combining relations: it leads to the reorganization of aggregation (composition) and generalization (subclass) hierarchies. A view mechanism in an OODB context is thus more intricate than its analogue in a relational system.

The main contribution of this paper is the definition of a view mechanism that can be integrated as a basic functionality for OODBs *at the schema level.* Starting from a (real) schema, a virtual schema is defined. A virtual base is obtained when a (real) base is attached to a virtual schema. We study the consequences of this simple assumption. In particular, we observe the differences between a real schema and a virtual one. We also consider an extension (that we call generic views) where it is necessary to specify *several* real bases to attach data to a virtual schema.

This paper is a continuation of the work presented in [1]. We further extend that proposal with additional capabilities. The presentation is mostly informal and leans on a number of examples. The data definition language is quite intuitive and is based on that of the O_2 system [2]. However, the concepts that we discuss clearly apply to other OODB systems as well.

* Partially supported by Esprit Project GoodStep.

** On leave from Departamento de Informática, Universidade Federal de Pernambuco, Brazil. Partially supported by CNPq grant number 200.803-92.1.

2 Virtual Schemas

In our approach a view is defined as a *virtual schema*. A virtual schema is, as a normal schema, an organizational unit meant to encapsulate a set of related definitions. The main difference is that a real schema describes the structure and behavior of real data stored in the database whereas a virtual schema refers to a virtual world.

A view is thus in our context a special kind of schema to which some constraints on its use and definitions are imposed. We will use the term *virtual schema* as a synonym of view in what follows and the term *real schema* will be used in contrast to virtual schema to avoid confusion.

Like a real schema, a view includes definitions of classes, methods, types, functions and named objects. It may also import and export definitions from other schemas. In addition to that, the view definition primitives, namely *virtual classes*, *imaginary classes*, *virtual attributes* and *hiding of properties*, can be used in a virtual schema. These primitives will be presented in the sequel.

We next illustrate the notion of virtual schema through an example.

Let us define a real (root) schema from which we will derive our first view. The schema is partially specified in Figure 1, where the O_2 data definition language [2] is used. Only relevant definitions are shown. Two classes, namely `Date` and `Person` are imported from other schemas. Two other classes, `C_Employee` and `Department` are defined in the schema along with two named sets which are roots of persistence for instances of the defined classes.

```
schema company_schema;

import schema o2kit class Date;
import schema general class
Person;


class C_Employee inherits Person
type tuple(salary:real,
       department:Department,
       date_of_admission:Date);
methods ...
end;
```

```
class Department
type tuple(name:string,
       boss:C_Employee);
methods ...
end;

name The_C_Employees:
set(C_Employee);
name The_Departments:
set(Department);
```

Fig. 1. Real schema `company_schema`

Figure 2 shows a virtual schema derived from schema `company_schema`. This example contains the main components of a view definition, which are explained in the sequel.

```
virtual schema company_view from company_schema;

import all;

virtual class Boss includes
    (select d.boss from d in The_Departments)

attribute number_of_employees:integer in class Department has value
  count(select e from e in The_C_Employees
        where e.department = self);

attribute subordinates:set(C_Employee) in class Boss has value
  ((select e from e in The_C_Employees
        where e.department = self->department) - set(self));

attribute employees:set(C_Employee) in class Department has value
  self.boss.subordinates;

attribute number_of_subordinates:integer in class Boss has value
  count(self.subordinates);

attribute boss:Boss in class C_Employee has value self.department.boss;

hide attribute salary,boss in class Boss;
```

Fig. 2. View `company_view` defined from schema `company_schema`

A virtual schema is always derived from another virtual or real schema, which will be called its *root schema*. The root schema of a view determines on which bases it can be activated, namely those bases instantiated from its root schema. The root schema of view `company_view` is `company_schema`, as declared in the virtual schema definition command through its `from` clause.

In a view, we can import definitions from other schemas and views as well. The command `import all` specifies that all definitions from the root schema are to be imported; that includes those definitions already imported to the root schema itself, as it is the case for class `Date` imported from schema `o2kit` to `company_schema`.

After creating the view through the `virtual schema` command and importing definitions from other schema(s), we have the appropriate framework for defining virtual data. Here, we follow the ideas of [1]. The core specification of the view therefore consists in the definitions of *virtual classes* and *imaginary classes* with their respective *virtual attributes* and in the *hiding* of properties.

We briefly describe virtual attributes and the hiding of definitions. We will next discuss in more detail the concepts of virtual and imaginary classes since they raise interesting issues.

Virtual Attributes A virtual attribute is a special kind of function whose returned value is viewed as part of the structure of an object. They can be defined in real, virtual and imaginary classes. In addition, they can be defined from other virtual attributes.

Class `Department`, for example, is extended with the addition of a virtual attribute to it, namely `number_of_employees`. The virtual attribute `employees` in class `Department`, in turn, makes use of virtual attribute `subordinates` defined in virtual class `Boss`.

Hiding Definitions Let us assume that `company_view` is a view intended to be publicly available and that salaries of bosses are considered confidential. For this reason, attribute `salary` in class `Boss` is hidden.

Confidentiality is provided by the hiding mechanism. Not only attributes, but also methods and classes can be hidden. It is important to notice that hiding an attribute has a different effect from declaring it as private. In O_2, for instance, encapsulation provides modularity and enhances code maintainability, but it can be broken in the interactive (*ad hoc*) query mode, thus it cannot be used to implement authorization constraints.

Authorization must be provided at the view level through the combined use of the hiding and importing mechanisms as well as the definition of appropriate access rights to views. O_2 allows the definition of user groups to which read and write access rights can be granted with respect to schemas and bases. Such a mechanism is naturally extended to cope with virtual schemas and bases.

Virtual Classes Virtual classes can be defined from other classes through two virtualization processes, namely *specialization* and *generalization*. The current example considers specialization. Generalization will be discussed later on.

A virtual class can be defined from another (real, virtual or imaginary) class, which is called its *base class*. The definition of a virtual class includes the specification of its extension (population), i.e. the set of objects belonging to it, which is specified through a query expression[3]. Such query expression is called the *defining query* of the virtual class.

The definition of a virtual class has the following general format:

virtual class *class_name* **includes** *query_expression*

The class `Boss` defined in Figure 2, is a specialization of class `C_Employee`. Every instance of `Boss` is actually an instance of `C_Employee`.

Many different virtual classes can be defined from a given class through specialization by using different queries stating different (and not necessarily mutually excluding) properties. This approach has been considered by [1, 3, 16] among others and it leads to some basic issues:

Where should the virtual classes be placed in the global class hierarchy? The motivation for integrating virtual classes in the global class hierarchy is based on the need for sharing properties (intentional data) and object instances (extensional data), since virtual classes are defined from real classes and are populated with their instances.

If virtual classes are placed in the global class hierarchy, a number of problems arise. These problems are related to conflicts between the position of the type of the virtual class in the global type hierarchy and the position of the extension of the virtual class in the extension graph defined by the set containment relationship among class extensions.

At first glance, a virtual class defined by specialization is a subclass of its base class. Taking the view defined in Figure 2, we are intuitively led to consider that an

[3] The query language of O_2 is called O_2SQL and is, as its name suggests, an SQL based declarative query language.

instance of **Boss** is a **C_Employee**. This "*is_a*" relation is the conventional subclassing relationship. In the O_2 data model, although there is a distinction between class and type, the type of a given class C is a subtype of the type(s) of the superclass(es) of C, if any. But class **Boss**, for instance, has the attribute **salary** projected out through the hiding operator and its type is not a subtype of the type of **C_Employee**.

Approaches to the integration of new classes in the hierarchy includes that of [14], where an algorithm is shown, and of [4], where the concept of ***non-strict inheritance*** is used. Other alternatives include the maintenance of a separate hierarchy for virtual classes, and the definition of a new relationship between virtual and real classes (which is not that of composition nor of inheritance). This last alternative is the one adopted here.

Virtual classes are linked to the class graph through a different kind of relationship. In other words, the class graph is extended with a new kind of edge which we call *may_be*, to distinguish it from the "*is_a*" conventional relationship. In that sense, an instance of the base class *may_be* an instance of a corresponding virtual class. The resolution mechanism is thus redefined to take this relationship into account so that properties (attributes and methods) of the base class can be shared by the virtual class and that properties of the former can be redefined by the latter. We will not pursue this issue here.

When should we compute the extension of a virtual class? We can make a distinction between two kinds of data models: those with class extensions (i.e. the set of all instances of a class) and those without them. Most systems support class extensions at least at the physical level (e.g., this is the case for O_2 although the class extensions are not available at the logical level). We will not argue for or against class extensions but consider what are the implications for the specifications of virtual classes. To see this, we consider an alternative definition for **Boss**:

```
virtual class Boss includes
    (select e from e in C_Employee
        where exists d in Departments:(d.boss = e))
```

Fig. 3. Definition for class **Boss** using class extension

If class extensions are available, we can use them to specify the population of **Boss** as in Figure 3. The difference between this definition and the one given in Figure 2 is that, in the original definition, the system must infer that the class **Boss** is derived from **C_Employee**, whereas this is explicitly specified in this new one. Indeed, for the definition given in Figure 3, one can interpret the **where** clause as the specification of the ***characteristic function***[4] of class **Boss** in class **C_Employee**.

Finally, one should note that in many cases, it could be more practical to define the characteristic function as a method (e.g., Figure 4) in particular to have access to private attributes of the object or to be able to refine it in subclasses.

The previous discussion suggests that a specification of the form **includes** *query_expression* is appropriate for models with class extensions, whereas the use of characteristic functions is more appropriate if class extensions are absent from

[4] The characteristic function tests the membership of an object in the extension of a given virtual class.

the model. Observe that in a context without class extension we need not have the extension of the view. Also, in all cases, it is crucial to be able to test membership in a view (i.e. to use the characteristic function) since this test is going to be at the core of the method resolution mechanism and is thus an essential component of the performance of the view system.

```
method body ℵ_Boss:boolean in class Employee {
  return(exists d in The_Departments:(d.boss = self));}
virtual class Boss includes e from e in Employee where e->ℵ_Boss
```

Fig. 4. Characteristic Function for Virtual Class Boss

How and when should an object be considered an instance of a virtual class? An interesting approach would be to have membership of an object in a virtual class automatically achieved (e.g. using a triggering mechanism). This way, as soon as a real object satisfied the appropriate conditions it would become a virtual object and automatically gain a new interface. This semantics will be from now on referred to as *dynamic interface resolution.*

Another possibility would be to let the user control when an object should become virtual and perform the relevant tests and convertions (like type casting) explicitly.

A combination of the two solutions would be to let the type of the references to an object (type of variables defined in programs, i.e. the context in which the object is manipulated) drive the interface resolution mechanism and have automatic virtual object construction activated every time a real object was pointed by a virtual reference.

In any case, it should be possible for the programmer to access the original interface of an object (including the hidden properties) when writing his or her applications. This could be achieved by type casting, for instance. From now on, we assume the dynamic interface resolution mechanism. Such mechanism can, however, be bypassed with type casting.

If an object is an instance of several classes in the same view, how do we solve the ambiguity? An object is an instance of one single real class but it can be an instance of many different virtual classes in the view.

Assuming the dynamic interface resolution mentioned above, when multiple virtual classes are defined from the same class, resolution conflicts may arise since an object may become an instance of more than one virtual class. Such conflicts resemble conflicts due to multiple inheritance. However, conflicts due to multiple inheritance can be detected at compile time whereas objects may become and cease to be an instance of a virtual class at run time as a consequence of an update, so the situation is more intricate for virtual classes.

Forbidding the overlap of virtual classes has been considered in some approaches but is clearly too restrictive. A possible solution would be to forbid the definition of more than one virtual classes from the same class in the same view, i.e. have at most one facet of an object active at a time, but this may lead to an explosion in the number of necessary auxiliary views.

There are (like for multiple inheritance) many alternatives based on type casting[5],

[5] Casting in O_2C, the O_2 programming language, is similar to that defined for C++.

user intervention and use of priority levels. Observe that priorities can be implicitly assigned through nested view activations. If, for instance, the employee facet of a person must prevail on his or her student facet then the view where the employee facet is defined can be derived from that where the student one is given. Nested view activation is analogous to functional composition, as it will be discussed later on.

Imaginary Classes An imaginary class is defined through a query which returns a set of tuples. To each tuple, a new object identifier is attached to construct the extension of the imaginary class. Imaginary objects are instances of imaginary classes.

The general format for the definition of an imaginary class is as follows:

`imaginary class` *class_name* `includes` *query_expression*

As for virtual classes, the defining query of an imaginary class is not evaluated (*a priori*) and imaginary objects are constructed only on demand.

Let us consider an example.

The class `Family` defined below combines two instances of class `Person` to construct a couple, to which the virtual attribute `children` is further attached.

```
imaginary class Family includes
    (select [husband:h, wife:w]
         from h in People
         where h.sex = "male" and h.spouse = w)

attribute children in class Family has value
    self.husband.children union self.wife.children
```

Fig. 5. Definition of Imaginary Class *Family. People* is a named set of Persons.

The value of an imaginary object, i.e. the tuple whose structure is inferred from the defining query, determines its identity. In other words, the object identity is a function of its value and when defining an imaginary class the user should be aware of that functional dependency in order to define the proper *core attributes*, i.e. the attributes composing the tuple value of the imaginary object and which are not virtual attributes. The first time an imaginary object is accessed, the attributes from which the identity of the object depends must be given so that the object can be properly constructed. Further accesses return the same object identifier.

Different uses of imaginary objects determine different policies to be applied as far as object updates are concerned. Imaginary objects are intended to be mostly used to combine different objects in a new structure, like a join in the relational algebra.

The identifiers of the original objects composing the new structure are kept so that updates performed to the imaginary object can be propagated to the original ones. But such updates can also invalidate the imaginary object, since the property stated in the defining query may no longer hold after some update. This is also the case for relational joins, where tuples from different relations are glued based on a relationship among some of their attributes.

Sometimes, imaginary objects are used only for reading purposes and there is no update involved. In such cases, there is no need to activate any kind of policy for checking consistency and propagating updates. When updates are intended to be performed on imaginary objects, it is the responsibility of the class designer to define "safe" updates only. A safe update is an update which does not affect the identity nor the consistency of an imaginary object. The values of the core attributes may change but their object identifiers must remain the same. In addition, changes to attribute values must preserve the class invariant implicitly stated in the defining query expression.

The definition of **Family** above states that there are two core attributes, namely **husband** and **wife**, and the identity of its instances depends on them. Changing the value of attributes **husband** or **wife** is dangerous and it is preferable to disallow such changes in the imaginary class interface. But the nested attributes, i.e. the attributes of **husband** and **wife** may be updated through that interface. Observe that the update of the nested attribute **husband.spouse** may lead to an inconsistency. The relationship between **husband** and **wife** should be viewed as an invariant.

The restriction above is not sufficient to guarantee the consistency of imaginary objects, since the original objects may still be updated through their original interfaces, e.g. the **husband** object may be updated through its **Person** interface, and the instance of **Family** where it occurs may disappear as a result of this update (e.g. as a result of a divorce). Imaginary objects can therefore become obsolete due to side effects and the system must keep track of this[6].

It is important to notice that imaginary objects do not exist in the database but only in the view. They result usually from the combination of smaller objects into an aggregate object, or from decomposition of a large object into several smaller objects. Other uses include the creation of an object-oriented view of a relational database and the transformation of complex values into objects.

3 Virtual Bases

Let us see how a view can be activated and consider the differences between a real base and a virtual one.

Let us assume the existence of a base named **company_base** which has been instantiated from schema **company_schema**. The view **company_view** can be activated on such a base as follows:

```
set base company_base; /* base activation */
set schema company_view; /* view activation */
```

This is a valid view activation since the root schema of **company_view** is the schema from which the current base **company_base** has been instantiated. Once a virtual schema is set, a virtual base is automatically activated. This virtual base becomes the current base and its root schema, i.e. **company_view**, the current schema.

A virtual base can also be given a name after it has been activated. The names of virtual bases are persistent and can be used as a shorthand for further view activations on the same base. Another more elaborate use of named virtual bases

[6] This problem also occurs with virtual objects as well as the values of virtual attributes. In any case, a triggering mechanism could be used to propagate and/or prevent updates so as to keep objects in the view consistent.

will be illustrated in Section 4, where they are passed as parameters to generic view activations.

Figure 6 illustrates the activation of **company_view** on base **company_base**. Triangles denote schemas whereas cylinders denote bases. Dotted triangles and cylinders denote virtual schemas and virtual bases respectively.

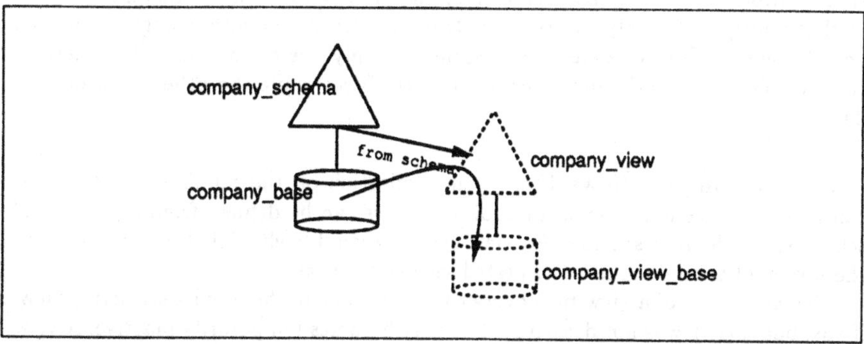

Fig. 6. Relationship between Real and Virtual Entities

Conceptually, a virtual base is created every time a view is activated. From an implementation point of view, however, this does not imply the physical creation of any virtual object. The concept of a virtual base is implemented through the activation of a more sophisticated interface resolution mechanism in charge of testing whether instances of real classes are also instances of a virtual class (using system derived characteristic functions) and performing the appropriate bindings as well as constructing the temporary virtual structures (dynamic interface resolution). Virtual data are therefore dynamically derived on demand.

It must be noticed that the view approach proposed here is different from that defined in relational systems. In such systems, view names (which denote virtual relations) are used in the query language as a shorthand for user convenience. When a query using a view name is computed, the view is dynamically evaluated and query optimization plays an important role in assuring a good performance. In our approach, view names are used for switching context. A good performance depends on efficient evaluation of the status that an object must acquire relatively to the currently active view at run time.

The system must keep track of dependencies between virtual attributes and the attributes they are derived from so as to be able to automatically update virtual attributes for those objects whose representations are mapped on the screen. In addition, since virtual class membership and consequent changes in structure and behavior for a given object may depend on its value, data updates must be controlled so that object interfaces be always consistent.

When **company_view** is active, i.e. when it is the current schema, every instance of class **C_Employee** which is also a virtual instance of class **Boss** gains a new virtual structure with two additional attributes, namely **subordinates** and **number_of_subordinates**. In addition, every instance of **C_Employee** also has an additional attribute, namely **boss**, but for instances of **C_Employee** which are also virtual instances of `Boss` this attribute is hidden. Instances of `Department` were also given two new attributes, namely `employees` and `number_of_employees`.

The new structure defined for a virtual object must not be confused with the creation of a new object. The object identifier of a virtual object is the same as that of its corresponding real object. Actually they are the same object, but have multiple interfaces. Related approaches are described in [18, 13], but they differ in that multiple copies of an instance variable are allowed to occur within an object [18] or that multiple explicitly constructed structures are stored with a single associated object identifier [13], whereas in our approach, only one of the multiple structures corresponds to the real (and possibly stored) object while the others add derived data.

Simple Nesting of Views There is no limitation on the number of views that can be defined from a schema. In addition, views can be defined from other virtual schemas, i.e. the root schema of a view can be virtual itself. This leads naturally to the notion of a valid sequence of nested view activations.

The activation of a view may overwrite definitions in the previously active view, if any, but this view is not deactivated, it only becomes temporarily inactive. A view activation stack is thus maintained and when a view is activated it is pushed onto the stack. The currently active view is always on the top of the stack. The bottom of the stack is always a real schema, the root of the schema dependency tree associated to the sequence of view activations recorded in the stack.

A more subtle way of nesting view activations is by passing virtual bases as parameters to a *generic view*. This will be considered in Section 4.

Real vs. Virtual Schemas Many constraints imposed on views come from the following essential principle: *Stored data and views must be independent.* In other words, views can be discarded or changed without compromising stored data. This is not true for real schemas. (The destruction of a schema in O_2 may happen only when all bases corresponding to this schema have been deleted.) The independence of stored data with respect to views is important for many reasons. It allows data structure and behavior to be described based only on real, i.e. conceptual schemas. As a consequence, views can be used for simulating schema evolution and different schema changes can be experimented without loss of data.

The following constraints distinguish virtual and real schemas:

1. To guarantee the independence of stored data with respect to views, real schemas cannot import definitions from virtual schemas. On the other hand, virtual schemas can import definitions from any other real or virtual schema.
2. Named objects defined in a virtual schema are virtual, i.e. they exist only during a view activation and are not persistent. Again for assuring database independence with respect to views.
3. Virtual classes cannot be explicitly instantiated via the `new` operator, available for object creation. Only instances of real classes can be explicitly created. Real instances are able to become virtual instances as a result of a view activation.
4. Imported classes can be redefined in a virtual schema but cannot be redefined in a real schema.

4 Generic Views and Database Integration

In this section, we consider a mechanism which provides more flexibility in nesting views, namely the generic views. The primary use of this mechanism is for integration of databases.

Database integration through views has been considered in a number of recent publications [11, 17, 6, 8, 1, 5]. Our approach is based on the use of *generic virtual schemas* and *class generalization.*

Let us assume the existence of bases `company_base` and `university_base`, instantiated from schemas `company_schema` and `uni_schema` respectively. We are interested in viewing the two heterogeneous bases as a single homogeneous base.

Class `C_Employee` is defined in `company_schema` shown in Figure 1, whereas `U_Employee` is defined in `uni_schema`, as shown in Figure 7. Both are subclasses of class `Person` and therefore share some attributes but each of them defines additional different attributes.

```
schema uni_schema;

import schema general class Person;

class U_Employee inherits Person...end;

name The_U_Employees: set(U_Employee);
```

```
virtual schema comp_uni_view from company_schema;

import all;
import schema uni_schema class U_Employee;
import base university_base name The_U_Employees;
virtual class Comp_Uni_Employee includes The_U_Employees, The_C_Employees;
```

Fig. 7. Database Integration through Generalization

The class `Comp_Uni_Employee` is defined as a generalization of `C_Employee` and `U_Employee`. The relevant definitions of `uni_schema` and the virtual schema `comp_uni_view`, where the generalization is defined, are given in Figure 7. The dissymmetry of the definition is due to the existence of a root schema which is a useful notion in general but leads here to some inelegance. The dissymmetry can be however eliminated. One might prefer, for instance, to use `general_schema` as the root schema and import the two other schemas for symmetry.

O_2 allows a schema to import names (roots of persistence) from different bases instead of importing them exclusively from other schemas. By importing a name from a schema, the user imports only its definition, no data being involved. When a name is imported from a base, however, all data which can be accessed from that named entry point in the imported base will be able to be accessed from the importing schema.

From the definition above we can derive the characteristic function. Indeed this could be combined with selective characteristic functions in definitions such as the one below, where we have a combined use of generalization and specialization:

```
virtual class Comp_Uni_Employee includes
        U_Employee where condition1,
        C_Employee where condition2
```

In the previous example, the import of names from foreign bases makes explicit reference to base names and commits programs defined in applications on the importing schema to a given base or set of bases. This is in contradiction to our philosophy so far to separate code (methods and application programs) from actual data.

We now introduce a mechanism to do this generically. In particular, we would like to be able to run the programs on different bases provided only at view activation.

View **comp_uni_view** defined in Figure 7 can be used to integrate no matter which base instantiated from schema **company_schema** (its root schema), but only with a single base, namely **university_base**, instantiated from schema **uni_schema**, since **The_U_Employees** was imported from it.

We want to modify the definition of **comp_uni_view** so that it can be used for the integration of any pair of bases instantiated from **company_schema** and **uni_schema** respectively.

This motivates the definition of a generic view, whose formal parameters must be replaced at view activation by actual parameters, namely the bases on which the view is to be activated[7]. The type of a formal view parameter is the name of a schema that determines the set of valid bases to be bound to that parameter when the view is activated. Thus, a database integration application can be written as a generic program and be applied to different structurally equivalent tuples of bases.

The generic definition of virtual schema **comp_uni_view** is given in Figure 8. View **comp_uni_view** can be activated on any base instantiated from **company_schema** (its root schema), but at view activation an additional base must be provided, which will be bound to the formal parameter **uni_base**. The named set **The_U_Employees** is then imported from this additional base, which must have been instantiated from schema **uni_schema**, as declared in the signature of the generic view. Also in Figure 8, we give an example of a valid generic view activation.

```
virtual schema comp_uni_view(uni_base:uni_schema) from company_schema;

import all;
import schema uni_schema class U_Employee;
import base uni_base name The_U_Employees;

virtual class Comp_Uni_Employee includes The_U_Employees, The_C_Employees;
```

```
set base company_base;
set view comp_uni_view(university_base);
```

Fig. 8. Definition and Activation of a Generic View

[7] The base instantiated from the root schema of the view and on which the view is activated can be seen as an implicit parameter, a reasoning similar to that of considering a message receiver in a message passing mechanism as an implicit parameter passed to the method implementing the message.

5 The Prototype O_2Views

A first prototype of the view mechanism described here has been implemented on top of the O_2 system.

The prototype is called O_2Views and encompasses a view definition language compiler. In O_2Views, virtual schemas can be defined using most of the features described above (generic views are not yet implemented). A view schema can be loaded into an O_2 system and the views can be used to query and update the database. Updates are performed in a restricted basis and must be further investigated.

Application programs can be developed for the view in the standard O_2 programming language O_2C. A graphical interface for the view specification has also been implemented.

This is a preliminary work. Applications are being written to test and validate the mechanism. The implementation is likely to change as the specification of the view mechanism evolves. Nevertheless, the specification of the system has attained a reasonable degree of maturity and we believe that the analysis of implementation aspects will play an important role in the definition of further extensions.

6 Conclusion

We have informally presented the functionality of a view mechanism for object-oriented databases. The approach is intended to favor the dynamic nature of intensional and extensional data by allowing it to be easily and intensively explored.

A virtual schema defines a context on which application programs can operate. Its activation, which results in the creation of a virtual base, represents a context switch and provides a means for dealing with the dynamics of database applications which is not favored by conventional object-oriented models.

There are yet several issues not yet fully resolved such as the placement of virtual classes in the hierarchy, strategies for solving resolution conflicts, or the lazy evaluation of virtual and imaginary extensions. Furthermore, it is necessary to explore how the view mechanism can be used in several contexts such as schema updates, object versionning, integrity constraint verification, and active databases. In particular, the use of deductive capabilities in conjunction with a view mechanism seems to be a promissing approach which remains to be studied.

Acknowledgments: Bernd Amann and Sophie Cluet are thanked for their valuable comments on earlier versions of this paper. We also would like to thank the referees for their comments and suggestions.

References

1. S. Abiteboul and A. Bonner. Objects and Views. In *Proc. ACM SIGMOD Conference on Management of Data*, pages 238–247, 1991.
2. F. Bancilhon, C. Delobel, and P. Kannelakis. *Building an Object-Oriented Database System - The Story of O_2*. Morgan Kaufmann, 1992.

3. Elisa Bertino. A View Mechanism for Object-Oriented Databases. In *International Conference on Extending Data Base Technology*, pages 136–151, Vienna, March 1991.
4. Alexander Borgida. Modeling Class Hierarchies with Contradictions. Technical report, Rutgers University, New Brunswick (NJ US), 1988.
5. W. Gotthard, P. C. Lockermann, and A. Neufeld. System-Guided View Integration for Object-Oriented Databases. *IEEE Transaction on Knowledge and Data Engineering*, 4(1), Feb. 1991.
6. Stephen Hayne and Sudha Ram. Multi-user view integration system (muvis): An expert system for view integration. *IEEE Data Engineering*, pages 402–409, July 1990.
7. S. Heiler and S.B. Zdonik. Object Views: Extending the Vision. In *IEEE Data Engineering Conference*, pages 86–93, Los Angeles, 1990.
8. M. Kaul, K. Drosten, and E.J. Neuhold. ViewSystem: Integrating Heterogeneous Information Bases by Object-Oriented Views. *IEEE Data Engineering*, pages 2–10, July 1990.
9. Henry Lieberman. Using Prototypical Objects to Implement Shared Behavior in Object-Oriented Systems. In *Proc. OOPSLA, Portland, OR*, 1986.
10. Guido Moerkotte and Andreas Zachmann. Multiple Substitutability without Affecting the Taxonomy. In *International Conference on Extending Data Base Technology*, 1992.
11. Amihai Motro. Superviews: Virtual Integration of Multiple Databases. *IEEE Transactions on Software Engineering*, 13(7):785–798, July 1987.
12. ANSI/X3/SPARC Study Group on Database Management Systems. Interim report. *ACM SIGMOD Bulletin 7,N2*, 1975.
13. Joel Richardson and Peter Schwarz. Aspects: Extending Objects to Support Multiple, Independent Roles. In *Proc. ACM SIGMOD Conference on Management of Data*, pages 298–307, 1991.
14. Elke Rundensteiner. A Class Integration Algorithm and Its Application for Supporting Consistent Object Views. Technical Report 92-50, Department of Information and Computer Science, University of Califoria, Irvine, May 1992.
15. Elke Rundensteiner and Lubomir Bic. Automatic View Schema Generation in Object-Oriented Databases. Technical Report 92-15, Department of Information and Computer Science, University of Califoria, Irvine, Jan. 1992.
16. M. H. Scholl, Christian Laasch, and Markus Tresch. Updatable Views in Object-Oriented Databases. In *Proc. DOOD, Munich, Germany*, 1991.
17. Michael Schrefl and Erich J. Neuhold. Object Class Definition by Generalization Using Upward Inheritance. In *Proc. IEEE Data Engineering Conf.*, pages 4–13, Los Angeles, Feb. 1988.
18. John J. Shilling and Peter F. Sweeney. Three Steps to Views: Extending the Object-Oriented Paradigm. In *Proc. OOPSLA, New Orleans, Louisiana*, 1989.
19. Katsumi Tanaka, Masatoshi Yoshikawa, and Kozo Ishihara. Schema Virtualization in Object-Oriented Databases. In *Proc. IEEE Data Engineering Conf.*, pages 23–30, Los Angeles, Feb. 1988.
20. Kazuyuki Tsuda, Kensaku Yamamoto, Masahito Hirakawa, Minoru Tanaka, and Tadao Ichikawa. MORE: An Object-Oriented Data Model with Facility for Changing Object Structures. *IEEE Transactions on Knowledge and Data Engineering*, 3(4):444–460, Dec. 1991.

Role-based Query Processing in Multidatabase Systems

Peter Scheuermann and Eugene Inseok Chong

Department of Electrical Engineering and Computer Science
Northwestern University
Evanston, IL 60208, USA

Abstract. We address the problem of data integration and query processing in multidatabase systems in the presence of conflicting values for the attributes that correspond to different instances of the same real-world object appearing in multiple roles. We present a new method for schema and data integration in multidatabase systems that presents the answer to the query as a set of sets representing the distinct intersections between the relations representing the various roles of interest. We present extensions to MSQL that allow us to express role-sets and quantifiers applied to them. We further develop a strategy for query processing based on our role-based model. Our method allows for local selection for all queries with/without aggregation and thus reduces the amount of data transmitted. In addition, it makes efficient use of merge-sort techniques to generate the role-sets and compute joins at the global query site.

1 Introduction

The integration of a number of databases into a multidatabase or federated system adds two new dimensions to the existing problems in heterogeneous systems, namely volume and autonomy [19,23]. The large volume of databases that need to be integrated in a federation implies in most cases that the construction of a global schema is not feasible. Autonomy means that different systems maintain control over their design and execution strategies. Whether partial or local integration needs to be performed, this system or user-defined process is usually carried out in two steps, namely schema integration [2,11,20] and data integration [2,10]. Schema integration deals with the resolution of naming conflicts (homonyms and synonyms), scale differences, and structural differences. Structural differences are resolved usually by performing an outerjoin operation [8,21] or via generalization [10,11,14]. However, the outerjoin method generates unnecessary null values. In order to avoid this problem, integration based on generalization introduces a generalized entity set which possesses the attributes common to all local databases. For example, assuming two local databases consisting of one relation each, FACULTY(ID,institution,salary,office) and STUDENT(ID,institution,salary,degree), the multidatabase would consist of the generalized entity set PERSON(ID,institution,salary).

We shall discuss now the implication of schema integration to data integration and show the deficiencies of current approaches.

1.1 The Impact of Schema Integration on Data Integration

When data integration is performed according to a generalization scheme a problem is encountered when the same real-world object has different values for the same attribute. Using the sample databases given above, the same real-world object may have two different salaries, one as a FACULTY and the other as a STUDENT. This inconsistency was solved in [10,11,14] by defining an aggregate function such as average over the overlapping local data values. This problem is also encountered in the data integration approach based on outerjoin when the same join attribute has different values.

There are a couple of problems with this approach. First, we are not dealing here with real inconsistencies, but rather with different values that an attribute can take for *distinct roles* played by the same real-world entity. By presenting the global user with an aggregate value, he/she may lose valuable information residing in the local databases. We view this as a violation of local autonomy [23]. The second related problem is another restriction placed on the global view. The global user has no access to the attributes specific only to some local databases, such as student degree and faculty office in our example.

An alternative approach, based on user-defined schema integration, has been presented in [17,18]. Assuming that the relational model is used as the common interface for the local databases and for the global presentation level, this approach extends the relational one by presenting the answer as a set of sets as opposed to a single set. Thus, in response to the query: 'retrieve all persons with a salary value greater than 30,000,' the answer will consist of two tables FACULTY and STUDENT. The problem with this approach is that tuples corresponding to real-world objects who are FACULTY and STUDENT will be scattered through the tables FACULTY and STUDENT and it is difficult for the user to visualize the two salary values for the same real-world object. Although it is possible in this approach to define a function that combines all tuples of the same real-world object [17], this is an operation applied after all other processing is finished and one that introduces null values since it requires an outerjoin.

In this paper, we present a new conceptual framework to schema and data integration in multidatabase systems and a related query processing strategy. Our approach, first suggested in [24], is based on the idea of presenting the answer to a query as a set of sets representing the *distinct intersections* between the relations corresponding to the various roles. We shall denote this set as a *role-set*. Thus, in response to the query given above, our answer will consist of three sets: the set of qualifying persons who appear only in the role FACULTY, the set of qualifying persons who appear only in the role STUDENT and the set of people who play both roles, FACULTY and STUDENT. This approach eliminates the problems discussed above. It is easy for the user to see the two salary values for the real-world objects that are in the set FACULTY & STUDENT. It does not introduce any null values; in addition, for the tuples that appear in both roles we can present also the office and degree information with no difficulty. Note that this approach can also be applied for objects that have a single role but appear in multiple instances across different local databases. We observe here that our approach requires the capability to identify instances of the same real-world object in different local databases. The object identification problem [15,16] is beyond the scope of this paper; we assume in this paper the existence of global object identifiers that can be used for this purpose.

1.2 Query Processing and Optimizations

MSQL [18] was the first multidatabase language proposed as an extension to SQL. MSQL manipulates multirelations which are sets of relations dynamically created by a query. The relations of a multirelation come in most cases from different local databases of a multidatabase and they may differ in degree, attribute name, and domain types. The answer to a query in MSQL is also a multirelation. Multirelational algebra and calculus were defined in [13] and it was shown how they be used to optimize MSQL queries. We provide in this paper a number of extensions to MSQL which allow us to present the answer as a role-set. In addition, our extensions provide more expressive power via the use of universal quantifiers for role-sets.

Query optimization in multidatabase systems is largely based on the approaches used for distributed database systems [1,3,4,7,29]. In distributed database systems, a user query is processed in three phases [26]. During the local processing phase, all local operations including selections and projections are performed using conventional query optimization techniques [5,6,25]. In the reduction phase, the size of the relations to be shipped to the final destination is further reduced, usually by applying semijoins [1,3,4,29]. In the final processing phase the reduced relations are sent to the final site where any remaining joins are performed. While most approaches concentrate on minimizing the data transmission costs, a number of algorithms have been proposed that aim at minimizing the processing time by using fragmentation and replication [27,28].

Query processing in multidatabase systems has to deal with additional problems due to heterogeneity and autonomy [12,14,22,24]. One aspect of autonomy is related to the resolution of inconsistencies between the local systems. A second aspect, is that now the global site can do very little as far as enforcing specific plans at the local sites. The multidatabase query processing approach proposed in [10,11,14] has a number of drawbacks. In addition to the violation of autonomy mentioned earlier, resolving inconsistencies via aggregate functions has the effect that local selections cannot be performed for aggregate queries. This increases the data transmission costs and places a heavy load on the global site where outerjoins and aggregation need to be performed for select queries. Since most relations handled at the global site are intermediate results for which no auxiliary access paths are available, it is important to devise a query processing strategy for the global site aimed at processing efficiently this type of data. The role-based query processing strategy that we present in this paper makes efficient use of merge-sort to generating the role-sets and compute the resulting joins at the query site.

The remainder of this paper is organized as follows. In section 2, we describe the role-based model and our extensions to MSQL. Section 3 describes our algorithm for query processing based on merge-sort. We conclude in Section 4.

2 Model Definitions and MSQL Extensions

We consider here multidatabases that are collections of a number of relational databases, denoted as local databases. The functions of the global data manager are duplicated at each site. In addition, each site maintains its own local database system. Hence, for a given query any site can act as the global, or assembly site; this is the site where the query is entered and the final answer is received. Our model supports user defined schema integration. As in MSQL the local databases participating in the federation are defined dynamically at query time. In addition, the user has the option to specify what strategy to use in order to deal with data inconsistencies, namely whether to use an aggregation based approach or not. We shall assume that in each local database an ID (key) uniquely identifies a tuple in a relation and, furthermore, that the same ID can serve as a global object identifier. While the unique key assumption has been used in other systems [10,11] too, the attribute(s) used to identify the instances of the same real-world object does not have to be a key, and the keys are not necessarily in the same format. If this is the case, we assume that a method similar to the one proposed in [16] is employed first for entity identification. We also make two additional assumptions for the ease of presentation only. The first is that a real-world object can have only one role in each local database. The second is that an object has only one materialization for each distinct role. Our model can easily be extended to remove these restrictions [9].

Definition 1: Let $R_1, R_2, ..., R_n$ be relations corresponding to distinct roles. Each relation R_i consists of all the materializations of real-world objects in a given role across the local databases. *Role-Set($R_1, R_2, ..., R_n$)* is the set of disjoint intersections between relations $R_1, R_2, ..., R_n$. For example, role-set(A,B,C) is the set {{A-B-C},{B-C-A},{C-A-B},{($A \cap B$)-C},{($B \cap C$)-A},{($A \cap C$) - B},{$A \cap B \cap C$}}. The number of elements in the role-set is $2^n - 1$.
Note: we define an intersection $R_1 \cap R_2 \cap ... \cap R_n$ so as to contain all the tuples representing distinct materializations of the same real world object. Qualification phrases can be expressed against role-sets resulting in an extended definition of a select statement.

MSQL Extension 1: *MULTISELECT attributes* and *USING field* are added for generating a role-set using *field* as the identifier for the same real-world object. For example,

MULTISELECT * USING *ID* FROM *X*, *Y*

The query will generate the role-set of the relations X and Y using ID as the global identifier. If we have X(ID,A,B) and Y(ID,A,C), then the query above is translated into a set of queries using SQL as follows:

{X-Y}: SELECT *ID,A,B* FROM *X*
WHERE *ID* NOT IN (SELECT *ID* FROM *Y*)
{Y-X}: SELECT *ID,A,C* FROM *Y*
WHERE *ID* NOT IN (SELECT *ID* FROM *X*)
{X∩Y}: SELECT *X.ID,X.A,X.B,Y.ID,Y.A,Y.C* FROM *X,Y*
WHERE *X.ID = Y.ID*

Definition 2: (use of quantifiers for selection from role-set)
∃ *condition*: select all materializations of a real-world object in an intersection $R_1 \cap ... \cap R_n$ as long as one of them satisfies the selection criteria.
∀ *condition*: select condition has be satisfied by all materializations of the objects. In both cases the user is presented with all the materializations.

Example 1. Assume that relations R and S represent two different roles of an object and they contain tuples with attributes (ID,A). The current extensions are R = $(<1,50>,<2,250>,<3,120>)$ and S =$(<1,150>,(3,180>)$. The intersection of R∩S is performed with respect to IDs : $R \cap S = (<1,50>,<1,150>,<3,120>,<3,180>)$. A select(∃) with respect to the qualification A $>$ 100 will return the set $R \cap S$ since for each of the two objects at least one materialization qualifies. On the other hand, a select(∀) with respect to the same qualification will return the set $(R \cap S)' = (<3,120>,<3,180>)$ since one of the materializations of object with ID=1 does not qualify.

MSQL Extension 2: *WHERE EXIST(predicates)* and *WHERE FORALL(predicates)* are added for ∃ and ∀ conditions respectively. The syntax is:
MULTISELECT target list USING ID FROM ROLE-SET(O)
WHERE EXIST (FORALL) (predicate).
Note that the role-set of an object O can be specified explicitly or can be defined separately similar to the CREATE operation in MSQL [18].

MSQL Extension 3: **.<attribute> <operator> *.<attribute>* or *<function-name>(*.<attribute>) <operator> <function-name>(*.<attribute>)* is added as a predicate of role-set. '*' can be any element of the role-set. *<operator>* can be any relational operator and *<function-name>* can be any aggregate function. For example,
MULTISELECT * USING *ID* FROM *X,Y* WHERE **.A = *.A*
The query will select the tuples with the same A values. The possible joins among the role-set elements are:

1.(X-Y)⋈(X-Y)	2.(Y-X)⋈(Y-X)	3.(X-Y)⋈(Y-X)
4.(X-Y)⋈(X∩Y)	5.(Y-X)⋈(X∩Y)	6.(X∩Y)⋈(X∩Y)

Joins 1,2,3 above correspond to one-to-one joins, joins 4,5 represent one-to-many joins and join 6 is a many-to-many join. Note that joins 1,2,6 contain also recursive joins which are included here for the sake of completeness. As an example, the join 5 above can be translated into SQL query as follows: (We let YO denote {Y-X}, and XY denote {X ∩ Y})

(Y-X)⋈(X∩Y): SELECT * FROM *YO,XY*
WHERE *YO.A = XY.(X.A)* OR *YO.A = XY.(Y.A)*

3 A Strategy for Role-based Query Processing

We outline in this section our strategy for query processing with role-based sets that aims at minimizing the amount of data to be transmitted between the local sites and the global site as well as reducing the processing costs at the global site for dealing with intermediate data and producing the final joins. The intermediate data to be generated at the global site requires the generation of ***private*** and ***overlap*** parts of a query. These sets can be found efficiently by applying a merge-sort after the selection. During this step we also apply the quantifiers for non-aggregate queries. In the case of aggregate queries, we identify during this step the overlap data that does not satisfy the aggregate condition in order to prevent unnecessary data communication for the overlap part. We define the following parameters and symbols to formalize our algorithm.

n : number of local sites
R_{ji} : relation j at site i
A_{kji} : attribute k of relation j at site i
GS : global site
r : number of relations in the query
R_j: $\cup_i R_{ji}$
LS_i : local sites (i=1,..,n)

Definition 3: *ID Overlap(IO)* is a set of IDs materialized in more than one local database. *ID Private(IP)* is a set of IDs materialized in only one local database. From the example 1, ID {2} is in the ID private and IDs {1,3} are in the ID overlap.

Definition 4: *Aggregation Overlap(AO)* is a subset of the ID Overlap, which satisfies a certain aggregate function specified in the selection criteria. *Selection Overlap(SO)* is a subset of the ID Overlap, whose IDs satisfy the selection criteria at all their sites. *Selection Private(SP)* is a subset of the ID Private, whose IDs satisfy the selection criteria. The Aggregation Overlap is used when the user specifies an aggregation function in the query. The Selection Overlap and Selection Private are used in connection with the ∀ condition while ID overlap and ID private are used in connection with the ∃ condition.

3.1 Selection and Projection

Algorithm 1:

Step 1. A user sends a query to the global site.

user query: $\pi_P\ \sigma_F(R_1 \times R_2 \times ... \times R_r)$
P ∈ target attributes, F : selection formula

Step 2. The global site modifies this query into a set of local queries by referring to local database information. The global site sends the subqueries to each local site. If the query involves no aggregation, the user can specify either $\exists$ condition or $\forall$ condition. If the query specifies the $\forall$ or $\exists$ condition, each local site performs a selection and sends all its IDs to the global site, then the global site attaches an indicator(SI) to the IDs to represent whether it was selected or not. The selection indicators are used to process $\exists$ and $\forall$ condition and the join operation. If the user query involves an aggregation such as an average, the global site requests the IDs of data along with the aggregation attributes. This makes local selection possible later on and also reduces communication costs significantly.

case 1 : $\exists$ or $\forall$ condition
  Each LS_i performs a selection on R_{ji}.
    temp := $\pi_{ID}\ \sigma_F(R_{ji})$ (j=1,...,r)
  Each LS_i sends R_{ji}[ID] to GS.
  GS attaches SI. (SI = 1 if ID $\in$ temp, 0 otherwise)
case 2 : aggregation
  Each LS_i sends R_{ji}[ID,A_{kji}] to GS. (A_{kji}:aggregation attribute)

Step 3. The global site merges all the IDs of the relations and sorts them(merge-sort method). The ID overlap part is then found among the relations by scanning each relation once using pointers that are advanced in interleaved fashion. There may be more than one overlap part. For example, if we have 3 relations A, B, and C, we have overlap parts (A $\cap$ B)-C, (A $\cap$ C)-B, (B $\cap$ C)-A, and A $\cap$ B $\cap$ C. If the query involves an aggregation, we perform the aggregation function simultaneously on aggregation attributes, and if the aggregation satisfies the selection criteria, we save the IDs. This constitutes the *aggregation overlap*. If the query specifies a $\forall$ condition, we check if an ID was selected at all its sites. If the ID was not selected at any of its sites, then disregard that ID. Otherwise, we save the ID. This constitutes the *selection overlap*. If the ID belongs to only one site, we save it in *selection private*. If the query specifies an $\exists$ condition, then the processing will be the same as the case of $\forall$ condition except that we check if an ID is selected at any of its sites. If it is, we save it in the *selection overlap*. The global site sends the ID overlap, selection overlap, and aggregation overlap information, as needed, to each local site.

case 1: $\exists$ condition
  GS finds selection private SP and selection overlap SO.
    $temp_j := (R_{j1}[ID], SI) \cup (R_{j2}[ID], SI) \cup ... \cup (R_{jn}[ID], SI)$ (j=1,..,r)
    $SO(R_{a1}, R_{a2}, .., R_{ah}) := temp_{a1}[ID] \cap temp_{a2}[ID] \cap ... \cap temp_{ah}[ID]$
      if $\exists$ SI=1, (a1,a2,..,ah $\in$ {1,..,r})
    $SP := \cup_j temp_j[ID]$ if ID $\in temp_j$ and ID $\notin temp_m$, $\forall m \neq j$ and
      SI=1
  GS sends SP and SO($R_{a1}, R_{a2}, .., R_{ah}$) to LS_i.
case 2: $\forall$ condition

GS finds selection private SP and selection overlap SO.

$temp_j := (R_{j1}[ID], SI) \cup (R_{j2}[ID], SI) \cup ... \cup (R_{jn}[ID], SI)$ (j=1,..,r)

$SO(R_{a1}, R_{a2}, .., R_{ah}) := temp_{a1}[ID] \cap temp_{a2}[ID] \cap ... \cap temp_{ah}[ID]$ if all SI=1, (a1,a2,..,ah $\in \{1,..,r\}$)

$SP := \cup_j temp_j[ID]$ *if* $ID \in temp_j$ *and* $ID \notin temp_m, \forall m \neq j$ and SI=1

GS sends SP and SO($R_{a1}, R_{a2}, .., R_{ah}$) to LS_i.

case 3: aggregation

GS finds ID overlap IO and aggregation overlap AO.

$temp_j := R_{j1}[ID, A_{kj1}] \cup R_{j2}[ID, A_{kj2}] \cup ... \cup R_{jn}[ID, A_{kjn}]$ (j=1,..,r)

$IO(R_{a1}, R_{a2}, .., R_{ah}) := temp_{a1}[ID] \cap temp_{a2}[ID] \cap ... \cap temp_{ah}[ID]$ (a1,a2,..,ah $\in \{1,..,r\}$)

$AO := \cup IO(R_{a1}, R_{a2}, .., R_{ah})$ if ID satisfies aggregation condition.

GS sends IO($R_{a1}, R_{a2}, .., R_{ah}$) and AO to LS_i.

Step 4. For the $\exists$ or the $\forall$ condition, each local site performs projection for both the selection private and selection overlap. For aggregation, each local site performs selection and projection for ID private part and projection for aggregation overlap. Each local site sends the retrieved data to the global site.

case 1: $\exists$ or $\forall$ condition

For selection private SP and overlap part SO:

Each LS_i performs projection.

$temp1_{ij} := \pi_P(R_{ji})$, (j=1,..,r), $\forall ID \in SP$

$temp2_{ij} := \pi_P(R_{ji})$, (j=1,..,r), $\forall ID \in SO$

Each LS_i sends $temp1_{ij}$ and $temp2_{ij}$ to GS.

case 2: aggregation

For ID private part IP:

Each LS_i performs selection and projection.

$temp1_{ij} := \pi_P\ \sigma_F(R_{ji})$, (j=1,..,r), $\forall ID \in IP$

Each LS_i sends $temp1_{ij}$ to GS.

For Aggregation overlap part AO:

Each LS_i performs projection.

$temp2_{ij} := \pi_P(R_{ji})$, (j=1,..,r), $\forall ID \in AO$

Each LS_i sends $temp2_{ij}$ to GS.

Step 5. The global site merges the data collected from each local site.

$private_j := \cup_i\ temp1_{ij}$

$overlap(R_{a1}, R_{a2}, .., R_{ah}) := \cup_{i,j}\ temp2_{ij}$ (j=a1,a2,..,ah)

result := $\{private_j\ , overlap(R_{a1}, R_{a2}, .., R_{ah})\}$

Example 2 ($\exists$ condition). Let us consider a multidatabase system consisting of two sites. The schema definition for each local database(LDB) is as follows and the corresponding relations are given in Table 1 and 2.

Site 1: Faculty: FAC(ID,NAME,SALARY,OFFICE)
Student: STU(ID,NAME,SALARY,DEGREE)
Site 2: Faculty: FAC(ID,NAME,SALARY,OFFICE)
Student: STU(ID,NAME,SALARY,DEGREE)

Note that the schema definition for the relation representing the same real-world object such as FAC could be different in each local database. Also their attribute names could be different. FAC and STU are multiple identifiers [17], meaning that FAC and STU identify more than one relation (FAC identifies FAC in site 1 and 2, and STU identifies STU in site 1 and 2). For a user query, 'retrieve ID, NAME, SALARY for a person whose salary is ≥ 150 from faculty and student,' the extended MSQL query is as follows: (We assume that the user specifies the ∃ condition.)

Table 1. LDB1.FAC and LDB1.STU

ID	NAME	SALARY	OFFICE
1	John	300	H-100
2	Mike	250	H-101
3	John	350	H-102
4	Mike	250	H-103

ID	NAME	SALARY	DEGREE
5	Mary	120	PhD
6	Nancy	100	MS
7	Mike	150	PhD

Table 2. LDB2.FAC and LDB2.STU

ID	NAME	SALARY	OFFICE
5	Mary	330	Y-100
7	Mike	250	Y-101

ID	NAME	SALARY	DEGREE
1	John	100	MS
3	John	150	PhD
8	Smith	170	MS

MULTISELECT *ID, NAME, SALARY* USING *ID*
FROM *FAC, STU* WHERE EXIST($SALARY \geq 150$)

The global site modifies this user query into subqueries for each local database and sends them to corresponding local sites. Notice that since the user query does not involve any aggregation, we need to request only IDs. Now, each local site performs a selection and sends the IDs for FAC and STU to the global site. The global site receives the IDs from the local sites, attaches the selection indicators and merge-sorts them(Table 3). Note that merge-scan allows us to obtain all overlap parts by scanning each relation only once simultaneously independent of the number of roles.[1] In this example, the overlap part between FAC and STU is {1,3,5,7}. The global site sends this information to each local site and each local site performs a projection. Each local site sends the results to the global site for a merge of these results. The final results are given in Table 4-5.

[1] If the amount of data is too large to fit in the main memory available, we need to swap in and out some portion of the data between main memory and secondary storage such as a disk. This is exactly the same as the external sorting method.

Table 3. FAC and STU

ID	SI
1	1
2	1
3	1
4	1
5	1
7	1

ID	SI
1	0
3	1
5	0
6	0
7	1
8	1

Table 4. (FAC-STU) and (STU-FAC)

ID	NAME	SALARY
2	Mike	250
4	Mike	250

ID	NAME	SALARY
8	Smith	170

Table 5. FAC ∩ STU

ID	NAME	FAC.SALARY	STU.SALARY
1	John	300	100
3	John	350	150
5	Mary	330	120
7	Mike	250	150

Example 3 (∀ condition). Consider the following query.

MULTISELECT * USING *ID* FROM *FAC, STU*
WHERE FORALL(*SALARY* ≥ 150)

In the case that the user specifies the ∀ condition, the global site requests IDs from each local site. Each local site first performs a selection and then sends IDs to the global site where these data are merged(Table 3). The global site finds the selection private and selection overlap. In this example the selection private is {2,4,8}, and the selection overlap is {3,7}. The global site sends these results to each local site. Each local site performs a projection for both selection private and selection overlap parts, and sends the results to the global site where these results are merged(Table 6 and 7).

Example 4 (Aggregation). For the query 'retrieve ID, NAME, SALARY for persons whose total salary in roles faculty and students ≥ 450.' The MSQL query is:

MULTISELECT *ID, NAME, SALARY* USING *ID*
FROM *FAC, STU* MGROUP BY *ID* HAVING MSUM(*SALARY*) ≥ 450

The global site requests each local site to send its IDs and the values of the aggregation attribute SALARY; it then merge-sorts these data (Table 8). The global site finds the overlap part, computes aggregate values simultaneously, and checks if they satisfy the aggregation condition. This results in an overlap part consisting of {1,3,5,7} and an aggregation overlap part consisting of {3,5}. The global site sends these results to each local site, and each local site performs selection and projection for the private part and projection for the aggregation overlap part. Each local site sends the results to the global site where a merge is performed to produce the final results(Table 9). Notice that sets (FAC-STU) and (STU-FAC) are empty in this example.

Table 6. (FAC-STU) and (STU-FAC)

ID	NAME	SALARY	OFFICE
2	Mike	250	H-101
4	Mike	250	H-103

ID	NAME	SALARY	DEGREE
8	Smith	170	MS

Table 7. FAC ∩ STU

ID	NAME	FAC.SALARY	OFFICE	STU.SALARY	DEGREE
3	John	350	H-102	150	PhD
7	Mike	250	Y-101	150	PhD

Table 8. FAC and STU

ID	SALARY
1	300
2	250
3	350
4	250
5	330
7	250

ID	SALARY
1	100
3	150
5	120
6	100
7	150
8	170

Table 9. FAC ∩ STU

ID	NAME	FAC.SALARY	STU.SALARY
3	John	350	150
5	Mary	330	120

3.2 Join

The join operation is performed after the selection so that we can reduce the costs. The processing steps of the join operation after the selection with $\exists, \forall$, or aggregation will be the same. Since we need to generate the results as a role-set, we proceed with our join operation as follows:

Algorithm 2:

Step 1. After the selection, the global site has the ID information about the selected tuples. The global site sends the IDs to each local site. Then each local site sends to the global site the join attributes corresponding to each ID.

Step 2. At the global site we merge-sort on the join attributes of each relation. If the join condition involves an aggregation, then we compute the aggregate values for join attributes, and use the aggregate values during a join.

Step 3. Using the same approach as in the selection process, we can find a role-set by scanning each relation once comparing join attribute values. The tuples with the same join attribute values are stored in the buffer so that we do not need to retrieve those tuples again when we actually perform a join.

Example 5 (Join without aggregation). Consider the following join query:

MULTISELECT *ID, SALARY* USING *ID* FROM *FAC, STU*
WHERE EXIST(*SALARY* $\geq$ 150) AND *FAC.NAME = STU.NAME*

As can be seen from the example 2, we get the IDs {1,2,3,4,5,7,8} among which the overlap part is {1,3,5,7} after the selection. After receiving the ID information from the global site each local site sends the joining attribute NAME and target attribute SALARY values to the global site. The global site merge-sorts on the NAME values received from local sites(Table 10). In this example since the relations STU and FAC are involved, we can get as a set of sets joins (STU-FAC) ⋈ (STU-FAC), (FAC-STU) ⋈ (FAC-STU), (STU-FAC) ⋈ (FAC-STU), (STU-FAC) ⋈ (STU ∩ FAC), (FAC-STU) ⋈ (STU ∩ FAC), and (STU ∩ FAC) ⋈ (STU ∩ FAC). Since the join is done between FAC and STU only, the answer would exclude the joins (STU-FAC) ⋈ (STU-FAC) and (FAC-STU) ⋈ (FAC-STU). The answer set can be found by keeping a pointer to each relation and comparing NAMEs for FAC and STU. This process is described below.

We keep a buffer for each relation. During the scan the IDs with the same join attribute values are kept in the buffer until a different value is encountered at which time we generate joins using IDs in two buffers. Let us assume that Buffer1 is assigned to FAC and Buffer2 is assigned to STU. The IDs with selection indicator 0 are skipped because these tuples are not involved in the join at all. Their existence enables us to present all the values of the object and perform an aggregation function if needed. Buffer1 would have IDs {1,3} with a value John and Buffer2 would have {3} with the same value. We have a join {(1,3)} assuming that we do not join between the same objects. The {(1,3)} will be put in the join (STU ∩ FAC) ⋈ (STU ∩ FAC) because IDs 1 and 3 are in the overlap part. After that Buffer1 would have {5} without any match. Buffer2 would have {7} with a value Mike and Buffer1 would have {2,4,7} with the same value. Then generate a join {(2,7),(4,7)} in the set (FAC-STU) ⋈ (STU ∩ FAC) and {(2,4)} in the set (FAC-STU) ⋈ (FAC-STU) since ID 7 is in the overlap part and IDs 2 and 4 are in the private part. The final results are given in Table 11 and 12. The sets (STU-FAC) ⋈ (FAC-STU) and (STU-FAC) ⋈ (STU ∩ FAC) are empty in the example. If the query involves a recursive join, then we generate a join between IDs in the same buffer. From the example above, to compute (FAC-STU) ⋈ (FAC-STU) we perform a join between IDs 2 and 4 when Buffer1 has {2,4,7} with a value Mike since IDs 2 and 4 belong to FAC private part.

4 Conclusion

We have introduced the concept of a role-set which provides an attractive alternative for data presentation in multidatabase systems. Using role-sets we have developed a new method for data integration that maintains the materialization autonomy of local database systems and provides users with more accurate information if they so desire. We have provided appropriate extensions to MSQL to enable users to manipulate role-sets and express different universal quantifiers with respect to them. We have developed a new strategy for query processing based on role-sets that makes use of merge-sort in order to compute the various overlaps and to perform the joins at the global site.

The merge-sort method is well-suited to handle large amounts of intermediate data efficiently. We have performed a number of experimental studies to compare our method to that of Dayal [10,11,14]. Our method outperforms Dayal's in

Table 10. FAC and STU

ID	NAME	SALARY	SI	ID	NAME	SALARY	SI
1	John	300	1	1	John	100	0
3	John	350	1	3	John	150	1
5	Mary	330	1	5	Mary	120	0
2	Mike	250	1	7	Mike	150	1
4	Mike	250	1	6	Nancy	100	0
7	Mike	250	1	8	Smith	170	1

Table 11. (FAC-STU) ⋈ (STU ∩ FAC)

ID	SALARY	ID	FAC.SALARY	STU.SALARY
2	250	7	250	150
4	250	7	250	150

Table 12. (STU ∩ FAC) ⋈ (STU ∩ FAC)

ID	FAC.SALARY	STU.SALARY	ID	FAC.SALARY	STU.SALARY
3	350	150	1	300	100

terms of transmission time as well as local processing time [9]. Dayal's method requires expensive semijoins in order to find the private and overlap parts, which is much more efficiently done via a merge-sort. In addition, our method reduces data movement between sites by allowing local selections to be performed for all queries with/without aggregation.

References

1. Apers, P.M.G., Hevner, A.R., and Yao, S.B.: Optimization algorithms for distributed queries. IEEE Trans. on Soft. Eng. (1983) 57–68
2. Apers, P. and Scheuermann, P.: Schema architectures and their relationship to transaction processing in distributed database systems. Information Sciences **54** (1991) 41–66
3. Bernstein, P.A. and Chiu, D.: Using semijoins to solve relational queries. JACM (1981) 25–40
4. Bernstein, P.A., Goodman, N., Wong, E., Reeve, C., and Rothnie, J.B.: Query processing in a system for distributed databases(SDD-1). ACM Trans. on Database Systems (1981) 602–625
5. Blasgen, M.W. and Eswaran, K.P.: Storage and access in relational data bases. IBM Systems Journal (1977) 363–377
6. Bratbergsengen, K.: Hashing methods and relational algebra operations. Proc. Tenth Intl. Conf. on Very Large Data Bases (1984) 323–333
7. Ceri, S. and Pelagatti, G.: Distributed Databases: Principles and Systems. McGraw-Hill (1984)
8. Chen, A.L.P.: Outerjoin optimization in multidatabase systems. Proc. IEEE 2nd Intl. Symp. on Databases in Parallel and Distributed Systems (1990) 211–218

9. Chong, E.I.: Query optimization in distributed database systems and multidatabase systems. Ph.D. Dissertation, Dept. of Elec. Eng. and Computer Science, Northwestern University (in preparation)
10. Dayal, U.: Query processing in a multidatabase system. In: W. Kim, et al.(eds.): Query Processing: Database Systems. New York: Springer 1985, pp.81–108
11. Dayal, U. and Hwang, H.Y.: View definition and generalization for database integration in a multidatabase system. IEEE Trans. on Software Engineering **10** (1984) 628–644
12. Du, W., Krishnamurthy, R., and Shan, M.-C.: Query optimization in heterogeneous DBMS. Proc. 18th Intl. Conf. on Very Large Data Bases (1992) 277–291
13. Grant, J., Litwin, W., Roussopoulos, N., and Sellis, T.: Query languages for relational multidatabases. VLDB Journal **2** (1993) 153–171
14. Hwang, H.Y., Dayal, U. and Gouda,M.: Using semiouterjoins to process queries in multidatabase systems. Proc. Third ACM SIGACT-SIGMOD Symp. on Principles of Database Systems (1984) 153–162
15. Kent, W.: The breakdown of the information model in multi-database systems. ACM SIGMOD Record **20** (1991) 10–15
16. Lim, E., Srivastava, J., Prabhakar, S., and Richardson, J.: Entity identification in database integration. Proc. IEEE Intl. Conf. on Data Engineering (1993) 294–301
17. Litwin, W. and Abdellatif, A.: Multidatabase Interoperability. IEEE Computer **19** (1986) 10–18
18. Litwin, W., Abdellatif, A., Zeroual, A., Nicolas, B., and Vigier, P.: MSQL: A multidatabase language. Information Sciences **49** (1989) 59–101
19. Litwin, W., Mark, L., and Roussopoulos, N.: Interoperability of multiple autonomous databases. ACM Computing Surveys **33** (1990) 267-293
20. Position Papers. Workshop on Heterogeneous Databases, Northwestern University, Evanston, IL. (1989)
21. Rosenthal, A. and Reiner, D.: Extending the algebraic framework of query processing to handle outerjoins. Proc. Tenth Intl. Conf. on Very Large Data Bases (1984) 334–343
22. Rusinkiewicz, M. and Czejdo, B.: An approach to query processing in federated database systems. Proc. 20th Hawaii Intl. Conf. on System Sciences (1987) 430–440
23. Scheuermann, P. (editor): Report of the workshop on heterogeneous database systems held at Northwestern University. ACM SIGMOD Record **19** (1989)
24. Scheuermann, P. and Chong, E.I.: Query processing in multidatabase systems. Proc. IEEE Intl. Conf. on Systems, Man, and Cybernetics (1992) 1250–1254
25. Selinger, P.G., Astrahan, M.M., Chamberlin, D.D., Lorie, R.A., and Price, T.G.: Access path selection in a relational database management system. Proc. ACM SIGMOD Intl. Conf. on Management of Data (1979) 23–34
26. Yu, C.T. and Chang, C.C.: Distributed Query Processing. ACM Computing Surveys **16** (1984) 399–433
27. Yu, C.T., et al.: Query processing in a fragmented relational distributed system:MERMAID. IEEE Trans. on Soft. Eng. (1985) 795–810
28. Yu, C.T., et al.: Partition strategy for distributed query processing in fast local networks. IEEE Trans. on Soft. Eng. (1989) 780–793
29. Yu, C.T., et al.: On the design of a distributed query processing algorithms. Proc. ACM SIGMOD Intl. Conf. on Management of Data (1983) 30–39

Content Routing for Distributed Information Servers

Mark A. Sheldon[1], Andrzej Duda[1,2], Ron Weiss[1]
James W. O'Toole, Jr.[1], David K. Gifford[1]

[1] Programming Systems Research Group, MIT Laboratory for Computer Science, Cambridge, MA 02139, USA
[2] Bull-IMAG Systèmes, 38610 Gières, France

Abstract. We describe a system that provides query based associative access to the contents of distributed information servers. In typical distributed information systems there are so many objects that underconstrained queries can produce large result sets and extraordinary processing costs. To deal with this scaling problem we use *content labels* to permit users to learn about available resources and to formulate queries with adequate discriminatory power. We have implemented associative access to a distributed set of information servers in the *content routing system*. A content routing system is a hierarchy of servers called *content routers* that present a single query based image of a distributed information system. We have successfully used a prototype content routing system to locate documents on several user file systems and on a large number of information servers.

1 Introduction

The Internet contains over one million hosts that provide file service and other information servers specializing in topics such as news, technical reports, biology, geography, and politics. The Internet's vast collection of servers can be viewed as a distributed database containing a wealth of information. Unfortunately, this information is relatively inaccessible because there is no mechanism for browsing and searching it associatively.

The difficulty of providing associative access to a large number of distributed information servers lies primarily in problems of scale. The scale of the Internet, which is today only a fraction of its eventual size, is so great as to render infeasible any comprehensive indexing plan based on a single global index. In addition, the cost of distributing a query throughout the Internet is prohibitive. Finally, in very large scale systems, the number of results to a typical user query is incomprehensibly large. For these reasons, we expect that efficient associative access will require both *content routing* and *query refinement*. Content routing is the process of directing user queries to appropriate servers. Query refinement helps a user formulate meaningful queries. These query services can be implemented by a *content routing system* that will:

- Support a uniform query interface that allows progressive discovery of network contents and guides users in formulating queries of adequate discriminatory power.
- Propagate descriptions of server contents through a hierarchy of information servers.

- Route individual queries to available servers based on the expected relevance of the server to the query.

This paper explores the thesis that *content labels* can be used to organize the semantics of associative access to a distributed set of information servers, and that *content routers* based on the content labels can serve as the implementation basis of distributed associative access. We have implemented a prototype system that uses content labels to describe the contents of individual servers. The system contains content routers that provide associative access to underlying information servers. From the user's perspective, browsing and searching can be performed without regard to the location of individual data objects.

Using a prototype system, we have explored the automatic construction of content labels, tested their use in routing queries to information servers, and examined the basic performance characteristics of a multi-layered content routing system. We have used the system to locate documents on file systems and information servers. Initial experience suggests that a content routing system is an effective tool for exploring and searching a large network of information servers.

Unlike previous systems for locating and accessing information in a network, content routing provides a uniform, hierarchical framework combining associative access at two levels: associative access to sets of servers and associative access to documents on the servers. Important advances offered by our architecture include:

- **Usability:** Content labels can be used to provide feedback to users, enabling them to learn about available resources and formulate queries. Thus content labels organize the search space and enable navigation and discovery.
- **Scalability:** Content routing provides a uniform way to access large networks of information servers based on their contents. Layered content routing provides a scalable system architecture by maintaining limited knowledge of the attributes at the information servers.
- **Efficiency:** Users can efficiently search a network of servers using a content routing system. Content labels distill the content of information servers so that queries can be routed to appropriate servers.

In the remainder of this paper we review related work (Section 2), discuss the Content Routing System design (Section 3), discuss issues in constructing content labels (Section 4), describe the prototype implementation (Section 5), report on our experience (Section 6), and outline conclusions based on our experience (Section 7).

2 Related work

Previous work can be categorized as: distributed naming systems, network navigation systems and network-based information retrieval systems. No previous system combines a coherent architecture for associative access to distributed, heterogeneous information servers with query-specific feedback to help the user organize the search space.

Distributed naming systems such as X.500 [4], Profile [16], the Networked Resource Discovery Project [17], and Nomenclator [14] provide attribute-based access to a wide variety of objects; however, they do not support the hierarchical relationship between servers and data that our system achieves through its use of content labels.

Network navigation systems such as the Gopher system [1] and the World-Wide Web [3] provide a means for organizing servers to allow navigating among and browsing through remote information. Gopher provides the equivalent of a distributed file service, and World-Wide Web provides distributed hypertext documents. Discovering and locating information in these systems is difficult because these systems do not support query routing. Veronica [10] is a discovery system that maintains an index of document titles from Gopher menus.

Network-based information retrieval systems provide access to information on remote servers. The Wide Area Information Service (WAIS) [11, 19] provides a uniform means of access to information servers on a network. However, the user must choose appropriate servers from a directory of services. The Archie system [7] polls FTP sites on the Internet and indexes the files by name. A query yields a set of host/filename pairs which may be used to retrieve the relevant files manually. The Conit system [12, 13] provides a uniform user interface to a large number of databases accessible from several retrieval systems. There is no support for the automatic selection of relevant databases for a query. The Distributed Indexing mechanism [5] is based on precomputed indices of databases that summarize the holdings on particular topics of other databases. The architecture has a fixed three layer structure that is not flexible enough for content based access to heterogeneous information servers. Simpson and Alonso propose a querying architecture for a network of autonomous databases [18] that forwards user queries to known information sources. This approach has a probabilistic query semantics and does not support browsing with query refinement. The Information Brokers of the MITL Gold project [2] do not provide access to objects directly. Rather, they return descriptions of an object's location and the method that may be used to retrieve the object.

The concepts of query routing and query refinement were introduced in [9]. A query is routed to one or more databases that contains the result set of the query.

3 The Content Routing System

In this section we present the semantics and architecture of content routing systems. The overall job of a content routing system is to direct user requests to appropriate servers (content routing) and to help a user formulate meaningful queries (query refinement). Both of these tasks require a content routing system to employ detailed knowledge about what information is available and where it is located.

It is not feasible for a content routing system to maintain a detailed, single, global index of all information, nor is it practical to ask servers what they contain on a query-by-query basis. A single, detailed, global index would be quite large and costly to maintain in real time. Querying servers on a query-by-query basis is very expensive and would lead to substantial delays when there are thousands of servers.

Our system uses *content labels* as a compact and efficient means of describing server contents. As we will describe in detail, content labels allow a content routing system to implement both content routing and query refinement. The remainder of this section describes how the content routing system organizes the search space of a distributed information system (Section 3.1), provides a detailed description of the system operations that comprise the system's interface and semantics (Section 3.2), and illustrates the intended use of the system through examples (Section 3.3).

3.1 System Organization

A content routing system extends a traditional information retrieval system to a distributed and hierarchical network of information servers. It supports conventional document types, such as text, electronic mail, and video, along with conventional operations on those documents. A content routing system defines a new document type, called a *collection*, that supports new operations designed to enable users to browse and search a large distributed information system.

A *collection* document consists of a set of documents (possibly including other collection documents) together with a description of the set called a *content label.* Because a collection document contains other documents including collections, it can be viewed as a hierarchical arrangement of documents in a directed acyclic graph (see Figure 1). A content label is a compact representation of the set of member documents in the form of a query predicate. All the documents of a collection must satisfy the content label of that collection interpreted as a predicate.

A content routing system is a network of information servers that provides a distributed search space organized by content labels. Leaf nodes in the network are endpoint information servers that store conventional documents. The hierarchical network of internal nodes is composed of *content routers*, which are information servers that support collection documents. The structure of the network mirrors the collection hierarchy of Figure 1, where the server underlying each collection stores the conventional documents and content labels of the layer below.

A content router implements a collection as an information retrieval service (which in general runs remotely) and a content label. User query and retrieval operations can be applied to content labels or routed to the servers that implement the collections. If an operation is forwarded to multiple servers then the results are merged. A content router may elect to forward operations to servers or to refuse to do so depending on the cost effectiveness or expense of that operation.

An information server registers with content routers by providing a content label and an interface for the content router system operations. Our design does not limit the form of content labels. In principle, a content label could consist of the disjunction of all of the attributes that appear in a collection. Alternatively, a content label could simply be the name of the host that contains a set of files. In practice, we expect content labels to lie between these two extremes, containing attributes including host names, domains, authors, libraries, priorities, and subjects. Pragmatic issues in the construction of content labels are explored in Section 4.

The system operations interface includes operations for query, document retrieval, and query refinement requests (see section 3.2). Servers may be organized by administrative domain (e.g., all the servers at MIT), by a subject hierarchy (e.g., based on the Library of Congress categorization scheme), or by a mechanism in which servers

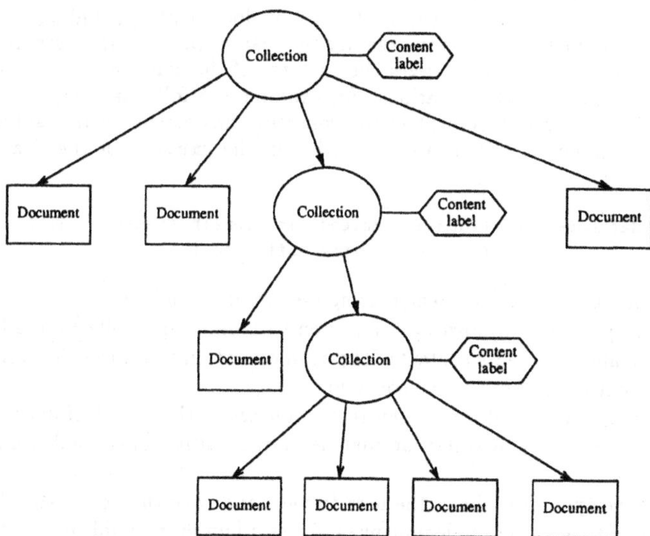

Fig. 1. A content routing system provides access to a hierarchy of collections.

target particular information markets. To support query refinement, a content router may extract term relationship information from its registered collections.

3.2 System Operations

A content routing system supports operations for query, document retrieval, and query refinement, in addition to conventional document operations. A user may *select* a set of documents from the collection using a query, *list results* of a selection, and *retrieve* an individual document. For collection documents, the system interface also supports the new operations *show fields*, *show values*, *expand*, and *search*, which are described below. Together, these services are designed for browsing and searching large distributed information systems.

For the purposes of this paper and our prototype system, we have chosen a simple predicate data model. *Documents*, which may be text files, directories, digital video or any other data objects, are associated with sets of *attributes*. Each attribute consists of a *field* name and a *value*. Typical attributes are `text:database` and `author:ullman`. Some field names have predefined semantics, e.g., `author`, and may or may not make use of a controlled vocabulary. Other fields may have semantics that vary from domain to domain, e.g., `category`. Individual documents may also export their own field names, thus the set of fields is extensible. Values can assume a variety of types, including integers and dates. In our current prototype however, values are strings.

A *query* is a boolean combination of attributes. When a query is applied to a set of documents, the subset of documents that satisfies the query is called a *query result set*.

A collection document, consisting of a set of documents (including other collections) and a content label, helps to organize the search space for the user. Because the content label accurately characterizes the contents of the collection, it can be used by the system to guide search operations. For example the following very small content label implies that every document of the collection has attribute **subject:database** and **collection-type:software** and is either in the **cmu.edu** or the **stanford.edu** domains.

```
[ (subject:database) and ((domain:cmu.edu) or (domain:stanford.edu))
                      and (collection-type:software) ]
```

The basic operations of the content routing system are as follows:

The *open* operation initializes a connection to a particular collection, allowing the user to search and browse its contents. The open operation initializes the current result set to be the entire contents of the collection.

The *select* operation reduces the current result set to the subset of documents that matches the given query. A collection matches a query if its content label matches the query.

The *retrieve* operation allows the user to view and save the document. A retrieval request applied to a collection document produces a human-readable description of the contents of that collection.

The *search* operation allows the user to submit a query to the content routing system for query routing. The routing system automatically forwards the query to relevant information servers. To a user specifying search queries, the system appears as a single large virtual information server. This virtual information server contains all the conventional documents that are reachable from the currently open collection.

The *expand* operation allows the user to access the contents of a collection or set of collections. When a collection from a query result set is expanded, the query is applied to the components of the collection and matching components are added to the result set. The expansion operation does not affect a conventional document. Expanding a set of documents results in the union of the expansion of every document in the set. The resulting documents may then be queried, retrieved, or expanded. When a result set has been expanded, the user has access to new query terms, namely, those attributes arising from the component documents of the collections.

While composing a query, a user can learn about possible terms by using the *query refinement* feature. The user can learn from the system the set of available fields, and the system will also suggest potentially interesting values for fields based on the query fragment the user has presented.

The *show fields* operation displays the set of attribute field names known to the currently open collection. Ideally, the set of fields displayed should be limited to those found in the documents of the current result set.

The *show values* operation suggests information rich values for a given field that are related to the documents in the current result set. Our design leaves the precise behavior of this operation as an implementation issue.

The *list results* operation enumerates the documents in the current result set.

These operations for guiding query formulation help the user manage the complexity of the search space. A user browses documents by alternately broadening and narrowing queries. Typically users start with broad queries. The set of documents to peruse becomes smaller as a query is refined. The user refines queries either by using system recommended completions or by using attributes discovered in interesting content labels. When a query is sufficiently narrowed, its collection documents may be expanded. This process continues in a pattern of contracting selections alternating with expansions.

3.3 An Example

This section contains a simple, extended example of how a content routing system might work, and in fact comes from our running implementation. However, these examples are illustrative and are not intended to limit future implementations. For pedagogical reasons, we use a simple textual interface, although our system provides a graphical browser.

The user can perform a search that will automatically retrieve relevant documents from the information servers in the system. First, the user opens a collection of WAIS collections, lists the fields available for query construction, and defines a query. The user then refines the query by inquiring about possible query completion values, and then incorporates the system's suggestions into a new query. Finally, the user displays the result set that matches the refined query, and retrieves a particular document.

```
=> open-collection crs-wais
=> show-fields
   administrator:       field:          label:       port:
   collection-type:     hostaddress:    location:    text:
   cost:                hostname:       owner:
=> search text:buddhism
=> show-values text:
   academic    chinese     data      religion     society
   asian       cultural    omni      religions    tibetan
   bases       culture     raw       resource     zen
=> search text:buddhism and text:tibetan
=> list-results
   ANU-Asian-Religions:Bibliographical_reference.1
   ...
   ANU-Asian-Religions:Bibliographical_reference.26
   ANU-Shamanism-Studies:Samuel_Geoffrey_In_press_Ci.1
   ANU-SocSci-Netlore:TIBETAN_FONTS_FOR_MACINTOSHES.1
   Tantric-News:File_STS1089.1
   ...
   Tantric-News:File_News_184.6
=> retrieve ANU-Asian-Religions:Bibliographical_reference.26
   TIBETAN SHAMANISM & BUDDHISM Bibliography [Last updated: 19 Feb 1992]
   ---------------------------------------------------------------------
   Wylie, Turrell V. 1978. 'Reincarnation: a political innovation in
   Tibetan Buddhism.' Ligeti 1978: 579-586.
```

Alternatively, the user can browse the system and progressively explore the network resources. In the following example, the user opens a collection, selects all the collection documents that contain a specific attribute, and displays the content label for one of these collections.

```
=> open-collection crs-wais
=> select  text:buddhism
=> list-results
   ANU-Asian-Religions      ANU-Thai-Yunnan              lists
   ANU-Shamanism-Studies    ANU-ZenBuddhism-Calendar     mailing-lists
   ANU-SocSci-Netlore       file-archive-uunet           Tantric-News
=> retrieve  Tantric-News
   (hostname: sunsite.unc.edu) and (hostaddress: 152.2.22.81) and
   (collection: Tantric-News) and (label: server) and (label: WAIS) and
   ...
   (text: Society) and (text: Tantric) and (text: Studies)
   ...
```

When the user discovers collections that may contain relevant information, the user can **expand** the current query to retrieve matching documents from these collections.

```
=> select  text:buddhism and text:tibetan
=> list-results
   ANU-Asian-Religions     ANU-SocSci-Netlore     Tantric-News
   ANU-Shamanism-Studies   file-archive-uunet
=> expand
=> list-results
   ANU-Asian-Religions:Bibliographical_reference.1
   ...
   ANU-Asian-Religions:Bibliographical_reference.26
   ANU-Shamanism-Studies:Samuel_Geoffrey_In_press_Ci.1
   ANU-SocSci-Netlore:TIBETAN_FONTS_FOR_MACINTOSHES.1
```

Note that after the **expand** operation above, the user will get the set of fields defined in the selected collections. Since all the documents in the expanded result set above were collections, the fields from the original collection may no longer be available.

```
=> show-fields
   author:     date:      imports:   owner:      subject:   title:
   category:   exports:   name:      priority:   text:      type:
```

4 Constructing Content Labels

A good content label will contain two kinds of attributes:

- Administratively determined *value added* attributes that describe a collection but may or may not appear in the documents themselves. For example, an administrator may want to advertise that a server has the attribute `collection-type:software`.
- Attributes automatically derived from the collection contents, possibly using various statistical tools. For example, frequently occurring descriptive terms are good candidates for content labels.

If desired, it is possible to enforce a uniform meaning for a given field name across servers and document types. For example, **owner** could always refer to the owner of a document. It is also possible to allow the meaning of field names to be defined differently for different servers or document types.

Content labels represent a compromise for a scalable architecture, since there are practical limits on the size of content labels. Limiting content label size not only helps manage local resources, but also encourages administrators of remote information servers to make effective use of their content label advertising budget. A budget scheme will give priority to specialized servers when users submit more specific queries.

Server	*# of attributes*	*Server size (MB)*	*Index size (MB)*
comp	564493	65	50.5
rec	309473	43	29.5
users1	247914	184	29.5
nyt	165678	174	29.3
users2	99451	28	15.6
ap	36620	29	3.9
total	1423629	403	158.3
unique	1077522		

Table 1. Information servers statistics

In order to explore how content labels can be generated automatically for large collections of objects, we have gathered some attribute statistics on six information servers. Table 1 gives the characteristics of the servers: the number of distinct attributes, the server size (total size of documents in the database in megabytes), and the index size (size of the index data structures). *Comp* is the USENET **comp** newsgroup hierarchy, *rec* is the **rec** newsgroup hierarchy, *users1* and *users2* are two user file systems, *nyt* is a database of New York Times articles, and *ap* is a database of Associated Press articles.

Figure 2 plots the total number of unique attributes versus the number of servers. It shows that **text** comprises a majority of the attributes and that the number of distinct attributes is large. A content label containing all attributes (or even all **text** attributes) would be infeasible. However, some information-rich attributes such as **author**, **title** and **subject** have a small set of information-rich values and are thus good candidates for content labels.

Content labels must reconcile two conflicting objectives. On one hand, they must contain terms that characterize the collection as a whole (typically high frequency terms), and on the other hand, they must be able to distinguish servers with respect to each other. To evaluate the discriminatory power of attributes, we gathered data on the distribution of attributes over servers. Figure 3 shows for a given number of servers how many attributes appear only on that many servers. For example, there were 10 **category** attributes that appeared on three servers. If a given attribute has a narrow distribution, that is, it identifies a small number of servers, then it can used for routing. Wide distribution terms are useful for describing collections for browsing. As shown in the figure, low frequency attributes such as **owner**, **category**, and **type**

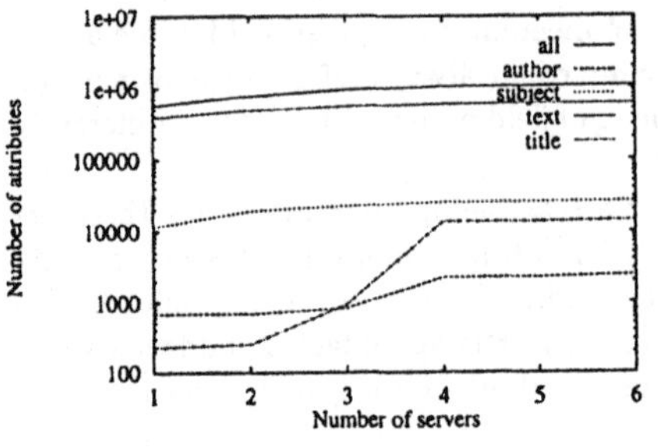

Fig. 2. Cumulative number of attributes

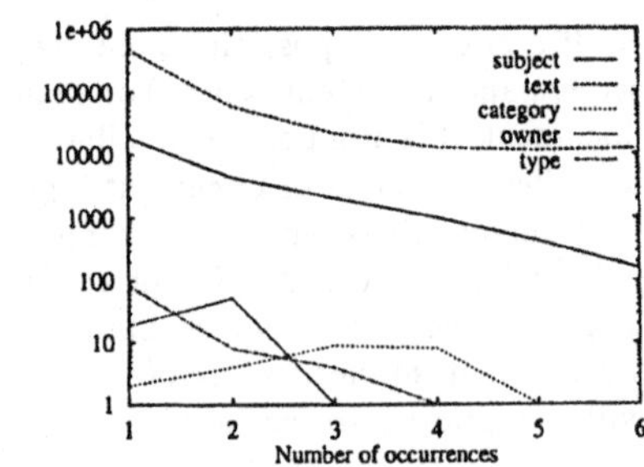

Fig. 3. Attribute histogram

have discriminatory power over servers and can be used for content routing. Higher frequency attribute fields like `text` and `subject` are more common so that the most frequent terms can be used for categorizing the collection as a whole and propagated to upper routing layers.

5 Implementation

We have built a prototype implementation of a content routing system that provides query routing to an extensible number of servers. The system uses the Semantic File System interface [8] for both information servers and content routers. Because it is implemented as an SFS server, our content router is a user level NFS server that may be mounted by any NFS client. Figure 4 shows the architecture of our prototype content router implementation.

Path names that pass through the NFS interface to the server are interpreted as queries and results are returned in dynamically created *virtual directories*. On demand, the server computes the contents of virtual directories. Queries at the content router apply to the content labels for the collections registered there. The content router uses the query to determine the set of collections. Our implementation constructs suggested refinements for a given query by identifying terms frequently collocated with the terms appearing in the query.

The server performs an expand operation by forwarding the query (and subsequent query refinements) to the set of servers whose content labels match the query. The merged results are presented to the user. Our current implementation of the search operation uses syntactic hints embedded in queries. These hints indicate to the router which terms should apply to content labels. We use these hints because we are still experimenting with various routing algorithms.

Our content router interposes itself between a client and an information server during query processing when results from more than one server must be combined.

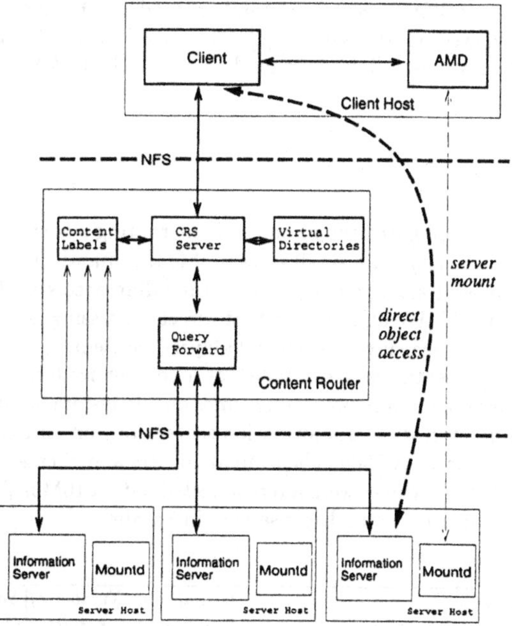

Fig. 4. A prototype content router.

We call this approach *mediated processing* because the content router mediates the responses from multiple information servers to present a collective result.

When only a single server is sent a query or once a document of interest is identified, a client is instructed to bypass the content router and contact the end-point server directly. We call this approach *direct processing.* Direct processing allows a client to obtain maximum performance from the end-point server and also minimizes content router load. In our architecture, client to server forwarding is implemented by having the content router return a symbolic link tc a client in response to a request for a virtual directory or file. The symbolic link returned refers to the end-point server and is dynamically resolved by the client with the help of an automount daemon [15].

The content router collects content labels from a set of servers to which it will provide access. We have experimented with two ways of creating content labels: for our SFS file systems, content labels are administratively determined and for WAIS servers content labels consist of disjunctions of attributes obtained from the individual WAIS source and catalog files. The WAIS catalog files contain headlines for each document (subject of a message or title of an article). Thus, they contain information-rich terms that characterize document content fairly well. From 492 existing WAIS servers, we have retrieved 371 catalog files which occupy 352.5 megabytes (MB) of disk space. As only part of catalog files (headlines) is used for constructing content labels and only unique terms are kept, the size of the resulting content labels is 12.4MB.

To provide access to WAIS servers, we implemented an SFS-WAIS gateway so that WAIS servers are viewed as SFS servers [6]. The SFS-WAIS gateway translates SFS queries into WAIS questions and uses the public domain client WAIS code for querying WAIS servers.

6 Experience

We have used several configurations of our content routing system. We measured the performance of query routing in a small system of four semantic file systems. We measured the performance of a single query router providing access to 492 WAIS servers located around the world. We also verified that direct processing achieve better performance than mediated processing in a multiple-layered system.

Table 2 shows representative performance of a content router. We expect that we will be able to further lower query processing times on our system because our prototype implementation is not tuned. The information servers run on an SGI 4D/320S and a heavily loaded DEC Microvax 3500. The content routers and clients were run on Sparc Station IPX's. All these machines were interconnected with a 10Mbit/s Ethernet. These tests did not process queries on multiple servers in parallel.

Example query	*Number of servers*	*Number of results*	*Search time (sequential)*
`library:users and owner:`	1	88	1.2s
`library:users and text:semantic and owner:sheldon`	1	22	0.6s
`library:users and text:semantic and text:library and owner:sheldon`	1	9	1.2s
`location:mit and extension:video`	2	60	2.6s
`location:mit and owner:gifford`	2	31	1.4s
`text:toys and text:williams`	4	27	9.9s

Table 2. Routed query performance on four local SFS servers

We also used our prototype to locate and access documents on a collection of 492 WAIS servers, and we gathered statistics on some example queries. The server in this case ran on an SGI 4D/320S, and the WAIS servers were distributed throughout the internet and ran on unknown types of machines. Since many public WAIS servers do not support conjunction, our SFS-WAIS gateway is forced to run a separate remote query for each term and compute result set intersections locally. This greatly increases processing times and encourages users to restrict themselves to highly specialized query terms. The statistics for some sample queries are presented in Table 3. We compare the content router conducting searches on different WAIS servers in parallel with sequential search using `waisq`, a program in the WAIS distribution. The `waisq` program was given the servers chosen by our content router. In general, parallel searching performs better than sequential. However, there is no linear speedup: latencies on different servers

Example query (all attributes are `text`*)*	*Number of servers*	*Number of results*	*Number of down servers*	*Search time (parallel)*	*Search time (sequential)*
`bosnia and clinton`	4	86	0	219.0s	1003.4s
`buddhism and tibetan`	5	71	0	397.7s	646.6s
`multimedia and maestro`	13	23	0	215.2s	233.3s
`perfect and hashing`	8	31	0	52.7s	147.6s
`transactions and nested`	7	13	1	46.5s	151.4s

Table 3. Example query performance routing to 492 WAIS servers

vary so that parallel search time is strongly limited by the slowest server. Some servers contain large databases, are accessed by many users, and have limited processing power. These servers limit the performance of any search. For example, the long search time for `buddhism` and `tibetan` was due almost entirely to the processing time at one server (`ANU-Asian-Religions`) that continued to run long after other servers had finished.

From our experience, we believe that query routing in a hierarchical collection of distributed servers is feasible. Demanding applications like digital video can achieve adequate throughput because content routers do not mediate object accesses. Our experience with using the content router for locating and accessing WAIS servers shows that supporting boolean operations on servers is crucial to efficient searching. However, we were pleasantly surprised at the efficacy of routing based on content labels derived from WAIS catalogs. With virtually no tuning based on high-level knowledge or sophisticated statistics, it was not difficult to explore a large set of information servers. In particular, we found query completion to be quite useful. Performance of the system is acceptable, though we would like to improve query performance and the handling of failures.

7 Conclusions

We have designed and implemented a content routing system that allows users to browse, locate, and access documents of interest in large, heterogeneous, distributed information systems. We have organized the search space using content labels describing servers. The scope of an initial query can be sufficiently narrowed and refined using a query completion feature so that the result set is efficiently computed.

We have built a prototype based on the semantic file system model. We have successfully used our system to locate data objects on servers in our laboratory and to locate documents on a large number of WAIS servers. Along with demonstrating the feasibility of our approach, the prototype shows interactive performance mainly limited by the processing time at end-point information servers. The most surprising result was that even with relatively poor information about remote server contents, content labels were quite useful for browsing and locating interesting information.

Future work will involve investigating more sophisticated techniques for constructing content labels, for organizing the network of servers, and for handling unreachable servers.

References

1. B. Alberti, F. Anklesaria, P. Linkner, M. McCahill, and D. Torrey. The Internet Gopher protocol: A distributed document search and retrieval protocol. University of Minesota Microcomputer and Workstation Networks Center, Spring 1991. Revised Spring 1992.
2. D. Barbara and C. Clifton. Information Brokers: Sharing knowledge in a heterogeneous distributed system. Technical Report MITL-TR-31-92, Matsushita Information Technology Laboratory, Princeton, NJ, Oct. 1992.
3. T. Berners-Lee, R. Cailliau, J.-F. Groff, and B. Pollermann. World-Wide Web: The information universe. *Electronic Networking*, 2(1):52–58, 1992.
4. CCITT. The Directory - Overview of Concepts, Models and Services. Recommendation X.500, 1988.
5. P. B. Danzig, S.-H. Li, and K. Obraczka. Distributed indexing of autonomous internet services. *Computing Systems*, 5(4), 1992.
6. A. Duda and M. A. Sheldon. Content routing in networks of WAIS servers. Submitted for publication, Sept. 1993.
7. A. Emtage and P. Deutsch. Archie – an electronic directory service for the Internet. In *USENIX Association Winter Conference Proceedings*, pages 93–110, San Francisco, Jan. 1992.
8. D. K. Gifford, P. Jouvelot, M. A. Sheldon, and J. W. O'Toole. Semantic file systems. In *Thirteenth ACM Symposium on Operating Systems Principles*. ACM, Oct. 1991. Available as *Operating Systems Review* Volume 25, Number 5.
9. D. K. Gifford, J. M. Lucassen, and S. T. Berlin. An architecture for large scale information systems. In *10th Symposium on Operating System Principles*, pages 161–170. ACM, Dec. 1985.
10. H. Hahn and R. Stout. *The Internet Complete Reference*. Osborne McGraw-Hill, Berkeley, California, 1994.
11. B. Kahle and A. Medlar. An information system for corporate users: Wide Area Information Servers. Technical Report TMC-199, Thinking Machines, Inc., Apr. 1991. Version 3.
12. R. S. Marcus. An experimental comparison of the effectiveness of computers and humans as search intermediaries. *Journal of the American Society for Information Science*, 34(6):381–404, Nov. 1983.
13. R. S. Marcus. Advanced retrieval assistance for the DGIS gateway. Technical Report LIDS R-1958, MIT Laboratory for Information and Decision Systems, Mar. 1990.
14. J. Ordille and B. Miller. Distributed active catalogs and meta-data caching in descriptive name services. In *Proceedings of the 13th Internatinoal Conference on Dsitributed Computing Systems*, pages 120–129. IEEE, 1993.
15. J.-S. Pendry and N. Williams. Amd: The 4.4 BSD automounter reference manual, Mar. 1991. Documentation for software revision 5.3 Alpha.
16. L. Peterson. The Profile Naming Service. *ACM Transactions on Computer Systems*, 6(4):341–364, Nov. 1988.
17. M. F. Schwartz. The Networked Resource Discovery Project. In *Proceedings of the IFIP XI World Congress*, pages 827–832. IFIP, Aug. 1989.
18. P. Simpson and R. Alonso. Querying a network of autonomous databases. Technical Report CS-TR-202-89, Princeton University, Princeton, NJ, Jan. 1989.
19. R. M. Stein. Browsing through terabytes: Wide-area information servers open a new frontier in personal and corporate information services. *Byte*, pages 157–164, May 1991.

A Unified Approach to Concurrency Control and Transaction Recovery * (Extended Abstract)

Gustavo Alonso[1], Radek Vingralek[2], Divyakant Agrawal[1], Yuri Breitbart[2], Amr El Abbadi[1], Hans Schek[3], Gerhard Weikum[3]

[1] Department of Computer Science,
University of California,
Santa Barbara, CA 93117
[2] Department of Computer Science,
University of Kentucky,
Lexington, KY 40506
[3] Department of Computer Science,
ETH Zurich
CH-8092 Zurich, Switzerland

1 Introduction

Conventional transaction management in shared databases is traditionally viewed as a combination of two orthogonal problems. One is to guarantee correctness when several transactions are executed concurrently. This is ensured by the concurrency control component of a transaction processing system. The other is to ensure the correctness of the database in spite of transaction aborts and system failures. This is ensured by the recovery mechanism. In both cases there are several criteria that impose increasing restrictions on executions, resulting in a hierarchy in which only the most restrictive criteria are chosen for implementing concurrency control and recovery mechanisms. The result is that the different criteria are incomparable except for the most restrictive criterion in each component. For instance, strict two phase locking and log based recovery with before images has become the de facto standard (i.e. rigorous schedules [BGRS91], once considered as a possible candidate for a unified treatment of concurrency control and transaction recovery).

Recently, Schek, Weikum and Ye [SWY93] have developed a unified theory for concurrency control and recovery. In this theory, the traditional concurrency control theory is expanded to include the actions of aborted transactions. As a result, the extended theory can be used to determine whether a given execution is correct both from a concurrency control as well as recovery points of view. A hierarchy of correctness classes is defined and the authors introduce a particular class, called *prefix-reducibility* (PRED). PRED is argued to be the most

* This material is based in part upon work supported by NSF grants IRI-9221947, IRI-9012902 and IRI-9117904 and by grant from Hewlett-Packard Corporation. This work has been performed while Y. Breitbart was on one year sabbatical and R. Vingralek was visiting for 8 months the database research group at ETH, Zurich.

permissive class of executions that are intuitively correct accounting for both concurrency and recovery in the system. The original paper left the construction of a scheduler based on PRED as an open problem.

In this paper, we analyze the characteristics of a scheduler to recognize the class of PRED executions. We start by proposing an equivalent definition for PRED. The original definition of PRED was stated in a non-procedural manner, which hinders its use for the development of dynamic schedulers. Our definition is procedural, and provides us with easy, graph testing protocols for recognizing all PRED executions. We also develop efficient schedulers based on a new class of locks.

Following a suggestion of the program committee of the EDBT'94 conference, this paper combines the results of [AAE93] and [VBSW93] in which closely related results have been developed independently and in parallel.

2 Model

A database is a collection of data objects. Users interact with the database by issuing transactions. A transaction is a partial order of read and write operations followed by either an abort or a commit operation. Two operations of different transactions conflict if they are performed on the same data object and one of them is a write. History H over a set of transactions T is a partial order of all the operations in the transactions from T such that this partial order must be in agreement with the partial order of each transaction from T and any two conflicting operations in H are ordered. In history H we also allow a set-oriented *group abort* operation $a(T_{i_1}, \ldots, T_{i_k})$, where $T_{i_1}, \ldots, T_{i_k}$ are from the transaction set T. This operation indicates that an abort should be executed for each transaction from $T_{i_1}, \ldots, T_{i_k}$. However, the execution of these aborts is conducted concurrently.

A projection of a history H on a set of transactions T is a history that contains only operations of transactions from T. A committed projection of history H is the history $C(H)$ that contains only operations of committed transactions in H. A *complete* history H over a set of transactions T is a history in which each transaction from T is either committed or aborted. In what follows we will use the standard notions of serializability, recoverability, avoidance of cascading aborts, and strictness [BHG87].

In order to handle aborted transactions explicitly in the history we replace a transaction abort statement with a sequence of the transaction's undo operations. Each operation of an aborted transaction T_i that changes the database state, i.e. a write operation in our model, is replaced in the history with its inverse operation denoted by o_i^{-1}. On the other hand, the operations of T_i that do not impact the database state, in our case read operations, can be safely discarded from the history since the returned values are rendered invalid by the abort. Thus, if the scheduler produces a serializable history of transactions operations for committed transactions and undo operations for aborted transactions by discarding read operations of aborted transactions, then issues of serializability and recovery are treated by such a scheduler in a uniform way. To guarantee correct recovery, it is assumed that active transactions (i.e., transactions that neither commit nor abort in H) will abort. These ideas proposed in [SWY93] lead to the following definition of an *expanded history*:

Definition 1. Expanded Histories

Let $H = (A, <)$ be a history. Its expansion $\tilde{H}$, or expanded history $\tilde{H}$, is a tuple $(\tilde{A}, \tilde{<})$ where:

1. $\tilde{A}$ is a set of actions which is derived from A in the following way:
   (a) For each transaction $T_i \in H$, if $o_i \in T_i$ and o_i is not an abort operation, then $o_i \in \tilde{H}$
   (b) Active transactions are treated as aborted transactions, by adding a set-oriented abort $a(T_{i_1} \ldots T_{i_k})$ at the end of H, where $T_{i_1} \ldots T_{i_k}$ are all active transactions in H.
   (c) For each aborted transaction $T_j \in H$ and for every write operation $w_j(x) \in T_j$, there exists an inverse write $w_j^{-1}(x) \in \tilde{H}$, which is used to undo the effects of the corresponding write operation. An abort operation $a_j \in H$ is changed to $c_j \in \tilde{H}$.
2. The partial order, $\tilde{<}$, is determined as follows:
   (a) For every two operations, o_i and o_j, if $o_i < o_j$ in H then $o_i \tilde{<} o_j$ in $\tilde{H}$.
   (b) If $a(T_{i_1}, \ldots, T_{i_k}) \in H$, then every two conflicting undo operations of transactions from the set $\{T_{i_1}, \ldots, T_{i_k}\}$ are in $\tilde{H}$ in a reverse order of the two corresponding write operations in H.
   (c) All undo operations of every transaction T_i that does not commit in H follow the T_i original actions and must precede c_i in $\tilde{H}$.
   (d) Whenever $o_n < a(T_{i_1}, \ldots, T_{i_k}) < o_m$ and some undo operation o_j^{-1} ($j \in \{i_1, \ldots, i_k\}$) conflicts with o_m (o_n), then it must be true that $o_j^{-1} \tilde{<} o_m$ ($o_n \tilde{<} o_j^{-1}$).
   (e) Whenever $a(\ldots, T_i, \ldots) < a(\ldots, T_j, \ldots)$ for some $i \neq j$, then for all conflicting undo operations of T_i and T_j, o_i^{-1} and o_j^{-1}, it must be true that $o_i^{-1} \tilde{<} o_j^{-1}$.

Note that this definition of expanded histories is more restrictive than that in [SWY93]. With the original definition, the expansion of the history $w_1[x]w_2[x]a_1a_2$ could be either $w_1[x]w_2[x]w_1^{-1}[x]c_1w_2^{-1}[x]c_2$ or $w_1[x]w_2[x]w_2^{-1}[x]c_2w_1^{-1}[x]c_1$. The intuitively correct expansion is the first one and so is assumed in [SWY93]. However, the definition provided did not rule out the second expansion, which is undesirable because it delays the abort operation issued by T_1.

A history H is *reducible* (RED) if its expansion $\tilde{H}$ can be transformed to a serial history by applying the following three transformation rules finitely many times.

1. **Commutativity Rule.** If two operations o_i and o_j do not conflict, and there is no o_k such that $o_i \tilde{<} o_k \tilde{<} o_j$, then the ordering $o_i \tilde{<} o_j$ can be replaced by $o_j \tilde{<} o_i$

2. **Undo Rule.** If $w_i[x]$ and $w_i^{-1}[x]$ are in $\tilde{H}$ and $w_i[x] \tilde{<} w_i^{-1}[x]$ and there is no o_j such that $w_i[x] \tilde{<} o_j \tilde{<} w_i^{-1}[x]$, then $w_i[x]$ and $w_i^{-1}[x]$ can be omitted from the expanded history
3. **Null Action Rule.** Read operations of aborted or active transactions in H can be omitted from $\tilde{H}$.

Unfortunately, the class RED is not prefix-closed and hence cannot be used for on line scheduling of transactions. This is resolved by further restricting this class of histories. In particular, a history H is *prefix reducible* (PRED) if every prefix of H is reducible. If we use the term SR-RC for the class of histories that are both serializable and recoverable, it can be shown that PRED $\subset$ SR-RC. Similarly, if by SR-ST we denote the class of histories that are both serializable and strict, SR-ST $\subset$ PRED [SWY93].

3 Serializability with Ordered Termination

We start this section by describing in more detail the standard recovery mechanism [HR83, BHG87, GR93], which is also assumed in the model proposed in [SWY93]. In this model, a *log* is maintained on stable storage for recovery purposes. Note that virtually all commercial systems employ a log-based recovery method [GR93], whereas deferred update methods have not been adopted in practice for performance reasons. The log is composed of a set of log records, each corresponding to a write operation. The log is used for two main purposes. First, when a transaction aborts, it is used to retrieve the transaction's log records for undoing the updates of the transaction. Second, after recovery from failures, the log is traversed by a special restart routine that redoes missing updates of all committed transactions and undoes the updates of all aborted or active transactions. A common implementation technique for transaction undo and redo is the restoration of before-images and after-images of the database objects; however, undo and redo may also be based on more general operations at the storage level.

We now consider the various restrictions that are imposed by log-based recovery on the order in which transactions may terminate. In particular, we are interested in the restrictions, if any, imposed on the commitment or abortion of transactions when they execute conflicting operations, i.e., wr, ww, and rw conflicts. These restrictions are as follows. To guarantee recoverable histories, if $w_1[x] < r_2[x]$ then $c_1 < c_2$. Transaction undo involves the invocation of undo steps that reinstall the state of database objects as of the time before the update that is undone; the order of the undo steps is the reverse of the order of the corresponding forward operations. Thus, if $w_1[x] < w_2[x]$ then if both transactions abort, $a_2 < a_1$ or $a(T_1, T_2)$; if T_1 aborts then T_2 cannot commit; and if T_1 commits and T_2 aborts, then there is no restriction on the termination order. Finally, the fact that commit decisions must be made on-line without knowing the future outcome of active transactions forces that if $w_1[x] < w_2[x]$ then $c_1 < c_2$; otherwise, if T_2 committed first, then a subsequent abort of T_1 could not be realized properly by means of log-based undo steps. These restrictions are formalized in the following definition.

Definition 2. Serializability with Ordered Termination (SOT)
A history H is SOT if it is recoverable, serializable, and for every pair of conflicting operations w_i and w_j in H such that w_i precedes w_j and a_i cannot appear before w_j, the following conditions hold:

1. if T_j commits then it commits after T_i commits and
2. If T_i aborts then either it aborts after T_j aborts or H contains a group abort $a(\ldots T_i \ldots T_j \ldots)$.

Note that in the definition of SOT, serializability is with respect to the committed projection of the history, while the constraints on the termination of transactions are in terms of both committed as well as aborted transactions in the history. In [AVA+94] we prove the following theorem.

Theorem 3. *The class of histories SOT is equivalent to the class of histories PRED.*

Although intuitively PRED is the largest class of executions that is correct from both the concurrency control and the recovery points of view [SWY93], PRED executions may result in cascading aborts. Traditionally, cascading aborts occur when transactions are allowed to read uncommitted data. PRED executions may also result in cascading aborts when transactions write on uncommitted data. In particular, consider the following execution:

$$w_1[x]w_2[x]a_1$$

The abort of T_1 forces the abort of T_2 and a_2 must precede a_1 or they must be executed concurrently.

When restricted to the traditional methods of restoring before images, it can be shown that the class of strict and serializable histories is the maximal subclass of PRED that avoids cascading aborts [AVA+94]. To overcome this limitation, the next step is to modify the underlying recovery mechanism to expand the class of valid histories and still avoid cascading aborts. In [AVA+94] we extend log-based recovery to avoid cascading aborts due to write-write conflicts and to allow transactions to abort regardless of the status of other transactions with which they may conflict.

4 Scheduling Protocols

The theorem in the previous section is fundamental since it provides a constructive characterization of PRED executions. This characterization serves to develop efficient protocols for enforcing PRED executions.

4.1 Serialization Graph Testing

Let H be a history. We expand the notion of the serialization graph $SG(H)$ of history H by considering direct conflicts between any two transactions. The edges of the graph are annotated with the type of conflict between the two transactions (rw, wr, or ww). To guarantee SOT histories, the execution of transactions has the following three constraints: $SG(H)$ must be acyclic, if $T_i \rightarrow^{wr} T_j$ in $SG(H)$ then T_i must commit before T_j can commit, and if $T_i \rightarrow^{ww} T_j$ in H then either T_i commits before T_j terminates or T_j aborts before T_i terminates or both transactions abort concurrently.

These constraints imply that in case of a wr or ww conflicts there might be cascading aborts (note that the traditional notion of cascading aborts only applies to wr conflicts).

From the above constraints we derive the following serialization graph testing algorithm that recognizes SOT histories.

Let PRECEDE(T_j) be the set of transactions T_i such that $T_i \rightarrow^{wr/ww} T_j$. Let FOLLOW($T_j$) be the set of transactions T_k such that $T_j \rightarrow^{wr/ww} \ldots \rightarrow^{wr/ww} T_k$.

1. When an operation o_i that is not abort nor commit is submitted, add a node for T_i to the serialization graph, if it is not already there. Then add all corresponding ww, wr, and rw edges. If a cycle appears, a_i is submitted.
2. When c_i is submitted, the protocol checks whether PRECEDE(T_i) is empty. If this is not the case, c_i is delayed until all transactions in PRECEDE(T_i) have committed. Otherwise, c_i is executed. Once committed, T_i is removed from the graph and from all FOLLOW and PRECEDE lists.
3. When a_i is submitted, all transactions in FOLLOW(T_i) must also be aborted. If FOLLOW(T_i) is empty then a_i is executed. Otherwise, a(T_i FOLLOW(T_i)) is executed. This implies that undo operations to all write operations of all transactions in (T_i, FOLLOW(T_i)) are performed in reverse order than that in which they appear in the history . All aborted transactions are removed from the serialization graph, and from all immediate FOLLOW and PRECEDE lists.

Note that it is possible that an abort operation is issued when the transaction has already been aborted as a result of cascading aborts. In this case, the abort operation is acknowledged immediately without further action. We also assume that the scheduler has some mechanism ensuring that no two scheduled conflicting operations are processed at the same time.

The previous protocol is pessimistic. To reduce overhead, an optimistic protocol could be used. Its formulation is the same as above except that the graph is tested for cycles only when c_i is submitted. If there are no cycles, c_i gets processed in the same way as in the pessimistic protocol. Otherwise, c_i is rejected and a group abort is submitted that includes all transactions involved in a cycle. The detailed description and proofs of the correctness of these algorithms appear in [AVA+94].

4.2 Ordered Sharing Locking Protocol

Although the serialization graph testing approach recognizes, in general, all correct executions, it may incur unacceptable overhead. Many widely used concurrency control protocols use *locking* as a basic primitive for synchronization. Traditionally, there are two types of relationships between locks: shared and non-shared. For example, read locks can be shared but a write lock cannot be shared with any other lock. Two phase locking [BHG87] is the most widely accepted concurrency control protocol. Recently in [AE90], a new locking primitive was introduced that allows a new relationship, referred to as ***ordered sharing***. Ordered sharing can be used with two phase locking to eliminate the blocking between read and write operations. For example, in order to eliminate read-write blocking, a transaction T_j can be granted a write lock on an object even if a transaction T_i holds a read lock on the same object. We say that there is an *ordered shared relationship* from T_i's read lock to T_j's write lock. The advantage of using ordered sharing is that it eliminates blocking between read and write operations, and it can be used to restrict the execution of commit or abort operations. To ensure SOT executions, the two phase locking with ordered sharing must observe the following rules:

1. *Lock Rule.* A transaction must obtain a read (write) lock on an object before executing a read (write) operation on that object.
2. *Two Phase Rule.* A transaction must not acquire any locks once it has released a single lock.
3. *Lock Acquisition Rule.* If T_j acquires a lock with an ordered shared relationship with respect to a lock held by another transaction T_i, the corresponding operation of T_j must be executed after that of T_i.
4. *Lock Relinquish Rule.* If transaction T_j acquired a lock with an ordered shared relationship with respect to a lock held by transaction T_i and T_i has not released *any* of its locks, then T_j cannot release any of its locks.
5. *Delayed commitment and abortion.* If T_j reads from T_i then T_j can commit only if T_i has committed and if T_j overwrites a value written by T_i then T_j does not commit before T_i terminates and T_i does not abort before T_j terminates.

The ordered sharing of locks is necessary because SOT does not impose any restriction on the order in which the operations are executed, as long as the overall history is serializable. With basic two phase locking, histories such as $w_1[x]w_2[x]w_1[y]w_2[y]$ are not possible, however they are correct and valid according to SOT. The rules of two-phase locking with ordered sharing guarantee the serializability of the committed projection of the history. The delayed commitment and abortion rule ensures that the expanded history is SOT. This protocol accepts a strict subset of SOT. However, we note that the SOT histories that are not accepted by this protocol are not order-preserving serializable histories[4].

[4] Order-preserving serializable histories maintain the order of non-interleaved transactions in the equivalent serial history [BSW79, BBG89].

5 Conclusions

In this paper, we have addressed an open problem posed by [SWY93]: how to characterize the class of histories PRED in a constructive way so that unified scheduling protocols can be derived from it. We have slightly modified the original definitions of expanded histories and PRED to account for certain executions, and we have provided an equivalent class, SOT, with a more constructive definition. This new class is used as the basis for several protocols that implement unified concurrency control and recovery in an efficient manner.

So far, our model is restricted to read and write operations. However, both the model and the developed protocols can be generalized to transactions with semantically rich operations where recovery is based on compensating operations.

References

[AE90] D. Agrawal and A. El Abbadi. Locks with Constrained Sharing. In *Proceedings of the Ninth ACM Symposium on Principles of Database Systems*, pages 85–93, April 1990. To appear in Journal of Computer and System Sciences.

[AAE93] G. Alonso, D. Agrawal, A. El Abbadi. A Unified Implementation of Concurrency Control and Recovery. Technical Report, Department of Computer Science, University of California at Santa Barbara, TRCS93-19, October 1993

[AVA+94] G. Alonso, R. Vingralek, D. Agrawal, Y. Breitbart, A. El Abbadi, H. Schek, and G. Weikum. Unifying concurrency control and recovery of transactions. *Information Systems*, 1994. to appear in the special EDBT'94 issue.

[BBG89] C. Beeri, P. A. Bernstein, and N. Goodman. A Model for Concurrency in Nested Transactions Systems. *Journal of the ACM*, 36(2):230–269, April 1989.

[BGRS91] Y. Breitbart, D. Georgakopoulos, M. Rusinkiewisz, and A. Silberschatz. On rigorous transaction scheduling. *IEEE Transaction on Software Engineering*, 17(9), 1991.

[BHG87] P. A. Bernstein, V. Hadzilacos, and N. Goodman. *Concurrency control and recovery in database systems*. Addison-Wesley, 1987.

[BSW79] P. A. Bernstein, D. W. Shipman, and W. S. Wong. Formal Aspects of Serializability in Database Concurrency Control. *IEEE Transactions on Software Engineering*, 5(5):203–216, May 1979.

[GR93] J. Gray and A. Reuter. *Transaction Processing: Concepts and Techniques*. Morgan Kaufmann, 1993.

[HR83] T. Härder and A. Reuter. Principles of Transaction-Oriented Database Recovery. *ACM Computing Surveys*, 15(4):287–317, December 1983.

[SWY93] H. J. Schek, G. Weikum, and H. Ye. Towards a Unified Theory of Concurrency Control and Recovery. In *Proceedings of the ACM Symposium on Principles of Database Systems*, pages 300–311, June 1993.

[VBSW93] R. Vingralek, Y. Breitbart, H.-J. Schek, G. Weikum. Concurrency Control Protocols Guaranteeing Atomicity and Serializability. Technical Report 199, Department of Computer Science, ETH Zurich, July 1993.

Algorithms for Flexible Space Management in Transaction Systems Supporting Fine-Granularity Locking

C. Mohan, Don Haderle*

IBM Almaden Research Center, San Jose, CA 95120, USA
*IBM Santa Teresa Laboratory, 555 Bailey Avenue, San Jose, CA 95161, USA
mohan@almaden.ibm.com, haderle@stlvm14.vnet.ibm.com

Abstract We present several methods which relate to space management in a transaction system supporting fine-granularity (e.g., record) locking. These methods enable varying length records to be supported efficiently by permitting garbage collection to be performed within a page without the moved records having to be locked or the movements having to be logged. We present methods to do the following: (1) When a transaction releases space, efficiently prevent that space from being consumed by other transactions until that transaction terminates, while allowing the same transaction to reuse the space it freed. (2) Under the correct circumstances, avoid reading a totally empty deallocated page from disk during page reallocation. (3) Updating and logging of free space inventory pages' (FSIPs') changes for correct recovery. (4) Reduce locking during a table scan by a transaction using the isolation level of cursor stability. Our methods improve concurrency and space utilization, and provide I/O and CPU savings. Our space reservation and FSIP logging methods have been implemented in DB2 V3 in preparation for DB2's support of record locking.

1. Introduction

Storage management issues for records (tuples) have not received that much attention in the database research literature. In this paper, we focus on them with respect to concurrency control, recovery and performance. The methods presented in this paper enable storage and manipulation of varying length records to be supported efficiently (e.g., as in System R [Astr76] and DB2™ [Moha93a]). *Flexible storage management* permits garbage collection (i.e., page compaction) to be performed within a page to consolidate free space in a contiguous area of the page without the records moved as a result of the garbage collection having to be locked or the movements having to be logged. This leads to improved storage utilization and higher levels of concurrency. It reduces the need for frequent offline data reorganizations which affect data availability. Avoidance of locking and logging of the moved records is possible because locking of data and logging of updates are done in a logical, rather than physical, manner [MHLPS92].

1.1. Space Reservation

In a transaction processing system (e.g., a relational DBMS), it is necessary to support rollback or undo of part or all of the actions executed as part of a transaction [MHLPS92]. When a transaction's action which may need to be undone has freed some storage space (e.g., by deleting a record or contracting a record) on a particular page, that space cannot be consumed by the actions of *other* transactions without compromising the system's ability to undo on the *same page* the action which freed the space. In order to guarantee the atomicity property of transactions, we cannot compromise that ability if undo has to be performed on the same page. A transaction is allowed to consume space that it itself has freed, because a rollback to the point where the freed space would be needed must also include undoing the actions which consumed the space.

In the case of storage organizations like the System R one, which has been adopted by all IBM and many nonIBM RDBMSs, records are stored in a set of data pages and indexes contain key values and identifiers of records (RIDs) which contain those key values. A RID contains a page number which normally is the ID of the page in which the record is stored. Sometimes, the RID may actually be that of a *pointer record* which in turn contains the RID which refers to the page where the user's record (*overflow record*) is now stored. This kind of indirection happens when a record is expanded during an update and there is no place in the original page for the longer record. Since RIDs are used for a variety of purposes (e.g., locking, maintaining scan positions during table and index scans), we cannot easily afford to change the RID of a record. It is for those reasons and others relating to complications during recovery that undo of a data page change (as opposed to an index change - see [MoLe92]) has to be performed on the *same page* where the original action was performed. Hence the need for methods like the ones described in this paper. When locking and logging are not physical in nature, the (logical) locks obtained on records are not sufficient to ensure that space freed by one transaction is not consumed by other transactions.[1] Something more needs to be done to *reserve* uncommitted freed space. In section 3, we describe methods for doing space reservation. In section 7, we contrast them with other methods that we are aware of.

1.2. Space Tracking

Typically, each file containing records has a few pages called free space inventory pages (***FSIPs***). They are called space map pages (SMPs) in DB2. Each FSIP describes the space information relating to a large number of data or index pages. FSIPs allow searches for space to be done efficiently during record inserts and updates which cause overflows. FSIPs also permit some optimizations like avoiding reading of empty pages from disk to be performed (e.g., when a page deallocated during a page delete operation of an index is being reallocated during a page split operation [Moha90b, MoLe92]). If multiples tables are stored in a single file, but on a given page not more than one table's records are stored and FSIPs track which pages contain which table's records (e.g., as in segmented tablespaces of DB2 [CrHT90]), then FSIPs also permit dropping a table or mass deletion (i.e., delete all records of a table [CrHT90, HaSe89]) to be performed very efficiently by just marking the FISP entries for the table's pages as being deallocated. There is no need to visit the individual pages themselves and make changes to them to indicate that they don't contain any records (i.e., physically delete the records and log the deletions). In segmented tablespaces, FSIPs are also consulted during table scan oper-

™ DB2, DB2/2, DB2/6000, IBM and OS/2 are trademarks of the International Business Machines Corp.

ations to identify which pages of the file contain records of a particular table so that only those pages are accessed.

An FSIP keeps only approximate information (e.g., information like at least 25% of the page is full, at least 50% is full, etc.) to make sure that not every space-freeing or space-consuming operation to a data page requires an update to the space information in the corresponding FSIP. But there are some pieces of information which have to be tracked precisely (e.g., whether a page is empty or not) since such information may be relied upon to be accurate to implement optimizations like the ones mentioned above. To avoid special handling of the recovery of the FSIPs during redo and undo, and also to provide *recovery independence* [MHLPS92], it is highly advisable that updates to the FSIPs also be logged. Later, we discuss issues concerning how this logging is done and present methods which guarantee correct recovery and which also support the previously-mentioned optimizations.

2. Assumptions

We make the following assumptions about the transaction system:

- The granularity of locking is something finer than a page (e.g., a record).
- The lock manager, while returning from processing a lock-request call, will indicate whether the lock was already being held by this transaction at the time of the current call and if the lock was held then the mode in which the lock was held [Moha90b]. It will also indicate whether the lock is currently held by any *other* transaction.
- Each log record relates to only updates of a single page.
- Transaction identifiers (IDs) are monotonically increasing. ***MyID*** represents the ID of the current transaction.
- On whatever pages space reservation is needed, an operation which was originally performed on a given page during ***forward processing*** (i.e., when the transaction is not rolling back) will affect the same page if that operation is undone. This is typically the case with data pages (see [MHLPS92]). This is to be contrasted with high-concurrency indexes in which due to logical undos the page affected during undo may be different from the one affected during forward processing (see [Moha90b, MoLe92]). No space reservation is done for such objects and the handling of the running-out-of-space condition for such objects is discussed in [MoLe92].
- Every record in a data page has an associated record identifier (***RID***). A RID consists of a page ID concatenated with an index into an array (***pointer array***) that is present in the corresponding data page. Each nonzero element of the array contains a pointer to the corresponding record on the page. This level of indirection allows records to be moved around within a page, during garbage collection and record updates, without the RID being changed. This permits index entries to remain unmodified when such operations are performed. This is the storage organization used in systems like System R, DB2, DB2/2™, DB2/6000™ and SQL/DS [Moha93a].

---

1 In contrast, in IMS, where *physical* locking and logging are done, the locks obtained on a deleted object are sufficient to protect the freed space. Even there, when locking is done on *records* rather than on *segments*, special logic is needed to reserve the space freed by deleting a segment.

• There are two fields in each page called ***TFS*** (Total Free Space) and ***CFS*** (Contiguous Free Space) which keep track of space availability on the page. The CFS area is generally the free space that begins after the last record on the page and extends until the beginning of the trailer of the page. The ***NFS*** (noncontiguous free space) is scattered in the area which begins after the header of the page and ends at the beginning of the last record on the page. The total size of the NFS area is (TFS-CFS). The different segments of free space that constitute the NFS may be chained together to easily locate them.

3. Space Reservation Methods

The important data structures that we use in our space reservation methods are the following:

• There are 2 bits on every page to track the information relating to space reservation. We call them ***RSB1*** (Reserved Space Bit 1) and ***RSB2***. RSB1 has a value of '1' if some of the free space in NFS is in the reserved state. RSB2 has a value of '1' if some of the free space in the CFS area is in the reserved state. We never let RSB2 be equal to '1' when RSB1 = '0'.

• With each page in the buffer pool, the buffer manager associates a ***BCB*** (Buffer Control Block). The BCB has a field called ***RT*** (Reserving Transaction). If BCB.RT < > '0', then that means that only the transaction whose identifier is equal to the current value of RT could possibly have some space reserved on the corresponding page. If BCB.RT = '0', then it implies that either (1) there is no reserved space on the page (RSB1 = '0') or (2) there are possibly many transactions which have reserved space on the page (RSB1 = '1'). The buffer manager on reading a page from disk initializes the value of BCB.RT to '0'. This is a conservative action and is necessitated by the fact that pages with uncommitted changes may be written back to disk which will cause the original (true) values of BCB.RT to be lost.

Our objectives in proposing our methods are: (1) Maximize space utilization - e.g., try to allow a transaction which has already reserved space on a page to reuse that space during a subsequent space-consuming operation involving the same page. (2) Since, even with record locking in force, it is unlikely that there would be too many times when more than one transaction would have uncommitted updates on a given page at the same time, optimize for the case where there is only one reserver on a page. This will minimize the space management overhead. (3) Minimize the space and execution overhead of the space management logic - e.g., avoid tracking explicitly all the pages in which a transaction had reserved some space and at transaction termination time making the transaction visit those pages just to update the reservation information.

The methods presented below use locks for space reservation purposes. They exploit the information tracked in the BCB and the page, and the facilities of the lock manager, described in the section "2. Assumptions", to reduce the number of times locks are requested and to detect when only one transaction has reserved space on a given page. They also exploit the Commit_LSN idea described in [Moha90a, Moha93b, Moha93c]. Commit_LSN is the LSN of the first log record of the *oldest* update transaction still executing in the transaction system. The usefulness of this value comes from the observation that all the data in pages with page_LSN *less than* Commit_LSN must be committed data. The exploitation of the Commit_LSN idea is not required for the presented methods to work. Use of Commit_LSN helps avoid locking under certain conditions.

The method followed by a transaction which **frees B bytes** of space due to a space-freeing operation (e.g., record delete or record contraction) on page P during the transaction's **forward processing** is presented in Figure 1. In this method, a transaction which needs to reserve some space on a page obtains an IX mode reservation lock on the page. The choice of the IX mode permits multiple transactions to be able to concurrently reserve space on the same page since IX is compatible with IX. In addition to getting that lock, the reserver also sets (='1') the RSB1 bit on the page if the freed space is going to remain in the NFS area. If the space is merged with the CFS area, then RSB2 must also be set. If no other transaction is already a reserver on this page, then the current transaction leaves its MyID in BCB.RT. If there is at least one other reserver, then the current transaction sets BCB.RT to zero. The current transaction can determine whether other reservers for this page exist by checking the return code from the lock manager when the IX lock call returns. RSB1 and RSB2 can be reset immediately on noticing that page_LSN is less than Commit_LSN since the latter implies that the transactions which had earlier reserved space on the current page must have terminated.

The method followed by a transaction which **needs B bytes** of space for its space-consuming operation (e.g., record insert or record expansion) on page P during the transaction's **forward processing** is given in Figure 2. In this method, the transaction first tries to see if Commit_LSN can be used to reset RSB1 and RSB2. Then, it checks if any space on the page is reserved by examining RSB1. If RSB1 is not set, then it can use any of the free space after, optionally, performing garbage collection. If RSB1 is set but RSB2 is not set, then space in the CFS area is available for use. But, in this case, in order to help other transactions, if BCB.RT says that the current transaction is the only reserver, then NFS, if sufficient, is used. This way, CFS will still be available to other transactions. Otherwise, if

```
X latch P                          /* get exclusive access to page   */
IF page_LSN < Commit_LSN THEN      /* no uncommitted data on page    */
  set RSB1, RSB2 = '0'             /* could garbage collect now      */
IF BCB.RT <> myID THEN             /* may not be a reserver already  */
  get IX lock on page              /* get reservation lock           */
  IF no other transaction holds reservation lock THEN
    IF I did not already hold lock THEN /* no reservers so far   */
      set RSB1, RSB2 = '0'         /* could garbage collect now      */
    set BCB.RT = myID              /* I will be the only reserver now*/
  ELSE
    BCB.RT = 0                     /* at least 2 reservers now       */
  set RSB1 = '1'                   /* indicate some space is reserved*/
ELSE                               /* I am the only reserver already;*/
  no need to get reservation lock /* RSB1 must be '1' already     */
perform space-freeing operation
add freed space to NFS             /* space not merged with CFS      */
TFS = TFS + B
```

Figure 1: Method for Freeing Space

```
X latch P                          /* get exclusive access to page    */
IF page_LSN < Commit_LSN THEN      /* no uncommitted data on page     */
  set RSB1, RSB2 = '0'             /* could garbage collect now       */
IF TFS < B THEN                    /* not enough free space on page   */
  unlatch P, exit and go to another page
IF RSB1 = '0' THEN                 /* no reserved space on page       */
  perform space-consuming operation
  adjust TFS (set TFS = TFS - B) & possibly CFS
  unlatch P and exit
ELSE                               /* RSB1 = '1'; RSB2 = '1' or '0'   */
  IF RSB2 = '0' THEN               /* CFS is not reserved             */
    IF BCB.RT = myID THEN          /* I am the only reserver          */
      IF enough space is available together in NFS area THEN
        do operation using space in NFS
        adjust TFS
        unlatch P and exit
    IF CFS >= B THEN               /* CFS is sufficient               */
      do operation using space in CFS
      adjust TFS & CFS
      unlatch P and exit
    ELSE                           /* CFS is not sufficient           */
  ELSE                             /* RSB1 = '1' and RSB2 = '1'       */
IF BCB.RT = myID THEN              /* I am the only reserver          */
  If necessary perform garbage collection
  IF garbage collection is performed THEN/* NFS becomes part of CFS*/
    set RSB2 = '1'
  do operation using any space
  adjust TFS & possibly CFS
  unlatch P and exit
ELSE                               /* there may be many reservers     */
  Conditionally Instant X lock P/* check if the reservers are gone*/
  IF lock granted THEN             /* no other reservers              */
    IF I already held lock THEN /* I am a reserver                    */
      set BCB.RT = myID            /* remember I am the only reserver*/
      If necessary perform garbage collection
      IF garbage collection is performed THEN
        set RSB2 = '1'             /* NFS becomes part of CFS         */
    ELSE                           /* I am not a reserver             */
      RSB1 = '0'                   /* no space on page is reserved    */
    do space-consuming operation
    adjust TFS & possibly CFS
    unlatch P
  ELSE                             /* other reservers still exist     */
    unlatch P and go to another page to perform operation
```

Figure 2: Method for Consuming Space

sufficient, CFS is used. If RSB1 is set, RSB2 is not set and BCB.RT ≠ MyID, but CFS is not sufficient, then the transaction has to request the page reservation lock in the S mode to see if there is any other reserver. The lock would be grantable if there is no other reserver. Whether or not the current transaction itself had earlier reserved space on the page would be determined by examining the return code from the lock manager. RSB1 can be reset (='0') if the lock is grantable and the current transaction is not a reserver on that page. If the former is true but the latter is false, then the transaction can set BCB.RT to MyID since the current transaction is the only reserver on the page. If the lock is not grantable immediately, then, in order not to decrease concurrency by making the transaction wait, the transaction is made to go to another page to find space.

During restart *redo* and normal/restart *undo* of a transaction's updates, RSB2 should be set if RSB1 is already set and space is consumed after doing garbage collection. Otherwise, RSB1 and RSB2 values are left undisturbed assuming that whenever space is freed it is *not* added to CFS. During restart recovery, whenever a space-freeing operation of an *in-doubt* (*prepared*) distributed transaction is redone, RSB1 is set to '1'. The IX mode reservation lock would have to be reacquired for an in-doubt transaction if it had performed any space-freeing operation on a page.

4. Logging Updates to Free Space Inventory Pages

In the section "1.2. Space Tracking", we introduced the reader to free space inventory pages (FSIPs). In this section, we discuss them further and then present methods to perform logging and recovery correctly for them.

To understand the recovery implications relating to FSIPs, let's consider an execution scenario. Transaction T1 might cause the space on a data page to change from being 48% full to 52% full, thereby requiring an update to the FSIP entry for that page to change it from the at least 25% full state to at least 50% full state. Later, T2 might cause the space to go to 60% full, which does not require an update to the FSIP since the FSIP tracks space only approximately and hence cares about only some state transitions. Now, if T1 were to rollback, then the space would change to 56% full and this should *not* cause an update to the FSIP since it is not an interesting state transition. If T1 had written its FSIP change log record as a *redo-undo* record, then T1's rollback would cause the FSIP entry to say 25% full, which would be wrong, given the *current* state of the data page. This scenario points to the need for logging the changes to the FSIP as *redo-only* changes and for the need to do ***logical undos*** with respect to the FSIP updates. That is, while undoing a data page update, the system has to determine whether that data page undo operation causes the free space information to have a state transition and if it does cause a transition, then update the FSIP and write a *redo-only* log record which describes the change to the FSIP.

We can easily construct an example in which a transaction does not perform an update to the FSIP during forward processing, but needs to perform an update to the FSIP during rollback. We can also construct an example in which the FSIP update performed during forward processing is not the exact inverse of the FSIP update performed during the rollback. These are possible due to fine-granularity (e.g., record) locking which allows other transactions to change the available space on a page between the time one transaction performs an update and the time that transaction undoes that update.

In the rest of this section, we describe methods for logging the updates to FSIPs so that recovery will be done correctly. Since an FSIP update may cause a data page's state to be set to the empty state (i.e., there are no records on the page), the proper ordering of the logging of the updates to the data and FSIP pages is important. The ordering requirement turns out to be nontrivial and it depends on whether the transaction is going forward or is rolling back!

During **forward processing**, the following method is used.

```
X latch data page
Perform data page update, log it, update page_LSN
Check if FSIP update is needed
If yes then
  X latch appropriate FSIP²
  Perform FSIP update, log using redo-only log record, update page_LSN
  Release FSIP latch
Unlatch data page
```

Note that during forward processing, the logging of the data page's update is done *before* that of the FSIP's update, if any. The opposite order might cause problems if a failure were to happen after the logging of the FSIP update but before the logging of the data page update. Then, during restart recovery, the FSIP update will not be undone due to the logging of that update using a *redo-only* log record. Such a scenario could result in the FSIP saying that a data page is empty when in fact it is not. The latter could cause a table scan to skip that data page, thereby returning incorrect results (see the section "6. A Method for Reducing Locking").

During (normal and restart) **undo processing**, the following method is used.

```
X latch data page
Perform data page update
Check if FSIP update is needed
If yes then
  X latch appropriate FSIP
  Perform FSIP update, log using redo-only log record, update page_LSN
  Release FSIP latch
Log data page update using a compensation log record, update page_LSN
Unlatch data page
```

Note that during undo processing, the logging of the data page's update is done *after* that of the FSIP's update, if any. The opposite order might cause problems if a failure were to happen after the logging of the data page update but before the logging of the FSIP update. Then, during restart recovery, the FSIP update will not be performed due to the logging of the data page update using a compensation log record (CLR). CLRs are redo-only records in ARIES [MHLPS92]. Further, in ARIES, a CLR contains a field called UndoNxtLSN which points to the predecessor of the log record whose undo caused the CLR to be written. As a result of this, when a CLR is encountered during undo, the next record that is processed is the one pointed to by UndoNxtLSN. This way an already-undone log record is not even encountered during the undo processing. If we had not already taken

---

2 If latching of FSIPs causes contention since FSIPs are normally hot spots, then, to support concurrent updates of an FSIP, latching can be substituted with *compare and swap* logic (atomic update instructions) to update the relevant FSIP entry and the page_LSN field. The latter should be updated only if the already existing value is less than the new value. The existing value may be higher if a second concurrent transaction had logged its FSIP update *after* the first transaction but had updated the page_LSN *before* the first transaction. DB2 avoids latching/locking FSIPs to provide higher concurrency.

care of the FSIP update *before* writing the CLR as part of undoing the data page update, then, if we were to fail right after logging the CLR alone to disk, then during restart recovery we will not realize that the FSIP needs to be updated. Such a scenario could result in the FSIP saying that a data page is empty when in fact it is not! The latter could cause a table scan to skip that data page, thereby returning incorrect results.

It should be noted that in both forward and undo processing the data page latch is held while the FSIP is updated. This ensures that two different transactions' updates to the same data page and FSIP do not get done in different sequences between the data page and the FSIP thereby introducing an inconsistency between the data page's actual state and its state as reflected in the FSIP.

It is interesting to contrast the above solution to the FSIP-logging problem with what DB2 does today where DB2 supports only page as the smallest granularity of locking. Page locking guarantees that if a transaction made a data page change which caused an FSIP change and subsequently that data page change is rolled back, then that FSIP change would also have to be undone. Consequently, DB2 logs FSIP log records as *redo-undo* records and it does not have to think about FSIP updates while undoing a data page update (i.e., there is no need to logically undo FSIP changes based on rollback-time state of the data page). As part of introducing record locking support into DB2, we have changed DB2's FSIP logging method to the one described above in the latest release of the product (DB2 V3).

5. A Method for Reducing I/Os

In this section, we describe a method (see Figure 3) for use during a record insert operation when a transaction is in forward processing. This method, under certain conditions, avoids having to read from disk a page whose FSIP entry says that the page is empty. If the page does not have to be read, then a buffer slot can be allocated for that page and formatted as needed (e.g., RSB1 and RSB2 will be set to '0'). Thus, one synchronous I/O operation can be saved which can lead to less load on the I/O device, save the CPU overhead of initiating an I/O and performing a process

```
FSIP says data page K is empty
Request conditional X (reservation) lock on K
If lock granted and lock not already held by current transaction Then
  If FSIP entry still says K is empty Then
    Allocate an empty slot in buffer pool for K
    Format slot and log formatting action
    Follow normal insert logic (insert, log data and FSIP changes, ...)
    Release lock on K
  Else
    Release lock on K
    Follow normal insert logic (read page, check RSB bits, ...)
Else
  If lock granted then release lock on K
  Follow normal insert logic (read page, check RSB bits, ...)
```

Figure 3: Method for Page Reallocation Without Disk Read

switch, improved response time and reduced lock hold time. Just because the FSIP entry says that the page is empty, we cannot always ignore the disk version of the page since there may be some *uncommitted* deletes involving that page. In that case, the RSB1 and RSB2's settings should not be disturbed which means that the page would have to be read to see if there is any *unreserved* free space. Otherwise, the reserved space might get consumed by some transactions other than the reserving transactions and the reserving transactions would be in trouble if they choose to roll back or they have to be rolled back due to deadlocks, system failures, etc. Hence, to do this optimization correctly, we use the reservation lock to determine whether the page's empty state is the *committed* state.

Our method for doing the above is shown in Figure 3. We have assumed that the FSIP page latch is not acquired while accessing the FSIP in the interest of permitting high concurrency. The method holds on to the space reservation lock for a while to prevent multiple transactions from reformatting the same page. It also rechecks the status of the FSIP entry for that page *after* acquiring the reservation lock to be sure that another transaction had not already allocated it and inserted data into it. We also have to make sure that we do not set the page status to the allocated state *before* the buffer slot for the reallocated page is formatted. Otherwise, a table scanner (or an inserter) might notice that the page is allocated and access it before it is formatted. The problem with that is that the deallocated state might not be a page with no records in it (i.e., an empty page), but might actually be a page which has some old records which had been *deleted* via a mass delete operation (see the section "1.2. Space Tracking" and [CrHT90, HaSe89]). Such records should not be read since they are logically no longer part of the table. Note that in instances like this avoiding the read of the old version of a deallocated page is a *requirement* rather than an optimization.

6. A Method for Reducing Locking

In this section, we describe a method (see Figure 4) for reducing locking when a *cursor stability* [Moha90a] table scan is being performed and record locking is in effect. In this case, the table is usually locked in the IS mode and the individual records are locked in S mode, assuming only reads are being done. The straightforward implementation of the table scan operation would require that every empty and *nonempty* RID pointer array element in a data page be locked to ensure that the scan does not bypass or skip ("jump over") uncommitted deletes. Such locking of empty elements can be very expensive in terms of CPU overhead. In Figure 4, we present a more efficient implementation of this operation. That method also avoids reading and processing empty pages under certain conditions.

We avoid reading and processing an empty page if we find that no *other* transaction has any uncommitted updates on it. The latter is determined by obtaining the reservation lock in S mode (we could use Commit_LSN with FSIP's page_LSN to try to avoid this lock). The current transaction may have some uncommitted deletes on the page, which of course can be ignored. In the case of nonempty pages, if RSB1 is set, then we see if it can be reset using the Commit_LSN optimization. If the latter does not help and the current transaction is not the only reserver (if it is a reserver at all), then we request the reservation lock and wait for the other reservers to terminate. Once we obtain the lock or if we find that the current trans-

```
Processing for each page of interest found by looking at FSIP:

If the FSIP entry for data page P says that P is empty Then
  request (reservation) instant S lock on P/*uncond req; may cause wait*/
  If the FSIP entry still says that the page is empty Then
    skip page              /* note that I may have uncommitted deletes*/
    go to FSIP, process entry for next data page /* on this empty page */
Read and S latch P
If page_LSN < Commit_LSN Then          /* no uncommitted updates on page */
  set RSB1, RSB2 = '0'
If RSB1 = '1' and BCB.RT <> myID Then
  request instant S (reservation) lock on P
  If I did not hold reservation lock before Then
    set RSB1 = '0'
  Else BCB.RT = myID                   /* I am the sole reserver          */
Lock only nonempty slots of RID pointer array and read pointed-to records
   (usual logic used to avoid deadlocks and to read record at a time)
Unlatch P
```

Figure 4: Method for Reducing Locking During Table Scans

action is the only reserver, then we process only the nonempty pointer array elements. If RSB1 is set and the reservation lock is not immediately obtainable, then an alternative, which can lead to higher concurrency at a higher locking cost, is to lock every element of the RID pointer array.

7. Related Work

In this section, we discuss related methods about which we have enough information.

7.1. System R Method

The System R method (which is the basis for the SQL/DS scheme) has the following features.

When record level locking is being done, space freed by a transaction is kept reserved at least until that transaction terminates by actually retaining a space of the desired length containing the RID of the record that that space constituted before the space was freed. That RID would have been locked by that transaction before it freed the space. Such a space is referred to as a *locked hole*. Sometimes, the freed space may not be large enough to contain the RID. Such a hole is called a *small hole*! In this case, the RID associated with the small hole is the RID of the record immediately physically preceding it on the page. This means that when garbage collection is done it must be ensured that the small hole and the record preceding it are treated as a unit and moved together! A small locked hole is created when an existing record is updated and the updated version of the record has to be put on a different page due to unavailability of enough free space on the original page. In this case, the original record's prefix area is turned into a pointer to the overflowed record on the other page and the rest of the original record becomes a hole. If the latter is less than 4 bytes, then it becomes a small hole.

A transaction does not use space that it reserved at the time of a delete or an update during subsequent insert or update operations. In fact, even during the undo of a delete it does not necessarily reuse the space that the delete operation originally reserved! The reuse happens only if the unreserved free space on the page is not enough for the deleted record to be reinserted.

The space reserved by one terminated transaction might get carried over as the reservation of another transaction! This is possible since the RID released by one transaction (through the delete of the corresponding record) might be reused to identify a newly inserted record of another transaction. If the latter transaction did not use the space released by the former while inserting that record, then that space will not be available to anyone until the latter transaction terminates. If, after the second transaction commits, a third transaction were to delete the newly inserted record, then there will be 2 locked holes with the same RID! The sizes of these holes might be different. If the third transaction were to rollback later and there is no unreserved free space to put back the record, then the right locked hole must be reused. This is done by comparing the lengths of the locked holes with the length of the record that must be reinserted!

During garbage collection, holes are moved around. For each locked hole, a check is made to see if the corresponding RID is still locked. If it is not, then that space becomes unlocked. Otherwise, it remains locked. Garbage collection moves the records and locked holes to the beginning of the page and makes all the free space contiguous. No effort is made to put all the locked holes in a contiguous area. The net result is that in System R more garbage collections will be required than in our method. Even locked holes get moved around, resulting in more copying operations. Additionally, garbage collection has to worry about reservations and treat small and big holes differently. Our garbage collection does not have to worry about reservations in this fashion at all, beyond setting RSB2 if RSB1 is set.

During an update operation, the update is done in-place in the original record's space only if none of the fields' length is being changed and no new fields are being added to the record. For all other types of updates, new space is used to contain the updated record and the old record's space is put in the reserved state! The net result is that even updates that shrink or expand a record a little bit could cause overflow of the updated record to a new page! The situation could be especially bad if the record size is a significant fraction of the page size.

7.2. Starburst Method

DB2/2 (formerly called OS/2™ Extended Edition Database Manager), DB2/6000 and Starburst use the method described in [LiMP86, LiMR90]. That method maintains, on each page a free space counter (FREE) and a reserved space descriptor consisting of (1) a reserved space count (RSVD), (2) the ID of the *youngest* (most recent) transaction contributing to the reserved space (TRANS), and (3) the amount of reserved space contributed by the youngest transaction to reserved space (TRSVD). FREE is the total amount of free space on the page. The unreserved (i.e., immediately usable) free space is FREE - RSVD. TRANS is the transaction ID of the youngest transaction to reserve space on the page. If the youngest transaction that reserved space on the page and all transactions older than that have terminated, then all the reserved space on the page can be unreserved because all transactions that could have possibly reserved space on that page have terminated. Space is reserved by incrementing the reserved space count (RSVD) and by setting the transaction ID (TRANS) to the *maximum* of its current value and the transaction ID of the transaction reserving the space.

When attempting to consume space on a page, only FREE - RSVD space is available. This insures that enough space remains to allow uncommitted transactions to rollback deletions from the page. If TRANS is less than the transaction ID of all active transactions, the reserved space (RSVD) can be reset to zero prior to checking for available space. The space TRSVD is available to the transaction TRANS. If TRANS is younger than the transaction undoing a space consuming operation, then RSVD must be incremented because the allocation being undone *may* have used reserved space (i.e., decremented RSVD). Instead of waiting for TRANS and all transactions older than TRANS to terminate before unreserving all the RSVD space, Starburst uses a locking scheme similar to the one described in this paper.

8. Summary

From our experience with IBM products and prototypes, we have learnt that a badly-designed space management scheme can lead to enormous overheads, inefficiencies and difficult code maintenance. Unobvious negative implications of badly-designed schemes have shown up during the executions of even benchmarks like TPC-B [Serl91].

Our method requires very little space overhead on every page of the database. It uses only 2 bits. In contrast, the Starburst method uses many *words* of storage on every page, whether or not there is currently any reserved space. On every data page, it explicitly keeps track of the total amount of reserved free space, the amount of free space reserved by the youngest transaction and the name of the youngest transaction to reserve space on the page. Our two bits track whether or not there is reserved space in the contiguous and noncontiguous free spaces.

Further, the logic used in the other methods during normal and undo processing is very complicated since they explicitly keep track of the *amount* of reserved free space. Our method's logic is much simpler.

The other methods exploit information about the youngest transaction to reserve space on a page and/or space-reservation locks obtained on pages to determine when all reserved space can be reused. We use locking and/or the log sequence number on the page to make that determination. Instead of keeping the youngest transaction information on the page itself and incurring the permanent space overhead, we keep that information in the buffer control block for the page. Even if the page is removed from the buffer, we initialize that field appropriately to avoid errors.

We described a method for avoiding reading of a totally empty page from disk. This saves a synchronous disk I/O and avoids task switching. The idea of avoiding the read of a previously deallocated page during its reallocation is not new. The manner in which we did it in combination with all the other related methods of this paper is what is new. This is a nontrivial piece of logic when there is concurrent activity and record locking is in effect.

We also described methods for correctly handling the updating and logging of free space inventory pages' (FSIPs') changes when each log record describes only updates to a single page, as is the case in most DBMSs.

This is a nontrivial piece of logic when record locking is in effect (during normal processing data page change is logged first and then the FSIP's change; during rollback processing, the opposite order must be followed). This method is independent of the particular space reservation method in use.

We also described a method for reducing locking during a table scan by a transaction using the isolation level of cursor stability. By exploiting the information being tracked (2 bits on every page) for space reservation purposes, it can avoid having to lock the record identifiers (RIDs) of currently *nonexisting* records. In the absence of our method, the latter must be done to avoid skipping over uncommitted deleted records. This is an important optimization since in practice cursor stability is used very often by customers. To our knowledge, such a method is not described anywhere in the literature. This method is easily adaptable to the Starburst-style space reservation methods also.

Our space reservation and FSIP logging methods have been implemented in DB2 V3 [Moha93a] in preparation for DB2's support of record locking. Commit_LSN is also implemented there.

Acknowledgements Our thanks go to our colleagues who implemented our ideas in DB2.

9. References

Astr76 Astrahan, M., et al. *System R: Relational Approach to Data Base Management*, **ACM Transactions on Database Systems**, Vol. 1, No. 2, June 1976.

CrHT90 Crus, R., Haderle, D., Teng, J. *Method for Minimizing Locking and Reading in a Segmented Storage Space*, **U.S. Patent 4,961,134**, IBM, October 1990.

HaSe89 Haderle, D., Seppi, K. *Mass Delete of Index Structures*, **IBM Technical Disclosure Bulletin**, August 1989.

LiMP86 Lindsay, B., Mohan, C., Pirahesh, H. *Method for Reserving Space Needed for "Rollback" Actions*, **IBM Technical Disclosure Bulletin**, Vol. 29, No. 6, November 1986.

LiMR90 Lindsay, B., Mohan, C., Rodriguez, R.A. *Method for Updating Free Space Allocation Records in OS/2 DBM Table Data Files*, **IBM Technical Disclosure Bulletin**, Vol. 33, No. 6A, November 1990.

MHLPS92 Mohan, C., Haderle, D., Lindsay, B., Pirahesh, H., Schwarz, P. *ARIES: A Transaction Recovery Method Supporting Fine-Granularity Locking and Partial Rollbacks Using Write-Ahead Logging*, **ACM Transactions on Database Systems**, Vol. 17, No. 1, March 1992.

Moha90a Mohan, C. *Commit_LSN: A Novel and Simple Method for Reducing Locking and Latching in Transaction Processing Systems*, **Proc. 16th International Conference on Very Large Data Bases**, Brisbane, August 1990.

Moha90b Mohan, C. *ARIES/KVL: A Key-Value Locking Method for Concurrency Control of Multiaction Transactions Operating on B-Tree Indexes*, **Proc. 16th International Conference on Very Large Data Bases**, Brisbane, August 1990. A different version of this paper is available as **IBM Research Report RJ7008**, IBM Almaden Research Center, September 1989.

Moha93a Mohan, C. *IBM's Relational DBMS Products: Features and Technologies*, **Proc. SIGMOD International Conference on Management of Data**, Washington, May 1993.

Moha93b Mohan, C. *A Cost-Effective Method for Providing Improved Data Availability During DBMS Restart Recovery After a Failure*, **Proc. 19th International Conference on Very Large Data Bases**, Dublin, August 1993.

Moha93c Mohan, C. *Transaction Processing System and Method With Reduced Locking*, **United States Patent 5,247,672**, IBM, September 1993.

MoLe92 Mohan, C., Levine, F. *ARIES/IM: An Efficient and High Concurrency Index Management Method Using Write-Ahead Logging*, **Proc. ACM SIGMOD International Conference on Management of Data**, San Diego, June 1992. A longer version of this paper is available as **IBM Research Report RJ6846**, IBM Almaden Research Center, August 1989.

Serl91 Serlin, O. *The History of DebitCredit and the TPC*, Chapter 2 in **The Benchmark Handbook for Database and Transaction Processing Systems**, J. Gray (Ed.), Morgan Kaufmann Publishing, Inc., 1991.

Indexing Alternatives for Multiversion Locking*

Paul M. Bober** and Michael J. Carey

Computer Sciences Department, University of Wisconsin, Madison WI 53706, USA

Abstract. In this paper, we present several options for extending single-version indexing schemes for use with multiversion two-phase locking. The proposed options are orthogonal to the underlying indexing structure (e.g., hashing or B+ trees). The options differ in where they place references to individual versions; this version selection information is placed either with the data or in the leaf entries of one or more indices. We also briefly summarize the results of a performance study showing that storing version selection information with the data is usually the best option because it keeps indices smaller, thus enabling a larger fraction of the indices to remain cached in the buffer pool.

1 INTRODUCTION

Due to the adoption of relational database technology and the increasing ability of database systems to efficiently execute ad-hoc queries, query processing is becoming an increasingly important function of transaction processing systems. The concurrency control algorithm found in most commercial database systems, two-phase locking (2PL) [14], however, does not efficiently support on-line query processing. With 2PL, queries can lock large regions of data for long periods of time, causing update transactions to suffer long delays. As a result, many applications run queries without obtaining locks or using only short-term locks, allowing the queries to see transaction-inconsistent answers. These approaches are referred to as GO processing and cursor stability locking, respectively.

To solve this data contention problem while providing consistent answers to queries, a multiversion extension to two-phase locking was proposed and implemented in a system developed at Prime in the early 1980s [12]. This extension was also used in a system developed at Computer Corporation of America (CCA) [10, 11], and it has subsequently been incorporated in DEC's Rdb product [22]. In multiversion two-phase locking (MV2PL), a timestamp mechanism is used in conjunction with the temporary retention of prior versions of data so that a read-only query can serialize before all update transactions that were active during any portion of its lifetime. In MV2PL, read-only queries do not contribute to data contention since they do not have to set or wait for locks. This form of versioning, where old copies of data are retained temporarily for concurrency control purposes (as opposed to long-term retention for historical queries), has been referred to as *transient versioning* [21].

Since indexes are important for good performance in database systems, it is important to to determine how they may coexist with MV2PL. Conventional

* This research was partially supported by an IBM Research Initiation Grant

** Author's current address: Transarc Corporation, The Gulf Tower, 707 Grant Street, Pittsburgh, PA 15219

single-version indexing structures such as B+ trees and hashing are not entirely compatible with MV2PL in their current forms, as they support searches on key value alone (not on both key value and timestamp together). Without timestamp information encoded in the index, a given query will have no way of knowing if an entry with a matching key references a version that it should see without first retrieving the version and examining its timestamp information. Thus, frequent *false drops* may occur since not all retrieved tuples are actually needed. Furthermore since false drops are possible, the use of *index-only plans*, a common relational query processing optimization that avoids retrieving actual tuples when only indexed attribute values are needed, is ruled out.[3]

To support efficient query processing, it is clear that an MV2PL system must utilize an indexing scheme specifically designed for multiversion data. One approach, taken in DEC's Rdb system, is to treat index nodes like data records at the storage level, including having MV2PL applied to them [16]. While this approach supports index-only plans, it is not compatible with the use of high performance non-2PL B+ tree concurrency control algorithms such as those proposed in [3, 20, 21]. Because (non-2PL) B-tree concurrency control algorithms are widely viewed as being important to achieving acceptable performance, we do not consider the Rdb approach further.

A number of other multiversion indexing approaches have been proposed in the literature; examples include [13, 27, 17, 19, 21]. With the exception of [21], however, these schemes are designed to support historical databases, where out-of-date versions are retained for an arbitrary length of time. In contrast to transient versioning databases, historical databases may have a large number of versions of each tuple (some of which may have been migrated to tertiary storage, e.g., optical disk). Because of this, the basic indexing design tradeoffs are different for the two types of versioning. For example, while it might be reasonable in a transient versioning system to require a query to traverse the entire length of a (short) linked list of tuple versions, this would not be reasonable in a historical versioning system. Furthermore, it is likely that a historical versioning system will be required to store pieces of its indexes on tertiary store, as the indexes may grow very large. Lastly, efficient garbage collection is very important in a transient versioning system, as versions are not needed for very long once they have been replaced by a more current version.

In this paper, we compare a range of possible multiversion indexing approaches that are designed specifically for MV2PL. This paper is an extension of our previous work, where we proposed and studied the *on-page caching* scheme for placing transient multiversion data on secondary storage [7]; that scheme is a refinement of CCA's version pool scheme [10]. Each of the multiversion indexing approaches that we study in this paper are integrated with on-page caching to present a complete version placement and indexing solution for MV2PL.

The remainder of the paper is organized as follows: In Section 2 we review

---

[3] e.g., using an index-only plan, a query computing the average salary of a group of employees can compute the average by simply scanning the leaves of the employee salary index (if one exists).

the MV2PL algorithm, the CCA version pool scheme, and our on-page caching refinement. In Section 3 we describe four multiversion indexing schemes, and discuss potential performance tradeoffs between them. In Section 4, we briefly summarize the results of a performance study that compares the indexing schemes in terms of their I/O costs for queries and update transactions. Lastly, we present our conclusions in Section 5.

2 BACKGROUND

In this section we set the stage for the discussion of multiversion indexing approaches by reviewing the MV2PL algorithm, the CCA version pool scheme for managing storage for multiple versions of data, and our on-page caching refinement to the CCA version pool scheme.

MV2PL is only one of a number of published multiversion concurrency control algorithms. Because it is a direct extension of the de facto industry standard, 2PL, we are primarily concerned with indexing in the context of MV2PL in this work. For completeness, however, we wish to identify some of the other proposals here. To the best of our knowledge, Reed's distributed timestamp ordering scheme [23] was actually the first multiversion concurrency control algorithm proposal. Several 2PL-based algorithms that retain at most two versions of data in order to reduce blocking due to read/write conflicts have also been proposed [5, 26]. Other multiversion extensions of single-version concurrency control algorithms include: multiversion optimistic validation [24, 9, 18] multiversion timestamp ordering [2], and the multiversion tree protocol [25]. Finally, in [7], we presented a generalization of MV2PL that provides queries with a tradeoff between consistency and performance.

2.1 Multiversion Two-Phase Locking (MV2PL)

In MV2PL, each transaction T is assigned a startup timestamp, $T_S(T)$, when it begins to run, and a commit timestamp, $T_C(T)$, when it reaches its commit point. Transactions are classified at startup time as being either ***read-only*** or ***update*** transactions. When an update transaction reads or writes a page[4] it locks the page, as in traditional 2PL, and then accesses the current version. Update transactions must block when lock conflicts occur. When a page is written, a new version is created and stamped with the commit timestamp of its creator; this timestamp is referred to as the version's create timestamp (CTS).[5] When a read-only query Q wishes to access a page, on the other hand, it simply reads the most recent version of the page with a timestamp less than or equal to $T_S(Q)$. Since each version is stamped with the commit timestamp of its creator, Q will only read versions written by transactions that committed before Q began running. Thus, Q will be serialized after all transactions that committed prior to its startup, but before all transactions that are active during any portion of

[4] MV2PL utilized page-level locking in its original form.

[5] Actually, to reduce commit-time processing, the page is stamped with the creator's transaction id, and a separate list is used to map transaction ids to commit timestamps [10].

its lifetime—as though it ran instantaneously at its starting time. As a result, read-only transactions never have to set or wait for locks in MV2PL.

When an update transaction deletes a page in MV2PL, the prior versions of the page must persist until all queries which may require them have completed. Deletes may thus be handled by assigning a *delete timestamp* (DTS) to the last version of each page. Initially, the DTS of the most recent version is infinite, signifying that it is in the current database. When a page is deleted, the commit timestamp of the deleter is assigned to the DTS of the current version (denoting that it is no longer part of the current database). Update transactions should access a page only if it has a current version. Likewise, a query may access a page only if the query's startup timestamp is less than the DTS of the most recent version (i.e., only if the page was not deleted as of the query's arrival).

2.2 The CCA Version Pool Organization

To maintain the set of versions needed by ongoing queries, the CCA scheme divides the stored database into two parts: the main segment and the version pool. The main segment contains the current version of every page in the database, and the version pool contains prior versions of pages. The version pool is organized as a circular buffer, much like the log in a traditional recovery manager [15]. The CCA design chains the versions in reverse chronological order; in Section 3, we discuss other ways of organizing sets of versions. Three attractive properties of the version pool are that (i) updates are performed in-place, allowing clustering of current versions to be maintained, (ii) version pool writes are sequential (i.e., similar to log writes) and (iii) storage reclamation is relatively straightforward.

Figure 1 depicts the main segment of the database, the version pool, the pointers used to manage version pool space, and the version chain for a page X.

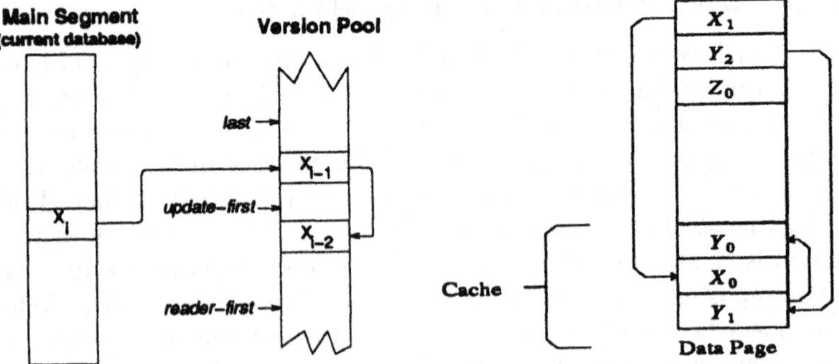

Fig. 1. CCA Version Pool Org. **Fig. 2.** A Data Page with a Cache

Version pool entries between *reader-first* and *last* in the figure contain versions that may be needed to satisfy read requests for ongoing queries. Entries between *update-first* and *last* contain page versions recorded by ongoing (or recently committed) update transactions.

Garbage collection in the version pool is done when the oldest query finishes, thus allowing the *reader-first* pointer to move. Garbage collection is simple due to the sequential nature of this deallocation process; however, a problem with the CCA scheme is that a very long running query may hold up the reclamation of version pool space. Another problem is that the ordinary sequential I/O patterns of queries may become disrupted by random I/O operations to the version pool. Moreover, because a query must read successively older versions (relative to the current database) as it ages, the number of version pool I/O operations that it must make to read a given page increases with time. As a result, queries may begin to thrash if they are sufficiently large [6]. The on-page version caching refinement discussed next was designed to alleviate these problems.

2.3 On-Page Version Caching

In [6], we presented and studied a record-level refinement to the CCA version pool scheme in which versions are maintained on records (as opposed to pages) and a small portion of each main segment (i.e., data) page is reserved for caching prior versions. Such an on-page cache reduces the number of read operations required for accessing prior versions. Another benefit is that versions may "die" (i.e., become unnecessary for maintaining the view of a current query) while still in an on-page cache and thus not have to be appended to the version pool at all. We review the concepts of the on-page cache here so that we may show how it can be integrated with the various indexing approaches. Figure 2 shows a data page with records X, Y, and Z, and a cache size of 3. Prior versions of these records are resident in the on-page cache in the figure.

With on-page caching, updates to records are handled in the following manner: When a tuple is updated, the current version is copied[6] into the cache before it is replaced by the new version. Likewise, when a tuple is deleted, the current version is also copied into the cache. If the cache is already full, *garbage collection* is attempted on the page. Garbage collection examines each entry in the cache to determine whether or not it is needed to construct the view of any current query. If garbage collection is unsuccessful in freeing a cache slot, then some prior version is chosen for replacement. The replacement algorithm chooses the least recently updated entry for replacement (i.e., the entry which has resided in the cache the longest is moved to the version pool).

In addition to the cache replacement policy, there is also a write policy that determines when a cached prior version should be appended to the version pool. The *write-one* policy appends a version only when it is chosen to be replaced in the cache. This policy attempts to minimize the size of the version pool by 1) keeping only one copy of each prior version and 2) allowing a prior version the maximum chance of being garbage-collected before being written to the version pool. In contrast, the *write-all* policy appends *all* of the prior versions in a page's cache to the version pool at once; this is done when a cache overflow occurs and the least recently updated entry has not yet been appended to the version pool. In this scheme, a version chain will actually contain two copies of those versions

[6] In practice, copying a version into the on-page cache simply means moving its entry in the page's slot table. The cache does not have to be a physically contiguous region of the page; cache overflows can be detected by maintaining a count of bytes occupied by prior versions.

that have been written to the version pool but not yet replaced from the cache. The write-all policy introduces a degree of positional clustering in the version pool by attempting to cluster versions from the same main segment page; this benefits queries that sequentially scan the data by increasing their locality of reference to the version pool. Because of the added positional clustering, the write-all policy was shown to be able to complete queries at a faster rate than write-one [6]. Despite having to replicate some prior versions under write-all, the more rapid completion of queries under this policy was also shown in many cases to lead to a significantly lower overall storage cost than under write-one; in other cases, the storage cost was not appreciably higher.

As we pointed out earlier, a very long running query may hold up the reclamation of version pool space. In contrast, versions that reside in an on-page cache may be garbage-collected soon after they become unnecessary. Also, on-page garbage collection is done whenever an update occurs on a page whose cache is full, at which time each prior version in the cache is examined to determine whether it is still needed. Since such update operations dirty the data anyway, on-page garbage collection is essentially free. For further details about version garbage collection and other aspects of on-page caching, see [6].

3 MULTIVERSION INDEXING APPROACHES

In this section, we discuss options for extending single-version indexing schemes to handle multiversion data. We outline four different approaches and discuss their performance tradeoffs. The approaches include: Chaining (CH), Data Page Version Selection (DP), Primary Index Version Selection (PI), and All Index Version Selection (AI). These basic approaches are largely orthogonal to both the version placement scheme employed and to the underlying indexing structure (e.g., hashing or B+ trees). We describe the approaches here as they would work with the on-page caching method for storing prior versions (as described in Section 2) and the B+ tree indexing method [4].

We used several criterion to select the schemes that we will be considering here. First, to be practical, we decided that the schemes should involve only relatively simple changes to proven indexing methods. Furthermore, because versions come and go rapidly in transient versioning, garbage collection should be relatively inexpensive. Lastly, we decided that index-only plans should be supported since they are an important optimization in many existing systems.

The multiversion indexing schemes that we consider differ in how they accomplish *version selection*, the mechanism by which the appropriate version of a tuple is located in the collection of existing versions. Version selection information is either placed with the data or with the index entries of one or more of the indices. In all of the schemes, we assume that relations have a single primary key index and zero or more secondary key indices, and that tuples are stored separately from the indices. For purposes of presentation, we further assume that primary key values cannot be updated.

3.1 Chaining (CH)

In the Chaining (CH) versioning selection scheme, each index leaf entry simply references the most recent version of a tuple; the remainder of the versions are chained behind the current version in reverse chronological order, as in the CCA scheme [10]. The organization of data pages (with on-page caching) and the version pool was discussed in the previous section. As described earlier, each version of a tuple has a *create timestamp* (CTS) which is the commit timestamp of the transaction that wrote the version. The most recent version also has a *delete timestamp* (DTS) which is the commit timestamp of the transaction that deleted the tuple; its value is infinity if the tuple exists in the current database.

Figure 3 illustrates this scheme by showing an example of how a single tuple is stored and indexed both on the primary key and on a secondary key. Interior nodes of the index are not shown since they are identical to those in a single-

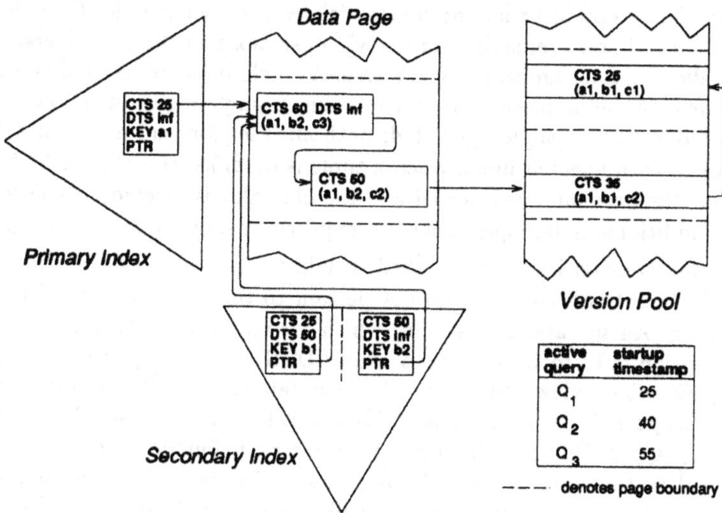

Fig. 3. Chaining

version B+ tree, as in all of the schemes that will be considered here. The tuple in Figure 3 has four versions: (a1, b1, c1) with CTS 25, (a1, b1, c2) with CTS 35, (a1, b2, c2) with CTS 50, and (a1, b2, c3) with CTS 60. The primary key index is built on the first attribute, with the secondary key index on the second. Currently, there are three queries running in the system: Q_1 with a startup timestamp of 25, Q_2 with startup timestamp 40, and Q_3 with startup timestamp 55. The existence of these queries necessitates the retention of all of the prior versions shown in the figure.

As shown in the figure, index leaf page entries in the CH scheme consist of a key, a tuple pointer, a create timestamp (CTS), and a delete timestamp (DTS). The CTS field contains the timestamp of the transaction which inserted the key into the index, and the DTS field contains the timestamp of the transaction that (logically) deleted the key from the index. Together, the CTS and DTS fields represent the range of time over which an index entry's key value matches some version of the referenced tuple. For example, in Figure 3, the CTS and DTS fields in the secondary index entry with key b denote that all versions of the illustrated tuple with timestamps greater than or equal to 25 and less than 50 have b1 as the value of their second attribute; likewise the CTS and DTS fields in the entry with key b2 denote that all versions with timestamps greater than or equal to an 50 have an indexed attribute value of b2. Note that the entries that reference a given tuple (from within the same index) have non-overlapping timestamp ranges since each version may have only one key value at a time. Delete operations do not physically remove leaf entries because they may be needed by queries to provide access paths to prior versions of tuples. We will discuss shortly how the index is searched and how leaf entries are eventually garbage-collected when they are no longer needed.

With the exception of having logical deletes (i.e., setting the DTS field instead of immediately removing an entry), operations on the multiversion B+ tree parallel those on an ordinary B+ tree. A single insertion is made into each index when a tuple is inserted into a relation; a single logical deletion is made in each index when a tuple is deleted; both an insertion and a logical deletion are made in each affected index when a tuple is modified (i.e., for each changed key value, the new value is inserted and the old value is deleted). Later we will see that additional index operations are required in some of the other schemes.

The multiversion index is searched just like a B+ tree, except that transactions filter out entries which do not pertain to the database state that they are viewing. An update transaction, which views the current database state, pays attention only to index entries whose DTS is infinity (*inf* in the figure). A query Q, which views the state of the database as of its arrival, pays attention only to index entries whose CTS and DTS values satisfy the inequality $CTS \leq T_S(Q) < DTS$. Such entries were inserted, but not yet deleted, as of Q's arrival in the system. By following these rules, false drops do not occur, and therefore index-only plans may be utilized when applicable. In the example shown in Figure 3, queries Q_1 and Q_2 must follow the secondary index entry with key b1, while Q_3 must follow the entry with key b2.

As in all of the schemes that we will be discussing, *garbage collection* within an index leaf page is invoked when the page overflows. Since the page is already dirty and pinned in the buffer pool at such times, index garbage collection does not require any additional I/O operations. The garbage collection process examines each logically deleted entry (i.e., each one with a finite DTS) to determine whether or not it is still needed for some active query. Specifically, an entry is still needed if there exists a query Q ∈ active queries such that $CTS \leq T_S(Q) < DTS$ (as described above). A logically deleted entry is physically removed if it is not needed for any active query; such an entry will never be needed later for a subsequently arriving query, as such queries will be assigned startup timestamps that are greater than or equal to the entry's DTS.

To minimize the additional storage overhead due to versioning, *compression* of the timestamp information (CTS and DTS) is possible. This will be especially important for indices with small keys. To this end, a single bit may be used to encode a DTS value of infinity. Likewise, a single bit may also be used to encode any CTS value that is less than the startup timestamp of all active queries, as all that matters is the fact that the entry preceded their arrival. (In practice, these two bits together will require extending index entries by a whole byte.) If a tuple requires only one leaf entry in some index, the entry may have both fields compressed. This occurs when the index key value in the tuple has remained constant since the arrival of the oldest active query, which is likely to be a common case. In the example in Figure 3, the CTS of the secondary leaf entry having key b1 may be compressed, and likewise for the DTS of the entry having key b2. Thus, an index on an attribute that is rarely changed will remain close in size to a single-version B+ tree. Furthermore, during periods when queries are not run, the indices may be gradually compressed down towards the size of ordinary B+ trees (with the exception of the additional byte per entry) by merging pages during garbage collection; when queries reenter the system, the indices will gradually expand as needed. The main disadvantage of compressing the timestamps is the added overhead of maintaining growing and shrinking index entries, but code to handle this should already be part of any B+ tree implementation that supports variable-length keys.

3.2 Data Page Version Selection (DP)

A drawback of the chaining approach used in CH is that a long-running query may have to read a large number of pages to reach the version of a tuple that it needs. The data page (DP) version selection scheme is a modification of CH that limits the number of pages that a query must read to two (exclusive of index pages). It accomplishes this by recording the addresses and timestamps of each version of a tuple in a small table known as a *version selection table* (VST).[7]

The VST is located on the data page that contains the current version of the tuple (or in the case of a deleted tuple, on the page that contained the final version). Rather than referencing the current version of a tuple, an index leaf entry references the tuple's VST. Figure 4 illustrates the DP scheme by modifying the example used to illustrate the CH scheme. From the figure, it can

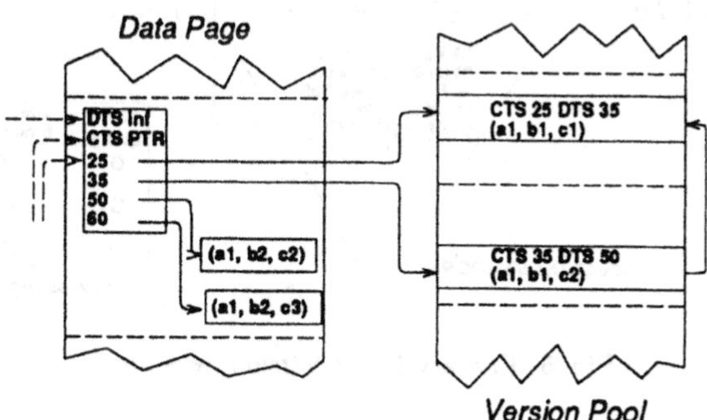

Fig. 4. Data Page Version Selection

[7] For versions that are replicated under the write-all cache write policy, this scheme would list their replicated versions in the VST twice (i.e., once for their on-page cache copy and once for the version pool copy).

be seen that a query must now read at most two pages (a data page and a version pool page) to locate any tuple. In contrast, to locate the version with CTS 25 in Figure 3 under the DP scheme, a query would have to read three pages.

A disadvantage of DP over CH is the additional room on data pages consumed by the VST entries of versions that have migrated to the version pool. However, since VST entries are small, this is not likely to have a significant impact unless the tuples themselves are small in size.

3.3 Primary Index Version Selection (PI)

The Primary Index (PI) version selection scheme is a modification of DP that stores the version selection table together with the tuple's primary index leaf page entry (instead of on a data page). It is similar[8] to the scheme presented in [21], which is the only previously published indexing scheme for multiversion locking that we are aware of. Figure 5 illustrates the PI scheme by adapting the running example. Note that a versioned tuple has only one entry in the primary index because primary index keys cannot be changed.

The motivation for placing VSTs in the primary index is that it enables queries to retrieve versions through the primary index by reading only a single data page or version pool page. One drawback to this approach, however, is that the pointer to a version from its VST must also be updated when the version is migrated to the version pool. If on-page caching is used, this increases the path

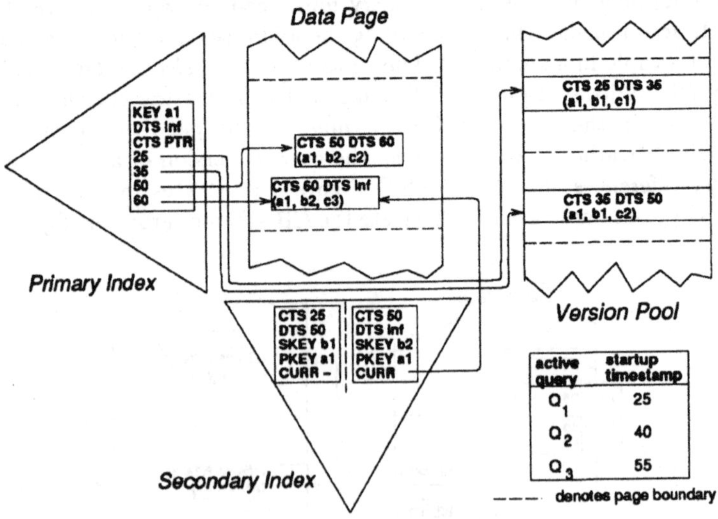

Fig. 5. Primary Index Version Selection

length of update transactions that need to free cache space in order to modify or delete a tuple. Another drawback is that the presence of the VSTs on primary index leaf pages will lead to a larger primary index.

[8] The overall versioning scheme in [21] differs in that it bounds the number of versions per tuple by essentially restricting the number of query startup timestamps in use.

The largest drawback with placing the VSTs in the primary index is that secondary indices no longer provide queries with direct access to the data. Instead, secondary indices provide a mapping from secondary key to primary key, with the data being retrieved through the primary index. As a potentially important optimization for update transactions, however, a secondary index entry for the *current* version of a tuple can store the address of the current version. This shortcut is illustrated in Figure 5 by the presence of the CURR field in each secondary index entry. However, this optimization can be used only if the current version of a given tuple is always stored in a fixed location (determined when the tuple is created). Furthermore, read-only queries cannot use this optimization because they cannot tell which version of a tuple to retrieve without first examining the tuple's VST in the primary index.

Finally, in terms of performance, requiring all read-only queries to access data through the primary index is likely to be problematic unless most queries are primary index scans anyway or a large fraction of the primary index remains resident in the buffer pool. Otherwise, if the buffer pool is not sufficiently large, a secondary index scan will generate a random I/O pattern in the primary index. Thus, even if the data were ordered (clustered) on the relevant secondary index key, the query's I/O pattern would be partially random. As a result, it appears unlikely that this scheme can perform well for queries using a secondary index.

3.4 All Index Version Selection (AI)

In the PI scheme, the primary index is an efficient access method for primary key queries because its leaves contain the addresses of all tuple versions; secondary indices are inefficient for queries, however, because accesses must additionally go through the primary index. The all index (AI) version selection scheme is a modification of PI that places VSTs in the leaf entries of *all* indices (secondary as well as primary). This allows direct access to the data from each index, thus removing the aforementioned inefficiency.

Figure 6 illustrates the AI scheme by adapting the running example one last time. The figure shows the addition of a VST in each secondary index leaf entry, providing a direct access path for queries from the secondary indices to the data. However, a drawback of this modification is that placing additional information in the secondary indices increases the size of all indices. Another serious drawback of the AI scheme is the additional path length that it imposes on update transactions when versions are created or migrated to the version pool. In the AI scheme, when a new version is created as a result of a tuple modification, *all* secondary indices must be updated—even if the associated key value was unaffected by the modification. In contrast, in the other multiversion indexing schemes, a secondary index does not have to be updated if the modification does not change the indexed attribute value. For example, in Figure 6, the creation of the versions (a1, b1, c2), and (a1, b2, c3) required placing their addresses in the secondary index VSTs; in the other schemes, the creation of these versions did not require updating the secondary index at all. Likewise, when a version is migrated to the version pool, all of the references to the version must be updated.

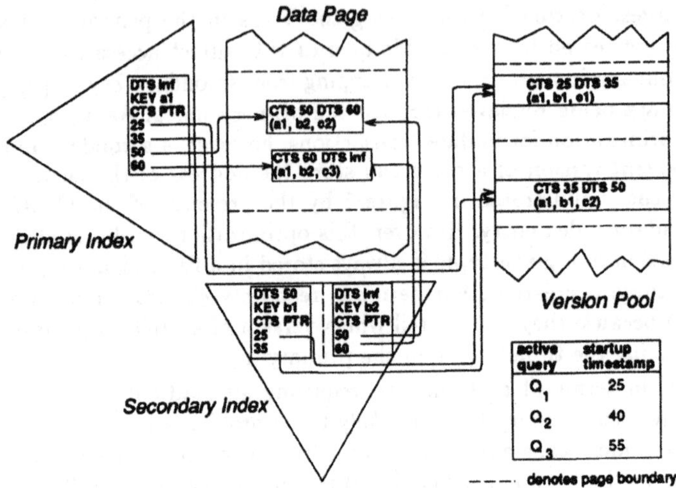

Fig. 6. All Index Version Selection

3.5 Summary of Multiversion Indexing Approaches

In this section we have outlined a range of B+ tree based multiversion indexing schemes, with each scheme differing in how it supports version selection. In CH, version selection is supported by chaining versions in reverse chronological order, while in DP, version selection is accomplished via the use of a VST that is stored together with the current version of a tuple. In PI, VSTs are stored in the primary index instead, and in AI, VSTs are stored in all of the indices. The advantage of placing version selection information in an index is that it allows queries to directly access the versions that they need from the index without having to go through one or more intermediate data pages for each version that has been migrated to the version pool. A drawback to placing version selection information in an index is that when a tuple is modified (i.e., a new version of the tuple is created), version selection information for the tuple must be updated in the index—even if the key value for that index was not affected by the change.

4 PERFORMANCE RESULTS

We have conducted a simulation study of the alternative multiversion indexing schemes to compare the schemes in terms of their I/O costs for queries and update transactions. Due to space limitations in the proceedings, we can only summarize the results of the study here, and we direct the reader to [8] for full details of the study.

Despite having the advantage of direct references from index entries to individual versions, we found in the study that the PI and AI schemes have the same or higher I/O costs for queries when the buffer pool is not large enough to hold all of the index pages. This is because the version selection information in the index entries consumes critical buffer pool space, thus lowering the buffer pool hit rate. As a result, the I/O cost for update transactions under PI and AI is higher than DP and CH under these conditions as well. If the buffer pool is instead large enough to hold all of the index pages, version selection information in the indices will contribute to a lower query I/O cost, but only for *unclustered* index scans. Since the data pages of a relation are scanned sequentially in a *clustered* index scan, having version selection information in the indices eliminates only a few consecutive accesses to each data page, which does not reduce the number of physical I/O operations.

Finally, we saw that the I/O costs for queries under CH and DP are normally about the same since queries typically access the most-recent or second-most-recent version of each record. When queries begin to thrash, however, CH's I/O cost rises relative to that of DP's since queries access older versions. In short, the results show that DP and CH perform considerably better than PI and AI, and that DP is less susceptible to query thrashing than CH.

5 CONCLUSIONS

In this paper, we have presented and compared four basic schemes for extending single-version indexing structures to handle multiversion data. Although B+ trees were used to illustrate the different multiversion indexing approaches, they can all be combined with any existing database index structure. The resulting multiversion indexing schemes differ in where version selection information is located. In the AI scheme, version selection information is placed in all of the indices, whereas in the PI approach, the information is placed only in the primary index. In contrast, the DP and CH approaches place version selection information with the data instead. DP and CH differ in that DP maintains a table to locate all of the versions of a tuple, while CH chains the versions in reverse chronological order. The results of a performance study, which we summarized briefly, indicate that DP is the version indexing approach of choice, with CH being a close second.

References

1. Agrawal, D., A. Bernstein, P. Gupta and S. Sengupta, "Distributed Multiversion Optimistic Concurrency Control with Reduced Rollback," *Journal of Distributed Computing*, Springer-Verlag, 2(1), January 1987.
2. Agrawal, D. and S. Sengupta, "Modular Synchronization in Multiversion Databases: Version Control and Concurrency Control," *Proc. 1989 SIGMOD Conference*, 1989.
3. Bayer, R. and M. Schkolnick, "Concurrency of Operations on B-trees," *Acta Informatica*, September 1977.
4. Bayer, R. and E. M. McCreight, "Organization and Maintenance of Large Ordered Indicies," *Acta Informatica*, Volume 1, Number 3, 1972.
5. Bayer, et al., "Parallelism and Recovery in Database Systems," *ACM Trans. on Database Sys.*, 5(2), June 1980.
6. Bober, P. and M. Carey, "On Mixing Queries and Transactions via Multiversion Locking," *Proc. of the Eighth IEEE Data Engineering Conf.*, 1992.
7. Bober, P. and M. Carey, "Multiversion Query Locking," *Proc. of the Eighteenth International Conference on Very Large Databases*, 1992.

8. Bober, P. and M. Carey, *Indexing Alternatives for Multiversion Locking,* Tech. Report #1184, University of Wisconsin—Madison, November 1993.
9. Carey, M. J., *Modeling and Evaluation of Database Concurrency Control Algorithms,* Ph.D. Thesis, Comp. Sci., U. of California, Berkeley, 1983.
10. Chan, A., S. Fox, W. Lin, A. Nori, and Ries, D., "The Implementation of an Integrated Concurrency Control and Recovery Scheme," *Proc. 1982 ACM SIGMOD Conf.*, 1982.
11. Chan, A., and R. Gray, "Implementing Distributed Read-Only Transactions," *IEEE Trans. on Software Eng.*, SE-11(2), Feb 1985.
12. DuBourdieu, D., "Implementation of Distributed Transactions," *Proc. 6th Berkeley Workshop on Distributed Data Management and Computer Networks*, 1982.
13. Easton, M., "Key-Sequence Data Sets on Indelible Storage," *IBM Journal of Research and Development*, May 1986.
14. Eswaran, K., J. Gray, R. Lorie, I. Traiger, "The Notions of Consistency and Predicate Locks in a Database System," *CACM* 19(11), 1976.
15. Gray, J., "Notes on Database Operating Systems," in *Operating Systems: An Advanced Course*, Springer-Verlag, 1979.
16. Joshi, Ashok, *Personal Communication.*
17. Kolovson, C. and M. Stonebraker, "Indexing Techniques for Multiversion Databases," *Proc. of the Fifth IEEE Int'l Conf. on Data Engineering*, 1989.
18. Lai, M. and K. Wilkinson, "Distributed Transaction Management in Jasmin," *Proc. of 10th International Conference on Very Large Database Systems*, 1984.
19. Lomet, D. and B. Salzberg, "Access Methods for Multiversion Data," *Proc. 1989 ACM SIGMOD Conf.*, 1989.
20. Lehman, P. and S. Yao, "Efficient Locking for Concurrent Operations on B-trees," *ACM Transactions on Database Systems*, 6(4), December 1981.
21. Mohan, C., H. Pirahesh, and R. Lorie, "Efficient and Flexible Methods for Transient Versioning of Records to Avoid Locking by Read-Only Transactions," *Proc. 1992 ACM SIGMOD Conf.*, 1992.
22. Raghavan, A., and T.K. Rengarajan, "Database Availability for Transaction Processing," *Digital Technical Journal* 3(1), Winter 1991.
23. Reed, D., "Implementing Atomic Actions on Decentralized Data," *ACM Transactions on Computer Systems*, 1(1), February 1983.
24. Robinson, J., *Design of Concurrency Controls for Transaction Processing Systems*, Ph.D. Thesis, Comp. Sci. Tech. Rep. No. CMU-CS-82-114, 1982.
25. Silberschatz, A. "A Multi-Version Concurrency Control Scheme With No Rollbacks," *ACM-SIGACT-SIGOPS Symposium on Principles of Distributed Computing*, August 1982.
26. Stearns, R. and D. Rosenkrantz, "Distributed Database Concurrency Control Using Before-Values," *Proc. of the 1981 ACM SIGMOD Conf.*, 1981.
27. Stonebraker, M., "The Design of the Postgres Storage System," *Proc. Thirteenth International Conference on Very Large Database Systems*, 1987.

A Rule-Based Approach for the Design and Implementation of Information Systems

Ilias Petrounias and Pericles Loucopoulos
Information Systems Group, Department of Computation
UMIST
P.O. Box 88 , Manchester M60 1QD, U.K.
e-mail: {ilias, pl}@sna.co.umist.ac.uk

Abstract. This paper presents the design, implementation and evaluation of an application following the deductive approach. The application concerns a safety critical system and for modelling the application domain two conceptual models, developed within the ESPRIT project TEMPORA, were used: the Entity Relationship Time (ERT) for the structural part and the Conceptual Rule Language (CRL) for constraints, derivation and event-action rules. The mapping from the conceptual level to the deductive DBMS platform, namely MegaLog, is described with some sample results. An overview of the system, along with a simple user interface for creating different application scenarios are presented and are followed by some statistic results of a real life case study and an evaluation of the proposed approach.

1 Introduction

Application programs using traditional and fourth generation languages have increased in size and complexity. In order to facilitate complex application development, to avoid code redundancies and multiple developments of similar programs with closed functionalities and to support reasoning capabilities on symbolic data, it is often desirable and beneficial to *integrate* into the database itself a definition of common knowledge shared by different users [6]. As a result a new trend emerged within the database research community: database systems that are based on logic. Research on the relationship between the database theory and logic goes back to the 1970s [4] and has grown over the last few years ([5], [10], [11], [13]), although, unfortunately it has not yet resulted in many commercial products and the available ones have not yet really been tested. Traditional database systems manage the data and meta-data which comprise the *extensional* knowledge that is embedded in facts and instances. The *intentional* knowledge is identified as the knowledge beyond the factual content of the database and this kind of knowledge can be fully specified in the form of rules in a rule base *before* the database is established [3]. A deductive database system then integrates data manipulation functions and deductive functions into a single system to support *derived* knowledge, in which extensional and intentional knowledge are mixed in order to define derived relations which are often a generalisation of the view concept. The objective of such systems is the integration of as much knowledge as possible in the intentional database so that application programs remain efficient, small and easy to write and to maintain, and the management in a consistent and efficient way of the rules and data and finally the provision of retrieval and manipulation functions to query and update both the extensional and intentional relations.

This paper attempts to summarise some of the results of the use of a deductive system in designing and implementing a safety critical application. Additionally it attempts to evaluate the use of the conceptual models developed within the TEMPORA project in designing and implementing an application. The proposed approach as a framework for application development can also be very useful as part of a validation process and especially semantic prototyping which is a top-down approach which refines the various aspects of a conceptual schema as inconsistencies are discovered and enables the business people to assist in validating the schema by identifying them and by suggesting modifications [12]. Results from the model-theoretic semantics of logic [1] can be used in semantic prototyping to test a schema's correctness and to overcome the problem of validating the conceptual schema. The proposed approach is well suited for logic based semantic prototyping. A conceptual schema in MegaLog corresponds to a logic theory and can be proved for formal properties. The contribution of the PROLOG language and its supporting environments has been demonstrated in [16].

The whole paper uses a particular case study as a pilot, in order to show the feasibility of the approach and the behaviour of the deductive platform, both in terms of functionality and performance for such a role. Section 2 describes the case study which is the development of a safety critical system, more specifically the handling of a possible attack against a ship, while section 3 describes the conceptual modelling formalisms that were used to model the application domain. Section 4 describes the reasons for choosing a deductive platform for the case study and section 5 presents deductive platform that was used (MegaLog). Section 6 presents the mapping algorithms from the conceptual level to MegaLog. Section 7 presents some of the design and implementation considerations, a user interface for the system for creating different scenarios, provides some statistical results from a real life case study and presents the advantages and disadvantages of the approach that was followed. Finally section 8 draws some conclusions.

2 The Case Study

OWN_SHIP is located in an area with certain co-ordinates and is travelling with some speed following a particular course. Its location in this area is given by its longitude and latitude and the area in which it is located has some environmental data at the time of interest. The ship's engines have certain capabilities (i.e. power, propulsion etc.). The ship has a number of weapon systems to defend itself against a possible attack each one with certain capabilities and characteristics (i.e. guns, missiles), information providers (i.e. radars) to detect such an attack, logistic information (i.e. status of available fuel) and data concerning possible damages in OWN_SHIP's systems.

At some point in time OWN_SHIP's information providers locate one or more tracks which have certain characteristics (certain type, travelling speed etc.). A system located on the ship will have -based on the information provided- to decide whether or not the detected tracks should be considered as threats to the ship and if they are to formulate a plan in order to prepare a defend against them. In doing so it will have to take into account that the available defence resources might be limited due to possible damages in weapon systems or because the number of threats is too great to defend against or even because some weapons are not usable in the particular situation. Therefore, the system will have to assign priorities to the tracks -depending on their type, distance from OWN_SHIP etc.- in order to deal firstly and be able to use the best available weapons against those that are considered to be the most dangerous ones. Additionally, and because different information providers might give slightly different information about the same tracks, the system after following each track's history must be able to distinguish between 'real' and duplicate tracks. After distinguishing between them the system will only be interested in the 'real' ones.

3 Conceptual Models

Three major categories of information about the world can be identified: Structural *knowledge* describing the objects of the application domain and their interrelationships. *Dynamic knowledge* describing the various functions (processes) of the domain, which change the state of the objects. *Declarative knowledge* which is concerned with the actual rules that govern both the structural and the dynamic knowledge.

3.1 The Entity-Relationship-Time Model (ERT)

The ERT model [17] uses as its basic structure the Entity-Relationship approach in order to preserve the well known advantages of this approach. The basic mechanism differs from the original ER model [2] in that it regards any association between objects in the unified form of a relationship. Thus, the conceptually unnecessary distinction between attributeships and relationships is avoided. The ERT accommodates explicit modelling of time, taxonomic hierarchies and complex objects. Different aspects of data abstraction that are dealt with in the ERT are: classification, generalisation, aggregation and grouping. The most primitive concept in ERT is that of a *class* which is defined as a collection of individual objects that have common properties. Every relationship is viewed as a named set of two (entity or value, role) pairs where each role expresses the way that a specific entity or value is involved in a relationship. Time is introduced in ERT as a distinguished class called time period class. Each time varying entity class and each time varying relationship class is timestamped with a time period class, i.e. for each entity class, a time period might be associated which represents the period of time during which an entity is modelled. This is referred to as the *existence period* of an entity. The same applies also to relationships and is referred to as the *validity period* of a relationship. A distinction is made between different variations of ISA hierarchies. These are based on two constraints that are usually included in any ISA semantics namely, the *partial/total* ISA constraint and the *disjoint/overlapping* ISA constraint [18]. Thus, four kinds of ISA relationships are supported: Partial Disjoint ISA, Total Disjoint ISA, Partial Overlapping ISA and Total Overlapping ISA. In ERT, *physical part hierarchies* as well as *logical part hierarchies* are accommodated [9]. The ERT schema for the previously described case study is shown in Figure 1.

3.2 The Conceptual Rule Language

The Conceptual Rule Language (CRL) [8] provides the means for controlling the behaviour of a domain in terms of rules. CRL allows us to express the external rules (that the user views) as manipulating data in the ERT model, but have our executable rules manipulate data in the database model, and thus be more efficient to execute. Three different types of CRL rules have been distinguished: constraint, derivation and event-action rules.

Every CRL rule accesses the ERT model at least once. The expression that accesses the model is named *static class reference*. Every static class reference selects a (sub)set of instances of an entity class or a value class of the model and returns the set of instances of the first entity or value class in the expression. For example, figure 2 depicts the relationship between the entities WEAPON and POSITION; the class reference

```
WEAPON is_located_at POSITION
```

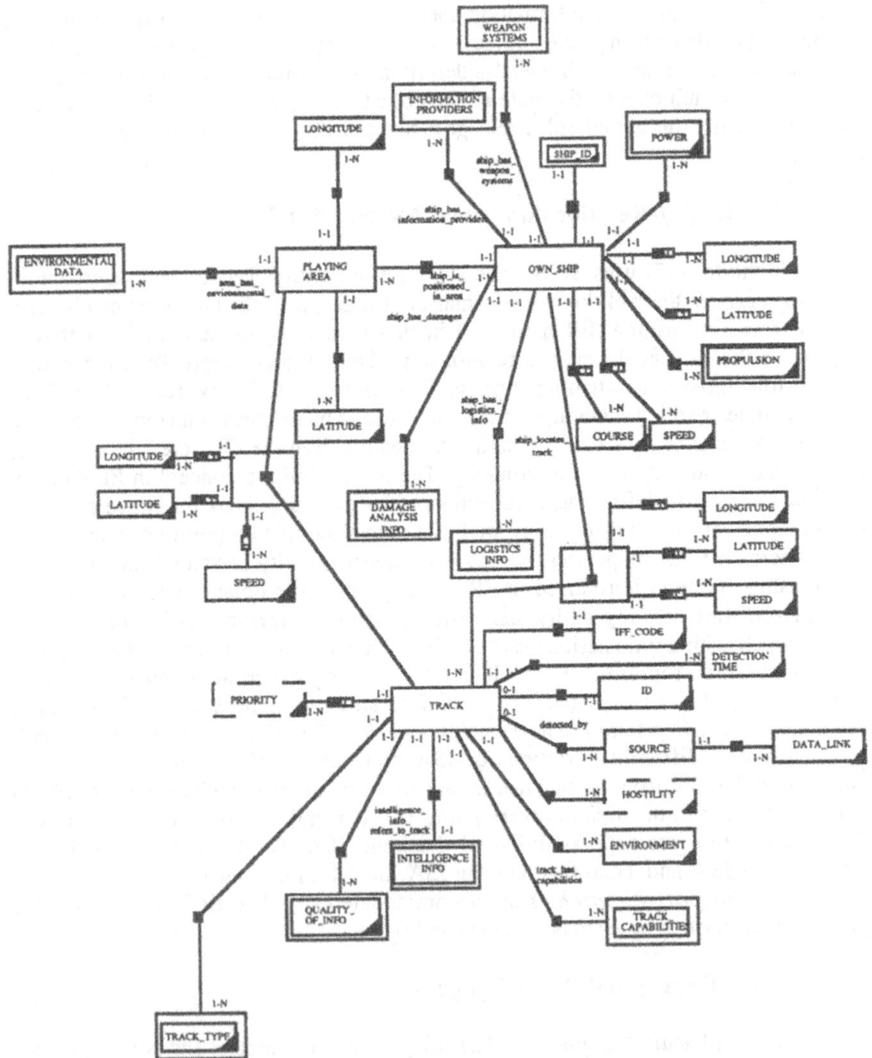

Figure 1. The ERT schema of the application domain

selects all the weapons that are located in a specific position, thus returning, for example, the set $[W_1, W_2, W_4, W_5]$. Entity and value classes may be instantiated thus binding instances of sets when the same instance is used more than once in the same constraint rule. For example, if the relationship of Figure 2 is considered, the static class reference

```
WEAPON is_located_at POSITION.P
```

can be interpreted as "For every Weapon find the Positions that it is located in" and the result will be, for example, the sets [W_1, W_4], [W_2], [W_5]. A second type of static class reference is used when an entity is referenced more than once in the constraint, in which case all references are connected through either AND (represented as ",") or OR (represented as "|").

Figure 2. Example ERT schema and instantiation of it

Constraint Rules. Two types of constraint rules are distinguished: static constraints and transition constraints. *Static constraints* represent conditions which must hold at every state of the database and are time-independent. *Transition constraints* define valid state transitions in the database, thus specifying restrictions on the behaviour of the system. Such types of constraints do not refer to the current state of the database; they rather reflect a part of business policy across time and they represent the connections between database states, as they develop across time. An example is given below stating that when OWN_SHIP has started its journey then the number of available weapon systems cannot increase (they can only decrease):

```
WEAPON_SYSTEMS belong_to OWN_SHIP at [now, X] is_less_than
WEAPON_SYSTEMS belong_to OWN_SHIP at [Y, now]
```

Derivation Rules. Derivation rules specify a way by which one can obtain the value of an ERT component when needed, instead of having it explicitly stored. For example, in Figure 1 derived value class HOSTILITY could be defined as follows (depending on the distance of a track from OWN_SHIP and on the value of its code):

```
HOSTILE (X) is_derived_as TRACK[has Iff_code where
Iff_code="unknown", has Longitude(L1), has Latitude(LL1)] and L1 ≤
min_distance + {L2|OWN_SHIP has Longitude(L2)} and LL1 ≤ min_distance
+ {LL2|OWN_SHIP has Latitude(LL2)}
```

Event-Action Rules. Event-action rules express reactions when certain situations occur; they control the processes that the system is required to perform. The situations correspond to *events* and to *conditions* (preconditions) that must hold on the model. The reaction corresponds to *processes* the execution of which will create a new state of the model. The general format of an event-action (e-a) rule is as follows:

```
WHEN <event> [IF <precondition>] THEN <action>
```

and described as WHEN an event is detected, IF a certain condition holds, THEN an action will be performed. An event-action rule is applied on a schema's view and manipulates objects of that view. For example, the case that when a new threat is detected a new plan will have to be formulated is represented as:

```
WHEN new_threat(Iff_code, Environment, SOURCE, ID, Type]
THEN assess_threat (TRACK, hostile_tracks)
```

The WHEN part of an e-a rule corresponds to an event, which if detected, the rule is triggered. Events are of three types: external, internal and temporal. External events are happenings perceived in the environment and have some importance for the system [15]. An external event has a name and some parameters, each of which corresponds to some object in the ERT. Internal events are state transitions [15]. Temporal events are special types of internal events that refer to time. The IF part of an e-a rule expresses a condition on the model. Once the rule is triggered, this condition (expressed similarly to static constraints) must be true for the action to take place. The IF part of a rule may be omitted, in which case the condition is supposed to be TRUE. The THEN part of an event-action rule expresses the actions to be performed after the firing of an event-action rule in order to reach a new state of the model, a state transition. External actions are results and/or messages forwarded to the external world. They always emit the model's data retrieved or modified by the rule.

4 Why Deductive Capabilities were Required for the Case Study

The application described in section 2 required a certain amount of intentional knowledge to be represented in order to be able to derive new information from the facts stored in the database. For example, some types of tracks might be considered more dangerous than others and this has to be reflected in the priority assigned to each one of them in order for the ship to defend against them firstly. In addition, certain weapons are considered better than others in defending against particular tracks. It is also known beforehand that certain defence weapons cannot be used in all situations (i.e. a torpedo is useless against an aircraft). Finally, different types of weapon systems need different times in order to be prepared for use. The first kind of knowledge is to be used in deciding a track's priority, the second in allocating the best of the available weapons against a track and the third one will exclude from the available weapons the ones that are not usable against a certain track's attack but may be used to defend against others. The last one is needed when deciding if a weapon that is currently in use can be considered as a later time option of defence. These types of knowledge are more easily and naturally represented in a deductive environment where they will be implemented either as facts (not stored in the database) or rules. Additionally they can be externalised from the actual programming code and thus become easy to handle and maintain.

Other information can be derived from the facts that are stored in the database and need not be explicitly stored. For example, the priority of a track is determined by the environment in which the track is located, the track's type, make and distance from the ship. In a traditional database system (i.e. relational) these parts would have to be implemented in a more complicated manner as part of the actual application programming code where in a deductive environment the user has only to supply the rules and the system will provide the matching.

5 The Implementation Platform: MegaLog

The MegaLog persistent programming environment has been developed within the Knowledge Bases Group at the European Computer-Industry Research Centre (ECRC) and was designed as a support platform for the next generation of database management systems (DBMSs). MegaLog offers a deductive database system, that is, a system with all the functionalities of a traditional DBMS but enhanced with an additional, integral, deductive capability. MegaLog supports in an entirely transparent and symmetric way the persistent (disk) storage and the access and update of rules as well as data [7]. As a result the number of stored rules is not any more limited by the available main memory. Newly acquired rules are interactively and incrementally compiled into a rellocatable form in order to avoid overheads of interpretation on execution. Transaction handling, along with recovery and concurrent operations in a multi-user environment are also provided. The environment is based on an abstract machine containing three major components: an inference engine based on a derivative of the Warren Abstract Machine (WAM), a relational engine that has been built over a file management system and is capable of directly indexing complex objects and logical clausal structures and a main memory management subsystem performing full incremental garbage collection and providing full support for dynamic allocation of memory on demand.

The design of MegaLog has been based on the observation that unification in logic can be viewed as an extension of addressing by content in traditional database systems. There is no impedance mismatch problem between the database language and the programming language because there is no distinction between the two of them in a persistent logic programming environment. The programming language interface is a full implementation of PROLOG extended with arrays and global variables and with an integrated set of relational operations. Both tuple and set oriented operations are provided. MegaLog can, therefore, support a relational system as a special case of its more generalised logic formalism. The incorporation of the garbage collector fulfils a requirement that is fundamental to database systems -continuous operation- which is however not normally supported by PROLOG systems. The efficiency of the system is claimed to be of the same order as that of current commercial relational systems, for the same class of relational operations. Beyond that, we know of no other that is widely available at the moment and can offer comparable functionality.

6 Transformation from the Conceptual Level to the Deductive Platform

In order for the chosen platform to be proven useful there must be an easy and direct mapping from the data and rules at the conceptual level to statements in the run-time platform. The first subsection describes the mapping from the ERT constructs to MegaLog while the next one presents the mapping from CRL to MegaLog. The examples that are used are from the case study and in some cases only the part that is referred to is presented. The complete algorithms for mapping ERT and CRL to MegaLog can be found in [14].

6.1 Mapping from ERT to MegaLog

Every simple entity can be represented as a predicate having as arguments all the entity's attributes that appear on the ERT model, for example
`track(Id, Iff_Code,Environment, Speed, ...).`
Complex attributes have the same form as entities, but they are not represented explicitly; they appear only as part of the entity to which they belong, i.e. :
`own_ship(has(ship_id(hasComponent(...))`
When a timestamp appears as part of an entity or relationship we need to add a new part to the entity or relationship that will have the form time(Start_time, End_time), i.e. if entity customer was timestamped:
`own_ship(has(Latitude,time(Start_time,End_time))`

Depending on whether the ISA relationship represents a partial disjoint, a total disjoint, a partial overlap or a total overlap we need to describe what the entity is allowed to be and/or what it is not allowed to be. In all cases and because of the entity predicates described at the beginning of this paragraph the missile and torpedo predicates will exist and will have at least all the attributes of weapon. For example, if missiles and torpedoes are the only weapons (total) and they are not overlapping, then they can be described as:

```
weapon(..,..):-missile(..,..,),not(torpedo(..,..,)).
weapon(...,...):-torpedo(...,...),not(missile(...,...)).
```

The assertion that two entities are connected through a relationship is represented by a predicate having as arguments the keys of these entities. The validated fact assertion depends on the existence of the connected entities, i.e.:

```
detected_by(Track_id,Source_id).
detected_by(Track_id,Source_id):source(Source_id,..),Track(Id,..,..)
```

Complex entities can represented in the same way simple entities where every simple entity that appears within the complex one has the same form as a complex attribute; the only difference is that because of the previously mentioned rules simple entities and relationships (apart from relationships indicating attributes) between them are represented explicitly too. When a uniqueness or cardinality constraint appears on the ERT we need to add a new clause in the entity's or relationship's assertion that will not permit more than the allowed number of same values to exist. These constraints are to be checked every time upon insertion, deletion and update.

6.2 Mapping from CRL to MegaLog

Every static constraint is composed by multiple accesses to an ERT diagram which are connected via set operators (union, intersection, difference) or set comparisons (subset_of, disjoint_from, equal_to). The first way in which an ERT access can be performed is when every entity or value is referenced only once, i.e.:

TRACK is_located_by SOURCE has Data_Link

which will return a set of all tracks working for which all of the above apply. Such an ERT access consists of triplets that in the simplest of cases have the form

ENTITY relationship ENTITY

or VALUE in the place of entities, but no two values can exist in the same triplet. Each triplet can be represented with three clauses -one for every part of the triplet- within a predicate that will return the required result. The last part of a triplet can be the first one of the next, as is the case in the previous example, in which case the clause representing it need not be repeated. The ERT access will return a set containing all existing entities (or values) of the type that is referenced first within the ERT access; in the example the result will be a set of employees. Therefore the key of the first entity (or the first value) will be the argument of the predicate that will be used, i.e.

```
ert_access(Track_id):-        track(Track_id,_,_,...),
                        is_located_by(Track_id, Source_id),
                        source(Source_id, Data_Link,_,...).
```

The above predicate will return every track that satisfies the selected criteria; because a set is expected another predicate will be needed to collect the results of the above one:

```
ert_access1(Result):-findall(Track_id, ert_access(Track_id), Result).
```

If the ERT access requested a value instead of entity the value would be requested both as the output of the first predicate (also it has to be referred as a variable in the owner's entity clause) and in the collecting statement. When a value appears in an ERT access the value and the relationship ('has' or its inverse 'is_of') connecting it to the 'owner' entity are ignored and the three clauses are reduced to just one, that of the 'owner' entity. If the value class is followed by a statement with an expression providing a value, then the value is inserted as a constant (in case of comparisons an additional predicate will be required) in the entity's predicate. For example, the ERT access

```
        SOURCE has Data_Link where Data_Link = 'xxx'
```

will be represented as

```
        Source(Source_id,_,..., xxx,...).
```

In the case where an entity or value class is referenced more than once in an ERT access the treatment is the same as before bearing in mind that role names in CRL refer to what is outside the brackets and therefore the first part of several triplets will be the same. If, however, an OR is reached within the brackets then more predicates will be required for representing alternatives, bearing in mind, however, that the part outside the brackets is the same for all expressions included in them. For example, the ERT access

```
WEAPON_SYSTEM[is_located_at POSITION | has Quantity where Quantity=5]
```

will be represented as

```
new_access(Weapon_id):-    weapon_syst(Weapon_id,_,...,_),
                        is_located_at(Weapon_id, Position_id).
new_access(Weapon_id):-    weapon_syst(Weapon_id,_ , 5,_,...).
```

In cases of instantiations the clauses that represent the target entity or value and the relationship are substituted by a collecting statement for the first clause on the first relationship appearing in the ERT access and will be inserted at the end of the predicate. This happens because of interest are the results for every instantiation and not for every entity or value class that participates in the ERT access. For example,

```
        WEAPON is_located_at POSITION.P
```

is requested to return for every position the set of weapons that are located there and therefore it will be represented as:

```
third_ert_access(Result):-   position(Position_id, _,...),
        findall(Weapon_id,is_located_at(Weapon_id,Position_id),
             Result).
```

If the constraint refers to enumerated sets of ERT data then the result of the collection of values an aggregate operator (number_of, average etc.) that is easily implemented will be applied. For example, in the example that was used in the beginning of the paragraph if the ERT access was of the form

```
        number_of(WEAPON is_located_at POSITION )
```

the ert_access would have the form:

```
last_ert_access1(Final_Result):-
                      findall(Weapon_id,ert_access(Weapon_id), Result),
                      number_of (Result, Final_Result).
```

Implemented explicit or implicit temporal operators are applied to the results of the ERT accesses and then two ERT accesses are compared or transformed via set operators or set comparisons:

```
ERT access1    set comparison or set operation      ERT access2
```

Derivation rules use an ERT access format to define a object and therefore their representation in MegaLog is straightforward. Every time that is needed a predicate that will return the derived object will be called to perform the specific ERT access that will calculate the derived object's value. Finally, for the event-action rules we require one predicate for each rule which in turn will be comprised by three others. The first one of these three will either be a system call (to determine whether or not an external event happened) or a checking predicate upon an affected relation (for internal events). The second one will be the precondition part of the event-action rule which is treated in the same way as static constraints and the third one defines the action to be taken as a consequence of the firing of the rule. This will eventually correspond to a process that will need to be implemented.

Both the transformation algorithms that have been described in this section have been fully implemented (along with a parser for the CRL) providing an automatic route from the editors used for the capture and representation of requirements to the actual run-time system.

7 Design and Implementation Issues

The main processes that the system is required to perform are shown in Figure 3. The rounded boxes represent the processes, the lines with the arrows the triggers (or output) of the processes and finally for each process it is shown whether or not it requires to read something from the data model.

A user interface has been specified and implemented for the interactive introduction of different scenarios in order to test various system. The user is provided with the opportunity to create different scenarios by interactively changing the parameters of the objects that are displayed on the screen. This is done by including facilities of automatically inserting and deleting information about the ship's position, speed, power, damages, etc. as well as for the detected tracks interactively to provide for a different scenario. An example layout screen, displaying all information about the ship's positioning and located tracks is shown in Figure 4.

7.1 Statistics, Comparison with other DBMSs, Evaluation of the Approach

The safety critical system that was described before and was implemented in MegaLog was used in a real life case study and some statistical results are presented in Table 1. The first case that is presented in this table corresponds to 60 initial tracks reduced to 9 while the second one to the 250 reduced to 25. In this table the time is expressed in milliseconds. TIME TAKEN indicates the actual time that the system required in each case in order to produce the required defence plan. USER CPU TIME is the amount of time that the CPU spent in user mode, while SYSTEM CPU TIME is the amount of time that the CPU spent in system mode. PAGE RECLAIMS, PAGE FAULTS and SWAPS provide information about paging and swapping from the operating system (UNIX). Heap statistics include information about the usage of the heap in MegaLog while the rest indications provide information about symbol table usage and performed system table garbage collections (note that in this last case the results i.e. total number of bytes collected are added together after each run of the application, thus the number appearing in the table does not demonstrate the real situation after each time the system runs. This is achieved with the *bytes collected on last run* data).

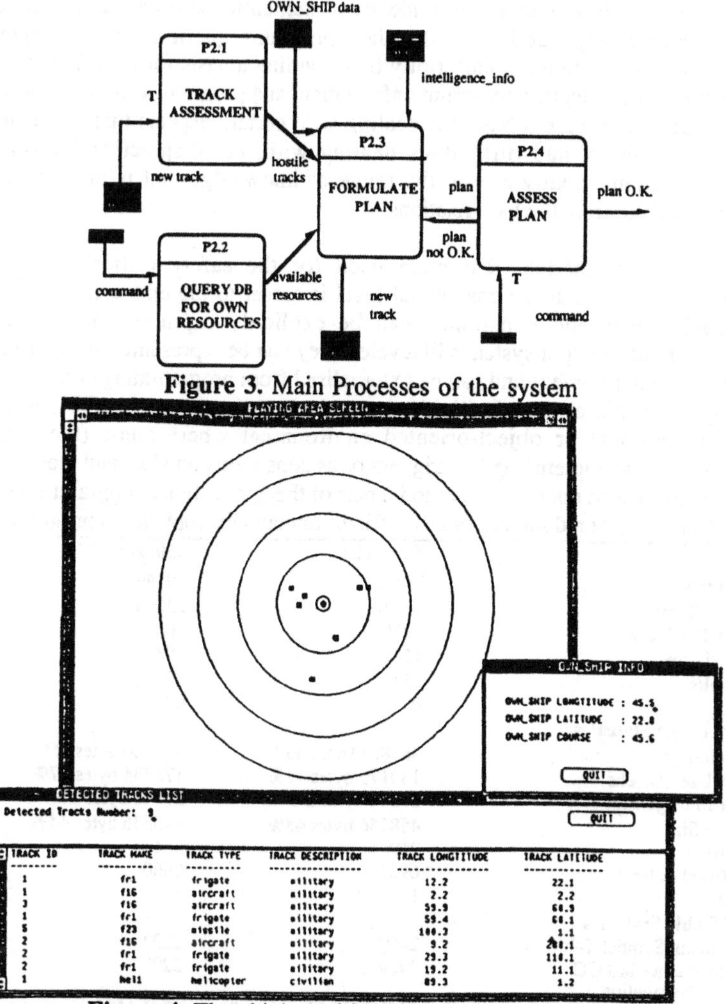

Figure 3. Main Processes of the system

Figure 4. The ship's positioning and the located tracks

The deductive DBMS platform seemed to behave very well when the application data scaled up with the large amounts of input that were provided. These figures are comparable (in fact somewhat better) than when the same application was tried on a relational DBMS. Especially, as far as the garbage collection is concerned, the database that was created using the relational DBMS had to be emptied and reloaded with two or three sample runs of the application; this problem did not occur with the deductive platform. However, the time required for the development of the system was in the case of the relational DBMS greater and especially in the parts that were identified before as those that originally required the deductive capabilities of the underlying DBMS.

Deductive database systems represent a new direction in database technology and have first order logic as their theoretical foundation. This approach has several desirable properties. Logic itself has a well-understood semantics and can be employed to provide a uniform language for defining data, programs, queries, views and integrity constraints and an operational uniformity by providing a basis for a unified attack on query optimisation, integrity constraint enforcement and program correctness proofs. It can, additionally, provide a basis for dealing with certain aspects that the relational approach has always had difficulties dealing with, i.e. disjunctive information. Deductive relations greatly extend the range of knowledge that is included in the database or derived from the base relations.

In the conceptual models that were used for the safety critical system the representation of rules at the conceptual level is closer to the end user's perception. Additionally, rules and constraints can be explicitly captured and maintained throughout an information system's lifecycle. They can be represented straightforward in a deductive environment and can be externalised from programming code (and kept separately in one place), thus facilitating easy access and maintenance. This is not the case in a relational or object-oriented environment where some (the simplest constraints) can be implemented as triggers or as constraints on slots and methods, but the more complicated ones will have to be part of the application's programming code, thus resulting in code redundancies and difficult to maintain application programs.

	60 tracks	**250 tracks**
Time Taken	74148	101400
User CPU Time	18310	33060
System CPU Time	7250	10820
Page Reclaims	1542	808
Page Faults	234	69
Swaps	0	0
Memory Usage Statistics		
Used Memory	381801 bytes 36%	372166 bytes 35%
Waste in Used Blocks	180175 bytes 17%	178334 bytes 17%
Used for Management	27844 bytes 2%	27440 bytes 2%
Total Free Size	458756 bytes 43%	470636 bytes 44%
Blocks(free)	219	361
Blocks (used & free)	6961	6860
Segments	1	1
Symbol Table Statistics		
Valid Items in Symbol Table	2409	2293
Items added since last GC	2409	2293
Hash Key Distribution (0,1,2,3,>3,>10)	8261 1591 311 46 14 0	8351 1523 291 44 14 0
Garbage Collection Statistics		
Number of collections of Global Stack	89	82
Total Number of Bytes Collected	8867456	8137088
Bytes Collected on Last Run	100904	100360

Table 1. Sample Statistics of the Case Study

The approach that was used in this case study demonstrates the feasibility of an automatic implementation from conceptual models. This is useful in approaches, such as semantic prototyping [12], which is a top down experimental approach refining the various aspects of a conceptual model as inconsistencies are discovered. It tries to prove that a conceptual model is incorrect by proving that it is inconsistent, and also to increase the possibility that the conceptual model is correct (with respect to the modelled reality) by testing it against realistic situations. The mapping mechanism, transforming specifications to MegaLog expressions, makes it possible for conceptual specifications, which represent objects and business rules, to be executed. Thus, since the expressions of the conceptual modelling language have been mapped to executable code, they can result in a prototype of the system under development, and through its execution they can be checked for their correctness and consistency. Prototyping in this sense is not concerned with screen and dialogue specifications. All intentional knowledge is checked through corresponding extensional knowledge. A run-time environment developed for checking, compiling and executing MegaLog programs can be used as an animation tool for executing the MegaLog code that represents a conceptual model originally defined in ERT and CRL. The main advantage that this approach offers is direct executability leading to an architecture such as in Figure 5:

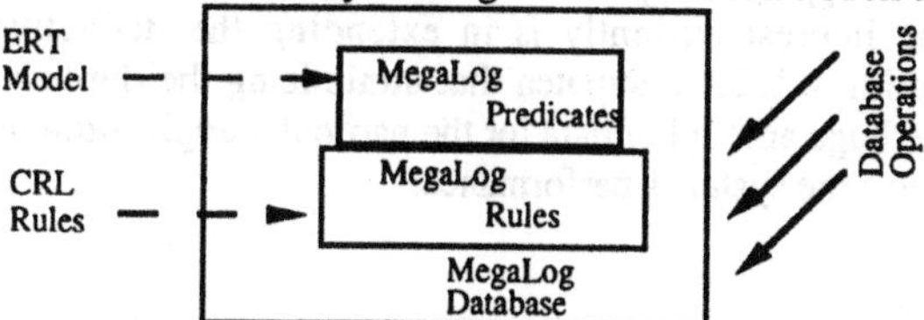

Figure 5. The proposed architecture

Most of the disadvantages faced during the application of the case study come from the fact that deductive technology is still more or less in a research stage. Not many commercially available products exist so that they can be tested in real life applications to fully explore their capabilities and shortcomings. MegaLog, for example, because it is based on logic does not offer the ***update*** operation found in relational databases. Also the insert operation when not all values for all the attributes are supplied (in case they are not known at the time of insertion) is not supplied. In this case the handling of values becomes difficult because a default value -'null' for example- will be treated as a constant by MegaLog (and not as a special kind of value as is the case in relational systems). At the same time the insertion of variables in the place of unknown values causes greater manipulation problems, because PROLOG will match the variables with anything. This means that this 'incomplete' insert will be followed by an update (which essentially is a delete and an insert operation) and not by another insertion for the previously unknown values. In other cases, however, the manipulation of the database contents is easier, i.e. with the provision of the *project* operation that it is not part of standard SQL. While every relation in a MegaLog database requires at least one key to be defined, these are only used for indexing and the system will accept the insertion of a different tuple with the same value for the key. This might be an advantage in applications that do not require the usual management of primary keys (i.e. temporal databases) offered by relational systems but leads to finding artificial ways in preserving the uniqueness of key values in a relation.

8 Conclusions

The design, implementation and evaluation of an application that was carried out in a deductive environment was presented in the previous sections. The advantages and shortcomings of the approach that was followed were reported along with a comparison with relational technology. Deductive database systems offer more expressive power than the traditional ones along with the ability to deduce new facts from explicitly stored ones. They can offer many advantages to potential users and the uniformity they provide is a very attractive idea. The MegaLog logic programming environment with some additional relational operations (i.e. updates, inserts with not all values provided) was proven very useful in the application of the case study that was chosen and it is one of the few products that are widely available - despite some shortcomings - to offer both database and logic programming functionalities integrated.

The application of the conceptual models that were used in a deductive environment demonstrates that, because the processes, their control and the checking for the consistency of data were be represented as rules and goals and kept outside programming code, application programs can become smaller and easier to write and to maintain. The interest currently is in extending the deductive platform with distributed capabilities. It is anticipated that minimising the duplication of processes and especially the huge amount of data for the particular application that was described will greatly enhance the system's performance.

References

1. Budde, R. (ed.) *Approaches to prototyping*, Springer-Verlag, 1984.
2. Chen P.P-C. *The Entity-Relationship Model-Toward a Unified View of Data* ACM TODS vol.1 no.1, pp.9-36, March 1976.
3. Elmasri, R. and Navathe, S.B. *Fundamentals of Database Systems*, The Benjamin/Cummings Publishing Company, Inc. 1989.
4. Gallaire, H. and Minker, J. (eds) *Logic and Databases*, Plenum Press, 1978.
5. Gallaire, H., Minker, J. and Nicolas, J.M. *Logic and Databases: A Deductive Approach*, Computing Surveys, Vol 16., No. 2, June 1984.
6. Gardarin, G. and Valduriez, P. *Relational Databases and Knowledge Bases*, Addison-Wesley Publishing Company, Inc., 1989.
7. Horsfield, T., Bocca, J. and Dahmen, M., *MegaLog User Guide*, 1990.
8. Katsouli, E., Papastamatiou, G.,Petrounias, I.,Loucopoulos,P.,Theodoulidis, B., *Revision of the Rule Language of TEMPORA*, E2469/UMIST/NT1.1/1/Draft, 1992.
9. Kim W., Banerjee J., Chou H.T., Garza J.F., Woelk D. *Composite Object Support in Object-Oriented Database Systems*, Proc. 2nd Int. Conf. on Object-Oriented Programming Systems, Languages and Applications, Orlando, 1987.
10. Lloyd, J.W. and Topor, B.W. *A Basis for Deductive Database Systems*, The Journal of Logic Programming, 1985(2), pp 93-109.
11. Lloyd, J.W. and Topor, B.W. *A Basis for Deductive Database Systems II*, The Journal of Logic Programming, 1986(5), pp 55-67.
12. Loucopoulos, P.,Karakostas, V.,*Modelling and Validating office information systems: an object and logic oriented approach*, Software Engineering Journal, March 1989.
13. Minker, J. (ed). Foundations of Deductive Databases and Logic Programming, Morgan Kaufmann Publishers, Inc., 1988.
14. Petrounias, I., Loucopoulos, P. Design, Implementation & Evaluation of an Application following the Deductive Approach, 4th DAISD'93, Catalonia, 1993.
15. Rolland, C. and C. Richard, *The REMORA Methodology for Information Systems Development and Management*, Conference on Comparative Review of Information System Design Methodologies, North Holland, 1982.
16. Tarski, A. *Logic semantics and metamathematics*, Oxford University Press, 1956.
17. Theodoulidis, C., Wangler, B. and Loucopoulos, P. *Requirements Specification in TEMPORA*, Proceedings CAiSE'90, Kista, Sweden, 1990.

On Behavioral Schema Evolution in Object-Oriented Databases *

Magdi M. A. Morsi[1] Shamkant B. Navathe[2] John Shilling[2]

[1] IBM Santa Teresa Laboratory, San Jose, CA 95141, USA
[2] College of Computing, Georgia Tech, Atlanta, GA 30332, USA
e-mail: magdi@vnet.ibm.com, sham@cc.gatech.edu

Abstract. This paper describes the effect of schema evolution operations on the implementation of methods. The effect of these operations is captured as temporary inconsistencies. Extensions for handling these temporary inconsistencies in our Graphical Object-Oriented Schema Environment prototype, called *GOOSE* are described. In *GOOSE*, the schema information is maintained as a set of system objects of system defined classes. In order to maintain these temporary inconsistencies, the system classes have been augmented with two classes, namely *Uses* and *Stubs*, as specialization of the system class *Class*. Furthermore, schema evolution operations for explicitly resolving these inconsistencies are defined.

1 Introduction

The schema evolution operations enable a user to modify the database schema and propagate these changes to the affected objects. However, the consistency of the database state should not only ensure the consistency of the structural component but also its behavioral component (methods.) Also, the class hierarchy in an object-oriented database captures the different applications of an enterprise. The notion of subclassing in a class hierarchy supports the inheritance of both properties and extensions among classes. This paper addresses the effect of schema evolution operations on the behavioral components of the database schema. Our notion of the behavioral components is based on the implementation of methods. We consider the method signature as representative of the method behavior.

We also address the notion of consistency of method implementations in terms of the signature of the methods used in their invocation. Moreover, the violation of these consistencies are maintained as temporary inconsistencies which may be subsequently resolved by either the side effect of schema evolution operations or explicitly through other operations. In addition, the effect of some schema evolution operations may be propagated to the method implementations, such as renaming of classes, instance variables, and methods.

* This work is partially supported by NSF grants number IRI-9010120 and CDA-9114359 and the Army Center of Excellence in Information System grant number DAAL03-92-G0377.

This paper describes a framework for maintaining the inconsistencies that may arise as a side effect of schema evolution operations on method implementations. These inconsistencies are maintained as temporary inconsistencies which can be resolved as a side effect of subsequent schema evolution operations. In addition other schema evolution operations are defined to resolve these inconsistencies. Section 2 describes the terms used and the different inconsistencies which may arise as a side effect of schema evolution operations. Section 3 describes our support for method implementation. The set of schema evolution operations on methods is in Section 4. The relationship of this framework to previous works appears in Section 5. Finally, Section 6 contains a summary and conclusion.

2 An object-oriented data model

In this section we describe the core concepts of object-oriented data models with which our model is consistent. The adopted data model maintains its implementation components as well as user-defined classes as a part of the overall schema definitions. We use the term *object* to represent an encapsulation of values for its instance variables, called its *state*, and methods for manipulating it. *Classes* are used to describe object types, as defined by their instance variables and methods. The *properties* of a class connote its instance variables and methods. Objects communicate via *messages*. The *domain* of an instance variable is the set of values it might have from its class type, which is called the *domain class*.

Definition 1. The database schema consists of a set of classes $\mathcal{C}$. Each class $c \in \mathcal{C}$ has a set of properties (instance variables and methods) associated with it. The function $\mathcal{IV}(c)$ returns the set of instance variables in c. Similarly, the function $\mathcal{M}(c)$ returns the methods of c. □

Inheritance is a mechanism used for defining specialization relationships between classes. *Multiple inheritance* allows a class to inherit properties from several superclasses.

Definition 2. The set of classes $\mathcal{C}$ are related through class-subclass relationship. That is, each class $c \in \mathcal{C}$ has a set of superclasses associated with it. The function $\mathcal{SP}(c)$ returns the set of superclasses of c. Similarly, the function $\mathcal{SB}(c)$ returns the set of subclasses of c. The function $\mathcal{SP}^{+}$ ($\mathcal{SB}^{+}$) returns recursively the set of superclasses (subclasses) of a class. Similarly, the function $\mathcal{SP}^{*}(c)$ is defined as $\mathcal{SP}^{+}(c) \bigcup \{c\}$ (and the function $\mathcal{SB}^{*}(c) = (\mathcal{SB}^{+}(c) \bigcup \{c\}$.) □

We use the notion of *full forced inheritance* (*FFI*). Under *FFI*, even if there is a naming conflict among inherited properties, all of these properties must be inherited and none should be rejected. To resolve the naming conflict (whenever it arises), the property name is prefixed with the name of the class in which it is locally defined (its class of origin.)

Definition 3. Under *full forced inheritance*, the properties of a class is a subset of the properties of its subclass. That is, for each class c, the $\mathcal{IV}(c) \subseteq \mathcal{IV}(s)$ and $\mathcal{M}(c) \subseteq \mathcal{M}(s)$ where $s \in \mathcal{SB}(c)$. □

The *ISA* relationship captures the relationship between a class and its superclass and is represented in a class hierarchy.

Definition 4. The $\mathcal{SB}$ relates the classes $\mathcal{C}$ in a directed acyclic graph. That is, for each class $c \in \mathcal{C}$, $c \notin \mathcal{SB}^{+}(c)$. Also, the root class **Object** $\in \mathcal{SP}^{*}(c)$ for all $c \in \mathcal{C}$. Moreover, if a class s is a subclass of c ($s \in \mathcal{SB}^{*}(c)$), then the class c cannot be a subclass of s ($c \notin \mathcal{SB}^{*}(s)$ where $s \neq c$) followed from inheritance *DAG*. □

The *extension* of a class C contains all objects that are visible through C which consist of all objects of type C as well as those of the subclasses of C. The *direct extension* of a class C contains all objects in the extension of C which are not in the extension of any subclass of C.

Definition 5. The database state consists of a set of objects $\mathcal{O}$. The function $\mathcal{DE}(c)$ returns the set of objects in the *direct extension* of the class c. Moreover, every object $o \in \mathcal{O}$ is a member of the *direct extension* of a single class. That is, $\mathcal{DE}(c) \bigcap \mathcal{DE}(s) = \Phi$ where $c, s \in \mathcal{C}$ and $s \neq c$.
Similarly, the function $\mathcal{E}(c)$ returns the *extension* of the class c, where $\mathcal{E}(c) = \bigcup_s \mathcal{DE}(s)$ for all $s \in \mathcal{SB}^{*}(c)$. □

The database schema is represented as a class hierarchy (lattice) that captures two inheritance relationships, namely the inheritance of properties from a class to its subclasses and the inclusion of the class extension into extension of its superclasses.

Definition 6. The *reference* relationship among the interface of the structural component of the database schema captures the relationship between an instance variable and its domain class. The type closure of the structural component requires that the domain class of each instance variable to be an existing class in the database schema. That is, for all $i \in \mathcal{IV}(c)$ where $c \in \mathcal{C}$, the domain of i (denoted $\mathcal{D}(i)$) is $\in \mathcal{C}$. □

The value of an unconstrained instance variable is an object in the extension of its domain class.

Definition 7. The *reference* relationship among the interface of the behavioral component of the database schema captures the relationship between a method parameter and its domain (parameter type.) The type closure of the behavioral component requires that the domain class of the formal parameter be part of the schema. The actual domain of the parameter depends of the parameter *mode* (`in`, `out`, `inout`.) The domain of the `inout` parameter includes the direct extension of the domain class. The domain of the `out` parameter includes the objects in the direct extension of its superclasses. The domain of the `in` parameter includes the extension of the domain class. □

The rest of this section describes our abstraction of method implementation and the relationship between the different components of the schema.

2.1 Method implementation

The components of the database schema are related through the properties of its classes. Each class may have associated with it a set of instance variables. An instance variable has a unique name. Also, each instance variable is typed where the relationship between an instance variable and its type is captured through the *hasDomain* relationship. In addition, each class has a set of methods associated with it. The *interface* of a method is used to validate the method invocation which is captured in the method signature. The method signature consists of its name, class of origin, and set of parameters. The definition of each parameter includes its name, domain class, and *mode* (e.g. **input, output, inout**.) That is, the full method signature is constructed by prefixing the result of the **signature** function (defined in Definition 10) with the method name and the name of its class of origin. The relationship between a method and its parameter types are captured through *hasParameterOfType* relationship. These relationships capture in the type closure defined in the previous section.

A method implementation is considered as a sequence of method invocation on objects. These objects are either instance variables, formal parameters, or local variables. Each of these objects are typed objects. This can be represented as follows:

c::m (p_1 PT_1 PC_1, ... , p_n PT_n PC_n)
{ VC_1 v_1; ... ; VC_m v_m ;
O_i-> m_j (o_1,..., o_j) ;
⋮
O_h-> m_p (o_1,..., o_p) ; } ;

The method header includes its class name, method name, and method parameters. Each method parameter includes the parameter name (p_r), mode (PT_r) which can be either **in, out,** or **inout**, and class (PC_r). The local variables are declared using a C notation where each variable definition includes its name (v_i) and its domain class (VC_i). A method code is abstracted as a sequence of method invocations. That is, each statement is a method invocation on a recipient object O_q. The set of object references are names of either a parameter, an instance variable, a local variable, or $Self$ (invocation of another locally defined method in the same class c.) Also, other classes are used as type for its parameters or locally defined variables. We enforce a notion of encapsulation where an instance variable is visible to only its class of origin and its subclasses. In our abstraction, the order of method invocation is considered irrelevant. Consider the following example:

Example 1. The database schema shown in Figure 1, consists of four classes, namely C_1, C_2, C_3,and C_4, which are named *CN1, CN2, CN3,* and *CN4*, respectively. That is, in our model the classes are instance of the system class **Class**

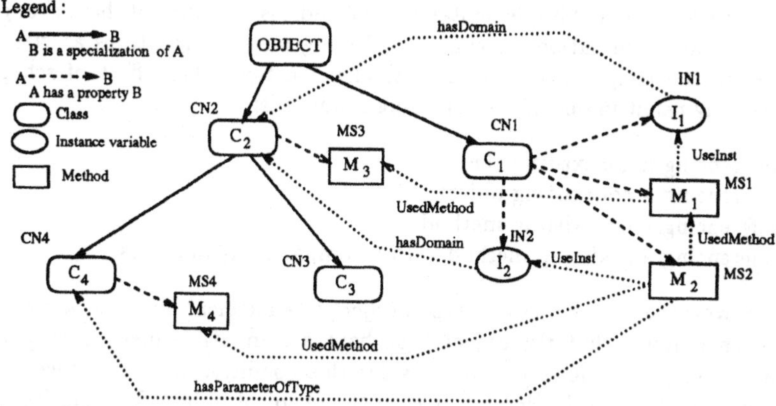

Fig. 1. Example of a method implementation

and class names are attributes of these classes. The class C_1 has two locally defined instance variables I_1 and I_2 named (*IN1* and *IN2*) as well as two methods M_1 and M_2 having the method signatures *MS1* and *MS2*, respectively. Similarly, each of the classes C_2 and C_4 has a locally defined method M_3 and M_4. The relationship *hasDomain* captures the domain class of an instance variable. That is, the domain of class of I_1 and I_2 is the class C_2. Similarly, the relationship *hasParameterOfType* captures the type of the formal parameters of a method. That is, the method M_2 has a parameter of type C_4.

The implementation of a method includes two *uses* relationships, namely *UseInst* and *UsedMethod.* The *UseInst* relationship captures the set of instance variables used in the implementation of a method. In this example schema, the implementation of the methods M_1 and M_2 use the instance variables I_1 and I_2, respectively. The *UsedMethod* relationship captures the set of methods used in the implementation of a method. In this example schema, the implementation of M_1 uses the method M_3. The implementation of the method M_2 uses the methods M_1 and M_4. □

The behavioral consistency is an important issue that has to be addressed in object-oriented databases. The run-time errors may lead to a system failure of the database management which is not acceptable. The inconsistency of the behavioral component of the database can be due to several reasons. Moreover, the fragmentation of the method implementation and the several relationships (illustrated in the previous example) complicate the problem of tracking down the source of an error. In this section, we address some of the sources which may lead to run-time errors. We define a set of properties associated with method implementations. The violation of these properties are detected and maintained as temporary inconsistencies.

In order to address the effect of schema changes on the behavioral components, we use method signatures as representation of the behavioral components. The schema evolution operations, described in [9, 7], support a wide range of dynamic changes on the database schema. In order to address the effect of these changes of method implementations, we address the effect of these changes on method implementations as changes affecting method signatures as well as changes on the recipient objects of method invocations. The effect of schema changes may result in one of the following conditions:

1. Referencing a nonexisting class.
2. Referencing a nonexisting object.
3. Referencing a nonexisting method.
4. Referencing an existing method with incompatible parameters.

Moreover, the referencing to a typed object as a recipient object in a method invocation requires that the object type have a compatible method with the specified invocation. However, we consider this condition as a reference to a nonexisting method in the domain class of the recipient object. The consistency of the behavioral component of an object-oriented database schema should guarantee the following:

Type closure: The type of either an instance variable, a formal parameter, or a local variable referenced in a method should be an existing class in the class hierarchy.
Object references: A named object in a method implementation should be either an formal parameter, an instance variable name, or a local variable.
Existence of methods: The set of methods invoked on a named object should exist in their corresponding type (class) and be uniquely identifiable.
Compatible invocation: The set of methods invoked on a named object should be compatible with their signatures.

Our approach for supporting these consistency constraints is based on *invalidating* the method implementation where these consistencies are violated. Moreover, the user is notified of potential inconsistency that may arise as a side effect of schema evolution operations.

3 Support for method implementation

In this section, we describe the support for method implementation using a set of system classes, namely *UsedIn* and *Stub*. The schema evolution operations on methods are described along with other operations to explicitly resolve temporary inconsistencies. We also describe the effect of schema evolution operations on these classes.

We define the interface of a method implementation as the set of variables externally defined. This set includes its *formal parameters* and *instance variables* referenced. Also, the set of local variables used represents an additional internal naming space.

Definition 8. The object named in a method implementation *MI* consists of three sets, namely the set *IN* containing the names of the instance variables used, the set *FP* containing the names of its formal parameters, and the set

LV containing its local variables. The value of the set FP is computed from the method definition. The values of the sets LV and IN are computed by scanning the source code of the method implementation. We also assume that these sets are disjoint, such that $IN \bigcap FP = \Phi$, $IN \bigcap LV = \Phi$, and $LV \bigcap FP = \Phi$. The set of names used MN in a consistent method implementation is the union of the above three sets. That is, $MN = IN \bigcup FP \bigcup LV$. □

The above assumption is too restrictive for practical use. However, it simplifies the presentation where the notion of a variable scope is ignored. In the following definition, we introduce the implementation of a method as a sequence of statements where each represents a method invocation.

Definition 9. The implementation of a method M, denoted by MI, consists of a sequence of method invocations s_i, where $0 \leq i \leq n$, of the following format:

$$O_i\text{->}\ m_{i_j}\ (o_{i_1}, \ldots, o_{i_k})\ ;$$

Each invocation is on a named object O_i, called the *recipient object*. The method invoked is defined by a method name m_{i_j}. The parameters of a method consist of a sequence of objects (values) or named objects represented by the o_{i_k}. The consistency of a method implementation MI requires that every recipient object O_i is an element of its naming space. This is described as the following invariant.

$$\forall O_i \in MI \Longrightarrow (O_i \in MN) \vee (O_i = Self)$$

Moreover, every parameter in a method invocation has to be a named object or a typed constant. The introduction of a typed constant refers to a value where its type can be uniquely identified from its representation by the parser. This set of values is a subset of the set of atomic objects O_A. This is described as the following invariant:

$$\forall o_{i_j} \in MI \Longrightarrow (o_{i_j} \in MN) \vee (o_{i_j} \in \mathbf{O_A})$$

The above two invariants capture the notion of *object reference*. □

The type closure of a method implementation requires the following: every referenced class as a type must be either (i) an element in its naming space or (ii) a constant.

Definition 10. The set of classes used UC in the implementation of a method MI consists of the types of its referenced instance variables, formal parameters, its local variables, and constants. The type of the variables used are explicitly defined. The type of the constants are computed by the parser. The consistency of a method implementation requires that every used class as a type be an existing class in the database schema. That is,

$$\forall c \in UC \Longrightarrow c \in C$$

where C is the set of existing classes defined in the database schema. □

In order to address the compatibility of method invocation, we introduce the function **substitute**. The **substitute** function takes as its input a method invocation and returns a partial signature of a method where the *mode* of its parameters are not included.

Definition 11. A *partial signature* of a method has the following format:

$c\text{->} m\ (c_1, \ldots, c_k)$

where c is the recipient class, m is a method name, and c_i for $1 \le i \le k$ are the classes of its parameters. The **substitute** functions is defined as follows:

substitute :: invocation : **String** ⟶ **String**

The **substitute** function returns a string in which the named objects and the typed constants in its input string are replaced by their types (classes.) □

For a consistent method implementation, the *partial signature* of each method invocation has to uniquely identify a method in its recipient class. Moreover, using the *partial signature* of a consistent method implementation, we can construct the interface of a method which is a specialization of the identified method.

A method implementation includes several *Uses* relationships. These *Uses* relationships capture the set of referenced objects in a method implementation, called *structural* relationships, as well as the set of methods invoked on these referenced objects, called *behavioral* relationships. The *structural* relationships include three relationships, namely *UseInst*, *UseParameter*, and *UseLocal*. The *UseInst* relationship captures the set of instance variables referenced in a method implementation. The *UseParameter* relationship captures the set of formal parameters referenced in the method implementation. The *UseLocal* relationship captures the set of local variables referenced in an implementation. These reslationships are constructed as described in the following definition.

Definition 12. The *Uses* relationships of a method implementation *MI* are constructed by associating each named object in the set *MN* with a set of *partial signatures*. The structural definition of a *Uses* relationship is as follows:

class **Uses**
  objectName : **String** ;
  signature : { **String** } ;
end **Uses** ;

UseInst, *UseParameter*, and *UseLocal* are sets of the type *Uses*. The set of *UseInst* relationships for a method implementation *MI* locally defined in a class c is constructed as follows:

UseInst:: methodImpl : **String**, c : **Class** ⟶ { **Uses** }
  returns { m | ∃ i ∈ *IN* ∧ m.objectName = i ∧
    $\forall\ O_i\text{->}\ m_{i_j}\ (o_{i_1}, \ldots, o_{i_k}) \in$ methodImpl
    $\wedge\ O_i = \mathrm{i}\ \wedge$ **substitute**($O_i\text{->}\ m_{i_j}\ (o_{i_1}, \ldots, o_{i_k})$) ∈ m.signature }

The *UseInst* is constructed by associating each instance variable, that is the recipient object of a method invocation, with its set of partial signatures.

Similarly, the sets *UseLocal* and *UseParameter* for a method implementation *MI* are computed. The only difference is that the named objects should be elements in the sets *LV* and *FP*, respectively. □

A class may have several locally method implementations associated in it. These method implementations include at most one implementation for each method in its schema. The union of the *Uses* relationship is defined as follows:

Definition 13. The *Uses* relationships of a class, which have a set of locally defined method implementations, are constructed using the *Uses* relationships associated with each method. Instance variables are uniquely named and identically referenced in method implementations. The set of *UseInst* relationships associated with a class is defined as follows:

UseInst:: c : **Class** ⟶ { **Uses** }
returns { m | (∃ i, m_i) $m_i \in$ *c.methodImpl* ∧ i ∈ *UseInst* (m_i, c) ∧
m.objectName = i.objectName ∧ ∀$m_j \in$ *c.methodImpl* ∧
∃ q ∈ *UseInst* (m_j, c) ∧ q.objectName = i.objectName ∧
∀s_q ∈ q.signature ⇒ s_q ∈ m.signature }

The structure of the *UseInst* relationship is similar to a nested relation. That is, the *UseInst* relationship of a class is constructed by applying the *unnest* operation followed by *nest* operation on the union of the set *UseInst* relationship associated with its locally defined method implementations in a class.

Similarly, the sets *UseLocal* and *UseParameter* are computed using the union of their corresponding *Uses* relationships where the *objectNames* are prefixed with their method names. □

The above *Uses* relationships which are used to define the set of used methods of a class reference a the domain class of either an instance variable, formal parameter, or local variable in a method implementation. This set of methods is constructed by replacing the object references with their types (classes.)

We use the term **method schema** to represent the set of referenced classes and properties visible in a method implementation. We also use the term *client class* C of a class S to capture the relationship between a class S and its referencing class C. For each entry in the set *UsedMethod* relationship, the defined class will have a system class *UsedIn* as its subclass which captures the set of methods used in a client class. The *UsedIn* classes are similar to any other class, with the exception that they do not inherit all the properties defined in their superclasses. That is, the *Used* classes do not follow the notion of *full forced inheritance* of regular classes in the database schema. This is illustrated in the following example.

Example 2. The database schema, shown in Figure 2, consists of three classes, C_1, C_2, and C_4. The class C_4 has a locally defined method $M2$ along with its

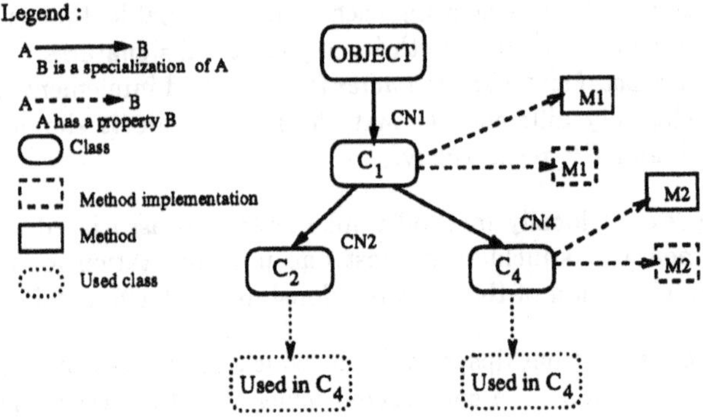

Fig. 2. Example of the *Used* system classes

implementation. The method $M2$ has a formal parameter which has as its type the class C_2. Also, the method implementation of $M2$ invokes a method on the meta variable *Self*. As a result of adding a method implementation for $M2$ in the class C_4, the *UsedIn* system class is created as a subclass of the class C_2 which has a set of method signatures for each method invoked on a recipient object of type C_2 in the implementation of $M2$. Also, another *UsedIn* system class is created as as a subclass of C_4 containing the set of methods and instance variables referenced in the implementation of $M2$ in C_4. □

The *UsedIn* system class represents a specialization of its associated class which contains a specialization of a subset of the methods defined in that class. The *UsedIn* class associated with the class which has a set of locally defined method implementations, such as the *UsedIn* C_4 class associated with C_4 in the above example, contains a specialization of a subset of the methods defined in its schema as well as the set of instance variables referenced in its locally defined method implementations.

The *UsedIn* classes associated with a class C, as described above, capture the set of methods used by the client classes of C. However, they do not capture the client classes which do not invoke any method on their named objects. These client classes may have either a locally defined instance variable, a formal parameter, or a locally defined variable which is not referenced in any method invocation of its locally defined method implementations. Specifically, some named objects are not the recipient objects of any method invocation. In order to account for these references, the computation of *UseInst* and *UseParameter* relationships is augmented with every class used as a domain for a locally defined instance variable or a type of a formal parameter for locally defined method, respectively. The set of method signatures associated with these *Uses* relationships are empty sets. Similarly, the *UseLocal* relationship is modified to include the domain classes of locally defined variables in a method implementation.

Also, in order to capture the relationship between methods in the schema of a class (either inherited or locally defined) and their corresponding method implementations, we define a system relationship, called *implementedAs*. This relationship associates each method in the schema of a class with another class where the method implementation is locally defined. This *implementedAs* relationship exists only if there is no locally defined implementation of a method. For each method defined in a class, it should have either a locally defined implementation or a reference of a superclass where an implementation exists.

In order to capture the references to nonexisting classes, we introduce another system class type, called *Stub*, which has no locally defined property. However, it may have a set of *UsedIn* classes associated with it. A *Stub* class is a place holder for a reference to a nonexistent class. A *Stub* class may be created as a side effect of dropping a class from the database schema and will have the name of the dropped class. It can be removed as a side effect of adding a class with the same name.

4 Schema evolution operations on methods

In this section, we describe additional schema evolution operations on methods and their implementations. Due to space limitation, the details of some of these operations are not included in the paper. These operations include adding, dropping, and modifying a method. Also, the operations on method implementations include adding and replacing a method implementation. We also describe the semantics associated with these operations and their effect on the *UsedIn* system classes. The effect of these operations on method implementations and additional operations to explicitly resolve temporary inconsistencies which may arise as a side effect of dynamic schema changes are also described. The syntax of adding a method to a class is defined as follows:

Add Method <*methodName*> To <*className*>
[With Parameters <*parameterList*>]

Effect on the *UsedIn* **classes:** The *UsedIn* classes associated with the class *className* may include locally defined methods indicating the existence of a temporary inconsistency. That is, a locally defined method in a *UsedIn* class is considered that of an undefined method. If there exists a locally defined method in a *UsedIn* class which has a compatible signature, the *nonexistent* method is replaced with the newly added method. There may exist at most one method with such characteristics. However, this method may include several specializations. The *nonexistent* method would be resolved only if all its specializations are compatible. Otherwise, the *nonexistent* method is retained with its subset of unresolved specializations. The resolution of a *nonexistent* method takes place not only at the class *className* but also at its subclasses.

The effect of reducing the method naming space is detected at the class *className* and its subclasses. The *UsedIn* classes are used to propagate the modified method name to their client classes. □

The method interface defined in an **Add Method** operation can subsequently be modified using **Modify Method** operation described in [9]. Also, methods can be dropped using **Drop Method** operation which has the following syntax:

Drop Method <*methodInterface*> From <*className*>
[Retain Implementation In <*localImplementationClass*>
With Label <*methodLabel*>] [Drop All]
[Drop Implementation In <*localImplementationClass*>]

The **Drop Method** operation should contain a clause for each implementation of the specified method, unless the `Drop All` clause is specified. The option of retaining a method implementation enables the user to keep unused source code in the system as instances of the class **MethodCode**. These methods can be reused for other defined methods with or without modification. The details for maintaining these pieces of code are described in [9].

Effect on the *UsedIn* classes: This operation affects the *UsedIn* classes associated with the class *className* by introducing temporary inconsistencies. That is, if the dropped method is defined in any of the *UsedIn* classes associated with the class *className* or any of its subclasses, this method is considered as a temporary inconsistency (as a missing method.) This would result in creating a new locally defined method in each *Used in* class containing the dropped method in its schema. □

Add Implementation For <*methodInterface*> At <*className*>
[As <*sourceCode*>] [As Abstract]
[As That In <*localImplementationClass*>]
[As That Labeled <*methodLabel*>]

The implementation of a method can be inherited from the class *localImplementationClass* which is a superclass of the class *className*. The constraint on the inheritance of a method implementation requires that the class *localImplementationClass* should not have a subclass *C* which has a local implementation of the defined method where the class *C* is also a superclass of the class *className*. That is, the class containing the locally inherited method has to be one of the lowest superclasses of the class *className* which has a locally defined method implementation. Also, if the implementation of the defined method in the class *className* is declared as an `Abstract`, then all the superclasses of the class *className* should have their locally defined method implementation be of type `Abstract`.

Effect on the *UsedIn* classes: This operation would not affect the *UsedIn* classes associated with the class *className*. However, if defined method implementation is either defined by its source code or an object label, this may result in either creating new *UsedIn* classes for the classes that are referenced in the implementation, or it may add methods to an existing *UsedIn* class. □

Temporary inconsistencies may arise due to a *nonexistent* of a method or an instance variable. The above operations enable the user to implicitly resolve either one of these inconsistencies. However, other operations, described in [9], enable the user to explicitly resolve these inconsistencies, such as **Modify Method** operation may be used for either. The effect of these operation on the method implementation and *UsedIn* system classes are similar to that of the previously described operations. However, the modification of method invocation can be restricted to a specific referenced object, a specific class, or a specific class hierarchy rooted by a specified class. The syntax and semantics of these operations are described in [9].

The description of the effect of the structural schema evolution operations on the behavioral component of the database schema can be found in [9]. This includes their effects of the *UsedIn* classes, temporary inconsistencies, and method implementations.

5 Relationship to previous work

The effect of schema evolution operations in *Orion* on the components of the database schema have been addressed in [1]. The *Orion* object-oriented database system supports more than twenty different schema evolution operations. The *Orion* approach is based on a set of rules for describing *what constitute a consistent database schema.* The enforcement of these rules are captured in the semantics of the database schema operations. However, these rules do not distinguish between the schema level and the object level.

The semantics of the schema evolution operations in *GemStone*, as described in [2], constrain the set of applicable operations on the database schema. This approach is similar to the *Orion* approach. However, the set of applicable operations as well as the consistency rules are different. This is due to their support for strong object identity. That is, each reference to object is guaranteed that the referenced object exists.

The effect of schema evolution operation at the instance level and schema level have been addressed by Nguyen and Rieu in [3, 4]. The completeness of the schema evolution operations at the schema level does not imply completeness at the instance level. For example, *changing the class of origin* of an instance variable is equivalent to dropping and adding an instance variable at the schema level. At the instance level these operations are not equivalent.

Another approach for maintaining consistency of the database schema in the O_2 ODBMS is described in [5, 6], using a separate tool, called *Integrity Consistency Checker* (ICC.) The integrity consistency checker in O_2 ensures the consistency of the database schema. The O_2 data model handles naming conflict as merging of the properties with the same name. The compatibility of the type of the merged properties is a must. In order to maintain these relationships between a property and its origin class, additional edges are maintained, called *virtual edges.* However, the consistency of the behavioral components of the method implementation is not addressed.

6 Summary and conclusion

Work on schema evolution in object-oriented databases, particularly dealing with behavior in the form of method, has been lacking. In this paper we have concentrated on the effect of the changes to the behavioral component in object-oriented databases.

The support for behavioral component is provided using a set of schema evolution operations on the methods and their implementations. Also, the effect of these operations on the method schemas have been addressed. As a result of schema evolution operations, temporary inconsistencies may arise as a side effect of these operations. In order to address temporary inconsistency, we describe a framework for maintaining and resolving these inconsistencies using a set of system classes, namely *Stub* and *UsedIn*. The *Stub* classes are used to capture the references to non-existing classes. The *UsedIn* classes capture the references to non-existing methods and instance variables in method implementations. We also provide operations for explicitly resolving these inconsistencies.

The approach adopted for our data model is based on a *full fledged object-oriented design and implementation* of the database components. A prototype has been developed using this approach for a graphical object-oriented schema environment (*GOOSE*.) The set of schema evolution operations supported in *GOOSE* includes a subset of the operations described in [7, 8, 9]. The support for these operations is captured in a set of persistent system classes.

References

1. J. Banerjee, W. Kim, H.-J. Kim, and H. Korth, "Semantics and implementation of schema evolution in object-oriented databases," in *Proceedings of the International Conference on Management of Data,* San Francisco, CA, pp. 311–322, May 1987.
2. D. Penney and J. Stein, "Class modification in the GemStone Object-Oriented DBMS," in *Proceedings of the Second Conference on Object Oriented Programming Systems, Languages, and Applications*, Kissimmee, Florida, pp. 111–117, October 1987.
3. G.-T. Nguyen and D. Rieu, "Expert database support for consistent dynamic objects," in *Proceedings of the Thirteenth Conference on Very Large Databases*, Brighton, UK, pp. 493–500, September 1987.
4. G.-T. Nguyen and D. Rieu, "Schema evolution in object-oriented database systems," Tech. Rep. TR No. 947, INRIA Laboratoire de Genie Informatique, France, December 1988.
5. R. Zicari, "A framework for schema updates in an object-oriented database system," in *Proceedings of the Seventh International Conference on Data Engineering*, Kobe, Japan, pp. 2–13, April 1991.
6. C. Delcourt and R. Zicari, "The Design of an Integrity Consistency Checker (ICC) for an Object-Oriented Database System," in *Proceedings of the European Conference on the Object-Oriented Programming,* P. America, ed., Geneva, Switzerland, pp. 95–117, Springer-Verlag, July 1991.
7. M. Morsi, S. Navathe, and H.-J. Kim, "A Schema Management and Prototyping Interface for an Object-Oriented Database Environment," in *Proceedings of the IFIP working conference on the Object Oriented Approach in Information Systems*, Quebec City, Canada, pp. 157–181, North Holland Publishers, Inc., October 1991.
8. M. Morsi, S. Navathe, and H.-J. Kim, "An Extensible Object-Oriented Database Testbed," in *Proceedings of the Eighth International Conference on Data Engineering*, Pheonix, Arizona, pp. 150–157, February 1992.
9. M. Morsi, *Extensible Object-Oriented Database with Dynamic Schemas.* PhD thesis, College of Computing, Georgia Institute of Technology, Atlanta, GA, September 1992.

Representing and Using Performance Requirements During the Development of Information Systems

Brian A. Nixon

Department of Computer Science, University of Toronto
Toronto, Ontario, Canada M5S 1A4

Abstract. We are concerned with dealing with performance requirements, such as "achieve good time performance for retrieving tax appeals," during the development of information systems. We adapt a framework for *non-functional requirements* (global quality requirements) by treating (potentially conflicting or synergistic) performance requirements as goals. Our *Performance Framework* helps a developer to *refine* goals, *select* among competing implementation alternatives, *justify* implementation decisions, and *evaluate* the degree to which requirements are met. For manageability of development, we *represent* and *organise* knowledge about information systems and their design, implementation and performance. This paper further organises methods for dealing with performance goals, with some focus on implementation of long-term processes and integrity constraints. We illustrate the framework using some actual workload descriptions of a taxation appeals system, and describe a prototype development tool, currently under development.

1 Introduction

Performance is a central issue for information systems. We are concerned with dealing with performance requirements during the development of information systems, which range from credit card systems to income tax systems, and typically have a relatively large processing volume, conceptual design, and number of entities. To aid a developer deal with performance requirements, e.g., "achieve good space performance for information on income tax appeals" we propose a *Performance Framework* to help select from implementation alternatives with varying performance characteristics, while also considering the system's design (e.g., definitions of taxpayers), and workload (e.g., the number of appeals).

Our Performance Framework adapts to performance a framework for dealing with *non-functional requirements (NFRs,* global quality requirements). The *NFR Framework* was applied to several NFRs, including accuracy [12], then refined [14, 27] and applied to security [15] and performance [33, 34].

The framework treats performance requirements as (interrelated, potentially conflicting or synergistic) *goals,* which are refined through refinement methods, used as criteria for selecting among competing implementation alternatives, and evaluated to determine the degree to which a set of performance requirements is supported. Both performance requirements (which constrain *how* a system operates) and functional requirements (which state *what* a system does) [13] are considered during the implementation process, in which performance goals, decisions, and their effect on goals are organised into a *goal-graph structure*, in the spirit of AND/OR trees [29]. This helps a developer *select* among alternatives and *justify* implementation decisions, by explaining why a particular requirement is (or is not) met by a system. The developer can selectively focus attention, thus controlling goal-graph expansion. Since goals representing NFRs are rarely "satisfied" in a clear-cut sense, but decisions do contribute to, or hinder, a particular goal, we use goal *satisficing* [42] to suggest that generated software is expected to satisfy NFRs within acceptable limits, rather than absolutely.

We treat performance requirements during the implementation phase of system development, in which *designs* (expressed in a conceptual design language, such as is offered by semantic data models [18, 36], e.g., TaxisDL [5]) generate *implementations* (expressed in a (relational) database implementation language, e.g., DBPL [4]). Implementation of the design languages can be difficult, as they have several implementation techniques (for issues including record layout for entities and attributes with inheritance [9, 30, 3], constraint enforcement [8, 20], and process scheduling [11]) with varying performance characteristics.

To manageably deal with performance of information systems, the Performance Framework takes the NFR Framework, and then represents, in an organised way, knowledge about information system design, implementation and performance. This uses results from semantic data models, object-oriented systems, databases, and software performance engineering [43]. An early paper [33] provides a *layered* [19] conceptual framework for performance prediction and implementation selection. A recent paper [34] provides the basic Performance Framework, by adapting the NFR Framework, and illustrates selection.

This paper refines the Performance Framework by further organising performance goal refinement methods, with some focus on refinement methods for selecting implementations of long-term processes and integrity constraints. These are illustrated in a realistic setting of a tax appeal system and its actual workload. We describe a *Performance Assistant* tool, currently under development, intended to aid a developer use the framework.

1.1 The Performance Sort and Layered Performance Structures

A starting point for understanding good system performance is the set of standard definitions from computer systems theory (e.g., [24]). The *Performance Sort* (Fig. 1 (a)) provides a vocabulary for a set of performance concepts. Performance can be specialised into time and space performance, which in turn can be further specialised. Good time performance means seeking fast response and high throughput, while good space performance means decreased or low usage.

To further organise performance considerations, we use a *layered structure* (Fig. 1 (b)). Each layer deals with one main issue. Development starts at the top, the source (design) language. Issues are considered one-at-a-time, and eliminated by decisions which have an impact upon lower layers, where the system

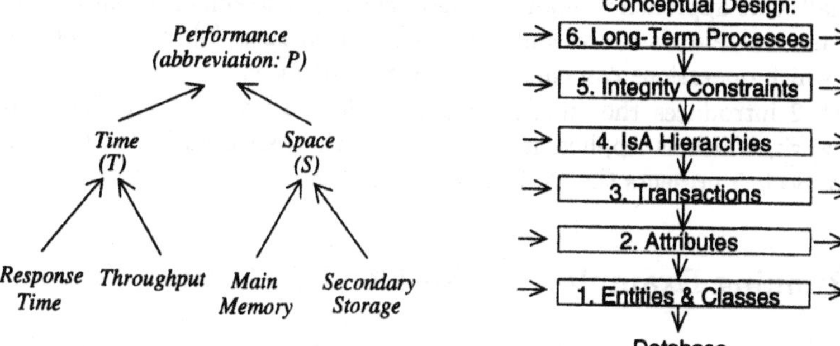

Fig. 1. **(a)** Performance Sort.

Fig. 1. **(b)** Performance Layering.

is represented in more detail using successively simpler models. Finally, results are expressed in the target (implementation) language. This approach (both for selecting implementations and predicting their performance) is adapted from a model for relational database performance prediction [19], which was motivated by several database performance models based on multiple layers.

Our particular layering, which focusses on data model features of conceptual designs, was motivated in part by our experience [32] that such features often *interact* with implementation and performance considerations. While any layering can help control the number of concepts considered at a time, our particular choice of features and their ordering permits some existing data models to be represented by subsets of layers. For example, by removing Layers 5 and 6, we have basic features of semantic data models such as Taxis [30]; by then removing Layers 3 and 4, we have basic features of Entity-Relationship models [10]. Of course, a different ordering may well be used in *developing* a design.

1.2 Related Work

The NFR Framework was influenced by work on decision support systems, e.g., [25], which in representing design rationale makes explicit the goals presupposed by arguments. It was also influenced by the DAIDA environment for information system development [21] [4] which also addresses implementation of conceptual designs. DAIDA, and the TI transformation-based system [2], focus on correctness requirements. While recognising the importance of non-functional and functional requirements, Bubenko [7] also emphasises acquiring a goal-directed enterprise model. Other goal-directed work early in the software lifecycle includes requirements acquisition [17] and organisation modelling [44].

A framework for performance engineering [35] also focusses on information system development, with an emphasis on performance prediction, tools and case studies [6]. For automating physical database design, Rozen [41] offers a framework and a tool. In an automatic programming setting, Kant [23] provides performance-based selection of structures and procedures for programming-in-the-small. One approach to maintaining integrity constraints is to automatically repair inconsistent database states via production rules [8]; the system determines which operations can cause a constraint violation.

Sect. 2 introduces the running example. Sect. 3 presents the Performance Framework, which is applied in Sect. 4 to performance goals for the sample system. Sect. 5 presents the Performance Assistant.

2 Running Example and Workload Statistics

As a running example for this paper, we consider an information system for income tax appeals, which manages the handling of appeals by taxpayers who disagree with decisions made by the Canadian Department of National Revenue.

We have used available operational procedure manuals and statistics [37, 38, 39, 40] which partially describe the appeals system (However, a system specification of the existing appeals database is not available to us). After the Department receives an appeal, the case is assigned to an appeals officer, who may then repeatedly examine the taxpayer's account, and consult with the taxpayer. Departmental policy requires an appeals officer to discuss the matter with the taxpayer within 50 days of receipt of the appeal, and complete the review within 90 days, resulting in a decision within 120 days.

Currently, an inventory control database handles enquiries and prepares reports on case disposition and time spent by staff. However, workload control and the supervision of the progress of appeals cases are not automated. As an enhanced, partially automated follow-up service would be helpful to departmental operations[1] we wish to develop a system with such a service to track appeals. We have added some functional requirements and system performance requirements which could reasonably be expected for such a system.

Characteristics of the application domain guide our choice of design language. We choose TaxisDL, as its features (including long-term processes, integrity constraints, and IsA hierarchies) can naturally represent the appeals process, which is consultative and interactive, is subject to legislative and policy constraints, and has many classifications of taxpayers, decisions, etc. Fig. 2 is a simplified representation of a portion of the long-term appeals process, represented as a TaxisDL *script*. Scripts [11] are augmented Petri nets [45]. Control flows between *locations* (represented as nodes), along directed *transitions* (arcs). The actions to be accomplished along a transition are specified by the *goals*[2] of a transition.

Actual *workload statistics* [40, 38] are used here. Approximately 18 000 000 tax returns are filed annually. For the year ended March 31, 1992, some 57 072 appeals were concluded, in an average of 104 days, and 38 532 appeals were unresolved at year-end. In the 4 quarters of the year, between 64% and 84% of decisions were made within 60 days, and 18% to 55% were issued within 30 days.

[1] Letter from F. Livernoche, Dept. of National Revenue, Taxation, Nov. 19, 1992.

[2] When not qualified, "goal" will refer to a component of a goal-graph structure, rather than a goal of a script transition.

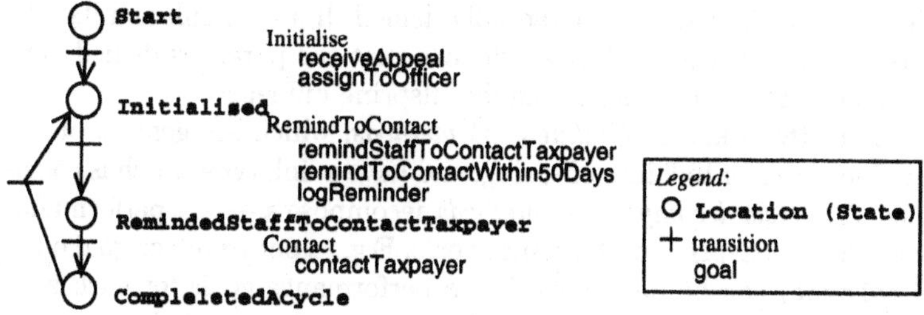

Fig. 2. Portion of a script for tax appeals.

However, approximately 4% of the cases took longer than the service standard, leaving at year-end 5 378 cases outstanding for over 120 days.

3 Performance Framework

This section describes the Performance Framework. We introduce the NFR Framework, and describe our representation of performance knowledge.

3.1 NFR Framework

The Performance Framework builds on the NFR Framework [14, 27], which includes goals, link types, and refinement methods.

There are three classes of *goals,* each with an associated sort, parameters, and a parameter indicating the layer at which a goal is stated. *(1.) Performance goals* are stated by the developer, or are produced by refining other goals. An example is *Time*[List,2], where the sort is *Time* (an instance of the *Performance* sort), the parameter is List, and the layer parameter is 2. The interpretation of this goal is that there should be good time performance for a list; the goal is stated at Layer 2 which deals with attributes. *(2.) Satisficing goals* represent implementation decisions adopted to satisfice performance goals. E.g., one way to satisfice the above time goal is to not compress list data stored in the system; this is written: *UncompressedFormat*[List,2]. Sorts range over categories of implementation decisions. *(3.) Argumentation goals* state evidence for or against other goals or refinements. E.g., *InformalClaim*["List is frequently accessed",2] supports using an uncompressed format, to get good time performance.

Performance requirements are used as criteria for selecting among competing implementation alternatives, and can be refined to satisficing goals. Development proceeds by refining each goal, the parent, into a set of offspring. Unlike AND/OR trees, there are several *link types* [14, 27] relating the satisficing of the offspring (or failure thereof) to the satisficing of the parent; links may also relate other links to argumentation goals. If an *AND* link and all its offspring are satisficed, the parent is potentially satisficed, but if any offspring is denied (unsatisficeable), the parent is potentially denied. If a *sub* link is satisficed, but the offspring denied, the parent is potentially denied. If a *-sub* link and its offspring are satisficed, there is inconclusive evidence that the parent is denied. The *und* link type indicates undetermined parent-offspring influence.

There are three kinds of *refinement methods,* which are generic procedures which refine a goal or link into offspring, and have a link type which is considered satisficed. *(1.) Goal decomposition methods* decompose a parent performance goal into one or more offspring performance goals. E.g., a performance goal on a class (e.g., `Employee`) can be decomposed into performance goals for each attribute of the class; here an *AND link* is used. Also common are *sub* links conveying the sense of a (single) offspring contributing partially to the satisficing of a parent. *(2.) Goal satisficing methods* refine goals into satisficing goals, making a commitment to particular implementation decisions. *(3.) Argumentation methods* refine a goal or a link into an argumentation goal, thereby indicating evidence for or against the satisficing of a goal.

3.2 Organisation of Performance Goal Refinement Methods

There are a number of performance goal decomposition methods (GDMs). How do we organise them? Goals have sorts, parameters, layer parameters, and additional attributes (such as criticality and dominance). Decomposition methods can refine goals along each of these dimensions. We can form broad groups of methods for each of these dimensions, which are shown as the second row of Fig. 3, and can be further sub-divided. For example, the layer-based methods can be specialised into groups of methods for each layer (bottom right of Fig. 3).

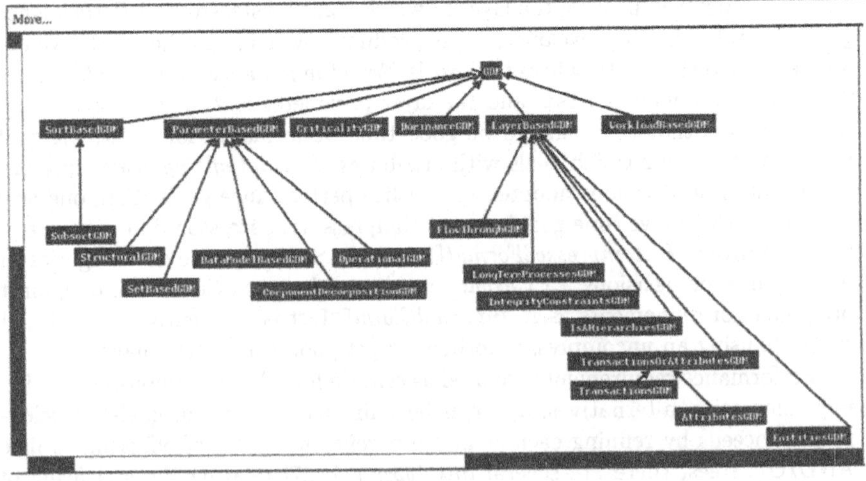

Fig. 3. Organisation of Performance Goal Decomposition Methods.

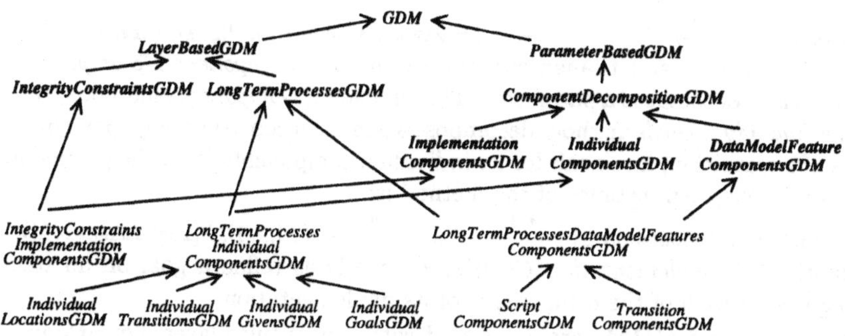

Fig. 4. Some Decomposition Methods for Layers 6 and 5.

Many of the refinement methods are formed by multiple inheritance, from two or more broad groups shown in Fig. 3. E.g., the *Transition Components* method (lower right of Fig. 4) is a specialisation of both the *Layer-Based* method for long-term processes and the *Parameter-Based* method for data model feature component decomposition. This arrangement should help the developer in understanding, representing and using a fairly large number of methods, since: the groupings can help a developer focus attention on a smaller number of methods; a developer who understands general groups of methods will understand some characteristics of more specific groups and their individual methods, as well as those formed by multiple inheritance from known groups; and the groupings can provide some guidance when new methods are defined.

Similarly, goal *satisficing* methods (GSMs) are arranged into broad groups, again including sorts, parameters and layers, but also sources of satisficing methods. These include implementation techniques from semantic data modelling, object-oriented systems, and database systems, as well as principles for achieving responsiveness. Multiple inheritance again defines more specific methods.

3.3 Performance Goal Decomposition Methods

We now describe some performance GDMs, some of which are shown in Fig. 4. The presentation follows the organisation shown in Fig. 3.

Sort-Based GDMs refine a goal with a sort into goals with its sub-sorts. For example, the *Time-Space* method decomposes a *Performance* goal into two goals, one dealing with *Time*, the other with *Space*.

Parameter-Based GDMs decompose a goal based on its parameter. *(1.) Data Model Feature methods,* such as the *Transition Components* method,[3] decompose a goal on a feature (here, a script's transition, e.g., `RemindToContact`) into goals for its constituent constructs (e.g., preconditions and postconditions):

[3] Some methods have a refinement with a *sub* link, followed by one with an *AND* link; this is helpful when the conjuncts are incomplete, or have different degrees of importance. Here, such *sub* refinements are omitted from definitions, and not named.

$P[\texttt{transn}, \texttt{l}] \xrightarrow{sub} \ldots \xrightarrow{AND} \{P[\texttt{givens(transn)}, \texttt{l}], P[\texttt{goals(transn)}, \texttt{l}]\}$, where l is a layer and transn is a transition. *(2.) Component Decomposition methods* also decompose a parameter. The *Individual Components* methods, such as the *Individual Goals* method, decompose a goal on a construct (e.g., postconditions of a transition) into goals for its individual components (e.g., the particular postconditions). An instance of the method is:

$P[\texttt{goals(RemindToContact)}, \texttt{l}] \xrightarrow{sub} \ldots \xrightarrow{AND} \{P[\ldots, \texttt{l}], P[\texttt{logReminder}, \texttt{l}]\}$
Similarly, the *Implementation Components* methods refine a goal on an item into goals for each of the components of its implementation.

Layer-Based GDMs are associated with a particular layer. For example, *Long-Term Processes* methods (Layer 6) include the *Transition Components* and *Individual Transitions* methods. The *Flow Through* method relates goals at different layers, using an *inter-layer link.*

Goal-Attribute–Based GDMs indicate the critical and dominant parts of the workload, by adding an attribute to the goal.

3.4 Performance Goal Satisficing Methods

There are many GSMs from implementation of semantic data models and object-oriented systems. For example, there are implementations of temporal integrity constraints with varying performance characteristics, including *cyclic checking* [45] (exhaustive circular examination of all entities with a particular constraint) and a *trigger mechanism* (event-driven selective checking [11] as in active databases) which can often be more efficient.

Some GSMs come from the area of systems performance engineering [43], which provides principles for achieving system *responsiveness* to users. For example, a *compressed format* for attributes saves space, but at the cost of extra time for repeated uncompression and compression of data. This is an example of *early fixing,* the mapping, as early as possible, of functions and information to the instructions and structures which achieve them.

3.5 Argumentation Methods

A developer may argue, by the *Vital Few* argumentation method, that particular goals are much more important to satisfice than others.

4 Illustration: Goal-Graph Structures for Tax System

We illustrate how a system developer would use the Performance Framework to deal with time and space goals for the tax appeal system, using some of the aforementioned methods, at a few layers, as well as workload statistics.

4.1 A Time Goal for Long-Term Processes

The developer desire good time performance for the actions of the tax appeal process. As actions are performed along script transitions, the developer states at Layer 6 (long-term processes) a goal of good time performance for the transitions (top centre of Fig. 5). By the *Individual Transitions* decomposition method,[4] the goal is refined into goals for each individual transition of the script. The developer chooses to refine the goal by data model components. Focussing on the transition which reminds staff to contact the taxpayer, the *Transition Components* decomposition method produces goals for the transition's preconditions and postconditions. A further refinement yields goals for each of the transition's postconditions (goals), one of which reminds staff to contact the taxpayer within 50 days of the filing of the appeal. This in turn is realised by a combination of *Implementation Components,* one of which is a *constraint* (at Layer 5, related by an inter-layer link to Layer 6) that the system issue a reminder to staff within 40 days, if the taxpayer has not already been contacted.

To quickly issue the reminder, the developer considers several satisficing methods (See, e.g., the implementation techniques for temporal constraints in [11]). One option is *cyclic checking,* whereby each transition of each taxpayer's script is sequentially examined; if it is 40 days since the appeal was filed, a reminder is sent to staff. This gives reasonable performance with a small number of script instances; otherwise, the time overhead of repeatedly checking each script is too great, since only a few scripts will meet the temporal condition. As the workload statistics [40] indicate there are many (recently 38 532) appeals pending, the developer argues that the criterion for using cyclic checking is not met. The elimination of this satisficing method is recorded in the goal-graph structure by denying a claim that the criterion is met; this denies the *link* from the cyclic-checking satisfying goal to its parent.

The developer considers another satisficing method for temporal constraints, the *Time-Ordered List* [11], which keeps script instances in a list, sorted by the time at which they need to be activated. Here, this offers efficient time access: we only examine the front of the list; scripts with the appropriate date are removed from the list, and reminders are issued. More specialised structures can be considered. A queue structure would offer time and space advantages if reminders are issued for every appeal on the 40th day, as removal operations can be restricted to the front. However, the queue is ruled out because the workload patterns show that reminders are not always needed: some cases are resolved within 30 days, and a majority are resolved within 60 days; hence, many cases are concluded before the 40th day, and in some others the taxpayer has been contacted before then. An implication for implementation is that entries need to be able to be efficiently removed in advance of the normal time. The developer instead chooses a list structure which allows early removal.

Justification links (bottom of Fig. 5) relate satisficing goals to the selected implementation, while *dependency links* (right of Fig. 5) relate functional re-

[4] When link types are omitted from figures, generally a *sub* link is assumed if there is only one offspring; otherwise an *AND* link is assumed.

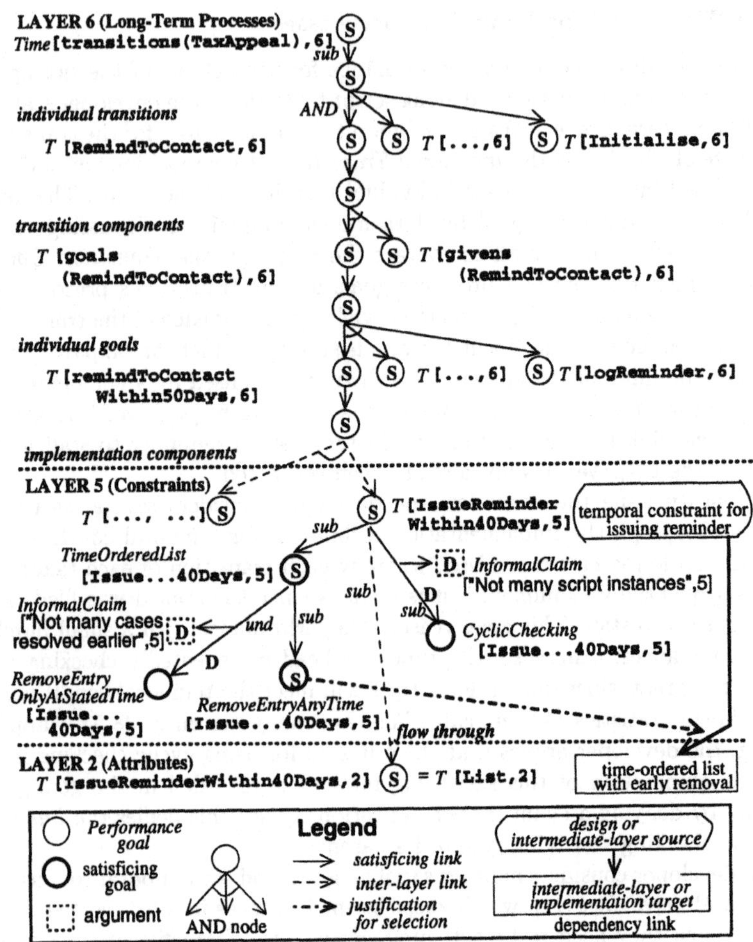

Fig. 5. A goal-graph structure for long-term processes.

quirements to an implementation. At Layer 2, we will consider storage of the attributes of the list structure which was chosen at Layer 5 to meet the integrity constraint. The *Flow Through* method relates the two layers via an inter-layer link, producing the goal T[`IssueReminderWithin40Days`,2] (bottom of Fig. 5), which is renamed for ease of presentation as T[`List`,2] (top left of Fig. 6).

4.2 Time and Space Goals for Attributes

The developer also requires good *space* performance for the list's attributes (top right of Fig. 6), which may conflict with the above time goal. Both the time and space goals for the list are partioned, by the *Subset* method, into goals for the front (where many accesses are made) and the end (remainder) of the list. The

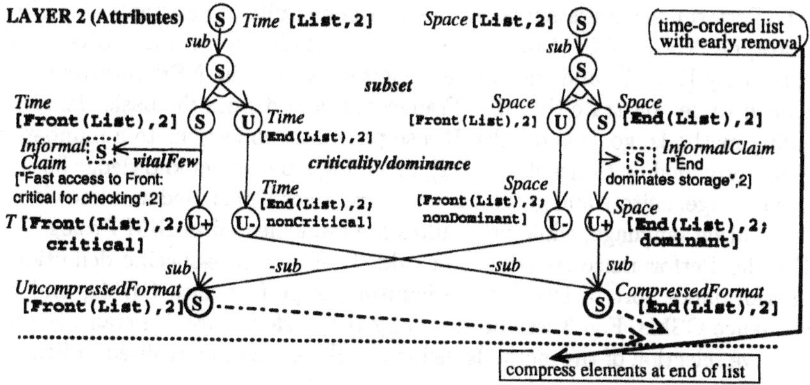

Fig. 6. A goal-graph structure for attributes of a list.

developer argues that the end dominates storage, but that access to the front is critical for fast constraint checking. Now compressing attributes saves space, but requires extra time for uncompression. Thus the developer chooses to only compress attributes at the end of the list, resulting in fast access time to the front, which is critical, and efficient space usage for the end, which dominates storage. However, the storage goal for the (non-dominant) front is not met; neither is the (non-critical) time goal for access to the end.

To establish which goals are satisficed, a labelling algorithm [27] examines labels of leaves of the goal-graph to see if they are satisficed. Results propagate upwards, by combining label values while considering link types according to a set of rules; in addition, the developer can determine results when values are conflicting or indefinite. A node or link of the graph is labelled: *satisficed* (or *S*); *denied* (or *D*); *conflicting* (or *C*) if it is both potentially satisficed and denied; and *undetermined* (or *U*) if it is neither. Results are propagated via inter-layer links to higher layers.

The result for the list's time and space goals (Fig. 6) is that the critical and dominant goals are satisficed. This is in accordance with principles for achieving responsiveness [43]. When a satisficed critical goal is combined with an unsatisficed non-critical one, the developer can adjust the label values of a non-critical (or non-dominant) goal, so that the overall goal is considered satisficed.

5 Performance Assistant

The *Performance Assistant* is intended to aid a developer use the framework. The cataloguing and displaying of available methods shows developers their options, helping them prevent things from being overlooked, and aiding them in identifying and dealing with tradeoffs. The system records decisions, maintaining goal graphs, and evaluating whether goals have been satisficed. Also, facilities for recording arguments can increase developers' awareness of design rationale.

The Performance Assistant is one member of a family of Assistants for NFRs. A prototype "core" *NFR Assistant* [14] been extended to several NFRs: accuracy, security [14, 15], and (in progress) performance. The NFR Assistant was developed to demonstrate the NFR Framework, and defines the basic elements, including methods, goals and links. It also provides connections to a number of facilities, provided by ConceptBase [22], including a persistent knowledge base, a query language, editors and graphical browsers. Telos [26] is used as a knowledge representation language, while procedures are implemented in BIM Prolog [1].

For the Performance Assistant, we added performance-specific definitions: the Performance sort, a layering mechanism, 59 performance GDMs, and 56 performance GSMs. Fig. 3 was produced by the Performance Assistant. A representative selection of the methods defined in Telos are to be realised in Prolog.

6 Conclusions

A framework for treating performance requirements in the development of information systems has been presented, and refined by further organising the representation of performance goal refinement methods, and describing methods for long-term processes and integrity constraints. This work was then applied to treat performance requirements of a sample information system using some actual workload descriptions. The resultant goal-graph structure showed that critical and dominant goals were satisficed, consistent with principles for generating responsive software. We presented the Performance Assistant tool, currently under development. The Performance Framework and Assistant, and case studies [16], offer further evidence for the usefulness of the NFR Framework.

There are several aspects to future work. Additional quantitative measures can be added to the framework, e.g., performance prediction results could be used in arguments. The study of the sample system has raised some issues, such as the relationship between a satisficing goal and performance goals at lower layers. After completing the implementation of the Performance Assistant, we need to test it on realistic examples. Furthermore, it would be interesting to see if the basic components of the Performance Framework would apply using different assumptions. For example, if other design and implementation language families were used, would the layering approach be applicable? If performance is not considered is during implementation, how applicable would the present organisation of methods be? Answers would also help indicate whether our treatment is too dependent on conceptual design features. Finally, the study of other actual systems will help demonstrate the applicability of the Performance Framework to a wide variety of performance requirements, system designs, and workloads.

Acknowledgements. My sincere gratitude to Prof. J. Mylopoulos, L. Chung and E. Yu for ongoing discussions, and assistance in preparing this paper. The NFR Assistant was implemented in cooperation with L. Chung, with assistance from I. Maione, T. Rose and D. Lauzon. Many thanks to F. Livernoche and G. Venner of the Dept. of National Revenue, Taxation for information on the tax appeals process. My thanks to the referees for their excellent suggestions.

References

1. *BIM Prolog 2.4 Manual.* BIM sa/nv, Belgium (1989)
2. R. Balzer: A 15 Year Perspective on Automatic Programming. TSE **11** (1985)
3. V. Benzaken: An Evaluation Model for Clustering Strategies in the O_2 Object-Oriented Database System. Proc. 3rd Int. Conf. Database Theory (1990) 126–140
4. A. Borgida, J. Mylopoulos, J. W. Schmidt, I. Wetzel: Support for Data-Intensive Applications: Conceptual Design and Software Development. Proc. Second Int. Workshop on Database Programming Languages (1989) 258–280
5. A. Borgida, J. Mylopoulos, J. W. Schmidt: The TaxisDL Software Description Language. In M. Jarke (Ed.): *Database Application Engineering with DAIDA*. Berlin: Springer-Verlag (1993)
6. G. Brataas, A. L. Opdahl, V. Vetland, A. Sølvberg: Information Systems: Final Evaluation of the IMSE. Report, SINTEF, Univ. of Trondheim (1992)
7. J. Bubenko jr: Towards a Corporate Knowledge Repository. SYSLAB Report 91–023–DSV, Stockholm University (1991)
8. S. Ceri, J. Widom: Deriving Production Rules for Constraint Management. Proc. 16th Int. Conf. Very Large Data Bases (1990) 566–577
9. A. Chan et al.: Storage and Access Structures to Support a Semantic Data Model. Proc. Eighth Int. Conf. Very Large Data Bases (1982) 122–130
10. P. Chen: The Entity-Relationship Model — Toward a Unified View of Data. ACM TODS **1** (1976) 9–36
11. K. L. Chung, D. Rios-Zertuche, B. A. Nixon, J. Mylopoulos: Process Management and Assertion Enforcement for a Semantic Data Model. Proc., Int. Conf. Extending Database Technology (1988) 469–487
12. L. Chung: Representation and Utilization of Non-Functional Requirements for Information System Design. Proc. Third Int. Conf. CAiSE '91 (1991) 5–30
13. K. L. Chung, P. Katalagarianos, M. Marakakis, M. Mertikas, J. Mylopoulos, Y. Vassiliou: From Information System Requirements to Designs: A Mapping Framework. Information Systems **16** (1991) 429–461
14. K. L. Chung: Representing and Using Non-Functional Requirements: A Process-Oriented Approach. Ph.D. Thesis, Dept. Comp. Sci., Univ. Toronto (1993). Also Report DKBS–TR–93–1
15. L. Chung: Dealing With Security Requirements During the Development of Information Systems. Proc. Fifth Int. Conf. CAiSE '93 (1993) 234–251
16. L. Chung, B. Nixon: Dealing with Non-Functional Requirements: Three Case Studies. Manuscript, Dept. Comp. Sci., Univ. Toronto (1993)
17. A. Dardenne, A. van Lamsweerde, S. Fickas: Goal-directed Requirements Acquisition. Science of Computer Programming **20** (1993) 3–50
18. R. Hull, R. King: Semantic Database Modeling: Survey, Applications, and Research Issues. Computing Surveys **19** (1987) 201–260
19. W. F. Hyslop: Performance Prediction of Relational Database Management Systems. Ph.D. Thesis, Dept. of Computer Science, Univ. of Toronto (1991)
20. H. V. Jagadish, X. Qian: Integrity Maintenance in an Object-Oriented Database. Proc. 18th Conf. Very Large Data Bases (1992) 469–480
21. M. Jarke, J. Mylopoulos, J. W. Schmidt, Y. Vassiliou: DAIDA: An Environment for Evolving Information Systems. ACM Trans. Information Systems **10** (1992)
22. Matthias Jarke (Ed.): ConceptBase V3.1 User Manual. Univ. of Passau (1992)
23. E. Kant: On the Efficient Synthesis of Efficient Programs. Artif. Intell. **20** (1983)

24. E. D. Lazowska, J. Zahorjan, G. S. Graham, K. C. Sevcik: *Quantitative System Performance*. Englewood Cliffs, NJ: Prentice-Hall (1984)
25. J. Lee: Extending the Potts and Bruns Model for Recording Design Rationale. Proc. 13th Int. Conf. Softw. Eng. (1991) 114–125
26. J. Mylopoulos, A. Borgida, M. Jarke, M. Koubarakis: Telos: Representing Knowledge about Information Systems. ACM Trans. Information Systems **8** (1990)
27. J. Mylopoulos, L. Chung, B. Nixon: Representing and Using Non-Functional Requirements: A Process-Oriented Approach. IEEE TSE **18** (1992) 483–497
28. J. Mylopoulos, L. Chung, E. Yu, B. Nixon: Requirements Engineering 1993: Selected Papers. Report DKBS–TR–93–2, Dept. Comp. Sci. Univ. Toronto (1993)
29. N. Nilsson: *Problem-Solving Methods in Artificial Intelligence*. McGraw-Hill (1971)
30. B. Nixon, L. Chung, D. Lauzon, A. Borgida, J. Mylopoulos, M. Stanley: Implementation of a Compiler for a Semantic Data Model: Experiences with Taxis. Proc. ACM SIGMOD (1987) 118–131
31. B. A. Nixon, K. L. Chung, D. Lauzon, A. Borgida, J. Mylopoulos, M. Stanley: Design of a Compiler for a Semantic Data Model. In J. W. Schmidt, C. Thanos (Eds.): *Foundations of Knowledge Base Management*. Springer-Verlag (1989)
32. B. Nixon, J. Mylopoulos: Integration Issues in Implementing Semantic Data Models. In F. Bancilhon, P. Buneman (Eds.): *Advances in Database Programming Languages*. New York: ACM Press (1990) 187–217
33. B. Nixon: Implementation of Information System Design Specifications: A Performance Perspective. In P. Kanellakis, J. W. Schmidt (Eds.): *Database Programming Languages: Bulk Types & Persistent Data — The Third International Workshop* (1991) 149–168. San Mateo, CA: Morgan Kaufmann
34. B. A. Nixon: Dealing with Performance Requirements During the Development of Information Systems. Proc. IEEE Int. Symp. on Requirements Eng. (1993) 42–49
35. A. L. Opdahl: Performance Engineering During Information System Development. Dr.ing. thesis, Fac. Comp. Sci. & Elec. Eng., Norwegian Inst. Technology (1992)
36. J. Peckham, F. Maryanski: Semantic Data Models. Comp. Surveys **20** (1988)
37. Revenue Canada, Taxation: Objections and Appeals. Ottawa (1980)
38. Revenue Canada, Taxation: 1991 Taxation Statistics, Ottawa (1991)
39. Revenue Canada, Taxation: Taxation Operations Manual **70** (1992)
40. Dept. of National Revenue, Taxation, Appeals Branch: Quarterly Statistical Reports for the Periods Ended June 2 & Sept. 27, 1991; Jan. 3 & Mar. 31, 1992. Number of days to reassesss Notices of Objection for reassessments between Jan. 1 & Mar. 31, 1992. Also for periods ending: Dec. 31, 1991; June 26 & Sept. 25, 1992
41. S. Rozen: Automating Physical Database Design: An Extensible Approach. Ph.D. Dissertation, Dept. Comp. Sci., New York Univ. (1993)
42. H. A. Simon: *The Sciences of the Artificial*, 2nd Ed. MIT Press (1981)
43. C. Smith: *Performance Engineering of Software Systems*. Addison-Wesley (1990)
44. E. Yu: An Organization Modelling Framework for Information Systems Requirements Engineering. Ph.D. Thesis, Dept. Comp. Sci., Univ. Toronto (forthcoming)
45. M. D. Zisman: Use of Production Systems for Modeling Concurrent Processes. In D. A. Waterman, F. Hayes-Roth (Eds.): *Pattern-Directed Inference Systems*. New York: Academic Press (1978) 53–68

A Model-Theoretic Semantics of the Multilevel Relational Model *

Xiaolei Qian
Computer Science Laboratory, SRI International
333 Ravenswood Avenue, Menlo Park, CA 94025

Abstract

A multilevel relational database represents information in a multilevel state of the world, which is the knowledge of the truth value of a statement with respect to a classification level in a security lattice. We develop a model-theoretic semantics of the multilevel relational model with tuple-level classification, which formalizes the notion of validity in multilevel relational databases. We also identify the multilevel security constraints that precisely characterize the validity of multilevel relational databases.

1 Introduction

A *state of the world* could be envisioned as a set of elements linked together by relationships. Information in a state of the world is the knowledge of the truth value of a statement [9], which could be either an elementary fact as "Enterprise is on mission #101 to Rigel" or a general law as "every starship has a unique destination".

A *relational database* captures a finite set of elements linked together by relationships. Elementary facts are represented as tuples in relations, and general laws are represented as integrity constraints. These are the only information explicitly captured by a relational database, from which implicit information could be derived. For example, from the explicit elementary fact "Enterprise is on mission #101 to Rigel" represented by the tuple "(Enterprise, 101, Rigel)", we could derive the implicit information "there is a starship Enterprise". A relational database is *valid* if the relations form a model of the integrity constraints [9].

A *multilevel state of the world* is a state of the world together with a *classification mapping*: every piece of information — either an elementary fact or a general law — is mapped to a set of classification levels in a security lattice.

***This work was supported by U.S. Department of Defense Advanced Research Projects Agency and U.S. Air Force Rome Laboratory under contracts F30602-91-C-0092 and F30602-92-C-0140.**

Information in a multilevel state of the world is the knowledge of the truth value of a statement with respect to a classification level [14], which could be either a classified elementary fact as "it is top-secret that Enterprise is on mission #101 to Rigel", or a classified general law as "it is confidential that every starship has a unique destination".[1]

A ***multilevel relational database*** with ***tuple-level classification*** is a relational database together with a ***tuple classification scheme***, which maps every tuple in every relation to a set of classification levels in a security lattice, and every integrity constraint to the bottom level in the lattice (i.e., integrity constraints are not classified). The tuple classification scheme of a multilevel relational database is intended to represent the classification mapping of a multilevel state of the world.

Access by processes to a multilevel relational database is controlled by a *security policy*, which is an interpretation of the mandatory access control policies employed in manual systems. A well-accepted security policy is the Bell-LaPadula model [4]. In this model, every process is assigned a clearance level in the security lattice of the multilevel relational database. The security policy has two important properties which ensure that information does not flow down the lattice:

- *The Simple Security Property* A process is allowed a read access to a tuple only if the former's clearance level is identical to or higher than the latter's classification level in the security lattice.
- *The *-Property* A process is allowed a write access to a tuple only if the former's clearance level is identical to or lower than the latter's classification level in the security lattice.

The notion of integrity is problematic for multilevel relational databases. Existing approaches attempt to enforce integrity across multiple classification levels [1, 8, 15]. If a low tuple contradicts some high tuple with respect to the integrity constraints, then allowing both tuples would violate integrity, disallowing the low tuple would introduce a signaling channel — a signal to low users about the existence of the high tuple, and disallowing the high tuple would cause loss of high information. For example, the low tuple "(Enterprise, 102, Rigel)" contradicts the high tuple "(Enterprise, 101, Rigel)" with respect to the constraint "every starship has a unique mission". Disallowing the low tuple would signal to low users that Enterprise is on a high mission. In fact, Burns [1] has noticed that such integrity enforcement is in fundamental conflict with secrecy enforcement: no multilevel relational databases could simultaneously satisfy both integrity and secrecy requirements. This problem is known as *polyinstantiation* in the limited context where integrity constraints consist of key-based

[1] The notion of a multilevel state of the world captures the knowledge at various classification levels, but not the *metaknowledge* that relates the knowledge at multiple classification levels, such as the polyinstantiation and referential security properties to be introduced in Section 3. Although we provide a characterization of the validity of multilevel relational databases using polyinstantiation and referential security properties, a thorough treatment of such metaknowledge is out of the scope of this paper.

functional dependencies only, which has been the subject of continuous debate in the literature [2, 5, 6, 12].

According to the Bell-LaPadula model, low tuples are always accessible high. However, *accèssibility* is different from *believability*. Integrity should be enforced at every classification level only on those tuples believable at that level, and believability should be maximized to allow maximum sharing across classification levels.

The filter function proposed in the literature [2, 3, 7] takes the extreme by equating believability to accessibility, thus maximizing believability. However, integrity is compromised if a low tuple contradicts some high tuples with respect to the integrity constraints, in which case the filter function would result in an invalid high database. For example, both the low tuple "(Enterprise, 102, Rigel)" and the high tuple "(Enterprise, 101, Rigel)" would be in the high database computed by the filter function, which is invalid with respect to the constraint "every starship has a unique mission".

Smith and Winslett proposed a belief-based semantics of the multilevel relational model [13], which defines a multilevel relational database as a set of single-level relational databases, one for every classification level. They distinguished between accessibility and believability, and took the other extreme by allowing no low tuples to be believable high, thus minimizing believability. Although integrity is straightforward to enforce, a multilevel relational database that directly employs such a semantics would no longer be multilevel — it would be a set of single-level relational databases in which there is no sharing across classification levels.

Thuraisingham proposed a proof-theoretic semantics of the multilevel relational model [14], in which a low tuple is believable high only if it does not contradict any integrity constraints when combined with high tuples. Given two low tuples classified incomparably, what happens if either tuple is believable high without contradicting the integrity constraints, but inconsistency would arise when both tuples are believable high? To determine what is believable high, the result of Thuraisingham's approach would depend on the (random) order in which the nonmonotonic inference rule is applied to these two tuples, which introduces ambiguity. It should be noticed that such problems occur even with a totally-ordered security lattice, if we allow arbitrary integrity constraints. For example, an integrity constraint could state that there should be no more than two starships going to Rigel. If we have one high tuple "(Enterprise, 101, Rigel)" together with two low tuples "(Voyager, 102, Rigel)" and "(Discovery, 103, Rigel)", then at most one low tuple is believable high, but it is unclear which one should.

The paper is organized as follows. The standard relational model is defined in Section 2, together with a characterization of the information content of relational databases. In Section 3 we develop a model-theoretic semantics of the multilevel relational model with tuple-level classification, and identify the multilevel security constraints that precisely characterize the validity of multilevel relational databases. Finally, Section 4 provides some concluding remarks. Due to space limitations, formal proofs are not included. Interested readers could read [10] for proofs and a treatment of integrity enforcement.

2 Relational Model

We give a formal definition of the relational model, and characterize the information content of relational databases in terms of atomic decomposition. We then define filtering functions, which will be used in the next section to formalize the validity of multilevel relational databases.

2.1 Basic Notations

Following the practice of most existing approaches, we consider the relational model extended with two important classes of integrity constraints: key-based functional and referential dependencies. Extensions to more general classes of integrity constraints are left to another paper.

Let U be a finite set of *attributes*. If X, Y are subsets of U, then XY denotes the union of X, Y. If $A \in U$, then XA denotes $X\{A\}$. A *relation scheme* (in fourth normal form) $R[X, K]$ is a set of attributes $X \subseteq U$ named R with nonempty *primary key* $K \subseteq X$. A *database schema* is a pair $(\mathcal{R}, \mathcal{C})$, where $\mathcal{R} = \{R_i[X_i, K_i]\}_{1 \leq i \leq n}$ is a family of relation schemes and $\mathcal{C}$ is a set of *key-based referential dependencies*:

- every referential dependency in $\mathcal{C}$ has the form $R_i[Y] \hookrightarrow R_j$, where $1 \leq i, j \leq n$, $Y = K_i$ or $Y \subseteq X - K_i$, and $|Y| = |K_j|$; and
- $Y = Z$ or $Y \cap Z = \emptyset$ for $1 \leq i, j, k \leq n$ and $R_i[Y] \hookrightarrow R_j, R_i[Z] \hookrightarrow R_k$ in $\mathcal{C}$.

For referential dependency $R_i[Y] \hookrightarrow R_j$ in $\mathcal{C}$, Y is a *foreign key* in R_i to R_j. For relation scheme $R_i[X_i, K_i]$ in $\mathcal{R}$ and attribute $A \in X_i$, A is a *nonkey* attribute if $A \notin K_i$ and $A \notin Y$ for any foreign key Y in R_i. Figure 1 shows a schema with two relation schemes SMD and MT, where boxes represent relation schemes, attributes to the left of double lines form primary keys, and arrows between boxes represent referential dependencies.

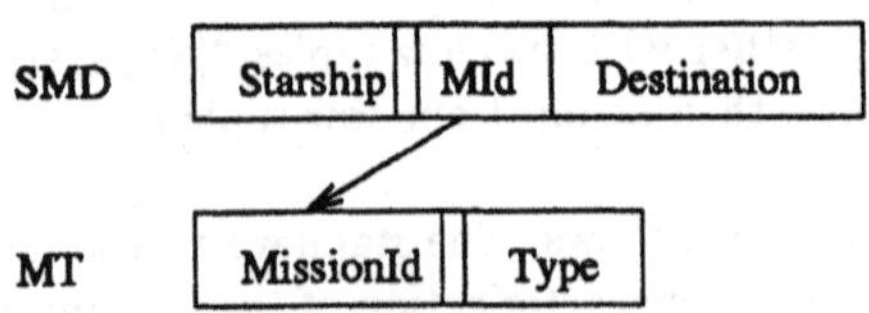

Figure 1: A Schema

Let $\mathcal{D}$ be a (possibly infinite) set of values. A *tuple* over attributes X is a partial mapping $t[X]: X \mapsto \mathcal{D}$ that assigns values from $\mathcal{D}$ to attributes in

X. For attribute $A \in X$, $t[A]$ denotes the value assigned to A by $t[X]$, and $t[A] = \perp$ denotes that $t[A]$ is undefined. For attributes $Y \subseteq X$, $t[Y]$ denotes the partial mapping whose domain is restricted to attributes in Y. For tuple t over X, $t[X] = \perp$ denotes that t is empty: $t[A] = \perp$ for all attribute $A \in X$; and $t[X] \neq \perp$ denotes that t is total: $t[A] \neq \perp$ for all attribute $A \in X$. A ***relation*** r over relation scheme $R[X, K]$ is a set of tuples over X such that $t[K] \neq \perp$ for tuple $t \in r$. For attributes $Y \subseteq X$, $r[Y]$ denotes the set of tuples $t[Y]$ where $t \in r$; and the ***total projection*** of relation r to Y, denoted as $\Pi_Y r$, is the set of tuples $t[Y]$ such that $t[Y] \in r[Y]$ and $t[Y] \neq \perp$. Relation r is ***valid*** if it satisfies the ***key integrity property***: for every pair of tuples $t, t' \in r$, $t[K] = t'[K]$ implies $t = t'$. In other words, tuples with the same primary key value should be identical.

A ***database*** b over database schema $(\mathcal{R}, \mathcal{C})$, where $\mathcal{R} = \{R_i[X_i, K_i]\}_{1 \leq i \leq n}$, is a family of relations $\{r_i\}_{1 \leq i \leq n}$, where r_i is a relation over $R_i[X_i, K_i]$, such that either $t[Y] = \perp$ or $t[Y] \neq \perp$ for every foreign key Y in R_i, relation $r_i \in b$, tuple $t \in r_i$, and $1 \leq i \leq n$. It is ***r-valid*** if every relation in b is valid. It is ***valid*** if it is r-valid and satisfies the ***referential integrity property***: for every referential dependency $R_i[Y] \hookrightarrow R_j$ in $\mathcal{C}$ and tuple $t \in r_i$, if $t[Y] \neq \perp$ then there is a tuple $t' \in r_j$ such that $t[Y] = t'[K_j]$. In other words, every foreign key value refers to an existing primary key value. $\mathcal{D}$ is the ***universe*** of b. Below is a database over the schema of Figure 1.

Starship	MId	Destination
Enterprise	101	Rigel
Voyager	102	Talos
Discovery	103	Rigel

MissionId	Type
101	spy
102	explore
103	mine

Given databases b, b' over schema $(\mathcal{R}, \mathcal{C})$ with relations $\{r_i\}_{1 \leq i \leq n}, \{r'_i\}_{1 \leq i \leq n}$ respectively, $b \cup b'$ denotes the database $\{r_i \cup r'_i\}_{1 \leq i \leq n}$ over the same schema; and b is a ***subdatabase*** of b', denoted as $b \subseteq b'$, if $r_i \subseteq r'_i$ for $1 \leq i \leq n$.

2.2 Atomic Decomposition

Every tuple in a database represents an elementary fact. Often, the elementary fact represented by a tuple is a conjunction of several ***smaller*** elementary facts. For example, tuple "(Enterprise, 101, Rigel)" represents the elementary fact "Enterprise is on mission #101 to Rigel", which is the conjunction of two smaller elementary facts "Enterprise is on mission #101" and "Enterprise goes to Rigel".

Let $\mathcal{B} = (\mathcal{R}, \mathcal{C})$ be a schema where $\mathcal{R} = \{R_i[X_i, K_i]\}_{1 \leq i \leq n}$. The ***atomic decomposition*** of $\mathcal{B}$ is a schema consisting of the following set of relation schemes $\mathcal{R}^a$:

- $R_i^K[K_i, K_i]$ for every $R_i[X_i, K_i]$ in $\mathcal{R}$,

- $R_i^Y[K_iY, K_i]$ for every $R_i[X_i, K_i]$ in $\mathcal{R}$ and foreign key Y in R_i where $Y \subseteq X_i - K_i$, and
- $R_i^A[K_iA, K_i]$ for every $R_i[X_i, K_i]$ in $\mathcal{R}$ and nonkey attribute $A \in X_i - K_i$;

and the following set of key-based referential dependencies $\mathcal{C}^a$:

- $R_i^Y[K_i] \hookrightarrow R_i^K$ and $R_i^A[K_i] \hookrightarrow R_i^K$ for every $R_i^K[K_i, K_i], R_i^Y[K_iY, K_i]$, and $R_i^A[K_iA, K_i]$,
- $R_i^K[K_i] \hookrightarrow R_j^K$ if K_i is a foreign key in R_i to R_j, and
- $R_i^Y[Y] \hookrightarrow R_j^K$ for every foreign key Y in R_i to R_j where $Y \subseteq X_i - K_i$.

From every database b over $\mathcal{B}$ we could construct a unique database b^a over the atomic decomposition $\mathcal{B}^a$ of $\mathcal{B}$ as follows. From every relation $r_i \in b$ over $R_i[X_i, K_i]$ in $\mathcal{B}$, we construct relations $r_i^K = \Pi_{K_i} r_i, r_i^Y = \Pi_{K_iY} r_i$, and $r_i^A = \Pi_{K_iA} r_i$ in b^a over R_i^K, R_i^Y, and R_i^A respectively.

Since b and b^a captures the same elementary facts, $\mathcal{B}$ and its atomic decomposition $\mathcal{B}^a$ are semantically equivalent [11]. Notice that every tuple in b is in general broken into several *smaller* tuples in b^a. Therefore every elementary fact captured by b is equivalent to a conjunction of perhaps several smaller elementary facts captured by b^a.

Furthermore, the atomic decomposition of $\mathcal{B}$ into $\mathcal{B}^a$ is the *finest* possible decomposition, in the sense that every tuple in b^a represents an *atomic* elementary fact whose further decomposition leads to loss of information. For example, tuple "(Enterprise, 101)" represents the elementary fact "Enterprise is on mission #101", while tuples "(Enterprise)" and "(101)" represent the elementary facts "there is a starship Enterprise" and "there is a starship on mission #101" respectively. The conjunction of the latter two is not equivalent to the former. Below is the atomic decomposition of the schema of Figure 1.

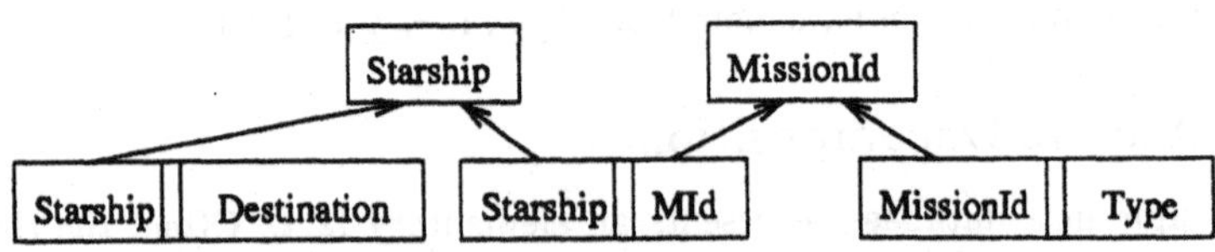

Given two databases b, b' over schema $\mathcal{B}$ with relations $\{r_i\}_{1 \leq i \leq n}, \{r_i'\}_{1 \leq i \leq n}$ respectively, b' is *more informative* than b, denoted as $b \sqsubseteq b'$, if the atomic decomposition of b is a subdatabase of the atomic decomposition of b'. In other words, b' is more informative than b if every atomic tuple in b is also an atomic tuple in b'.

2.3 Filtering Functions

Let v, v' be either values in $\mathcal{D}$ or $\perp$. We define the operators $\otimes, \oslash$ on v, v' as follows, where $v \otimes v'$ computes the nonconflicting information in v, v', and $v \oslash v'$

computes the information in v and the nonconflicting information in v':

$$v \otimes v' = \begin{cases} v & \text{if } v = v' \text{ or } v' = \bot \\ v' & \text{if } v = \bot \\ \bot & \text{otherwise} \end{cases}$$

$$v \oslash v' = \begin{cases} v & \text{if } v \neq \bot \\ v' & \text{otherwise} \end{cases}$$

Let t, t' be tuples over X. We define the operators $\otimes, \oslash$ on t, t' as follows, where $t \otimes t'$ computes the nonconflicting information in t, t', and $t \oslash t'$ computes the information in t and the nonconflicting information in t':

$$t \otimes t' = \begin{cases} t & \text{if } t = t' \text{ or } t' = \bot \\ t' & \text{if } t = \bot \\ \bot & \text{otherwise} \end{cases}$$

$$t \oslash t' = \begin{cases} t & \text{if } t \neq \bot \\ t' & \text{otherwise} \end{cases}$$

Let $\mathcal{B} = (\mathcal{R}, \mathcal{C})$ be a schema where $\mathcal{R} = \{R_i[X_i, K_i]\}_{1 \leq i \leq n}$. Given relation r_i over $R_i[X_i, K_i]$ and tuples $t, t' \in r_i$, we define the operators $\oplus, \ominus$ on t, t' as follows, where $t \oplus t'$ computes a tuple over X_i that contains the nonconflicting atomic tuples in t, t', and $t \ominus t'$ computes a tuple over X_i that contains the atomic tuples in t and the nonconflicting atomic tuples in t'. Suppose that Z is either K_i, or foreign key Y in R_i, or nonkey attribute $A \in X_i$:

$$(t \oplus t')[Z] = t[Z] \otimes t'[Z]$$
$$(t \ominus t')[Z] = t[Z] \oslash t'[Z]$$

Given two relations r_i, r'_i over $R_i[X_i, K_i]$, let $r_i \oplus r'_i$ denote the following relation over $R_i[X_i, K_i]$, which computes the nonconflicting information in r_i, r'_i:

$$\{t \oplus t' | t \in r_i \wedge t' \in r'_i \wedge t[K_i] = t'[K_i]\}$$
$$\cup \{t | t \in r_i \wedge \neg(\exists t')(t' \in r'_i \wedge t'[K_i] = t[K_i])\}$$
$$\cup \{t' | t' \in r'_i \wedge \neg(\exists t)(t \in r_i \wedge t[K_i] = t'[K_i])\}$$

and let $r_i \ominus r'_i$ denote the following relation over $R_i[X_i, K_i]$, which computes the information in r_i and the nonconflicting information in r'_i:

$$\{t \ominus t' | t \in r_i \wedge t' \in r'_i \wedge t[K_i] = t'[K_i]\}$$
$$\cup \{t | t \in r_i \wedge \neg(\exists t')(t' \in r'_i \wedge t'[K_i] = t[K_i])\}$$
$$\cup \{t' | t' \in r'_i \wedge \neg(\exists t)(t \in r_i \wedge t[K_i] = t'[K_i])\}$$

Given two databases $b = \{r_i\}_{1 \leq i \leq n}$ and $b' = \{r'_i\}_{1 \leq i \leq n}$ over $\mathcal{B}$, let $b \oplus b'$ and $b \ominus b'$ denote respectively the databases $\{r_i \oplus r'_i\}_{1 \leq i \leq n}$ and $\{r_i \ominus r'_i\}_{1 \leq i \leq n}$ over $\mathcal{B}$. Figure 2 shows two relations SMD_1 and SMD_2 over the relation scheme SMD of Figure 1, together with $\text{SMD}_1 \oplus \text{SMD}_2$ and $\text{SMD}_1 \ominus \text{SMD}_2$.

SMD$_1$

Starship	MId	Destination
Enterprise	101	Rigel
Voyager	102	Talos

SMD$_2$

Starship	MId	Destination
Enterprise	102	Rigel
Discovery	103	Rigel

SMD$_1 \oplus$ SMD$_2$

Starship	MId	Destination
Enterprise	$\perp$	Rigel
Voyager	102	Talos
Discovery	103	Rigel

SMD$_1 \ominus$ SMD$_2$

Starship	MId	Destination
Enterprise	101	Rigel
Voyager	102	Talos
Discovery	103	Rigel

Figure 2: Filtering Functions

Theorem 1 *For r-valid databases b, b' over $\mathcal{B}$, $b \ominus b'$ is an r-valid database over $\mathcal{B}$ such that $b \sqsubseteq b \ominus b' \sqsubseteq b \cup b'$, and $c \sqsubseteq b \ominus b'$ for every r-valid database c over $\mathcal{B}$ where $b \sqsubseteq c \sqsubseteq b \cup b'$.*

Theorem 1 tells us that $b \ominus b'$ is an r-valid database more informative than b but less informative then $b \cup b'$, and is the (unique) most informative such database.[2] In Figure 2, SMD$_1 \ominus$ SMD$_2$ is more informative than SMD$_1$ because it contains the tuple "(Discovery, 103, Rigel)". It is less informative than SMD$_1 \cup$ SMD$_2$ because it does not contain the atomic tuple "(Enterprise, 102)".

Theorem 2 *For r-valid databases b, b' over $\mathcal{B}$, $b \oplus b'$ is an r-valid database over $\mathcal{B}$ such that $b \oplus b' \sqsubseteq b \cup b'$. For every r-valid database c over $\mathcal{B}$ where $b \oplus b' \sqsubset c \sqsubseteq b \cup b'$, there is an r-valid database c' over $\mathcal{B}$ where $b \oplus b' \sqsubset c' \sqsubseteq b \cup b'$, such that neither $c \sqsubseteq c'$ nor $c' \sqsubseteq c$.*

Theorem 2 tells us that $b \oplus b'$ is an r-valid database less informative than $b \cup b'$. Moreover, any such database that is strictly more informative than $b \oplus b'$ has to involve a random choice: there is another such database that is incomparable in information content. In other words, $b \oplus b'$ is the (unique) most informative such database that does not involve random choices.[2] In Figure 2, SMD$_1 \oplus$ SMD$_2$ is less informative than SMD$_1 \cup$ SMD$_2$ because the MId of Enterprise is missing. Any r-valid database strictly more informative than SMD$_1 \oplus$ SMD$_2$ but no more informative than SMD$_1 \cup$ SMD$_2$ has to contain either "(Enterprise, 101)" or "(Enterprise, 102)" but not both, which involves a random choice between the two.

3 A Model-Theoretic Semantics

We give a formal definition of the multilevel relational model with tuple-level classification. We then formalize the validity of multilevel relational databases,

[2] By restricting ourselves to key-based functional and referential dependencies, such a database always exists, which is not the case for more general integrity constraints.

and identify the multilevel security constraints that precisely characterize the validity.

3.1 Multilevel Relational Model

A *security lattice* $\mathcal{L}$ is a lattice $(L, \preceq)$, where L is a set of *classification levels* and $\preceq$ is the *dominance relation*. A *multilevel relation scheme* is a pair $(R[X, K], \mathcal{L})$, where $R[X, K]$ is a relation scheme and $\mathcal{L}$ is a security lattice. A *multilevel database schema* is a pair $(\mathcal{B}, \mathcal{L})$, where $\mathcal{B}$ is a database schema and $\mathcal{L}$ is a security lattice. Figure 3 shows a security lattice that we use in the rest of the paper.

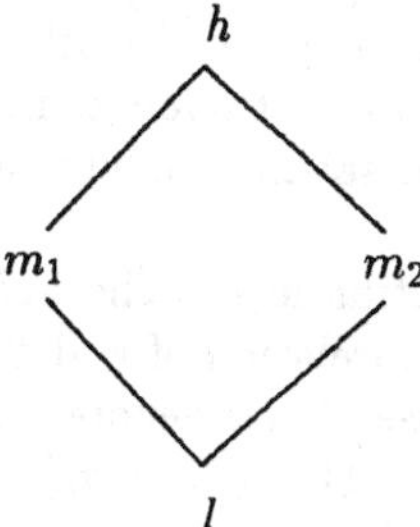

Figure 3: Security Lattice

Let $(\mathcal{B}, \mathcal{L})$ be a multilevel schema where $\mathcal{B} = (\mathcal{R}, \mathcal{C})$, $\mathcal{R} = \{R_i[X_i, K_i]\}_{1 \le i \le n}$, and $\mathcal{L} = (L, \preceq)$. A *multilevel relation* over the multilevel relation scheme $(R_i[X_i, K_i], \mathcal{L})$ is a pair (r_i, κ_i), where r_i is a relation over $R_i[X_i, K_i]$ and κ_i is a mapping from tuples over X_i to sets of classification levels in L, such that $\kappa_i(t) = \{\}$ iff $t \notin r_i$, and $l \in \kappa_i(t)$ if t is classified at $l \in L$. A *multilevel database* over multilevel database schema $(\mathcal{B}, \mathcal{L})$ is a family of multilevel relations $\{(r_i, \kappa_i)\}_{1 \le i \le n}$, where (r_i, κ_i) is a multilevel relation over $(R_i[X_i, K_i], \mathcal{L})$. We denote it by the pair (b, κ), where $b = \{r_i\}_{1 \le i \le n}$ is a database over $\mathcal{B}$, and $\kappa = \{\kappa_i\}_{1 \le i \le n}$ is a family of mappings. Figure 4 shows a multilevel database over the schema of Figure 1 and the security lattice of Figure 3. The classification level of every tuple is listed to the right of that tuple.[3]

A multilevel relation (r_i, κ_i) satisfies the *polyinstantiation security property* if for every pair of tuples $t, t' \in r_i$ and classification level l where $l \in \kappa_i(t), l \in \kappa_i(t')$, we have that $t[K_i] = t'[K_i]$ implies $t = t'$. In other words, tuples classified at the same level should satisfy all the functional dependencies. A multilevel database (b, κ) satisfies the polyinstantiation security property if every multilevel relation in (b, κ) does.

A multilevel relation (r_i, κ_i) satisfies the *referential security property* if, for every referential dependency $R_i[Y] \hookrightarrow R_j$ in $\mathcal{C}$, tuple $t \in r_i$, and classification

[3] A tuple could in general be classified at multiple levels, although every tuple is classified at exactly one level in this example.

Starship	MId	Destination	
Enterprise	101	$\perp$	h
Enterprise	102	Rigel	m_1
Enterprise	103	Rigel	m_2
Voyager	102	Rigel	m_1
Voyager	102	Talos	m_2
Discovery	103	Rigel	l

MissionId	Type	
101	spy	m_1
102	explore	l
103	mine	l

Figure 4: A Multilevel Database

level $l \in \kappa_i(t)$, there is a tuple $t' \in r_j$ and a classification level $l' \in \kappa_j(t')$ such that $t[Y] = t'[K_j]$ and $l' \preceq^* l$. In other words, every foreign key value dominates the primary key value it refers to in terms of classification. The multilevel database of Figure 4 satisfies polyinstantiation and referential security properties.

Let $l \in L$ be a classification level. The *l-slice* of multilevel relation (r_i, κ_i), denoted as $\sigma_l(r_i, \kappa_i)$, is a subrelation of r_i defined as $\{t | t \in r_i \wedge l \in \kappa_i(t)\}$. The *l-slice* of multilevel database (b, κ), denoted as $\sigma_l(b, \kappa)$, is a subdatabase of b defined as $\{\sigma_l(r_i, \kappa_i)\}_{1 \leq i \leq n}$. The l-slices $\sigma_l(r_i, \kappa_i)$ and $\sigma_l(b, \kappa)$ are respectively a single-level relation and database collecting all tuples in r_i and b that are classified at l. The h-slice of the multilevel database of Figure 4 consists of the first tuple in SMD and no tuples of MT.

3.2 Validity and Views

Intuitively a database represents one view of a state of the world (perceived world [9]), while a multilevel database represents multiple views of a multilevel state of the world — one for every classification level. Furthermore, these multiple views are related by the security lattice. Contained in the view at a level are tuples believable at that level. Consequently integrity should be enforced within each view, rather than across multiple views.

What tuples belong to the view at a classification level? First, all tuples classified at that level should be part of the view. Second, for tuples classified below that level, as many of them as possible should be part of the view as long as integrity is preserved, in order to maximize sharing. Third, in case that either but not both of two low tuples could be in a high view, neither of them should be in the high view, because the high view lacks further information to justify the preference of one over the other. In other words, integrity constraints serve as a filter on how much low data could flow high.

Formally let $(b, \kappa) = \{(r_i, \kappa_i)\}_{1 \leq i \leq n}$ be a multilevel database over multilevel schema $(\mathcal{B}, \mathcal{L})$ where $\mathcal{B} = (\mathcal{R}, \mathcal{C}), \mathcal{R} = \{R_i[X_i, K_i]\}_{1 \leq i \leq n}$, and $\mathcal{L} = (L, \preceq)$. Also let $l \in L$ be a classification level. The *l-validity* of (b, κ) and the *l-view* of (b, κ), denoted as $\varsigma_l(b, \kappa) = \{\varsigma_l(r_i, \kappa_i)\}_{1 \leq i \leq n}$ where $\varsigma_l(r_i, \kappa_i)$ is the *l-view* of (r_i, κ_i), are defined recursively as follows.

- Suppose that l is the bottom level of $\mathcal{L}$. Define $\varsigma_l(b,\kappa) = \sigma_l(b,\kappa)$. If $\sigma_l(b,\kappa)$ is valid, then (b,κ) is l-valid. Otherwise (b,κ) is not l-valid.

- Suppose that l is not the bottom level of $\mathcal{L}$. Let b_H be $\sigma_l(b,\kappa)$ and b_L be $\oplus_{l' \prec_l} \varsigma_{l'}(b,\kappa)$. Also let b_U be $b_H \ominus b_L$. Define $\varsigma_l(b,\kappa) = b_U$. If b_U is valid then (b,κ) is l-valid. Otherwise (b,κ) is not l-valid.

Multilevel database (b,κ) is *valid* if it is l-valid for every classification level $l \in L$. Notice that the l-views of (r_i, κ_i) and (b,κ) are respectively a single-level relation and database.

The above definition formalizes our intuition about views. All atomic tuples classified at level l are part of the l-view since $b_H \sqsubseteq \varsigma_l(b,\kappa)$ according to Theorem 1. For atomic tuples classified below level l, as many of them as possible are part of the l-view since they are part of b_U according to Theorem 1. In case that either but not both of two atomic tuples classified below level l could be in the l-view, neither is in the l-view since neither would be in b_L according to Theorem 2. The multilevel database of Figure 4 is valid, and its h-view is shown in Figure 5.

Starship	MId	Destination
Enterprise	101	Rigel
Voyager	102	$\perp$
Discovery	103	Rigel

MissionId	Type
101	spy
102	explore
103	mine

Figure 5: h-view

Our model-theoretic semantics coincides with the Bell-LaPadula model for primary key values, in the sense that all low primary key values are part of the high view. In the extreme case that there are no integrity constraints (i.e., $X_i = K_i$ for $1 \le i \le n$ and C is empty), our model-theoretic semantics completely coincides with the Bell-LaPadula model, in the sense that all low tuples are part of the high view, since $\varsigma_l(b,\kappa) = \bigcup_{l' \preceq^* l} \sigma_{l'}(b,\kappa)$.

Our model-theoretic semantics of the multilevel relational model is an extension of the Bell-LaPadula model, in the sense that we distinguish between two kinds of low data: those that are believable high (e.g., the atomic tuple "(Enterprise, Rigel)"), and those that are accessible but not believable high (because they violate integrity constraints when combined with high data) (e.g., the atomic tuple "(Enterprise, 102)"). Integrity is enforced only on believable low data.

Let f_l be the number of levels immediately dominated by l, and f be $\max\{f_l | l \in L\}$. For multilevel relation (r_i, κ_i), the size of its l-slice $\sigma_l(r_i, \kappa_i)$ and l-view $\varsigma_l(r_i, \kappa_i)$ is bounded by $O(|r_i|)$. The cost of computing $\varsigma_l(r_i, \kappa_i)$ for bottom level is bounded by $O(|L| \times |r_i|)$. For nonbottom level l, the cost of computing b_H is bounded by $O(|L| \times |r_i|)$, the cost of computing b_L is bounded by $O(|r_i|^f)$, and the cost of computing b_U is bounded by $O(|r_i|^2)$. Assuming that $|L| \ll |r_i|$ and $2 \ll f$, the cost of computing $\varsigma_l(r_i, \kappa_i)$ is bounded by $O(|L_l| \times |r_i|^f)$, where L_l is the set of levels dominated by l.

3.3 Validity Checking

Given a multilevel database, straightforward validity checking based on the recursive definition of validity is likely to be expensive, because it involves computing views for all classification levels and checking their validity. Luckily, multilevel validity could be equivalently characterized by multilevel security properties, whose computation is comparable in complexity to integrity checking in single-level databases.

Let $(\mathcal{B}, \mathcal{L})$ be a multilevel schema where $\mathcal{B} = (\mathcal{R}, \mathcal{C})$, $\mathcal{R} = \{R_i[X_i, K_i]\}_{1 \leq i \leq n}$, and $\mathcal{L} = (L, \preceq)$. Also let $l \in L$, and $(b, \kappa) = \{(r_i, \kappa_i)\}_{1 \leq i \leq n}$ be a multilevel database over $(\mathcal{B}, \mathcal{L})$ where (r_i, κ_i) is a multilevel relation over $(R_i[X_i, K_i], \mathcal{L})$.

Lemma 3 *Suppose that $\varsigma_l(b, \kappa) = \{r_i^l\}_{1 \leq i \leq n}$. For every $t \in r_i^l$, there is $t' \in r_i$ and $l' \in \kappa_i(t')$ such that $t[K_i] = t'[K_i]$ and $l' \preceq^* l$.*

Lemma 3 tells us that every primary key value in an l-view comes from some tuple classified at or below l. In other words, if a tuple is not classified at or below l, then its primary key value could not appear in the l-view. For example, the primary key value "Discovery" in the h-view of Figure 5 comes from the tuple "(Discovery, 103, Rigel)" of Figure 4, which is classified at l.

Theorem 4 *A multilevel database is valid iff it satisfies polyinstantiation and referential security properties.*

Theorem 4 tells us that view computation is not necessary for validity checking. For example, the multilevel database of Figure 4 is valid because it satisfies polyinstantiation and referential security properties. Furthermore, validity checking in multilevel databases is comparable in complexity to that in single-level databases. The cost of checking polyinstantiation security in multilevel relation (r_i, κ_i) is bounded by $O(|L|^2 \times |r_i|^2)$, while the cost of checking key integrity in single-level relation r_i is bounded by $O(|r_i|^2)$. For $R_i[Y] \hookrightarrow R_j$ in $\mathcal{C}$, the cost of checking referential security in multilevel database (b, κ) is bounded by $O(|L|^3 \times |r_i| \times |r_j|)$, while the cost of checking referential integrity in single-level database b is bounded by $O(|r_i| \times |r_j|)$.

4 Conclusion

We developed a model-theoretic semantics of the multilevel relational model with tuple-level classification, which formalizes the notion of validity in multilevel relational databases for the limited but most common class of integrity constraints — key-based functional and referential dependencies. We also identified the multilevel security constraints that precisely characterize the validity of multilevel relational databases. Our model-theoretic semantics is consistent with, and extends, the Bell-LaPadula model. Compared with existing approaches, our model-theoretic semantics maximizes believability without compromising integrity or introducing ambiguity.

Contrary to the claim that integrity and secrecy are in fundamental conflict [1, 8, 15], our results demonstrate that integrity and secrecy could live harmoniously with each other: a multilevel relational database does not have to sacrifice one for the other. Moreover, validity checking in multilevel relational databases is comparable to that in single-level relational databases in terms of complexity. Instead of developing special-purpose integrity techniques for multilevel databases, we could readily adopt those from single-level databases.

Several logical extensions of this work are possible. First of all, we could consider classes of integrity constraints that are more general than key-based functional and referential dependencies. Such extensions must be made with great care however, since it might become impossible to maximize believability without choosing arbitrarily what low tuples to believe at high, as we can see from the examples in Section 1. Secondly, information in a multilevel state of the world might include the metaknowledge that relates the knowledge at multiple classification levels, such as the polyinstantiation and referential security properties of Section 3. The notion of validity needs to be extended. A view at a classification level should not only be valid in terms of the knowledge at that level, but also be consistent with views at other levels in terms of the metaknowledge. The complexity of validity checking is likely to increase significantly, because cross-level metaknowledge interacts with single-level knowledge in complicated ways, as Theorem 4 shows. Finally, we could extend our approach to the multilevel relational model with element-level classification, based on the connection between the two classification schemes established in [11].

Acknowledgment

The author is indebted to Teresa Lunt, Tom Garvey, Mark Stickel, Marianne Winslett, Ken Smith, and Bhavani Thuraisingham for helpful discussions.

References

[1] R. K. Burns, "Integrity and Secrecy: Fundamental Conflicts in the Database Environment"; *Proceedings of the Third RADC Database Security Workshop*, 1990, 37-40.

[2] S. Jajodia and R. Sandhu, "Polyinstantiation Integrity in Multilevel Relations"; *Proceedings of the 1990 IEEE Symposium on Security and Privacy*, 1990, 104-115.

[3] S. Jajodia and R. Sandhu, "Toward a Multilevel Secure Relational Data Model"; *Proceedings of the ACM SIGMOD International Conference on Management of Data*, 1991, 50-59.

[4] C. E. Landwehr, "Formal Models for Computer Security"; *ACM Computing Surveys* **13**:3, September 1981, 247-278.

[5] T. F. Lunt, "The True Meaning of Polyinstantiation: Proposal for an Operational Semantics for a Multilevel Relational Database System"; *Proceedings of the Third RADC Database Security Workshop*, 1990, 26-36.

[6] T. F. Lunt, "Polyinstantiation: An Inevitable Part of a Multilevel World"; *Proceedings of the Fourth IEEE Workshop on Computer Security Foundations*, 1991, 236-238.

[7] T. F. Lunt, D. E. Denning, R. R. Schell, M. Heckman, and W. R. Shockley, "The SeaView Security Model"; *IEEE Transactions on Software Engineering* **16**:6, June 1990, 593-607.

[8] C. Meadows and S. Jajodia, "Integrity versus Security in Multilevel Secure Databases"; *Database Security: Status and Prospects*, C. E. Landwehr (editor), North-Holland, 1988, 89-101.

[9] J-M. Nicolas and H. Gallaire, "Data Base: Theory vs. Interpretation"; *Logic and Databases*, H. Gallaire and J. Minker (editors), Plenum Press, 1978, 33-54.

[10] X. Qian, "A Model-Theoretic Semantics of the Multilevel Secure Relational Model"; *Technical Report*, Computer Science Laboratory, SRI International, 1993.

[11] X. Qian and T. F. Lunt, "Tuple-Level vs. Element-Level Classification"; *Database Security, VI: Status and Prospects*, B. M. Thuraisingham and C. E. Landwehr (editors), North-Holland, 1993, 301-315.

[12] R. Sandhu, S. Jajodia, and T. F. Lunt, "A New Polyinstantiation Integrity Constraint for Multilevel Relations"; *Proceedings of the Third IEEE Workshop on Computer Security Foundations*, 1990, 159-165.

[13] K. Smith and M. Winslett, "Entity Modeling in the MLS Relational Model"; *Proceedings of the Eighteenth International Conference on Very Large Data Bases*, 1992, 199-210.

[14] B. M. Thuraisingham, "A Nonmonotonic Typed Multilevel Logic for Multilevel Secure Database/Knowledge-Base Management Systems"; *Proceedings of the Fourth IEEE Workshop on Computer Security Foundations*, 1991, 127-138.

[15] S. Wiseman, "The Control of Integrity in Databases"; *Database Security, IV: Status and Prospects*, S. Jajodia and C. E. Landwehr (editors), North-Holland, 1991, 191-204.

On the Semantics of (Bi)Temporal Variable Databases

James Clifford and Tomás Isakowitz

Leonard N. Stern School of Business
New York University, New York, NY 10012-1126

Abstract. Numerous proposals for extending the relational data model to incorporate the temporal dimension of data have appeared during the past several years. These have ranged from *historical data models*, incorporating a *valid time* dimension, to *rollback data models*, incorporating a *transaction time* dimension, to *bitemporal data models*, incorporating both of these temporal dimensions. Many of these models have been presented in a non-traditional fashion, allowing the use of *variables* at the instance level. Unfortunately, the precise semantics of these database objects, e.g. tuples, with variables has not been made clear. In this paper we propose a framework for providing a formal specification of the precise semantics of this type of database, which we call a *variable database*. In addition, since more than one possible interpretation can be given to the specific temporal variables , such as *now* and ∞, which have appeared in the literature, we discuss several alternative semantics that can be given to these *temporal variable databases* incorporating one or more of these variables. We also present a constraint on the way such databases are allowed to evolve in time if they are to support a rollback operator.

1 Introduction

There have been numerous temporal database models proposed in the literature, incorporating one and sometimes two of the temporal dimensions to data which have been identified as important in data modeling of temporal information. These two temporal dimensions to data are defined in [13] as follows. The *valid time* of a fact is defined as the time when the fact is true in the modeled reality, and the *transaction time* of a database fact as the time when the fact is stored in the database. The majority of these models (e.g. [16, 2, 7, 1, 25, 4, 18, 21, 24, 10, 23]) have incorporated only the valid time dimension. A far fewer number, the *transaction-time* or *rollback* data models, have incorporated only the transaction time dimension (e.g. [11, 17].) Finally, the *bitemporal* data models, such as [2, 24, 19, 9], have incorporated both dimensions,

In examining all of these temporal database proposals, it is clear that two different *types* of models have been proposed. The first type, which we call *extensional* models, have been presented in the traditional manner. These models have either been presented as logical models directly, such as [5], or have been presented in such a way that their logical model was clear. This type of model essentially accords with the view expressed in [22] that a relational database can be seen as a set of ground first-order formulae, for which there is a minimal model.

However, many of the proposed models have not been specified in this tradition. Rather than being presented as a set of *ground atomic formulae*, these models have been presented a set of formulae some of which are ground, but others of which have included one or more *free variables*. Chief among these variables have been "*now*" (used, for example in [4, 10, 6]) and "∞" (used in [24]), but "*uc*" (in [26]) and "*forever*" have also been used or proposed. Clearly, these approaches have advantages at the implementation level, namely, they are space efficient and avoid the need for updates at every moment in time. However, nowhere have we found a clear exposition of these symbols, i.e., nowhere has the semantics of this type of database – a database with free variables – been formally specified so that the logical model represented by the database was clear. Because the symbols chosen already suggest an *intuitive* meaning to many readers, their informal use has led many to suppose that they understood their semantics. However, this reliance on intuition has led to much confusion, as we shall discuss in Section 2. Moreover, such data models generally include a query language and data manipulation language, whose semantics are generally specified in terms of an algorithm that generate a resulting relation. The question naturally arises, what is the correctness criterion for this algorithm if the precise semantics of neither the data model nor the language is provided?

We would like to call these models with free variables *intensional* models (because that is essentially what they are) but hesitate to use this already overloaded term. Instead we call them *variable databases*. The lack of a formal specification of the semantics of these *variable databases* is the chief motivation for this paper. In order to provide a precise semantics for these variable databases, we introduce a fully extensional bitemporal data model in Section 3. This model is fully ground, i.e. it does not admit variables. It is clearly space inefficient, and thus we emphasize that it is *not intended to be used as an implementation* of bitemporal databases. We then show how this fully extensional logical model can serve as the reference point to provide this semantics for these variable database models, and establish the correctness criterion for their query languages, as shown in Figure 1.

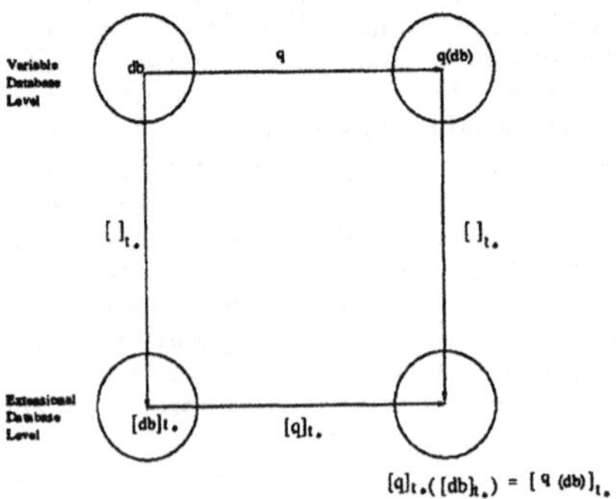

Fig. 1. Relationship Between Variable Database and Extensional Database

The top level of the figure, labeled *Variable Database Level*, represents some variable database model, e.g., TQuel ([24]). The presentation of many of these models has focussed on the structure of a database *db* in the model, and the definition of some query language for the model. In the Figure we see a particular variable database *db* being mapped by some query q to another variable database $q(db)$ (or, alternatively, by some operation Θ to another variable database $\Theta(db)$). The lower half of the figure, labeled *Extensional Database Level*, represents our fully extensional bitemporal data model, whose semantics is well-specified in the standard tradition of a first-order logical framework. In order for the semantics of variable databases (such as *db*) and queries or operations (q or Θ) on variable databases to be well-specified, a mapping between the two levels needs to be defined. This mapping, which we call $[]_{t_*}$, is a mapping from variable databases to extensional databases. At any particular time t_*, which we call the *reference time* (see Section 5), it provides the interpretation of any variable symbols (such as *now*) which are allowed at the Variable Database Level, and establishes the correctness criterion for the operational semantics at the Variable Database Level, namely, that the diagram in Figure 1 must commute, i.e., $[q]_{t_*}([db]_{t_*}) = [q(db)]_{t_*}$

In the remainder of this paper we will address the issues that we have touched upon in this introduction.

2 Problems with Variable Databases

In the literature of temporal database models, two different *types* of models have been proposed. Those models which we call *extensional* models, have been presented in the traditional manner. For example, in the traditional relational database model a database consists of a set of relation schemas such as **FACULTY** (*NAME RANK*), and a set of *base domains* for every attributes in every relation scheme. The **FACULTY** relation scheme would admit relations consisting of tuples such as $< Jane, Full >$ and $< Merrie, Assistant >$. An historical data model defined in the relational framework might allow for relation schemes such as **FACULTY** (*NAME RANK TIME*) and therefore admit relations consisting of tuples such as $< Jane, Full, 11\text{-}80 >$ and $< Merrie, Assistant, 9\text{-}77 >$. These models are fully *extensional* – each relation consists of a set of tuples *all of whose values come from some base domain.* In his classic work relating databases to first-order logic, [22] shows how such a (relational) database can be seen as a set of ground first-order formulae, for which there is a minimal model.

If, however, a model admits tuples such as $< X, Full, 11\text{-}80 >$ or $< Jane, X, 11\text{-}80 >$, or $< Jane, Full, X >$, then in order to understand the semantics of such tuples with *variables* it is necessary to state the exact interpretation of these variables. Unfortunately, the literature of temporal database abounds with proposals for models that include temporal variables, without a precise explication of their semantics.

Moreover, such data models generally include a query language and data manipulation language, whose semantics are generally specified in terms of an algorithm that generates a resulting relation. The question naturally arises, what is the correctness criterion for this algorithm if the precise semantics of neither the data model nor the language are provided? A fully extensional logical model is needed as the reference point to provide this semantics, in the manner illustrated in Figure 1.

Consider, for example, a typical bitemporal relation as shown in Figure 2. (This particular example is taken from [24], and is intended only to serve as a generic example of a bitemporal database with variables.) Note that it makes use of the special variable symbol "∞" in both the transaction time and valid time dimensions. Several problems arise with the use of the ∞ variable.

FACULTY					
		VALID-TIME		TRANS-TIME	
NAME	RANK	(from)	(to)	(start)	(stop)
Jane	*Assistant*	*9-71*	*12-76*	*9-71*	∞
Jane	*Associate*	*12-76*	*11-80*	*12-76*	∞
Jane	*Full*	*11-80*	∞	*10-80*	∞
Merrie	*Assistant*	*9-77*	*12-82*	*8-77*	∞
Merrie	*Associate*	*12-82*	∞	*12-82*	∞
Tom	*Associate*	*9-75*	∞	*8-75*	*10-75*
Tom	*Assistant*	*9-75*	*12-80*	*10-75*	∞
Tom	*Associate*	*12-80*	∞	*11-80*	∞

Fig. 2. The Faculty Relation

First, the meaning of the "∞" variable is not clear. At an intuitive level, ∞ conveys the meaning of *forever*. It would seem that the symbol "∞" in the valid time predicts that Jane will be a Full Professor throughout eternity. The use of "∞" in the transaction time seems to anticipate future database transactions. Obviously, neither of these two interpretations is intended. Second, although the same notation is used both for *valid time* and for *transaction time*, they are different variables. In the valid time dimension, "∞", probably means "up to the present moment", whereas the intention of "∞" in transaction time is "until further notice." The use of the same variable in both dimensions is confusing, since it implies that they mean the same thing. Lastly, since the meaning of the variables is given indirectly through the definitions of database operators rather than declaratively, it is not clear whether the database operations (insert, delete, update) are well specified or, indeed, correct. For example, looking at the tuple $< Merrie, Assistant, 9\text{-}77, 12\text{-}82, 8\text{-}77, \infty >$ it is not clear what the database recorded at time 8-77. Did the database predict that *Merrie* would no longer be an *Assistant* professor in *December of 82*? Or did this only become known in *December of 82*, when the tuple $< Merrie, Associate, 12\text{-}82, \infty, 12\text{-}82, \infty >$ was added?

In this paper we present a formal model that resolves the first two issues, and by doing so also creates a framework within which to resolve the third issue. We also define a Rollback Evolution Constraint that database operations should satisfy in order to enable rollbacks to past database states. We define a timeslice operator and prove that under this constraint it can serve as such a rollback operator. We will have frequent occasion to refer to this Faculty example. Since it is notationally simpler to work with integer times (1, 2, 3, etc.) instead of dates, we will refer throughout the rest of the paper to Figure 3, which represents the same information as Figure 2, but with the dates replaced by an integer.

FACULTY					
		VALID-TIME		*TRANS-TIME*	
NAME	*RANK*	*(from)*	*(to)*	*(start)*	*(stop)*
Jane	Assistant	1	5	1	∞
Jane	Associate	5	9	5	∞
Jane	Full	9	∞	8	∞
Merrie	Assistant	7	11	6	∞
Merrie	Associate	11	∞	11	∞
Tom	Associate	3	∞	2	4
Tom	Assistant	3	10	4	∞
Tom	Associate	10	∞	9	∞

Fig. 3. The Faculty Relation Recast

3 An Extensional Model for Bitemporal Databases

In order to provide a model that treats valid time, transaction time and the relationships between them, we need to have one, underlying notion of time to serve as our temporal universe. The granularity of the two time dimensions may be different, but it would not make sense to have completely different models of time for these two dimensions, for example, to view one of these as discrete and the other as continuous. For in such a case it would not be possible to express queries about the interaction between these two temporal dimensions – for example, *Which faculty members received a retroactive change in rank?*, i.e., for whom the valid time of their change in rank precedes the transaction time recording the change. Such queries are clearly one of the goals of using a bitemporal database. Since most database researchers have adopted the view that valid time in a database is best viewed as discrete, and every database transaction model that we are aware of has this property, we will adopt a discrete model of time here.

3.1 The Temporal Universe

Let T be our *temporal universe*, and let T satisfy the following properties:

1. T is countably infinite,
2. T is totally ordered by a relation, which we will symbolize by $<$.
3. T contains distinguished elements, $\top$ and $\bot$, such that $\forall t \in T[\bot \leq t \leq \top]$. Intuitively, $\bot$ and $\top$ correspond to $-\infty$ and ∞.

In other words, T is isomorphic to the set of integers $I = \{\bot\} \cup \{\ldots, -2, -1, 0, +1, +2, \ldots\} \cup \{\top\}$. (If an infinite past is not required, the natural numbers N could be used instead of the integers.)

A bitemporal database needs domains for two temporal universes, the ***valid time universe*** and the ***transaction time universe***, and it may be desirable or convenient to restrict them to some subset of T. Therefore, let

- $T_{VT} \subseteq T$ denote the *valid time universe* of our database, and
- $T_{TT} \subseteq T$ denote its *transaction time universe*.

Whenever we discuss a particular database instance, three moments in time are of particular interest. The first of these is what we may call the *birth* of the database, i.e., that time in T_{TT} when the first transaction occurs for the database. We can, if we like, think of this as the transaction that inserts the first tuple, or even as the transaction that creates the database schema. Let us denote this time by t_0. The second moment in time is the *reference time*, denoted by t_*, used to refer to the state of the database at some particular time in its history. The time t_0 is important because it constrains the time t_*. To simplify the discussion that follows, we will assume that t_0 is a *single* value for all of the relations in any given database. The third moment in time of special interest is the moment at which we issue some operation or query on the database. We denote this time by t_{now}. Clearly, we have the following constraints on these three times: $\bot \leq t_* \leq \top$, and $\bot \leq t_0 \leq t_{now} \leq \top$. More specifically, for references to transaction time, (i) $t_0 \leq t_* \leq t_{now}$, and for references to valid time, (ii) $\bot \leq t_* \leq \top$

Note that t_{now} is the time at which an operation or query is performed, whereas t_* is the time at which we would like to evaluate or "observe" the database.

3.2 Extensional Representation of Bitemporal Values

A simple and convenient extensional representation for bitemporal attribute values can be obtained by using sets of *ground* tuples of the form < vt,tt,a >. In order to do this, however, we need to understand the meaning of any variable symbols that may appear in our database. The set of triplets in Table 1 represents the value of the *RANK* attribute for all of Tom's tuples in the **FACULTY** relation of Figure 3. We will call the set of all of these tuples for a given "object" in a relation (e.g., "Tom") an ***attribute history***[1]. Although the representation does not make it explicit, the value **r** of *RANK* is a function of *tt* and *vt*, i.e., for each pair of values < *vt*, *tt* > there is exactly one entry (vt,tt,r) in the table. This representation provides a homogeneous treatment of the transaction time and valid time dimensions.

(3,2,Associate)
(4,2,Associate)
(5,2,Associate)
...
(⊤,2,Associate)
(3,3,Associate)
(4,3,Associate)
(5,3,Associate)
...
(⊤,3,Associate)
(3,4,Assistant)
(4,4,Assistant)
...
(9,4,Assistant)
etc.

Table 1. The extensional representation of Tom's rank.

Note that the table represents the value of just one attribute, *RANK*, of one tuple in the **FACULTY** relation. The complete tuple for Tom is portrayed by two such tables, the one for *RANK* we just discussed, and another one for *NAME*. The complete **FACULTY** relation, therefore, would be represented in this fashion by a set of these *NAME* and *RANK* table pairs, one pair for each faculty member.

Whenever we want to refer to the value of an attribute *A* in a tuple *t* in a bitemporal relation *r*, we use the notation: *r.t.A*. Hence, an attribute history is given by *r.t.A*, which

[1] We oversimplify here, and ignore the distinction made in [5] between grouped and ungrouped temporal data models. For simplicity we assume, as in [24], that the key attribute *NAME* does not change over time, and therefore can serve to locate all of the tuples for a given "object" such as, here, a faculty member.

consists of a set of triples of the form (vt, tt, a). Using this notation, Table 1 represents the attribute history **FACULTY**.*tom.rank*, where *tom* denotes the tuple for Tom.

Taken literally, the use of "∞" in the definition of the **FACULTY** relation results in an infinite set of triplets for Tom's *RANK* attribute. As is apparent from this discussion, the use of symbols such as "∞" complicates the ground model. It is not clear at all that the representation of Table 1 is correct, i.e., that it accurately represents the information implied in the database by the variable symbol "∞".

We will call a representation of the database at this level an *extensional database*, in contrast to the *extensional level* shown in Figures 2 and 3. Thus, at the extensional level, the database contains sets of ground tuples. This is consistent with current semantic models for databases [22] and is useful in defining the behavior of the database. A central concern of this paper is the development, in Section 5, of the relationship between the variable and extensional views of a database.

3.3 Graphical Representation of Bitemporal Relations

In our investigations on bitemporal databases, we have found the graphical notation that we are about to explain quite useful for various reasons. Firstly, its visual appeal is intuitive, and this makes bitemporal concepts easier to grasp. Each time dimension corresponds to an axis: transaction time is the X-axis, valid time is the Y-axis. This allows us to represent passage of time as spatial displacement, and provides a visual representation for interesting phenomena such as history changes and predictions about the future. Secondly, the graphs explicitly provide a uniform representation of both time dimensions. Thirdly, the graphical representation makes explicit the differences in various treatments of time in temporal databases. As we will see in Section 5.1, the graphical representation clearly shows that the assumptions that values hold until *now*, or until *infinity* or *until-changed* are quite different. Lastly, although it may be hard to visualize graphs with more than two dimensions, the uniform treatment we present here can be nonetheless easily extended to more dimensions. Thus, our framework can be extended to encompass multi-dimensional temporal databases, for example indexical databases ([3]). A variation of these graphs has been independently explored by Jensen and Snodgrass [15, 12].

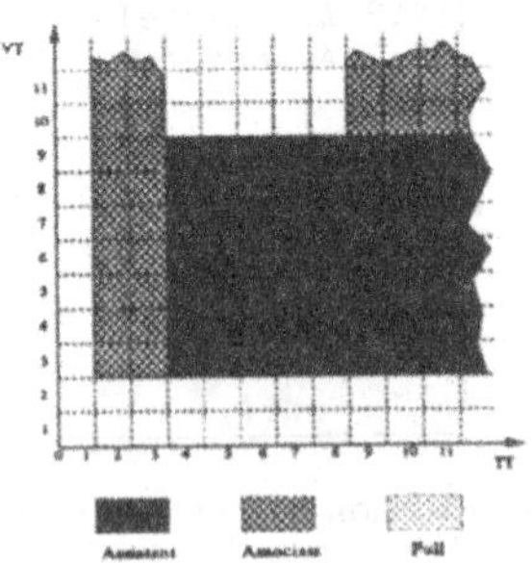

Fig. 4. A graphical representation of the bitemporal *rank* attribute for Tom in the **FACULTY** relation.

Figure 4 represents the *RANK* attribute history of Tom in the **FACULTY** relation. The ragged edges in a particular dimension indicate that the area extends in that dimension to *"infinity"*. In the graphical representation, each attribute history is assigned a graph. Thus the information about an object such as faculty member Tom is viewed with two graphs: one for the *NAME* attribute and another for the *RANK*. Alternatively, different colors can be used for the various attributes, thereby plotting all attributes onto the same graph[2]. For the purposes of this paper, it will suffice to concentrate on one attribute at a time.

[2] This would only be possible in a *homogeneous* model which assumes that all attributes in a tuple have the same lifespan.

Each cell in the graph stands for a particular transaction time, tt, and a particular valid time, vt. As indicated in the "key" to Figure 4, the cell's hue of grey represents the value of the $RANK$ corresponding to the $< vt, tt >$ combination. For example, at $tt = 2, vt = 3$, Tom's rank is **Associate**; and for $tt = 8, vt = 9$ it is **Assistant**. In fact, although the graph is bi-dimensional, it represents tri-dimensional information since it plots points of the form $< vt, tt, rank >$, where the domain of $rank$ is $\{Assistant, Associate, Full\}$.

The vertical dimension, valid time, represents historical data, namely how the value of an attribute changed over time in the real world. A vertical column, for example, the column for $tt = 11$, shows the attribute's history as recorded by the database. In this case, at $tt = 11$, the database recorded that Tom was an Assistant Professor from time 3 through 9, and an Associate from time 10 onwards.

The horizontal dimension, transaction time, captures the changing database perceptions about a particular time in the real world. For example, the horizontal row for $vt = 3$ shows that for transaction times 2 through 3, the database recorded Tom's rank as **Associate**, but subsequently recorded it as **Assistant**, through *"infinity"*. The change in hue along the horizontal row for $vt = 3$ captures this change in perception.

The diagonal of the graph, which corresponds to (tt, vt) where $tt = vt = x$, captures information about what the database records at time x about time x in the real world. (This is what is captured by the so called *snapshot* databases.) Any cells above the diagonal represent predictions, because the tt is earlier than the vt. Any cells below the diagonal record database perceptions about the past, because the vt is earlier than the tt. Not all graphs for bitemporal relations need to correspond to contiguous rectangular shapes. Jensen and Snodgrass [14] provide a more detailed analysis of the various regions in this space, introducing a comprehensive taxonomy of the spatial representation of various temporal concepts.

4 The Variable and Extensional Database Levels

For at least two reasons, temporal database models presented in the literature have tended to utilize *variables* such as ∞ in their representation schemes. In the valid time dimension, these variables have been used because the values of many attributes frequently do not change over long periods of time. In the transaction time dimension, they have been used because as the reference time moves inexorably forward – as the clock on the wall "ticks" – for most of these "ticks" the database does not change state, and so it is inefficient to store multiple copies of the same, unchanged information.

While there have been various schemes proposed in the literature for this, it is unfortunate that the semantics of these schemes has seldom been clearly presented. It has therefore been unclear whether and how these schemes differ, or if in fact some of them are the same. Figure 5 presents a number of these schemes, namely: interval representations, *now*, ∞, and *uc*.

NAME	*RANK*	*VALID-TIME*	*TRANS-TIME*
Tom	Assistant	$[3, 10)$	$[4, 10)$
Mary	Associate	$[3, \infty)$	$[2, 4)$
Mary	Assistant	$[3, 10)$	$[4, \infty)$
Henry	Associate	$[3, now)$	$[2, 4)$
Henry	Assistant	$[3, 10)$	$[4, now)$
Patricia	Associate	$[3, uc)$	$[2, 4)$
Patricia	Assistant	$[3, 10)$	$[4, uc)$

Fig. 5. Shorthand Representation Schemes

It is logic that can provide an answer to the question of what, precisely, these various notations mean. Specifically, we want to look at the *extensional model* that is intended by each of these representation shorthands, for on this level we are able to deal with questions of truth and validity. In order to do this we need to understand the role of the variables in these representations.

An extensional model specifies the value of every predicate, *for every moment* in the universe of times T. If a shorthand notation is used, with special symbols such as *now*, the model is *incompletely specified* unless the meaning of these symbols is given, i.e., unless it is possible to uniquely determine what *extensional model* is being defined. For this reason, we will introduce the *extensionalization* mapping, $[]_{t_*}$, depicted in Figure 1 of Section 1. This mapping transforms a variable database db into an extensional database $[db]_{t_*}$ for a particular time t_*.

Given our universe of times T, linearly ordered and discrete, it is clear that the first tuple in Figure 5, which uses no variables, corresponds to the extensional model given in Figure 6. The interpretation of the other tuples, which *do* utilize variable symbols, is more problematic. Earlier, in Table 1, we showed what we assumed to be the extensional model for Tom's rank in Figure 2, using the ∞ scheme.

(3,4,Assistant)
(4,4,Assistant)
(3,5,Assistant)
(4,5,Assistant)
(5,5,Assistant)
(3,6,Assistant)
...
(9,9,Assistant)

Fig. 6. Extensional Model of Intervals

4.1 Reference Time

There is one additional time that needs to be introduced, a time we shall call the *reference time*, a term analogous to the *indices* or "points of reference" in intensional logic (Montague [20]), and discussed more recently in the context of historical databases in [8]. Like all databases, a temporal database exists in time. When we want to refer to the state of the database at some particular time in its history, we call this time the *reference time*, which we denote by t_*. The intent is to be able to denote what an observer looking at the database at time t_* would see. For the same reason that motivates the comparability of transaction times with valid times, we will also want the reference times to be drawn from our same universe of times.

It is useful to view temporal database – and indeed each relation in it – as "indexed" by time, i.e., the to view the database as a trajectory of database states (or instances) through time: $db_{t_0} \rightarrow db_{t_0+1} \rightarrow \cdots \rightarrow db_{t_{now}}$ Moreover, each relation r can likewise be viewed as: $r_{t_0} \rightarrow r_{t_0+1} \rightarrow \cdots \rightarrow r_{t_{now}}$, as depicted at the top in Figure 7. As the Figure also shows, each such state of the variable database, db_{t_i}, has an extension denoted by $[db_{t_i}]_{t_i}$, i.e. the extension of database db_{t_i} at time t_i. Most of the time the stored database $db_{t_{i+1}}$ will be the same as the stored database db_{t_i}, except in the case where a transaction is COMMITted at time t_{i+1}. However unless the database is completely extensional, it is possible (indeed, typical), to have $db_{t_{i+1}} = db_{t_i}$ while $[db_{t_{i+1}}]_{t_{i+1}} \neq [db_{t_i}]_{t_i}$, i.e., $[db_{t_i}]_{t_{i+1}} \neq [db_{t_i}]_{t_i}$.

Whenever we observe the database at a time t_x, we see db_{t_x}, i.e., the contents of the variable database at time t_x. In contrast, we use the notation $[db_{t_x}]_{t_*}$ to denote the *extensional interpretation* of database db_{t_x} with respect to reference time t_*. It is very common to evaluate the current database $db_{t_{now}}$ at the current reference time t_{now}, i.e. to look at $[db_{t_{now}}]_{t_{now}}$. However, one might also want to interpret the current (or any) database $db_{t_{now}}$ with respect to some earlier (or later) time t_*, i.e., to see $[db_{t_{now}}]_{t_*}$. Such an operation is related to the concept of *rollback*, as discussed in Section 6.

We can extend this notation to subsets of the database in the obvious way. When we refer, for example, to $r.t.A_{t_x}$, we are referring to the value of attribute A in tuple t in the relation r as stored in the database at time t_x, i.e., at the variable level. By contrast, when we refer to $[r.t.A_{t_x}]_{t_*}$, we are referring to the the extensional level of this attribute value, i.e. its logical interpretation. Indeed, if q is a query in some query language L for our data model, $q(db_{t_x})_{t_*}$ and $[q(db)b_{t_x}]_{t_*}$ denote the result of that query, at the variable level and its extensional interpretation, respectively, when asked at reference time t_*. We point out that, in the literature, many models, such as the one in [5], have been presented completely extensionally; they did not present an operational model at the variable level, and thus did not make use of any variable symbols requiring further interpretation.

However, since the meaning of symbols such as ∞ depends on the reference time t_*, it time-dependent $r.t.A_{t_*}$ in general *cannot* equal $[r.t.A_{t_*}]_{t_*}$, since the latter is a purely extensional set of *ground* tuples. Moreover, given $r.t.A_{t_*}$, it is not entirely clear what $[r.t.A]_{t_*}$ is. In what follows we explore these issues and propose well defined translation mappings from $r.t.A_{t_*}$ to $[r.t.A_{t_*}]_{t_*}$. In the context of Figure 1, we will be providing the details of the mapping $[]_{t_*}$ between the variable and extensional database levels.

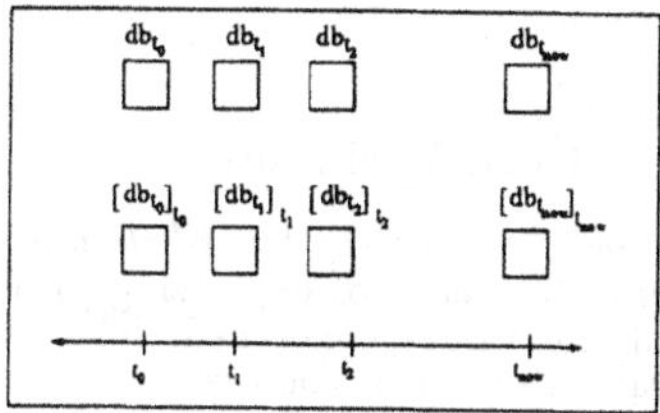

Fig. 7. Database Evolution in Reference Time

5 Extensionalization of Variable Databases

This $[]_{t_*}$ transformation takes place in two steps. First, all variables appearing in *db* are instantiated, for example, the variable *now* is to be bound to the time t_* at which the extensionalization is performed. Secondly, tuples that refer to time intervals are *expanded* into a set of tuples in the extensional model. This follows the same principle used in logic, where the semantics of a formula is determined by first providing a *variable assignment* that grounds the variables, and then using a semantics defined on ground formulae. In addition, we will have to provide an extensionalization for *operators*, so that queries with variables that are to operate on the variable level, are transformed into queries *without* variables that operate on the extensional level. Our focus will be mostly on the extensionalization of the variable databases.

The use of interval notation to denote time spans, shown in all cases of Figure 5, has been extensively used in the literature. When time is discrete, however, time intervals are merely shorthand for a finite set of extensional facts. A simple way of mapping a *ground* database, i.e. a database without variables, into the extensional model consists of *expanding* time intervals. This is how the extensional model given in Figure 6 was obtained from the first tuple in Figure 5.

Values at the variable level of the form $< [t_1, t_2) \mapsto a >$ are therefore shorthand for the set of tuples: $\{(t_1, a), (t_1 + 1, a), \ldots, (t_2 - 1, a)\}$. Hence $[t_1, t_2)$ stands for an open-closed interval, and $[t_1, t_2]$ for a closed-closed one. If the temporal universe T is discrete, we can use solely closed intervals, for example, $[t_1, t_2 - 1]$ can be used instead of $[t_1, t_2)$. Whenever, the special symbols ∞, *now*, *forever* and *uc* appear as interval endpoints, it is necessary first to bind these variables to ground temporal values so that the intervals can then be expanded.

The special symbols $\perp$ or $\top$ are treated in the obvious way:

- $(\perp, t_1) \mapsto a$ is the infinite set $\{(t, a) | t < t_1\}$.
- $[t_1, \top) \mapsto a$ is the infinite set $\{(t, a) | t \geq t_1\}$.

Tuples in bitemporal variable databases contain two kinds of time intervals: transaction-time intervals and valid-time intervals. It is not clear how to *combine* these two intervals. One possibility is to represent the combination with a *Cartesian Product* ($\times$). Consider for example the following tuple: $< Merrie, Assistant, 9\text{-}77, 12\text{-}82, 8\text{-}77, \infty >$. A Cartesian Product interpretation states that Merrie has the status Assistant for all the times in $[9\text{-}77, 12\text{-}82) \times [8\text{-}77, \infty]$. That is, the above tuple is shorthand notation for the set: $\{< Merrie, Assistant, vt, tt > \mid 9\text{-}77 \leq vt < 12\text{-}82 \text{ and } 8\text{-}77 \leq tt < \top\}$. However, this interpretation seems to be incorrect. For example, it indicates that at time 8-77 the database predicted Merrie's rank from 9-77 through 12-82. A different interpretation can be given by a *Step-wise Cartesian Product* ($\otimes$) defined as follows:

$$[x_1, x_2] \otimes [y_1, y_2] = \{(x, y) | x_1 \leq x \leq min(x_2, y) \wedge y_1 \leq y \leq y_2\} \quad (1)$$

In the context of the tuple for Merrie, this combination results in

$$\{< Merrie, Assistant, vt, tt > \mid \text{9-77} \leq vt < min(\text{12-82}, tt) \text{ and } \text{8-77} \leq tt < \top\}$$

As we will see, the use of $\otimes$ to combine the transaction and valid time intervals is more adequate than the first one.

5.1 Extensionalization of the Variables

The special symbols "∞", "*now*", "*forever*" and *until changed*("*uc*") are notational aids at the variable level, that provide means of expressing an evolving database without explicitly enumerating all of the values concerned. These special symbols ∞, *now*, *forever* and *uc* denote interval endpoints as follows:

- $[t_1, \infty)$: From time t_1 (including t_1) onwards.
- $[t_1, now]$: From time t_1 (including t_1) up until (and including) the current time.
- $[t_1, forever)$: From time t_1 (including t_1) onwards (this the same as ∞.)
- $[t_1, uc)$: From time t_1 (including t_1) onwards until there is a change.

It appears to us that ∞ and *forever*, used in different models, have the same meaning. Since, as pointed out in Section 1, ∞ has been used in the literature with various meanings, we will use the symbol *forever* here. The semantics of *uc* will be discussed at the end of this section. However, let us note at this point, that, when only one time dimension is considered, there does not appear to be a difference between *uc* and *forever*. This follows from the fact that until the symbol *uc* is changed, it does have the same meaning as *forever*. Once a transaction changes the symbol, it no longer appears in the database where it used to, and hence the issue of its semantics vanishes.

At the level of variables, we can think of the mapping $[]_{t_*}$ as a *variable assignment* $[]_{t_*} : Var \mapsto T$, where Var is the set of variables in our language and T is the universe of times. Thus, if $[now]_{t_*} = 55$, then the interval $[t_1, now]$ is mapped by $[]_{t_*}$ to $[t_1, 55]$. As we shall see, certain restrictions apply to the functions $[]_{t_*}$. The fact that these restrictions depend upon the reference time t_* at which we wish to observe the database explains the use of the subscript t_* in $[]_{t_*}$.

The variable assignment $[]_{t_*}$ for the special variables might differ for rollback and historical databases. In order to distinguish among the various variables, we will use subscripts as follows: now_{tt} and $forever_{tt}$, for rollback databases, and now_{vt} and $forever_{vt}$, for historical databases. We now explore what the variable assignments should be for rollback, historical and temporal databases.

Rollback Databases When only the transaction time dimension of the data is incorporated into the database, the symbols now_{tt} and $forever_{tt}$ are used to prescribe the evolution of the database. The semantics of transaction time do not allow predictions into the future. This means that the right endpoint of every interval must be less than or equal to t_{now}. This results in the following variable assignment $[]_{t_*}$: $[now_{tt}]_{t_*} = t_*$ and $[forever_{tt}]_{t_*} = t_*$ Because of the restricted nature of transaction times — they are set by the system to be equal to the time of the operation — in this dimension t_* is subject to the following restriction: $t_0 \leq t_* \leq t_{now}$.

Therefore, the symbols now_{tt} and $forever_{tt}$ have the same meaning in rollback databases, and so only one of them is needed. In the remainder of this paper we will use the symbol now_{tt}.

The extensionalization of a variable rollback database is obtained by expanding the intervals that result from applying the variable assignments. Table 2 shows the extensionalization of attribute histories. Notice that the first entry (**r1**) explicitly excludes entries for times beyond t_*.

Recall that even when the database itself does not change at time t_*, its extension interpretation might be different. As an example, consider the *RANK* attribute history

	Variable Database	Extensional Database
r1	$[t_1, t_2) \mapsto a$	$[A]_{t_*} = \{(tt, a) \mid t_1 \leq tt < min(t_*, t_2)\}$
r2	$[t_1, now_{tt}] \mapsto a$	$[A]_{t_*} = \{(tt, a) \mid t_1 \leq tt \leq t_*\}$
r3	$[t_1, forever_{tt}) \mapsto a$	$[A]_{t_*} = \{(tt, a) \mid t_1 \leq tt \leq t_*\}$

Table 2. Extensionalization of Rollback Databases.

denoted by $[5, now] \mapsto$ *Assistant*. Suppose that this is added to the database at time 5. The extensional database at reference time 5 is obtained from $[now_{tt}]_5 = 5$, hence $[rank]_5 = \{(5, \mathit{Assistant})\}$. Assuming that no transaction is committed at time $tt = 6$, the extensional database as observed at reference time 6 is derived from $[now_{tt}]_6 = 6$, yielding $[rank]_6 = \{(5, \texttt{Assistant}), (6, \texttt{Assistant})\}$. Hence, even though no transaction changed the state of the database at times 5 and 6, the extensional databases differ.

	Variable Database	Extensional Database
h1	$[t_1, t_2) \mapsto a$	$[A]_{t_*} = \{(vt, a) \mid t_1 \leq vt < t_2\}$
h2	$[t_1, now_{vt}] \mapsto a$	$[A]_{t_*} = \{(vt, a) \mid t_1 \leq vt \leq t_*\}$
h3	$[t_1, forever_{vt}) \mapsto a$	$[A]_{t_*} = \{(vt, a) \mid t_1 \leq vt\}$

Table 3. Extensionalization of Historical Databases.

Historical Databases When only the valid-time dimension of the data is incorporated into the database, the symbols now_{vt} and $forever_{vt}$ are used in a tuple to allow it to express the values of attributes over some period of time, perhaps encompassing the past or even the future. Thus, we have the following variable assignment: $[now_{vt}]_{t_*} = t_*$, and $[forever_{vt}]_{t_*} = \top$. Here, $\top$ is the special element in T that is greater than any other time in T. As a consequence, we point out that the symbol $forever_{vt}$ is in fact not a variable, but a constant. The result of expanding intervals is shown in Table 3. In contrast to rollback databases, future times are allowed because it is possible to make predictions in historical databases.

Bitemporal Databases When valid time and transaction time are combined, there might be interactions between the two times. The variable assignment follows naturally from the rollback and historical cases as follows: $[now_{tt}]_{t_*} = t_*$, $[now_{vt}]_{t_*} = t_*$, and $[forever_{vt}]_{t_*} = \top$ (also a constant). The extensionalization of time intervals now involves combining transaction-time and valid-time intervals. It is not clear how exactly such combinations should be dealt with. In Table 4 we provide denotations for the six combinations obtained by using the cartesian product from the analyses of the rollback and historical cases, namely one of $\{\mathbf{r1}, \mathbf{r2}\}$ with one of $\{\mathbf{h1}, \mathbf{h2}, \mathbf{h3}\}$.

	VT	TT	Extensional View
r1×h1	$[vt_1, vt_2)$	$[tt_1, tt_2) \mapsto a$	$[A]_{t_*} = \{(vt, tt, a) \mid tt_1 \leq tt < min(t_*, tt_2) \wedge vt_1 \leq vt < vt_2\}$
r1×h2	$[vt_1, now_{vt}]$	$[tt_1, tt_2) \mapsto a$	$[A]_{t_*} = \{(vt, tt, a) \mid tt_1 \leq tt < min(t_*, tt_2) \wedge vt_1 \leq vt \leq t_*\}$
r1× h3	$[vt_1, forever_{vt}]$	$[tt_1, tt_2) \mapsto a$	$[A]_{t_*} = \{(vt, tt, a) \mid tt_1 \leq tt < min(t_*, tt_2) \wedge vt_1 \leq vt\}$
r2× h1	$[vt_1, vt_2)$	$[tt_1, now_{tt}] \mapsto a$	$[A]_{t_*} = \{(vt, tt, a) \mid tt_1 \leq tt \leq t_* \wedge vt_1 \leq vt < vt_2\}$
r2× h2	$[vt_1, now_{vt}]$	$[tt_1, now_{tt}] \mapsto a$	$[A]_{t_*} = \{(vt, tt, a) \mid tt_1 \leq tt \leq t_* \wedge vt_1 \leq vt \leq t_*\}$
r2× h3	$[vt_1, forever_{vt}]$	$[tt_1, now_{tt}] \mapsto a$	$[A]_{t_*} = \{(vt, tt, a) \mid tt_1 \leq tt \leq t_* \wedge vt_1 \leq vt\}$

Table 4. Extensionalization of Bitemporal Databases.

Until Changed Interpreting the combinations of transaction-time intervals and a valid-time intervals as Cartesian Products results in an interpretation that is graphically represented as rectangular areas or in unions of rectangular areas. However, it is quite unlikely that this captures the desired meaning of the notation. Consider for example, the value for Jane's *rank* inserted into the database at *transaction time* 1, as: $[1, now_{tt})[1, forever_{vt}) \mapsto$ *Assistant*. The interpretation as a Cartesian Product implies that Jane will be an Assistant Professor forever, i.e. at valid times $2, 3, 4, \ldots$. This can hardly be an accurate representation of the world where, in fact, it is not known for sure how long she will remain in her position. Moreover, the tenure process dictates that, in any case, she will not be remain Assistant Professor beyond her evaluation for tenure, e.g. seven years after her hiring date. Thus the information conveyed by the database when interpreted as a Cartesian Product is inaccurate!

The intended meaning of the above entry is more likely to be: *"Jane will be an Assistant as long as she is not promoted or quits her job, i.e. until changed."* No prediction is made about her rank at times beyond valid time = 1. However, if at reference time 2, this value is still in the database, then it would state that at Jane is still an Assistant at valid time = 2.

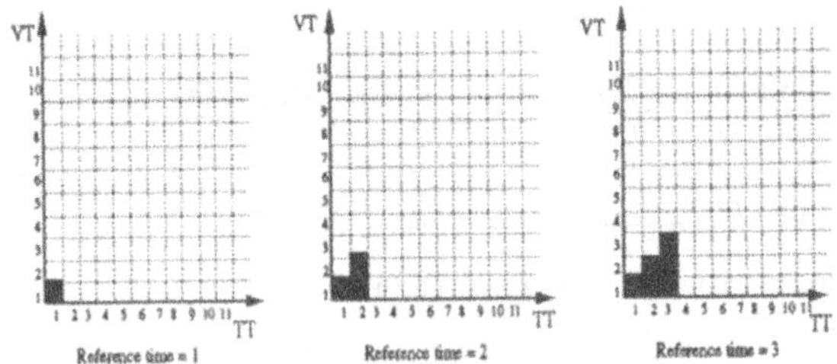

Fig. 8. How Jane's rank evolved.

How can we capture this semantics for *until changed* in our extensional model? The intended evolution of the information about Jane's rank is depicted in the stepwise pattern of Figure 8. Since the shaded areas in the Figure are not rectangular, the intended meaning of the combination of the intervals cannot be that of a Cartesian Product. We propose the use of a new symbol uc_{vt} to indicate the use of the $\otimes$ operator to combine the intervals. Recall the definition of $\otimes$, in equation (1). The resulting semantics are shown in Table 5. The meaning of the first two entries in the Table coincides with Figure 8. The role of the second component of the unions in the table is to allow explicit predictions to be made. For example, if at reference time 2, it is predicted that Tom will start as an Associate at time 3, his tuple would be $< [3, uc)[2, now) \mapsto$ `Associate` $>$. Hence the triplet $(3, 2,$ `Associate`$)$, a prediction, is in the extensional view. Based on these definitions of the variable symbols, we are in a position to recast the original **FACULTY** relation of [24] as shown in Figure 9.

	VT	TT	Extensional Database
r1⊗ h2'	$[vt_1, uc_{vt}]$	$[tt_1, tt_2) \mapsto a$	$[A]_{t_*} = \{(vt, tt, a) \mid tt_1 \leq tt < min(t_*, tt_2) \wedge vt_1 \leq vt \leq tt\}$ $\bigcup \{(vt_1, tt, a) \mid tt_1 \leq tt < min(t_*, tt_2)\}$
r2⊗ h2'	$[vt_1, uc_{vt}]$	$[tt_1, now_{tt}] \mapsto a$	$[A]_{t_*} = \{(vt, tt, a) \mid tt_1 \leq tt \leq t_* \wedge vt_1 \leq vt \leq tt\}$ $\bigcup \{(vt_1, tt, a) \mid tt_1 \leq tt \leq tt_*\}$
r2'⊗ h1	$[vt_1, vt_2)$	$[tt_1, uc_{tt}] \mapsto a$	$[A]_{t_*} = \{(vt, tt, a) \mid tt_1 \leq tt \leq vt \wedge vt_1 \leq vt < vt_2\}$ $\bigcup \{(vt, tt_1, a) \mid vt_1 \leq vt < vt_2\}$
r2'⊗ h2	$[vt_1, now_{vt}]$	$[tt_1, uc_{tt}] \mapsto a$	$[A]_{t_*} = \{(vt, tt, a) \mid tt_1 \leq tt \leq vt \wedge vt_1 \leq vt \leq t_*\}$ $\bigcup \{(vt, tt_1, a) \mid vt_1 \leq vt \leq t_*\}$

Table 5. A Possible Meaning for *until changed*.

FACULTY					
		VALID-TIME		TRANS-TIME	
NAME	RANK	(from)	(to)	(start)	(stop)
Jane	Assistant	1	uc_{vt}	1	5
Jane	Associate	5	uc_{vt}	5	8
Jane	Full	9	uc_{vt}	8	now_{tt}
Merrie	Assistant	7	uc_{vt}	6	11
Merrie	Associate	11	uc_{vt}	11	now_{tt}
Tom	Associate	3	uc_{vt}	2	4
Tom	Assistant	3	uc_{vt}	4	9
Tom	Associate	10	uc_{vt}	9	now_{tt}

Fig. 9. A Fresh View of the Faculty Relation

The last two rows in Table 5 present the symmetric case where the transaction time is bound by the valid time. In this case, the database *forgets* about transactions that affect valid dates if these are committed after that date. We include them here for completeness. It is not clear whether or not they have any applicability to real-world problems.

To summarize, in this section we have dealt with the extensionalization of variable databases by providing a mapping $[]_{t_*}$ which first assigns temporal values to the various temporal variables, and then proceeds to expand the resulting intervals into full extensional models. We have prescribed specific variable assignment to be used in rollback, historical and bitemporal databases, and we have explained the reasons for such choices. This has led us to establish clear distinctions among the following variables $now_{tt}, now_{vt}, forever_{vt}, forever_{tt}, uc_{tt}$ and uc_{vt} and to provide meanings to all of them.

6 Rollbacks

Rollbacks are a fundamental operation on temporal databases that enable returning to an earlier database state. As a database evolving over time is characterized by its states:

$$db_{t_0} \rightarrow db_{t_1} \rightarrow \ldots \rightarrow db_{t_\alpha} \ldots \rightarrow db_{t_{now}}$$

Rolling back from a database state db_{t_x} to time t_α entails obtaining information that pertains to db_{t_α}. We differentiate between two kinds of rollback operators as follows.

Definition. A *strong rollback operator* is a two place operator ϕ such that: $(\forall \alpha \geq t_0)(\forall x \geq \alpha)\ \phi(db_{t_x}, t_\alpha) = db_{t_\alpha}$.

Definition. A *weak rollback operator* is a two place operator ω such that: $(\forall \alpha \geq t_0)(\forall x \geq \alpha)\ \omega(db_{t_x}, t_\alpha) = [db_{t_\alpha}]_{t_\alpha}$.

The difference between strong and weak rollbacks is that the strong rollback returns the actual state of the variable database, db_{t_α}, whereas the weak rollback only returns its extension, which is given by $[db_{t_\alpha}]_{t_\alpha}$.

6.1 The Rollback Evolution Constraint

Rollback operators can exist provided that, in some way, the database "keeps" information about earlier states. That is, the operational semantics of the database operators has to be constrained so that "older" states are recoverable. We propose the following constraint as a reasonable one, and we will show that it leads to the existence of a weak rollback operator.

Rollback Evolution Constraint:

As a database evolves from state t_α to state t_x, it should always be possible to recover, from t_x, the database extension as of reference time t_α, i.e. $(\forall \alpha \geq t_0)(\forall x \geq \alpha)\ [db_{t_x}]_{t_\alpha} = [db_{t_\alpha}]_{t_\alpha}$.

Diagrammatically, the rollback evolution constraint prescribes the commutativity of the upper triangle in Figure 10. We now define a rollback operator and we show that it is a *weak rollback*.

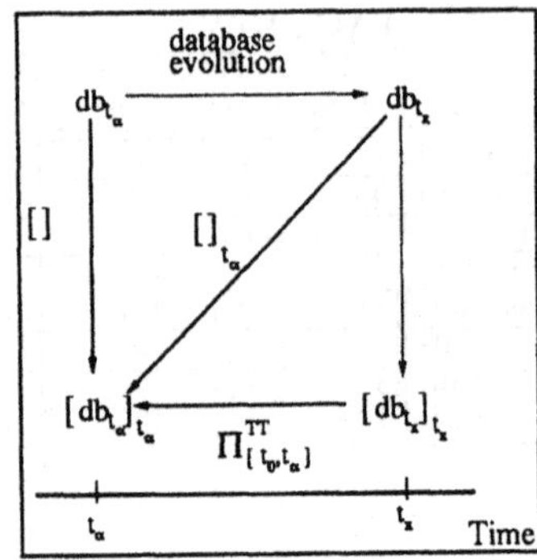

Fig. 10. Relating rollbacks across database levels.

6.2 Timeslice Operators

At the extensional database level, we can define *timeslice* operations, analogous to *projections* in the temporal dimension. The valid-time timeslice, which we denote by Π^{VT}, projects the database onto some subset of its valid times. The transaction-time timeslice, denoted Π^{TT}, projects the database onto some subset of its transaction times.

Definition. The *valid time timeslice* of an attribute value $r.t.A$ at valid time vt_i is given by: $\Pi^{VT}_{vt_i}(r.t.A) = \{(vt_i, tt, a) \mid (vt_i, tt, a) \in r.t.A\}$.

Definition. The *valid time timeslice* of $r.t.A$ at a set of valid times $S = \{vt_{i_1}, \ldots, vt_{i_n}\}$ is given by: $\Pi^{VT}_S(r.t.A) = \{(vt, tt, a) \mid (vt, tt, a) \in r.t.A \wedge vt \in S\}$.
Note that a frequent type of set S of interest is an interval, such as $[t_i, t_j)$.

Definition. The *transaction time timeslice* of $r.t.A$ at transaction time tt_i is given by: $\Pi^{TT}_{t_i}(r.t.A) = \{(vt, tt_i, a) \mid (vt, tt_i, a) \in r.t.A\}$.

Definition. The *transaction time timeslice* of $r.t.A$ at a set of transaction times $S = \{tt_{i_1}, \ldots, tt_{i_n}\}$ is given by: $\Pi^{TT}_S(r.t.A) = \{(vt, tt, a) \mid (vt, tt, a) \in r.t.A \wedge tt \in S\}$.

At the extensional level, without any variables, the definition of these operators is straightforward. Intuitively, a valid time timeslice represents information the database contains about a particular time period, e.g. "What was Tom's salary between 1975 and 1983?" The transaction time timeslice however, represents information about what was recorded during a particular time period in the databases, e.g. "What did database record during the period 1975-1983 about Tom's salary?" Hence, timeslicing along the valid time dimension deals with historical information while transaction time timeslicing is related to rollbacks. However, these relationships between a syntactic level (timeslices) and a semantic level (history, rollback) cannot be taken for granted.

From the above definitions and from the semantics given to $[]_{t_x}$, the following Lemma is easily proven.

Lemma The timeslice operator $\Pi^{TT}_{[t_1,t_2]}$ performs the equivalent of evaluating the database at a different time. i.e.: $(\forall \alpha \geq t_0)(\forall x \geq \alpha)\ [db_{t_x}]_{t_\alpha} = \Pi^{TT}_{[t_0,t_\alpha]}([db_{t_x}]_{t_x})$.

In terms of the diagram in Figure 10, the Lemma states that the lower triangle commutes. We are now in a position to define a weak rollback operator: $\Pi^{TT}_{[t_0,t_\alpha]} \circ []_{t_x}$. As the diagram in Figure 10 shows, the rollback evolution constraint and the previous Lemma result in the following Theorem.

Theorem The operator defined as $\Pi^{TT}_{[t_0,t_\alpha]} \circ [\,]_{t_x}$ is a *weak rollback*. That is, $(\forall \alpha \geq t_0)(\forall x \geq \alpha)\ \Pi^{TT}_{[t_0,t_\alpha]} \circ [\,]_{t_x}(db_{t_x}) = [db_{t_\alpha}]_{t_\alpha}$.

We point out in passing that the graphical notation for attribute histories provides a useful way to visualize these timeslice operators. A transaction-time timeslice at a time t_i would correspond to viewing *only* the column in the graph corresponding to $tt = t_i$. A transaction-time timeslice at a set of times $S = \{tt_{i_1}, \ldots, tt_{i_n}\}$ would correspond to viewing only those columns in the graph corresponding to each tt_j in S. A transaction-time timeslice at a set of times $S = \{tt_{i_1}, \ldots, tt_{i_n}\}$ which corresponds to a contiguous interval $[tt_{i_1}, tt_{i_n}]$ would correspond to viewing only those columns corresponding to a rectangle with lower and upper bounds of tt_{i_1} and tt_{i_n}, respectively. The same visualization of valid-time timeslicing can be made, with *"horizontal rows"* replacing *"vertical columns"* in the description, above.

7 Summary and Conclusions

In this paper we have explored the interactions between transaction time, valid time, and reference time in bitemporal databases. We began by pointing out several problems which have resulted from the widespread use in these data models of such variables as "∞", "*now*", and "*uc*", without a formally defined semantics. We have proposed a fully extensional model for bitemporal databases, and described how this model can be used as the reference point for providing such a precise semantics for these variable databases, as well as for providing the correctness criteria for the definition of the operations of their query language. We then addressed the question of what semantics can reasonably be given to the particular variable symbols which have appeared in the literature of bitemporal databases. To help clarify the different possible interpretations for these symbols, we introduced a two-dimensional, graphical representation for temporal objects. With this representation we illustrated a number of possible semantics for these two temporal dimensions, both independently and in combination. At the operational level, we presented a Rollback Evolution Constraint that database operations should satisfy in order to enable rollbacks to past database states. We then defined a timeslice operator and proved that under this constraint it can serve as such a rollback operator.

We are presently at work on a logic-based query language based on the semantic analysis presented here. Moreover, we believe that the precise semantics of several temporal models proposed in the literature could profitably be examined in light of the extensionalization framework presented in this paper.

Several additional research questions are posed by this work. While the step-wise growth semantics for *uc* in Section 5.1 seems reasonable, other possible combinations of these two temporal dimensions might also prove useful. In addition, the use of the bitemporal graph representation at the user interface – for displaying the results of queries, for the assertion of temporal integrity constraints, etc. – seems to us a promising one for further research. Finally, our analysis assumed that the variables such as *now* and *forever* were only used as the upper limit on an interval. Entries that are the temporal mirror-image of those we analyzed, such as $[now, t_1)$, for an entry that progressively *forgets* information as time passes, or $[past - forever, t_1)$, that records a fact as forever true *prior* to some time t_1, might also prove useful.

References

1. G. Ariav. A temporally oriented data model. *ACM Transactions on Database Systems*, 11(4):499–527, December 1986.
2. J. Ben-Zvi. *The Time Relational Model.* PhD thesis, University of California at Los Angeles, 1982.
3. J. Clifford. Indexical databases. In *Proceedings of Workshop on Current Issues in Database Systems*, Newark, N.J., October 1992. Rutgers University.
4. J. Clifford and A. Croker. The historical relational data model HRDM and algebra based on lifespans. In *Proc. Third International Conference on Data Engineering*, pages 528–537, Los Angeles, February 1987. IEEE.

5. J. Clifford, A. Croker, and A. Tuzhilin. On completeness of query languages for grouped and ungrouped historical data models. In A. Tansel, J. Clifford, S. Gadia, S. Jajodia, A. Segev, and R. Snodgrass, editors, *Temporal Databases*. Benjamin-Cummings, 1993.
6. J. Clifford and A.U. Tansel. On an algebra for historical relational databases: Two views. In S. Navathe, editor, *Proceedings of ACM SIGMOD Conference*, pages 247–265, Austin, TX, May 1985. ACM.
7. J. Clifford and D. S. Warren. Formal semantics for time in databases. *ACM Transactions on Database Systems*, 6(2):214–254, June 1983.
8. M. Finger. Handling database updates in two-dimensional temporal logic. *Journal of Applied Non-Classical Logics*, 2(2), 1992.
9. S. Gadia. A seamless generic extension of SQL for querying temporal data. Technical report, Iowa State University, 1992.
10. S. K. Gadia. A homogeneous relational model and query languages for temporal databases. *TODS*, 13(4):418–448, 1988.
11. C. S. Jensen, L. Mark, and N. Roussopoulos. Incremental implementation model for relational databases with transaction time. Technical Report UMIACS-TR-8963/CS-TR-2275, University of Maryland, College Park, MD, June 1989.
12. C. S. Jensen, R. T. Snodgrass, and M. D. Soo. Extending normal forms to temporal relations. TR 92-17, Department of Computer Science, University of Arizona, Tucson, AZ, July 1992.
13. C.S. Jensen, J. Clifford, S.K. Gaida, A. Segev, and R.T. Snodgrass. A glossary of temporal database concepts. *ACM SIGMOD Record*, 21(3), September 1992.
14. C.S. Jensen and R. Snodgrass. Temporal specialization. In F. Golshani, editor, *Proceedings of the International Conference on Data Engineering*, pages 594–603, Tempe, AZ, feb 1992. IEEE.
15. C.S Jensen and R.T. Snodgrass. Proposal of a data model for the temporal structured query language. TempIS Technical Report 37, Department of Computer Science, University of Arizona, Tucson, AZ, July 1992.
16. S. Jones and P.J. Mason. Handling the time dimension in a data base. In *Proc. International Conference on Data Bases*, pages 65–83, Heyden, July 1980. British Computer Society.
17. D. Lomet and B. Salzberg. Rollback databases. Technical Report NU-CCS-92-3, Northeastern University, 1992.
18. R.G. Lorentzos, N.A.; Johnson. TRA: A model for a temporal relational algebra. In *Proceedings of the Conference on Temporal Aspects in Information Systems*, pages 99–112, France, May 1987. AFCET.
19. E. McKenzie and R. Snodgrass. Supporting valid time in an historical relational algebra: Proofs and extensions. Technical Report TR–91–15, Department of Computer Science, University of Arizona, Tucson, AZ, August 1991.
20. R. Montague. *Formal Philosophy: Selected Papers of Richard Montague*. Yale University Press, New Haven, 1974.
21. S. B. Navathe and R. Ahmed. A temporal relational model and a query language. *Information Sciences*, 49(2):147–175, 1989.
22. R. Reiter. Towards a logical reconstruction of relational database theory. In *On Conceptual Modelling*, pages 191–233. Springer, 1984.
23. N.L. Sarda. Algebra and query language for a historical data model. *The Computer Journal*, 33(1):11–18, February 1990.
24. R. Snodgrass. The temporal query language TQuel. *ACM Transactions on Database Systems*, 12(2):247–298, June 1987.
25. A.U. Tansel. Adding time dimension to relational model and extending relational algebra. *Information Systems*, 11(4):343–355, 1986.
26. G. Wiederhold, S. Jajodia, and W. Litwin. Integrating temporal data in a heterogeneous environment. In A. Tansel, J. Clifford, S. Gadia, S. Jajodia, A. Segev, and R. Snodgrass, editors, *Temporal Databases*. Press, 1993.

Correctness of ISA Hierarchies in Object-Oriented Database Schemas

Anna Formica, Michele Missikoff

IASI CNR - Viale Manzoni 30, I-00185 Rome, Italy

Abstract. In Object-Oriented databases, ISA hierarchy provides a powerful modeling tool that, through the inheritance mechanism, yields a coincise description of the world. In this paper, we tackle the problem of the correctness of ISA hierarchies in Object-Oriented database schemas. In general, the inheritance mechanisms proposed in literature do not preserve subtyping, i.e. they are not sound. Strict inheritance has been proposed in order to guarantee subtyping after inheritance. However, strict inheritance is sound but fails to cope with a significant class of schemas. The problem relies on refinement rules. In the paper, we characterize the schemas for which strict inheritance is sound and complete and we present a methodology aimed at identifying such schemas. The problem is addressed using the Object-Oriented data definition language $\mathcal{TQL}$.

1 Introduction

Database design is a complex activity requiring skilled database experts. With the advent of expressive database models and, in particular, Object-Oriented databases [14], the design of correct database schemas becomes a critical and increasingly difficult activity [9]. In this perspective, new methodologies and tools are required to support the database design phase [13].

In this paper, the problem of Object-Oriented database (OODB) design is investigated, focusing in particular on the correctness of OODB schemas. OODBs are organized according to ISA hierarchies. An ISA hierarchy is used in the database schema to define *types* (also referred to as *class definitions*) in an incremental way, by refining the types previously introduced [2]. The types are defined as tuples of typed properties (attributes) that determine the structure of the objects state.

ISA hierarchy has a set inclusion semantics, i.e. the set of objects representing the extension of a given type is a subset of the extensions of all its supertypes, up in the hierarchy. There is a second important aspect of ISA related to *inheritance*. The ISA construct in a type can be seen as a "place holder" for the properties of the supertypes. The ISA construct can be expanded rewriting the type with all the inherited properties of its supertypes (in general, also the methods are inherited, but here we focus only on the database schema).

This research has been partially supported by "Progetto Finalizzato Sistemi Informatici e Calcolo Parallelo" of CNR, Subproject 5, Group Logidata+, and Subproject 6, Group Infokit.

Inheritance is a critical mechanism, in particular inheritance conflicts [3] (also referred to as *naming conflicts*) can arise when a property has been defined in the hierarchy more than once, differently typed. Inheritance conflicts can be internal or external. The former take place if a property has been defined in the subtype and in the supertype(s), as well. The latter take place in presence of *multiple inheritance.* The two kinds of inheritance conflicts are not mutually exclusive. In the literature, different solutions have been proposed to cope with inheritance conflicts. The first OODB systems, such as [3], [4], [18], introduced severe limitations, such as prohibiting multiple inheritance, or tended to leave to the designer the burden of resolving (or avoiding) inheritance conflicts. This unconstrained approach, referred to as *loose inheritance*, does not guarantee the correctness of the schema with respect to subtyping. In fact, after having applied inheritance, a type assumes a structure which is not a refinement of its supertypes, therefore there will be objects in the database that may not satisfy one or more supertypes.

To avoid this hierarchy anomaly, *strict inheritance* has been introduced [1], [16], [17]. Strict inheritance is based on the notion of *refinement.* Refinement rules have been used in the past to verify if, given two type definitions, one is subtype of the other [7].

In this paper, we focus on the verification of OODB schemas, with particular emphasis on ISA hierarchy and inheritance. This work has been carried out within the project Mosaico, an environment for the conceptual specification and rapid prototyping of OODB applications [15]. In Mosaico, the database schema, modeled using the language $\mathcal{TQL}$ [10], [11], is supplied to the Static Verification Module, which has the task of verifying its correctness. $\mathcal{TQL}$ is a strongly typed language and Mosaico applies strict inheritance. We discovered that the proposed approach could correctly process the majority of the schemas, by applying inheritance and by normalizing the types with ISA, or by rejecting incorrect schemas. However, there is a class of schemas that could not be handled by the proposed method: such schemas could not be proven correct nor incorrect. We introduced the notion of *ISA certifiable* schemas, for which it is possible to prove *strong correctness.* For the second class of schemas, we introduced the notion of *weak correctness.*

The remaining of this paper is organized as follows. In the next section, we briefly illustrate the language $\mathcal{TQL}$. In Section 3, we focus on *correct* $\mathcal{TQL}$ schemas in presence of ISA hierarchies. To this end, the notions of *consistent* schemas and *legal ISA hierarchies* are presented. Then, the *ISA certifiable* schemas are introduced and their characterization is given. Finally, in Section 4, the conclusion and some comments on future work are reported.

2 The Language $\mathcal{TQL}$

The language $\mathcal{TQL}$ has been conceived for conceptual modeling [6] of OODB schemas. In this perspective, it avoids all the technical details required in developing an industrial database application, while retaining all the basic features of the Object-Oriented approach. A second simplification is introduced by the possibility of defining a schema as a set of types. Classes in Mosaico are pure extensional entities, i.e., set of objects. Another restriction is represented by the fact that there is only one class for each type defined in the schema (similarly to relational systems, where there is one table for each relation declared in the schema). A set of type-definitions forming a $\mathcal{TQL}$ schema is shown below.

person := [name:str, age:(0..100), tel:{int}, addr:[street:str, city:str]]
student := **ISA** person [college:str, age:(17..29), vehicle:car]
car := [maker:(VW,Fiat,Saab), max_speed:int, owner: person] .

A type-definition is composed by a name (also referred to as *t_term*) and a tuple of typed properties. The **ISA** construct allows the declaration of supertypes. Properties (also referred to as *p_terms*) can be typed in different ways, by using: (i) basic types, such as integer (*int*) or string (*str*); (ii) explicit sets of values, given either by enumeration (like in the property *car.maker*) or specifying interval extremes (like in *student.age*); (iii) type labels, as in *car.owner*, establishing an explicit link between two types (association); (iv) nested tuple, such as in *person.addr*. Associations can form cycles, hence resulting in recursive types.

A property is considered single-valued, unless curly brackets are used. The use of curly brackets indicates multi-valued properties, on which it is possible to impose cardinality constraints. In absence of cardinality constraints, any number of distinct values is acceptable (as for *person.tel*).

In the following box, the formal syntax of $\mathcal{TQL}$ is presented: non-terminal symbols are in small plain characters, while terminal symbols are in bold. Symbols in italics are user-defined strings.

Definition 2.1 Syntax of $\mathcal{TQL}$.
<type-definition> ::= *t_term* := <type-sentence>
<type-sentence> ::= <body> | **ISA** *t_term* ... *t_term* <body>
<body> ::= *t_term* | <bt> | (<*value_set*>) | [<tp>,...,<tp>]
<bt> ::= **integer** | **real** | **boolean** | **string** | **TOP**
<tp> ::= *p_term*:{<body>}$_{m,M}$ $\quad$ $m,M \in \aleph_0 \cup \{\infty\}, m \leq M$

Note the presence of the basic type **TOP**, which represents the most general type. It plays a special role, as it will be clarified in the following subsection, where the formal semantics of the language is presented.
Before concluding this section, we give the formal definition of schema.

Definition 2.2 $\mathcal{TQL}$ schema.
A $\mathcal{TQL}$ schema is a non-empty set of type-definitions having no dangling t_terms. □

2.2 $\mathcal{TQL}$ Formal Semantics

The semantics of $\mathcal{TQL}$ reported here follows a pure denotational approach, inspired by the work developed for Terminological Systems [5], [12]. With this approach, a type-definition is a formula and a class is simply one of its possible extensions. Given an interpretation, there is a tight and immutable association between types and classes: given a type-definition, there is only one class that corresponds to it.

Definition 2.3 Semantics of *TQL* type-definitions.
Let Σ be a finite set of oids representing a given state of the Application Domain, T the set of *TQL type-sentences*, and P the set of p_terms. Consider a function $\mathcal{E}$ from T to the powerset $\wp(\Sigma)$:

$$\mathcal{E} : T \to \wp(\Sigma)$$

and a function Π from P to the powerset $\wp(\Sigma \times \Sigma)$:

$$\Pi : P \to \wp(\Sigma \times \Sigma).$$

Then, $\mathcal{E}$ is an *extension function* over Σ with respect to the type-definition:

t_term := type-sentence

iff the value of $\mathcal{E}$ on the type-sentence is defined starting from the values of its components as follows. The extension of a type-sentence is computed by following the structure of the syntax.

Semantics of type-sentences:

$\mathcal{E}\{$type-sentence$\}$ =

a) $\mathcal{E}\{$body$\}$

b) $\mathcal{E}\{$**ISA** *t_term ...t_term* body$\} = (\bigcap_i \mathcal{E}\{t_term_i\}) \cap \mathcal{E}\{body\}$

$\mathcal{E}\{$body$\}$ =

c) $\mathcal{E}\{t\_term\}$

d) $\mathcal{E}\{bt\}$

e) $\mathcal{E}\{(value\_set)\} = \{value\_set\} \cap \Sigma$

f) $\mathcal{E}\{[tp,...,tp]\} = \bigcap_j \mathcal{E}\{[tp_j]\}$

$\mathcal{E}\{$bt$\}$ =

g) $\mathcal{E}\{\textbf{integer}\} = \mathbb{Z} \cap \Sigma$

h) $\mathcal{E}\{\textbf{real}\} = \mathbb{R} \cap \Sigma$

i) $\mathcal{E}\{\textbf{boolean}\} = \{true,false\} \cap \Sigma$

l) $\mathcal{E}\{\textbf{string}\} = \mathbf{S} \cap \Sigma$

m) $\mathcal{E}\{\textbf{TOP}\} = \Sigma$

$\mathcal{E}\{[tp]\} = \mathcal{E}\{[p\_term:\{body\}_{m,M}]\} = E_1 \cap E_2$

where:

$E_1 = \{ x \in \Sigma \mid \forall\ y \in S_{p\_term,x} \Rightarrow y \in \mathcal{E}\{body\} \}$

$E_2 = \{ x \in \Sigma \mid m \le |S_{p\_term,x}| \le M \}$

and:

$S_{p\_term,x} = \{ y \in \Sigma \mid \langle x,y\rangle \in \Pi\{p\_term\} \}$

$m, M \in \aleph_0 \cup \{\infty\}$, and $|S_{p\_term,x}|$ represents the cardinality of the set $S_{p\_term,x}$.

Finally, the notions of an *interpretation* and a *model* of a *TQL* schema are given.

Definition 2.4 *Interpretation* of a *TQL* schema.
An *interpretation* of a *TQL* schema is a 3-tuple $\Im = \langle\Sigma,\mathcal{E},\Pi\rangle$, where Σ represents the current state of the Application Domain, Π is a function as defined above, and $\mathcal{E}$ is an extension function over Σ with respect to each type-definition of the schema. □

Definition 2.5 *Model* of a *TQL* schema.
A *model* of a *TQL* schema is an interpretation $\Im = \langle\Sigma,\mathcal{E},\Pi\rangle$ such that, for each type-definition in the schema:

t_term := type-sentence

it results:

$$\mathcal{E}\{t\_term\} = \mathcal{E}\{\text{type-sentence}\}. \square$$

Having defined the language $\mathcal{TQL}$, in the next section we focus on the correctness of $\mathcal{TQL}$ schemas and, in particular, on **ISA** hierarchies.

3 Correctness of $\mathcal{TQL}$ Schemas

The verification of the correctness of $\mathcal{TQL}$ schemas is the main goal of the work shown in this paper. The proposed solution represents the core of the Static Verifier implemented in the system Mosaico. Such a verification is performed by examining the type-definitions of the schema according to the following steps:

1) syntactic correctness:
   - well formed type-definitions (according to $\mathcal{TQL}$ grammar);
   - no dangling references (w.r.t. associations and **ISA** hierarchies);

2) semantic correctness:
   - local consistency:
   - **ISA** hierarchy:
     * acyclicity;
     * subtyping consistency;
     * legality.

In the following, we concentrate on the semantic verification of the correctness of a conceptual schema. In particular, we start investigating the consistency of a schema. The consistency is the main property of a schema: it is related to the possibility of defining, in the database, objects satisfying the types of the schema. We will see that inconsistent schemas result from the presence of local inconsistencies or subtyping inconsistencies. For what concerns **ISA** hierarchies, Mosaico requires not only consistency but also legality. Legality of **ISA** hierarchy is related to the set inclusion semantics of **ISA**: every object satisfying the definition of a type must also satisfy the definitions of its supertypes. Furthermore, since **ISA** implies inheritance, we will formally introduce the strict inheritance rules. If all the type-definitions of the schema can be normalized according to the strict inheritance rules, the legality of **ISA** hierarchy is guaranteed. Unfortunately, we will see that strict inheritance rules are not complete: there is a class of schemas for which inheritance and the normalization process does not terminate. For this class of schemas, the correctness must be axiomatically assumed since it cannot be proved by analyzing the structure of types. Thus, the notion of ***ISA** certifiable schema* is introduced. We will show that, in **ISA** certifiable schemas, strict inheritance is sound and complete. A main problem is the availability of a methodology that allows the characterization of such schemas. This issue will be investigated at the end of this section.

3.1 Consistent Schemas

Consistency is the primary property of a conceptual schema. A schema is consistent if there exists at least one database state for which every type-definition of the schema

has a non-empty class. Since in *TQL* cardinality constraints can be associated to multi-valued properties, it is possible to write the following type-definition:
vehicle := [model:str, color:{(red, blue,green)}4,5]
Obviously, it is not possible to construct a set having at least cardinality 4 if we have three elements.

In more formal terms, we start by defining the consistency of a type-definition, and then we extend such a notion to a schema.

Definition 3.2 *Consistent* type-definition.
A type-definition:

t_term := type-sentence

is *consistent* iff there exists at least one model $\Im = <\Sigma, \mathcal{E}, \Pi>$ such that:

$$\mathcal{E}\{t\_term\} \; (= \mathcal{E}\{\text{type-sentence}\}) \neq \emptyset. \; \square$$

In more practical terms, consistency means that the type-definition does not contain contradictions and, therefore, it is possible to construct objects of the given type. Hence, we have the following definition.

Definition 3.3 *Consistent* schema.
A schema S containing the type-definitions:

$$S = \{t\_term_i := \text{type-sentence}_i\} \qquad i = 1..n$$

is *consistent* iff there exists at least one model $\Im = <\Sigma, \mathcal{E}, \Pi>$ such that, for i = 1..n:

$$\mathcal{E}\{t\_term_i\} \; (= \mathcal{E}\{\text{type-sentence}_i\}) \neq \emptyset$$

i.e., all the type-definitions of the schema have non-empty extension. □

We refer to *local inconsistency*, when we are in presence of typings having incompatible value sets and cardinality constraints, as in the example at the beginning of this subsection. In the next subsections, we will show that inconsistency can be found also in presence of inheritance conflicts. We will refer to it as *subtyping inconsistency*. Furthermore, we will see that for what concerns **ISA** hierarchies, Mosaico requires more than the consistency. It requires legality. Given a type-definition with **ISA**, we require not only the possibility of constructing objects that satisfy such a hierarchy of types (consistency) but, furthermore, every object satisfying the definition of the type must also satisfy the definition of its supertypes, i.e. the set inclusion constraint represented by **ISA** must be satisfied (legality of the **ISA** hierarchy).
Before analyzing consistency and legality of **ISA** hierarchies in detail, in the next subsection, we report the *TQL* refinement rules.

3.2 Refinement Rules

Type refinement has been extensively investigated in the past. The rules reported here represent an extension of subtyping as defined in [7], extension due to the enhanced property typings of *TQL*. Essentially, in *TQL* two tuple types t and v are in refinement relationship if v is obtained from t by: (i) adding one or more properties to the properties of t, or (ii) refining the cardinality constraints (i.e. specifying sub-intervals) of one or more multi-valued properties of t, or (iii) refining one or more properties of t, by typing them with refined types.

In formal terms, we have that a type v is a refinement of a type t (v **REF** t) if one of the following conditions is satisfied:

1) $t \sqsupseteq v$;

where the relationship "$\sqsupseteq$" holds if either t and v are equal, t is the elementary type **TOP** and v is any type, or if v is an enumerated type and t is a built-in type of the same sort.

2) if t and v are both enumerated types:

$t = (t_1,...,t_n)$

$v = (v_1,...,v_m)$

and $\{v_1,...,v_m\} \subseteq \{t_1,...,t_n\}$.

3) if t and v are both type-definitions of the form:

$t = t' := [\, p_1,...,p_r \,]$

$v = v' := [\, q_1,...,q_s \,]$

where: $p_i = term\_p_i : \{body\_p_i\}_{m_i,M_i}$ for $i = 1...r$

$q_j = term\_q_j : \{body\_q_j\}_{k_j,K_j}$ for $j = 1...s$

and $\forall\, p_i,\ i = 1...r,\ \exists\, q_j,\ 1 \le j \le s$, such that:

a) $term\_p_i = term\_q_j$

b) $m_i \le k_j$ and $K_j \le M_i$

c) ($body\_q_j$ **REF** $body\_p_i$) or ($k_j = K_j = 0$).

□

Note that, refinement rules apply only to tuples of typed properties, i.e. to types in *normal form*.

3.3 The ISA Hierarchy

In Mosaico, we have three kinds of inheritance: absolute, composed, and refined. Inheritance is absolute if a property belongs to only one supertype and is not redefined in the subtype (there are no inheritance conflicts). Inheritance is composed if a property belongs to at least two supertypes (external inheritance conflicts). Finally, inheritance is refined if a property belongs to supertypes and is redefined in the subtype (internal inheritance conflicts). If inheritance is absolute, the typed properties are inherited without modifications. External conflicts are resolved by composition of the different typings. As we will show in the next subsections, such a composition is obtained by considering a type (if there exists) that is a refinement of the ones reported in each occurrence of the property. Finally, in case of internal conflicts, the typed properties of the supertypes will be overridden by the ones locally specified, if the latter are refinement of the former.

In applying the strict inheritance outlined above, the legality of **ISA** hierarchies is preserved. If the hierarchy is illegal, the process is stopped and an error message is returned. The issue will be formally addressed in the next subsections. Here, some examples are provided.

The following **ISA** hierarchy is legal:

person := [name:str, age:int]

parent := **ISA** person [age:(10..150), child:{person}$_{1,5}$] .

In fact, by applying the refined inheritance to the property *age*, the condition of refinement between the type *int* and the set of values specified in the tuple is satisfied.
The following subsections, that illustrate in formal terms the conditions for legal **ISA** hierarchies and the *TQL* strict inheritance rules, start with a few examples of inconsistent **ISA** hierarchies.

3.3.1 Inconsistent ISA Hierarchies

We have anticipated that inconsistency in **ISA** hierarchies (also referred to as subtyping inconsistency) is caused by inheritance conflicts. An example of subtyping inconsistency is the following:

person := [name:(Bob,Tom), age:(0..150)]
student := **ISA** person [name:(Susan,Ann)] .

The subtype *student* is not consistent with its supertype *person*. In fact, the typings of the property *name* not only are not in refinement, but they are also disjoint. It is not possible to define *student* objects which are *person* objects as well. Therefore, the extension of the subtype is always empty.
The following is another example of inconsistent schema due to another kind of inheritance conflict:

vehicle := [maker:str, speed:int, color:$\{$(red,green,blue)$\}_{2,3}$]
bicycle := **ISA** vehicle [maker:$\{$str$\}_{2,2}$] .

The inconsistency is due to the cardinality constraints on the property *maker*.

Obviously, if an **ISA** hierarchy is not consistent, it is also illegal. On the other hand, we will see in the following subsection that, for **ISA** hierarchies, consistency does not imply legality.

3.3.2 The *TQL* Strict Inheritance Mechanism

In this subsection, we give the formal definition of legal subtyping and, then, we formally define the *TQL* strict inheritance rules. A few examples will follow.

Definition 3.4 *Legal* **ISA** hierarchy (*Legal subtyping*).
Given a schema with **ISA** declarations, the **ISA** hierarchy (subtyping) of such a schema is *legal* if it is not cyclic and, for each type-definition in the schema with the **ISA** construct, the following conditions are verified:

Condition 1)

for each property p_term_h belonging to at least two supertypes and not belonging to the definition of the type, as in the following:

t_term := **ISA** t_term_1 ... t_term_r [...]
t_term_1 := [..., p_term_h:$\{body_1\}_{m1,M1}$, ...]
...
t_term_n := [..., p_term_h:$\{body_n\}_{mn,Mn}$, ...]

where $2 \leq n \leq r$, there exists $body_h$ such that:

- if $body_i$, i = 1..n, are basic types or sets of values, than:

$body_h = \bigcap_i body_i \neq \emptyset$
if $body_i$, i = i..n, are type labels or tuples, than $body_h$ is a type label of the schema, that is the greatest lower bound (glb) of $body_i$, i = 1..n, according to the partial order induced by the refinement relationship over types.

Furthermore, there exists an interval of cardinality, $[m_h, M_h]$, such that, for i = 1..n:

$[m_h, M_h] = \bigcap_i [m_i, M_i] \neq \emptyset$.

<u>Condition 2)</u>

for each property p_term$_h$ belonging to supertypes and to the definition of the subtype, as in the following:

t_term := **ISA** t_term$_1$ ... t_term$_r$ [..., p_term$_h$:{body$_h$}$_{mh,Mh}$, ...]
t_term$_i$:= [..., p_term$_h$:{body$_i$}$_{mi,Mi}$, ...]

where $1 \leq i \leq r$, it results:

- $body_h$ is a refinement of $body_i$.
- $m_i \leq m_h$ and $M_h \leq M_i$. □

From the above definition follows that if an **ISA** hierarchy is legal than every object satisfying the definition of a type satisfies also the definitions of its supertypes: set inclusion semantics is satisfied.

As already mentioned, legality of subtyping is more than consistency. In fact, if an **ISA** hierarchy is legal it is also consistent. On the other hand, it is possible to have consistent **ISA** hierarchies that are not legal. For instance, the following example is hierarchically consistent, but illegal:

vehicle := [maker:str, color:{(red,blue,green)}]
car := **ISA** vehicle [max_speed:int, color:{(yellow,red)}] .

In fact, the refinement condition for the typings of the property *color* is violated.

Now, we introduce the *TQL* strict inheritance rules. These rules perform the normalization of the type-definitions with **ISA**, in case of legal **ISA** hierarchy. Otherwise, in case of illegal subtyping, the normalization does not take place and the definition is rejected.

Definition 3.5 *Strict Inheritance Rules.*
Consider a schema having an **ISA** hierarchy. If the **ISA** hierarchy is legal, then each type-definition of the schema with the **ISA** construct can be normalized according to the following inheritance rules:

a) for each property belonging to only one supertype and not redefined in the type, the typed property is inherited as it is (absolute inheritance);
b) for each property p_term$_h$ belonging to at least two supertypes and not belonging to the definition of the type, the inherited typed property:
p_term$_h$:{body$_h$}$_{mh,Mh}$
is obtained according to the condition 1) of the definition 3.4.
c) for each property p_term$_h$ belonging to supertypes and to the definition of the type, the typed properties of the supertypes are overridden by the one in the definition of the type:

p_term_h:{$body_h$}$_{m_h,M_h}$
according to the condition 2) of the definition 3.4.

If a type-definition of the schema does not verify the conditions of the definitions 3.4, the normalization process is not performed and the definition is rejected. □

For instance, consider the following schema:

young := [name:str, age:(0..30)]
mother := [name:str, sex:(female), age:(10..50)]
youngMother := **ISA** young mother [age:(10..25)] .

Strict inheritance can be performed, yielding the normalized type:

youngMother := [name:str, sex:(female), age:(10..25)] .

In fact, the typings of the property *age* in the two occurrences in *young* and *mother* are overridden by the typing (10..25) specified locally in the subtype. The **ISA** hierarchy is legal.
On the other hand, the **ISA** hierarchy below is not legal:

person := [age:(0..150), vehicle:{car}$_{2,3}$, ssn:str]
student := [age:(18..40), vehicle:{car}$_{0,1}$, college:str]
gr_student := **ISA** person student [age:(23..40)]
car := [maker:str, color:str] .

In fact, while the property *age* can be correctly overridden, for what concerns the property *vehicle*, the composition of the cardinality intervals yields an empty intersection. Due to the empty intersection, this **ISA** hierarchy is also inconsistent.

Now that we have introduced the notion of legal subtyping, and we have defined the strict inheritance rules for $\mathcal{TQL}$, some questions arise. Is it always possible to to check the legality of **ISA** hierarchies and, therefore, to apply strict inheritance rules?
In the next subsection, we address this problem and introduce the notion of **ISA** certifiable schemas.

3.3.3 ISA Certifiable Schemas

Let us start this subsection with the following example. Consider the schema:

person := [name:str, friend:person] (1)
student := **ISA** person [friend:student] . (2)

In this example, there is an internal inheritance conflict due to the property *friend*. Is this **ISA** hierarchy legal? According to condition 2) of definition 3.4, this hierarchy is legal if *student* is a refinement of *person*. Since refinement applies only to tuples, we need first to normalize the type-definition *student*. But, in order to complete the normalization process, it is necessary to establish if the typing of the property *friend* in *student* (which is *student*) is a refinement of the corresponding typing in the supertype *person* (which is *person*). Briefly, normalization and refinement are recursively interwoven and the process does not terminate.

The example shows that there are schemas for which it is not possible to establish if the **ISA** hierarchy is legal, i.e. legality is not decidable. For such schemas, the legality of **ISA** cannot be established with strict inheritance: strict inheritance is not complete.
Therefore, we have the following theorem.

Theorem 3.1 Strict Inheritance rules are not complete.
Proof. See the preceding example. □

The problem just presented leads to the notion of **ISA** certifiable schemas. To this end, we first give the definition of *normal form reducible* type-definition. Then, we show that, for **ISA** certifiable schemas, strict inheritance is sound and complete. Finally, we provide the necessary and sufficient conditions that allow the identification of such a class of schemas.

Definition 3.6 *Normal form reducible* type-definition.
A type-definition with the **ISA** construct is *normal form reducible* (NF-reducible) if there exists another type-definition, in normal form, semantically equivalent to it. □

Note that, two type-definitions are semantically equivalent iff their type-sentences denote the same set of objects (i.e. classes) for all the interpretations. This notion of semantic equivalence follows directly from the formal semantics defined in Section 2.
Now, using the definition 3.6, we are able to introduce the definition of **ISA** certifiable schemas.

Definition 3.7 ***ISA*** *certifiable* schema.
A schema containing an **ISA** hierarchy is ***ISA*** *certifiable* iff *all* the type-definitions of the schema are NF-reducible. □

In the introduction, we mentioned that inheritance is sound if it preserves subtyping. Inheritance is also complete if the normalization process always terminates. The following theorem states that for **ISA** certifiable schemas strict inheritance is sound and complete.

Theorem 3.2 For **ISA** certifiable schemas strict inheritance is sound and complete.
Proof. Omitted for lack of space. □

In the following, we provide a methodology that allows the identification of **ISA** certifiable schemas. Let us define a *path* of a type-definition as a sequence of p_terms defined in its tuple and, eventually, in its associated types, recursively. A *cyclic path* is a path that reaches the type-definition from which it was originated.

Theorem 3.3 A schema is **ISA** certifiable iff in the schema there are no type-definitions in **ISA** having common cyclic paths.
Proof. Omitted for lack of space. □

For example, consider the following schema:

person := [name:str, age:(0..150)]
student := **ISA** person [age:(18..40), friend:student].

The second type-definition is recursive, nevertheless it is NF-reducible since it has no cyclic paths common to its supertype *person*. In particular, this **ISA** hierarchy is legal since the strict inheritance conditions are verified. The normalized type-definition is:

student' := [name:str, age:(18..40), friend:student']

that is semantically equivalent to *student*. Furthermore, it is easily verifiable, using refinement rules, that the normalization preserves subtyping.
Consider now the schema {(1),(2)} reported at the beginning of this subsection. In that case, the schema is not **ISA** certifiable: the type-definition (2) is not NF-reducible. In fact, the condition of theorem 3.3 is not verified: the type-definition (2) has the cyclic path *friend* that is common to its supertype *person*. Therefore, a type-definition in normal form, semantically equivalent to (2), does not exist. In fact, consider the following type-definition:

student' := [name:str, friend:student'] . (2')

This is not semantically equivalent to the original one (2), due to the loss of the subtyping constraint. In fact, expressions (1) and (2) require that, for all the interpretations, every object satisfying (2) also satisfies (1). On the contrary, considering definitions (1) and (2'), it is possible to define an interpretation such that an object satisfying (2') does not satisfies (1).
It is useful to draw a graphic representation of this example, where nodes and arcs represent types and property names, respectively. Note, in the figure, the cyclic path *friend* common to the two type-definitions.

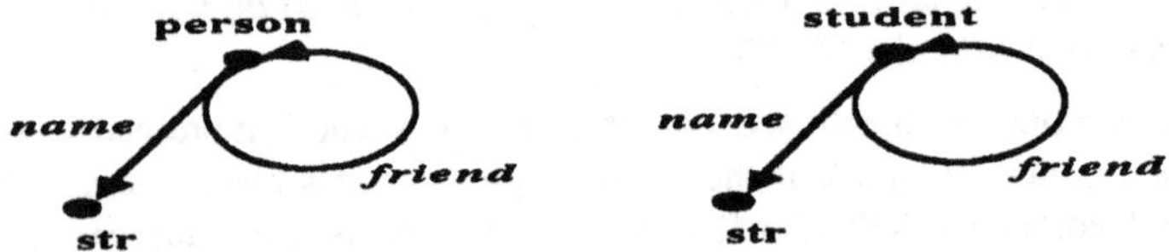

A further example of a type-definition that is not NF-reducible is given by the following schema:

employee := [manager:boss]
boss := [subordinate:{employee}]
seniorEmp := **ISA** employee [manager:seniorEmp, subordinate:{seniorEmp}].

In this case, *seniorEmp* is not NF-reducible: *manager.subordinate* is a cyclic path common to its supertype *employee*, as it is possible to see also in the following figure.

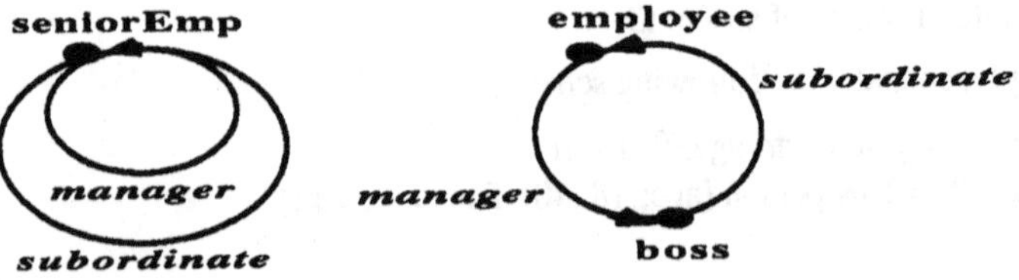

Note that, in analyzing paths we are only concerned with the arcs, although the types associated with corresponding nodes are in **ISA** hierarchy.

In conclusion, we refer to *strong correctness* when the normalization of **ISA** can be performed applying strict inheritance. In the cases in which strict inheritance does not terminate, a further assumption is necessary: *axiomatic subtyping*. Then, if no other contradictions arise, we can normalize the subtype. However, in order to guarantee the semantic equivalence, we need to keep a set inclusion constraint associated to the type-definition in normal form. In this latter case, we are in presence of *weak correctness*.

4 Conclusion and Future Work

The work presented in this paper focuses on the static verification of the schema of an Object-Oriented database. In our proposal, the verification is carried out within the process of type normalization, performed using strict inheritance. Strict inheritance has been conceived in order to resolve inheritance conflicts, by using the refinement rules. This approach guarantees that subtyping is preserved after normalization, for legal **ISA** hierarchies, or the process is stopped if illegal subtypings are identified. Unfortunately, there is a class of schemas that is not correctly handled by the methods based on the well known refinement rules proposed in literature. This class of schemas has been characterized and a criterion to process such schemas has been proposed.

The work presented is part of a larger activity carried out within the project Mosaico [15], an environment for the specification, verification, and rapid prototyping of OODB applications. Mosaico has been experimented on a specific application: the project PORT [8]. This application concerns a system for the management and control of railway traffic. Based on our experience, we believe that the result of this work can be applied to other complex applications. The experience on the project PORT gave us suggestions for future activity. After having completed the implementation of the Static Verifier Module, which embodies the results presented in this paper, the next goal is to verify the correctness of a schema enriched with explicit integrity constraints. To this end, a study on its feasibility, related to the expressive power of the language, is being carried out.

References

1. A.Albano, L.Cardelli, R.Orsini; "Galileo: A Strongly-Typed, Interactive Conceptual Language"; ACM Transactions on Database Systems; Vol.10, No.2, June 1985.
2. M.Atkinson, F.Bancilhon, D.DeWitt, K.Dittrich, D.Maier, S.Zdonik; "The Object-Oriented Database System Manifesto"; 1st Int. Conf. on Deductive and Object-Oriented Databases; W.Kim et al. (eds.), 1989, 40-57.

3. J.Banerjee, H.Chou, J.Garza, W.Kim, D.Woelk, N.Ballou; "Data Model Issues for Object-Oriented Applications"; in "Readings in Database Systems" ed. by M.Stonebraker; Morgan Kaufmann Pub.; San Mateo, CA, 1988.
4. A.Biliris, N.H.Gehani, N.V.Jagadish, W.D.Roome; "ODE Object Database & Environment"; AT&T Bell Laboratories, Technical Report, Murray Hill, New Jersey; 1992.
5. R.J.Brachman, H.J.Levesque; "The tractability of Subsumption in Frame-Based Description Languages"; Proc. of National Conference on Artificial Intelligence - AAAI 84, 34-37; Austin, 1984.
6. M.L.Brodie, J.Mylopoulos, J.W.Schmidt; "On Conceptual Modelling"; Springer-Verlag, 1984.
7. L.Cardelli; "A Semantics of Multiple Inheritance"; Readings in Object-Oriented Database Systems; ed. by S.B.Zdonik and D.Maier; 1990.
8. F.Camurri, M.Missikoff, G.Sissa; "An Object-Oriented Model for Railways Traffic Supervision"; Proc. of ANIPLA Conference, Genova, Sept. 1992.
9. C. Cauvet, C. Rolland, C. Proix; "Information System Design: an Expert System Approach"; in Advances in Database Technology - EDBT '88, J.W. Schmidt, S. Ceri, M. Missikoff (Eds.), LNCS 303, Springer-Verlag, 1988.
10. A.Formica, M.Missikoff; "Adding Integrity Constraints to Object-Oriented Database"; ISMM First International Conference on Information and Knowledge Management (CIKM-92), Baltimore, November 1992.
11. A.Formica, M.Missikoff; "Modeling Semantic Integrity Constraints in Object-Oriented Database Schemas"; "Logidata+: Deductive Databases with Complex Objects"; LNCS 701, P.Atzeni (Ed.), Springer Verlag, 1993.
12. A.Formica, M.Missikoff, S.Vazzana; "An Object-Oriented Data Model for Artificial Intelligence Applications"; Next Generation Information Systems Technology, LNCS 504, J.W.Schmidt, A.A.Stogny (Eds.), Springer Verlag, 1991.
13. M. Jarke; "DAIDA: Conceptual Modelling and Knowledge-Based Support for Information Systems"; Technique et Science Informatique, v.9 n.2, 1990.
14. W.Kim; "Object-Oriented Databases: Definition and Research Directions"; IEEE Trans. on Knowledge and Data Engineering; Vol.2, N.3; September 1990.
15. H.Lam, M.Missikoff; "Mosaico: A Specification and Rapid Prototyping Environment for Object-Oriented Database Applications"; Technical Note 1993.
16. C.Lecluse, P.Richard; "The O_2 Database Programming Language"; Proc. of VLDB Conference; 1989.
17. C.Lecluse, P.Richard, F.Velez; "O_2: an Object-Oriented Data Model"; Proc. of ACM SIGMOD Conference; Chicago, 1988.
18. D.Shipman; "The Functional Data Model and the Data Language DAPLEX"; Readings in Object-Oriented Database Systems; S.B.Zdonik and D.Maier (Eds.); 1990.

Power Efficient Filtering of Data on Air

T. Imielinski[1], S. Viswanathan and B. R. Badrinath[1]

Dept of Computer Science, Rutgers University
New Brunswick, NJ 08903

Abstract

Organizing massive amount of information on communication channels is a new challenge to the data management and telecommunication communities. In this paper, we consider wireless data broadcasting as a way of disseminating information to a massive number of battery powered palmtops. We show that different physical requirements of the wireless digital medium make the problem of organizing wireless broadcast data different from data organization on the disk. We demonstrate that providing index or hashing based access to the data transmitted over wireless is very important for extending battery life and can result in very significant improvement in battery utilization. We describe two methods (*Hashing* and *Flexible Indexing*) for organizing and accessing broadcast data in such a way that two basic parameters: tuning time, which affects battery life, and access time (waiting time for data) are minimized.

1 Introduction

In this paper, we consider wireless data broadcasting as a way of disseminating information to a massive number of battery powered palmtops. In this scenario the clients, equipped with palmtops will filter the incoming stream of information in order to match the pre-specified requests. Filtering will not involve transmitting any requests to the server - it will be a *receive only* activity targeted at monitoring and ad hoc querying of the data stream.

We show that different physical requirements of the wireless digital medium make the problem of organizing wireless broadcast data different from data organization on the disk. We demonstrate that providing index or hashing based access to the data transmitted over wireless is very important from the battery life point of view and can result in significant improvement in battery utilization, possibly of orders of magnitude. New technology can utilize and build upon some well known techniques (file organization and access). These traditional solutions cannot be applied directly though and need substantial modification because of the different physical limitations. New solutions require merging interdisciplinary expertise ranging from new communication protocols to file system and database design.

This paper and [3] provide different organization and access methods for the wireless broadcast data. In [3] we concentrate on indexing methods, with special emphasis on the access time, while in this paper we analyze a hashing scheme and an index based scheme with special emphasis on minimizing the tuning time. The schemes presented in this paper are flexible in the sense that, we can sacrifice access time for a gain in tuning time and vice versa. We will concentrate here on the wireless communication medium, although most of the presented work will also apply to the fixed network.

We will distinguish between two fundamental ways of providing users with information:

- *Data Broadcasting*: Periodic broadcasting of data on the channel. Accessing broadcasted data does not require uplink transmission and is "listen only."

[1]Work supported in part by NSF (SGER) award IRI-9307165

Querying is viewed as *filtering* of the incoming data *stream* according to the user specified "filter".

- *Interactive/On-Demand:* The client requests a piece of data on the uplink channel and the server responds by sending this piece of data to the client.

In practice, a mixture of the above two modes will be used. The most frequently demanded items (weather, stock, traffic) will be broadcasted. Since the cost of broadcast does not depend on the number of users who "listen" this method will scale up with no penalty when the number of requests grows. For example, if the weather information is broadcasted every minute, then it doesn't matter whether 10 or 10000 users are listening, the average access time will be 30 seconds. This would not be the case if the weather was provided on demand. The "on-demand" mode will have to be used for the less often requested items. Broadcasting them periodically would be a waste of bandwidth. However, even in the pure "on-demand" mode- it makes sense to batch similar requests together (multicast as opposed to unicast) and send the answer once rather than cater individually to each request. Periodic data broadcasting is the main topic of this paper.

MOTIVATION

Power conservation is a key issue for small palmtop units which typically run on small AA batteries [2]. The lifetime of a battery is expected to increase only 20% over the next 10 years [7]. A typical AA cell is rated to give 800 mA-Hr at 1.2 V (.96 W-Hr). The constraint of limited available energy is expected to drive all solutions to mobile computing on palmtops. Assuming that the power source of the palmtop to be 10 AA cells with a CD-ROM and a display, the constant power dissipation in a CD-ROM (for disk spinning) will be about 1 W. The power dissipation for display will be around 2.5 W. Thus the assumed power source will last for 2.7 Hrs. Thus to increase the longevity of the batteries, the CD-ROM and the display may have to be powered off most of the time. Apart from CD-ROM and display, the CPU and the memory of the palmtops also consume power. There is a growing pressure on hardware vendors to come up with the energy efficient processors and memories. The Hobbit chip from AT&T is such a processor which consumes only 250 mW in the full operation mode. The power in "doze" mode is only 50 μW (the ratio of power consumption in normal operating mode to doze mode is 5000). When the palmtop is listening to the channel, the CPU must be in active mode for examining data packets (finding, if they match the predefined data). This is a waste of energy since on an average only a very few data packets are of interest to the particular unit. It is definitely beneficial if the palmtop can slip into doze mode most of the time and "wake up" only when the data of interest is expected to arrive. This requires the ability of selective *tuning* which is discussed in detail in this paper. In our model we explore filtering of data from the data broadcast using selective tuning features. The mobile clients will remain in a doze mode most of the time and tune in periodically to get information which is broadcasted on the communication channel.

Wireless data broadcasting can be viewed as *storage on the air* - an extension of the client's memory. Because of its periodic nature, latency of broadcast (the period between two successive broadcasts) will serve as the access time of such a memory and will not depend on the number of users accessing it. Such "public" storage will actually outperform any traditional storage media, for a sufficiently large number of users (this is shown in [4]).

Broadcasting over a fast, fixed network has been investigated as an information dissemination mechanism in the past. In the Datacycle project [6] at Bellcore the database circulates on a high bandwidth network (140 Mb/s) and individual users query this data by filtering the relevant information using a special massively parallel transceiver capable of filtering up to 200 million predicates a second. The main difference between the broadcasting considered in this paper and the broadcasting model used in the Datacycle architecture is that battery life was of no concern at all in the Datacycle architecture and this precisely our concern.

Gifford in [5] describes a system where newspapers are broadcasted over the FM band and down loaded by a PC equipped with radio receivers. There is a single communication channel and tuning time plays little role since the PCs are connected to a continuous power supply.

In section 2, we discuss data organization methods suitable for broadcasting. In section 3 and in section 4 we discuss two indexing schemes for organizing and broadcasting data. In section 3 we discuss the ***hashing*** scheme and in section 4 ***flexible indexing*** is discussed; we also compare the performance of the two schemes in this section. In Section 5 we present conclusions and discuss future work.

2 Data Organization Basics of Broadcasting

Consider a file consisting of a number of records which are identified by keys. The file is not static and can be updated frequently so its size can grow and shrink at any time. Suppose that the server broadcasts this file periodically to a number of clients. The clients will only receive the broadcasted data and are interested in fetching individual records (identified by a key) from the file. Therefore fetching individual records from the broadcasted file will be performed *without* transmitting an uplink request but by *filtering* the incoming broadcasting *stream* for the given data item. Hence, queries will be answered only by *listening* to the channel. Data filtering is done by direct key matching.

Example *Consider the stock ticker tape broadcasted continuously. Each "edition" of the broadcast may include different groups of stocks; those which are currently "on the move". Stocks are identified by their symbols and the clients may be interested in monitoring pre-specified stocks or just in obtaining an isolated stock quotation.*

We would like to organize the broadcasted data in such a way that the following two parameters are minimized:

- *Access Time*: Time elapsed from the moment a client issues a query to the moment the answer is received by the client.

- *Tuning Time*: Amount of time spent by the client, listening to the channel.

Having these two parameters makes the data organization on the broadcast a problem which is different from the organization of the disk based files, where only one parameter - access time is taken into consideration. Here, we will have to optimize with respect to two parameters which work against each other.

If data is broadcasted without any form of directory, then the client in order to filter a data item, will have to tune to the channel on an average half of the time it takes to for the broadcast. As we will see, this is unacceptable as it requires the client's CPU to be active for a long time, consuming scarce battery resources. We would rather provide a selective tuning enabling the client to "wake up" only when data of interest is being broadcasted. We assume that the communication channel is the source of *all* information to the client including data as well as directories. We assume a *single channel* since multiple channels are really equivalent to a single channel with capacity (bit rate/bandwidth) equivalent to the combined capacity of the corresponding channels.

Selective tuning will require that the server broadcasts directory together with the data. The directory may be eventually cached by the client but new clients who have *no prior knowledge* of the broadcasted data organization will have to access it from the air. Besides, we will assume that the file will be changed by the server and can grow and shrink any time between successive broadcasts. The smallest logical unit of the broadcast will be called a *bucket.* The size of the bucket is a multiple of the size of a packet. Both access time and the tuning time will be measured in terms of number of buckets.

Broadcasts will contain successive versions of the file which will constitute (together with the directory) successive *bcasts* [2]. Each bucket of the current *bcast* will have a number called the *address* of the bucket - the sequence number of this bucket within the current *bcast.* Pointers to the specific buckets within the *bcast* will be provided by specifying the *offset* between the bucket which holds the pointer and

[2] a version of the broadcasting of the file along with any index or other control information

the bucket to which the pointer points to. The actual time of the broadcast for such a bucket will be calculated by multiplying ($offset$ - 1) by the time necessary to broadcast a single bucket (which depends on the bit rate of the channel and the size of the bucket).

A naive method of providing a directory would be to broadcast the index before each broadcast of the file. This, however, leads to an unacceptably large average access time (having to wait first for directory and then for the data). Hence, there is a need to interleave the directory with the data more often to reduce the initial waiting time. Then however, we increase the overall length of the broadcast.

We could also provide hashing based schemes to improve the direct access properties and reduce the tuning time. However, even if the hashing function is perfect we may end up with many buckets which are "half empty" - increasing the size of the broadcast and consequently the access time.

Notice that in the traditional I/O terms the tuning time roughly corresponds to the disk access time in terms of number of disk blocks being accessed. However, the tuning time is fixed per broadcasted bucket, while the access time to the disk block varies depending on the position of the read/write head. The broadcast access time, on the other hand, corresponds to *space* requirement of the data on the disk. The larger, the file size the longer broadcast access time. Therefore, adding a data directory (index or hash) improves the tuning time while it *increases* the access time[3].

In general, different types of users may need different tradeoffs between tuning time and access time. Some may value lower access time and may have more leverage in terms of the tuning time (larger, laptop machines which may have more powerful batteries), some others will prefer lower tuning time and will be ready to pay for it in terms of the access time. Thus we need *flexible* data organization methods capable of accommodating different classes of users[4]. Distributed indexing method provided in [3] is not flexible in this sense, since it does not benefit from a more lenient tuning time requirements. In this paper we introduce two data organization methods which can be used for different priorities in terms of tuning and access time. The hashing method makes it possible to trade tuning time for the access time by changing the size of the overflow area. The *flexible* indexing method is also parameterized in such a way that depending on the value of the parameter we may change the ratio of the access to tuning time.

3 HASHING

Hashing based schemes do not require a separate directory to be broadcasted together with the data. The hashing parameters are simply included in the data buckets. Each bucket has two parts : the *Data* part and the *Control part.* The control part is the "investment" which helps guide searches to minimize the access and listening times. Control part for the first N buckets (B) includes:

- Hash Function: h
- Shift: The pointer (i.e. the actual bucket number) to a bucket which contains keys K such that h(K) = address(B)

The shift function is necessary since most often the hashing function will not be perfect. In such a case there will be collisions and the colliding records will be stored immediately following the bucket assigned to them by the hashing function. This will create an offset for other buckets (pushing the rest of the file "down"). The control part of the rest of the buckets have an offset to the beginning of the next broadcast.

[3]Sounding really strange from the traditional file access point of view. It is obvious however, since broadcasting index increases the total size of the broadcast

[4]Notice this whole discussion arises because we have two basic performance parameters instead of just one as in the case of disk based files

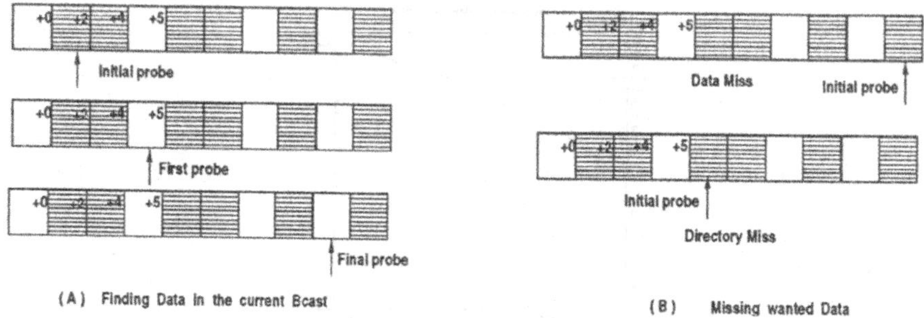

Figure 1: Hashing A

We will now present two hashing protocols: *Hashing A* and *Hashing B*. *Hashing B* will be an improvement of *Hashing A*. *Hashing B* will require maintaining some additional information.

3.1 Hashing A

The access protocol for record with key K is as follows:

- Probe the current bucket, read the control data from it and calculate $h(K)$.
- IF *Current bucket* $\# < h(K)$
  —THEN Go into *doze mode* and listen again to slot $h(K)$
  —ELSE wait till the beginning of the next *bcast*, repeat protocol again
- At $h(K)$, get the *Shift*, go into *doze mode* to wake up after *Shift* number of buckets
- This time listen until either the record with key K is found (successful) or with key L $(h(L) \neq h(K))$ is found (failure)

Figure 1(A)[5] illustrates a simple scenario of locating a key K = 15 in the file, hashed Modulo 4. Assuming that the initial probe takes place on the second physical bucket, the client reads the hashing function from the control part of the that bucket and proceeds with the first probe to the bucket number of four which, in case there is no overflow would contain the key K = 15, if it exists in the file. Since there is overflow, the keys are shifted and the client reads the value of the shift (5) and goes into the doze mode, and tunes in, in the final probe to the beginning of the "logical bucket" number four (to conclude whether the key K =15 is present it must look at all the overflow buckets of that bucket).

Figure 1(B) illustrates the cases when the client has to wait until the next broadcast in order to locate the given key K. This may occur either due to the *data miss* or due to the *directory miss*. In the data miss scenario the client's initial probe comes after the bucket containing the key which he wants. In the directory miss case, the client's initial probe comes before the bucket containing his key but *after* the bucket which contains a proper pointer (in this case the physical bucket number four). In such a case there is no way for the client to find out that the key which he is looking for is still to be broadcasted and the client has to wait until the next bcast.

[5]In all the figures, the buckets which are fully white denote the logical buckets (by a *logical bucket* of k, we mean the $h'(k)$ bucket) and the ones with bars denote the overflow buckets (of the preceding white bucket). The numbers in the right hand side top corners of some buckets denote the shift value in the control part of that bucket.

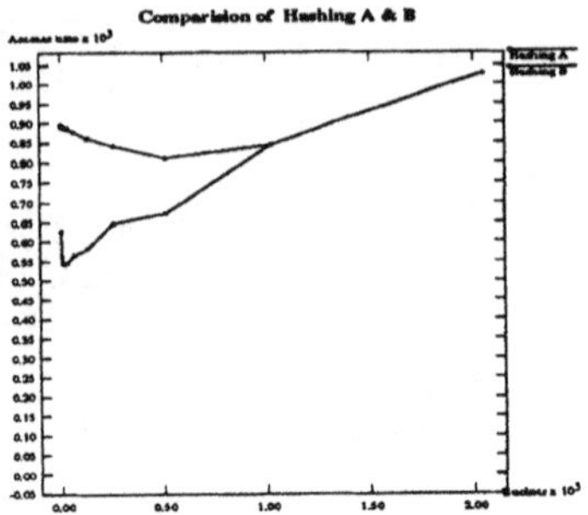

Figure 2: Comparison of Hashing A & Hashing B

Given the file, what is the hashing function minimizing the access time? For the disk based files the best function is the perfect hashing function (the one with no overflow). For the broadcasted files this is not the case. This critical difference comes from the fact that the total number of broadcasted buckets has immediate impact on the access time (the more one has to wait for the next version of the file). The perfect hashing function does not minimize the number of physical buckets necessary for the file bcast. On the contrary, the more overflow buckets are used, the smaller the total number of broadcasted buckets is. Indeed, the more overflow buckets the file has, the lesser "half-empty" buckets are broadcasted and this consequently results in better bucket utilization. The smaller the overflow area the lower is the tuning time which reaches minimum for the perfect hashing function. This further shows the basic differences between the file organization for broadcast and file organization for the disk storage. Hashing based scheme for the broadcasted file displays the *random access* behavior for the tuning time and the *sequential access* behavior for the access time (when the size of the file matters). Access schemes for the disk based files are only characterized by one parameter - the access time. Two parameters: tuning time and the access time are needed for the broadcasted files and the behavior of the access time for broadcasted files is drastically different from the access time for the disk based ones. For example, the perfect hashing function is not always "perfect" for the broadcasted files.

3.2 Hashing B

Hashing A can be further improved if we notice that the directory miss phenomenon may be significantly reduced with a minor modification to the hashing function. Assume that d is the size of the minimum overflow chain. We can now modify the hashing function h to

$$h'(K) \begin{cases} h(K) & \text{if } h(K) = 1 \\ (h(K)-1)(1+min\_overflow)+1 & \text{if } h(K) > 1 \end{cases}$$

and leave the rest of the scheme unchanged. In this way, the new hashing function h' takes under consideration the shift introduced by the overflow (taking under consideration the value of the minimum overflow).

Figure 2 illustrates the improvement, which is because the probability of a data miss is significantly reduced in case of *Hashing B*. If the sizes of the overflow chains per logical bucket do not differ much, then the reduction is substantial [6]. In the extreme case, when all buckets have the same size of the overflow chain, h' turns into the perfect hashing function for the file whose bucket size is increased by $(1+d)$ times.

[6]the hashing function over here is a uniform hashing function

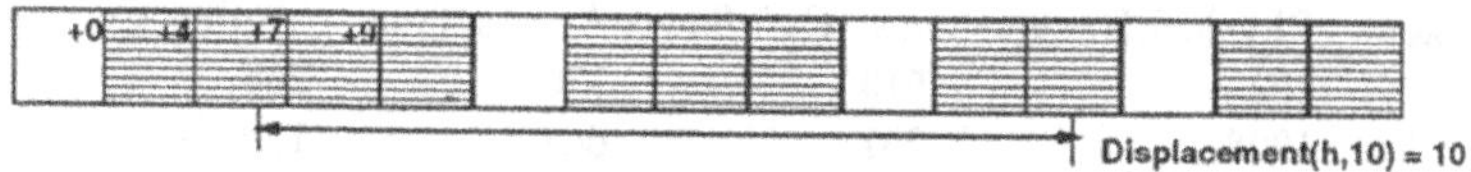

Missing directory for Hashing A

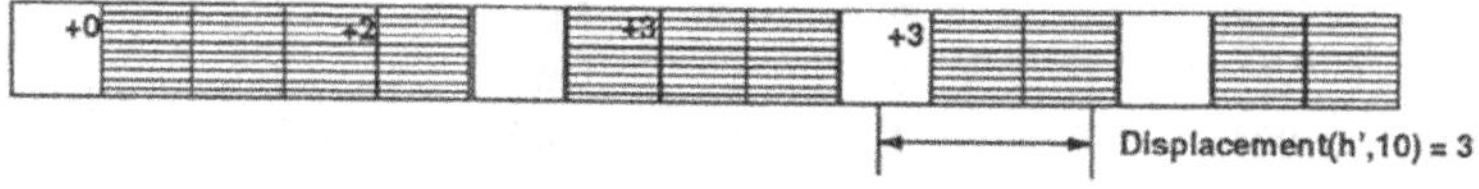

Missing directory for Hashing B

Logical buckets = 4 (h(k) = mod 4)

Figure 3: Displacement Comparison

The expected access time for the Hashing B can be calculated as follows. Let h' be the modified hashing function of h. By *Displacement*(h, K) we denote the difference between the address of the physical bucket where K resides (*Physical_bucket(k)*) and the designated bucket for k ($h'(k)$)computed as:

$Displacement(h, K) = Physical\_bucket(K) - h'(K)$

The expected access time is computed by calculating for each key K in the file, the access time "per key" and then averaging it out. The expected access time "per key" is the combination of two factors:

- If the initial probe is in the part of the broadcast between the designated bucket and the physical bucket of the key, then the data miss occurs despite of the fact that the key is still ahead in the current broadcast. Thus, the unit has to wait an extra revolution. This is calculated as[7]

  $(Displacement(h, K)/Data(h)) * (Data(h) + 1/2 * Displacement(h, K))$

- If the initial probe is outside of the displacement area then:

  $(1 - (Displacement(h, K)/Data(h))) * (Data(h) + Displacement(h, K))/2$

  Since in this case the unit has to wait, on average between the *Displacement*(h,K) and the file size.

The expected access time is computed as a sum of expected access times per key divided by the total number of keys in the file (again assuming that all query requests refer to the records in the file)

Figure 3 illustrates the source of the basic advantage of the hashing scheme B over the hashing scheme A. Given the same file and the same key K (K=10), the probability of the directory miss for the *Hashing B* is much smaller than that for *Hashing A*. This probability is proportional to the value of $Displacement(h, K)$ which is shown for both schemes and is demonstrated to be much smaller for the Hashing B. In both the Hashing schemes, getting a good hashing function depends on the distribution of the keys.

Table 1 illustrates how the expected access time and the tuning time depend on the hashing function used. The table shows the average access time and the average tuning time for the situation when there are 17 records per bucket (each record with 30 bytes of length). The size of "control part" is 24 bytes(per bucket). The size of the data file is 1024 buckets hence the total number of data records is 17408. Notice that

[7] *Data(h)* is the size of bcast for the given data file, for a given hash function h

Buckets	Physical.Buckets	Av. Overflow	Access Time	Tuning time
2	1025	513	770	258
4	1026	257	642	130
16	1032	65	549	34
32	1040	33	537	18
64	1056	17	537	10
128	1088	9	549	6
512	1280	3	642	3
2048	2048	1	1025	2

Table 1: Access time for Hashing Scheme B

the perfect hashing function which gives 1024 logical buckets (which corresponds to 2048, physical buckets) gives the access time (1025) which is far from optimal, thought the tuning time (of 3) was the minimum for this case. In fact the optimal access time is provided by the hashing function with 32 or 64 logical buckets, but here we compromise on the tuning time which is 18 or 10 times as much (respectively). This is a consequence of the small number of physical buckets. Notice that the lower level hashing functions have even smaller number of buckets but then the data miss probability due to hitting the first time the right logical bucket is too high (if this happens we have to wait for the next broadcasted version). Thus the higher the number of logical buckets the lower the tuning time. For lower number of logical buckets the access time is also high as the data miss is high.

Hence, *perfect hashing function does not provide the minimal access time for the broadcasted files*

In fact the minimal access time is achieved by the hashing functions with significantly smaller number of logical buckets than the perfect hashing function. Notice that the tuning time goes asymptotically down to 3 data accesses when the number of logical buckets grows (the minimum is achieved for the perfect hashing function).

There are a number of possible other hashing schemes which can be used as well for the broadcasted files, however in our view the hashing scheme presented above provides us with the best access time/tuning time profile. For instance, grouping all overflow buckets at the end of the file with each logical bucket having a pointer to its overflow area leads to alternative hashing scheme. Its access time will be comparable to the first of our hashing schemes since the data miss behavior in this case will be equivalent to the first of our schemes. The second scheme will provide better access time due to the reduced data miss.

Notice that hashing is a *flexible* method of organizing broadcasted data. Indeed, if we have more leverage in terms of the tuning time we can improve the access time by simply reducing the number of logical buckets (thus by increasing the overflow).

However, the price to be paid in case we want to minimize the tuning time in terms of the access time increase is rather high for hashing methods considered here (perfect or near perfect hashing increases the size of the broadcast and consequently the access time). A natural question is whether can improve the tuning time of hashing method without paying a high access time penalty same level? One way of achieving this goal is to provide a hybrid scheme mixing hashing and indexing: use hashing to reach the right logical bucket and then use indexing within each logical bucket to reach the right physical bucket. Statistically, there is some empty space in the "last" physical, overflow bucket of each logical bucket so we could *reuse* this extra space to store this local index. Unfortunately, the amount of this empty space is a statistical variable and cannot be guaranteed - hence additional indexing would almost surely increase the overall size of the broadcast and add to the access time.

In the next section we show a method which is not based on hashing but which can maintain its good access time characteristics while significantly lowering the tuning time.

instance, the index in the data bucket #25 specifies that for all key values which are smaller than 25 the client has to tune to the bucket that is 43 buckets away which is bucket # 1 of the next *bcast* (in this case the client simply missed the key and has to wait for the next broadcast). If the key is larger than 49 then the client has to tune again to the data bucket #49 (which the offset #= 25 indicates). This data bucket will provide an index to help the client further on. Similarly, if the searched key is larger than 33 (but not larger than 49) then the client should tune again 9 buckets ahead where he will use the index at the bucket 33. Not all data buckets contain the index though. Notice that if we go "further down" the index for the data bucket #25, we reach the tuple with (first field) 31. Here if, the key is between 31 and 33 then the client will not search the tuples that follow and will tune to the buckets between 31 and 33 in search of the key. Notice that the index information is *distributed* between different data buckets.

Formally, the control index can be divided into two parts: the *binary control* index and the *local index*. The *binary control index* and the *local index* together will be called *control index*. The control index consists of tuples. Each tuple has two fields. The first field is a key for a data record and the second field is a pointer to the data bucket containing that record. By a pointer we mean an $offset$ value, which denotes the relative position of the data bucket from this bucket. Each bucket has an $offset$ to the beginning of the next data segment.

The *binary control index* has $\lceil \log_2 i \rceil$ tuples. Where i is the number of data segments in front of this data segment (including this one).

- (a) The first tuple consists of the key of the first data record in the current data bucket and an offset to the beginning of the next broadcast
- (b) The k th tuple consists of the key of the first data record of the $\lfloor \log_2 i/2^{k-1} \rfloor + 1$ th data segment followed by an offset to the first data bucket of that data segment.

The *local index* consists of m tuples (m is a parameter which will depend on number of tuples a bucket can hold, the access time desired etc). The *local index* further partitions the data segment into $m+1$ data *subsegments* D_1, D_2,...,D_{m+1} and consists of the following m tuples :

- (a) The first tuple consists of the key of the first data record of the D_{m+1}. The specified offset points to the first data bucket of D_{m+1}.
- (b) The k th tuple consists of the key of the first data record of the D_{m+1-k} followed by an offset to the first data bucket of D_{m+1-k}.

The first bucket of each data segment stores control index as well as (if space allows) data records. The access protocol for a record with key k is as follows :

- (i) Make an initial probe and get the offset to the beginning of the next data segment and go into doze mode
- (ii) Tune in again to the beginning of the designated next data segment.
  - If the search key K is lesser than the first field of the first tuple in the *binary control index* then (the record has been missed) doze till the offset given by the second field and proceed as in step (ii) (else)
  - Search through the rest of the *binary control index* from the top to the bottom of the index to see if K is greater than or equal to the first field of each tuple, if the answer is positive follow the pointer of the first such tuple and proceeds as in step (ii) (else)

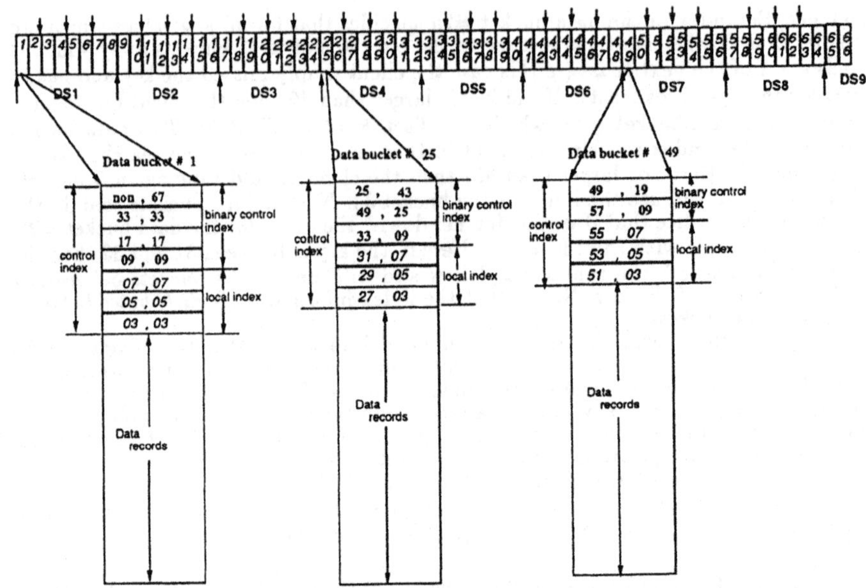

Figure 4: Example for Flexible Indexing

4 Flexible Indexing

We are now going to explore the fact that the file is completely known to the server prior to the broadcast. Notice that hashing divides the file into p logical buckets of statistically varying size. The sizes of each individual logical bucket vary and depend on the hashing function itself. Rather than using hashing we can simply divide the file into p segments and provide some indexing to help the user "navigate" and reduce the tuning time. The parameter p will make the indexing method proposed in this section *flexible* since depending on its value we will either get very good tuning time or very good access time.

We will assume that the data records are sorted in ascending (or descending) order. We divide the set of data buckets into p parts [8]. The data segments are numbered 1 through p. The first bucket in each of the data segment will contain a control part consisting of the *control index*. The control index is a binary index [9] which, for a given key K helps to locate the data bucket which contains that key.

Let us begin describing the technique with an example. Figure 4 shows a set of 66 data buckets[10]. Let $p = 9$, with the length of all but the last of the data segments be 8 buckets. The first bucket of each data segment contains an index. Three such buckets are illustrated in Figure 4. Each index entry is a pair which consists of the key value and the *offset* [11] showing the client when to tune again to find the searched key. For

[8] all but with the possible exception of the last, of the these parts are equal in length

[9] There is no other specific reason beyond simplicity for keeping the index binary

[10] the bucket number is also the key of the first record in that bucket

[11] as explained earlier *offset* denotes the relative distance of the bucket from this bucket (including this one)

- Search through the *local index* to see if K is greater than or equal to the first field of each tuple, if the answer is positive follow the pointer of the first such tuple, tune in at the designated bucket and proceeds as in (iii)

- (iii) Search the next $(L\_data\_segment/(m+1))$ buckets, sequentially to locate K, where *L_data_segment* denotes the length of a data segment.

Let us consider an example to illustrate the above protocol. Consider Figure 4 and let the key we are looking for be 54 and let the initial probe be made at bucket 20. The offset at bucket 20 will direct us to the beginning of the next data segment, in this case it is 25. The client tunes in at bucket 25. It checks to see if the query key (54) is lesser than 25, the answer is in negative. So the next tuple is checked. $54 > 49$ and hence the pointer 25 is selected. The client now tunes in after 25 data buckets to bucket 49. Searches through the control index in bucket 49, the comparison against the fourth tuple is successful ($54 > 53$) and hence the client tunes in at the fifth bucket. Then it searches sequentially through buckets 53 and 54 to find K.

4.1 Analysis

The tuning time[12] using the flexible indexing technique is : $\lceil \log_2 p \rceil + L\_data\_segment/(m+1)$ in the worst case. In general, the average tuning time is $\lceil \log_2 i \rceil + L\_data\_segment/2*(m+1)$ where i is the number of data segments in front of this data segment (including this one). This is because we require (atmost) $\lceil \log_2 p \rceil$ tunings after the initial probe to get to the relevant data segment. Once we get to the data segment that has the search key, then on an average we have to search $Data/(2*(m+1)*p)$ buckets sequentially [13]. Thus on an average the tuning time is

$$(\sum \lceil \log_2 i \rceil + Data/(2*(m+1)))/p$$

$\forall i \; 1 \leq i \leq p$ and *Data* being the size of the entire broadcast [14], thus upper bound on the average tuning time is

$$(\lceil \log_2 p \rceil + Data/(2*p*(m+1)))$$

Now, let us analyze the access time. Let the time required to get to the first bucket of the next data segment, on making an initial probe be called *probe wait*. On an average the probe wait is half the size of *L_data_segment*. After coming to the first bucket of the next data segment the client has to wait half the size of the *bcast* size (*Data*), on an average. This wait is called the *data wait*. The access time is the sum of the above two *waits*. Hence the access time is $0.5*(L\_data\_segment)+0.5*(Data)$ i.e.,

$$0.5 * Data * (1+p)/p$$

Let the size of the raw file (without the control index) be *File*. The total space(in terms of the number of buckets) occupied by the control index is
$(\sum \lceil \log_2 i \rceil + p*m)/n$, $\forall i \; 1 \leq i \leq p$
that is, $p*(\lceil \log_2 p \rceil + m)/n$ is an upper bound for the number of additional buckets due to the control index. Where n is the number of tuples that a bucket can hold.

The size of the final file (after the control index is added) is *Data* and $Data = File + p*(\lceil \log_2 p \rceil + m)/n$ Thus the access time using flexible indexing is :

$$0.5*(File + p*(\lceil \log_2 p \rceil + m)/n)*(1+p)/p$$

[12] we will ignore the initial probe and another first probe (if the former resulted in going to the next *bcast*) in the following discussion to convey the formula without confusion

[13] The half of the size of the data segment and $L\_data\_segment = Data/p$

[14] Data is the collection of all the data buckets and all of the control index

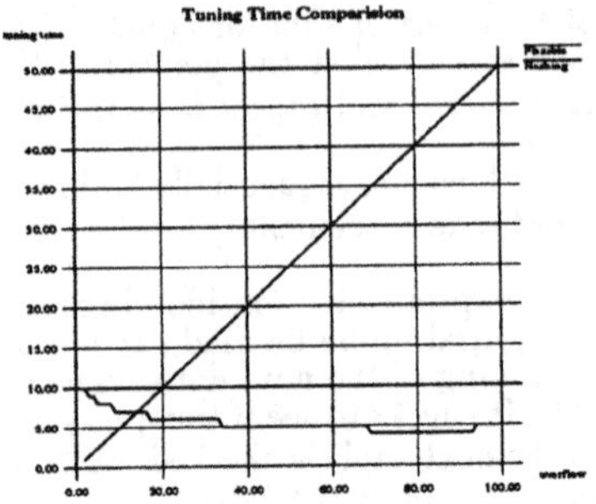

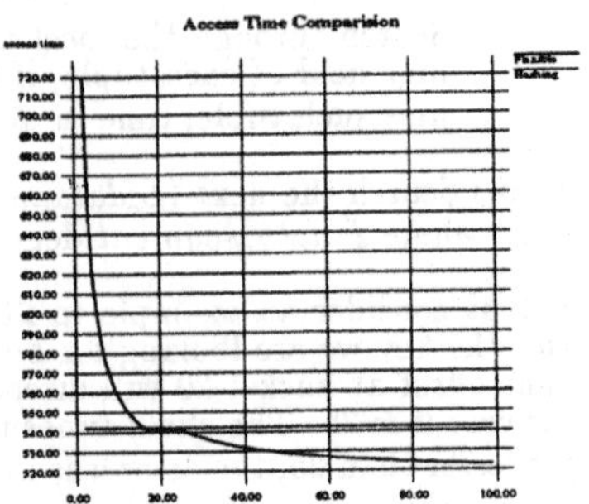

Figure 5: Comparison of Tuning Time & Access Time

4.2 Comparison of Hashing and Flexible Indexing

In the comparison we will consider a very good hashing function which will give us equal overflow (of length *over*) for all the values i.e., the minimum overflow and the average overflow are the same. Let the hashing function have p logical buckets i.e., the keys will be mapped into some number between 1 through p. To have a fair comparison we assume that *over* and the length of the data segment (*L_data_segment*) are the same. The hashing function divides the data buckets into p parts (each of length *L_data_segment*), as the overflow is the same for all the logical buckets.

The access time using hashing in this case is
$0.5 * (over) + 0.5 * (File + p/2)$ that is

$$0.5 * ((File + p/2) * (1 + p)/p)$$

and the average tuning time is $0.5 * (over)$ i.e.,

$$0.5 * (L\_data\_segment)$$

Let us first compare the tuning time using the two schemes. The tuning time due to flexible indexing is better when

$$(0.5 * (L\_data\_segment)) > (\log_2 p + Data/(2 * p * (m + 1))) \text{ i.e.,}$$

$$File > (2 * p * \log_2 p * m/(m + 1) - (\log_2 p + m) * p/n)$$

where the number of tuples in the *local index*, $m = min((n/2 - \log_2 p), (L\_data\_segment/2))$ when $(n/2 - \log_2 p) > 0$ else $m = 1$.

Figure 5(Left) illustrates a comparison of the tuning times using flexible indexing and hashing. The x-axis represents the length of *over* (overflow size which is equal to the size of the data segment) in terms of number of buckets. The number of data buckets in the file is 1024. The capacity of a bucket, n, was assumed to be 100. As the size of *over* increases, the number of data segments (p) decreases. In the hashing scheme the tuning time is half the data segment size and this grows linearly with the increase in the size of data segment. But in case of flexible indexing the tuning time grows very slowly and more over it is not a monotonically increasing function. Notice that when the size of data segment is less than 14 buckets (i.e., $Data < 2 * p * \log_2 p$) the tuning time using flexible indexing is larger than that of the hashing scheme. On the other hand, for for the sizes of data segment of more than 14, flexible indexing is a clear winner.

Let us now consider the access time comparison. Flexible indexing gives a better (lesser) access time when the following is true:
$0.5 * (File + p * (\lceil \log_2 p \rceil + m)/n) * (1 + p)/p \quad < \quad 0.5 * ((File + p/2) * (1 + p)/p)$

$$i.e., when \quad (\lceil \log_2 p \rceil + m) < n/2$$

As the capacity of buckets (n) increases the access time due to flexible indexing increases very slowly and the access time due to hashing increases quite fast. The difference between the access times due to flexible indexing and due to hashing is quite big for large values of p. Another important parameter that affects the access time is the capacity of the buckets i.e., the number of tuples a bucket can hold. Below a threshold of the capacity of buckets the access time of flexible indexing doesn't perform very well. This threshold is when $n/2 < \lceil \log_2 p \rceil + m$, where m is the number of data subsegments per data segment.

The graph in figure 5(Right) illustrates the point we made above. The number of data buckets ($File$) considered is 1024 and p, the number of data segments, is 100 (i.e., the overflow size is 10). The x-axis represents the values of n, the capacity of buckets and the y-axis the access time. When the value of n is small $n/2 < \lceil \log_2 100 \rceil + m$ [15], then hashing performs better than flexible indexing. For large values of n flexible indexing is better in terms of the access time. In the figure $\forall n, 1 \leq n < 16$, $(16/2 \not< (7+1))$ the access time due to hashing is better and $\forall n, 16 \leq n < 25$, $(25/2 \not< (7+5))$ both the methods are comparable in terms of their access times and and $\forall n, 25 \leq n$ flexible indexing performs better.

PRACTICAL IMPLICATIONS

Consider a stock market data of size 128 *Kbytes* that is being broadcasted in a channel of bandwidth 20 *Kbps*. Let the packet length be 128 *bytes*. It takes around 50 seconds to broadcast the whole file and 0.05 seconds to broadcast or tune into a single packet. Let the clients be equipped with the Hobbit Chip (AT&T). The power consumption of the chip in *doze mode* is 50 μW and the consumption in *active mode* is 250 mW.

The *tuning time* as well as the *access time*, if no indexing is used is 25 *seconds* (half of the *bcast* time). With *perfect hashing* we will have to tune into three buckets, resulting in a *tuning time* of 0.15 *seconds*. Thus the battery life is increased by 165 folds. But then the penalty is that the *access time* doubles to 50 seconds.

If we use *hashing B* with 20 logical buckets, then the *tuning time* is 53 buckets i.e., 2.65 *seconds*. Thus the battery life increases by almost 10 times at the cost of the *access time* increasing by just 1%. On using *flexible indexing*, for the same *access time* we can do by just tuning into just 6 ($\lceil log_2 20 \rceil + 1$) buckets. The *tuning time* is 0.3 *seconds*, thus the battery life increases by more than 80 times.

RESULTS

Our results can be summarized as :

- If the access time is of importance (of the two parameters) then if $n/2 < (\lceil \log_2 p \rceil + m)$ then use Hashing. i.e., if the capacity of the buckets are large use Flexible indexing else use Hashing.
- If the tuning time is of importance and if $Data > 2 * p * \log_2 p$ then use flexible indexing i.e., if the overflow is small use hashing else use flexible indexing.
- Hashing schemes should be used when the tuning time requirements are not rigid and when the key size is relatively large compared to the record size [3].
- Indexing schemes should be used when tuning time is restricted and the key size is relatively small compared to the record size [3].

[15] as specified before, $m = min((n/2 - \log_2 p), (L\_data\_segment/2))$ when $(n/2 - \log_2 p) > 0$ else $m = 1$

5 Conclusions

We have studied organization and access for broadcast data, taking a stand that periodic broadcasting is a form of storage. Data is stored "on the air" with the latency of access proportional to the duration of the *bcast*. Broadcasted data can be reorganized "on the fly" and refreshed (reflecting updates) between two successive *bcasts*. The main difference with the disk based files is that we need to minimize two parameters (access time and tuning time) contrary to just one (access time) for the disk based files. While broadcast tuning time roughly corresponds to disk access time, the broadcast access time is an equivalent of the disk space taken by the file.

We investigated two data organization methods namely *Hashing* and *flexible indexing* and we have demonstrated the relative advantages of both the schemes. In [3] which is orthogonal to this paper we also study data organization methods based on different types of indexing called $(1, m)$ *indexing* and *distributed indexing*. Distributed Indexing is better than any Hashing scheme for small key sizes. We provided evidence in [4] that hashing performs better then distributed indexing in case the key sizes are large.

There are a number of research questions which have to be investigated. If filtering has to be done by complex predicate matching then more sophisticated data organizations techniques are needed. In particular we would like to investigate further techniques of secondary indexing. There are a number of communication issues which have to be looked at in detail. How to achieve reliability of the broadcast in error prone environments such as wireless cellular? Since the clients are only listening there is no (or very limited) possibility of the acknowledgment. Multiple Access protocols which guarantee timely delivery of information are necessary for the broadcasting (and especially the directory) to work correctly. Finally, we view data broadcasted on the channel as another level of storage hierarchy, where data is literally "stored on the channel". This view allows us to look at data in a uniform way regardless of whether it is stored in one location or multicasted on the network.

References

[1] Rafael Alonso and Hank Korth, "Database issues in nomadic computing," MITL Technical Report, December 1992.

[2] David Cheriton, Dissemination-Oriented Communication Systems, Stanford University, Tech. Rept. 1992.

[3] T. Imielinski, S.Viswanathan and B.R. Badrinath, "Data on the Air - Organization and Access," Tech Report, DCS - Rutgers University – Oct 93.

[4] T. Imielinski, B. R. Badrinath and S.Viswanathan, "Data Dissemination in Wireless and Mobile Environment," Winlab – Rutgers University, Oct 93.

[5] David Gifford, John Lucassen, and Stephen Berlin, "The application of digital broadcast communication to large scale information systems," IEEE Journal on selected areas in communications, Vol 3, No. 3, May 1985, pp.457–467.

[6] T. F. Bowen et.al., "The Datacycle Architecture," Comm. of the ACM, Vol 35, No. 12, December 1992, pp. 71 – 81.

[7] Samuel Sheng, Ananth Chandrasekaran, and R. W. Broderson, "A portable multimedia terminal for personal communications," IEEE Communications Magazine, December 1992, pp. 64–75.

[8] Bob Ryan, "Communications get personal," BYTE, February 1993, pp. 169–176.

Video Information Contents and Architecture

Rune Hjelsvold

Norwegian Institute of Technology,
N-7034 TRONDHEIM, NORWAY

Abstract. As the use of digital audio and video is increasing so also is the need for a large scale database support of these new data types growing. Users want to share audio and video information and will like to use the same video information in several different presentations. To support video information sharing and reuse an architecture of video information and its contents is proposed. Three levels are defined: The presentation level consists of edited video presentations, the recording level consists of the basic recordings used in the different presentations, and the annotation level consists of descriptions of the contents of the individual recordings. The architecture will support applications in both creating and running a presentation, as well as in annotating and retrieving video information.

1 Introduction

Information access is a key component in everyday activities, ranging from professional activities to entertainment. To make it easy for people to find information various forms of information repositories have been made. In libraries, users may for instance find printed information like books, journals and newspapers, and in the electronic libraries "electronic books" can be found. In the last century, a growing part of the information that we receive is provided as film, television or radio. Unfortunately, the possibilities for users to search in this type of information are still very limited.

It is becoming technologically feasible to develope a system giving the users access to stored video information. At the end user side real-time digital video is supported on more and more platforms at a reasonable cost. Due to the progress in compression algorithms and to the advent of the MPEG standard [6], real-time digital video can be stored and transferred over networks at a resonable data rate (150 KBytes/sec). Several research projects have shown that these network capacities (see for instance [26]) and delivery rates (see [23], [22] and [20]) are, or will soon become, available. The progress in hardware technology will also have an impact of the DBMS [24] resulting in significantly higher performance and storage capacity.

The database community has not yet developed solutions for managing digital video in an uniform and efficient way. The alternatives today for storing digital video is mainly limited to CD-ROMS, small to medium scale hypermedia systems (like Hypercard [1]) and ordinary disks for storing small video files. As the use of digital multimedia increases, there will be a need for large scale multiuser solutions supporting both creation, analysis and retrieval of video information.

Current research in the area of multimedia has taken one of two approaches: the document approach and the hypertext approach. In [19] modelling of a multimedia document is discussed while in [12] the document metaphor has been used to develope a video document architecture. Hypertext is an interactive document allowing the user to browse through a document not by reading it sequentially but by following hyperlinks between hypernodes. The hypertext model is defined in [9] and many researchers are proposing extensions to this model to support video information. A video presentation based on the hypertext model will in this paper be termed "interactive presentations".

In cooperation with the National Library, Rana Branch (NBR), in Norway we will develope a video repository where users can access video information. NBR receives each year copies of all radio and television programs broadcast by the Norwegian Broadcasting Corporation. NBR is responsible for storing all this material under climatically perfect conditions *and for* making it accessible to the users. The goal with our project is to use network and database technologies to provide this access to the most valuable parts of the material.

Our work has not taken a hypertext approach. Instead our focus has been "narrative presentations" like traditional cinematic films and television programs. The approach has been based on cinematic film theory because the last century's research on cinematic film theory has resulted in an understanding of the complex structures of narrative films.

In cinematic film theory a differentiation is made between the composing of a scene (called "mise en scène) and the editing where scenes are put together to form the film (called "montage"). In our work we have made a similar division between *basic components* (equivalent to the scene composition) and *composite components* (equivalent to edited structures).

This paper is organised as follows: In Section 2 we give a short description of the applications which may use the video repository. In Section 3 we discuss the properties and the content descriptions of basic components. Section 4 gives a similar discussion of the composite components. In Section 5 we will give a short evaluation of the proposed architecture while Section 6 concludes the paper and points to areas for further research.

2 Video Applications

In this section we will briefly discuss the applications using the video repository. The applications will share the video information and will thus benefit from a common model of the content and architecture of the video information. Figure 1 illustrates how the different applications may share a common base of video information.

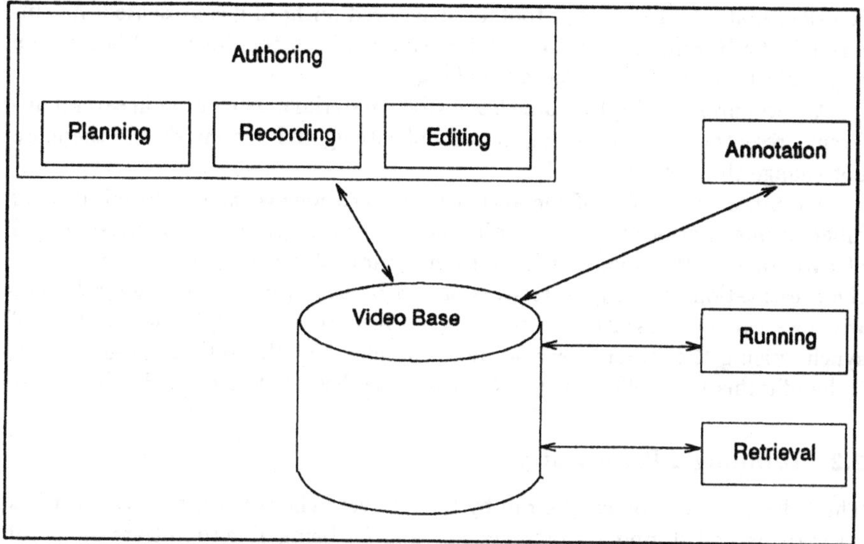

Fig. 1. Applications of the video repository

2.1 Presentation Authoring

Film and television making is a demanding task involving several professions. The process may be divided in different task as shown in Figure 1:

Planning The activites are often coordinated and directed by a set of plans. Plans are also made for the recording (in the context of cinematic film called shooting). During planning the architecture of the final result is often sketched and detailed descriptions of what is to be recorded are made. These plans will be used when the video is recorded and when the video presentation is edited.

Recording The video is normally recorded continuously by a video camera. In some cases, for instance when making animations, the video may be created in a frame-by-frame manner. When, and after, the video is recorded the film makers usually annotate the recorded video with relevant information for the editing task (for instance photographic techniques used, actors participating, and date of recording).

Editing In the editing task the final presentation is made out of the recorded video material. Traditionally the editing process has been cumberstone, demanding that the film maker step through the material to define the cutting point and then splice the pieces together. Digital video can be used to support the editing process by giving the video makers structured tools and easy access to the recorded material. In [10] one tool for structured authoring is presented. As emphasized by Hardman, such tools should support both top-down and bottom-up approaches for video presentation making.

As recognized in [18] the same basic video material may be used in several different presentations. The editing process of cutting and pasting should therefore not change the basic material.

An important aspect of the authoring applications is the synchronization of different information streams. Traditionally, the video presentation has consisted of two tracks - the image and the sound track. When computers are used as the presentation medium more streams can be used (for instance several video windows can be presented on the user's screen concurrently) and the task of synchronizing the stream become more complex and the authors need support to handle this in an efficient way. This topic is discussed in more detail in [10].

2.2 Running a Presentation

The video presentation can be run by the receiver. The receiver needs operations for starting and stopping a presentation, and for being able to initiate temporal pauses in the presentation. For interactive presentations the user needs operations for following hyperlinks between hypernodes and blocks of video information.

One significant problem related to sharing of digital video among several users is the problem of coding or compression techniques (see [14]). A number of compression techniques are already in use. It is so far not easy to translate video from one format to another in real time. When requesting a video presentation the user must therefore indicate which video format his/her computer can accept, and the video base must provide the information in the correct format.

2.3 Annotating Video

During the process of video presentation authoring the film maker wish to make detailed descriptions[1] of the contents of the video material. The same problem has been identified by for instance anthropologists (see [25] and [26]) who use video as a tool for documenting what they have experienced. Film companies normally have a huge collection of film material which they need to manage. Some of them have made database solutions for representing the contents of this material [29] but these solutions do normally not support the ability to make detailed descriptions of the contents.

2.4 Retrieving Video Information

As identified in [8] and [7] retrieving non-textual information must be supported by tools for querying and for browsing. In retrieving information from the video

[1] By detailed descriptions we mean descriptions that is directly related to an identified part of a recording - for instance saying that this part shows the Norwegian prime minister Gro Harlem Brundtland signing an international agreement.

base the user should be able to formulate a query related to the contents of the recordings or to the structure of the presentation. The user then need browsing tools to do detailed search through the retrieved video information. As discussed in [28] browsing of video information is difficult. Fast forward playing is one way of browsing but this is not a satisfactory tool in many cases. New techniques are required, for instance based on the video information structure and contents.

3 Basic Components

A video presentation is usually composed of a number of smaller pieces of video and audio. We have adopted the terminology used in cinematic film and have called the basic entities of video *shots*. In cinematic film, a shot is a single piece of film captured in one shot. In a video base, a shot is the term denoting a complete, single video object. In this paper we will also use the term *segment*. A video segment is a part of a shot including all frames in the shot appearing between a start and an end frame. In a similar manner, an *audio segment* is a continuous sequence of samples within an *audio recording*. The audio and video basic entities will be further described in the following section.

Traditionally, a video shot or an audio recording have been segmented, i.e. divided into non-overlapping segments. It should be noted that in our model different segments may very well overlap. The complete content description of a specific part of a video recording can be obtained by combining the descriptions of the segments that overlap

For retrieval of video information the conceptual models of the basic entities are needed. This conceptual model will include entities and relations describing the contents of the basic entitiess. Video shots and audio recordings are temporal objects and some of the entities may have properties which may undergo changes. This issue is discussed in [25] and in more detail in [26]. The conceptual model proposed will be further disussed in section 3.2

In [2] abstractions for audio and video are discussed and extensions for modelling basic audio and video structures are proposed. From this work we have adopted the following abstractions: *Quality Factors* used to represent the quality of the audio/video component, *Derivation Relationships* where the contents of one component is derived from another component of the same type, and *Temporal Composition* which is used to represent temporally correlated entities.

3.1 Object Description

In this section we will describe the attributes and operations applicable to a basic component. The attributes of a basic component are:

ObjectIdentity is used to uniquely identify the component.

SymbolicName is a text string that the author may optionally assign to the component to have a user-generated name for identifying the component.

Type defines a basic component as either a video shot, an audio recording, a video segment or an audio segment.

Coding defines the coding technique used during recording of audio (e.g. PCM audio or CD audio) and video (e.g. JPEG [30], MPEG [6], or px64 [15]).

Rate defines the number of frames or samples recorded per second (e.g. for European video the rate is 25 while for CD audio it is 44100).

QualityFactor defines the window resolution in pixels (width x heigth) and the depth of the colour plane (i.e. number of bits per pixel).

Icon is a reference to a raster image which can be used to represent the component.

NoOfFrames gives the total number of frames or samples in the component.

Data is a reference to the list of samples or frames. Each sample and frame has a numbered position in the list. The pair (ObjectIdcomponent,FrameNo) idcomponent one specific frame or sample. This attribute is not used in the segment types.

DerivedFrom is only used for the segment types and references the video shot or audio recording from which the segment is derived. A segment will in general have the same Rate, QualityFactor and Coding as the component from which it is derived. By defining other values to these attributes the segment may be redefine the Rate (e.g. from 25 to 10 frames per second) or QualityFactor (e.g. reducing the number of bits in the colour plane). A redefinition of the Coding attribute only makes sense if a code conversion module is available.

Synopsis is a textual description of the contents of this component.

The operations which apply to basic entities can be grouped in:

Frame/sample oriented

These operations are used for individual frames or samples. This includes methods for reading and updating single frames or samples and for stepping forewards or backwards in the list of frames or samples.

Continuous time oriented

This group includes operations for recording and playing audio or video. The operation is controlled by two parameteres defining the speed factor and the frame or sample number to be the first played. The speed factor has been proposed in [23] and is used to support fast or slow motion and reverse playing. A positive speed factor denotes playing forwards while a negative factor denotes reverse playing. A speed factor with absolute value less than 1 will result in slow motion while a value greater than 1 will result in fast motion. A pause operation will cause a temporary stop the play operation. The continue operation will restart the play operation.

Interrogation

An interrogation operation is used to request the number of the frame sample currently active. To modes are defined. In the instant mode the actual number is returned while in the continuous mode the number is continuously reported to the caller.

Administration

These operations are used to read and change the values of the attributes SymbolicName, Type, Coding, Rate, QualityFactor, Icon and Synopsis.

3.2 Semantics

Date and time semantics apply to video shots and audio recordings. Video and audio are recorded at some date and time. In addition to the time of recording there is a need for representing what can in film theory is called ***dramatic time.*** E.g. a video shot recorded in May 1993 may illustrate a situation or an event which happened in 1905. In the same way a distinction can be made between the location where the recording was done and the ***dramatic location.*** Real and dramatic time information is represented as attributes of video shots and audio recordings.

A description of the "technical contents" of an audio or video segment is also needed. For instance may audio information be classified as a comment, a dialogue (between two or more persons), music or real/effect sound (e.g. noise from an airport). This classification is represented as an attribute of an audio segment. To record video a number of photographing techniques may be used (e.g. zooming, panning or tilting). The techniques used to record a video shot are represented as attributes to video segments.

An explicit representation of the contents of a basic component is needed to support content based retrieval. The semantic entities identified are:

Person including attributes like Name, Date_of_birth, Nationality and Profession.
Location including attributes like country, State and Town.
Physical_Objects including attributes like Type_of_object and Object_ description.
Events including attributes like Type_of_event, Time, and Event_description.

The attributes listed above are considered as static in the sense that they are not changed frequently. Other attributes related to these entities, like a person's role or the presence attribute (indicating that the person is actually present in the segment) may change several times during a video shot or audio recording. In applications where video is used for analysis, most of the attributes are of this kind. In our model ***annotation*** is used as an abstraction for representing this information. An annotation represents a set of attributes of a semantic component that are valid only within a specific segment.

Figure 2 shows the general structure of the model. The purpose is to illustrate the ideas and not to give a complete description of it. Therefore, all attributes are excluded from it. The EER notation used to model the basic components is adopted from [4].

4 Composite Components

Composite components may be interactive or narrative. Interactive components components refers to some video and/or audio information which can be played by the user, and it identifies a number of hyperlinks which the user can follow to other composite (hyper-) components.

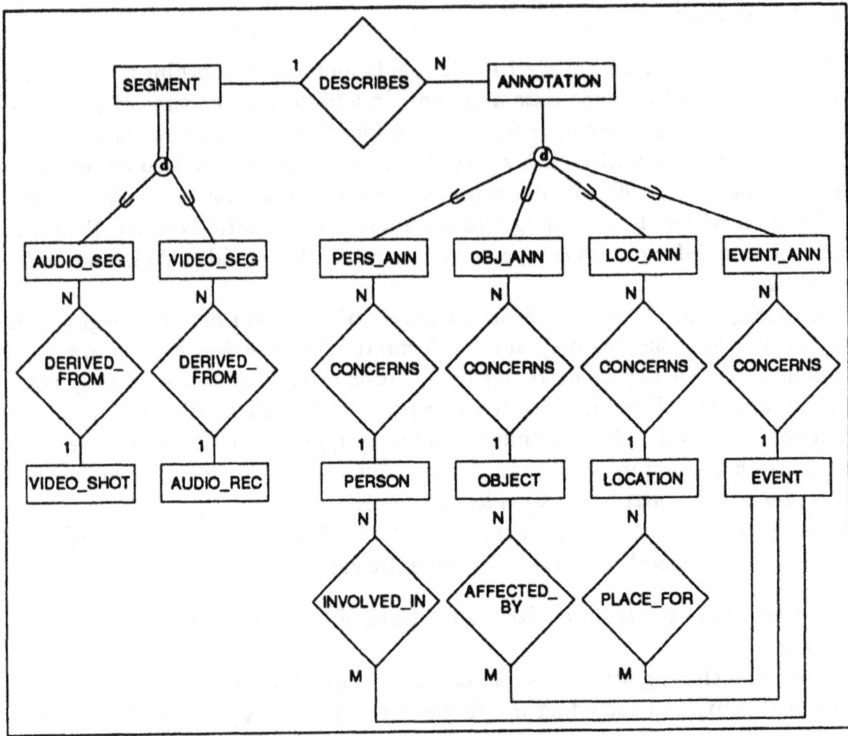

Fig. 2. EER diagram representing the contents of basic components

Video information is often termed as "unstructured information". From a semantic perspective this is not true for narrative presentations. A video presentation usually has a complex structure where the different video shots and audio recordings are related to each other in a hierarchical architecture. We use the term *story* for the composite objects. The author of a video presentation has a story to tell the receiver, and this story may be a collection of smaller stories. With the story concept the author (and the receiver) can identify and handle video and audio segments which are thematically or logically related, in a simple manner.

4.1 Object Description

In this section we will describe the attributes and operations applicable to a composite entities. The attributes of a composite component are:

ObjectIdentity is used to uniquely identify the component.

SymbolicName is a text string that the author may optionally assign to the component to have a user-generated name for identifying the component.

Type is either narrative or interactive.

ComponentArchitecture defines how the subcomponents are to be synchronized (e.g. in parallel in different windows or in sequence). Two different kinds of synchronization must be covered in the architecture both spatial (between different windows) and temporal. These issues are discussed in more detail in [10] and [17].

Synopsis is a textual description of the component.

The operations which apply to a composite component may be grouped in:

Running

This group includes the operations for playing, stopping, pausing and continuing as described in 3.1.

Architecture operations

This group includes operations for creating, modifying and deleting components in the component architecture and for manipulating the synchronization of components in a narrative presentation and the hyperlinks in an interactive presentation.

Administration

This group includes operations for reading and modifying the attributes SymbolicName and Synopsis.

4.2 Semantics

We have not extended the hypermedia model with new semantics but we have developed a model for a narrative presentation. In this model we are using different types of story entities, based on the work by the cinematic film theorist Christian Metz, [21]:

Scene

In [5] the scene is defined as "a complete, continuous chain of actions which take place in the same place at the same time". We have modelled the scene as a special type of segment.

Proper sequence

The term sequence is used to describe different structures. Here we define a proper sequence as a group of scenes linked together by a definable common thread of action.

Descriptive story

There are no temporal relations nor a common thread of action linking the subcomponents of a descriptive story. The subcomponents are semantically linked to each other because they describe different aspects of a the same thing. The headline news is an example of a descriptive story. They are linked together by describing different aspects of the afternoon news.

Interleaved story

Two or more stories may be intereleaved in time. This method is often used to give the viewers the a context for interpreting each the individual stories interleaved. In the news this may be used for alternating between studio and an reporter out in the fields.

Concurrent story
The subcomponents of a concurrent story are presented to the viewer concurrently.

In the model we have used the temporal composition relation (t_comp) described in [2]. This relation will also be used for deriving annotations to a story. The annotions made to segments which are covered by the story, will also apply to the story as such. The derivation of annotations is a useful support of queries.

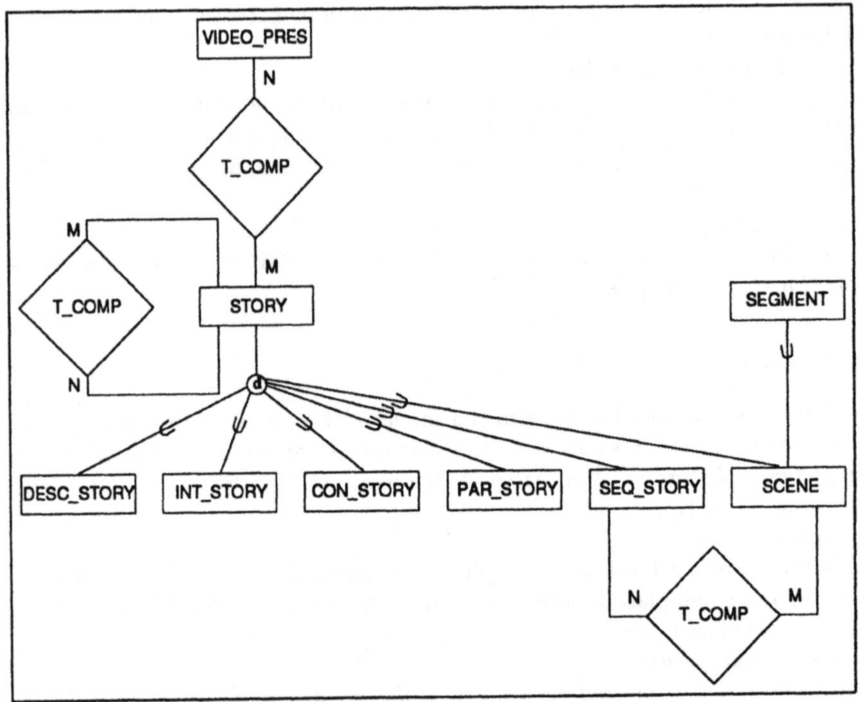

Fig. 3. EER diagram representing the video presentation structure

5 Evaluation of the Architecture

Our proposal for the video information architecture can be illustrated by Figure 4. The information contained in the video base can be divided in three: The video shots and audio recordings, the presentations and the annotations.

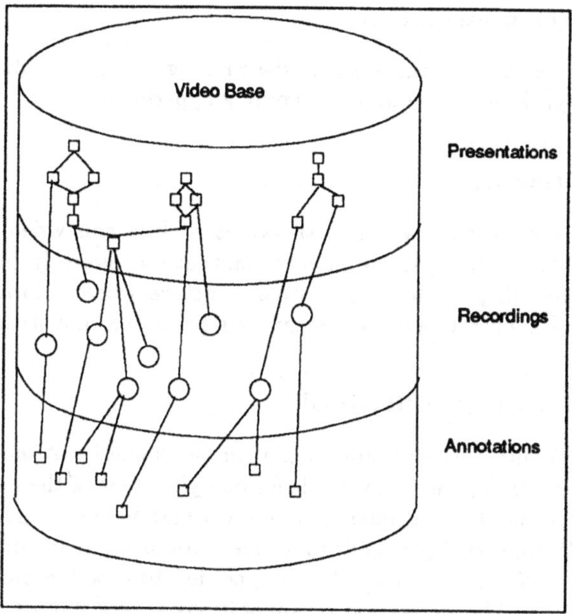

Fig. 4. The Video Base Contents

5.1 Presentation Authoring

The proposed architecture separates the presentation components from the "raw" video and audio material. This is a useful property in a multiuser environment where several video makers may use the same video and audio material in different presentations. It is also useful because both interactive and narrative presentations can coexist and use the same basic material.

The proposed architecture will also support structured authoring because of the definition of the different composite components. For instance, since interleaved story is a defined concept, the authoring tool may support the video maker in interleaving two video shots.

The proposed architecture will also support the various phases of the authoring task. In the planning the film maker may define the archictecture without having the video material available. Descriptions of the video shots and audio recordings can also be made before it is actually recorded. During recording, the video maker can access the video base to get the descriptions and to browse the proposed structure. During editing both the planned structure and the recorded material are available.

It may seem that the video base will put an extra burden on the video maker during the authoring. This will not be the case because the video maker is already doing most of these activities manually.

5.2 Running a presentation

The proposed architecture will support the running of a presentation by explicitly handling synchronization and by handling hyperlinks.

5.3 Annotating video

The proposed architecture will give the video makers and video analysts the flexibility to annotate any part of the material that they need. In the same time, the architecture will provide a conceptual structure where information about persons, locations, objects and events can be represented in a structured way.

5.4 Video Information Retrieval

The proposed architecture will support content based queries. Annotations made during the production phase is available for querying. One of the main problems for supporting content based queries in a video base is how to get the content descriptions. Within our framework these descriptions are made during the production phase and thus reducing the time needed to describe and classify the final presentation. The derivation of annotations makes it possible to search for composite components based on the description of a segment used within this component. It also allows the possibility of supporting traditional queries towards a hypermedia presentation.

The proposed architecture will support browsing both by using the concept of speed factor and by explicitly representing the architecture. Tools can be made for browsing the architecture based on this explicit representation .

6 Conclusion

6.1 Results

In this paper we propose an architecture that can be used for explicitly representing the contents and the complex structures of video information. Two models have been presented, one model of the contents of the video shots and audio recordings and one model of the structure. From a database point of view, digital video and audio are new data types. We have given a general description of the components and the operations that may be used to access these data types

6.2 Further Work

Much work reamins to be done in the field of audio and video databases. In this paper we have focused on modelling of video and audio contents and structure and much work remains to be done even in this more narrow field. As a first step we will design and test a prototype video base management system based on the ideas presented in this paper. In cooperation with Norwegian Broadcasting Corporation and the Nation Library, Rana Branch the appropriateness will be validated by users demanding data base support for video and audio information.

The basis for our work has been television and cinematic film. As digital video becomes available to almost every user of computers, new application areas for digital video will appear. In [28] the use of digital video for storing information from desktop video conferences is discussed. Education and distant learning is another example along the same line.

References

1. "HyperCard" authoring system for Macintosh, Cupertino, CA.
2. C. Breiteneder, S. Gibbs, and D. Tsichritzis, "Modelling of Audio/Video Data", In: Proceedings of the 11th International Conference on the Entity-Relationship Approach, Karlsruhe, October 7-9, 1992.
3. G. Davenport, T.G. Aguierre Smith, and N. Pincever, "Cinematic Primitives for Multimedia", IEEE Computer Graphics & Applications, July, 1991.
4. R. Elmasri and S.B. Navathe, Fundamentals of Database Systems, The Benjamin/Cummings Publishing Company, ISBN 0-8053-0145-3, 1989.
5. B. Foss, Dramaturgy: Narrative Technique and Dramaturgy in Film and Television, SVT Training, ISBN 91-630-1028-3, 1992.
6. D. Le Gall, "MPEG: A Video Compression Standard for Multimedia Applications". Communications of the ACM, Vol. 32, No. 4, 1991.
7. F. Garzotto, L. Mainetti, and P. Paolini, "Modelling Multimedia Data Bases: The Importance of Exploration v.s. Queries", Tech. Rep. 03-91, Dep. of Electronics, Politecnico di Milano, Italy, 1991.
8. C. Goble, M. O'Docherty, P. Crowther, M. Ireton, J. Oakley and C. Xydeas, "The Manchester Multimedia Information System". In: Proceedings of the 3rd international Conference on Extending Database Technology, Vienna, March 23-27, 1992.
9. F. Halasz and M Schwartz, "The Dexter Hypertext Reference Model", NIST Hypertext Standardization Workshop, Gaithersburg, MD, January 16-18, 1990.
10. L. Hardman, G. van Rossum and D.C.A. Bulterman, "Structured Multimedia Authoring". To appear in proceedings of the ACM Multimedia'93 Conference, Anaheim, August 4-6, 1993.
11. E.M. Hoffert and G. Gretsch, "The Digital News System at EDUCOM: A Convergence of Interactive Computing, Newspapers, Television and High-Speed Networks". Communications of the ACM, Vol. 32, No. 7, 1989.
12. W. Kameyama, T Hanamura and H. Tominaga, "A Proposal of Multimedia Document Architecture and Video Document Architecture". In: Proceedings of ICC '91 - the International Conference on Communications Conference Record, Denver, June 23-26, 1991.
13. M. Lesk, "Television Libraries for Workstations: an All-Digital Storage, Transmission and Display System for Low-Rate Video". In: Multimedia Information. Proceedings of a conference, Cambridge, July 15-18, 1991.
14. M. Liebholt and E.M. Hoffert, "Toward an Open Environment for Digital Video". Communications of the ACM, Vol. 32, No. 4, 1991.
15. M. Liou, "Overview of the px64 kbit/s Video Coding Standard". Communications of the ACM, Vol. 32, No. 4, 1991.

16. N. Lippis, "Multimedia Networking - Restructuring the Enterprise for Video Traffic". Data Communications, February, 1993.
17. T.D.C. Little and A. Ghafoor, "Spatio-Temporal Composition of Distributed Multimedia Objects for Value-Added Networks". IEEE Computer, October, 1991.
18. W.E. Mackay and G. Davenport, "Virtual Video Editing in Interactive Multimedia Applications", Communications of the ACM, Vol. 32, No. 7, 1989.
19. C. Meghini, F. Rabitti, and C. Thanos, "Conceptual Modeling of Multimedia Documents", IEEE Computer, October, 1991.
20. P.G. Milazzo "Shared Video under UNIX". In: Proceedings of the 1991 Summer USENIX Conference, Nashville, TN, 1991.
21. J. Monaco, How to Read a Film. The Art, Technology, Language, History and Theory of Film and Media, Oxford University Press, 1981.
22. M. Pasieka, P. Crumley, A. Marks and A. Infortuna, "Distributed Multimedia: How can Necessary Data Rates be Supported? In: Proceedings of the 1991 Summer USENIX Conference, Nashville, TN, 1991.
23. L.A. Rowe and B.C. Smith, "A Continuous Media Player", Proceedings of the Third International Wrokshop on Network and OS Support for Digital Audio and Video, San Diego CA, November, 1992.
24. P.G. Selinger, "The Impact of Hardware on Database Systems". In: Proceedings of the International Symposium on Database Systems of the 90s, Berlin, November 5-7, 1990.
25. T.G. Aguierre Smith and N.C. Pincever, "Parsing Movies in Context", In: Proceedings of the 1991 Summer USENIX Conference, Nashville, TN, 1991.
26. T.G. Aguierre Smith, If You Could See What I Mean... Descriptions of Video in an Anthropoligst's Video Notebook, Master Thesis, MIT, 1992.
27. K.H. Smith, "Accessing Multimedia Network Services". IEEE Communications Magazine, May, 1992.
28. S.M. Stevens, "Next Generation Network and Operating System Requirements for Continuous Time Media", In: Proceedings of the Second International Workshop for Network and Operating System Support for Digital Audio and Video, Heidelberg, November, 1991.
29. J. Turner, "Representing and accessing information in the stockshot database at the National Film Board of Canada". The Canadian Journal of Information Science, Vol. 15, No. 4, December, 1990.
30. G.K. Wallace, "The JPEG Still Picture Compression Standard". Communications of the ACM, Vol. 32, No. 4, 1991.

Optimizing Storage of Objects on Mass Storage Systems with Robotic Devices *

Ling Tony Chen and Doron Rotem**

Lawrence Berkeley Laboratory
Berkeley, CA 94720

Abstract. Automated robotic devices that mount and dismount tape cartridges and optical disks are an important component of a mass storage system. Optimizing database performance in such environments poses additional challenges as the response time to a query may involve several costly volume mounts and dismounts in addition to seek distances within a volume. In this paper we analyze some optimization problems concerning placement of data on such devices. We present a dynamic programming algorithm for optimal loading of data on a robotic device to minimize expected query response time. The method is general in the sense that it can be tailored to work for different hardware characteristics such as seek and mounting times. A variant of the method is also presented which achieves optimal response times subject to storage utilization constraints.

1 Introduction

Many data base applications such as multimedia databases, medical image management systems, high energy physics experiment databases, and climate modeling databases require storage and efficient access to terabytes of data. Mass storage systems are being developed as an economical solution to the ever growing demand on storage space generated by such applications. A typical mass storage system consists of a combination of storage devices arranged in a hierarchy. The following layers are commonly found according to [5, 6]

1. (Inline storage) RAM or SSD (solid state disk).
2. (Online storage) Magnetic disks.
3. (Nearline Storage) Robotic devices storing tape cartridges or optical disks.
4. (Offline Storage) Disks or tapes stored on shelves, or at alternative sites.

Specialized operating systems such as UNITREE or EPOCH [5] control the migration of files across the hierarchy such that files which are used more often are kept on the faster more expensive storage devices. The migration process is automatic and transparent to the user.

* The support of the Department of Energy under contract DE-AC03-76SF00098 is gratefully acknowledged.

** Also with Department of MIS, School of Business, San Jose State University

In order to build database systems that use mass storage systems efficiently, we need a better understanding of the costs involved in accessing data across the hierarchy. The least understood part of this hierarchy in terms of optimization, is the nearline storage layer consisting of robotic devices. These devices can pick tape cartridges or optical disks from some bin storage and place them into a drive.

The main focus of this paper is to study optimization strategies for initial data placement in the nearline storage layer of a mass storage system. Our work was initially motivated by a climate modeling application where terabytes of data are loaded into a mass storage system from large simulation programs performed on supercomputers. Various segments of the data are subsequently accessed by climate modelers for the purpose of visualization. Initial study of the system revealed that long delays for visualization queries are incurred by excessive mounts and dismounts of tapes. As access patterns are fairly well understood in this environment, we are interested in improving the response time of the system by a more efficient initial placement of the data on the tape cartridges.

Additional applications that may benefit from our approach are multimedia database systems needing to support the storage and access of very large objects. Such objects may include images, video, and audio data. Typical queries in such databases need to access long sequential streams of data which may reside on some kind of a robotic device [4, 9].

2 Problem Formulation and Notation

We will use the term volume to denote a physical unit (tape or optical disk) which may be mounted or dismounted in a single operation of the robotic device. We assume that the data to be loaded arrives as a stream of N atomic blocks (not necessarily of the same size). The data can be a sequence of frames from video data, an audio stream, an output of a simulation program, etc. As the order in which blocks arrive is very much application dependent, we assume it cannot be changed by the optimization program. We will discuss the implications of removing this assumption in Section 6.

The problem we consider here is that of breaking this long linear stream of N blocks, $C_1, C_2, .., C_N$, into segments such that each segment is assigned to a different volume. A break can occur anywhere between a pair of consecutive blocks but not in the middle of a block. We assume each query needs to access some subsequence of contiguous blocks from the stream $C_1, C_2, .., C_N$. There are two types of penalties to consider, namely, the volume mount penalty and the seek penalty.

As an example of the optimization problem we are studying here, let us consider the data and the queries represented in Figure 1. We can either place the blocks $C_1, C_2, .., C_N$ on one volume, or break them into two volumes right before C_i as indicated by the dashed line. As a result of this break, the queries Q_6 and Q_3 will incur an extra volume mount whereas the queries Q_7 and Q_4 will have a shorter seek distance as they are now much closer to the beginning

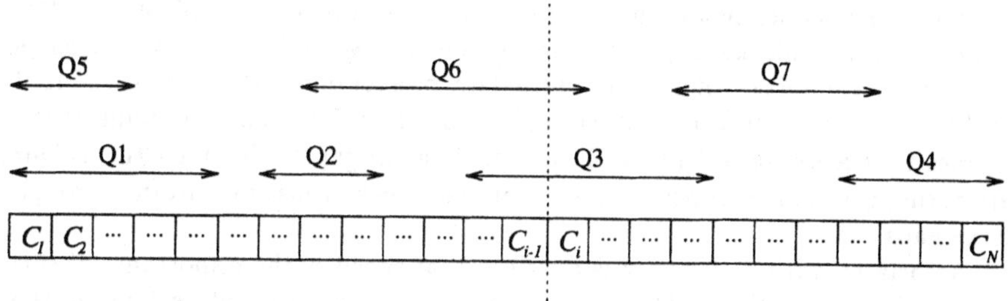

Fig. 1. Example of a stream of N blocks and queries on the blocks

of a volume. The queries Q_1, Q_2, and Q_5 are not affected by this break. The preferable option depends on the relative gain in seek time compared with the extra volume mounting needed.

Intuitively, we can see that breaking the data into many small segments will increase the chances of queries incurring many volume mounts. On the other hand, using very large segments may increase the chances of a long seek distance within a volume before the first byte of the answer to a query is found. The problem is to find an optimal set of break points such that the total expected penalty is minimized.

Initially we will present an algorithm to find this optimal solution which makes the assumption that the capacity of each volume is fixed and known (which excludes the case where on the fly compression is used), and that all volumes involved are of the same size. Furthermore, it makes the assumption that there is no restriction on the total number of volumes that can be used and that data will always be stored starting from the beginning of each volume. We also assume that there is only one drive available in this system. Thus to answer a query in which the answer is spread across n volumes, one would have to mount (and dismount) these volumes one after the other. The reason why we make this assumption is that although there may be many parallel drives in the system, in a multi-user environment it is impossible to predict how many of these drives will be available when the query needs to be serviced. Therefore minimizing the number of volume mounts needed is a reasonable strategy. We will discuss how to lift some of these restrictions later in Sections 5 and 6.

The following parameters are used to characterize the hardware system:

1. Each volume holds M bytes.
2. It takes T_m seconds to dismount a volume from the drive and mount as well as initialize a new volume.
3. It takes $T_s(x)$ seconds to seek to the x'th byte on a volume. It is assumed that $T_s(0) = 0$, any overhead involved in reading the first byte is counted in T_m, not T_s.

No restriction is imposed on the function $T_s(x)$ except that it should be computable in constant time. In Section 4 we will show how to improve the algorithm's running time when $T_s(x)$ is a linear function.

We also assume that each query accesses a contiguous set of blocks. The justification for this assumption is that this is a reasonable scenario for queries which require a portion of audio or video data, or a set of measurements produced within some time interval. In other applications this is just an approximation to queries that access a few block clusters with small gaps in between them. Our approximation thus ignores the potential possibility of fast forwarding through large gaps.

Associated with each query is a weight that specifies the importance of this query relative to others. This weight need not be normalized as long as the weights of all queries were determined using the same scale. The goal of our algorithm is to find a way of partitioning the input stream into volumes such that the sum of the weighted query response times over all queries is minimized.

The input is assumed to be an ordered vector of blocks C_1 through C_N in which the following information is given for each block C_i:

1. L_i: The length of the block (in bytes).
2. W_i: The weighted sum of all queries that read C_i.
3. B_i: The weighted sum of all queries that read both C_{i-1} and C_i.

The parameter B_i can be viewed as the penalty incurred by placing the blocks C_{i-1} and C_i on two different volumes. This is because if a volume break actually occurred between blocks C_{i-1} and C_i, all the queries counted in B_i would have an increased response time of T_m seconds, since a new volume would need to be mounted to answer the remaining part of the query.

The information about the values B_i and W_i may either come from statistics collected over the usage of the data or can be estimated from application dependent query patterns. For example, in the climate modeling application mentioned above, we found that queries asking to visualize temperatures measured during the month of January, or during the Spring season are much more likely to occur than visualizing the temperature between the 17th and the 19th of April. As another example, consider a multimedia application in which a previous Super-Bowl game is recorded in HDTV format, and users may request portions of it for reviewing. Although exact query positions may not be known, general rules can be used to estimate the regions in which queries are more likely to occur. For example, the time during actual plays as well as after the two minute warning will typically be accessed more frequently than timeout periods or injury waiting periods.

From the above information, we can easily compute in $O(N)$ time:

1. P_i: The starting position (in bytes) of block C_i measured from the beginning of C_1. It can be computed by letting $P_1 = 0$, and $P_i = P_{i-1} + L_{i-1}$.
2. S_i: The weighted sum of all queries that *start* reading from this block. This can be simply computed by $S_i = W_i - B_i$.

Note that the pair of numbers S_i and B_i, carry the exact same amount of information as W_i and B_i. Actually, in our algorithm, only S_i and B_i are used, whereas W_i is never used except for computing S_i.

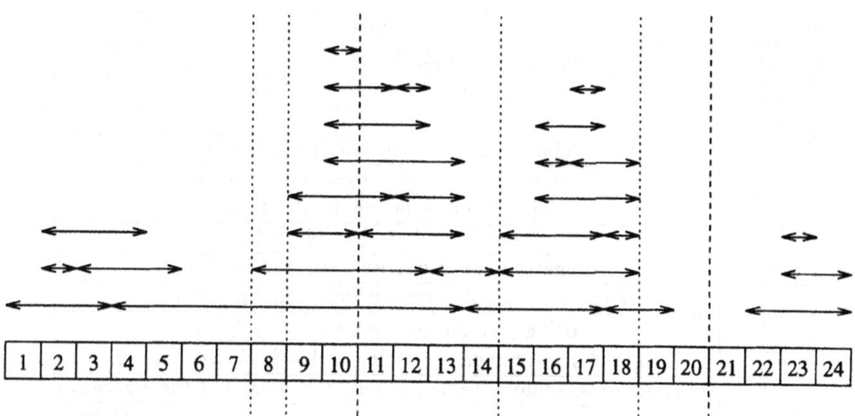

Fig. 2. Problem where 24 blocks must be broken into volumes of 10 blocks or less

As an example to the complexities involved in the problem we are tackling, consider a stream of 24 blocks as shown in Figure 2. This example is used to illustrate the fact that this problem is by no means a trivial problem where a good solution can be found by a simple glance at the data.

Assume that the queries on this stream of blocks are as shown on top of the blocks, and that all queries are of equal weight. Furthermore, assume that each volume can hold only 10 blocks. A naive and straightforward approach to this problem, is to simply put blocks 1 through 10 on the first volume, blocks 11 through 20 on the second, and blocks 21 through 24 on the last. This is obviously a bad solution since a lot of queries read both block 10 and block 11, and thus are split across 2 volumes in this approach. However, even if the straightforward approach was improved a little and we moved the breaks right before blocks 9 and 19, it still does not represent a very good solution since the blocks stored at the beginning of volume 3 (where seek time is small) are practically useless. A good solution would be to break volumes right before block 9 and 15. This way the heavy load of queries between block 15 through 18 ends up being at the beginning of volume 3, where seek time is typically much less than at the end of a volume. Even when breaking before block 15 is known to be the best thing to do, it is by no means obvious whether the first break should be before block 9 or block 8. Breaking before block 9 will have the benefit of reducing the seek time for a lot of queries, but will make one extra query cross a volume boundary. The decision on which break to use will involve a detailed comparison that considers the mounting time T_m as well as the seek speed T_s. At this point we hope the reader is convinced that using our O(N) or even O(N^2) time dynamic programming algorithm for finding an optimal solution is easier than coming up with a good suboptimal *hueristic* (which may take the same amount of time).

Table 1 lists all the major notations used in this paper along with their meaning. Some of them have already been defined, whereas others will be defined later in this paper.

Notation	Meaning
N	The number of blocks in the input stream
M	Capacity of a volume in bytes
Q_i	A query
T_m	Volume mounting and dismounting time
$T_s(x)$	Time needed to seek x bytes into a volume
C_i	The ith block in the input stream
L_i	Length (in bytes) of block C_i
W_i	Weighted sum of queries that read block C_i
B_i	Weighted sum of queries which read C_{i-1} and C_i
P_i	Starting position of block C_i (i.e. $\sum_{k=1}^{i-1} L_k$)
S_i	Weighted sum of queries starting at block C_i (i.e. $W_i - B_i$)
D_i	Dynamic programming value computed at stage i of the algorithm
$U(i,j)$	Change in seek time when blocks $C_i, .., C_{j-1}$ are on one volume
R_i	A pointer storing the j value that caused D_i to be minimal
Z_i	$\sum_{k=1}^{i-1} S_k$
J	Set of j values under consideration in the computation of D_i
$m(J,i)$	The element of J with minimal value for $D_j - Z_j \times T_s(P_i)$
X_j	The leftmost x position for which j is potentially $m(J,i)$
$IX(i,j)$	The x in which $D_i - Z_i \times T_s(x) = D_j - Z_j \times T_s(x)$
V	A limit on the number of volumes used

Table 1. List of all notations used in this paper

3 The $O(N^2)$ Dynamic Programming Algorithm

With all of the above terms defined, we are ready to describe the algorithm. The algorithm requires $O(N^2)$ time and uses dynamic programming. The algorithm is based on the observation that the location of a set of optimal breaking points placed on the right of C_i is independent of all queries with endpoints before C_i. This allows us to compute partial optimal solutions as we scan the stream from right to left. Stated more formally, assume that in an optimal solution there is a break placed between blocks C_i and C_{i-1} and let $OPT(C_i)$ be the set of optimal breaks to the right of C_i. Let us denote by $Q(C_i)$ the subset of the queries consisting only of queries whose endpoint is to the right of C_i. The principle of optimality that we are utilizing here is that *$OPT(C_i)$ is an optimal solution to the problem with input stream $C_i, C_{i+1}, .., C_N$ and query set $Q(C_i)$.*

Let us now describe the algorithm in more detail. Initially the algorithm assumes that all the blocks are on one long imaginary volume that can hold everything (i.e. the leftmost break is on the right of block C_N). Let the total weighted response time under this one volume configuration be some constant. Starting from the last block C_N, and working our way down to C_1, we compute a cost D_i, which is the minimal extra response time involved in a configuration in which:

1. There is a break between C_{i-1} and C_i.
2. There are no breaks between C_1 through C_{i-1}.
3. The other breaks between C_i through C_N have been chosen optimally, under the constraint that no volume contains more than M bytes.

Note that D_i could be a negative number, since it represents the gain or the loss in response time due to the placement of such breaks.

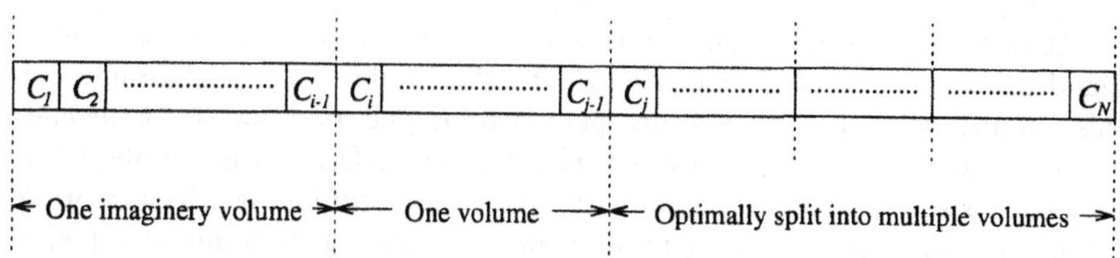

Fig. 3. Intermediate view of a block stream during dynamic programming

Dynamic programming can be employed efficiently because each D_i can be computed in O(N) time by only using D_j values where $j > i$ as we prove below.

Proposition 1. *The value of D_i can be computed by the following formula:*

$$D_i = B_i \times T_m + \min_{\substack{P_j - P_i \le M \\ i<j\le N+1}} (D_j - U(i,j)) \tag{1}$$

where

$$U(i,j) = \sum_{k=i}^{j-1} S_k \times (T_s(P_k) - T_s(P_k - P_i)) \tag{2}$$

Proof. Initially we set $D_{N+1} = 0$. Assume by induction that D_m is correctly computed for all $m > i$, i.e., D_m represents the additional cost of the optimal way to break blocks C_m through C_N into volumes. Given that there is a break between C_{i-1} and C_i, let the immediate break on the right of it be between C_{j-1} and C_j for some $j > i$. This implies that the blocks $C_i, C_{i+1}, \ldots, C_{j-2}, C_{j-1}$ will be placed on one volume. This is illustrated in Figure 3. The constraint $P_j - P_i \le M$ in the above equation guarantees that in computing the minimum, we are only considering values of j such that these blocks do in fact fit on one volume. The term $B_i \times T_m$ reflects the extra response time needed to mount a new volume for all the queries that access both C_{i-1} and C_i. On the other hand, $U(i,j)$ reflects the decrease in response time due to that fact that the seek time for all blocks C_k in the set $C_i, \ldots, C_{j-1}$ will now be reduced from $T_s(P_k)$ to $T_s(P_k - P_i)$ since C_i is now at the beginning of a volume. Note that this reduction in seek time only affects the queries that *start* reading from block C_k. This is because, a query only needs to seek once to the first block, and all other blocks are read consecutively without anymore seeks.

The fact that this formula will compute the relative response time of the optimal way to break the blocks from C_i through C_N, comes from the fact that all possible j's, in which block C_i through C_{j-1} can fit on one volume, are considered and that the D_j's have been correctly computed by the induction hypothesis.

Note that $U(i, j)$ can be accumulated while we are enumerating through the j's for each D_i, this reduces the running time of the algorithm to $O(N^2)$ instead of $O(N^3)$.

At each step in which a new D_i is computed for each i, we record the newly found minimal value of D_i and also record the j value j_{min}, that resulted in this minimal value. Let the recorded pointer be R_i (i.e. $R_i = j_{min}$). At the end, when we have finally computed the minimal value for D_1, we can simply follow the pointers starting from R_1, in order to find all the positions in which to break the blocks. Since this breaking resulted in D_1 obtaining its minimal value, it is guaranteed to be the optimal way to break the entire stream into multiple volumes.

4 The $O(N)$ Dynamic Programming Algorithm

In this section we will describe an even faster algorithm that can be applied under certain circumstances. Due to space limitations however, we will only describe the algorithm without any proof. If the function that describes the volume seek time $T_s(x)$ is either linear (i.e. $T_s(a + b) = T_s(a) + T_s(b)$) or constant, we can simplify the algorithm such that it requires only $O(N)$ time. This is very useful, since for typical problems N could be very large. The assumption that the seek time is either constant or linear with the seek distance is also very practical and is observed in many mass storage devices. The assumption $T_s = 0$ can also be used as a good approximation for optical disk jukeboxes where seek time is considered negligible compared to mounting time. Even for systems that have non-linear seek time, the seek function can usually be closely approximated by a linear function. Thus when one is willing to sacrifice absolute optimality for solving the problem faster, this approximation can be used.

The simplification comes from the fact that Equation (2) can be rewritten as:

$$U(i, j) = \sum_{k=i}^{j-1} S_k \times (T_s(P_k) - T_s(P_k - P_i)) = \sum_{k=i}^{j-1} S_k \times T_s(P_i) \tag{3}$$

when T_s is linear. When T_s is constant, the entire equation will become zero. This can be simply considered as a subcase of T_s being linear since it is equivalent to

$T_s(x) = 0$. In this section we will only discuss the algorithm under the general assumption that T_s is linear. The special case where $T_s(x) = 0$ follows easily.

We will maintain an array Z_i that holds the running sum of S_i (i.e. $Z_i = \sum_{k=1}^{i-1} S_k$). Thus Equation (3) can be further reduced to:

$$U(i,j) = (Z_j - Z_i) \times T_s(P_i) \tag{4}$$

which leads to Equation (1) being simplified to

$$D_i = B_i \times T_m + Z_i \times T_s(P_i) + \min_{\substack{P_j - P_i \leq M \\ i<j\leq N+1}} (D_j - Z_j \times T_s(P_i)) \tag{5}$$

If we can maintain a data structure in which the minimum in the above equation can be found in constant time, we would then be able to perform the entire algorithm in $O(N)$ time. Described more formally, we are faced with the problem of maintaining a set of integers j such that when presented with an integer i, we can in constant time identify the j in the set that has the minimal value for $D_j - Z_j \times T_s(P_i)$. We do, however, know that the i's presented to us will be a sequence of integers in decreasing order due to the dynamic programming procedure. Let the set of j's that needs to be considered at any time be called J. And let the element $j \in J$ that has the minimal value for $D_j - Z_j \times T_s(P_i)$ be called $m(J,i)$.

For a certain i, the three basic operations that need to be performed on the set J are:

1. Remove all $j \in J$ in which $P_j - P_i > M$.
2. Find $m(J,i)$.
3. Insert i into J.

In this section we shall describe a way to update and maintain J such that the second operation can be performed in constant time, and the total time for the first and third operation over all $1 \leq i \leq N$ can be performed in $O(N)$ time. But first we make the following observation:

Proposition 2. *If $j' = m(J,i')$, then for all future i values (i.e. $i < i'$), no $j > j'$ need ever be considered anymore.*

This theorem means that if we store J as an ordered set, whenever we find $j' = m(J,i')$ for a certain i', we can safely remove all $j > j'$ from J. Put in another way, if we scan the ordered set J starting from the largest element and while proceeding downwards we remove all elements that cannot possibly be $m(J,i)$ anymore. The first element that we end up not removing from the set must be $m(J,i)$. In order to be able to perform this scan we maintain a parameter X_j for each $j \in J$, that records the position along the x dimension in which to the left of X_j, it is no longer possible for j to be $m(J,i)$, and thus j should be removed from the set J. Initially for each j inserted into J, X_j is set to $P_j - M$ due to the volume size restriction. As the dynamic programming proceeds however, X_j may be moved to the right due to new elements i being inserted into J such that $D_i - Z_i \times T_s(x) < D_j - Z_j \times T_s(x)$ for x positions greater than X_j. In the following discussion, we shall use $IX(i,j)$ to abbreviate the x coordinate in which $D_i - Z_i \times T_s(x) = D_j - Z_j \times T_s(x)$. Since $T_s(x)$ is a linear function, this x value can be easily computed in constant time.

We are now ready to describe the $O(N)$ time dynamic programming algorithm:

- $D_{N+1} = 0$
- $J = \{N+1\}$
- $X_{N+1} = P_{N+1} - M$
- For $i = N$ downto 1
  1. Remove all $j \in J$ such that $P_i < X_j$
  2. Compute and store D_i and R_i based on the fact that $m(J,i)$ is simply the largest element in J
  3. Insert i into J as follows
     (a) Scan the elements of J from small through large, until an element k is found such that $IX(i,k)$ is smaller than X_k. Then let the largest element in J that is smaller than k be k' If no such k was found, however, we simply let k' be the largest element in J.
     (b) If k' exists, remove all elements of J that are smaller than k'.
     (c) If k' exists, and $IX(i,k')$ is smaller than X_k (or P_i, if k does not exist), then let $X_{k'} = IX(i,k')$, otherwise remove k' from J.
     (d) Insert i into J with $X_i = P_i - M$.
- Endfor

The ordered set J can be maintained by a simple queue data structure. The only operations that need to be performed on the queue are removing elements at both ends, and inserting elements at one end. Thus we can easily implement this queue using either a doublely linked list or a circular array. This guarantees that all the deletion and insertion operations can be performed in constant time. Using this data structure, we can see that all steps of the algorithm can be performed in constant time except for Steps 1, 3(a), and 3(b). For these three steps, although the running time for each iteration of the For loop could be longer than constant, the total running for these three steps throughout the entire loop must be $O(N)$ since at most N elements are inserted into J and thus at most N elements can be removed. This brings us to the conclusion that the entire algorithm requires only $O(N)$ time.

5 Variants of the Algorithm

The general dynamic programming algorithm presented in the previous sections can be modified in several ways to accommodate specific application or hardware device characteristics. In this section, we discuss some useful variants of the algorithm. Specifically we discuss here:

- Tailoring the algorithm to meet storage utilization requirements: This arises when there must be a high utilization of storage space on each volume.

- Variable but known volume capacities: This is important in a multiuser environment, where the data must be loaded on the remaining free space available on existing volumes.
- Uncertain volume capacity: This is important when on-the-fly compression is employed while data is written on each volume. In such a case, the actual capacity of a volume will not be known until the end of volume is encountered while attempting to write a block.

The first variation that we shall discuss is how to solve the problem of low storage utilization. Note that although the response time increases for each new volume that we use (due to queries that cross the breaking point), it also gets decreased because of smaller seek times on the queries that start on the newly broken off volume. Because of this it is quite possible that the optimal solution found by our dynamic programming algorithm will place a small number of blocks on each volume, and as a result, utilizes the storage of each volume very poorly.

There are three solutions to this problem. The first (and in the authors opinion the best) solution involves adding a large constant C to the right side of Equation (1). Qualitatively, this large constant will have the effect of making the dynamic programming algorithm find a solution that uses fewer volumes, since one C will be added to the final dynamic programming value for each extra volume that is used in the final solution. The larger the constant, the stronger the hint is for the algorithm to use fewer volumes. Quantitatively, this constant represents the extra amount of total weighted query response time one is willing to put up with, in order to use one less volume in the solution. One can also play around with this constant C (using perhaps a binary search method) to find a solution that uses a reasonable number of volumes without increasing the total response time too much.

The second solution involves placing a limit on the algorithm to use at most V volumes in the solution. Of course, for the problem to be solvable, the total storage capacity of the V volumes must be enough to hold all the blocks. The dynamic programming algorithm can be modified to obey this volume limit, by simply computing an array of D_i and R_i for each i, such that $D_i[v]$ represents the value of D_i if we used exactly v volumes up to now. When computing $D_i[v]$ at each iteration, $D_j[v-1]$ should be used on the right hand side of Equation (1). The final solution will be the one resulting in the minimal value of $D_1[v], \forall v \in \{1, 2, \ldots, V\}$. Both the $O(N^2)$ time algorithm as well as the $O(N)$ time algorithm can be modified in this manner to find the optimal solution under the V volume limit. The drawback of this method is that the total running time of the algorithm will increase by a factor of V, and that there is usually no good reason to set V at any particular number (unless it was specified by the application). For any V that we happen to use, it is always possible that by using $V+1$ volumes, the total response time could have been improved by a tremendous amount.

The third method is the least desirable method, but yet it still might be useful under some circumstances. It involves placing a minimum percentage limit (say

p), on the amount of storage that must be used per volume. The algorithm can be modified to obey this limit, by simply changing the *min* operator in Equation (1) to only consider j's is which $P_j - P_i \geq pM$ as well as $P_j - P_i \leq M$. This modification, however, can not be made on the O(N) time algorithm. Thus only the O(N^2) time algorithm can be used. This method also has the drawback that there is usually no good reason to set p at any particular value. For whatever p we select, it is always possible that by simply letting one of the volumes store slightly less than pM, all the other volumes can have a higher utilization factor without greatly increasing the total response time.

The second variation we shall discuss, is the case where volumes are of different but known sizes. We can prove that this variant of the problem is NP-complete by a transformation from the subset-sum problem. The complexity arises due to the exponential number of ways in which the volumes can be ordered during the scanning of the input stream. Thus for large number of volumes, some heuristic for ordering the volumes must be used before our dynamic programming algorithm can be utilized. For a small number of volumes, however, we can enumerate all possible permutations of volumes, and try each one of them individually with the dynamic programming algorithm. The final optimal solution will be the the one that yields the lowest value of D_1. The dynamic programming algorithm must be modified in this case to not only handle a fixed number of volumes V, but also each volume will have a different capacity $M[v]$, and possibly even a different seek function $T_s[v]$ (since blocks might be stored starting from the middle of a volume). The solution is to use the modified algorithm discussed previously, in which at most V volumes can be used. But also modify it such that Equation (1) uses a different value for M as well as T_s when computing different $D_i[v]$ values. The equation used should be:

$$D_i[v] = B_i \times T_m + \min_{\substack{P_j - P_i \leq M[v] \\ i<j\leq N+1}} (D_j[v-1] - U_v(i,j))$$

where $U_v(i,j)$ is the same as $U(i,j)$ except that $T_s[v]$ is used in place of T_s. Unfortunately, when this change to the algorithm is introduced, only the O(N^2) algorithm can be used.

The last variant we discuss is how to handle the case of uncertain volume sizes. For such a case it is impossible to precompute the optimal partition. To actually find the optimal partition would involve actually storing the data on the volumes in all the different possible ways, which would require a tremendous amount of time. The best practical thing that we can hope for, would be a good heuristic that could tell us how many blocks we should backtrack and move to the beginning of the next volume, when we encounter the end of a volume while writing a block. Let C_i be the first block written on this volume, and let C_j be the last block which was only partially written on this volume. Obviously, C_j needs to be moved to the beginning of the next volume, The question we now want to answer is: How many more blocks beside C_j should we also move to the beginning of the next volume in order to minimize the total query response time? Using the assumption that the volume capacity M is infinite, we can precompute all D values D_N down to D_{i+1}. If $D_k = \min(D_{i+1}, D_{i+2}, \ldots, D_j)$, then breaking the volume right before C_k, and moving blocks C_k through C_j onto the beginning of the next volume, would be a very good heuristic. The reason being that it represents the optimal position we can break off the next volume, under the assumption that the next volume can hold all of the remaining blocks. Since the amount of data that can be held in the next volume is unknown, this is a very practical assumption to make. Again, in this variant, we can also encounter the problem of low storage utilization. One way of solving this problem would be to add a penalizing weight to the right of Equation (1) that would increase proportional to $P_j - P_k$ as we compute D_k for $k < j$. The penalty is proportional to $P_j - P_k$, since it represents the capacity of the space left unused at the end of the volume. Another way to solve the problem would be to use a rule that says at most x blocks (or y bytes) can be backtracked.

6 Summary and Future Work

Both algorithms were implemented on a SPARCstation 10 for a large set of test problems. Run time results were analyzed to verify that the optimal solution is indeed found. We found that using this dynamic programming algorithm is very practical even for huge datasets found commonly in environments that use mass storage systems. On the Sparc 10, the $O(N^2)$ algorithm could find the optimal solution for $N = 10,000$ (with each volume holding 1000 blocks) in roughly 13 seconds. The $O(N)$ time algorithm could solve the problem for $N = 100,000$ in less than 1 second. In fact, for the $O(N)$ time algorithm, the delay caused by thrashing, due to shortage of memory to hold all the large arrays, is much more significant than the running time required by the algorithm itself.

In this paper we studied some optimization problems concerning placement of data on the nearline storage layer of a mass storage system. The results show that significant improvements in the access of data can be achieved by careful placement of the data on volumes based on application dependent access patterns. As is the case with all optimization schemes, more accurate information about access patterns may lead to more efficient placements. In the case that such patterns are not fully known in advance, some basic rules or even some general probability distribution information can be used as input to the program in order to avoid potential disasters which can be created by arbitrarily breaking the data into volumes.

This work is only a first step in the study of query optimization for databases which use mass storage systems. Additional problems we are currently investigating include:

- Response time for queries can be further minimized if we remove the restriction on the order of the blocks in the input stream. Efficient linear orderings of the data can lead to shorter "read distance" of queries as the total size of gaps between useful data read by the query are minimized. In general, this problem is NP-complete, but for specific applications some efficient orderings can be found. This problem was investigated in another context in [3].

- In environments where users can control the number of drives available for answering queries, we can take advantage of tape striping such that large queries can benefit from I/O parallelism [2]. The volume placement problem we solve here is still relevant but the computation of seek and mount penalties need to be changed for such environments, as multiple mounts are performed in parallel.
- In a multi-user environment, some multi-query optimization can be performed to avoid excessive mounts and dismount of volumes. By analyzing the volume requirements of queries currently in the queue a mount scheduler may devise an efficient mounting plan to minimize the total response time needed to satisfy all queries in the queue.

Acknowledgements

The authors wish to thank Arie Shoshani, head of the Data Management Group at LBL, for numerous ideas and comments throughout the design of these algorithms. We would also like to thank Bob Drach, Steve Louis, George Richmond, and Sue Hyer of the Lawrence Livermore National Laboratory, for their useful discussions regarding the motivation and results of this paper.

References

1. S. Coleman and S. W. Miller. *Mass Storage System Reference Model: version 4*. IEEE Technical Committee on Mass Storage Systems and Technology, 1990.
2. A. L. Drapeau and R. Katz. Striped Tape Arrays. In *Proceedings of the Twelfth IEEE Symposium on Mass Storage Sytems*, pages 257–266, April 1993.
3. S. Ghosh, Y. Kambayashi, and W. Lipski. *Data Base File Organizations, Theory and Application of the Consecutive Retrieval Property*. Academic Press, New York, 1983.
4. T.D.C. Little and A. Ghafour. Conceptual Models for Time-dependent Multimedia Data. In *Proceedings of Multimedia Information Systems*, pages 86–110, February 1992.
5. S. Ranade. *Mass Storage Technologies*. Meckler, Westport, London, 1991.
6. S. Ranade. *Jukebox and Robotic Libraries for Computer Mass Storage*. Meckler, Westport, London, 1992.
7. J. Wishner. The IEEE Storage System Standards Working Group Physical Volume Repository. In *Proceedings of the Twelfth IEEE Symposium on Mass Storage Sytems*, pages 87–100, April 1993.
8. C. K. Wong. *Algorithmic Studies in Mass Storage Systems*. Computer Science press, 1983.
9. C. Yu, W. Sun, D. Bitton, Q. Yang, R. Brunno, and J. Tullis. Efficient Placement of Audio on Optical Disks for Real-time Applications. *Communications of the ACM*, 32(7):862–871, 1989.

On the Estimation of Join Result Sizes

Arun Swami[1] and K. Bernhard Schiefer[2]

[1] IBM Almaden Research Center, 650 Harry Road, San Jose, CA 95120-6099
[2] IBM Toronto Lab, 895 Don Mills Road, North York, Ontario, Canada M3C 1W3

Abstract. Good estimates of join result sizes are critical for query optimization in relational database management systems. We address the problem of incrementally obtaining accurate and consistent estimates of join result sizes. We have invented a new rule for choosing join selectivities for estimating join result sizes. The rule is part of a new unified algorithm called Algorithm **ELS** (**E**quivalence and **L**argest **S**electivity). Prior to computing any result sizes, equivalence classes are determined for the join columns. The algorithm also takes into account the effect of local predicates on table and column cardinalities. These computations allow the correct selectivity values for each eligible join predicate to be computed. We show that the algorithm is correct and gives better estimates than current estimation algorithms.

1 Introduction

The join is an important operation in relational database management systems. When a user-generated query involves multiple joins, the cost of executing the query can vary dramatically depending on the query evaluation plan (QEP) chosen by the query optimizer. The join order and access methods used are important determinants of the lowest cost QEP.

The query optimizer estimates the eventual result size, or cardinality, of joining the specified tables and uses this information to choose between different join orders and access methods. Thus, the estimation of join result sizes in a query is an important problem, as the estimates have a significant influence on the QEP chosen.

A survey of the use of statistics and estimation techniques in query optimization is given in [7]. There has been a lot of work done on estimating selectivities, e.g., ([1, 10, 8]). In [6], a number of new selectivity estimation methods were proposed for highly skewed distributions such as Zipf distributions [17, 3]. Errors in the statistics maintained by the database system can affect the various estimates computed by the query optimizer. An analytical model was used in [4] to study the propagation of errors in the estimated size of join results as the number of joins increases in queries with a single equivalence class.

When more than two tables are involved, the query optimization algorithm often needs to estimate the join result sizes incrementally. Incremental estimation is used, for example, in the dynamic programming algorithm [13], the **AB** algorithm [15] and randomized algorithms [14, 5]. The optimizer first determines the join result size from joining the first two tables, then determines the join result size from the join with a third table, and so on. Thus, the query optimizer incrementally estimates the final join result size from the result sizes of the intermediate tables produced.

We have identified a number of problems with current practice in join size estimation. The problems include dealing with local predicates correctly, correct handling of multiple columns in a single table that belong to a single equivalence class, and correct incremental estimation of join result sizes. In this paper, we describe an algorithm called **ELS** that solves these problems and give arguments for the correctness of the solutions.

In the next section, we give a brief overview of the terminology and known results in join size estimation that are used in this paper. The reader knowlegeable in query optimization can skim Section 2. Section 3 describes some of the problems in current join size estimation practice. Algorithm **ELS** is outlined in Section 4. In [16] we also show how one can handle the case of multiple local predicates on a single column. In Sections 5, 6, and 7, we describe the techniques used in Algorithm **ELS** to address the problems described in Section 3. We illustrate the value of our algorithm in terms of execution time in Section 8. In Section 9 we summarize the contributions of this paper and indicate some directions for future work.

2 Background

The following assumptions are made by most query-processing cost models in practice and this paper:

1. *Independence*: Within each relation, values chosen from distinct columns that are involved in join predicates are independent.
2. *Uniformity of Attribute Values*: The distinct values in a join column appear equifrequently in the column.
3. *Containment*: When joining two tables, the set of values in the join column with the smaller column cardinality is a subset of the set of values in the join column with the larger column cardinality.

The implications of these and other assumptions are discussed in depth in [2].

Note that we need the uniformity assumption only for the join columns, i.e., we can use data distribution information for local predicate selectivities. Some work has been done ([1]) to relax some of these assumptions. However, this requires assuming a certain parametric model of the data (nonuniform Zipf distribution) and determination of the parameter values, or keeping a large amount of metadata (correlation statistics). There is a tradeoff between implementation complexity and possible gains in accuracy of estimates. Most query optimizers choose to work with the assumptions listed above. As in other work, we focus on *conjunctive* queries where the selection condition in the WHERE clause is a conjunction of predicates. These queries constitute the most important class of queries.

A table may participate in several join predicates. Let a table R be joined with another (possibly intermediate) table I. At this point in the join ordering, the query optimizer only needs to consider the predicates that link columns in table R with the corresponding columns in a second table S that is present in table I. These join predicates are termed *eligible* join predicates.

The query may include predicates that involve only a single table. Such predicates are called *local* predicates. The join result size is typically estimated as the product of the cardinalities of the operand tables after applying the local predicates (if any) and the join predicates [13]. When queries contain equality predicates (either local or join predicates), it is possible to derive additional implied predicates using transitive closure. (Similar derivations are possible for nonequality predicates too, but equality predicates are the most common and important class of predicates that generate implied predicates.) Transitive closure can be applied to two join predicates that share a common join column in order to obtain another join predicate.

Example 1a Suppose the following SQL statement is entered as a query [3]:

SELECT R_1.a
FROM R_1, R_2, R_3
WHERE $(R_1.\mathrm{x} = R_2.\mathrm{y})$ AND $(R_2.\mathrm{y} = R_3.\mathrm{z})$

We can use the principle of transitivity with the join predicates J1: $(R_1.\mathrm{x} = R_2.\mathrm{y})$ and J2: $(R_2.\mathrm{y} = R_3.\mathrm{z})$ to obtain the join predicate J3: $(R_1.x = R_3.z)$.

Performing this predicate transitive closure gives the optimizer maximum freedom to vary the join order and ensures that the same QEP is generated for equivalent queries independently of how the queries are specified. In the above example, without predicate J3, most query optimizers would avoid the join order beginning with $(R_1 \bowtie R_3)$ since this would be evaluated as a cartesian product, which is very expensive[4]. Since join predicates can share columns, the effects of applying them may not be independent. In the above example, once join predicates J1 and J2 have been evaluated, J3 has in effect been evaluated, and hence evaluating it separately can have no further effect on the size of the join result. Equivalence classes of join columns can be used to capture these dependencies.

Initially, each column is an equivalence class by itself. When an equality (local or join) predicate is seen during query optimization, the equivalence classes corresponding to the two columns on each side of the equality are merged. In the example above, given join predicate J1, columns x and y are in the same equivalence class. When join predicate J2 is seen, the equivalence classes of columns y and z are merged. Thus columns x, y and z are now in a single equivalence class. As we will see later, we can use the equivalence class structure to correctly take into account the effect of dependencies between join predicates. We will often use the terminology "x and y are *j-equivalent* (columns)" to denote that x and y belong to the same equivalence class.

Multiple equivalence classes can be handled using the independence assumption as follows. Since the join columns in different equivalence classes are assumed satisfy the independence assumption, the predicates involving columns

[3] In the rest of the paper, we show only the WHERE clause of SQL queries.
[4] We use $\bowtie$ as the symbol for the join operation

in one equivalence class reduce the join result size independent of the predicates involving columns in another equivalence class. Thus, in the rest of the paper, we can focus on the case of a single equivalence class.

Two kinds of statistics are typically important in query optimization. One statistic is the number of tuples contained in a single table. This value is known as the *table cardinality* and is denoted by $\|R\|$, wherein R is the table. The second statistic is the number of distinct values present in a column. This value is known as the *column cardinality* and is denoted by d_x, wherein x is the column. These two statistics are important because they are used to estimate the size of the results from different operations on the table data, which in turn helps to determine the cost of these operations.

Consider a join predicate (J:($R_1.x_1 = R_2.x_2$)), where the column cardinality of x_1 (x_2) of table R_1 (R_2) is d_1 (d_2). The size of the join result can be estimated [13] as:

$$\|(R_1 \bowtie R_2)\| = d_i \times \frac{\|R_1\| \times \|R_2\|}{d_1 \times d_2}, \quad \text{where } d_i = \min(d_1, d_2) \qquad \text{(Equation 1)}$$

Since $\min(d_1, d_2)/d_1 \times d_2 = 1/\max(d_1, d_2)$ Equation Equation 1 can be rewritten as:

$$\|(R_1 \bowtie R_2)\| = \|R_1\| \times \|R_2\| \times S_J, \quad \text{where } S_J = \frac{1}{\max(d_1, d_2)} \qquad \text{(Equation 2)}$$

where S_J is termed the *selectivity* of the join predicate J. In order to enable a more intuitive understanding of Equation 2, we will derive Equation 1 using the assumptions listed above. For each distinct value, there are $\|R_i\|/d_i$ tuples in R_i having that value in the join column (from the uniformity assumption). Using the containment assumption, we get that the number of distinct values that appear in the join columns of both the tables is $\min(d_1, d_2)$. But these are precisely the values for which the join takes place. Hence, the number of tuples in the intermediate result ($R_1 \bowtie R_2$) is:

$$\|(R_1 \bowtie R_2)\| = \min(d_1, d_2) \times \frac{\|R_1\|}{d_1} \times \frac{\|R_2\|}{d_2} = \|R_1\| \times \|R_2\| \times \frac{1}{\max(d_1, d_2)}$$

In [12], Rosenthal showed that Equation 1 holds even if the uniformity assumption is weakened to require expected uniformity for only one of the join columns.

Equation 1 can be generalized for n relations to get Equation 3 below. Let R_1^n denote the result of joining tables $R_1, R_2, \cdots, R_n$ on columns $x_1, x_2, \cdots, x_n$ respectively. Here there are equality predicates between each pair of columns and in the terminology of equivalence classes, all the $x_i s$ are in a single equivalence class, i.e., are j-equivalent. Denote the column cardinality of x_i by d_i for $i \in 1 \cdots n$. Let $d_{(1)}, d_{(2)}, \cdots, d_{(n)}$ be a rearrangement of $d_1, d_2, \cdots, d_n$ in increasing order as $d_{(1)} \leq d_{(2)} \leq \cdots \leq d_{(n)}$. Then, such that $d_{i_1}, d_{i_2}, \cdots, d_{i_n}$ are ordered in an ascending sequence. Then,

$$d_{(1)} = \min(d_{(1)}, d_{(2)}, \cdots, d_{(n)}) = \min(d_1, d_2, \cdots, d_n)$$

Then, using the assumptions listed above, it can be shown that the size of the intermediate result R_1^n is:

$$\|R_1^n\| = d_{(1)} \times \frac{\|R_1\|}{d_1} \times \frac{\|R_2\|}{d_2} \times \cdots \times \frac{\|R_n\|}{d_n}$$

$$= \frac{\|R_1\| \times \|R_2\| \times \cdots \times \|R_n\|}{d_{(2)} \times d_{(3)} \times \cdots \times d_{(n)}}, \quad \text{where } d_{(1)} = \min(d_1, d_2, \ldots, d_n) \quad \text{(Equation 3)}$$

that is, all column cardinalities except for the smallest one are present in the denominator.

Example 1b Continuing with Example 1a, let the statistics for the tables be as follows:

$\|R_1\| = 100$, $\|R_2\| = 1000$, $\|R_3\| = 1000$, $d_x = 10$, $d_y = 100$, $d_z = 1000$

The join selectivities from Equation 2 are:

J1: $S_{J1} = 1/\max(d_1, d_2) = 1/\max(10, 100) = 0.01$
J2: $S_{J2} = 1/\max(d_2, d_3) = 1/\max(100, 1000) = 0.001$
J3: $S_{J3} = 1/\max(d_1, d_3) = 1/\max(10, 1000) = 0.001$

If R_2 is joined with R_3, the size of the intermediate result table can be estimated using Equation 2:

$$\|R_2 \bowtie R_3\| = \|R_2\| \times \|R_3\| \times S_{J2} = 1000 \times 1000 \times 0.001 = 1000$$

Using Equation 3, the size of $(R_1 \bowtie R_2 \bowtie R_3)$ is estimated to be:

$$\|R_1 \bowtie R_2 \bowtie R_3\| = \frac{100 \times 1000 \times 1000}{100 \times 1000} = 1000$$

which is the correct answer.

3 Problems in Join Size Estimation

There are a number of problems with current practice in join size estimation. The problems include dealing with local predicates correctly, correct handling of multiple columns in a single table that belong a single equivalence class, and correct incremental estimation of join result sizes.

3.1 Effect of Local Predicates

If a local predicate is present, the local predicate may reduce the cardinality of the table. This reduced cardinality is called the *effective* cardinality of the table. It can be used in other cardinality calculations, such as for estimating join result sizes. When the local predicate is on a join column, the predicate can also reduce the column cardinality of the join column. Thus, it is clear that local predicates will affect join result sizes, since the predicates affect both the number of participating tuples and, possibly, the column cardinality of the join columns. It is evident that an algorithm is needed for taking into account the effect of local predicates when estimating join result sizes. We do not know of any algorithm that *correctly* takes into account both local predicates and join predicates. In Section 5, we describe how to correctly take into account the effect of local predicates in join size estimation.

3.2 Single Table J-Equivalent Columns

During the incremental calculation of join result sizes, it can happen that two or more of the eligible join predicates involve join columns of the next table that are j-equivalent. For example, consider a table R_1 joining with another table R_2 using the following join predicates: $(R_1.x = R_2.y)$ and $(R_1.x = R_2.z)$. By transitive closure, we get the predicate $(R_2.y = R_2.z)$. When R_1 is joined with R_2, all three predicates are eligible and involve columns y and z of R_2 that are j-equivalent by virtue of the predicate $(R_2.y = R_2.z)$.

Current query optimizers do not treat this as a special case and therefore, by default, the join selectivities of all such join predicates are used in calculating the join result sizes. However, using them produces an incorrect result because the join columns are not independent. In Section 6, we describe an algorithm that correctly handles the case when two or more of the join columns of a relation are j-equivalent.

3.3 J-Equivalent Columns from Different Tables

Another problem that arises in incremental computation is that the effect of all the eligible predicates involving different tables is not independent. In Example 1b, once join predicates J1 and J2 have been evaluated, J3 has in effect been evaluated and hence, evaluating it separately can have no further effect on the estimated size of the join result. Yet, in current practice, its selectivity will be included in the result size estimate.

In [13], the selectivities of all the eligible join predicates are multiplied together along with the product of the individual effective table cardinalities (as reduced by the selectivities of local predicates). We call this the ***multiplicative*** rule ($\mathcal{M}$). This rule can compute an incorrect join result size because all the join selectivities are used without accounting for dependencies. Rule $\mathcal{M}$ can dramatically underestimate the join result size as shown in Example 2.

Example 2 As in Example 1b, let R_2 and R_3 be joined first, and then R_1. From Example 1b, we have $\|R_2 \bowtie R_3\| = 1000$. When R_1 is joined, Rule $\mathcal{M}$ estimates the join result size to be:

$$\begin{aligned}\|R_2 \bowtie R_3 \bowtie R_1\| &= \|R_2 \bowtie R_3\| \times \|R_1\| \times S_{J1} \times S_{J3} \\ &= 1000 \times 100 \times 0.01 \times 0.001 = 1 \quad \text{(correct answer is 1000)}\end{aligned}$$

The problem of underestimation of join result sizes by Rule $\mathcal{M}$ suggests dividing the eligible join predicates into groups, with join predicates involving j-equivalent columns being grouped together, and then choosing for each group a single join selectivity. The problem appears to be analogous to the problem of picking among multiple local predicates on a single column [16]. Thus, one would expect to pick the ***smallest*** join selectivity value for each group. We refer to this idea as the smallest selectivity rule ($\mathcal{SS}$). Though this seems to be the intuitive choice, this choice of join selectivity can compute an incorrect join result size as shown in Example 3.

Example 3 As in Example 1b, let R_2 and R_3 be joined first, and then R_1. From Example 1b, we have $\|R_2 \bowtie R_3\| = 1000$. When R_1 is to be joined, Rule $\mathcal{SS}$ puts predicates J1 and J3 in a single group, since columns x, y and z are j-equivalent. Since $S_{J3} < S_{J1}$, it uses only predicate J3 in calculating the join result size. Thus, Rule $\mathcal{SS}$ estimates the join result size as follows:

$$\begin{aligned}\|R_2 \bowtie R_3 \bowtie R_1\| &= \|R_2 \bowtie R_3\| \times \|R_1\| \times S_{J3} \\ &= 1000 \times 100 \times 0.001 = 100 \quad \text{(correct answer is 1000)}\end{aligned}$$

A third procedure has been proposed but, to our knowledge, has not been implemented in any optimizer. The proposal is to assign a *representative* join selectivity to each equivalence class and to use that selectivity whenever join predicates in that equivalence class are being used. The problem with this proposal is that there is no certainty that a correct value for this representative join selectivity exists that will work in all cases. In our example query, if the representative selectivity is 0.01, the estimate for the final join result size will be 10000, which is too high. If the representative selectivity is 0.001, the estimate for the final join result size will be 100, which is too low. In Section 7, we describe a new rule for correctly choosing the join selectivities when undertaking an incremental estimation of join result sizes.

4 Algorithm ELS

We describe an algorithm called **ELS** (**E**quivalence and **L**argest **S**electivity) that solves the problems described in the previous section. Algorithm **ELS** consists of two phases. The first is a preliminary phase that is to be performed before any join result sizes are computed. In this phase, the predicates implied due to transitive closure are generated and join selectivities are calculated. The preliminary phase consists of steps 1 through 5. The second phase computes, incrementally, the join result sizes. The processing for this final phase is outlined in step 6.

1. Examine each given predicate.
   - Remove any predicate that is identical to another predicate, so that queries involving duplicate predicates such as (R_1.x > 500) AND (R_1.x > 500) can be handled.
   - Build equivalence classes for all columns that are participating in any of the predicates.
2. Generate all implied predicates using transitive closure. There are five variations:
   a. Two join predicates can imply another join predicate.
   $(R_1.\mathrm{x} = R_2.\mathrm{y})$ AND $(R_2.\mathrm{y} = R_3.\mathrm{z}) \Longrightarrow (R_1.\mathrm{x} = R_3.\mathrm{z})$
   b. Two join predicates can imply a local predicate.
   $(R_1.\mathrm{x} = R_2.\mathrm{y})$ AND $(R_1.\mathrm{x} = R_2.\mathrm{w}) \Longrightarrow (R_2.\mathrm{y} = R_2.\mathrm{w})$

c. Two local predicates can imply another local predicate.
$(R_1.\mathrm{x} = R_1.\mathrm{y})$ AND $(R_1.\mathrm{y} = R_1.\mathrm{z}) \Longrightarrow (R_1.\mathrm{x} = R_1.\mathrm{z})$
d. A join predicate and a local predicate can imply another join predicate.
$(R_1.\mathrm{x} = R_2.\mathrm{y})$ AND $(R_1.\mathrm{x} = R_1.\mathrm{v}) \Longrightarrow (R_2.\mathrm{y} = R_1.\mathrm{v})$
e. A join predicate and a local predicate can imply another local predicate. Here *op* denotes a comparison operator, and *c* is a constant.
$(R_1.\mathrm{x} = R_2.\mathrm{y})$ AND $(R_1.\mathrm{x}\ op\ c) \Longrightarrow (R_2.\mathrm{y}\ op\ c)$

3. Assign to each local predicate a selectivity estimate that incorporates any distribution statistics. In [16], we present a complete algorithm to handle the case of multiple local predicates on a single column. In essence, the most restrictive equality predicate is chosen if it exists, otherwise we chose a pair of range predicates which form the tightest bound.
4. For each table, compute an estimate of the table cardinality and the column cardinality of each column after all the local predicates have been included. We show that if these new estimates are correctly used in the computation of join selectivities and join result sizes, we do not need to concern ourselves with local predicates after this step. This is discussed further in Section 5.
5. Process each join predicate by computing its join selectivity. If two join columns from the same table are j-equivalent, special care is needed in the computation of the join selectivities. We describe an algorithm for handling this case in Section 6.
6. For each intermediate result of the join order, estimate the result size. We have invented a new rule, which is described in Section 7, to estimate the result size. We also prove that the rule is correct under the assumptions stated in Section 2.

5 Effect of Local Predicates on Join Result Sizes

In Section 3, we described the need to incorporate the effect of local predicates in the estimation of join result sizes. Let R be one of the tables participating in a join. Let a join column of R be x and let a local predicate involve column y of R. Here, y could be identical with x. Let $\|R\|$ be the cardinality of R before the local predicate is applied, and $\|R\|'$ be the cardinality of R after the local predicate is applied. Let d_x denote the column cardinality of join column x before the local predicate is applied, and d'_x denote the column cardinality of column x after the local predicate is applied. Similarly, we can define d_y and d'_y.

The estimates of $\|R\|'$, d'_x, and d'_y depend on the local predicate and the information available about the column y. For example, if the local predicate is of the form $y = a$ where a is a literal, we know that $d'_y = 1$. If we have distribution statistics on y, they can be used to accurately estimate $\|R\|'$. Otherwise, we can use the uniformity assumption (see Section 2) to estimate $\|R\|'$ (i.e., $\|R\|' = \|R\|/d_y$). For some other local predicate L involving y, if the local predicate selectivity S_L is known, we can estimate $\|R\|' = \|R\| \times S_L$ and $d_y{}' = d_y \times S_L$.

Now that we have estimated $\|R\|'$ and d'_y, we can estimate d'_x as follows. If y is identical with x, clearly $d'_x = d'_y$. If y and x are different columns, we use a simple urn model to estimate d'_x. The process is one of assigning $\|R\|'$

balls among d_x urns that are initially empty. Any of the urns can be chosen uniformly. The balls correspond to the selected tuples and the urns correspond to the distinct values in column x. The number of distinct values in x remaining after selection corresponds to the number of non-empty urns. We obtain the expected number of non-empty urns as follows, where $n = d_x$ and $k = \|R\|'$.

$$\begin{aligned}
&\text{Prob}\{\text{ball is put in urn } i\} &&= 1/n \\
&\text{Prob}\{\text{ball is not put in urn } i\} &&= (1 - 1/n) \\
&\text{Prob}\{\text{none of the } k \text{ balls is put in urn } i\} &&= (1 - 1/n)^k \\
&\text{Prob}\{\text{at least one of the } k \text{ balls is put in urn } i\} &&= (1 - (1 - 1/n)^k)
\end{aligned}$$

Then, the expected number of non-empty urns is given by $n \times (1 - (1 - 1/n)^k)$. Hence in the case where column x is distinct from column y, we have that

$$d'_x = \left\lceil d_x \times (1 - (1 - 1/d_x)^{\|R\|'}) \right\rceil$$

Note that if $\|R\|'$ is sufficiently large enough and approaches $\|R\|$, the term $(1-1/d_x)^{\|R\|'}$ will be close to 0 and $d'_x \approx d_x$. This estimate can be quite different from another common estimate $d'_x = d_x \times (\|R\|'/\|R\|)$. This can be seen from the following numerical example. Let $d_x = 10000$, $\|R\| = 100000$ and $\|R\|' = 50000$. Then the urn model estimate gives $d'_x = 9933$ whereas the other estimate gives $d'_x = 5000$. If $\|R\|' = \|R\|$, the estimate according to the urn model is $d'_x = 10000$.

At this point, the table and column cardinality estimates have already incorporated all local predicates. The rest of the estimation algorithm only has to deal with join predicates. We have thus taken into account the effect of local predicates and simplified subsequent processing. We can also take advantage of distribution statistics on columns that are involved in local predicates. This enables us to obtain more accurate estimates of join result sizes. The original, unreduced table and column cardinalities are retained for use in cost calculations before the local predicates have been applied, for example, when estimating the cost of accessing the table.

We have assumed that if the effect of a local predicate on the table cardinality and the column cardinalities of join columns is taken into account, then the local predicate is, in effect, applied before or together with the join predicates on this table. This being true, then the following argument shows that our approach to size estimation is correct. Consider all the local and join predicates being used to form an intermediate result. For the estimation of the result size, it does not matter in which order the predicates are applied. We can assume that the local predicates are applied first, evaluate their effects on the table statistics, and then compute the size obtained by applying the join predicates. Hence, in the following discussion, we will focus on join predicates and assume that local predicates can be handled as described above.

6 J-Equivalent Join Columns in a Single Table

Algorithm **ELS** needs to deal with the special case described in Section 3.2. Consider the following example query, involving columns from the same table that are j-equivalent.

WHERE (R_1.x = R_2.y) AND (R_1.x = R_2.w)

After transitive closure of predicates, we obtain the following tranformed query:

WHERE (R_1.x = R_2.y) AND (R_1.x = R_2.w) AND (R_2.y = R_2.w)

where the implied local predicate (R_2.y = R_2.w) is added using rule 2.a from Section 4. Let the statistics for the tables in the query be as follows: $\|R_1\| = 100$, $\|R_2\| = 1000$, $d_x = 100$, $d_y = 10$, $d_w = 50$. After transitive closure, R_2.y participates in every join in which R_2.w participates and vice versa. Hence, for computing join selectivities and join result sizes, we have to know the number of R_2 tuples that can qualify under the local predicate and also the number of distinct values that the qualifying tuples contain. We wish to quantify the effect of the local predicate on the effective cardinality of R_2 and the column cardinalities prior to evaluating the effect of the join predicates on the result sizes. To do so, we use a probabilistic argument as follows.

Without loss of generality, let $d_w >= d_y$. Let $\|R_2\|$ denote the table cardinality prior to join predicates being applied. We use the containment assumption for join columns (see Section 2) to infer that all the d_y distinct values are contained in the d_w distinct values. Now, consider any tuple of R_2. It has some value, say **q**, in column $R_2.y$. Assuming the independence and uniformity assumptions for columns $R_2.w$ and $R_2.y$, the probability that $R_2.w$ has the same value **q** is $1/d_w$. Since this is the case for every tuple of R_2, the effective cardinality of R_2 is given by $\|R_2\|'$, where

$$\|R_2\|' = \left\lceil \frac{\|R_2\|}{d_w} \right\rceil$$

Once this selection has been performed, only one of the columns needs to be joined since the evaluation of the local predicate has made the other join redundant. Using a simple urn model as in Section 5, we deduce that the column cardinality value that should be used for join selectivity computations is:

$$\left\lceil d_y \times (1 - (1 - 1/d_y)^{\|R_2\|'}) \right\rceil$$

that is, we pick the column with the most restrictive effect on the column cardinality. In our example query, $\|R_2\|' = \|R_2\|/d_w = 1000/50 = 20$. We pick R_2.y and the effective column cardinality in joins is hence,

$$\left\lceil d_y \times (1 - (1 - 1/d_y)^{\|R_2\|'}) \right\rceil = \lceil 10 \times (1 - (1 - 1/10)^{20}) \rceil = 9$$

The formulas given above can be generalized to the case of three or more join columns, from the same table, that are j-equivalent. Let $1, 2, \cdots, n$ be the equivalent join columns of table R, and let the column cardinalities be $d_1, d_2, \cdots, d_n$. Let $d_{(1)}, d_{(2)}, \cdots, d_{(n)}$ be a rearrangement of $d_1, d_2, \cdots, d_n$ in increasing order as $d_{(1)} \leq d_{(2)} \leq \cdots \leq d_{(n)}$. Then,

$$d_{(1)} = \min(d_{(1)}, d_{(2)}, \cdots, d_{(n)}) = \min(d_1, d_2, \cdots, d_n)$$

Using an argument similar to the one above, it follows that

$$\|R\|' = \left\lceil \frac{\|R\|}{d_{(2)} \times d_{(3)} \times \cdots \times d_{(n)}} \right\rceil$$

and that the effective column cardinality in joins is

$$\left\lceil d_{(1)} \times (1 - (1 - 1/d_{(1)})^{\|R\|'}) \right\rceil$$

7 Incremental Computation of Result Sizes

We saw in Section 3 that the "intuitive" rules currently used in query optimizers (Rule $\mathcal{M}$ and Rule $\mathcal{SS}$) do not correctly choose the join selectivities in the incremental estimation of join sizes. We present a new rule (called $\mathcal{LS}$) for picking one of the join selectivities for an equivalence class.

> $\mathcal{LS}$: *Given a choice of join selectivities for a single equivalence class, always pick the* **largest** *join selectivity.*

Rule $\mathcal{LS}$ appears counter-intuitive and a proof is provided in [16].

Multiple equivalence classes can be accommodated by using the independence assumption. Since the join columns in different equivalence classes are assumed to satisfy the independence assumption, each equivalence class independently reduces the join result size. The algorithm then determines the join selectivity for each equivalence class and multiplies them together to obtain the effective join selectivity.

Example 3 As in Example 1b, let R_2 and R_3 be joined first, and then R_1. From Example 1b, we have $\|R_2 \bowtie R_3\| = 1000$. When R_1 is to be joined, Rule $\mathcal{LS}$ puts predicates J1 and J3 in a single group, since columns x, y and z are j-equivalent. Since $S_{J3} < S_{J1}$, it uses only predicate J1 in calculating the join result size. Thus, Rule $\mathcal{LS}$ estimates the join result size as follows:

$$\begin{aligned} \|R_2 \bowtie R_3 \bowtie R_1\| &= \|R_2 \bowtie R_3\| \times \|R_1\| \times S_{J1} = 1000 \times 100 \times 0.01 \\ &= 1000 \quad \textbf{(correct)} \end{aligned}$$

As before, denote the result of joining tables $R_1, R_2, \cdots, R_n$ by R_1^n. Let us say that we have calculated the size of R_1^n. We now wish to join table R_{n+1} to obtain the result R_1^{n+1}. We now prove that Rule $\mathcal{LS}$ is correct by showing that the algorithm calculates the join result size in agreement with the size calculated by Equation 3 for a single equivalence class. Recall that we have already discussed how to handle multiple equivalence classes. The proof is by induction on the number of tables.

8 Experiment

We have presented Algorithm **ELS** and shown that it correctly estimates of join result sizes. In this section, we illustrate that correct estimation of join sizes can make a significant difference in query execution times. We use a straightforward select-project-join query that is shown below. For this query, Algorithm **ELS** can result in an order of magnitude improvement in query execution time.

SELECT COUNT()
FROM S, M, B, G
WHERE s = m AND m = b AND b = g AND s < 100

The tables used in the query are S (*s*mall), M (*m*edium), B (*b*ig) and G (*g*iant). A single column from each table participates in the query and is denoted by the table name in lower case, e.g., column s from table S. The query after transitive closure is transformed as follows.

SELECT COUNT()
FROM S, M, B, G
WHERE s = m AND m = b AND b = g AND s = b AND s = g AND
m = g AND s < 100 AND m < 100 AND b < 100 AND g < 100

The table and column cardinalites are given below.

$$\|S\| = 1000, \|M\| = 10000, \|B\| = 50000, \|G\| = 100000$$
$$d_s = 1000, d_m = 10000, d_b = 50000, d_g = 100000$$

The query optimizer in the Starburst DBMS [9] was modified to implement the multiplicative rule (Rule $\mathcal{M}$), the smallest selectivity rule (Rule $\mathcal{SS}$), and our Algorithm **ELS** (with Rule $\mathcal{LS}$). Predicate transitive closure (PTC) was implemented as a query rewrite rule [11] so that we could disable it as necessary for the experiments. Note that both Rule $\mathcal{SS}$ and Rule $\mathcal{LS}$ are sensible only when predicate transitive closure has been applied. No other changes were made to the optimizer and the optimizer's entire repertoire was enabled (including the Nested Loops and Sort Merge join methods).

The standard algorithm most commonly in use in current relational systems computes join selectivities independent of the effect of local predicates. Let Algorithm **SM** denote using Rule $\mathcal{M}$ with the standard algorithm. Similarly, let Algorithm **SSS** denote using Rule $\mathcal{SS}$ with the standard algorithm.

We ran four experiments. The original query, before predicate transitive closure, was run using Algorithm **SM**. Next, the query after predicate transitive closure was applied, was run with Algorithm **SM** and Algorithm **SSS**. Finally, the original query was run with Algorithm **ELS**. The results are shown in the table below which identifies the query and rewrite rule used, the algorithm used, the join order chosen by the algorithm, the result sizes estimated after each join, and the elapsed time for the chosen query evaluation plan (QEP) in seconds. Note that all the QEPs were executed using the same buffer size and that the access methods and join methods did not differ between the QEPs. Both Nested Loops and Sort Merge join methods were used in the QEPs.

Query	Algorithm	Join Order	Estimated Result Sizes	Time
Original	**SM**	$S \bowtie M \bowtie B \bowtie G$	(100, 100, 100)	610
Orig. + PTC	**SM**	$S \bowtie B \bowtie M \bowtie G$	$(0.2, 4 \times 10^{-8}, 4 \times 10^{-21})$	472
Orig. + PTC	**SSS**	$S \bowtie B \bowtie M \bowtie G$	$(0.2, 4 \times 10^{-4}, 4 \times 10^{-7})$	472
Orig.	**ELS**	$B \bowtie G \bowtie M \bowtie S$	(100, 100, 100)	50

We see that there is an improvement in query execution time when predicate transitive closure is used (see the first two rows in the above table). Predicate transitive closure is important because the additional predicates permit early selection and greater flexibility in the selection of the join order. This may result in the generation of better QEPs.

However, using predicate transitive closure is not enough. After predicate transitive closure is used, the QEPs chosen differ in the join order. This is due to the different estimates obtained for the intermediate join result sizes. The QEP chosen by **ELS** runs 9 - 12 times faster than the other QEPs.

The correct join result size after any subset of joins has been performed can be shown to be exactly 100. We can see in the second and third rows of the table that Algorithm **SM** and Algorithm **SSS** greatly underestimate the join result sizes. The optimizer estimates that the size of the 3-table composite result involving tables S, M, and B is extremely small. This misleads the optimizer into believing that table G will be accessed very infrequently. Thus, the optimizer puts table G last in the join order, which in turn leads to a poor QEP.

9 Summary

Accurate estimation of join result sizes is crucial in query optimization because the estimates have a significant influence on the query plans chosen. This paper described an algorithm (called **ELS**) for the correct incremental estimation of join result sizes. For each table, estimates of the table cardinality and the column cardinality of each column are computed, while taking into account the effect of local predicates and the case when two or more join columns in a table belong to the same equivalence class. These estimates are then used in the computation of join selectivities. For any intermediate result, Algorithm **ELS** chooses a correct subset of the eligible join predicates to determine the result size, while taking into account any dependencies between eligible join predicates. We proved the correctness of Algorithm **ELS**. We have shown that using the algorithm can make a significant difference in query execution time (possibly an order of magnitude or more).

Future work involves relaxing the assumptions that are used in this paper and in most of the work on join size estimation. We have already relaxed the uniformity assumption in the case of local predicates. Relaxing the assumption in the case of join predicates would enable query optimizers to account for important data distributions such as the Zipfian distribution. The independence assumption needs to be relaxed. All published work on estimation has dealt with the case of a single SQL query block. Estimation in nested SQL queries is a much harder problem. Work also needs to be done to extend the results in this paper to queries involving disjunctions.

Acknowledgements

We wish to thank Paul Bird, Philip Blair, Peter Haas, Richard Hedges, Bruce Lindsay, Guy Lohman, Sheila Richardson, Pat Selinger and Lori Strain for their comments on various drafts of this paper.

References

1. S. Christodoulakis. Estimating Block Transfers and Join Sizes. In *Proceedings of ACM-SIGMOD International Conference on Management of Data*, pages 40–54, 1983.
2. S. Christodoulakis. Implications of Certain Assumptions in Database Performance Evaluation. *ACM Transactions on Database Systems*, 9(2):163–186, June 1984.
3. C. Faloutsos and H. V. Jagadish. On B-tree Indices for Skewed Distributions. In *Proceedings of the Eighteenth International Conference on Very Large Data Bases*, pages 363–374, Vancouver, British Columbia, 1992. Morgan Kaufman.
4. Y. E. Ioannidis and S. Christodoulakis. On the Propogation of Errors in the Size of Join Results. In *Proceedings of ACM-SIGMOD International Conference on Management of Data*, pages 268–277, Denver, Colorado, 1991.
5. Y.C. Kang. *Randomized Algorithms for Query Optimization*. PhD thesis, University of Wisconsin-Madison, October 1991. TR 1053.
6. C. A. Lynch. Selectivity Estimation and Query Optimization in Large Databases with Highly Skewed Distributions of Column Values. In *Proceedings of the Fourteenth International Conference on Very Large Data Bases*, pages 240–251, Los Angeles, USA, 1988. Morgan Kaufman.
7. M. V. Mannino, P. Chu, and T. Sager. Statistical Profile Estimation in Database Systems. *ACM Computing Surveys*, 20(3):191–221, September 1988.
8. M. Muralikrishna and D. J. Dewitt. Equi-Depth Histograms for Estimating Selectivity Factors for Multi-Dimensional Queries. In *Proceedings of ACM-SIGMOD International Conference on Management of Data*, pages 28–36, Chicago, Illinois, 1988.
9. K. Ono and G. M. Lohman. Measuring the Complexity of Join Enumeration in Query Optimization. In *Proceedings of the Sixteenth International Conference on Very Large Data Bases*, pages 314–325, Brisbane, Australia, 1990. Morgan Kaufman.
10. G. Piatetsky-Shapiro and C. Connell. Accurate Estimation of the Number of Tuples Satisfying a Condition. In *Proceedings of ACM-SIGMOD International Conference on Management of Data*, pages 256–276, 1984.
11. H. Pirahesh, J. Hellerstein, and W. Hasan. Extensible/Rule Based Query Rewrite Optimization in Starburst. In *Proceedings of ACM-SIGMOD International Conference on Management of Data*, pages 39–48, San Diego, California, 1992.
12. A. Rosenthal. Note on the Expected Size of a Join. *ACM-SIGMOD Record*, pages 19–25, July 1981.
13. P. G. Selinger, M. M. Astrahan, D. D. Chamberlin, R. A. Lorie, and T. G. Price. Access Path Selection in a Relational Database Management System. In *Proceedings of ACM-SIGMOD International Conference on Management of Data*, pages 23–34, 1979.
14. A. Swami. *Optimization of Large Join Queries*. PhD thesis, Stanford University, June 1989. STAN-CS-89-1262.
15. A. Swami and B. Iyer. A Polynomial Time Algorithm for Optimizing Join Queries. In *Proceedings of IEEE Data Engineering Conference*, pages 345–354. IEEE Computer Society, April 1993.
16. A. Swami and K. B. Schiefer. On the Estimation of Join Result Sizes. Technical report, IBM Research Division, October 1993. IBM Research Report RJ 9569.
17. G. K. Zipf. *Human Behavior and the Principle of Least Effort*. Addison-Wesley, Reading, MA, 1949.

DBJ – A Dynamic Balancing Hash Join Algorithm in Multiprocessor Database Systems (Extended Abstract)

X. Zhao, R.G. Johnson, N.J. Martin

Department of Computer Science
Birkbeck College, University of London
London WC1E 7HX, UK

1 Introduction

Hash join algorithms are a popular query processing mechanism in parallel database systems. A number of papers have addressed the implementation of parallel hash join algorithms including [1], [2], [3], [4], [5], [6], [7], and [8]. Since selections or projections are often performed in advance of the later join operations in order to reduce data volumes, it is difficult to predict the distribution of input relations to a join operation. No hash function can guarantee a uniform output distribution without knowing the input distribution information [9]. The non-uniform output distribution of hash functions causes unbalanced workloads between processors. These unbalanced workloads can curtail scalability and degrade the performance. To take full advantage of parallel processing for a hash-based join algorithm, a workload balancing mechanism is necessary.

Data skew leading to unbalanced workloads may arise from several causes as noted by Walton et al. [8]. A number of skew-handling hash join algorithms have been proposed, including those of Kitsuregewa et al. [4], Hua et al. [3], Wolf et al. [10], and Dewitt et al. [2]. Most of them rely on obtaining knowledge of the source data distributions in order to reduce the unbalance arising from the join processing stages. The algorithms based on preprocessing to obtain the source data distribution result in a high cost. The DBJ algorithm presented needs no preprocessing and relies on no distribution assumptions. It detects the actual hash function output and corrects any unbalanced output dynamically. This is achieved without the need for a co-ordinating processor. This algorithm has been fully implemented in a multiprocessor database system.

2 The DBJ Algorithm

The DBJ algorithm is an architecture independent algorithm. We only assume in the following that certain processors, referred to as data servers, have directly attached disk drives and are used primarily for caching and organizing source relation data. Certain processors, referred to simply as processors, are used for the actual query processing. In fact a single physical processing component may act as both data server and processor.

The essence of hashing schemes is to use the key value of a tuple to compute the location for the further processing of that tuple. Let R and S be the two relations to be joined. These relations are assumed to be horizontally partitioned and uniformly distributed across all the data servers. Let R_d and S_d be the portion of R and S residing at the data server d and $|R_d|$ and $|S_d|$ be the cardinalities of each portion. Let $D+1$ be the number of data servers with the identifiers of the data servers being $0, 1, \ldots, D$. A hash function h partitions each R_d into $B+1$ number of buckets, R_d^0, R_d^1, ..., R_d^B. The identifiers of buckets are $0, 1, \ldots, B$. Suppose there are $P+1$ processors and their identifiers are $0, 1, \ldots, P$. Suppose at a timepoint the data server d has partitioned Q_d tuples and $q = Q_d/|R_d|$. Let C_{db}^{qp} be the number of tuples in bucket b which is allocated to processor p on the data server d at the moment when the ratio q of R_d's tuples has been partitioned. Each bucket is allocated to one processor and each processor may be allocated many buckets. Let function f map bucket identifiers to processor identifiers and $F(x)$ represent the set of the bucket identifiers with the same processor identifier x. The value C_{db}^{qp} gives the data distribution information during a partition phase.

On average there will be α buckets on each processor, where $\alpha = \lfloor (B+1)/(P+1) \rfloor$. The data servers initially allocate an equal number of buckets of R to each processor. The buckets, $R_d^{n(P+1)+p}$, $n = 0, 1, \ldots, \alpha$, are allocated to processor p initially by data server d, $d = 0, 1, \ldots, D$. At a timepoint before the partition phase finishes, each data server d has its own distribution information of $C_{dj}^{f(j)}$, $j = 0, 1, \ldots, B$. Each data server broadcasts this information to all other servers and the processors, thus allowing the entire current bucket distribution pattern, $C_j^{f(j)} = \sum_{i=0}^{D} C_{ij}^{f(j)}$, $j = 0, 1, \ldots, B$, to be organised on all the data servers and processors. The $\sum$ signifies that all C values with the same bucket identifier are added together. This distribution information also can be seen as a measure of the processor workloads, $C^k = \sum_{j \in F(k)} C_j^k$, $k = 0, 1, \ldots, P$. Since every data server and processor knows the distribution information, the balance check can take place on each of them independently and the balancing process can begin when it is necessary.

3 Dynamic Balance

The portion R_d on each data server is partitioned into $R_d^0, R_d^1, \ldots, R_d^B$ and moved to the $P+1$ processors. On each processor the buckets coming from different data servers are composed into complete single buckets, $R^j = \sum_{i=0}^{D} R_i^j$, $j = 0, 1, \ldots, B$. With the initial allocation of buckets, $B+1$ bucket buffers on each data server are assigned the processor identifiers, and each tuple is put into one of the buffers on the basis of its hashed key value. When the buffers are full, they are sent to the respective processors and the buffers are cleared for further use. Each data server d maintains the local counts $C_{dj}^{qf(j)}$, $j = 0, 1, \ldots, B$ and receives the counts $C_{ij}^{qf(j)}$, $i = 0, 1, \ldots, D$ where $i \neq d$, $j = 0, 1, \ldots, B$, from the other data servers. The processors receive all counts, $C_{ij}^{qf(j)}$ where $i = 0, 1, \ldots, D$ and $j = 0, 1, \ldots, B$. The overall distribution, $C^{qk} = \sum_{j \in F(k)} \sum_{i=0}^{D} C_{ij}^{qk}$, $k = 0, 1, \ldots, P$, is formed on all data servers and processors by broadcasting the counts from every data server.

A value β_d can be used to measure the progress of the partition phase on data server d. β_d represents the ratio of the amount of data that has been partitioned on data server d to the total amount of data that is going to be partitioned on d. Hence, β_d gives the percentage of the partition phase completed on each data server. When β_d reaches particular threshold values for the first time during the partition phase, a 'checkpoint' occurs and the data server d sends the bucket count information to the other servers and processors. Threshold values can be, for example, $10\%, 20\%, \ldots, 100\%$. At a checkpoint each data server has finished approximately the same amount of work. By basing the distribution of workload information on threshold values at each data server, it ensures that the workloads on each processor can be examined at the same point of the partition process. At a checkpoint, all β_d are the same, q approximately equals β_d, and C^{qk}, $k = 0, 1, \ldots, P$, gives the processor workloads.

The distribution information can be organized into an ordered list by per processor per entry. Each processor knows its own position in the list by its identity. Therefore each processor can act according to its own situation. When workloads are significantly different at a checkpoint, redistribution is possible and the balancing process begins. In the balancing process, the processor that has the biggest workload chooses the buckets whose size is closest to half of the difference between the biggest workload and the smallest workload, and ships these buckets to the processor which has the smallest workload. The processor transferring the buckets then changes the bucket addresses in the distribution information list. Since every other processor and data server has the same information and does the same calculation, they carry out the actions necessary for the balancing process without communication. All the data servers and other processors make the same changes to their bucket addresses simultaneously. When the data servers make the changes, the next partitioned data for the buckets will be sent to the new processor. The recalculation can take place based on the new distribution list in order to generate the new workload distribution.

4 Analysis

In order to compare the performance of the DBJ algorithm with that of other balancing algorithms, we develop a cost function with the same assumptions as those of Hua & Lee [3]. As there, we assume that the communication, disk I/O and CPU computation of each phase are perfectly overlapped, the two source relations have the same size and the same data distribution and are initially evenly distributed among disks, and the number of data servers equals the number of processors. Let N be $P+1$ for the number of processing components. In the join operation, we further assume as do Hua & Lee [3] that under the skew condition the relations are evenly distributed among all processors, except one which has excess data. It has $\sigma \times 100\%$ more tuples than each of the remaining processors. We have $|P_s| = \frac{|R|}{1+(N-1)(1-\sigma)}$ and $|P_u| = \frac{(1-\sigma)|R|}{1+(N-1)(1-\sigma)}$, where $|P_s|$ and $|P_u|$ are the cardinalities of the skewed partition and unskewed partitions respectively and $|R|$ is the cardinality of relation R. We assume that the overhead of the balancing process of the DBJ algorithm is 1% of the partition phase communication cost. Study of the implemented system in Section 5 suggests that this is an over estimate. The checkpoint β is set to 50% at the half way point of the partition phase.

The following additional parameters are used, following Hua & Lee [3]: t is the size in bytes of each tuple, ω_{io} is the I/O bandwidth of disk, ω_{comm} is the communcation bandwidth, M is the memory capacity, I_{cpu} is the CPU path-length for processing a tuple, and μ is the CPU processing rate in instructions per second. The join time of the DBJ algorithm can then be computed as follows (each cost being time in seconds):

$$T_{dbj} = T_{part} + T_{join}$$

The total cost equals the sum of the costs of the partition phase and join phase.

$$T_{part} = max(T_{pio}, T_{pcpu}, T_{pcomm})$$

The cost of the partition phase is dominated by the biggest cost of the communication, or CPU, or I/O operations.

$$T_{pio} = \frac{t|R|}{N\omega_{io}} + \frac{\frac{t|R|}{N} - M}{\omega_{io}}$$

The I/O cost in the partition phase is the sum of the costs of reading the first relation data from disk and writing data exceeding the memory capacity back to disk.

$$T_{pcpu} = |P_s| \times \frac{I_{cpu}}{\mu}$$

The processor with the skewed partition processes more data; processing this dominates the CPU cost in the partition phase.

$$T_{pcomm} = (\frac{N-1}{N}\frac{t|R|}{N\omega_{comm}} + T_{pextra})\frac{101}{100}$$

The communication cost equals the cost of normal data distribution plus the cost of the balancing process plus the cost of the balancing process overhead.

$$T_{pextra} = \frac{(|P_s| - |P_u|)\beta t}{\omega_{comm}}$$

The extra cost of the balancing process equals the cost of the excess data moving to other processors. Since the balancing process happens before the partition phase finished, only a portion of the excess data is moved.

$$T_{join} = \lceil \frac{t|R|}{NM} \rceil (T_{jhash} + T_{jprobe})$$

The cost of the join phase is the sum of the cost of building the hash table and the cost of probing the hash table multiplied by the number of time that is done.

$$T_{jhash} = max(\frac{M}{\omega_{io}}, \frac{M}{t}\frac{I_{cpu}}{\mu})$$

The cost of building the hash table is dominated by I/O cost or CPU cost for processing the data in fully utilized memory.

$$T_{jprobe} = T_{jlocal} + T_{jremote}$$

The cost of probing the hash table equals the cost of probing the local data and the cost of probing the remote data for the second relation.

$$T_{jlocal} = max(\frac{M}{N\omega_{io}}, \frac{M}{tN}\frac{I_{cpu}}{\mu})$$

N percent of the second relation data is local each time.

$$T_{jremote} = max(\frac{M(N-1)}{N\omega_{io}}, \frac{M(N-1)}{tN}\frac{I_{cpu}}{\mu}, \frac{M(N-1)}{N\omega_{comm}})$$

The rest of the second relation data is accessed via the network.

The cost functions of the GRACE, ABJ, and ABJ+ algorithms are given by Hua & Lee [3]. Using these cost functions we set parameters as follows: $N = 64$, $|R| = 1000000$, $T = 200$, $M = 2048000$, $\mu = 20000000$, $\omega_{io} = 4096000$, $\omega_{comm} = 4096000$, and $I_{cpu} = 1000$. The relative performance results are shown in Fig. 1 when σ varies from 0.1 to 0.9. We can see that under the cost model developed the DBJ algorithm gives better performance than either GRACE or ABJ algorithms, and better performance than ABJ+ for skew up to 85%, which covers most practical situations.

5 Implementation

It has been noted in Section 2 that the DBJ algorithm is architecture independent. It could be implemented on both shared nothing and shared memory architectures. In fact the algorithm has been fully implemented using the ADEPT machine [11]. This is a MIMD DBMS architecture, implemented at present on a T800 transputer-based Meiko Computing Surface.

Under the architecture, the transputers are divided into three groups: data servers, processors and the scheduler. The data servers, which are directly linked to disk drives, concentrate on caching and organizing source relation data. The processors do the actual query processing. The scheduler collects user queries, optimizes them and allocates them to a group of processors. The transputers are configured to be close together by using all available communication links, so data messages travel the minimum possible distance. A thirteen transputer architecture is used for illustration in this paper, consisting of three data servers, nine processors and one scheduler. The implementation of the DBJ algorithm has been in C and OCCAM 2: OCCAM 2 is used for implementing the communication functions and C is used for implementing the other functions. Remaining DBMS code comes from the previous work of the ADEPT project [11].

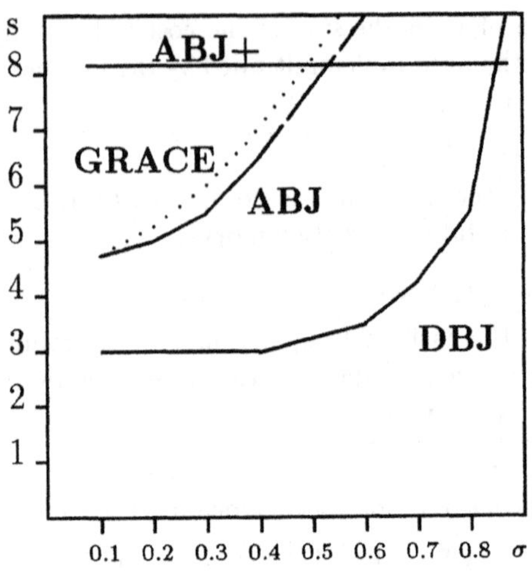

Fig. 1. Comparison

6 Experimental Results

In the following example, the relations are divided into 25 buckets and a join is carried out on 5 processors. The source relations are equally partitioned among three data servers and each tuple length is 70 bytes. Firstly, a description is given of how the real balancing process works in the algorithm. Suppose that relation R has 10200 tuples, with 3400 tuples being placed on each of three data servers; relation S has 20451 tuples and each data server has 6817 tuples, and a join operation joins the two relations on attributes $R.a$ and $S.b$. After the partition phase of the proposed hash join algorithm, the distribution of relation R without balancing is indicated in Table 1. Each column represents the distribution information for one processor. Suppose the first threshold value is at 70% of the partition phase and the average rate of growth of a bucket in the first 70% portion is maintained in the remaining 30% portion. The difference between the largest workload on processor 3 and the smallest workload on processor 1 is 720, and half of this is 360. This figure is bigger than 10% of the largest workload, and the gap will disappear if one of the smallest buckets is moved from processor 3 to processor 1. So the balancing process takes place by moving bucket 3 from processor 3 to processor 1 and the balanced distribution is showed in Table 1. Because the differences are now below the threshold value, no more balancing occurs.

Now compare the DBJ algorithm with an algorithm following the ABJ algorithm whereby the balancing process takes place statically after the partition phase, and which works as follows: each bucket of relation R is statically allocated to a processor in the partition phase, a designated coordinating processor collects the distribution information and reallocates the excess buckets to the

Initial Distribution					
Proc No	1	2	3	4	5
Load	1530	1800	2250	1800	1800
Buck No	1	2	3	4	5
Tuples	360	360	360	360	360
Buck No	6	7	8	9	10
Tuples	360	360	360	360	360
Buck No	11	12	13	14	15
Tuples	360	360	810	360	360
Buck No	16	17	18	19	20
Tuples	90	360	360	360	360
Buck No	21	22	23	24	25
Tuples	360	360	360	360	360

Balanced Distribution					
Proc No	1	2	3	4	5
Load	1890	1800	1890	1800	1800
Buck No	1	2	8	4	5
Tuples	360	360	360	360	360
Buck No	6	7	13	9	10
Tuples	360	360	810	360	360
Buck No	11	12	18	14	15
Tuples	360	360	360	360	360
Buck No	16	17	23	19	20
Tuples	90	360	360	360	360
Buck No	21	22		24	25
Tuples	360	360		360	360
Buck No	3				
Tuples	360				

Table 1. Distribution Balancing

underflow processor after the partition phase is complete and then each processor performs the join as in the DBJ algorithm. Since the authors' system does not have hard disks, the disk drives on the data servers have been simulated. The comparative performance of the algorithms is shown in Fig. 2. The vertical axis is the join execution time and its unit is a second; the horizontal line represents the size of the source relation R. The solid line represents the DBJ algorithm's performance with threshold values of 70%, 80%, 90% and 100%, the dotted line represents the static algorithm's performance. Fig. 2 demonstrates that the DBJ algorithm's performance is better.

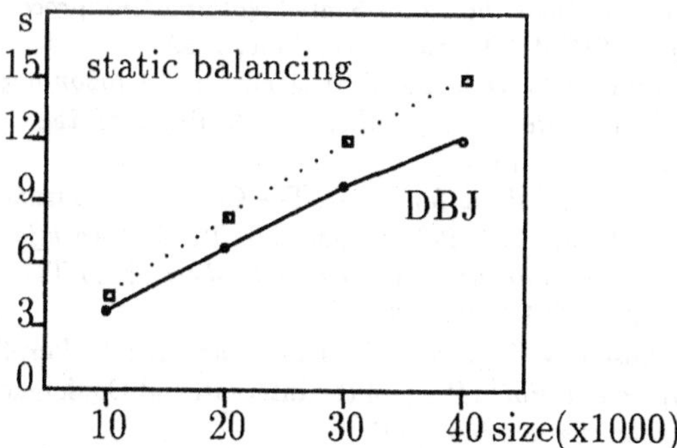

Fig. 2. Relation Size Influence

7 Conclusions

The *Dynamic Balancing Hash Join* (DBJ), has been proposed to handle the problem of skewed data in the join operation in multiprocessor database systems. The objective of this new algorithm is to avoid the high cost of preprocessing inherent in existing algorithms. The new algorithm only redistributes a small portion of the partitioned data and, thereby achieves a balanced output with little extra cost. This is achieved dynamically, without knowledge of the input distribution, nor any co-ordinating processor. A performance analysis shows that the new algorithm performs better than existing balancing hash join algorithms for a wide degree of skew.

References

1. David J. Dewitt, R. H. Gerber, "*Multiprocessor Hash Based Join Algorithms*", Proc. of the 11th VLDB Conference, Stockholm, Sweden, 1985.
2. David J. Dewitt, J.F. Naughton, D.A. Schneider, S. Seshadri, "*Practical Skew Handling in Parallel Joins*", Proc. of the 18th VLDB Conference, Vancouver, Canada, 1992.
3. Kien A. Hua, Chiang Lee, "*Handling Data Skew in Multiprocessor Database Computers Using Partition Tuning*", Proc. of the 17th VLDB Conference, Barcelona, Spain, 1991.
4. Kitsuregawa, M., Tanaka, H., and T. Motooka, "*Application of Hash to Data Base Machine and its Architecture*", New Generation Computing, Vol:1, No. 1, 1983.
5. M. Kitsuregawa and Y. Ogawa, "*Bucket Spreading Parallel Hash: A New Robust, Parallel Hash Join Method for Data Skew in the Super Database Computer(SDC)*", Proc. of 16th VLDB Conference, Brisbane, Australia, 1990.
6. Hongjun Lu, Kian-Lee Tan, Ming-Chien Shan, "*Hash Based Join Algorithms for Multiprocessor Computers with Shared Memory*", Proc. of the 16th VLDB Conference, Brisbane, Australia, 1990.
7. Donovan A. Schneider and David J Dewitt, "*A Performance Evaluation of Four Parallel Join Algorithms in a Shared Nothing Multiprocessor Environment*", Proc. of the 1989 SIGMOD Conference, June, 1989.
8. C.B. Walton, A.G. Dale and R.M. Jenevein, "*A taxonomy and performance model of data skew effects in parallel joins*", Proc. of the 17th VLDB Conference, Barcelona, Spain, 1991.
9. G. D. Knott, "*Hashing function*", The Computer Journal, Vol. 18, No 3, 1973.
10. J.L. Wolf, D.M. Dias, P.S. Yu and J.J. Turek, "*An effective algorithm for parallelizing hash join in the presence of data skew*", IBM T.J. Watson Research Center Tech Report RC 15510, 1990.
11. R. G. Johnson, N. J. Martin, X. Zhao, "*The ADEPT Parallel Database Architecture and Implementation*", Proc. of the International Conference on Parallel Computing '91, London, September, 1991.
12. Witold Litwin, Marie-Anne Neimat, and Donovan A. Schneider, "*LH* — Linear Hashing for Distributed Files*", Proc. of the 1993 SIGMOD Conference, June, 1993.

Tabu Search Optimization of Large Join Queries

Tadeusz Morzy[1], Maciej Matysiak[1], Silvio Salza[2,3]

[1] Institute of Computing Sciences, Technical University of Poznań, ul. Piotrowo 3A, 60-965 Poznań, Poland
[2] Dip.to di Informatica e Sistemistica, Università di Roma "La Sapienza", via Salaria 113, I-00198 Rome, Italy
[3] Istituto di Analisi dei Sistemi ed Informatica del CNR, viale Manzoni 30, I-00185 Roma, Italy

Abstract. Query optimization is a hard combinatorial optimization problem, which makes enumerative optimization strategies unacceptable as the query size grows. In order to cope with complex large join queries, combinatorial optimization algorithms, such as Simulating Annealing and Iterative Improvement were proposed as alternatives to traditional enumerative algorithms. In this paper, we propose to apply to optimization of complex large join queries the relatively new combinatorial optimization technique called Tabu Search. We have tested this technique on queries of different sizes and different types and have shown that Tabu Search obtains almost always better query execution plans than other combinatorial optimization techniques.

1 Introduction

The query optimizer in a relational database management system (*RDBMS*) translates a non-procedural query into a procedural execution plan, by selecting among the many alternative *query execution plans* (*QEP*), the one with the least estimated execution cost, according to a given cost function. The complexity of the optimization process is basically determined by the number of alternative *QEPs*, which in general grows quickly (exponentially) with the number of relations involved in the query, although several useful heuristics may be exploited to eliminate some of the alternatives [18]. Nevertheless *high* optimization costs may still be accepted, at least when compiling transactions that are expected to run many times.

Traditional query optimizers expect to deal with queries involving only a small number of relations, usually requiring less than 10 join operations. Therefore they can use *enumerative optimization strategies* which consider most of the alternatives *QEPs* [6, 7, 18, 16]. H owever new applications are now emerging, such as decision support systems, expert systems, knowledge base systems, object-oriented and deductive database systems, that are often built on top of relational systems, These applications typically require the processing of much more complex queries, involving many relations and with a large number of joins [15, 17, 2]. Such queries (with a number of joins ranging between 10 and 100) are usually referred to as *large join queries*. In these cases the enumerative optimization strategies become inadequate since they cannot face the combinatorial explosion of the number of alternative *QEPs* to evaluate.

To cope with such a hard combinatorial optimization problem, the use of randomized algorithms, such as *Iterative Improvement, Simulating Annealing* and *Genetic Search* has been proposed by several authors [5, 20, 19, 13, 11, 12]. The common idea behind all these strategies is to perform a random walk in the *state space*, where each state represents a possible *QEP*, starting from an *initial* state and trying to reach a *low cost* local minimum. Of course these strategies do not guarantee that the *global minimum*, i.e. the best execution plan, is attained, since only a small fraction of the state space is visited during the walk. Nevertheless they are of relevant practical interest, since the quality of the solution generally improves with the length of the search, and it is then possible to set up any suitable tradeoff between compilation cost and repeated execution cost.

Combinatorial strategies for query optimization were first described in [13], where Ioannidis and Wong applied Simulated Annealing (*SA*) to the optimization of recursive queries. In [20] Swami and Gupta investigated the problem of using Simulated Annealing and Iterative Improvement (*II*) f or optimization of large select-project-join queries. Later, Ioannidis and Kang [11, 12] proposed a new hybrid algorithm (called 2-Phase Optimization) that combines Iterative Improvement and Simulated Annealing. Recently, Swami and Iyer [21] have proposed a new polynomial time algorithm that combines combinatorial searching with the enumerative neighborhood search algorithm proposed earlier by Ibaraki and Kameda [10].

In this paper we propose to apply to optimization of large join queries the relatively new combinatorial optimization technique called Tabu Search (*TS*) [3, 8]. Based on simple ideas *TS* has been extremely efficient in getting almost optimal solutions for many types of difficult combinatorial optimization problems, e.g. problems related to graph coloring where it has shown better performance than Simulated Annealing [9]. As we will show later in the paper *TS* obtains better *QEPs* than other randomized algorithms. What differentiates the *TS* from previous randomized algorithms, like *II, SA* and *2PO*, is the neighborhood analysis, i.e the ability of searching repeatedly for a neighbor as good as possible. Unlike the *II, SA* and *2PO*, that tend to penetrate the search space by "visiting" as much states as possible, *TS* at each step of the general downward procedure generates a subset V^* of the states in the neighborhood $N(S)$ of the current state S, and then selects in it the best state S' and moves to it even if this would lead to an increase in the cost.

The major contribution of the paper is to prove that Tabu Search has a good performance on the large query optimization problem, when compared to other randomized algorithms that have been proposed for this problem, namely Simulated Annealing and Iterative Improvement. The analysis is carried out by performing an extensive set of experiments with respect to different query types (linear, star and bushy), different types of query execution plan types (left-deep, bushy trees), and different sizes of queries (from 10 to 100 joins). The results of the experiments show that Tabu Search performs better in almost all cases. Moreover the extensive parametric analysis we have performed allows to understand in which way each algorithm is sensitive to the main parameters that characterize the problem.

The paper is organized as follows. In Section 2, we formulate the problem of large join query optimization in terms of a combinatorial optimization problem. In section 3 we present the Tabu Search optimization technique, and the other randomized algorithms we want to compare to. In Section 4 we define the state space the set of moves and the cost function. In Section 5 we discuss the problems connected to the set up of the experiments, as query generation and database profiles. Finally the results of the experiments are presented in Section 6, and a discussion is given in Section 7.

2 Problem formulation

The execution cost of a relational query, i.e. time necessary to process the query, depends on the *query execution plan (QEP)*, i.e. on the particular sequence of relational operations that is selected to evaluate the query. For a given query there might be many alternative *QEPs*. The goal of query optimization is to find *QEP* with the lowest cost.

As in most of the literature we will restrict our work to queries involving only selection, projection and joins (*SPJ queries*). Traditional query optimizat ion algorithms process these queries by using an enumerative strategy, i.e. explorin g most of the solution space, but trying to restrict the search by the use of simple heuristics such as pushing down selections and projections, and avoiding unnecessary cartesian products [1, 14, 18].

As most systems implement the join operation as a 2-way join, the problem becomes that of determining the order in which to join the relations referenced in the query. In other words, the optimizer must select the best sequence of 2-way joins to achieve the N-way join requested by the query. In addition to that we need to select for each join in the sequence the performing method (nested-loop, sort-merge, hash-based, etc.). Effectiveness of a particular method depends on several factors, like cardinality of relations, availability of indexes, buffer size, etc. Finally, as some of the join methods (e.g. nested-loop) distinguish between the two operands, one being the *outer* relation and the other being the *inner* relation, this gives another option in the *QEP*.

Thus, we can reduce the query optimization problem to finding the order in which relations should be joined, together with the best join method for each 2-way join and the best arguments of each join. In the paper we consider *large join queries* for which the number of relations referenced by a single query is greater than 10.

3 Tabu Search Optimization Technique

3.1 Combinatorial Optimization Techniques

Each solution to a combinatorial optimization problem, in our case a *QEP*, is represented by a *state* in a *state* or *search* space. Each state S has a *cost* $cost(S)$ associated to it, which is given by some *cost function*. The goal of the optimization algorithm is to find the state with the globally minimum cost. Combinatorial optimization algorithms search for the "globally" optimum state by performing random walks in the state space. A walk consists of a sequence of *moves*, where each *move* is a transformation applied to a state to get another state. The states that can be reached in one move from a given state S are called *neighbors* of S. The move is called *downward* (*upward*) if the cost of the source state is higher (lower) than the cost of the destination state. A state is called *local minimum* if its cost is equal or lower than that of all its neighbors. There are usually many local minima, and only some of them are *global minima* i.e. have the lowest cost among all states in the state space. Finally we shall say that a state is on a*plateau* if it has no lower cost neighbor and it can reach states with the same cost without downward and upward moves. The optimal solution we are looking for is of course a global minimum.

Using the above terminology we now describe Tabu Search and the other combinatorial optimization techniques, that have been applied to the large join optimization problem, and to which we want to compare.

3.2 Tabu Search

Tabu Search is a general metaheuristic procedure for global optimization that has been proposed by Glover [3, 4], and independently by Hansen [8]. The main idea behind *TS* consists in performing an aggressive exploration of the state space that seeks to make at each step the best possible move, with the restriction that the move has to satisfy certain constraints. These constraints are contained in a cyclic list T (called *tabu list*), and are used to prevent the reversal, or sometimes repetition, of certain moves. Without such restrictions, the method could take a *best* move away from a local optimum (making an upward move), and then at the next step fall back into the local optimum. In general, the tabu restrictions are intended to prevent such cycling behavior and more broadly to induce the search to follow a new trajectory if cycling in a narrower sense occurs.

The Tabu Search algorithm is sketched in Figure 1. *TS* starts from a randomly generated initial state, and repeatedly performs moves from a state to a neighbor one. The critical step is choosing the best move from a state S to another state. At each iteration the procedure generates a subset V^* of the set $N(S)$ of the neighbors the current state S, from among the set of neighbors. A *best* solution S^* in V^* is determined and a move from S to S^* is made. The *TS* accepts both downward as well as upward moves, i.e. accepts moving from S to S^*, even if $cost(S)>cost(S^*)$. Upwared moves are accepted to avoid the possibility of being trapped in a local minimum which may be far away from the global minimum.

```
procedure TS()
S = initialize(); minS = S; /* Set an initial solution */
T = ∅; /* Set the tabu list */
while not ("stopping condition satisfied") do {
        generate the set V* ⊆ N(S) − T;
        choose the best solution S* ∈ V*;
        S = S*;
        T = (T − (oldest)) ⋃{S}; /* update the tabu list T */
        if cost(S) < cost(minS) then minS = S;
        }
return (minS);
```

Fig. 1. Basic Tabu Search Algorithm

At each move, in order to avoid cycling or at least to reduce the probability, a list T of already visited states (the tabu list) is updated. This forbids moves which should bring back to a previously (recently) visited state. Therefore, when the subset V^* of neighbor states has to be generated, we check that a candidate for membership of V^* is not in T. The procedure stops (*"stopping condition satisfied"*) if no improvement of the best solution $minS$ found so far has been made during a given number of iterations, or if there is no way of leaving state S because computing V^* with the tabu restrictions gives the empty set.

In our study, we adopt a modified version of *TS*. The first change concerns the initial state. Instead of starting directly from a randomly generated initial state, we improve it by running a local optimization algorithm until a local minimum is reached, and then take this as the initial state. A second change concerns the implementation of tabu list T. Actually keeping a list of states may be very space and time consuming, because of the frequent membership tests that are required by the algorithm. Therefore, instead of storing in T the set of recently visited states, we prefer to keep a set of moves. This considerably reduces the space and time needed to check the tabu restrictions. A last change concerns the stopping condition. In order to compare *TS* with other algorithms, we use a time limit instead of a number of iterations to stop optimization process.

3.3 Other Randomized Algorithms

In our study to analyze the performance of *TS* on the large query optimization problem, we compare it to two other randomized algorithms that have been proposed in the literature for this problem, namely the *Iterative Improvement* (*II*), and the *Simulated Annealing* (*SA*) [11, 12, 13, 20].

In Iterative Improvement the starting state is selected randomly. Then, II walks downward until it reaches a local minimum. Then a new starting state is randomly selected to get a new local optimum, and the procedure is iterated until a stopping condition (usually a time limit) is reached. The local minimum with the lowest cost found is returned.

In contrast to Iterative Improvement, Simulating Annealing investigates the state space by performing both downward and upward moves. It always accepts downward moves, but it accepts also upward moves with a probability which depends on the increase in cost entailed by making the move and on a parameter called the *temperature*. The probability of accepting an upward move is a monotonically increasing function of the temperature and a monotonically decreasing function of the cost difference. The higher the temperature or the smaller the cost difference, the more likely that an upward move will be accepted. Each walk through the state space ends when some condition is satisfied. The condition determines the number of states visited during the walk (called the chain length). Then, the temperature is reduced according to some function and another walk begins. The algorithm stops when the system is considered to be *frozen*, i.e when the temperature is equal to zero.

4 Application of Tabu Search to Query Optimization

In this section we discuss the application of Tabu Search and the other mentioned combinatorial optimization techniques to the optimization of large join queries. More precisely we specify the problem dependent features of the algorithms, such as the definition of the state space, the set of moves, the cost function, stopping conditions, etc.

4.1 State space

A single state in query optimization state space corresponds to a *query execution plan* of the query to be optimized. We use, as was mentioned in Section 2, the simple heuristics of pushing selections as down in the *QEP* as possible, performing projections as soon as possible and excluding inefficient cartesian products. So, we do not include selections and projections in our query execution plans – we simply assume that all possible selections and projections are already carried out. The remaining problem in the query optimization is to decide in which order to join the relations involved in the query and which join method to use for each join operation, together with the best arguments assignment for each join.

Each *QEP* can be concisely represented by a *binary join processing tree* (*BJPT*), whose leaves are base relations, internal nodes are join operators, and edges represent the flow of data. Each join operator in the *BJPT* has its own performing method. So, each internal node of *BJPT* is labeled by the appropriate method. Arguments of a join operator are distinguished by the labels "o" and "i", denoting, respectively, outer and inner relations. In our study, the state space consists of all possible *BJPTs* of the query, i.e. both linear and bushy *BJPTs*, and our aim is to find *BJPT* with the lowest cost.

4.2 Move set

A move is a single modification applied to a state to get another state. A set of applicable moves must ensure possibility of reaching every state in the state space. There are several sets of moves that ensure this requirement and from which one could choose. The one adopted in this study is the following. We use three types of moves:

- **Join method exchange**
  We consider two most popular join methods: ***nested-loop*** and ***sort-merge***. The move consists of changing the join method of a random selected join operator from nested-loop to sort-merge, or vice versa.
- **Join argument exchange**
  The move consists of exchanging arguments of a join with ***nested-loop*** method. So, the outer relation becomes the inner relation, or vice versa.
- **Change of join order**
  Let $R_1, R_2, \ldots, R_n$ denote base relations, $J_1, J_2, \ldots, J_m$ denote join operators, and o, i denote outer and inner arguments, respectively. Select at random one join operator, say, J_i from the *QEP*, but not the last one. Then, find another join, say J_j, in *QEP*, such that the result of J_i is an argument of J_j. We have three relations as the arguments. Two of them, R_1 and R_2, belong to J_i, and the third one, R_3, belongs to J_j. The move consists in changing the order of join operators in such way that the join J_j with relation R_3 will be carried out prior to the join J_i. Therefore, we have to decide which of J_i's arguments should be joined with the relation R_3. In order to do this, we search the query graph. Then, we carry out join J_j at first and its result becomes an argument for J_i – it may be either the outer or the inner argument.

We associate different probabilities with moves. Since the join order exchange enables us to faster investigate the state space, we assigned to this move the probability – 0.6. The change of the join method as well as the change of join arguments has the probability 0.2.

4.3 Cost Function

The cost of a state corresponds to the execution time of the query. The cost function that we used in our study takes into account both I/O as well as CPU processing required by each *QEP*. However, it is impossible to take into account all factors influencing the cost of *QEP*, mainly, because of the difficulty in specifying parameters of a computer system in which queries are performed. There are different cost formulas to be used depending on the kind of join method and availability of indexes. They are presented below.

Nested-loop joins with no index on the inner relation:

$$cost = C_{DISK} * (B_O + B_I * (B_O/(M/W)) + P_{IM}) + C_{CPU} * card_O * card_I$$

Nested-loop joins with B^+tree index on the inner relation:

$cost = C_{DISK} * (B_O + B_I + B_{NDX} + B_{IM}) + C_{CPU} * (card_O * card_I / k_{ndx})$

Sort-merge joins with no indexes:

$cost = C_O^{sort} + C_I^{sort} + C_{DISK} * (B_O + B_I + B_{IM}) + C_{CPU} * card_{IM}$

Sort-merge joins with a B^+tree index on the outer relation[4]:

$cost = C_{DISK} * B_{NDX} + C_I^{sort} + C_{DISK} * (B_O + B_I + B_{IM}) + C_{CPU} * card_{IM}$

where: C_{DISK} is the I/O transfer cost of a page to/from the disk, C_{CPU} is the processing cost needed to compare two tuples, M the size of available memory allocated for buffers, W is the size of a disk blocks, $card_O$ is the cardinality of the outer relation, $card_I$ is the cardinality of the inner relation, $card_{IM}$ is the cardinality of the intermediate join result, B_O, B_I, B_{IM} are sizes of outer, inner, and intermediate relations, respectively, B_{NDX} is the size of the index, C_O^{sort}, C_I^{sort} are costs of sorting outer, inner relations, respective ly.

The formulas are based on the following assumptions: i) there is no pipeline processing, i.e. all base relations are being fetched from a disk as well as all intermediate join results are materialized, ii) sizes of indexes are much smaller than sizes of associated relations, iii) minimal buffering for operations, iv) size of a disk page is 4KB, and v) I/O cost is an order of magnitude greater than CPU cost.

5 Parameters of the experiment

5.1 Algorithm Specific Parameters

There are several implementation specific features of the algorithms. These parameters influence performance of the algorithms and can be tuned to increase quality of the results. In Tables 5.1, 5.2 and 5.3 we summariz e the choices we have made in our experiments, for Tabu Search and the two other algorithms we are comparing.

parameters	value
initial state	first local minimum found
next state	the best neighbor, not on tabu list
local minimum	r-local minimum (20 neighbors)
stopping condition	time limit
length of tabu list	20

Table 5.1: Tabu Search parameters.

parameter	value
initial state	random state
next state	random neighbor
new starting state	random state
local minimum	r-local minimum (20 neighbors)
stopping condition	both time and local optimum

Table 5.2: Iterative Improvement parameters.

parameter	value
initial temperature	max_cost(R)-min_cost(R), where R is a set of 20 random states
temperature reduction	exponential according to time limit
initial state	random state
next state	random neighbor
inner-loop criterion	1/10 of a time limit
system has frozen	always at the end of time limit

Table 5.3: Simulated Annealing parameters.

In order to be able to compare results, we have set the same stopping condition for all the algorithms which is a time limit. However, since *II* finishes optimization always in local minimum, it may cause sometimes a little overstepping of a time limit. Instead of evaluating the cost of all neigbors of a given state, we consider a state to be a local minimum if none of r randomly chosen neighbors of it has lower cost. We call it *r-local minimum.*

To make a move in *TS*, 10 random neighbors of a current state are evaluated and the best one is selected. The tabu list holds 20 latest moves. To set an initial temperature in *SA* we test several random states. Initial temperature is equal to subtraction of highest and lowest cost. The shape of temperature reduction has an exponential form. The reductions of temperature are being made to freeze the system just before the time limit.

5.2 Query Generator

In our experiments we restricted to tree shaped queries with equality joins, a usual assumption in large query optimization [11, 12, 19, 20, 21]. We have been especially interested in analyzing how the shape of a query affects the performance of optimization algorithms. Therefore, the simulator we have built can generate different types of queries. By a query type we mean different shapes of the tree graph representing the query. More precisely we considered a full range of tree graphs, from linear trees to star graphs.

Each query graph is characterized by two parameters: N represents the *size* of the query i.e. the number of joins, and tt which represents the query *type*, i.e. the shape of the query tree, namely the number of successors of each internal node in the tree. The tt parameter takes values 1 through 10. The greater the value the greater the number of successors. e For tt equal 1, we get a linear query. For tt equal 10, we get a star query. For intermediate values, bushy query trees are generated.

In the experiments we kept the query size N ranging from 10 to 100 joins (the number of joining relations is $N+1$). Joining relations were randomly generated according to the database profile, and their joining attributes randomly selected.

5.3 Database Profile

The database profile we adopted is characterized by the following parameters; relation cardinalities: 100-1000 with probability 0.2, 1000-10000 with probability

0.6, 10000-50000 with probability 0.2; ballast: randomly chosen between 50 and 500; index flag: YES with probability 0.3, NO with probability 0.7; all joining attributes have the same width, each has randomly chosen domain cardinality.

We made the usual assumptions about uniform distribution of attribute values and independence of values in the join attributes [18]. We model a distribution of the relation cardinalities with a predominance of medium size relations (between 1000 and 10000 tuples). There are much fewer small and very large relations. The ballast parameter represents width of a relation without joining attributes. In other words, it represents attributes that must appear in the final result of a query. The index flag represents the availability of indexes for a relation. The flag refers to the entire relation and not to the single attribute. We assumed that, if there is an index for a relation, then all the joining attributes in that relation have an index.

6 Results of the Experiments

Due to the complexity of the query optimization problem, it is not feasible, at least for non-trivial values of N, to compute the global optimum, and hence to compare it with a solution given by a randomized algorithm. Therefore it is not possible to make an absolute statement on how good a given algorithm is. The only way to carry on the evaluation is to run a set of experiments, and to perform a parametric analysis to compare the solutions given by different algorithms, in a large range of situations. This would allow also to understand in which way every algorithm is sensitive to the main parameters that characterize the problem.

To run our experiments we implemented Tabu Search and the two other algorithms in C, and made all the runs on a dedicated Sun-4 workstation. More specifically in setting up the experiments we concentrated on three parameters:

1. N: number of joins ranging from 10 to 100;
2. tt: type of a tree graph ranging from linear to star query;
3. t_o: optimization time ranging from 5 seconds up to 20 minutes.

For any set of parameter values 50 different queries were generated. Each query was then optimized using all three algorithms. Then, in order to compare the relative performance of algorithms, cost of the solutions.were *scaled*, i.e. divided by the minimum solution cost found for that query among all algorithms.

A first series of results shows how the quality of the solution improves with the optimization time. In Figure 2 we consider a large query ($N = 100$) with average (bushy) structure ($tt = 5$). in the range between 10 and 20 seconds *TS* improves very much, then it stabilizes around 30 seconds, when it performs about 5 times better than *SA* and about 50 times better than *II*. A fairly different situation is depicted in Figure 3, where for a smaller query *TS* performs worse than *SA* and *II*, although the difference is not very large.

Apparently *TS* is better performing on larger queries. This trend is clearly confirmed in Figure 4 that shows how the size of the query affects the performance of the algorithms. For $N < 25$ *SA* has the best results, but *TS* becomes

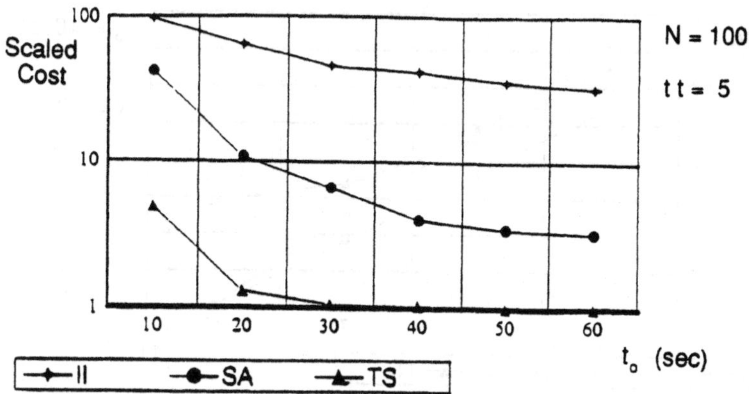

Fig. 2. Average scaled cost and optimization time (large queries)

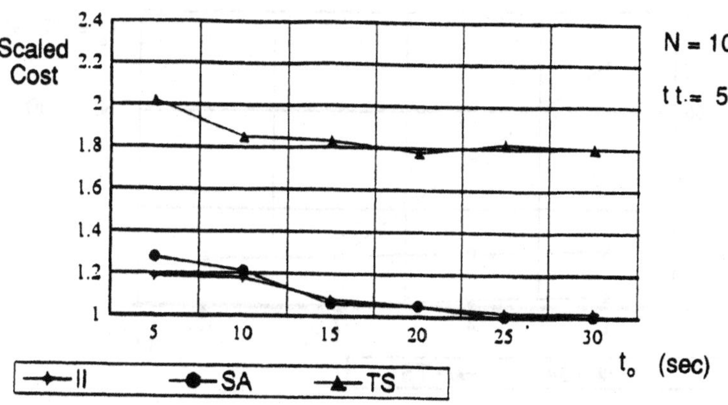

Fig. 3. Average scaled cost and optimization time (small queries)

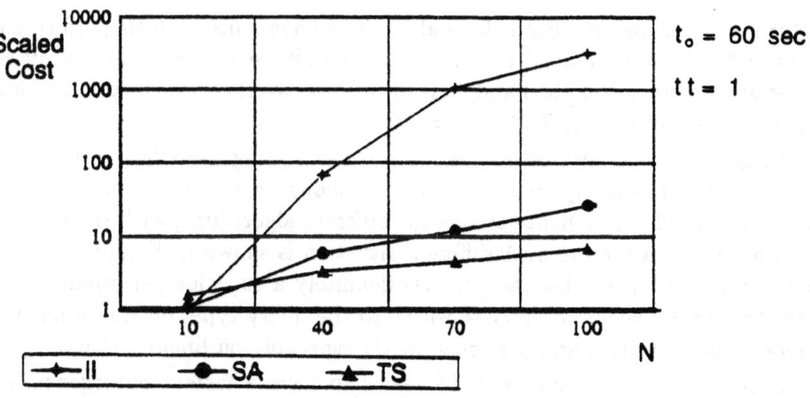

Fig. 4. Average scaled cost and query size

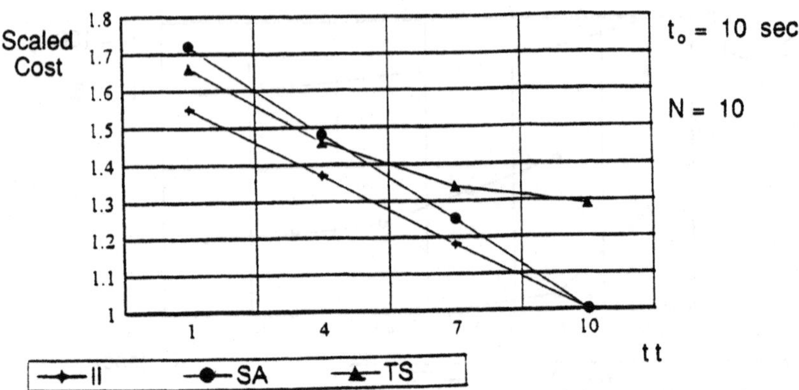

Fig. 5. Average scaled cost and query type (small queries)

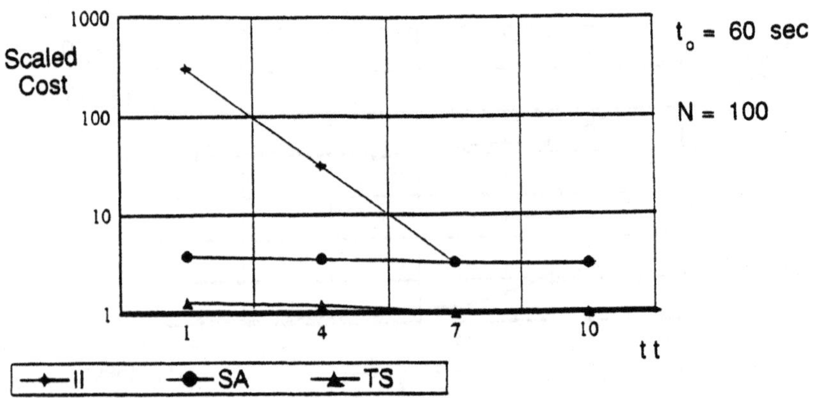

Fig. 6. Average scaled cost and query type (large queries)

better for larger queries. Both these algorithms have quite a *stable* performance on the whole range. Instead *II* appears to by quite sensitive to the query size (especially for linear queries) and ends up with an average scaled cost two order of magnitude worse than *TS* for $N = 100$.

We got also very interesting results when analyzing the effect of the query type. For rather small queries ($N = 10$), as shown in Figure 5, there is a very limited spread of performance among the different algorithms, with *II* constantly doing better than the other. A different situation is shown in Figure 6 for large queries ($N = 100$). In this case *TS* has definitely a superior performance, and both *TS* and *SA* seem not very sensitive to the query type, on the other hand *II* looks more sensitive and performs poorly especially on linear queries.

In all the cases we analyzed *TS* seems to have a faster convergence, and therefore its relative performance improves when the optimization time (i.e. the length of the search) is reduced. This trend is already clear from Figure 2.

7 Discussion

It emerges from the experimental results presented in the previous section that Tabu Search has, almost constantly, a superior performance with respect to Simulated Annealing and Iterative Improvement on the large query optimization problem. This is anyway in accordance with similar results that were obtained when dealing with other combinatorial optimization problems, as graph coloring and scheduling [9].

Two main aspects in the behavior of this algorithm seem to be particularly interesting. First it seems to converge on a low cost solution relatively faster than the other algorithms. This ensures that a fairly good solution may be found even in situations where the optimization time has to be limited.

Second, *TS* displays a very stable performance, when working on large queries, over all the range of query types, from linear trees to star queries. This property is actually shared with *SA*, and is possibly linked to the fact that both algorithms perform a long accurate search around the initial state, rather than many local optimizations as *II* does. This is an important feature as well, since the query optimizer in which the strategy is adopted may have to adapt to a variety of situations, as the structure of the query is concerned.

As usual when analyzing the performance of randomized algorithms is very difficu lt to give a formal explanation of their behavior. We believe that an explanation can be found by understanding the structure of the search space, since this in turn depends on the shape of the query tree. Such a kind of investigation has been carried out in [12] by Ioannidis and Kang, although with a different goal, i.e. analyze how restrictions on the shape of the execution plan may affect the performance of the algorithms and the quality of the solutions. We are now addressing this problem, in order to get a deeper understanding of our experimental results, and to propose extensions to the *TS* algorithm that would further improve its performance.

References

1. W. W. Chu and P. Hurley, *Optimal Query Processing for Distributed Database Systems*, IEEE Transactions on Computers C-31 (9), 1982, pp. 835-850.
2. D.H. Fishman, et. al., *IRIS: An Object-Oriented DBMS*, ACM Transactions on Office Information Systems, 5(1), 1987, pp. 48-69.
3. F. Glover, *Tabu Search-part I*, ORSA Journal on Computing 1(1989), pp.190-206.
4. F. Glover, *Tabu Search-part II*, ORSA Journal on Computing 2(1990), pp.4-32.
5. D. E. Goldberg, *Genetic Algorithms in Search, Optimization and Machine Learning*, Addison-Wesley, 1989.
6. G. Graefe, R. L. Cole, D. L. Davison, W. J. McKenna, and R. H. Wolniewicz, *Extensible Query Optimization and Parallel Execution in Volcano*, in *Query Processing for Advanced Database Applications* (eds. J. C. Freytag, G. Vossen and D. Maier), Morgan-Kaufman, San Mateo, CA, 1992.
7. G. Graefe and W. J. McKenna, *The Volcano Optimizer Generator: Extensibility and Efficient Search*, Proc. of the 9th Conference on Data Engineering, Vienna, Austria, 1993, pp. 209-218.

8. P. Hansen, B. Jaaumard, *Algorithms for the maximum satisfiability problem*, RUTCOR research report 43-87, Rutgers University, 1987.
9. A. Hertz, D. de Werra, *Using Tabu Search Techniques for Graph Coloring*, Computing, Vol. 39, pp. 345-351,1987.
10. T. Ibaraki and T. Kameda, *Optimal Nesting for Computing N-relational Joins*, ACM Transactions on Database Systems, 9(3), 1984, pp. 482-502.
11. Y. E. Ioannidis and Y. Kang, *Randomized Algorithms for Optimizing Large Join Queries*, Proc. of ACM-SIGMOD Conference on Management of Data, 1990, pp. 312-321.
12. Y. E. Ioannidis and Y. Kang, *Left-Deep vs. Bushy Trees: An Analysis of Strategy Spaces and its Implications for Query Optimization*, Proc. of ACM-SIGMOD Conference on Management of Data, 1991, pp. 168-177.
13. Y. E. Ioannidis and E. Wong, *Query Optimization by Simulated Annealing*, Proc. of ACM-SIGMOD Conference on Management of Data, 1987, pp. 9-22.
14. M. Jarke and J. Koch, *Query Optimization in Database Systems*, ACM Computing Surveys, Vol. 16, No. 2, 1984, pp. 111-152.
15. R. Krishnamurthy, H. Boral, and C. Zaniola, *Optimization of Nonrecursive Queries*, Proc. of the 12th VLDB Conference, Kyoto, Japan, 1986, pp. 128-137.
16. G.M. Lohman, C. Mohan, L.M. Haas, B.G. Lindsay, P.G. Salinger, P.F. Wilms, and D. Daniels, *Query Processing in R**, *Query Processing in Database Systems* (Kim, Batory, and Reiner (eds.), 1985), pp.31-47, Springer-Verlag Pub.
17. K. Ono and G. M. Lohman, *Measuring the Complexity of Join Enumeration in Query Optimization*, Proc. of the 16th VLDB Conference, Brisbane, Australia, 1990, pp. 314-325.
18. P.G. Selinger, M.M. Astrahan, D.D. Chamberlin, R.A. Lorie, and T.G. Price, *Access Path Selection in a Relational Database Management System*, Proc. of ACM-SIGMOD, 1979, pp. 23-34.
19. A. Swami, *Optimization of Large Join Queries: Combining Heuristics and Combinatorial Techniques*, Proc. of ACM- SIGMOD Conference on Management of Data, 1989, pp. 367-376.
20. A. Swami and A. Gupta, *Optimization of Large Join Queries*, Proc. of ACM-SIGMOD Conference on Management of Data, 1988, pp.8-17.
21. A. Swami and B. R. Iyer, *A Polynomial Time Algorithm for Optimizing Join Queries*, Proc. of the 9th IEEE Conference on Data Engineering, Vienna, Austria, 1993, pp. 345-354.

The Implementation and Performance Evaluation of the ADMS Query Optimizer: Integrating Query Result Caching and Matching*

ChungMin Melvin Chen and Nicholas Roussopoulos

Department of Computer Science
University of Maryland, College Park
MD 20742, USA

Abstract. In this paper, we describe the design and evaluation of the ADMS optimizer. Capitalizing on a structure called Logical Access Path Schema to model the derivation relationship among cached query results, the optimizer is able to perform query matching coincidently with the optimization and generate more efficient query plans using cached results. The optimizer also features data caching and pointer caching, alternative cache replacement strategies, and different cache update strategies. An extensive set of experiments were conducted and the results showed that pointer caching and dynamic cache update strategies substantially speedup query computations and, thus, increase query throughput under situations with fair query correlation and update load. The requirement of the cache space is relatively small and the extra computation overhead introduced by the caching and matching mechanism is more than offset by the time saved in query processing.

1 Introduction

The technology of caching query (intermediate) results for speeding up subsequent query processing has been studied widely in previous literature. The benefit of this technique is obtained from saving (part of) the subsequent query computations by utilizing the previous cached results. Applications of this technique can be found in different areas. In [Fin82, LY85, Rou91], cached query results were used in relational database systems to avoid repeated computations. [Sel87, Jhi88] addressed the problem of caching query results to support queries with procedures, rules and functions. In a client-server environment, caching query results on local workstation can not only parallelize query processing among clients, but also reduce the bus contention and the server request bottleneck [DR92]. Recently, this technique was also suggested to support query computations in extensible or object-oriented database systems where expensive computations are more likely to happen [HS93].

Different issues concerning the caching technique have also been studied. [AL80, Rou82b, Val87, Rou91] proposed alternative methods for storing the cached data, [Sel88, Jhi88] discussed the problem of selective caching and cache

* This research was sponsored partially by NSF under grant IRI-9057573 and GDR-85-00108, by NASA/USRA under contract FCPO-550-81, and by the University of Maryland Institute for Advanced Computer Studies (UMIACS).

replacement, and in [RK86, Han87, BLT86], different strategies for updating cached data are explored. Aside from the above work on cache management, the problem of how to identify the useful cached data for computing queries, referred as *query matching* problem, was addressed in [Fin82, LY85]. In their work, however, query optimization was not considered inclusively. This is not satisfactory because blindly using cached data in query computations without optimization may result in a query plan even worse than the one optimized from the original query without utilizing any cached results. Therefore, it is necessary to consider optimization at the same time of query matching. This issue was first discussed in [J+93]. However, since their work emphasized on supporting transaction time using differential techniques, the matching and optimization problem was not addressed sufficiently, and no performance evaluation was reported.

In this paper, we describe the design and implementation of the ADMS [2] Cache&Match Optimizer (CMO), and present a comprehensive performance evaluation. By caching previous query results on the disk, the CMO is able to perform the matching coincidently with the optimization, and generate an optimal plan using cached results. The integrated work is also enriched from the previous work that now it (1) can use multiple cached results in computing a query, (2) allows dynamic cache update strategies, depending on which is better, and (3) provides options for different cache management strategies. A variety of experiments were conducted to evaluate the performance of CMO, under alternative strategies and different situations. The results showed that with appropriate strategies, CMO can always improve substantially the performance.

The rest of this paper is organized as following. In Section 2, we discuss the framework of CMO and related issues. Section 3 describes the integration of query matching and optimization. Section 4 presents the experiment results from implementation. And finally in Section 5, we give the conclusion and future research direction.

2 The CMO Framework and Related Issues

The CMO mechanism consists of two major functional components: the *query matching optimizer* and the *cache manager*. Incoming queries are optimized through the matching optimizer, which capitalizes on a structure called LAPS (Logical Access Path Schema) in finding pertinent cached results, in order to generate more efficient plan. Query or intermediate results are saved on the disk and maintained by the cache manager, which keeps track of all the cached data and decides which to replace when the cache space is full. In the following, we discuss the concerned design issues for both modules, review the related work, and describe the approaches we adopted in the implementation.

2.1 Cache Management

Conventional relational database systems always allow users to save the final query results in relations [S+79, SWK76]. It is not uncommon that intermediate

[2] ADMS, the Advanced Database Management System, is a DBMS developed at the Department of Computer Science, University of Maryland, College Park [RES93].

results might also need to be produced to facilitate the query computations. Throughout this paper, we assume intermediate results are generated during query computations. Both intermediate and final query results are referred as *temporaries*. Though temporaries are mostly retained only within a query computation, it is not hard to keep them on disk over a longer time for potential reuse. In the following, we discuss some key issues regarding the management of cached temporaries.

How to store the cached temporaries ? Temporaries can be stored as actual data in relations called *materialized views* [AL80, BLT86]. Another approach is to store for each resulting tuple of the temporary, a number of *Tuple Identifiers (TID)*, instead of materialized values, which point to the corresponding tuples in the base relations, possibly through several levels, that constitute the resulting tuple. Variations of this *pointer based* approach have been proposed in [Rou82b, Val87, Rou91]. In contrast to materialized data caches, materializing pointer caches requires extra page references to higher level relations or temporaries. However, pointer caching is more space-effective since each tuple is represented by a small number of fixed length pointers. Besides, from the view of query matching, pointer caching is more versatile than data caching because (1) more temporaries can be retained in a limited cache space, and (2) unlike data caches which have only projected attributes, pointer caches virtually serve as indices to the base tuples and, thus, can select any attributes of the underlying relations whether or not used in the queries. Nevertheless, both pointer and data caching are implemented and evaluated in CMO.

What to cache ? In a system which provides unbounded disk space, we can simply cache everything generated and leave the decision of using these cached temporaries to the query optimizer. However, a more realistic situation is when we bound the available space for caching. In this situation, a *cache replacement strategy* must be employed to decide which temporaries to replace when the cache space is full. The problem of choosing a good replacement strategy so that the most profitable results can always be cached was addressed in [Sel88]. We incorporated some of the suggested cache replacement heuristics into CMO and experimented with them under different available cache space.

How to update outdated cached temporaries ? Cached temporaries become outdated when the underlying base relations are updated, and thus must be updated before they can be further used. Different strategies regarding *when* to update the outdated caches include: (1) *immediate update* (i.e., when relevant base relations are changed), (2) *periodical update*, and (3) *on-demand update* (i.e., only when they are requested). As for the cache update method, aside from updating via *re-execution*, the technique of *incremental update (*or *differential computation)* [LHM86, BLT86, Rou91] can efficiently update a temporary if only a little part of it is changed.

It was analyzed in [Han87] that none of the combinations of update strategy and update method is superior to all the others under all situations. As it is practically prohibitive to experiment with all possible combinations, on-demand strategy has been adopted in our implementation because it can batch consecutive updates into a single update (and thus reduce the excessive overhead of multiple smaller updates) and always prevents the unnecessary updates to never-used caches. The CMO, however, dynamically chooses between re-execution and incremental computations, depending on their corresponding estimated costs. The performance of CMO under different levels of relation update loads is evaluated in detail in the experiments.

How to keep track of the cached temporaries ? To facilitate the searching and matching against the cache pool, a LAPS structure is used in CMO to keep track of all the cached temporaries efficiently. Instead of recording each cached temporary independently, the LAPS integrates the cached temporaries along with their logical access paths which capture both the access methods and the derivation relationships. The integration of new cached temporaries and logical access paths into the LAPS is fairly direct and has been developed in [Rou82a].

2.2 Query Matching and Optimization

The task of generating the optimal plan, which may or may not use the cached temporaries, for a given query can be conceptually divided into two parts: matching and optimization.

Matching The problem of detecting if a cached temporary is useful for the computation of a query has been investigated in [Fin82, LY85]. We have adapted the method from [Fin82] to our use in the CMO optimizer. Besides, rather than using only one matched cache in a query, the CMO optimizer is capable of using multiple matched temporaries to answer the query more efficiently.

Optimization Optimization is required not only because there may be different combinations of matched caches from which the query can be computed, but also because it is not always beneficial to use caches. A possible solution, as suggested in [Fin82], is a *two phase* approach; during the first phase, the query is transformed into a number of equivalent queries using different cached temporaries, and during the second phase, all the revised queries are fed to a regular optimizer to produce an optimal plan. Without elaborate pruning, this approach may navigate an extremely large search space, even when only a few revised queries are produced from the first phase. A better alternative is to integrate the matching with the optimization and thus, unify the search spaces and avoid duplicate effort [J+93]. The CMO optimizer we implemented here belongs to the second approach.

In summary, the one-phase CMO provides the options of using different cache replacement strategies, data and/or pointer caches, and incremental and/or re-execution updates. In the next section, we describe the integration of matching and optimization in more detail.

3 Integrating Query Matching and Optimization

The matching mechanism only handles the class of *PJS-queries*— queries which involve only projection, selection and join. A PJS-query q is expressed in SQL as: **select** $\bar{a}_q$ **from** $\bar{r}_q$ **where** f_q, where $\bar{r}_q = r_1, r_2, \ldots, r_k$ are operand relations,

$\bar{a}_q = a_1, a_2, \ldots, a_l$ are projected attributes, and f_q is a boolean formula for which the resulting tuples must satisfy. We can therefore represent any query q as $q = (\bar{a}_q, \bar{r}_q, f_q)$. If $\bar{r}_q$ contains any derived relations, the query can be expanded to an expression which involves only base relations, we use $q = (\bar{A}_q, \bar{R}_q, F_q)$ to denote such *expanded* expression. With the same notations, we use $v = (\bar{a}_v, \bar{r}_v, f_v)$ to emphasize that temporary v is *directly* computed from the operand set $\bar{r}_v$ *without* producing any intermediate results in between. Similarly, the expanded notation for v is given by $v = (\bar{A}_v, \bar{R}_v, F_v)$.

In CMO, the query matching and optimization are integrated using a *graph searching* algorithm [Nil80] (referred as state transition network in [J+93, LW86]). The input to the optimizer includes an initial *query graph* (or *state*) which represents the uncomputed query, and a LAPS which models the cached temporaries. A state is *reduced* to a successive state when a part of the query is computed or matched by a cached temporary. Thus, starting from the initial state, successive states are generated until a final state, which represents the totally computed query, is reached. The path with the lowest cost leading to the final state is chosen as the optimal plan. In the following, we first define the LAPS and describe the steps of query matching, and then sketch out the unified CMO matching optimizer. More details about the algorithm and implementation can be found in a complete version of this paper [CR93].

3.1 The Logical Access Path Schema and Query Matching

Definition 1 A *Logical Access Path Schema* (LAPS) is a *directed* graph (N, E) where N is a set of nodes corresponding to base relations and cached temporaries, and E is a set of directed *hyperedges* corresponding to logical access paths such that for any temporary $v = (\bar{a}_v, \bar{r}_v, f_v) \in N$,

1. $x \in N,$ *for all* $x \in \bar{r}_v$, and
2. there is a hyperedge $e = (\bar{r}_v, v) \in E$ leading from the set of operand nodes $\bar{r}_v$ toward v, and labelled with f_v. □

Initially, the LAPS contains base relations only. When subsequent queries are processed and results are cached, it is augmented by integrating the cached temporaries along with their logical access paths[Rou82a]. The purpose of having LAPS is to facilitate the searching for qualified cached temporaries in parallel with the optimization.

We are now concerned about how to check if a cached temporary can be used in computing a query. A temporary is useful if itself alone can be used to compute a sub-query of the given query. Formally, we say a (sub-)query q is *derivable* from a cached temporary v (or v is a *match* of q) if there exist an attribute set A and a formula F such that, for any database instance d, $q(d) = \pi_A(\sigma_F(v(d)))$, where $q(d), v(d)$ denote the result of q and content of v under instance d, respectively. We list below without proof the conditions under which a temporary v is *sufficiently* qualified to be a match of a query q. In what follows, $x_1, \ldots, x_n$ denote the attributes in the corresponding formula; '$\rightarrow$', '$\leftrightarrow$' denote *logical implication* and *logical equivalent* respectively.

Condition 1 (Operand Coverability) $\bar{r}_v = \bar{r}_q$.

Condition 2 (Qualification Coverability) $\forall x_1, \ldots, x_n\ (f_q \rightarrow f_v)$, and, there exists a *restricting* formula f^r on v such that $\forall x_1, \ldots, x_n\ (f_q \leftrightarrow f_v \wedge f^r)$.

Condition 3 (Attribute Coverability) $\bar{a}_v \supseteq (\bar{a}_q \cup \alpha(f^r))$, where $\alpha(f^r)$ are attributes appearing in f^r.

Rather than using a looser condition $\bar{R}_v = \bar{R}_q$, Condition 1 requires the exactly same set of parent operands. However, this will not lose any generality when we capitalize on the LAPS to integrate the matching and optimization. Condition 2 guarantees that every tuple t in the result of q has a corresponding tuple t' in v such that t is a sub-tuple of t', and there exists a formula f^r through which these t' can be selected from v. Condition 3 assures that temporary v contains all the attributes that are projected in the target list of query q, as well as those required to evaluate f^r. The following lemma is a direct consequence of the above conditions.

Lemma 1. *v is a match of q if all the above three conditions are satisfied, in particular, $q(d) = \pi_{\bar{a}_q}(\sigma_{f^r}(v(d)))$ for all database instance d.*

This lemma basically states how to recognize a single cached temporary from which the result of a (sub-)query can be directly extracted. It does not, however, say anything about how to use multiple temporaries in computing a query. This is achieved by interleaving the optimization with the above steps of match checking in a unified searching algorithm and is described in the following subsection.

3.2 Integrating Matching with Optimization

The CMO optimizer can be viewed as a network of query graph reductions. A *query graph* (or *state*) represents the status of the original query as well as any partially processed queries during the optimization. A query graph is *reduced* to a new one by replacing a connected sub-graph with a single new node which corresponds to either a new intermediate result[3] or a matched temporary found in the LAPS. In the following, we formalize the query graph, reductions, and then describe the searching strategy.

Definition 2 (Query Graph) A *query graph* (or a *state*) is a connected, *undirected* graph $G(N, E)$ where

1. each node $n \in N$ denotes a relation, a cached temporary, or an intermediate result, and is associated with a schema $\alpha(n)$ and a projected attribute list $a(n) \subseteq \alpha(n)$,
2. each *hyperedge* $e \in E$ connects a subset of nodes $N(e) \subseteq N$, and is labelled with a formula $f(e)$. e is a *join edge (selection edge)* if $|N(e)| > 1\ (= 1)$. □

It is not hard to see that a query graph (N, E) actually represents a query $(\bar{a}_q, \bar{r}_q, f_q)$ where $\bar{a}_q = \cup_{n \in N} a(n), \bar{r}_q = N$, and $f_q = \wedge_{e \in E} f(e)$. Also note that since a formula can always be transformed into a conjunction of sub-formulas [CL73], every PJS-query can be represented by a query graph. Before we can define the reductions, we need to define *induced sub-query*. Given a state $q =$

[3] We use *intermediate results* to refer to those which are planned during the optimization but are not actually produced yet.

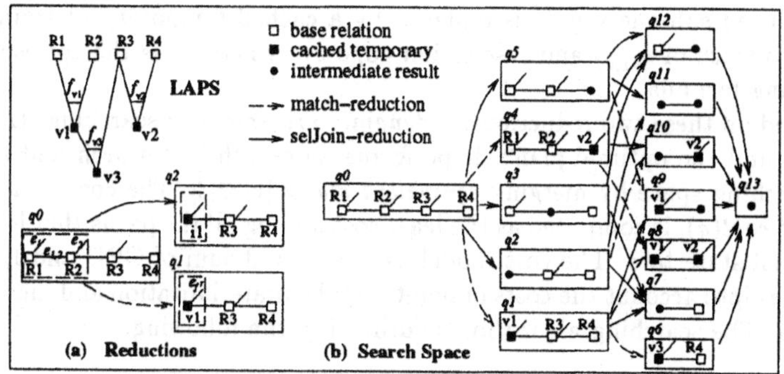

Fig. 1. State Reductions and Searching

(N, E) and an edge $e \in E$, let E^e_{ext} be the set of edges which connect at least one node from $N(e)$ with at least another node *not* from $N(e)$, and E^e_s be the selection edges incident on any node in $N(e)$, then the *sub-query* induced by e is a query $q_e(\bar{a}_{q_e}, \bar{r}_{q_e}, f_{q_e})$ such that

$$\bar{a}_{q_e} = a(N(e)) \cup (\alpha(N(e)) \wedge \alpha(E^e_{ext})), \quad \bar{r}_{q_e} = N(e), \quad f_{q_e} = f(e) \wedge f(E^e_s),$$

where $a(N(e)) = \cup_{n \in N(e)} a(n)$, $\alpha(N(e)) = \cup_{n \in N(e)} \alpha(n)$, $f(E^e_s) = \wedge_{e' \in E^e_s} f(e')$ and $\alpha(E^e_{ext})$ are the attributes appearing in the formula $f(E^e_{ext}) = \wedge_{e' \in E^e_{ext}} f(e')$.

Intuitively, a state is reduced by assigning an access path to the sub-query induced by one of its join edges. There are two different reductions, the *selJoin-reduction* corresponds to computing the induced sub-query directly from the operand relations of the sub-query; the *match-reduction* corresponds to using a matched cached temporary. We define both reductions below and demonstrate them using the example in Figure 1.(a).

Definition 3 (selJoin Reduction) State $q = (N, E)$ is *selJoin-reduced*, on a given join edge $e \in E$, to a new state $q' = (N', E')$ by constructing

1. $N' = N - N(e) \cup \{n'\}$, where $n' \notin N$ and $a(n') = a(N(e))$, $\alpha(n') = \bar{a}_{q_e}$,
2. $E' = E - \{e\} - E^e_s - E^e_{ext} \cup E^e_{ext'}$, where $E^e_{ext'}$ is a new set of edges formed from E^e_{ext} by replacing each occurrence of nodes from $N(e)$ with the new node n'. □

Definition 4 (Match Reduction) State $q = (N, E)$ is *match-reduced*, using a temporary $v(\bar{a}_v, \bar{r}_v, f_v) \in LAPS$ for a join edge $e \in E$, to a new state $q' = (N', E')$ if the induced sub-query q_e is *derivable* from v through a restricting formula f^r (as described in Lemma 1). In particular,

1. $N' = N - n(e) \cup \{n_v\}$, where $n_v \notin N$ and $a(n_v) = a(N(e)), \alpha(n_v) = a_{q_e}$.
2. $E' = E - \{e\} - E^e_s - E^e_{ext} \cup E^e_{ext'} \cup \{e_{f^r}\}$, where e_{f^r} is a new selection edge on n_v and is labelled with f^r. □

A selJoin-reduction is illustrated in Figure 1.(a), where state q_0 is selJoin-reduced to q_2 on edge $e_{1,2}$. Note the induced sub-graph $q_{e_{1,2}}$, bounded by a dashed rectangle in q_0, is replaced by a new intermediate result node $i1$ in q_2. A match-reduction is also shown, where state q_0 is reduced to q_1 on edge $e_{1,2}$.

The induced sub-query $q_{e_{1,2}}$ is replaced by a cached temporary $v1$ from LAPS ($v1$ is a match of $q_{e_{1,2}}$) and a selection edge e_{f^r} where f^r is the corresponding restricting formula.

Based on these two reductions, a *dynamic programming* searching strategy is used to find the optimal plan[4]. It performs a breadth-first search and restricts the searching space by merging *equivalent states* [CR93]. The cost of a state q, denoted $cost(q)$, is computed as the least cost among all the paths that lead from the initial state to q. The cost model uses weighted sum of CPU and I/O time and takes into account the costs of pointer cache materialization and incremental updates. The searching algorithm is outlined in the following.

Step 1 Let $q_0(N_0, E_0)$ be the initial state. $T := \{q_0\}$, $S := \emptyset$. Repeat Step 2 for $|N_0| - 1$ times.

Step 2 $S := T$, $T := \emptyset$. For each $q(N, E) \in S$, and each join edge $e \in E$, do

- **2.1** apply selJoin-reduction to q on e, let q_1 be the reduced state; apply match-reduction to q on e if applicable, let q_2 be the reduced state.
- **2.2** If there exists no $q' \in T$ equivalent to q_1, then $T := T \cup \{q_1\}$, otherwise if $cost(q') > cost(q_1)$ then $T := T - \{q'\} \cup \{q_1\}$. Do the same for q_2.

Step 3 Output the cheapest path leading from q_0 to the single final state in T as the optimal plan.

Continuing on the example of Figure 1.(a), its searching space is given in figure (b) where the selJoin-reduction and match-reductions are drawn in solid and dashed arrows respectively. Three iterations are performed, with a final state generated at the lowest level. Note that in this case, q_1 is further match-reduced to q_6 by using a matched temporary v_3, and q_8 corresponds to the state after using two matched temporaries v_1 and v_2. Merging of equivalent states are reflected by those arrows that come into the same state.

4 Experiments: Performance Evaluation

A CMO component has been incorporated in ADMS. It sits on top of the storage access module which provides alternative access methods to the relations. The access methods include sequential and index scan for single relation, and three join methods: nested loop, index, and hash joins. In the following, we present the experiments that were conducted to evaluate the performance of CMO.

4.1 The Experiment Environment

The experiments were carried out by running a centralized ADMS on a Sun SPARCstation 2. All the experiments were run under a single user stand-alone mode, so that the benefit from CMO can be measured in terms of elapsed time. Different databases and query loads were used throughout the experiments so that the impact from the CMO parameters as well as from the system's environment can be observed.

[4] An A* algorithm was used in an early version of the ADMS optimizer, however, experiments showed that it does not benefit much in reducing the searching space.

Relation	100	1k	2k	5k	10k
Cardinality	100	1,000	2,000	5,000	10,000
Size (KB)	20	208	408	1,008	2,016

Relation	100s	1ks	2ks	5ks	10ks
Cardinality	100	1,000	2,000	5,000	10,000
Size (KB)	10	95	200	496	976

Table 1. Synthetic Relations

Databases	Relations
DBMIX	1k, 2k, 5k, 10k
DBMIX-S	1ks, 2ks, 5ks, 10ks
DB100	100, 100′, 100″, 100‴
DB1k	1k, 1k′, 1k″, 1k‴
DB5k	5k, 5k′, 5k″, 5k‴

Table 2. Five Different Databases

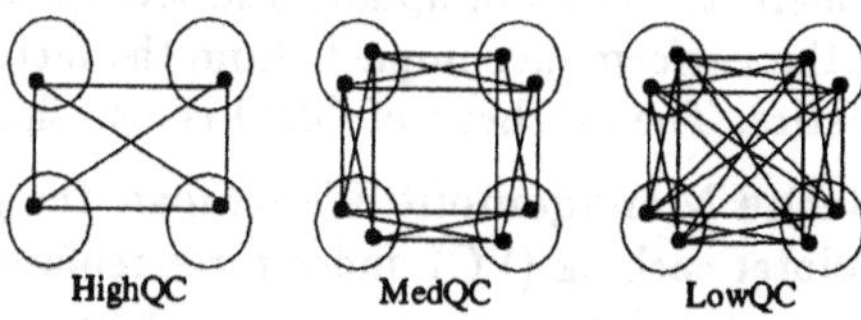

Fig. 2. Three Levels of Query Correlations

Databases Synthetic relations are generated according to the characteristics of the Wisconsin Benchmark [BDT83]. Table 1 outlines the cardinalities and sizes of each relation used in the experiments. Throughout the experiments, each tested database consists of four relations. Table 2 lists all the used databases, note that the primes (′) indicate the different relation instances of the same schema, cardinality and attribute value distributions.

Workload and Query Characteristics The query workload is generated by a customized random query generator. By specifying desired query characteristics, different copies of *query streams* can be generated that all satisfy the given characteristics. In the experiment, we restrict the number of join attributes so that common sub-expressions can recur in queries and, thus, the effectiveness of CMO can be observed. Informally, the *query correlation* among the queries of a query stream is measured as the number of distinct equal-join predicates appearing in it. Figure 2 shows three classes of query correlations used to generate the query streams. The circles denote the relations, the nodes denote the join attributes, and the edges denote the possible join predicates. Note that a maximum of 6, 16, and 24 distinct join predicates can be generated in HighQC, MedQC, and LowQC respectively.

Selection predicates are chosen from random attributes subject to the specified query selectivities. To allow best chance of data caching, every query is projected on all attributes of its participating relations. This makes no difference to pointer cache, but requires more space for data cache. Updates are restricted to certain attributes so that the cached temporaries will not change drastically in cardinality. However, the qualifying predicates in the update queries are randomly chosen from all attributes. Throughout the experiments, each query stream contains at least 50 queries. When not mentioned explicitly, the defaults for the database and the query correlation are DBMIX and MedQC respectively.

Performance Metrics The total *elapsed time* of a query stream execution, including query optimization and query computation time, is taken as the main metric for evaluating the performance outcome. Through the whole experiments, each run (query stream) was repeated several times and the average elapsed time was computed.

4.2 Experiment Results

Three major experiment sets were run to evaluate the CMO. The first set compared with different cache management strategies under different degrees of cached space availability. The second set of experiments were conducted to observe the performance degradation of CMO, under three different strategies of cache updates and different degrees of update selectivities and frequencies. And finally, we evaluated the performance impacts from the factors of database sizes and query characteristics. The overhead of CMO is also shown at the end.

4.2.1 Effect of Cache Management We compare the performance of data caching (DC) and pointer caching (PC) under three replacement strategies:

LRU: the least recently used — in case of a tie, LFU, LCS
LFU: the least frequently used — in case of a tie, LRU, LCS
LCS: the largest cache space required — in case of a tie, LRU, LFU

Two databases were tested (DBMIX, DBMIX-S) , the results are shown on the six curves labelled accordingly in Figure 3. As can be seen all PC curves are roughly the same but among them, PC/LCS is slightly better. In set DBMIX, the pointer caching runs faster than the data caching on all cache space ranges from 0 to 25 MB (we assume that disk space is sufficient for retaining intermediate results within a query). This suggests that when fair amount of intermediate results are generated and written to and read from the disk, the materialization cost of PC is compensated by its efficient write cost. Note that in this case, even with cache space more than 10MB, the performance of DC/LCS is still worse than that of PC/LCS with only 2MB. The inferiority of data caching can be attributed to the large overhead in writing and reading the intermediate results. To make it more competitive, the same experiment was performed again on a smaller database DBMIX-S within which the tuple length is now only around half of the original one. The results are shown in Figure 3.b, where DC now becomes closer to, though still inferior to, PC in performance.

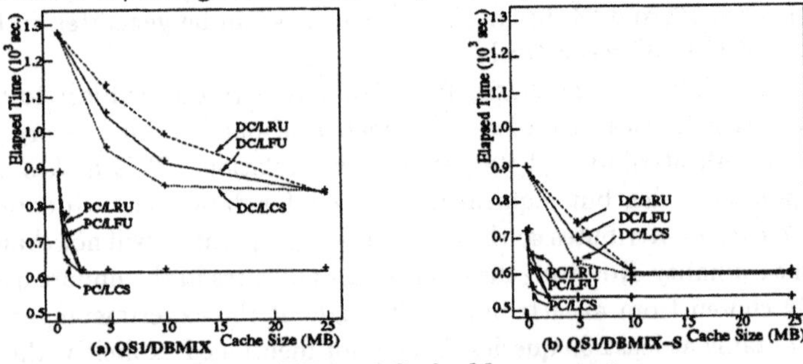

Fig. 3. Effect of Cache Management

It is fair to argue that some savings can be achieved in data caching by projecting out some of the non-useful attributes of the intermediate results. However, such a projection reduces the potential reuse of these intermediate results in other queries which may need these attributes. Thus, for data caching, there is a dilemma between reducing the intermediate size and enhancing the chance of cache reuse. Pointer cache, on the other hand, does not have this problem at all, since all attributes are implicitly inherited in the non-materialized cache. And for this reason, we believe that pointer caching is the proper choice in implementing a CMO-like mechanism. In the rest experiments, only pointer caching with LCS replacement is considered and the cache size is set to 4MB.

4.2.2 Effect of Relation Updates In this experiment, we evaluate the CMO performance degradation under relation updates. Three variations of CMO are evaluated under different degrees of update frequency and selectivities. CMO/INC uses incremental update only, CMO/REX uses re-execution update only, and CMO/DYN allows both methods and leave the decision to the optimizer. The performance of a regular optimizer (REG) without caching and matching technique is also included for comparison. Both relation update frequency (no. of update queries / no. of total queries) and update selectivity (no. of updated tuples / relation cardinality) are controlled. For each raw query stream (which contains no update queries), 15 variations are produced by interleaving it with update queries according to each combination of 5 different levels of update frequencies and 3 different levels of update selectivities. The frequencies range from 0%, 5%, 10%, 15% to 25%, and the update selectivities range from LS (1% – 5%), MS (6% – 10%) to HS (6% – 10% for 2/3 of the update queries, and 40% – 50% for the other 1/3).

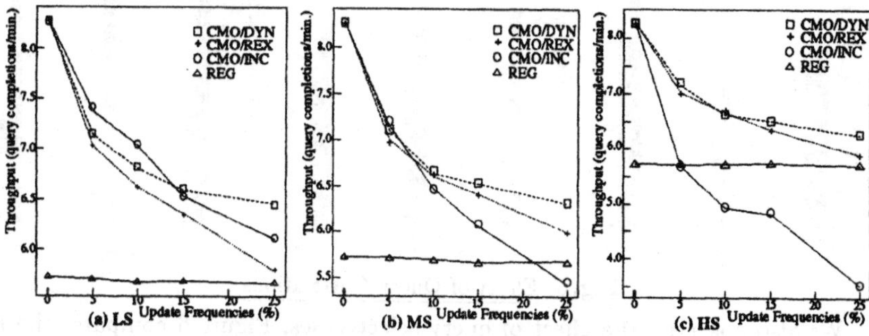

Fig. 4. Effect of Relation Updates

Four different query streams are experimented, Figure 4 depicts the average throughputs among all four query streams under different situations. The CMO curves, no matter what update strategies are used, perform better than REG in all LS, MS and HS sets (except CMO/INC in set HS), and decline elegantly as update frequency increases. This is no surprise since the cost of updating a outdated temporary is compensated by those subsequent queries that are able to use it before it becomes outdated again. In set LS, CMO/REX performs worse than the other two since re-execution update do not take advantage of incremental computation. CMO/INC is better than CMO/DYN at 5% and 10% update frequencies, but as the frequencies increase, it is outperformed by CMO/DYN. This is due to the increasing overhead of update log processing in CMO/INC. In set MS, except at 5% frequency, CMO/DYN performs the best; CMO/INC now swaps position with CMO/REX from LS. And finally in HS, CMO/INC declines drastically, and performs even worse than REG for frequencies greater than 10%. CMO/DYN still performs the best in this set.

The reader might wonder why CMO/DYN, which is supposed to be theoretically the best under all circumstances, is inferior to CMO/INC at update frequencies 5% and 10% in LS. We analyzed the statistical profile and found out that it is due to the problems of ***inaccurate cost estimation*** and the lack of ***global (multiple) query optimization***, which somtimes cause CMO/DYN to chose less efficient paths than CMO/INC and/or CMO/REX. Overall, though, CMO is cost effective in most environments where queries arrive in no ad hoc manner and, thus, there is no good way to predict what queries will appear in the stream.

4.2.3 Effect of Query Correlation and Database Sizes In this set of experiment, we observe the impact of the database environment on the CMO performance. Figure 5 shows the performance improvement of CMO over REG under three classes of query correlations: LowQC, MedQC, and HighQC. For each class, the results of three random generated query streams (QS1, QS2, QS3) are presented each of which consists of 70 queries. The portion below the horizontal dashed line denotes the total elapsed time of those queries that do not find any matched caches for use. It shows that CMO reduces the total elapsed time in all classes with a significant amount. And as query correlation increases, the improvement increases because of higher chance of match.

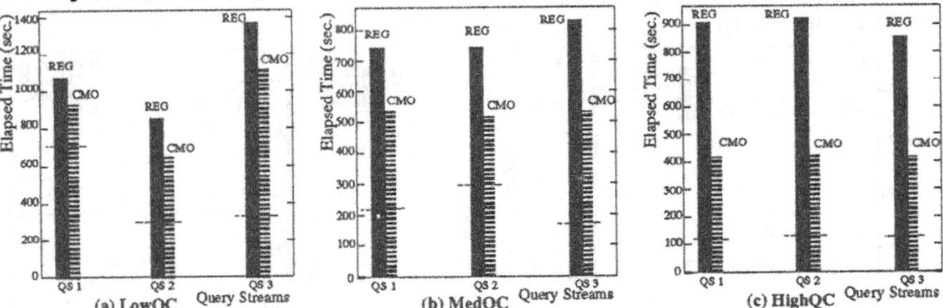

Fig. 5. Effect of Query Correlations

We also observed the effect of query selectivities. Figure 6 compares the results between two classes of query selectivities: low selectivities of 0.0001 – 0.05 (LS) and high selectivities of 0.0001 – 0.3 (HS). Intuitively, query matching should have been more advantageous in a large database with small selectivity queries, because it tends to save a large computation by caching a small amount of results. However, our results show that for the higher selectivity queries (HS), the relative improvement of CMO over REG is still as good as that in the lower selectivity one (LS), though elapsed time has almost doubled in HS.

To see the effect of database size, three different size databases were experimented in another set. We have adjusted the query selectivities for each query stream so that the query result sizes do not diverge too much among all three database sizes. The purpose of doing so is to observe the improvement trend for different size databases supposed that the query result sizes are fairly small and unchanged. Figure 7 shows the results, where CMO consistently shorten the

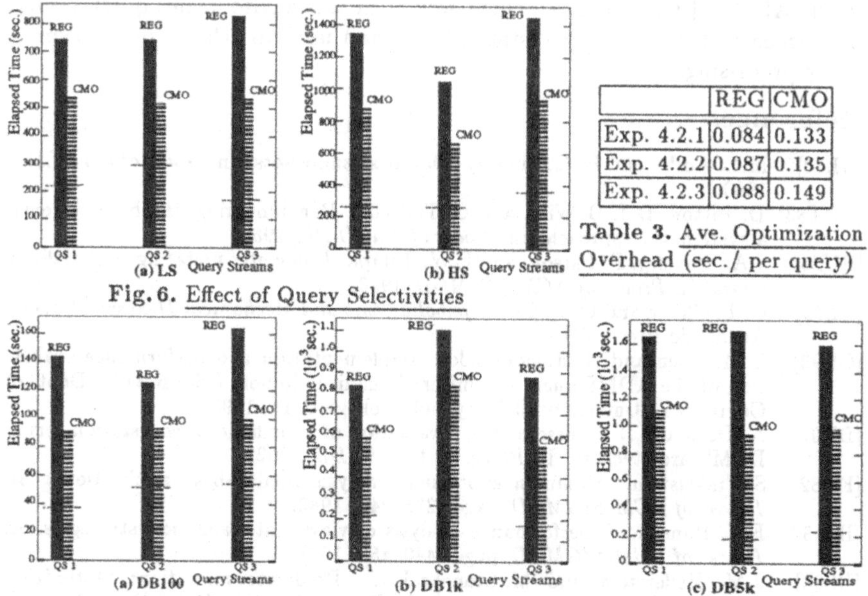

Fig. 6. Effect of Query Selectivities

	REG	CMO
Exp. 4.2.1	0.084	0.133
Exp. 4.2.2	0.087	0.135
Exp. 4.2.3	0.088	0.149

Table 3. Ave. Optimization Overhead (sec./ per query)

Fig. 7. Effect of Database Size

elapsed time from REG. However, no drastic differences in relative improvement can be told among the three database sizes.

Finally, we compare the optimization overhead of CMO with REG. Table 3 lists the average optimization time per query for each set of experiments we presented above. Though CMO has around 50% – 60% more optimization time than REG, the extra overhead introduced by CMO is relatively small when compared to and, thus, is compensated by the time saved in query computations.

5 Conclusion

This paper describes the ADMS query optimizer which matches and integrates in its execution plans query results cached in pointers or materialized views. The optimizer is based on the Logical Access Path Schema, a structure which models the derivation relationship among cached query results, for incrementally identifying the useful caches while generating the optimal plan. The optimizer features data caching and pointer caching, different cache replacement strategies, and different cache update strategies.

An extensive set of experiments were conducted and the results showed that pointer caching and dynamic cache update strategies substantially speedup query computations and, thus, increase query throughput under situations with fair query correlation and update load, The requirement of the cache space is relatively small and the extra computation overhead introduced by the caching and matching mechanism is more than offset by the time saved in query processing.

For the future research, we would like to extend the CMO techniques to concurrent queries and investigate how results cached from a query can be used in another concurrent query . Also we would like to adapt the CMO optimizer to the ADMS±[RK86, RES93] client-server. In this environment, query results are cached in local client workstation disks and used to achieve parallelism in query processing.

References

[AL80] M.E. Adiba and B. G. Lindsay. Database snapshots. In *Procs. of 6th VLDB*, 1980.

[BDT83] D. Bitton, D.J. DeWitt, and C. Turbyfill. Benchmarking database systems, a systematic approach. In *Procs. of 9th VLDB*, 1983.

[BLT86] J.A. Blakeley, P. Larson, and F.W. Tompa. Efficiently updating materialized views. In *Procs. of ACM-SIGMOD*, 1986.

[CL73] C. L. Chang and C. T. Lee. *Symbolic Logic and Mechanical Theorem Proving.* Academic Press, 1973.

[CR93] C.M. Chen and N. Roussopoulos. Implementation and performance evaluation of the ADMS query optimizer. Technical Report CS-TR-3159, Dept. of Comp. Sci., University of Maryland, College Park, 1993.

[DR92] A. Delis and N. Roussopoulos. Evaluation of an enhanced workstation-server DBMS architecture. In *Procs. of 18th VLDB*, 1992.

[Fin82] S. Finkelstein. Common expression analysis in database applications. In *Procs. of ACM-SIGMOD*, pages 235–245, 1982.

[Han87] E.N. Hanson. A performance analysis of view materialization strategies. In *Procs. of ACM-SIGMOD*, pages 440–453, 1987.

[HS93] J.M. Hellerstein and M. Stonebraker. Predicate migration: Optimizing queries with expensive predicates. In *Procs. of ACM-SIGMOD*, 1993.

[J+93] C. S. Jensen et al. Using differential techniques to efficiently support transaction time. *VLDB Journal*, 2(1):75–111, 1993.

[Jhi88] A. Jhingran. A performance study of query optimization algorithms on a database system supporting procedures. In *Procs. of 14th VLDB*, 1988.

[LHM86] B. Lindsay, L. Haas, and C. Mohan. A snapshot differential refresh algorithm. In *Procs. of ACM-SIGMOD*, pages 53–60, 1986.

[LW86] S. Lafortune and E. Wong. A state transition model for distributed query processing. *ACM TODS*, 11(3):294–322, 1986.

[LY85] P.-Å. Larson and H. Z. Yang. Computing queries from derived relations. In *Procs. of 11th VLDB*, pages 259–269, 1985.

[Nil80] N.J. Nilsson. *Principles of Artificial Intelligence.* Tioga Pub. Co., 1980.

[RES93] N. Roussopoulos, N. Economou, and A. Stamenas. ADMS: A testbed for incremental access methods. *To appear in IEEE Trans. on Knowledge and Data Engineering*, 1993.

[RK86] N. Roussopoulos and H. Kang. Principles and techniques in the design of ADMS±. *Computer*, 19(12):19–25, 1986.

[Rou82a] N. Roussopoulos. The logical access path schema of a database. *IEEE Trans. on Software Engineering*, SE-8(6):563–573, 1982.

[Rou82b] N. Roussopoulos. View indexing in relational databases. *ACM TODS*, 7(2):258–290, 1982.

[Rou91] N. Roussopoulos. An incremental access method for ViewCache: Concept, algorithms, and cost analysis. *ACM TODS*, 16(3):535–563, 1991.

[S+79] P. G. Selinger et al. Access path selection in a relational database management system. In *Procs. of ACM-SIGMOD*, pages 23–34, 1979.

[Sel87] T. Sellis. Efficiently supporting procedures in relational database systems. In *Procs. of ACM-SIGMOD*, 1987.

[Sel88] T. K. Sellis. Intelligent caching and indexing techniques for relational database systems. *Inform. Systems*, 13(2), 1988.

[SWK76] M. Stonebraker, E. Wong, and P. Kreps. The design and implementation of INGRES. *ACM TODS*, 1(3):189–222, 1976.

[Val87] P. Valduriez. Join indices. *ACM TODS*, 12(2):218–246, 1987.

Optimization of Nested Queries in a Complex Object Model

Hennie J. Steenhagen, Peter M.G. Apers, and Henk M. Blanken

Department of Computer Science, University of Twente,
PO Box 217, 7500 AE Enschede, The Netherlands

Abstract. Transformation of nested SQL queries into join queries is advantageous because a nested SQL query can be looked upon as a nested-loop join, which is just one of the several join implementations that may be available in a relational DBMS. In join queries, dangling (unmatched) operand tuples are lost, which causes a problem in transforming nested queries having the aggregate function COUNT between query blocks–a problem that has become well-known as the COUNT bug. In the relational context, the outerjoin has been employed to solve the COUNT bug. In complex object models supporting an SQL-like query language, transformation of nested queries into join queries is an important optimization issue as well. The COUNT bug turns out to be a special case of a general problem being revealed in a complex object model. To solve the more general problem, we introduce the *nestjoin* operator, which is a generalization of the outerjoin for complex objects.

1 Introduction

Currently, at the University of Twente, work is being done on the high-level object-oriented data model TM. TM is a database specification language incorporating standard object-oriented features such as classes and types, object identity, complex objects, and multiple inheritance of data, methods, and constraints. In TM, methods and constraints are specified in a high-level, declarative language of expressions. An important language construct is the SELECT-FROM-WHERE (SFW) construct. The SFW-construct of TM is comparable to the SFW-query block from HDBL, the query language of the experimental DBMS AIM [10]. HDBL is an orthogonal extension of SQL for extended NF^2 data structures. Optimization of TM SFW-expressions therefore has much in common with optimization of the SFW-expressions of SQL and HDBL.

Optimization of SQL queries has received quite some attention the last decade. An important problem in this area is the optimization of nested SQL queries [7, 5, 4, 8, 9]. SQL offers possibilities to formulate nested queries: SFW-query blocks containing other SFW-blocks in the WHERE clause. In [7], it was pointed out that it is advantageous to replace nested SQL queries by flat, or join queries. Flat SQL queries are SFW-blocks not containing subqueries in the WHERE clause. Replacing nested SQL queries by join queries is advantageous because a nested SQL query can be looked upon as a nested-loop join, which is just one of the several join implementations possible. After rewriting a nested query into a join query, the optimizer has better possibilities to choose the most appropriate join implementation.

In nested queries, inner operand tuples are grouped by the values of the outer operand tuples. Whenever aggregate functions occur between query blocks, the transformed, i.e. join query also requires grouping (expressed by means of the GROUP BY clause). In nested queries, dangling outer operand tuples, i.e. outer operand tuples that are not matched by any of the inner operand tuples, deliver a subquery result equal to the empty set. Transformation of a nested query into a join query causes the loss of dangling tuples. In the relational context, this may cause a problem when the aggregate function COUNT occurs between query blocks. As a solution to this problem (that has become well known as the COUNT bug), it has been proposed to use the outerjoin instead of the regular join [5].

In complex object models supporting an SQL-like query language, transformation of nested queries into join queries is just as important as in the relational context. However, in complex object models grouping of the inner operand is required not only if aggregate functions occur between query blocks, but in many other cases as well. The reason for this is that attributes may be set valued. Moreover, each time grouping is necessary, we have to deal with some kind of COUNT bug caused by the loss of dangling tuples, i.e. the COUNT bug is just a special case of a more general problem being revealed in a complex object model. An important result of this paper is that from the form of the predicate between query blocks it can easily be derived when grouping is not necessary. Nested queries that do not require grouping can be transformed into join queries; for the efficient and correct processing of nested queries that do require grouping a new join operator is introduced–the *nest join* operator.

Instead of producing the concatenation of every pair of matching tuples as in the regular join operation, in the nest join operation each left operand tuple is extended with the *set* of matching right operand tuples. This way two birds are killed with one stone: grouping is performed, and also dangling tuples are preserved. Implementation of the nest join operator is a simple modification of any common join implementation method, however, like the outerjoin operator, the nest join has limited rewrite possibilities compared to the regular join operator.

In general, in the logical optimization of a declarative query language, two approaches can be distinguished: (1) rewriting expressions in the query language itself and (2) translation into and rewriting in some intermediate language, for example an algebraic language. Also a combination of the two approaches is possible. For the logical optimization of TM, we have defined the language ADL, an algebra for complex objects which is an extension of the NF^2 algebra of [12]. This work will be used in the ESPRIT III project IMPRESS (Integrated, Multi-Paradigm, Reliable, and Extensible Storage System). The IMPRESS project started in 1992, and one of the subtasks is to translate (a subset of) the language TM into an algebra for complex objects resembling ADL. In this paper, our ideas with regard to query transformation will be presented using the language TM; we will not introduce the algebra for reasons of simplicity.

The structure of this paper is as follows. In Section 2, we briefly review the work that has been done with regard to nested SQL queries. In Section 3, we describe the language TM and the types of nested SFW-expressions that are of interest for the purpose of this paper. Nesting in the WHERE clause and in the SELECT clause are discussed in Sections 4 and 5, respectively, and we will see that in the transformation of nested queries into join queries in many cases grouping is needed, each case leading to some kind of COUNT bug if relational transformation techniques are used. Then, in Section 6, we introduce the nest join operator. The nest join is an operator that allows efficient processing of nested queries that cannot be transformed into join queries without grouping. Bugs are avoided by preserving dangling tuples. In Section 7 we show, for two-block queries, which types of nested queries can be transformed into join queries without problem. An example of query processing for an arbitrary linear nested query (having only one subquery per WHERE clause) is then given in Section 8. The paper is concluded by a section discussing future work.

2 Nested SQL Queries

In this section we briefly review the work that has been done on optimization of nested SQL queries. We do not give a complete overview; we merely indicate the ideas behind optimization of nested SQL queries with a view on the additional problems that come up with optimization of nested queries in a data model supporting complex objects.

Nested SQL queries are SFW-query blocks containing other (possibly nested) SFW-query blocks in the WHERE clause. For example, assume we have relation schemas $R(A, B, C)$ and $S(C, D)$, and consider the following SQL query:

```
SELECT *
FROM R
WHERE R.B IN SELECT S.D
             FROM S
             WHERE R.C = S.C
```

Disregarding duplicates, the nested query given above is easily transformed into the flat, or join query:

```
SELECT R.A, R.B, R.C
FROM R, S
WHERE R.B = S.D AND R.C = S.C
```

which, in relational algebra, is simply a join between tables R and S followed by a projection on R, i.e. a semijoin. The advantage of transforming nested queries to join queries is clear: a nested-loop join is just one of the several possible implementations of the join operator, and after transformation to a join query the optimizer can choose the most suitable join execution method. The method chosen may be a nested-loop join, but not necessarily–alternative join implementations are the sort-merge join, the hash join etc.

In [7], five types of nesting have been distinguished and an algorithm has been given to transform nested queries into join queries for each of these different types of nesting. In case aggregate functions occur between query blocks (one of the types of nesting) SQL's GROUP BY clause is employed to compute the aggregates needed. However, in [6] it has been shown that Kim's algorithm is not correct if the aggregate function COUNT occurs between query blocks. This flaw has become known as the COUNT bug. Consider the query:

```
SELECT *
FROM R
WHERE R.B = SELECT COUNT (*)
            FROM S
            WHERE R.C = S.C
```

Following Kim's algorithm, we get the following queries:

```
(1) T(C, CNT) = SELECT S.C, COUNT (*)
                FROM S
                GROUP BY S.C

    SELECT R.A, R.B, R.C
    FROM R, T
    WHERE R.B = T.CNT AND R.C = T.C
```

Alternatively, if the relation R does not contain duplicates, the nested query may be transformed into:

```
(2) SELECT R.A, R.B, R.C
    FROM R, S
    WHERE R.C = S.C
    GROUP BY R.A, R.B, R.C
    HAVING R.B = COUNT (S.C)
```

In the former, grouping of the inner operand and computation of the aggregate precedes the join operation; in the latter the join is executed first.

The queries resulting from the transformations do not give the correct result. In the original, nested query, dangling R-tuples for which $R.B = 0$, are included in the result; these tuples are lost in the join queries.

To solve the COUNT bug, it has been proposed in [5] to modify (2) by using outerjoins instead of joins in case the COUNT function occurs between query blocks. The right outerjoin operator preserves dangling tuples of the left join operand: unmatched left operand tuples are extended with NULL values in the right operand attribute positions.

As another solution, it has been proposed in [9] to modify (1), because in some cases (1) is more efficient than (2). It is proposed to have two types of join predicates in the second query of (1): a regular join predicate and an additional, so-called antijoin predicate, to be applied to the dangling tuples. In the example given above the antijoin predicate would be: $R.B = 0$. In Kim's second query the join is replaced by an outerjoin operation with join predicate $R.C = T.C$; to the tuples that match the predicate $R.B = T.CNT$ is applied, and to the unmatched tuples in R the antijoin predicate $R.B = 0$ is applied.

3 Nested TM Queries

3.1 General Description of TM

In this section we describe the features of TM that are important for the purpose of this paper–support for complex objects and the SELECT-FROM-WHERE construct. For a more comprehensive description of TM we refer the reader to [1, 2, 3].

TM is a high-level, object-oriented database specification language. It is formally founded in the language FM, a typed lambda calculus allowing for subtyping and multiple inheritance. Characteristic features of TM are the distinction between types, classes, and sorts, support for object identity and complex objects, and multiple inheritance of attributes, methods, and constraints. In TM, attribute types may be arbitrarily complex: the type constructors supported are the tuple, variant, set, and list type constructor; type constructors may be arbitrarily nested. Besides basic types, class names may be used in type specifications. Sets do not contain duplicates.

In constraint and method specifications we may use the SELECT-FROM-WHERE construct, having the following general format:

SELECT <result expression>
FROM <operand expression> <variable>
WHERE <predicate>

The meaning of the SFW-expression is as follows. The operand expression is evaluated; a variable is iterated over the resulting set; for each value of the variable it is determined whether the predicate holds, and if so, the result expression is evaluated and this value is included in the resulting set.

3.2 Types of Nesting in TM

One important difference between SQL on the one hand, and TM and HDBL on the other is that TM and HDBL are *orthogonal* languages. The operand and result expression of the SFW-query block of TM may be arbitrary expressions, also containing other (nested) SFW-expressions, provided they are correctly typed. The predicate may also be built up from arbitrary expressions (including quantifiers FORALL and EXISTS), as long as it delivers a Boolean result.

We give some examples of SFW-expressions. Assume we have specified classes 'Employee' and 'Department':

```
CLASS Employee WITH EXTENSION EMP
ATTRIBUTES
        name : STRING,
        address : Address,
        sal : INT,
        children : ℙ⟨name : STRING, age : INT⟩
END Employee

CLASS Department WITH EXTENSION DEPT
ATTRIBUTES
        name : STRING,
        address : Address,
        emps : ℙEmployee
END Department

SORT Address
TYPE ⟨street : STRING, nr : STRING, city : STRING⟩
END Address
```

The symbol $\mathbb{P}$ denotes the set type constructor, brackets $\langle\rangle$ denote the tuple type constructor. In TM, class extensions are explicitly named. The class 'Employee' has four attributes, of which the attribute 'address' has a complex type specified as a sort. Sorts are used to describe commonly used types such as 'Address', 'Date', 'Time' etc.

Q1: Select the departments that have at least one employee living in the same street the department is located.

```
SELECT d
FROM DEPT d
WHERE ⟨s = d.address.street, c = d.address.city⟩
        IN SELECT ⟨s = e.address.street, c = e.address.city⟩
           FROM d.emps e
```

Q2: Select for all departments the names of the departments and the employees living in the same city the department is located.

```
SELECT ⟨dname = d.name, emps = SELECT e
                               FROM EMP e
                               WHERE e.address.city = d.address.city⟩
FROM DEPT d
```

We make a distinction in the types of nested queries. In a SFW-expression, other SFW-expressions may occur in the SELECT clause (query $Q2$), in the FROM clause, and in the WHERE clause (query $Q1$). In this paper, the expressions of interest are nested SFW-expressions having subqueries in which free variables (correlated subqueries) occur; subqueries without free variables simply are constants. We do not consider SFW-expressions with subqueries in the FROM clause, because these can be rewritten easily. Furthermore, operands of subqueries may be either set-valued attributes, as in query Q1, or distinct tables, as in query Q2. Only if subquery operands are distinct tables, transformation to join queries is desirable. There is no use to flatten nested queries in which subquery operands are set-valued attributes, because set-valued attributes are stored with the objects themselves (as materialized joins), at least conceptually.

In short, the nested queries of interest are SFW-expressions having subqueries in the SELECT- and/or WHERE clause containing free variables and having distinct tables as operands. Initially, we will restrict ourselves to two-block queries. In Section 8 we will briefly discuss queries with multiple nesting levels.

4 Nesting in the WHERE Clause

Assume we have a two-block query with one-level deep nesting. The general format of such a query is:

```
SELECT F(x)
FROM X x
WHERE P(x, z)
        WITH z = SELECT G(x, y)
                 FROM Y y
                 WHERE Q(x, y)
```

The WITH clause is a TM construct enabling local definitions, used here to facilitate the description of the syntactical form of the predicate P. In this paper, we do not consider multiple subqueries, $P(x, z)$ contains only one occurrence of z.

We want to transform the nested query into a join query of the following format (remember that, in SQL, grouping is necessary only if aggregate functions occur between query blocks):

SELECT $F(x)$
FROM $X\ x, Y\ y$
WHERE $P'(x, v) \wedge Q(x, y)$
WITH $v = G(x, y)$

For notational convenience, also the expression $G(x, y)$ has been named by means of a WITH clause.

The goal of the transformation process is to transform the predicate $P(x, z)$, whose second argument z is set valued, into a predicate $P'(x, v)$, where values v are the members of z. The types of P and P' clearly differ: from the second argument of P a set constructor is removed, resulting in predicate P'.

4.1 Example Predicates

Assume that the predicate P only involves attribute a of the outer operand X and z, the subquery result. Because the attribute a may be set valued, this (already restricted) predicate between query blocks may take many different forms. We may have for instance[1]:

- $x.a$ *OP* z with *OP* $\in \{\in, \subset, \subseteq, =, \supseteq, \supset, \ni\}$,
- expressions involving quantifiers, for example $\exists s \in z\ (s = x.a)$,
- $x.a$ *OP* $H(z)$ with H an aggregate function and *OP* an arithmetical comparison operator,
- expressions involving set operators, for example $x.a \cap z = \emptyset$, or
- negations of expressions listed above.

Predicates can be divided into two groups: predicates that require grouping of the inner operand tuples and the predicates that do not. In Section 7, we give a formal characterization of predicates that do and do not require grouping; below, the need for grouping is discussed more informally.

Grouping is not necessary if the question whether outer operand tuples belong to the result or not (whether, for some outer operand tuple, the predicate evaluates to *true* or *false*) can be answered on the basis of the individual members of the subquery result, i.e. by *scanning* the subquery result. For example, consider the expression $x.a \in z$. The moment we encounter a tuple y in the inner operand Y such that the condition $Q(x, y)$ holds and $x.a$ equals the value of v, we know that tuple x belongs to the result. If no such v is found in the end, the predicate evaluates to *false*.

[1] In the rest of the paper we will use the common set-theoretical notation for comparison operators and boolean connectives occurring in TM-predicates because of its conciseness.

Grouping is necessary if the subquery result has to be available *as a whole* to decide whether the predicate holds. In this case, all tuples belonging to the subquery result must be kept, because the predicate can only be evaluated having all values in the subquery result at hand. An obvious example of a predicate requiring grouping is the expression $x.a = \text{COUNT}(z)$: not until the entire subquery result is at our disposal it is possible to compute (or output, if accumulated) the cardinality of the subquery result. Another predicate requiring grouping is for example the expression $x.a \subseteq z$.

Whenever a predicate needs grouping, we have to deal with some sort of COUNT bug if the nested query is transformed according to the algorithm of [7]. For example, the nested query:

```
SELECT x
FROM X x
WHERE x.a ⊆ z WITH z = SELECT y.a
                       FROM Y y
                       WHERE x.b = y.b
```

is, following the ideas of [7], transformed into the following TM queries:

```
T = SELECT ⟨b = y.b, as = SELECT y'.a
                          FROM Y y'
                          WHERE y'.b = y.b⟩
    FROM Y y

SELECT x
FROM X x, T t
WHERE x.b = t.b ∧ x.a ⊆ t.as
```

The first query groups the set of $y.a$ values by the values of the attribute b (cf. the operator nest (ν) from the NF^2 algebra [12]). The transformed query also suffers from a bug (which we might call the SUBSETEQ bug in this case): X-tuples for which $x.a = \emptyset$ that are not matched by any t-tuple on the condition $x.b = t.b$ are lost.

In summary, in TM grouping of the inner operand is required not only if aggregate functions occur between query blocks, but in many other cases too. If Kim's solution is chosen, the transformed query will suffer from a bug each time grouping is needed. We will not use the outerjoin operator to solve these bugs. Instead, in Section 6, we will introduce the nest join operator, which is a much cleaner solution in a model supporting complex objects.

5 Nesting in the SELECT Clause

In this section, we will show that, with one notable exception, nesting in the SELECT clause always requires grouping of the inner operand. SFW-expressions having subqueries in the SELECT clause are not new. In HDBL, it is also allowed to have SFW-query blocks in the SELECT clause. SFW-expressions nested in the SELECT clause commonly describe nested results, as in query Q2 from Section 3.2 where employees are grouped by departments. Consider the general format of a two-block query with nesting in the SELECT clause:

```
SELECT F(x, z)
        WITH z = SELECT G(x, y)
                 FROM Y y
                 WHERE Q(x, y)
FROM X x
WHERE P(x)
```

If this query is to be transformed into a join query, the inner operand values have to be grouped by the outer operand values. Grouping may take place preceding or following the join. In both cases again dangling tuples are lost.

With regard to nesting in the SELECT clause, there is one special case in which grouping can be avoided. In TM, a SFW-expression may be nested directly in the SELECT clause, meaning the result is a set of sets. This set of sets may be 'collapsed' by applying the operator UNNEST, which is defined as UNNEST$(S) = \bigcup\{s \mid s \in S\}$. Consider the following query:

```
UNNEST (SELECT (SELECT ⟨a = x.a, b = y.b⟩
                FROM Y y
                WHERE x.b = y.a)
        FROM X x
```

This nested query is equivalent to the join query:

```
SELECT ⟨a = x.a, b = y.b⟩
FROM X x, Y y
WHERE x.b = y.a
```

6 The Nest Join Operator

In the previous sections we have shown that in a complex object model, in many cases grouping seems to be an essential step in the transformation of nested queries to join queries. Queries requiring grouping may always be handled by means of nested-loop processing, which gives correct results but may be very inefficient. If we, though, choose to transform nested queries into join queries, we have to take special measures when queries need grouping because dangling tuples are lost. In the relational model the outerjoin is used to take care of dangling tuples: for subqueries that deliver empty sets the NULL is used to represent the empty set. In a complex object model, however, we do not have to represent the empty set: *the empty set is part of the model.*

Definition

The nest join operator, denoted by the symbol Δ, is simply a modification of the join operator. Instead of producing the concatenation of every pair of matching tuples, for each left operand tuple a set is created to hold the (possibly modified) right operand tuples that match. The nest join of two tables X and Y on predicate Q with function G (the function applied to the right-hand tuples satisfying the join predicate) is defined as:

$$X \underset{x,y:Q,G;a}{\triangle} Y \stackrel{d}{=} \{x \mathbin{++} \langle a = z\rangle \mid x \in X \wedge z = \{G(x,y) \mid y \in Y \wedge Q(x,y)\}\}$$

In this expression, x++$\langle a = z\rangle$ denotes the concatenation of the tuple x and the unary tuple $\langle a = z\rangle$, in which a is an arbitrary label not occurring on the top level of X. An example of the nest join operation is found in Table 1, where flat relations X and Y are equijoined on the second attribute (the join function is the identity function). Note that for dangling tuples $x \in X$, the tuple x ++ $\langle a = \emptyset\rangle$ is present in the result. The nest join operation is a neatly defined operation. Grouping, which is performed during the join, is made explicit by means of a set-valued attribute. Because dangling tuples are preserved, bugs like the COUNT bug are prevented.

a	b
1	1
1	2
2	3

c	d
1	1
2	1
3	3

a	b	s(c, d)
1	1	{(1,1), (2,1)}
1	2	$\emptyset$
2	3	{(3,3)}

Table 1. X, Y, and the nest equijoin of X and Y on the second attribute

Algebraic Properties

Assuming the nest join function is identity, the nest join can be expressed using the outerjoin, denoted by the symbol $\odot$, and the nest operator ν^*:

$$X \underset{x,y:Q,id;a}{\triangle} Y \equiv \nu^*_{X;a}(X \underset{x,y:Q}{\odot} Y)$$

In this algebraic expression, the operator ν^* is a slightly modified version of the standard nest operator performing nesting in the usual way, and then mapping nested sets consisting of a NULL-tuple to the empty set [13]. By using the nest join instead of the outerjoin followed by the nest operator, we do not have to resort to NULLs to avoid the loss of dangling tuples.

A disadvantage of the nest join operator is that it, like the outerjoin, has less pleasant algebraic properties. For example, the nest join operation is neither commutative nor associative. As another example, the nest join does not always associate with the regular join: $X \triangle (Y \bowtie Z)$ is not equivalent to $(X \triangle Y) \bowtie Z$, the two expressions already being typed differently. Below we list some examples of algebraic equivalences concerning the nest join operator.

Let $X \triangle_p Y$ denote a nest join operation on predicate p in which the nest join function equals the identity function (for simplicity omitting variable names and the nest join label). Let $r(a, b)$ denote a predicate referencing attributes in tables A and B (and no other), then we have:

- $\pi_X(X \triangle Y) \equiv X$
- $(X \bowtie_{r(x,y)} Y) \triangle_{r(x,z)} Z \equiv (X \triangle_{r(x,z)} Z) \bowtie_{r(x,y)} Y)$
- $(X \bowtie_{r(x,y)} Y) \triangle_{r(y,z)} Z \equiv X \bowtie_{r(x,y)} (Y \triangle_{r(y,z)} Z)$

Implementation

To implement the nest join, common join implementation methods like the sort-merge join, or the hash join can be used. However, some restrictions hold. First, in nest join implementations, an output tuple can be produced not until the entire set of matching right operand tuples has been found. Second, because in the nest join operation the output has to be grouped according to the values of the left operand tuples, the choice for outer and inner loop operand is restricted. For example, in a (simple) hash join implementation, if the join attribute does not form a key attribute of the right join operand, only the right join operand may be the build table. (For the regular join, usually the smaller operand is chosen as the build table.)

Use

The nest join operation can be employed to process queries with nesting in the SELECT- as well in the WHERE clause. Queries having subqueries in the SELECT clause often describe nested results, so processing by means of the nest join operation will be an appropriate method of processing. For queries with nesting in the WHERE clause, however, sometimes there are other, more efficient possibilities. In the following section we show in which cases grouping certainly is not necessary, so that, instead of the nest join operator, we may employ some flat join operator to obtain the results needed.

7 The Need for Grouping

In this section, we present a class of predicate expressions for which it is known that grouping is *not* necessary. Again consider the general format of a two-block query with nesting in the WHERE clause given in Section 4, then we have:

Theorem 1. *Grouping is* not *necessary if the predicate expression $P(x, z)$ can be rewritten into a calculus expression of the form (1) $\exists v \in z\ (P'(x, v))$ or (2) $\nexists v \in z\ (P'(x, v))$. In this expression, $P'(x, v)$ may be arbitrary.*

Proof of Theorem 1 is omitted due to lack of space. It is an open question whether grouping is always necessary in case predicate P cannot be rewritten into one of the two forms given above.

Generally, a nested query may be processed by applying nest join operators, possibly followed by (nested) function applications (e.g. projections) and selections. However, sometimes nest join operators may be replaced by flat join operators. For a two-block query, in case the predicate between the two blocks can be rewritten into a calculus expression of the first format, involving a non-negated existential quantifier, a semijoin operation will provide the correct result. If it is possible to rewrite the predicate into a calculus expression involving a negated existential quantifier, then the flat join operation needed is the antijoin operation. The join predicate is $P'(x, G(x, y)) \wedge Q(x, y)$. (Remember that the semi-and antijoin operations are defined as follows. Let X and Y be tables (sets of tuples having possibly complex attributes), and let P be a predicate, then the semijoin operation $X \ltimes_{x,y:P} Y$ is defined as $\{x \mid x \in X \wedge \exists y \in Y\ (P(x, y))\}$

and the antijoin operation $X \triangleright_{x,y:P} Y$ as $\{x \mid x \in X \wedge \nexists y \in Y\,(P(x,y))\}$.)

Examples of predicates that may or may not be rewritten into the desired format are listed in Table 2. Predicates above the separation line are predicates that may occur in SQL (being a subset of TM); predicates below the separation line are specific TM predicates involving set-valued attributes.

$P(x,z)$	$P'(x,v)$
$z = \emptyset$	$\nexists v \in z\,(true)$
$z \neq \emptyset$	$\exists v \in z\,(true)$
$count(z) = 0$	$\nexists v \in z\,(true)$
$x.a = count(z)$	
$x.a \in z$	$\exists v \in z\,(v = x.a)$
$x.a \notin z$	$\nexists v \in z\,(v = x.a)$
$x.a \subset z$	
$x.a \supset z$	
$x.a \subseteq z$	
$x.a \supseteq z$	$\nexists v \in z\,(v \notin x.a)$
$x.a \not\supseteq z$	$\exists v \in z\,(v \notin x.a)$
$x.a = z$	
$x.a \cap z = \emptyset$	$\nexists v \in z\,(v \in x.a)$
$x.a \cap z \neq \emptyset$	$\exists v \in z\,(v \in x.a)$
$x.a \ni z$	
$\forall w \in x.a\,(w \subseteq z)$	
$\forall w \in x.a\,(w \supseteq z)$	$\nexists v \in z\,(\exists w \in x.a : (v \notin w))$

Table 2. Rewriting TM predicates

8 Query Processing Example

In this section, we illustrate our ideas by means of an example concerning an acyclic query with nesting in the WHERE clause in which correlation predicates are all neighbour predicates (having free variables declared in the immediately surrounding block).

In a preprocessing phase, predicates between query blocks are rewritten into calculus expressions if possible. The purpose of this rewrite phase is to determine whether nest join operations may be replaced by flat join operations (semi- or antijoin), as indicated in the previous section.

Nested queries are processed by performing a number of join operations and executing a number of function applications (for example projections) and selections on the join results. If predicates between query blocks require grouping, a nest join operator is applied; if predicates do not need grouping a flat join operation is executed. Replacement of a nest join operator by a semijoin or antijoin operator is advantageous because the semi- and antijoin can be implemented more efficiently than the nest (or regular) join operator. Note that, like the semijoin, the antijoin operation may be implemented as a modification of the regular join. Consider the following query:

```
SELECT x
FROM X x
WHERE x.a ⊆ SELECT y.a   (P1)
            FROM Y y
            WHERE x.b = y.b ∧
                  y.c ⊆ SELECT z.c   (P2)
                        FROM Z z
                        WHERE y.d = z.d
```

Predicates P_1 and P_2 between query blocks do require grouping (see Table 2), so we may have the following execution strategy:

(1) A nest join with operands Y and Z on join predicate $y.d = z.d$. Each element of Z satisfying the join predicate is projected on the c attribute. The result of this step is the set: $T_1 = \{y \mathbin{++} \langle zs = \{z.c \mid z \in Z \wedge y.d = z.d\}\rangle \mid y \in Y\}$. Note zs is an arbitrary label.
(2) The result of (1) is restricted such that $y.c \subseteq y.zs$: $\{y \mid y \in T_1 \wedge y.c \subseteq y.zs\}$.
(3) The result of (2) is nest joined with X on join predicate $x.b = y.b$ and projected on attribute a. (A projection of (2) on attributes a and b may proceed the nest join operation.) We now have: $T_3 = \{x \mathbin{++} \langle ys = \{y.a \mid y \in T_2 \wedge x.b = y.b\}\rangle \mid x \in X\}$. Again, label ys is arbitrary.
(4) Finally, the result of (3) is restricted such that $x.a \subseteq x.ys$ and projected on the attributes of X (attributes a and b): $T_4 = \{\langle a = x.a, b = x.b\rangle \mid x \in T_3 \wedge x.a \subseteq x.ys\}$.

Now assume that the operators $\subseteq$ in predicates P_1 and P_2 are changed in $\in$ and $\notin$, respectively, then the nest join operation in (1) may be replaced by an antijoin operation, and the nest join in (3) may be replaced by a semijoin operation. The additional join predicates are $y.c = z.c$ and $x.a = y.a$, respectively.

9 Conclusions and Future Work

As in relational systems supporting SQL, in complex object models supporting an SQL-like query language optimization of nested queries is an important issue. A naive way to handle nested queries is by nested-loop processing. However, it is better to transform nested queries into flat, or join queries, because join queries can be implemented in many different ways. In a complex object model, it is not always possible to flatten nested queries–in this paper, we have described a class of nested SFW-expressions that can be flattened without problem. For those nested queries that cannot be transformed into join queries we have introduced the nest join operator, allowing correct and efficient processing of general nested queries.

Future work concerns a number of issues. We need a formal algorithm to translate general SFW-query blocks of TM into the algebra, also taking into account nesting in the SELECT clause, multiple subqueries, and multiple nesting levels (including cyclic queries). Logical optimization (rewriting algebraic expressions) may follow the translation process. Therefore, the algebraic properties of the nest join operator have to be further investigated, by analogy with for example the work of [11] concerning the outerjoin operator.

Acknowledgements

We thank our colleagues Rolf de By and Paul Grefen for comments on earlier drafts of this paper.

References

1. Bal, R. et al.: The TM Manual version 2.0. University of Twente, Enschede (1993)
2. Balsters, H., de By, R.A., and Zicari, R.: Typed Sets as a Basis for Object-Oriented Database Schemas. Proceedings ECOOP, Kaiserslautern (1993)
3. Balsters, H. and de Vreeze, C.C.: A Semantics of Object-Oriented Sets. Proceedings 3rd International Workshop on Database Programming Languages, Nafplion, Greece (1991)
4. Dayal, U.: Of Nests and Trees: A Unified Approach to Processing Queries That Contain Nested Subqueries, Aggregates, and Quantifiers. Proceedings VLDB, Brighton (1987)
5. Ganski, R.A. and Wong, A.K.T.: Optimization of Nested SQL Queries Revisited. Proceedings SIGMOD (1987)
6. Kiesling, W.: SQL-like and QUEL-like Correlation Queries with Aggregates Revisited. Memorandum UCB/ERL 84/75, Berkeley (1984)
7. Kim, W.: On Optimizing an SQL-like Nested Query. ACM Transactions on Database Systems 7 3 (1982) 443–469
8. Muralikrishna, M.: Optimization and Dataflow Algorithms for Nested Tree Queries. Proceedings VLDB, Amsterdam (1989)
9. Muralikrishna, M.: Improved Unnesting Algorithms for Join Aggregate SQL Queries. Proceedings VLDB. Vancouver, 1992.
10. Pistor, P. and Andersen, F.: Designing a Generalized NF^2 Model with an SQL-type Language Interface. Proceedings VLDB, Kyoto (1986)
11. Rosenthal, A. and Galindo-Legaria, C.: Query Graphs, Implementing Trees, and Freely-Reorderable Outerjoins. Proceedings SIGMOD, Atlantic City (1990)
12. Schek, H.J. and Scholl, M.H.,: The Relational Model with Relation-Valued Attributes. Information Systems 11 2 (1986) 137–147
13. Scholl, M.H.: Theoretical Foundations of Algebraic Optimization Utilizing Unnormalized Relations. Proceedings First International Conference on Database Theory. LNCS 243, Springer-Verlag (1986)

A Multi-Threaded Architecture for Prefetching in Object Bases

Carsten A. Gerlhof and Alfons Kemper

Universität Passau, Lehrstuhl für Dialogorientierte Systeme,
Fakultät für Mathematik und Informatik, D-94030 Passau, Germany,
[*gerlhof* | *kemper*]@db.fmi.uni-passau.de

Abstract. We propose a generic architectural framework, a *multi-threaded* run-time system for client/server architectures, which facilitates the integration, exchange and extension of various prefetching techniques. To demonstrate the viability of this architecture two prefetching techniques are incorporated: a *predictor-based* technique—which consists of a separate predictor component in the run-time system—and a *code-based* technique—which provides an explicit prefetch statement at the programming interface. Our quantitative analysis indicates that (static) code-based techniques are a promising alternative to expensive monitoring-based predictors.

1 Introduction

The fate of object-oriented database systems will largely depend on their performance compared to currently employed database technology. Database management systems bridge the gap between the two-level memory hierarchy by transferring objects between (volatile) main memory and (persistent) secondary storage. Unfortunately, the gap between disks and high-speed memories has widened. Therefore paging is now less effective than it used to be. As Wilkes [Wil92] already pointed out, there is an urgent need to reexamine memory management at a fundamental level. This holds definitely for client/server systems where the I/O costs are mainly determined by network latency and server utilization. To illustrate this problem we adapt an example from [KL91]. Consider a client/server system where the appropriate CPU costs for a regular buffer miss are 200 high-level statements. Assuming an application with 1000 statements and read or write operations every four statements, the application will be blocked over 30% of the time, even with 99% buffer hit ratio.

Prefetching is an optimization technique which loads pages in the database buffer *before* the application requests them. The goal of prefetching is to minimize buffer miss latency by overlapping computations and I/O. In the above example 500 program statements can be overlapped if we prefetch the fault pages timely, thus, we would save 30% running time in total. Prefetching techniques have already been proposed and investigated for virtual memory systems a long time ago [Jos70, BS76]. But in database management systems prefetching has not yet received enough attention. There are two reasons for that:

- For database applications prediction of page/object sequences is more complicated because of the overall complex structure of databases.
- Implementation of a software prefetching mechanism is not a trivial task. Only for microprocessors solutions are well-known [BC91, FP91, KL91, RL92].

Although some promising prefetching techniques have recently been proposed for database systems [WZ86, PZ91, CKV93], most of these techniques still have to prove their viability in a *real* system environment For this purpose, we propose a generic architectural framework, a *multi-threaded* run-time system for client/server architectures, which facilitates the integration, exchange and extension of various prefetching techniques. Threads can easily be exchanged or added to satisfy different requirements of different prefetching techniques. To demonstrate the viability of this architecture two prefetching techniques are incorporated: a *predictor-based* technique—which consists of a separate predictor component in the run-time system—and a *code-based* technique—which provides an explicit prefetch statement at the programming interface.

The paper is organized as follows. In Section 2 we first present a classification scheme for prefetching techniques and we give an overview of related work. Section 3 introduces the multi-threaded prefetching architecture and its implementation. In Section 4 benchmark results for a large variety of parameters for the two most promising prefetching techniques [MLG92, CKV93] are presented. The pros and cons of both approaches and some remaining open problems are summarized in Section 5. Section 6 concludes the paper.

2 Classification of Prefetching Techniques

Prefetching techniques can be classified along two dimensions: The *prediction mechanism* and the *unit of prediction*. Methods for predicting future references will be surveyed first.

Most of the prefetching techniques found in the literature use a separate *predictor component* to determine the application's behavior in the near future. Predictors can either be *strategy-based* [Jos70, Tri76, KE90, FP91] or *training-based* [BS76, Smi78, BC91, PZ91, CKV93] or *structure-based* [CK89, KGM91, Gem91]. *Strategy-based* predictors incorporate an explicit programmed strategy whereas *training-based* predictors require extensive *monitoring* for consolidating the statistics during run-time. Future references of an application are predicted by exploiting the reference patterns obtained in the past. *Structure-based* predictors are represented directly by the object net itself together with one common traversal (e.g., depth-first). In contrast, code-based techniques make use of an explicit non-blocking (i.e., *asynchronously*) working, prefetch statement at the user level, which the run-time system must provide. Generally, the insertion of such an instruction in the application's source code is left to the user. For compiler optimization, however, there already exist some promising proposals for automatically generating the prefetch statements in combination with *code motion*. But none of theses techniques—as far as the authors know—has yet been implemented and investigated for database systems.

The other dimension concerns the *unit of prediction*. Many techniques used in the past—mainly in operating systems—predict sequences of *pages* whereas in the last years some techniques were proposed for database systems which try to predict sequences of *objects*.

The following table shows the related work according to the classification scheme:

Prediction mechanism	Unit of prediction	
	Objects	Pages
Predictor-based	[CK89, KGM91] [BC91, Gem91, PZ91]	[Jos70, BS76, Tri76, Smi78] [FP91, KE90, CKV93]
Code-based	[WZ86, KL91, CKP91] [RL92, CB92, MLG92]	UNIX *madvise*

Predictor-Based Prefetching Techniques. One essential characteristic of predictor based prefetching techniques is the *time of prefetching*. Basically, there exist two classes of prefetching policies: (1) prefetching at every reference and (2) prefetching only at buffer misses. The prediction component is represented by an universal predictor $\mathcal{P}$. We divide predictors in two classes: fast predictors and slow predictors. Fast predictors employ a simple table lookup or they are strategy-based [Jos70, BS76, Smi78, Tri76, KE90]. Slow predictors require more prediction time [CK89, KGM91, Gem91, PZ91, CKV93]. Therefore, in the latter case prediction should take place in a separate *coroutine* to overlap computation with I/O caused by the buffer miss.

Code-Based Prefetching Techniques. As already mentioned in [BC91, KL91] complex data structures like linked lists or binary trees are a hard challenge for code-based prefetching techniques because the reference stream is entirely data dependent. The same holds for object-oriented database applications where mainly path expressions (reference chains) are traversed. In the following example below we show how an iteration through a list of part objects can be supported by code-based prefetching:

(a) Original Code

```
for(i := 0; i < len; i++) begin
  list.n_th[ i ].access;
end for;
```

(b) Transformed Code

```
P1: prefetch(list.n_th[ k ]);
P2: for(i := 0; i < len − k; i++) begin
      prefetch(list.n_th[ i + k + 1 ]);
      list.n_th[ i ].access;
    end for;
P3: for(i := len − k; i < len; i++) begin
      list.n_th[ len − 1 ].access;
    end for;
```

Here, we prefetch one object k iterations ahead. Therefore, we split the loop in three parts [MLG92]: the first part (P1) does the initial prefetching, in the second part (P2) references and prefetching is done and the third part (P3) constitutes the trailer of the loop without any prefetching.

Prefetching Performance Measures. As the previous discussion motivates, the *prediction accuracy* [PZ91] would be an intuitive way to measure the performance of prefetching techniques. Unfortunately, there is no guarantee that prefetched objects/pages are resident in the buffer by the time they are really accessed. Therefore, a more realistic measure is the ***reduction of buffer faults*** [Jos70, BS76, Smi78, PZ91, CKV93]. But there are some disadvantages when considering only buffer faults:

- When a prefetched item is pending, the application ***stalls*** until the item is available. This waiting time reduces the total running time and is not reflected by buffer faults.
- The computation for prediction can be very expensive, especially for space-consuming predictors which do not fit entirely in main memory.
- Operating system implementation details (size of the internal socket buffers, implementation of TCP/IP protocol, asynchronous notification) have a great impact on running time because they affect the total overhead of prefetching; e.g., the more items arrive asynchronously the more the CPU overhead is increased.
- The additional network traffic caused by prefetching also affects a regular demand fetch. Therefore, prefetching can increase the costs for regular buffer faults [BC91, KL91].

Summarizing the above arguments we conclude that buffer faults alone do not suffice to assess prefetching [KE90, KL91, MLG92]. Instead, the ***total running time (RT)*** of an application or the ***speed-up factor*** [FP91] seem to be the only practical evaluation criteria for prefetching. Consequently, in this paper we used the relative ***savings in running time*** which is computed as follows:

$$savings = \frac{(RT_{no\ prefetching} - RT_{with\ prefetching})}{RT_{no\ prefetching}} * 100$$

3 A Multi-Threaded Client/Server Architecture

In this section we focus on the general architecture for prefetching in object bases. First, we give an overview by outlining the new components which are essential for the realization of prefetching in a client/server environment. Afterwards, we discuss some intrinsic details of the basic threads and their interaction.

Lightweight processes (threads) are independent units of control within a regular (heavyweight) process. Context switches between threads are much faster than that of processes and cooperation primitives—like concepts for mutual exclusion—can be realized very efficiently at the user level, thus avoiding expensive calls to the operating system [Mue93]. In the following we present how threads can be used for prefetching and how they could be integrated in a page server architecture:

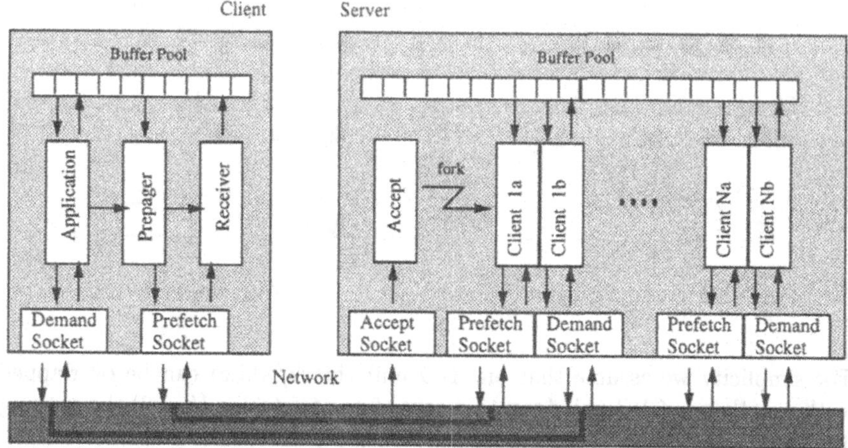

The server maintains two separate sockets with two associated threads for every connected client: one socket/thread for demand requests and one socket/thread for prefetch requests. In contrast to [PZ91], both sockets are given the same priority. We believe—and empirically verified—that the benefits from prefetching strongly depend on timely satisfaction of prefetch requests. Therefore, we don't want to run the risk that regular demands *overtake* prefetch requests. This becomes all the more likely if many clients are present and the demand requests are given higher priority. Otherwise, the gain achieved by prefetching becomes negligible.

At the client side predictor-based prefetching is implemented by three threads: the *application thread*, the *prepage thread*, and the *receiver thread*. The prepager is responsible for predicting and requesting pages. At buffer fault time the application thread notifies the prepager about the page number causing the fault and some special information about the current context (e.g., the working set). After the application thread has requested the faulting page from the server it will block on its next receive operation causing the prepager to be scheduled next. The prepager now computes the set of non-resident pages according to its page predictor $\mathcal{P}$ and sends the entire request to the server. Asynchronously incoming pages are handled by the receiver. For code-based prefetching we omitted the *prefetch thread* because, in this case, it seems more natural to let the prefetch statements directly be executed by the application thread. The buffer policy is similiar to [PZ91, CKV93]; i.e., prefetched pages are moved to the top of an LRU buffer as if they were demand fetched.

Because the implementation of the reception of a *set* of pages is more important than it seems to be on first glance, we will spend a little more attention on it. There are two major aspects: (1) The server has to maintain the ordering of page requests and (2) the receiver thread must give back control to the application thread as soon as it has received an entire prefetched page. Otherwise, the application thread cannot continue and, thus, computation cannot be overlapped with I/O. To explain this in more detail consider the next figure:

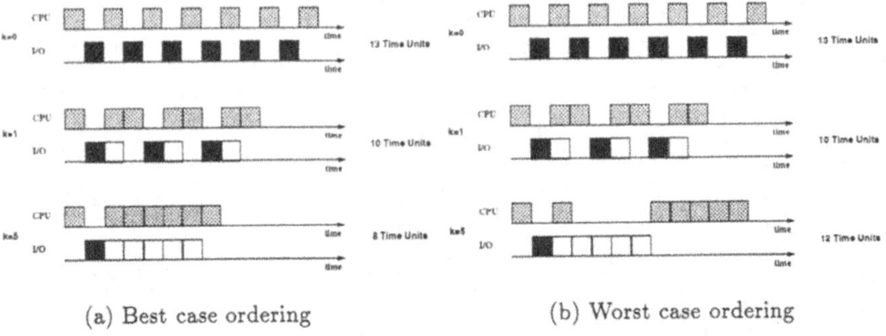

(a) Best case ordering (b) Worst case ordering

For simplicity we assume that one I/O unit (black/white) can be overlapped with exactly one CPU unit (grey). In case of no prefetching ($k = 0$) the running time is 13 time units. If we prefetch $k = 5$ pages (white) at page fault time and the server keeps ordering (case (a)), these I/O units overlap with computation, thus 5 units of running time are saved in total. If the ordering is reverse, i.e., the next (faulting) page comes last and the last page comes first, the application would block until *all* prefetched pages are received (case (b)). This shows that receiving a set of prefetched pages must be *interruptable*. Otherwise, if we receive all pages en bloc this would have the same effect as worst case ordering.

In our implementation a prefetch request is forced to be executed in any case. Therefore, pages are given different *states* according to a traffic light sequence: Resident pages are *green*, prefetched pages which are pending are assigned the color *red*. If the application tries to access a page in state *red*, the page's state changes to *yellow* and the application thread is blocked. As soon as the page becomes available the state changes to green, the receiving thread unblocks the waiting thread and gives up control in favor of the application thread.

The multi-threaded architecture is implemented with the LWP-package included in the SunOS 4.1.3 operating system. The implementation of prefetching in UNIX is currently affected by several problems: (1) There is still no efficient operating system support for threads, (2) the UNIX (stream) file system completely lacks support for *multiple* asynchronous notifications of incoming data and (3) the socket interface lacks operations to manipulate the internal buffer. As already pointed out in [Sto81] modern operating systems should evolute towards supporting database management functions more efficiently. We stress that an efficient implementation of prefetching will strongly depend on the capabilities of the underlying operating system.

4 Assessment of Prefetching Techniques

In this section we present some typical results of our extensive benchmarking. Our goal was to assess the basic prefetching principles—i.e. predictor-based and code-based techniques—and not to investigate the quality of the prediction mechanism. The following aspects are subject to a closer investigation: (1) the impact of clustering on prefetching, (2) the effect of physical versus logical OIDs on prefetching, (3) the effect of varying computation peaks, (4) the overhead of prefetching induced by high locality, and (5) the network traffic in a multi-client environment.

4.1 Benchmark Environment

Prefetching is affected by many parameters. Therefore, it is very important to use a simple benchmark for obtaining meaningful results. More complicated benchmarks have irregular structures (making prediction difficult) or are indeterministic (making interpretation of results difficult).

The structure of our database constitutes a list object containing 10000 objects. The size of the objects are uniformly 300 bytes, the page size is 4096 bytes. We performed a linear scan through all elements of the list. Note that after every time an element in the list is accessed, we return to the list object to obtain the reference to the next element. Thus, the trace looks like this: $id_0, id_1, id_0, id_2, \ldots, id_0, id_n$, where $id_1, \ldots, id_n$ are the OIDs of the element objects of the list id_0. The quality of the following techniques is compared:

- predictor-based prefetching using a Markov predictor for pages [CKV93],
- code-based prefetching using the technique proposed in [MLG92], and
- no prefetching, applying only a standard LRU buffer policy.

The Markov predictor constitutes a *page transition graph* which is constructed by monitoring the page accesses only of the element objects.[1] E.g., if we assume that two objects fit into a page and the database is clustered, then we would get the following (linear) sequence of pages: $S_0, S_0, S_1, S_1, \ldots$ If we have no clustering—that is the objects are randomly distributed over the pages—then the sequence will form a general graph, thus, making prediction more difficult. In our predictor-based technique we prefetched 1 page ahead and in the code-based prefetching we prefetched 1 object 1 iteration ahead, if not stated otherwise. The clustering algorithm used in this paper is a *greedy graph partitioning* (*GGP*) algorithm which yields good-quality clustering under acceptable running time for object bases [GKKM93].

4.2 Prefetching under Different Clusters

In this experiment we investigate the influence of different storage characteristics on prefetching assuming physical OIDs. Because the time between two object references is very crucial for prefetching (for overlapping with I/O), we plotted the *inter-reference time* (*IRT*) in microseconds against the x-axis. The inter-reference time is artificially generated by an appropriate **loop**-statement in our applications. Having no significant inter-reference time ($IRT \approx 0$) often means that—apart from the fact that there is a constant system overhead—in case

[1] If we had monitored the list object, too, we would have needed a second-order Markov predictor.

of no clustering "staccato-like" sequences of page faults will be generated. The main observation in Fig. 1(a) is that both prefetching techniques perform better than LRU—in almost all cases. With good clustering code-based techniques suffer from unnecessary requests for already resident objects; thus, increasing running-time. As IRT increases the code-based technique is able to overlap I/O with more computations and, finally, outperforms the predictor-based technique. Note that overlaps are well indicated by a lower gradient compared to the LRU curve. Remember that in the predictor case we prefetch only at page fault times whereas in the code-based technique prefetching is independent from any page accesses; therefore, reducing memory latency for every page fault uniformly. It is just these little savings accumulated step by step that makes the code-based technique superior at the end. The maximal savings in running-time are 27% for the predictor-based ($IRT = 0$) and 10% for the code-based technique ($IRT = 1500$).[2] Fig. 1(b) exhibits that techniques that are based on prediction of pages are very sensitive to clustering. Here, the Markov graph formed by the cluster is not precise enough to predict the exact pages. The need for a Markov Predictor of an order higher than 1 is evident. But it is difficult to determine the best order for all applications and all clusters in advance. In contrast, the prediction accuracy of the code-based technique is 100% and nearly every prefetch request results in requesting a non-resident page, thereby eliminating unnecessary prefetching requests. However, for applications with *high locality* this does not hold. The maximum savings for the code-based technique are 28% ($IRT = 1500$). But Fig. 1(b) also indicates that at $IRT = 0$ we have a small penalty. Therefore, the curve of the code-based technique needs a more detailed explanation. Let IPT be the inter-page-fault time, let T_{Pref} denote the CPU overhead induced by the prefetch statement and let T_{Fault} denote the time for a buffer miss. Then, we classify the effect of prefetching into three cases:

- Case 1: $IPT < T_{Pref} \leq T_{Fault}$. There is a loss of $T_{Pref} - IPT$.[3]
- Case 2: $T_{Pref} < IPT \leq T_{Fault}$. There is a gain of $IPT - T_{Pref}$.
- Case 3: $T_{Pref} < T_{Fault} \leq IPT$. There is a gain of $T_{Fault} - T_{Pref}$.

In the case of an inter-page-fault time of zero, i.e., no locality and no significant inter-reference time, there cannot be any gain through prefetching because there is no CPU time to overlap. This corresponds to Case 1. Case 2 occurs as soon as there are some computations which exceed the prefetch CPU overhead ($T_{Pref} \leq IPT$). Then, we have a reduction in running-time. Additionally, due to random buffer hits some prefetch requests could be executed completely; therefore, we save the next request message to the server and the running time is further reduced. However, as soon as the maximum overlap is reached increasing IRT also increases running-time.

[2] Note that with increasing inter-reference time, computations dominate over I/O—thus, reducing the savings in running-time achievable by prefetching.

[3] Because the code-based techniques do not prefetch exactly at page fault times, taking the IPT corresponds to the best case.

4.3 Prefetching With Logical Object Identifiers

To investigate the impact of the additional overhead induced by mapping logical OIDs to physical addresses we conducted the same experiment as in the preceding section for an object model utilizing logical OIDs (Fig. 2). Compared to Fig. 1 the overhead for code-based techniques substantially increases when relying on logical OIDs. This is exactly what we expected. Under good clustering, the benefits of code-based techniques—compared to LRU—are turned into the opposite: the running-time increases by up to 50%. However the gradient is much lower than for the LRU curve. This indicates that the "break-even point" becomes more unfavorable in terms of inter-reference time. For random clustering I/O waiting time dominates. Thus, the additional computations induced by the mapping can easily be compensated for. Note that for $IRT = 0$ there is, in reality, not an inter-reference time of zero because the mapping consumes some CPU time. Additionally, we have some random buffer hits (remember that we have poor clustering but a large buffer), thus the mapping causes a further prolongation of the inter-page-fault time. This is indeed the reason why here is—compared to Fig. 1(b)—a saving in running-time because the extra computations suffice to execute some overlapping prefetches. On the other hand, the predictor-based technique is not affected by the translation of logical OIDs because the prediction is independent of that mapping. This is, of course, only true for page-oriented predictors. When the predictor is object-oriented it would suffer just as severely as the code-based technique.

4.4 Prefetching under Varying Computation Peaks

The benefits of prefetching are based on overlapping computations with I/O; i.e., the *inter-page-fault time* must be "well behaved". In our experiments we controlled the inter-page-fault time by varying the inter-reference time. In real applications the inter-page-fault time is generally not constant, e.g., it is highly influenced by the buffer size and the locality of an application. In practice, this will reduce the performance gain achieved by prefetching. To study these effects we introduced *cycles* of computation peaks. We varied the inter-reference time for the i-th reference according to the following formula:

$$\mathrm{IRT}(i) = \begin{cases} cycle * peak & : \text{ if } \imath \bmod cycle = 0 \\ 0 & : \text{ otherwise} \end{cases}$$

Fig. 3 shows the running-time for random clustering, physical OIDs, and for $peak = 500, 1000, 1500$. We omitted the predictor-based technique here because the last experiments showed no improvement. As expected, computations cannot as easily be overlapped as in the uniform case. For all peak levels a substantial increase in running-time can be observed with increasing cycle length. But in most cases the running-time still remains below the corresponding LRU curve. Under good clustering no significant differences can be observed between the code-based and the predictor-based technique, because many subsequent hits on the same page leave the inter-page-fault time nearly invariant.

4.5 Prefetching under High Locality

In the previous subsections we only investigated prefetching under strict (logical) sequentiality. In this experiment we used a nested loop join over two lists of 300 elements. Because of the repeated scanning of the inner list, very high locality is provided. We simulated different scenarios, i.e., joining small or large lists, by using two buffer sizes: a small buffer (75% of the working set) and a large buffer (125% of the working set). Here, the working set basically consists of the set of pages in the inner list. Dependent on the buffer size we used three prefetching schemes for the code-based technique: prefetching for both lists, prefetching only for the outer loop in the case of a small buffer, and prefetching only for the inner loop in the case of a large buffer. The other remaining cases make no sense. We omitted this variant for the predictor-based technique, since the monitored sequences are independent of the buffer size.[4] The inter-reference time was set to 0 because a comparison inside a join loop is very fast. The savings in running-time are shown in the following table:

Working Set	Predictor-based	Code-based		
		Both	Inner	Outer
125%	-23%	-63%		+18%
75%	+17%	-17%	-16%	

Only in 2 out of 6 cases prefetching achieves savings in running-time. Surprisingly, the predictor-based technique suffers under high locality—there is a prolongation of running-time by 23%. The reason is that in this benchmark the prediction always suggests pages which are already resident: because we prefetch only on page fault times there cannot be any gain because the entire inner list fits into the buffer. The next page fault can only occur in the outer loop. The overhead induced under high locality is more evident for the code-based technique: the negative "savings" by 63% indicates that prefetching here must be considered harmful. Only after elimination of unnecessary prefetch requests, i.e. for the inner loop, the code-based technique can achieve reasonable savings (18%). In case of no locality, we have similar results to Fig. 1(a): the predictor-based technique outperforms the code-based technique at $IRT = 0$.

4.6 Prefetching in a Multi-Client Environment

The cost of a buffer fault essentially depends on the network traffic and on the number of clients connected to the server. In this experiment we focus on the performance of prefetching in presence of many heavy I/O-weighted clients. Therefore, we ran up to 5 additional special-purpose clients in parallel which produced 10000 page requests without any computations in between two page accesses. We used the same configuration as in Fig. 1(a) with $IRT = 1500$. To

[4] Note that there is no (trivial) mapping of monitored sequences to high-level statements.

study the effect of requesting a set of pages, i.e., lower tag-along costs for the additionally requested pages, we prefetched up to 15 pages in this experiment. For the code-based technique we prefetched $k_o = 1, 195$ objects per iteration ahead, the predictor-based technique prefetched $k_p = 1, 15$ pages ahead. Assuming that 13 objects fit into a page, prefetching 195 objects is comparable to prefetching 15 pages in the predictor case. Fig. 4 shows that both prefetching techniques perform clearly better than LRU. Consider the $k_o = k_p = 1$ case first. The predictor-based technique clearly outperforms the code-based technique when more than one client is connected to the server. Prefetching one object one iteration ahead does not suffice to cover buffer miss latency. Remember that in this experiment we have high temporal locality through good clustering. If the code-based technique discovers a non-resident object, it is usually too late. The predictor-based technique "looks" more than one object ahead because it is based on entire pages. Subsequent buffer hits on the current demand page suffice to hide latency. Prefetching a large set of objects/pages is more advantageous in a multi-client environment. The reason can be found in the low tag-along costs for a single set-request. From this experiment we conclude that the inter-reference time is not as important as in the dedicated single-client case. Here, the inter-page-fault time is mainly influenced by the increased server response time.

5 Discussion

In the preceding section we benchmarked the two most promising prefetching techniques in our experimental system architecture: a predictor-based page-oriented technique and a code-based object-oriented technique. Both techniques can substantially reduce the running-time of an application. However, the positive effect cannot be obtained in all cases. We conclude that the advantage of one technique may turn out as the disadvantage of the other technique and vice versa.

The most important parameter on prefetching is clustering. Prefetching tries to fill the "holes" still left by clustering. The first goal, however, should be to maximize locality by clustering. If this does not suffice to achieve reasonable performance—e.g. when clustering according to many diverging access patterns clustering is less effective than supporting only a single application—then prefetching is the method of choice. As our preceding quantitative analysis indicates, the degree of locality is an important hint for the applicability of prefetching techniques. For applications with high locality, when running on a well clustered database, prefetching often achieves only negligible gains. The most cost effective factor here is the residency check.

The prediction of the access behavior of non-standard database applications is very difficult. In further experiments we observed that the prediction accuracy for page-oriented predictors drops significantly when the page capacity (in objects) is large and, in addition, the *degree of sharing* is high or when the database is accessed through many different *entry points*. Accessing many shared objects through different objects within the same application makes monitoring less accurate.

Our analysis yields that *no* prefetching technique performs superior for *all* cases. Further pros and cons of both techniques are summarized in the table below.

Predictor-Based Page-Oriented	**Code-Based Object-Oriented**
+ Adaptive and variable prefetching via feedback at run-time possible.	– Fix compile-time made scheduling distance to hide memory latency.
– – Prediction accuracy very sensitive towards cluster quality.	+ Independent of storage structure.
– Prefetching only possible for monitored sequences.	++ No monitoring. Prefetching possible for all program paths.
+ Prediction of long sequences very easy.	– Only limited look-ahead.
+ Small overhead in case of high locality and large buffers.	– Many unnecessary prefetch statements. High overhead.

6 Conclusion

In this paper we distinguished two dimensions for classifying prefetching techniques: (1) the prediction mechanism and (2) the unit of prediction. Along the first dimension we distinguished *predictor-based* versus *code-based* techniques, along the second dimension we distinguished *object-oriented* versus *page-oriented* prefetching techniques. To prove the viability of prefetching techniques we proposed a generic architectural framework, a *multi-threaded* run-time system architecture, which facilitates the integration, exchange and extension of prefetching techniques. We outlined the realization of the two most promising techniques, a predictor-based page-oriented technique and a code-based object-oriented technique, in our architecture. Our extensive quantitative analysis—only a part of which could be presented in this paper—indicates that *no* prefetching technique performs superior in *all* cases. However, (static) code-based techniques are a promising alternative to (dynamic) predictor-based techniques:

- monitoring sequences of pages/objects requires an extensive "training" phase during which the statistics have to become consolidated.
- static code-based prefetching enables prefetching for all program paths, especially when a training phase is not possible, e.g. for CIM applications bound to technical processes.

In conclusion, we showed that prefetching in database management systems is feasible by today's software technology.

Acknowledgement This work was supported by the German Research Council DFG under contract Ke 401/6-1. We thank T. Jansen for his help in the implementation and extensive benchmarking of the various prefetching techniques.

References

[BC91] J.-L. Baer and T.-F. Chen. An effective on-chip preloading scheme to reduce data access penalty. In *Proc. of Supercomputing*, pages 176–186, 1991.

[BS76] J.-L. Baier and G.R. Sager. Dynamic improvement of locality in virtual memory systems. *IEEE Trans. Software Eng.*, 2(1):54–62, 1976.

[CB92] T.-F. Chen and J.-L. Baer. Reducing memory latency via non-blocking and prefetching caches. In *Proc. on Architectural Support for Programming Languages and Operating Systems* (ASPLOS), pages 51–61, Oct 1992.

[CK89] E. E. Chang and R. H. Katz. Exploiting inheritance and structure semantics for effective clustering and buffering in an object-oriented DBMS. In *Proc. of the ACM SIGMOD Conf. on Management of Data*, pages 348–357, Portland, OR, May 1989.

[CKP91] D. Callahan, K. Kennedy, and A. Portfield. Software prefetching. In *ASPLOS*, pages 40–52, Santa Clara, California, Apr 1991.

[CKV93] K. M. Curewitz, P. Krishnan, and J. S. Vitter. Practical prefetching via data compression. In *ACM SIGMOD*, pages 43–53, Washington, DC, May 1993.

[FP91] J. W. C. Fu and J. H. Patel. Data prefetching in multiprocessor vector cache memories. In *Proc. of the Intl. Symp. on Computer Architecture*, pages 54–63, May 1991.

[Gem91] GemStone. *Product Overview.* Servio Logic Corporation, 1420 Harbor Bay Parkway, Suite 100, Alameda, CA 94501, U.S.A., Feb 1991.

[GKKM93] C. Gerlhof, A. Kemper, C. Kilger, and G. Moerkotte. Partition-based clustering in object bases: From theory to practice. In *Proc. of the Intl. Conf. on Foundations of Data Organization and Algorithms (FODO)*, volume 730 of *Lecture Notes in Computer Science (LNCS)*, pages 301–316, Chicago, Illinois, Oct 1993, Springer-Verlag.

[Jos70] M. Joseph. An analysis of paging and program behaviour. *Computer Journal*, 13(1):48–54, 1970.

[KE90] D. F. Kotz and C. S. Ellis. Prefetching in file systems for MIMD multiprocessors. *IEEE Trans. on Parallel and Distributed Systems*, 1(2):218–230, Apr 1990.

[KGM91] T. Keller, G. Graefe, and D. Maier. Efficient assembly of complex objects. In *ACM SIGMOD*, pages 148–158, Denver, CO, May 1991.

[KL91] A. C. Klaiber and H. M. Levy. An architecture for software-controlled data prefetching. In *Proc. of the Intl. Symp. on Computer Architecture*, pages 43–53, May 1991.

[MLG92] T. C. Mowry, M. S. Lam, and A. Gupta. Design and evaluation of a compiler algorithm for prefetching. In *ASPLOS*, pages 62–73, Oct 1992.

[Mue93] F. Mueller. A library implementation of POSIX threads under UNIX. In *USENIX*, San Diego, CA, Winter 1993.

[PZ91] M. Palmer and S. B. Zdonik. Fido: A cache that learns to fetch. In *Proc. of the Conf. on Very Large Data Bases (VLDB)*, pages 255–264, Barcelona, Sep 1991.

[RL92] A. Rogers and K. Li. Software support for speculative loads. In *ASPLOS*, pages 38–50, Oct 1992.

[Smi78] A. J. Smith. Sequentiality and prefetching in database systems. *ACM Trans. on Database Systems*, 3(3):223–247, 1978.

[Sto81] M. Stonebraker. Operating system support for database management. *Communications of the ACM*, 24(7):412–418, Jul 1981.

[Tri76] K. S. Trivedi. Prepaging and applications to array algorithms. *IEEE Trans. on Comp.*, 25(9):915–921, Sep 1976.

[Wil92] M. V. Wilkes. The long-term future of operating systems. *Communications of the ACM*, 35(11):23–24/112, Nov 1992.

[WZ86] H. Wedeking and G. Zörntlein. Prefetching in realtime database applications. In *ACM SIGMOD*, pages 215–226, Washington, D.C., 1986.

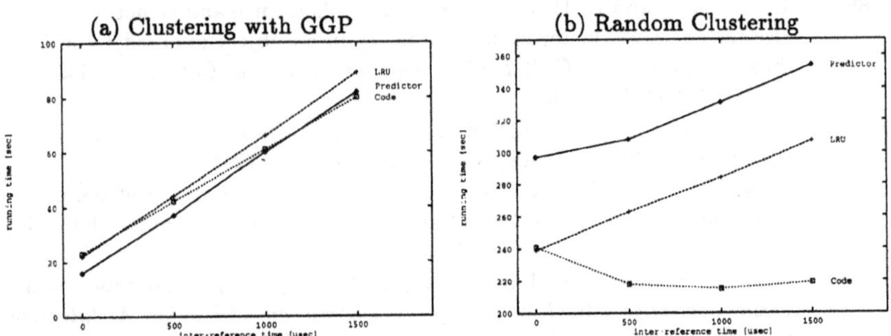

Fig. 1. Performance of Prefetching Techniques with Physical Object Identifiers

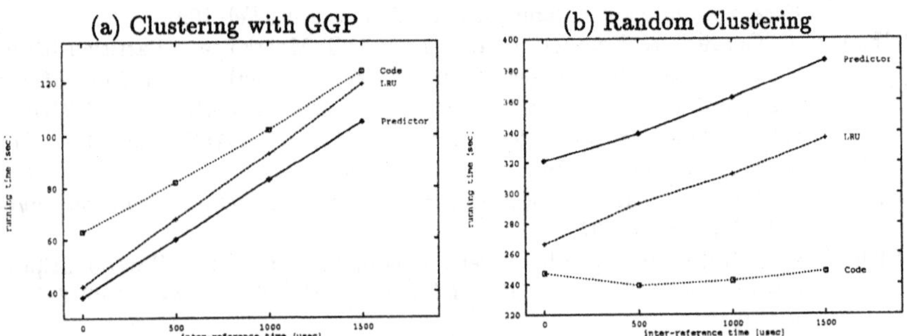

Fig. 2. Performance of Prefetching Techniques with Logical Object Identifiers

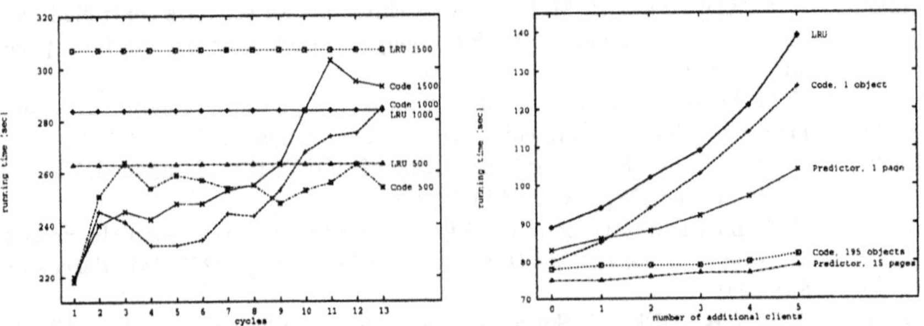

Fig. 3. Performance of the Code-Based Technique under Varying Computation Peaks

Fig. 4. Performance of Prefetching Techniques in a Multi-Client Environment

Supporting Full-Text Information Retrieval with a Persistent Object Store*

Eric W. Brown, James P. Callan, W. Bruce Croft, J. Eliot B. Moss

Department of Computer Science, University of Massachusetts, Amherst, MA 01003, USA

Abstract. The inverted file index common to many full-text information retrieval systems presents unusual and challenging data management requirements. These requirements are usually met with custom data management software. Rather than build this custom software, we would prefer to use an existing database management system. Attempts to do this with traditional (e.g., relational) database management systems have produced discouraging results. Instead, we have used a persistent object store, Mneme, to support the inverted file of a full-text information retrieval system, INQUERY. The result is an improvement in performance along with opportunities for INQUERY to take advantage of the standard data management services provided by Mneme. We describe our implementation, present performance results on a variety of document collections, and discuss the advantages of using a persistent object store to support information retrieval.

1 Introduction

The task of a full-text information retrieval (IR) system is to satisfy a user's information need by identifying the documents in a collection of documents that contain the desired information. This identification process requires a means of locating documents based on their content. A well known mechanism for providing such means is the inverted file index [15].

An inverted file index consists of a record, or inverted list, for each term that appears in the document collection. A term's record contains an entry for every occurrence of the term in the document collection, identifying the document and possibly giving the location of the occurrence or a weight associated with the occurrence. Inverted file indices can become quite large. Some commercial systems contain millions of full-text documents, occupying gigabytes of disk space. An inverted file index for such a collection will contain hundreds of thousands of records, ranging in size from just a few bytes to millions of bytes.

Typically, an IR system that depends on an inverted file index will use custom data management software built from scratch to support the index. An advantage of this approach is that the software is designed specifically to meet the requirements of the particular information retrieval strategy used in the system. A disadvantage is that building such software is difficult and tedious, particularly if it must provide sophisticated features such as concurrency control or recovery.

* This work is supported by the NSF Center for Intelligent Information Retrieval at the University of Massachusetts. Email: {brown, callan, croft, moss}@cs.umass.edu

Instead, we propose using an "off-the-shelf" data management facility, in the form of a persistent object store, to provide the inverted file index service. We have taken the INQUERY full-text retrieval system [20, 3], which originally used a custom B-tree package to provide the inverted file index support, and replaced the B-tree package with the Mneme persistent object store [14]. The result is a system that reaps the benefits of using an existing data management facility without sacrificing performance or functionality. The integrated system actually demonstrates a performance improvement, and the features of the persistent object store offer potential solutions to some of the difficult problems associated with inverted list management.

In the next section we take a closer look at the characteristics of inverted files that make them difficult to support. Next, we describe our integrated software architecture, including details of INQUERY and Mneme. Following that, we present a performance evaluation of the integrated system and discuss the results. In the last two sections we review previous and related work, and offer some concluding remarks. The principle contribution of our work is a demonstration that data management facilities for IR systems need not be custom built in order to obtain superior performance. Additionally, we show how the size distribution characteristics of records in an inverted file index, along with the characteristics of inverted file record access during query processing, can be used to guide decisions regarding persistent store organization and buffer management policy selection.

2 Inverted File Indices

There are three basic operations performed on an inverted file index: creation, lookup, and modification. The operation performed most often is lookup. As the IR system processes queries a lookup is typically performed at least once for each term in the query. Modifications occur less frequently as new documents are added to the collection and old or irrelevant documents are retired from the collection. Creation occurs once when a document collection is first indexed by the IR system, although it may be considered a special case of modification where a number of document additions are batched together.

If we optimize for the common case, lookup should be given the most careful consideration. Efficient lookup requires knowing the size distribution of the records in the file and a characterization of the record access patterns. The size of an inverted list depends on the number of occurrences of the associated term in the document collection. Zipf [23] observed that if the terms in a document collection are ranked by decreasing number of occurrences (i.e., starting with the term that occurs most frequently), there is a constant for the collection that is approximately equal to the product of any given term's frequency and rank order number. The implication is that nearly half of the terms have only one or two occurrences, while a few terms occur very many times.

Figure 1 shows the distribution of inverted list sizes for the TIPSTER document collection used in our performance evaluation below (see Table 1). For a given inverted list size, the figure shows how many records in the inverted file are less than or equal to that size, and how much those records contribute to the total file size. The figure also shows the distribution of sizes for the inverted lists accessed by TIPSTER query set 1.

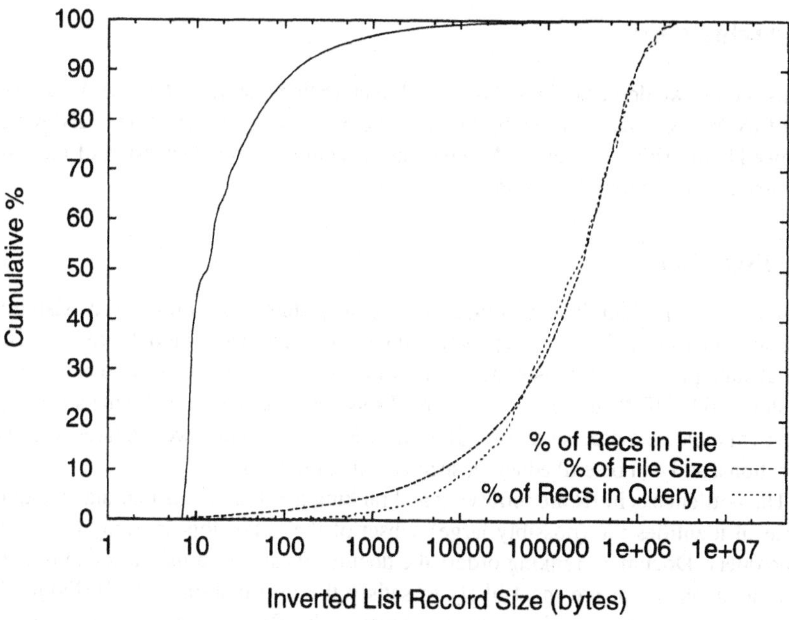

Fig. 1. Cumulative distributions over inverted list size for TIPSTER

The majority of the records accessed are between 10 Kbytes and 1 Mbyte. This size range represents a small percentage of the total number of records in the file, but a large percentage of the total file size. Therefore, we must be prepared to provide efficient access to the majority of the raw data in the file. The strong similarity between the inverted file distribution as a percentage of file size and the query distribution indicates that the former might be used to predict the latter. The same plots for the other collections used in the performance evaluation (not shown here) have similar shapes.

We also observe that there is significant repetition of the terms used from query to query. This can be expected for two reasons. First, a user of an IR system may iteratively refine a query to obtain the desired set of documents. As the query is refined to more precisely represent the user's information need, terms from earlier queries will reappear in later queries. Second, IR systems are often used on specialized collections where every document is related to a particular subject. In this case, there will be terms that are common to a large number of queries, even across multiple users.

Support for modification has traditionally been lacking in IR systems due to their archival nature. The recent trend, however, is towards incremental and dynamic update of document collections and associated index structures. Frequent addition of documents to a collection and modification of existing documents in a collection pose challenging problems for inverted list management. These operations require sophisticated database management features such as concurrency control and versioning, lending further credence to the approach we take below.

3 Architecture

In this section we describe the software architecture that resulted when the B-tree package of INQUERY was replaced by Mneme. We begin with a description of INQUERY, followed by a brief overview of Mneme, and conclude with a discussion of the issues addressed during integration of the two systems.

3.1 INQUERY

INQUERY is a probabilistic information retrieval system based upon a Bayesian inference network model [20, 3]. The power of the inference network model is the consistent formalism it provides for reasoning about evidence of differing types. Extensive testing has shown INQUERY to be one of the best IR systems, as measured by the standard IR metrics of recall and precision [10, 20]. INQUERY is fast, scales well to large document collections, and can be embedded in specialized applications.

The bottlenecks in IR are retrieving and ranking the documents that match a query. Retrieval identifies the (possibly large) subset of the collection that may be relevant to the query. Document ranking orders the documents so that a user can examine first those documents that are most likely to satisfy the information need. In INQUERY, document ranking is a sorting problem, because the Bayesian method of combining evidence assigns a numeric value to each document. Other functionality, for example sophisticated query processing and presentation of results, generally does not affect the speed of the system.

Two of INQUERY's data storage facilities affect the speed of retrieval: a hash dictionary and an inverted file index. INQUERY uses an open-chaining hash dictionary to map text strings (words) to unique integers called *term ids*. The hash dictionary also stores summary statistics for each string and resides entirely in main memory. The inverted file index is organized as a keyed file, using term ids as keys and a B-tree index. There is one record per term. A record has a header containing summary statistics about the term, followed by a list of the documents, and the locations within each document, where the term occurs. The record is stored as a vector of integers in a compressed format. The average compression rate for the four collections in Table 1 is about 60%.

During retrieval, INQUERY performs "term-at-a-time" processing of evidence. That is, it reads the complete record for one term and merges the evidence from that term with the evidence it is accumulating for each document. Then it processes the next term. This approach is fast because it minimizes I/O. However, it requires large amounts of memory for large collections because several inverted lists must be kept in memory simultaneously. A "document-at-a-time" approach, which gathered all of the evidence for one document before proceeding to the next, might scale better to large collections. However, it would be cumbersome with the current custom B-tree package.

3.2 Mneme

The Mneme persistent object store [14] was designed to be efficient and extensible. The basic services provided by Mneme are storage and retrieval of objects, where an object is a chunk of contiguous bytes that has been assigned a unique identifier. Mneme has no notion of type or class for objects. The only structure Mneme is aware of is that objects may contain the identifiers of other objects, resulting in inter-object references.

Objects are grouped into files supported by the operating system. An object's identifier is unique only within the object's file. Multiple files may be open simultaneously, however, so object identifiers are mapped to globally unique identifiers when the objects are accessed. This allows a potentially unlimited number of objects to be created by allocating a new file when the previous file's object identifiers have been exhausted. The number of objects that may be accessed *simultaneously* is bounded by the number of globally unique identifiers (currently 2^{28}).

Objects are physically grouped into *physical segments* within a file. A physical segment is the unit of transfer between disk and main memory and is of arbitrary size. Objects are also logically grouped into *pools*, where a pool defines a number of management policies for the objects contained in the pool, such as how large the physical segments are, how the objects are laid out in a physical segment, how objects are located within a file, and how objects are created. Note that physical segments are not shared between pools. Pools are also required to locate for Mneme any identifiers stored in the objects managed by the pool. This would be necessary, for instance, during garbage collection of the persistent store. Since the pool provides the interface between Mneme and the contents of an object, object format is determined by the pool, allowing objects to be stored in the format required by the application that uses the objects (modulo any translation that may be required for persistent storage, such as conversion of main memory pointers to object identifiers). Pools provide the primary extensibility mechanism in Mneme. By implementing new pool routines, the system can be significantly customized.

The base system provides a number of fundamental mechanisms and tools for building pool routines, including a suite of standard pool routines for file and auxiliary table management. Object lookup is facilitated by *logical segments*, which contain 255 objects logically grouped together to assist in identification, indexing, and location. A hash table is provided that takes an object identifier and efficiently determines if the object is resident in main memory. Support for sophisticated buffer management is provided by an extensible buffering mechanism. Buffers may be defined by supplying a number of standard buffer operations (e.g., allocate and free) in a system defined format. How these operations are implemented determines the policies used to manage the buffer. A pool *attaches* to a buffer in order to make use of the buffer. Mneme then maps the standard buffer operation calls made by the pool to the specific routines supplied by the attached buffer. Additionally, the pool is required to provide a number of "call-back" routines, such as a modified segment save routine, which may be called by a buffer routine.

3.3 The Integrated System

The Mneme version of the inverted index was created by allocating an object for each inverted list in the B-tree file. The Mneme identifier assigned to the object was stored in the INQUERY hash dictionary entry for the associated term. When the inverted list for a term is needed by the query processor, the object identifier for the list is retrieved from the hash dictionary and used to obtain the desired object.

Based on the analysis in Sect. 2 and the features of Mneme, we created three distinct groups of inverted list objects. First, in all of the test collections, approximately 50% of the inverted lists are 12 bytes or less. By allocating a 16 byte object (4 bytes for a size field) for every inverted list less than or equal to 12 bytes, we can conveniently fit a whole logical segment (255 objects) in one 4 Kbyte physical segment. This simplifies both the indexing strategy used to locate these objects in the file and the buffer management strategy for these segments. Inverted lists in this category were allocated in a *small object pool*. Second, a number of inverted lists are so large it is not reasonable to cluster them with other objects in the same physical segment. Instead, these lists are allocated in their own physical segment. All inverted lists larger than 4 Kbytes were allocated in this fashion in a *large object pool*. The remaining inverted lists form the third group of objects and were allocated in a *medium object pool*. These objects are packed into 8 Kbyte physical segments. The physical segment size is based on the disk I/O block size and a desire to keep the segments relatively small so as to reduce the number of unused objects retrieved with each segment.

This partitioning of the objects allows the indexing and buffer management strategies for each group to be customized. Each object pool was attached to a separate buffer, allowing the global buffer space to be divided between the object pools based on expected access patterns and memory requirements. The buffer replacement policy for all of the pools is least recently used (LRU) with a slight optimization. As queries are parsed by INQUERY, a tree is constructed that represents the query in an internal form. Before the tree is processed, we scan it and "reserve" any objects required by the query that are already resident, potentially avoiding a bad replacement choice.

With the above partitioning, the large object pool will still contain a huge range of object sizes. We experimented with further partitioning the large object buffer, but found the best hit rates were achieved with a single buffer of the same total size.

4 Performance Evaluation

We evaluated the persistent object store based INQUERY system by comparing it with the original system. Traditionally, IR system performance has been measured in terms of recall and precision. The portion of the system that determines those factors is fixed across the two systems we are comparing. Instead, we are concerned with execution time, which we measured on a variety of document collections and query sets. Below we describe the execution environment, the experiments, and the results.

4.1 Platform

All of the experiments were run in single user mode on a DECstation 5000/240 (MIPS R3000 CPU[2] clocked at 40 MHz) running ULTRIX[3] V4.2A. The machine was configured with 64 Mbytes of main memory, a 426 Mbyte RZ25 SCSI disk, and a 1.35 Gbyte RZ58 SCSI disk. The machine mounts many of its bin files from another host via NFS,

[2] MIPS and R3000 are trademarks of MIPS Computer Systems.

[3] DECstation and ULTRIX are registered trademarks of Digital Equipment Corporation.

Table 1. Document collection statistics and Mneme buffer sizes (all sizes are in Kbytes)

Collection	# of Docs	Collection Size	# of Terms	Inverted File Size B-Tree	Inverted File Size Mneme	Object Buffer Sizes Small	Object Buffer Sizes Med	Object Buffer Sizes Large
CACM	3204	2136	5944	641	556	12.7	24.4	24
Legal	11953	290529	142721	65840	71296	12.7	97.7	1098
TIPSTER 1	510887	1225712	627078	460836	476904	12.7	341.8	4596
TIPSTER	742358	2103574	846331	768406	789344	12.7	702.5	7806

and so could not be isolated from the network. In fact, the INQUERY system executables were stored on a remote host, although all of the data files accessed during the experiments were stored locally on the 1.35 Gbyte disk. The INQUERY system was compiled with the GNU C compiler (gcc) version 2.3.2 at optimization level 2.

4.2 Experiments

We measured the execution time of both systems on a number of query sets using the document collections described in Table 1. The documents in CACM [8] are abstracts and titles of articles that appeared in *Communications of the ACM* from 1958 to 1979. The three query sets used with CACM are different representations of the same 50 queries. TIPSTER is volumes 1 and 2 of the *TIPSTER* document collection, containing full-text news articles and abstracts on a variety of topics from news wire services, newspapers, Federal Register announcements, and magazines. The query set was generated locally from *TIPSTER topics 51-100* using automatic and semi-automatic methods. TIPSTER 1 consists of volume 1 only and uses the same query set. Both TIPSTER and CACM are standard test collections in the IR community. Legal is a privately obtained collection of legal case descriptions. The first query set for the Legal collection was supplied with the collection. The second query set was generated locally by supplementing the first query set with dictionary terms, phrases, and weights. In all cases the query sets are designed to evaluate an IR system's recall and precision and are representative of queries that would be asked by real users.

Each query set was processed by the two versions of INQUERY in batch mode, using appropriate relevance and stop words files. A relevance file lists the documents that should have been retrieved for each query and is required for determining recall and precision. A stop words file lists words that are not worth indexing because they occur so frequently or are not significantly meaningful.

Since the B-tree version of INQUERY does no user space main memory caching of inverted lists across record accesses, we measured the Mneme based version of INQUERY both with and without inverted list caching. For the version with caching, the main memory buffer sizes are shown in Table 1 and were determined for each collection as follows. The large object buffer size was 3 times the size of the largest inverted list in the collection. This heuristic was meant to allocate a reasonable amount of buffer space, in a somewhat regulated fashion, for each collection. Merely allocating a percentage of the total inverted file size would be inappropriate given the range of

Table 2. Wall-clock times (all times are in seconds)

Collection	Query Set	B-Tree	Mneme, No Cache	Mneme, Cache	Improvement
CACM	1	6.49	6.02	5.93	9%
	2	7.41	6.40	6.37	14%
	3	11.73	9.34	8.32	29%
Legal	1	62.84	51.36	50.55	20%
	2	65.82	53.46	52.01	21%
TIPSTER 1	1	2683.20	2568.24	2519.55	6%
TIPSTER	1	4132.34	3973.45	3894.74	6%

inverted file sizes. For the three larger collections, the medium object buffer size was 9% of the size of the large object buffer. This allocation was based on object access behavior observed during query processing, where the number of accesses to medium objects equaled roughly 9% of the number of accesses to large objects. For the CACM collection, 9% of the large object buffer would not have been large enough to hold a single medium object segment. Therefore, we made the CACM medium object buffer large enough to hold 3 medium object segments. The small object buffer was made large enough to hold 3 small object segments since small object access was insignificant.

Timings were made using the system clock via calls to ftime() and getrusage(). Timing was begun just before query processing started, after all files had been opened and any initialization was complete. Timing ended when the query set had been processed, before any files were closed. Each query set was run 6 times, and mean times from all six runs are reported below. In all cases, the result of any particular run differed from the mean by less than 1% of the mean. Before each query set was run, a 32 Mbyte "chill file" was read to purge the operating system file buffers and guarantee that no inverted file data was cached by the file system across runs. The measured I/O inputs for each run indicate that this was accomplished.

4.3 Results

Table 2 shows the wall-clock time required by the different versions of INQUERY to process each of the query sets. The Mneme version without caching achieves a noticeable improvement in performance over the B-tree version. The addition of caching to the Mneme version increases the performance further, yielding the improvements shown in the final column of the table. Improvement is calculated as (B-tree time – Mneme with cache time) / B-tree time.

A more precise measure of the portion of the system that varies across the different versions is system CPU time plus time spent waiting for I/O to complete. This was obtained by subtracting user CPU time from the wall-clock time. User CPU time approximates the time spent in the inference engine. This time should be comparable for all versions, and in fact varies by less than 1% across the versions. System CPU plus

Table 3. System CPU plus I/O times (all times are in seconds)

Collection	Query Set	B-Tree	Mneme, No Cache	Mneme, Cache	Improvement
CACM	1	1.97	1.48	1.41	28%
	2	2.56	1.53	1.52	41%
	3	5.22	2.82	1.90	64%
Legal	1	24.59	13.67	12.77	48%
	2	26.38	14.70	13.21	50%
TIPSTER 1	1	586.12	479.86	430.58	27%
TIPSTER	1	861.75	723.00	646.92	25%

I/O time is reported in Table 3. Again, the Mneme version without caching is faster than the B-tree version, and the Mneme version with caching is fastest.

For the end user, the reduction in wall-clock time is most significant. However, our goal was to demonstrate that the inverted file sub-system of an IR system could be efficiently supported by an "off-the-shelf" data management system. The system plus I/O times represent the time spent in the sub-system we have replaced, and the significant improvement shows that we have met our goal. It is also apparent from Tables 2 and 3 that as the collection becomes larger, the time spent in the inference engine starts to dominate the overall time, reducing the impact of improvements in system and I/O time.

To help explain the performance improvement of the Mneme versions, Table 4 gives some I/O statistics for each query set and INQUERY version. "I" is the number of I/O inputs measured with getrusage(), which counts the number of 8 Kbyte blocks actually read from disk. "A" is the average number of file accesses per inverted list lookup. Note that this does not represent actual disk activity since some file accesses are satisfied by the Ultrix file system cache. "B" is the total number of Kbytes read from the inverted list file during query processing. Again, this does not represent actual bytes read from disk since some file accesses are satisfied by the Ultrix file system cache.

We can make a number of observations from this table. The Mneme version without caching is faster than the B-tree version because it makes fewer accesses to the file (therefore fewer system calls) and, more importantly, fewer accesses to the disk. The B-tree version does limited and unsophisticated caching of index nodes, such that every record lookup requires more than one disk access. This problem gets worse as the file grows and the height of the index tree increases. Mneme, however, requires close to 1 file access per record lookup. Mneme locates objects based on their logical segments using compact multi-level hash tables. This lookup mechanism requires slightly more computation, but the reduced table size allows the auxiliary tables to remain permanently cached after their first access[4]. It is interesting to note that the Mneme version reads substantially more bytes from the file for the CACM queries than does the B-tree version. This is because the CACM queries generate more activity in the small and medium object pools, which have multiple objects clustered in physical segments. Accessing a given

[4] The TIPSTER collection requires only 512 Kbytes to cache all of the auxiliary tables.

Table 4. I/O statistics: I = I/O inputs, A = ave. file accesses / record lookup, B = total Kbytes read from file

Collection	Query Set	B-Tree			Mneme, No Cache			Mneme, Cache		
		I	A	B	I	A	B	I	A	B
CACM	1	82	1.89	585	63	1.02	1700	64	0.89	1496
	2	82	1.89	940	64	1.01	2430	64	0.85	2056
	3	83	1.44	2030	65	1.00	7890	65	0.45	3600
Legal	1	2747	2.92	20700	1626	1.07	20652	1625	0.96	17346
	2	2776	2.61	24526	1626	1.06	24668	1626	0.80	18594
TIPSTER 1	1	68280	2.89	503546	61308	1.03	503520	59917	0.60	271272
TIPSTER	1	96352	3.09	841304	87876	1.04	841516	84568	0.61	456062

object will cause the entire physical segment to be read in. This is less expensive than it appears because the physical segment size is tuned to the disk block transfer size. Each disk access causes 8 Kbytes to be read from disk, so in fact, based on the number of I/O inputs, the B-tree version transfers more raw bytes from disk even though it attempts to read far fewer bytes in the file.

Caching of inverted lists increases the performance of the Mneme version by further reducing the number of file and disk accesses. For CACM and Legal, the file system cache is able to satisfy enough file accesses so that there is no difference in "I" between the two Mneme versions. However, the reductions in "A" and "B" mean fewer system calls, less data copying between system and user memory space, and a savings in system CPU time. The TIPSTER collections are large enough that the Mneme version with inverted list record caching requires fewer I/O inputs than the versions that have file system caching only.

It is clear that caching of inverted lists to reduce disk accesses is advantageous, whether provided by the file system cache or the data management subsystem. It is also clear (and well known [17]) that caching provided by the file system is an inferior solution for data management problems. The buffer management requirements of inverted list data are better satisfied by the custom, domain tailored mechanisms in Mneme. The effectiveness of these caching mechanisms can be seen in Table 5, which shows the hit rates achieved in each of the buffers for each of the queries. The hit rates are fairly significant given that the buffer sizes allocated could be considered modest.

To further investigate the effects of buffer size, we measured the hit rates achieved in the large object buffer over a range of buffer sizes for the TIPSTER query set (see Fig. 2). The figure shows that increasing the buffer size gradually produces diminishing returns, but the knee of the curve can be used to guide buffer allocation.

5 Related Work

A great deal of work has been done in the area of supporting IR with a relational database management system (RDBMS). Some of the earliest work was done by Crawford and

Table 5. Buffer hit rates for the query sets

Collection	Query Set	Small Obj Buffer			Medium Obj Buffer			Large Obj Buffer		
		Refs	Hits	Rate	Refs	Hits	Rate	Refs	Hits	Rate
CACM	1	15	4	0.27	191	16	0.08	14	9	0.64
	2	11	2	0.18	191	17	0.09	25	17	0.68
	3	5	3	0.60	221	109	0.49	30	25	0.83
Legal	1	0	0	0.00	29	2	0.07	296	33	0.11
	2	0	0	0.00	35	9	0.26	366	95	0.26
TIPSTER 1	1	1	0	0.00	158	36	0.23	2112	938	0.44
TIPSTER	1	0	0	0.00	106	25	0.24	2137	923	0.43

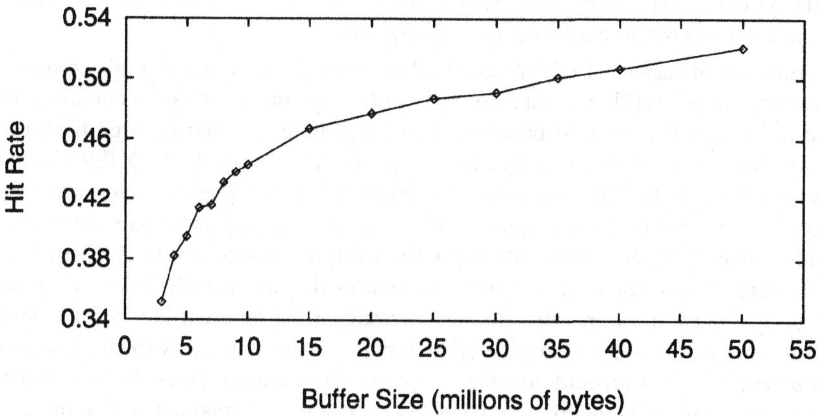

Fig. 2. Large object buffer hit rates for the TIPSTER query set

MacLeod [5, 12, 4, 13], who describe how to use the relational model to store document data and construct information retrieval queries. Similar work was presented more recently by Blair [1] and Grossman and Driscoll [9]. Others have chosen to extend the relational model to allow better support for IR. Lynch and Stonebraker [11] show how a relational model extended with abstract data types can be used to better support the queries that are typical of an IR system.

In spite of evidence demonstrating the feasibility of using a standard or extended RDBMS to support information retrieval, IR system builders have still chosen to build production systems from scratch. This is due to the belief that superior performance can be achieved with a custom system, a belief which is substantiated by a lack of results proving otherwise and anecdotal evidence. Additionally, most of the work described above deals only with document titles, author lists, and abstracts. Techniques used to support this relatively constrained data collection may not scale to true full-text retrieval systems. We desire to support full-text retrieval with high performance. Our approach, while similar in spirit to the above work, differs in both the data management technology chosen to support IR and the extent to which it is applied for that task. The data management technology we use is a persistent object store, and currently it is only used to manage an inverted file index.

Other work in this area has attempted to integrate information retrieval with database management [6, 16]. The services provided by a database management system (DBMS) and an IR system are distinct but complementary, making an integrated system very attractive. The integrated architecture consists of a DBMS component and a custom IR system component. There is a single user interface to both systems, and a preprocessor is used to delegate user queries to the appropriate subsystem. Additionally, the DBMS is used to support the low level file management requirements of the whole system. This architecture is similar to ours in that a separate data management system is used to support the file management requirements of the IR system. However, our data management system is a persistent object store and we focus on supporting high performance IR, with no support for traditional data management.

Efficient management of full-text database indices has received a fair amount of attention. Faloutsos [7] gives an early survey of the common indexing techniques. The two techniques that seem to predominate are signature files and inverted files, each of which implies a different query processing algorithm. Since the INQUERY system uses an inverted file index, and we are not interested in changing the query processing algorithm, we do not discuss signature files. Zobel et al. [24] investigate the efficient implementation of an inverted file index for a full-text database system. Their focus is on compression techniques to limit the size of the inverted file index. They also address updates to the inverted file and investigate the different inverted file index record formats necessary to satisfy certain types of queries. In our work, the format of the inverted file index records and the compression techniques applied to those records are pre-determined by the existing INQUERY system. Our approach is to replace the subsystem that manages these records, without changing the format of the records.

Tomasic and Garcia-Molina [19] study inverted file index performance in a distributed shared-nothing environment. Their simulation results show that caching inverted file index records in main memory can significantly improve performance. This is consistent with our results obtained from measuring an actual system, where the performance improvement of INQUERY integrated with Mneme is partly due to caching. This result implies that there is significant repetition of terms from query to query. This fact has severe implications for any IR study which assumes a uniform distribution over the term vocabulary when selecting query terms, such as the study in [18].

Properly modeling the size distribution of inverted file index records and the frequency of use of terms in queries is addressed by Wolfram in [21, 22]. He suggests that the informetric characteristics of document databases should be taken into consideration when designing the files used by an IR system. We have tried to take this advice to heart by developing appropriate file organization and buffer management policies based on the characteristics of the data and the data access patterns.

Buckley and Lewit [2] studied the effects of query optimization on an IR system and found that it can reduce the amount of data read from the inverted file. Reduced I/O could change the cache hit rates for the Mneme version of our IR system or alter the size distribution of inverted lists read by the system. We believe that these effects might require some adjustments in Mneme buffer sizes, but would not reduce the advantage of Mneme over the B-tree package.

6 Conclusions

Information retrieval systems development is reaching a point where further progress requires the use of more sophisticated data management services, such as concurrency control, dynamic update, and a complex data model. IR system builders are faced with the choice of developing these services themselves, or looking to "off-the-shelf" products to provide these services. Previous attempts at using standard DBMSs to provide these services have produced discouraging results due to poor performance. We have shown here that with the proper data management technology, sophisticated data management services can be supplied to an IR system by an "off-the-shelf" data management system without a performance penalty. In fact, the performance measurement results presented in Sect. 4 demonstrate that a performance improvement can be obtained.

Much of the performance improvement enjoyed by the Mneme version can be attributed to careful file allocation sympathetic to the device transfer block size and intelligent caching of auxiliary tables and inverted lists. While these features could be added to the B-tree package to achieve a similar improvement, it is exactly this type of effort we are trying to avoid by using an existing data management package.

Mneme offers other advantages besides data caching and smart file allocation. The extensibility of Mneme allows customization based on the characteristics of the data being stored. This capability is a clear advantage in an environment where the data management requirements are non-traditional, and was mandatory for satisfying the individual management needs of the different object groups in the inverted file. The more standard data management services provided by Mneme include recovery and support for a richer data model. Inter-object references allow structures such as linked lists to be used to break large objects into more manageable pieces. This could provide better support for inverted list updates and allow incremental retrieval of large lists.

The current version of Mneme is a prototype and does not provide all of the services one might expect from a mature data management system, such as concurrency control and transaction support. However, the nature of access to the data we are supporting here is predominately read-only. We expect that the addition of these services would not introduce excessive overhead or change the results reported above.

For future work we plan to implement some of the standard data management services not currently provided by Mneme and verify the above claim. We will also make use of the services that are currently provided by Mneme but not used to advantage above, such as the richer data model. Furthermore, it would be worthwhile to investigate other store and buffer organizations, looking for more opportunities to tune the system to the unique data management requirements of information retrieval.

References

1. D. C. Blair. An extended relational document retrieval model. *Inf. Process. & Mgmnt.*, 24(3):349–371, 1988.

2. C. Buckley and A. F. Lewit. Optimization of inverted vector searches. In *Proc. of the 8th Inter. ACM SIGIR Conf. on Res. and Develop. in Infor. Retr.*, pages 97–110, June 1985.
3. J. P. Callan, W. B. Croft, and S. M. Harding. The INQUERY retrieval system. In *Proc. of the 3rd Inter. Conf. on Database and Expert Sys. Apps.*, Sept. 1992.
4. R. G. Crawford. The relational model in information retrieval. *J. Amer. Soc. Inf. Sci.*, 32(1):51–64, 1981.
5. R. G. Crawford and I. A. MacLeod. A relational approach to modular information retrieval systems design. In *Proc. of the 41st Conf. of the Amer. Soc. for Inf. Sci.*, 1978.
6. J. S. Deogun and V. V. Raghavan. Integration of information retrieval and database management systems. *Inf. Process. & Mgmnt.*, 24(3):303–313, 1988.
7. C. Faloutsos. Access methods for text. *ACM Comput. Surv.*, 17:50–74, 1985.
8. E. A. Fox. Characterization of two new experimental collections in computer and information science containing textual and bibliographic concepts. Technical Report 83-561, Cornell University, Ithaca, NY, Sept. 1983.
9. D. A. Grossman and J. R. Driscoll. Structuring text within a relational system. In *Proc. of the 3rd Inter. Conf. on Database and Expert Sys. Apps.*, pages 72–77, Sept. 1992.
10. D. Harman, editor. *The First Text REtrieval Conference (TREC1).* National Institute of Standards and Technology Special Publication 200-207, Gaithersburg, MD, 1992.
11. C. A. Lynch and M. Stonebraker. Extended user-defined indexing with application to textual databases. In *Proc. of the 14th Inter. Conf. on VLDB*, pages 306–317, 1988.
12. I. A. MacLeod. SEQUEL as a language for document retrieval. *J. Amer. Soc. Inf. Sci.*, 30(5):243–249, 1979.
13. I. A. MacLeod and R. G. Crawford. Document retrieval as a database application. *Inf. Tech.: Res. Dev.*, 2(1):43–60, 1983.
14. J. E. B. Moss. Design of the Mneme persistent object store. *ACM Trans. Inf. Syst.*, 8(2):103–139, Apr. 1990.
15. G. Salton and M. J. McGill. *Introduction to Modern Information Retrieval.* McGraw-Hill, New York, 1983.
16. L. V. Saxton and V. V. Raghavan. Design of an integrated information retrieval/database management system. *IEEE Trans. Know. Data Eng.*, 2(2):210–219, June 1990.
17. M. Stonebraker. Operating system support for database management. *Commun. ACM*, 24(7):412–418, July 1981.
18. A. Tomasic and H. Garcia-Molina. Performance of inverted indices in distributed text document retrieval systems. Technical Report STAN-CS-92-1434, Stanford University Department of Computer Science, 1992.
19. A. Tomasic and H. Garcia-Molina. Caching and database scaling in distributed shared-nothing information retrieval systems. In *Proc. of the ACM SIGMOD Inter. Conf. on Management of Data*, Washington, D.C., May 1993.
20. H. Turtle and W. B. Croft. Evaluation of an inference network-based retrieval model. *ACM Trans. Inf. Syst.*, 9(3):187–222, July 1991.
21. D. Wolfram. Applying informetric characteristics of databases to IR system file design, Part I: informetric models. *Inf. Process. & Mgmnt.*, 28(1):121–133, 1992.
22. D. Wolfram. Applying informetric characteristics of databases to IR system file design, Part II: simulation comparisons. *Inf. Process. & Mgmnt.*, 28(1):135–151, 1992.
23. G. K. Zipf. *Human Behavior and the Principle of Least Effort.* Addison-Wesley Press, 1949.
24. J. Zobel, A. Moffat, and R. Sacks-Davis. An efficient indexing technique for full-text database systems. In *Proc. of the 18th Inter. Conf. on VLDB*, Vancouver, 1992.

Bit-Sliced Signature Files for Very Large Text Databases on a Parallel Machine Architecture

*George Panagopoulos and Christos Faloutsos**

Department of Computer Science
and Institute for Systems Research (ISR)
University of Maryland, College Park, MD 20742

Abstract. Free text retrieval is an important problem which can significantly benefit from a parallel architecture. Signature methods have been proposed to answer text retrieval queries in parallel machines [Sta88, LF92], under the assumption that the main memory is sufficient to hold the entire signature file. We propose the use of a Parallel Bit-Sliced Signature File method on a SIMD machine architecture when the size of the signature file exceeds the available memory. We propose that we need not examine all the bit slices; instead we use a *partial fetch* slice swapping algorithm. This method achieves graceful performance degradation according to the database size. We provide formulae for the optimal number of signature slices to fetch and match with the query signature. Arithmetic examples show that our method can handle a 128GB database with a 2sec response time on a machine with the characteristics of the Connection Machine.

1 Introduction

Free text retrieval in large text databases is an important problem involved in numerous applications, for example electronic office filing [TC83], computerized libraries [SM83], and electronic encyclopedias. Text databases are traditionally large, unstructured and archival in nature. Retrieval methods based on inverted indices introduce large space overhead (typically 50%–300% [Has81]) and large insertion cost. Signature-based text retrieval methods [CF84, FC87, Fal90] constitute an alternative between fast but space-expensive inversion methods and full text scanning. Signature methods have been shown to have a modest space overhead (typically 10%–15%), to be efficient in text retrieval and insertion, and to be well suited to the archival nature of text databases.

The signature methods also seem to be well suited to the concept of parallelism introduced with the development of massively parallel machine architectures. In signature methods, queries are answered using a two-stage retrieval

* This research was sponsored partially by the Institute for Advanced Computer Studies (UMIACS), by the National Science Foundation under the grants IRI-8719458, IRI-8958546 and IRI-9205273, by a donation by EMPRESS Software Inc., and by a donation by Thinking Machines Inc.

mechanism: first, the query signature is compared with the set of stored document signatures in a bit matching operation which identifies the documents that have a high probability of containing the required query words; then a detailed character matching procedure is invoked for the documents that qualify in the first stage. Large text database applications would benefit significantly by parallelism, especially in the bit matching step, as previous work has suggested [Sta88, Lin92].

The paper in [Sta88] presented a parallel signature-based algorithm for high-speed interactive querying of a text database on a SIMD computer, the Connection Machine. The results were based on the assumption that the main memory was sufficient to hold all the document signatures. In fact the algorithm does not extend well to the case of larger databases that do not fit in the Connection Machine memory. The Sequential Signature File method used in the paper requires the loading of the entire signature file, which makes retrieval prohibitively expensive for interactive applications.

Our motivation was to investigate the applicability of signature methods in SIMD architectures for very large text database applications, in which the signature file size exceeds the memory capacity of the computer system. The main contribution of this paper is the presentation of a parallel signature method that fits better to a SIMD architecture for large database applications. This method is based on the Bit-Sliced Signature File (BSSF) method as described in [FC88]. When the signature size exceeds the available main memory of the computer system in use, we propose the use of *partial fetch slice swapping*. The idea is to examine the bit slices already in memory and to fetch as many from the disk as necessary. Another contribution is a derived formula for the optimal number of signature slices to fetch and match against the query. Furthermore, we provide a performance analysis of the proposed method and we investigate it for various database sizes and other parameters of the application and the system architecture. We show that the proposed scheme on a machine with the characteristics of the Connection Machine can handle interactive text retrieval on databases of size in the order of 50GB. Finally, we show that the method is general enough to be also applicable on uniprocessor machines.

This paper is organized as follows. Section 2 is an introduction to the terminology used and a review of the Bit-Sliced Signature File method. Section 3 contains a description of the parallel system architecture model used and the proposed Parallel BSSF method. Section 4 contains the results of an analytic performance evaluation of the proposed retrieval algorithm. In section 5 we discuss the performance of the method for various application and system parameters. Finally, section 6 contains our conclusions.

2 Background

In this section we will present our terminology and review the Bit-Sliced Signature File text retrieval method [FC88]. The algorithms for insertion and retrieval will be presented.

For the purposes of signature construction, each document is considered here as a set of words. The words that appear in queries are called ***terms*** and are the only ones that take part in the construction of the document signatures. Each term in a document is hashed by m independent hash functions to m bit positions (not necessarily distinct) in a bit vector of length F. The corresponding bits will be set to 1, all the others being set to 0. The resulting value of the bit vector is the ***term signature***. The ***document signature*** is constructed by superimposing the term signatures, in other words by logically OR'ing them together. The following table illustrates the method for an example document that consists of two terms, with $F = 9$ bits per signature and $m = 3$ bits per word:

Word	Signature
`free`	001 000 110
`text`	000 010 101
Document	001 010 111

Suppose that there are N documents. The collection of the N document signatures forms an $F \times N$ bit matrix, called the ***signature matrix***, which will be stored in the ***signature file***. The signature file contains only the document signatures. The actual document text data are stored in a ***text file***. For every document the method maintains a ***posting***, which is a pointer to the beginning of the document in the text file. All postings are stored in a separate ***postings file***.

The ***insertion algorithm*** simply constructs a signature for each document inserted by superimposing the signatures of the contained terms, and appends the resulting document signatures to the signature file.

The ***retrieval algorithm*** answers queries, which are boolean formulae with terms as literals. During the first step of the retrieval algorithm, the query signature is constructed by applying the same hashing functions to the terms of the query. Then a bit matching operation is performed with the signatures stored in the signature file. A document potentially qualifies with respect to a query term if all the signature bits set in a query term are also set in the document signature. Every query term produces a list of documents that potentially contain this term. Then these lists are merged according to the boolean operators contained in the query.

The exact algorithms for insertion and retrieval of the documents depend on the organization of the signature file. In the *Sequential Signature File (SSF)* method, which is the basic organization, signatures are stored sequentially. This organization is useful for small database applications only, because retrieval requires the sequential search of the entire signature file. In the *Bit-Sliced Signature File (BSSF)* method [FC88], on the other hand, the signature matrix is vertically partitioned in F bit slices. Each bit slice is stored in consecutive disk blocks. Since only the bit slices relevant to the query need to be examined, the BSSF method permits the loading of only the relevant disk blocks of the signature file. For example, only at most m bit slices are required for a single word query. BSSF is more efficient than SSF in retrieval because of the smaller amount of data that needs to be loaded from the signature file.

The signature methods effectively perform a filtering of the entire set of the documents, eliminating the ones whose signature does not match the query signature. By an efficient application of this method, most of the non-qualifying documents will be eliminated without being read at all. Some of these documents may pass the filter, though, because of the superimposed coding. In the signature example above, if a word happens to have a signature "001 010 100", a query on it will retrieve the illustrated document in the answer, even if the word is not contained in the document. These cases are called *false drops*. The retrieval algorithm must eliminate the false drops by retrieving the actual documents and checking them against the query. This false drop elimination step can impose a very serious performance overhead if the design parameters allow for a large proportion of false drops. Therefore a major design criterion for the efficiency of a signature method is a small false drop probability. The latter is defined as the fraction of irrelevant documents whose signatures match the query signature.

3 The Proposed Parallel BSSF Method

In this section we will describe the application of the Bit-Sliced Signature File method on a SIMD parallel machine architecture. We will first present the architecture model of the underlying hardware. Then we will describe the application of the Parallel BSSF method on the architecture model used.

3.1 The System Architecture Model

The architecture model that we will use follows the parallel processor model in [Sto87]. The model corresponds to a SIMD machine architecture like the Connection Machine. It contains an array of P *parallel processors*, each with its own local memory of size M bits. The operation of the parallel processors is synchronized by a *host processor*, which also works as a front-end for the users. The host processor is equipped with its own (serial) I/O system.

The model includes a *parallel I/O bus* and a *parallel I/O system*. A file stored in this I/O system is not a single stream of bits, like in a serial I/O architecture, but a multiple stream of bits, one stream per processor. Such a *parallel file* is assumed to be formatted in a way that reflects the processor array structure. It can be depicted as a stream of P-bit vectors; each vector corresponds to a parallel bit array stored along the P processor memories. During an I/O transfer, each processor p will access bit p of the bit vector at the current file position. The file is said to have *width* equal to P, the size of this bit array.

In the following, we will use the term *processor* to mean one of the parallel processors, unless explicitly stated otherwise. These processors can execute *local operations* (e.g. ALU-associated), *global operations* (global maximum, global logical AND, broadcast and other similar operations over the entire array of processors) and *I/O operations* (parallel transfer from or to the parallel I/O system).

3.2 The Application Model

In this paper we are mostly concerned with conjunctive queries. The desired result is a list of documents that contain all the query terms. It is easy to extend the basic retrieval algorithm to accommodate more general boolean queries with no negated terms. One can simply convert the query in disjunctive normal form and merge the lists of documents that qualify for each conjunct. As in previous papers (see for example [FC88]) we will assume that the database consists of N documents with D terms on the average. When very long documents exist in the database, they can be broken down into "logical blocks", each with D terms.

3.3 The Data Structures

The modification of the serial BSSF method to the parallel architecture of our system model is straightforward. The text file will be kept in the host processor I/O system, while the signature file will be stored in the parallel external storage in bit-slice form, and appropriate portions of it will be loaded into the processor memories on demand, by a "slice replacement" algorithm.

We will assume that M bits of every processor's memory can be allocated for storage of signature bits[2]. Figure 1(a) illustrates our proposed implementation with an example consisting of a database with $N = 8$ documents and a system with $P = 4$ processors. Each processor has $M = 4$ bits of memory available for signatures, and will be assigned $V = \lceil N/P \rceil$ document signatures.

A simplified view of the allocation scheme is to consider each processor as a ***physical processor*** that corresponds to V ***virtual processors***, which are assigned one document each. These V virtual processors share the resources of the physical processor, i.e. they execute in round-robin fashion and each has $R = \lfloor M/V \rfloor$ bits of memory available for signatures. This scheme is equivalent to the virtual processor scheme of the Connection Machine. It permits us to view the system as if it really consisted of $V \cdot P$ processors, each having R bits of main memory. In the following we will adopt this scheme and by ***processor*** we will mean ***virtual processor***, except when we explicitly state ***physical processor***. In figure 1(b) we denote the virtual processors by VP_0, VP_1, etc. Note that the physical processor P_0 corresponds to the virtual processors VP_0 and VP_4. In general, if there are P physical processors, the physical processor P_i corresponds to the virtual processors VP_i, VP_{i+P}, etc. Since the virtual processors run in successive fashion and not in parallel, the algorithm steps below are meant to iterate V times in each physical processor. We will call V the ***virtual processor ratio*** of the system.

At every instance of time during text retrieval, we keep R bit slices of the signature file resident in main memory. A resident slice occupies one bit of each processor's memory. We will refer to the set of these bits storing a single slice as a ***frame***. There are R frames in the parallel computer system. In figure 1(b) we have only $R = 2$ frames; frame 0 holds slice 0 and frame 1 holds slice 3.

[2] The algorithm requires some additional parallel memory for other data structures, but this additional requirements are small enough to be safely ignored in our performance analysis.

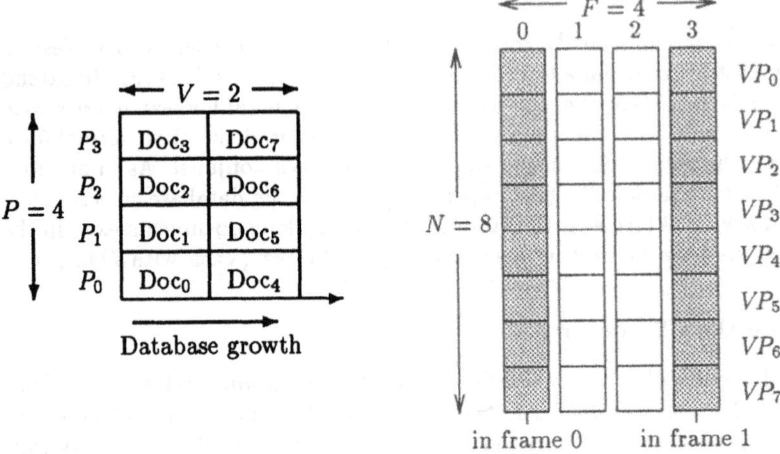

Fig. 1. Signature file in PBSSF method ($N = 8$ documents, $F = 4$ bits per signature, $P = 4$ physical processors, $M = 4$ bits per processor): (a) Allocation of documents to processors; each physical processor is assigned $V = 2$ documents (b) Signature file storage in parallel memory; 8 virtual processors, $R = 2$ resident slices (slices 0 and 3)

The resident bits of the signature file in each processor p form a *slice bit vector* of length R, which we will denote by $B_p[R]$. The relevant bits of the slice bit vectors are matched in each processor with the relevant bits of the query signature into a *response bit* R_p. The response bit R_p in processor p will be set at the end of the computation if and only if the signature document p matches the query signature.

3.4 The Parallel BSSF Algorithms

The *insertion algorithm* for the Parallel Bit-Sliced Signature File method is more efficiently executed in batches. It simply constructs the new document signatures and then appends the new bits to the signature file, slice by slice.

The *retrieval algorithm* is shown in figure 2. Given a conjunctive query, it produces a list of documents that match the query signature. It proceeds by constructing the query signature, then matching it against the document signatures stored in the database; finally, false drops are eliminated.

Step [R3] involves a decision of how may slices to fetch in memory, as well as a slice victim selection and replacement policy. We will call this procedure the *fetch policy*. If we consider the set of resident slices as the *state* of the memory, the fetch policy decides the next state given the current one and a set of slices references in the last query. The fetch policy can be quite general. It may take account of some or all of the past references and states, in addition to the current memory state.

Algorithm **Parallel BSSF Retrieval**

[R1] CONSTRUCT QUERY SIGNATURE: For every term w_i in the query, construct term signature s_i; then superimpose all term signatures on query signature S

[R2] INITIALIZE PARALLEL MEMORY: Initialize all response bits R_p to 1

[R3] MATCH DOCUMENT SIGNATURES: Decide how many and which, if any, slice faults to service by fetching the corresponding bit slices in main memory *(fetch policy)*; For every signature bit i that is resident in some frame r and must be matched, if the document signature bit $B_p[r]$ is 0, clear the response bit R_p; For every signature bit slice i that must be loaded, invoke a slice replacement algorithm to choose a frame for replacement and load slice i in that frame; then proceed as above to match the document signature bit with the query signature bit

[R4] OUTPUT MATCHING DOCUMENT ID'S: Find all processors p with $R_p = 1$

[R5] ELIMINATE FALSE DROPS: For each document to be retrieved, read document text from text file and scan text to check it against query

Fig. 2. The Parallel BSSF retrieval algorithm

We will call a *total fetch (TF)* policy one that always fetches all the referenced non-resident slices in memory and performs a complete signature match on all bits referenced by the query. An alternative policy is a *partial fetch (PF)* policy, which considers fetching a subset of these slices, in order to minimize the expected response time by reducing the cost of step [R3].

4 Performance Analysis

In this section we will present the results of an analytic evaluation of the expected response time of the retrieval algorithm for a query of c terms. The details of the analysis can be found in [Pan92].

We will assume that the cost of a local operation in each processor is t_{op} and the cost of a global operation is t_{glob}. The cost t_{slice} of an I/O operation that reads a slice of V bits in each processor's memory is:

$$t_{slice} = t_{seek} + V \cdot P \cdot t_{xfer}$$

where t_{seek} is the seek time for the parallel I/O storage device and t_{xfer} is the reciprocal of the maximum sustained transfer rate (measured in bits/sec) between the processor memories and the I/O system. For the host processor, let us define t_{hash} to be the cost of one hash function call, t_{scan} the scan cost per document block, and t_{doc} the cost of an I/O operation in the host processor that reads the text of one document from the text file, where:

$$t_{doc} = t_{seek} + b \cdot t_{blk}$$

where b is the average size of a document in blocks and t_{blk} is the cost of loading a disk block in memory. Here we assume similar characteristics for the serial and parallel disk systems.

Let s_q be the number of distinct bits set in the query signature, s_{res} the number of slice hits caused by the query, s_{fetch} the number of slices that the fetch policy decides to fetch into memory, and s_{match} the number of bits on which the signature match is performed (thus $s_{match} = s_{res} + s_{fetch}$). On the average:

$$s_q = F\cdot(1-(1-\tfrac{1}{F})^{cm}) \simeq c\cdot m$$
$$s_{res} \simeq c\cdot m\cdot \tfrac{R}{F}$$

The approximations work for $c\cdot m \ll F$. The false drop probability is:

$$F_d = w^{s_{match}}$$

where w is the average weight of the document signature, i.e. the probability that a signature bit in the signature file is set to 1. The value of w is [Sti60]:

$$w = 1-(1-\frac{1}{F})^{mD} \simeq 1-e^{-mD/F} \simeq \frac{m\cdot D}{F}$$

The last approximation works for $m\cdot D \ll F$.

We will define as *response time* t_{retr} of the retrieval algorithm the time until the first qualifying document appears, and will pessimistically assume that all the false drops are encountered before any qualifying document appears. Therefore we will include all the overhead cost due to the false drops in the response time of the algorithm:

$$t_{retr} = c\cdot m\cdot t_{hash} + V\cdot t_{op} + s_{fetch}\cdot t_{slice} + s_{match}\cdot V\cdot t_{op} + w^{s_{match}}\cdot N\cdot(t_{glob} + t_{doc} + b\cdot t_{scan}) \tag{1}$$

In the total fetch policy case, all slice faults cause the corresponding slices to be fetched in memory, therefore we simply have $s_{match,TF} = s_q$.

Now consider a partial fetch policy. Such a policy in general decides to bring a subset of the slice faults in memory. The policy should minimize the expected t_{retr} with respect to s_{match}, given the values of s_q and s_{res}. Solving $\partial t_{retr}/\partial s_{match} = 0$ in equation (1) above we have:

$$s_{match,PF} = \frac{1}{\ln w}\cdot\ln\frac{t_{slice}}{N\cdot(-\ln w)\cdot(t_{doc} + b\cdot t_{scan})} \tag{2}$$

assuming $V\cdot t_{op} \ll t_{slice}$ and $t_{glob} \ll t_{doc}$ (of course keeping $s_{res} \leq s_{match} \leq s_q$).

5 Arithmetic Examples and Discussion

In the graphs that follow we will present and discuss some analytical results derived from formulae (1)-(2). We have assumed a database that consists of single-block documents ($b = 1$, for a block size of 4Kbytes), where each document contains $D = 100$ terms. The signature file parameters have been tuned for optimal expected response time.

We assumed an architecture with characteristics similar to that of a fully configured CM-2 [Thi89]. We have used the following parameter values: $t_{seek} =$ 25ms, $t_{xfer} =$ 5ns (i.e. transfer rate of the Parallel I/O system 200Mbits/sec), $t_{op} =$ 10ns, $t_{glob} =$ 100ns, $t_{hash} =$ 0.8ms, $t_{blk} =$ 1ms and $t_{scan} =$ 1ms.

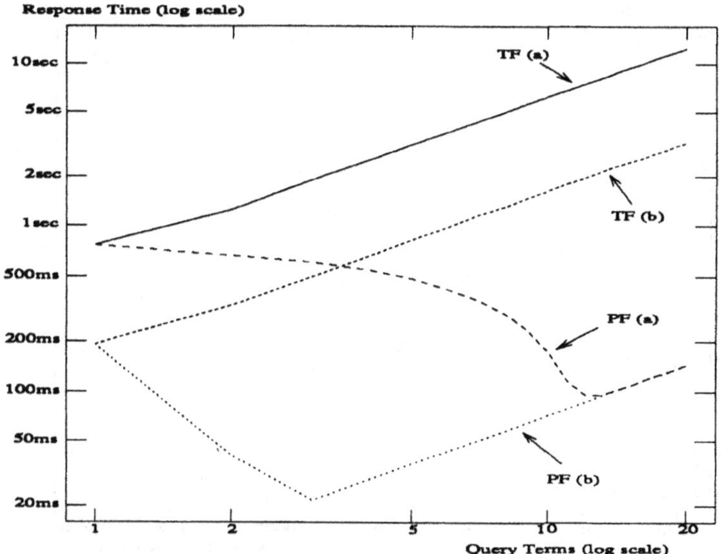

Fig. 3. Comparison of TF and PF policies (P = 64K processors, M = 64Kbits per processor) in log-log scale: (a) N = 10 million documents, 40GB database (b) N = 2 million documents, 8GB database

5.1 Comparison of Total and Partial Fetch Policies

Figure 3 compares the total fetch and partial fetch policies for different query sizes and for two database sizes. In case (a) we have assumed a 40GB database consisting of N = 10 million documents. The system consists of P = 64K processors, each with M = 64Kbits of memory available for signature slices. Both policies tended to select large signature lengths which produce small false drop probabilities. We chose to keep the upper limit of 4Kbits for signature lengths in order to keep a reasonable storage overhead (12.5% of the actual text file size) for the signature file. This signature length was chosen as the optimal by both TF and PF algorithms. The optimal value $m = 9$ was calculated for both policies. This gave a document signature weight $w \simeq 20\%$, as opposed to the required 50% in serial methods. The memory capacity is enough to hold only 10% of the signature file.

In the TF algorithm the false drop elimination cost quickly becomes negligible because of very small false drop probability as the query size grows larger. Almost all of the cost is signature slice I/O, which grows at a rate almost linear to the query size. The PF policy corrects this imbalance. Since the signature weight is very low, fewer slices need to be fetched for matching, while the false drop probability remains small enough to contribute very little to the retrieval cost. In fact, for queries with more than about 12 terms, the PF policy decides to fetch almost no slices at all on the average. Therefore, even though the percent-

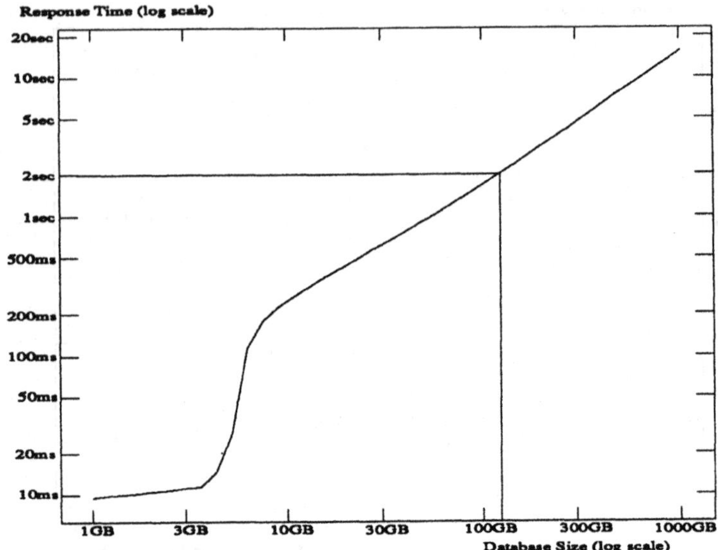

Fig. 4. Response time vs. database size (P = 64K processors, M = 64Kbits per processor, $c = 1$ terms per query, PF policy) in log-log scale

age of referenced non-resident slices increases with larger queries, the retrieval cost does not increase; the increase in response time accounts for the small (some milliseconds) increase in CPU time due to initial hash computations (construction of the query signature). The advantage of the partial fetch policy is clear and becomes even greater for multiple-word queries.

Case (b) in figure 3 shows that the same behavior can be expected from applications with relatively smaller database sizes. Here we have assumed a 8GB database consisting of $N = 2$ million documents. Both methods optimized the design for a signature length of $F = 4096$ bits and $m = 9$ bits set by each term. Now 50% of the total size of the signature file can be memory resident at any time. Again the PF policy performs much better than the TF policy. In the following graphs we use partial fetch for the PBSSF retrieval algorithm.

5.2 Effect of Database Size

Figure 4 shows the performance of the algorithm on a system with 64K processors, with 64Kbits memory each, for various database sizes and single-word queries. The database size ranges from 1GB (250,000 documents) to 1000GB (250 million documents). The diagram depicts the performance with optimal values of the design parameters F and m for the corresponding database size[3].

[3] It can also be shown (see [Pan92]) that the PBSSF method behaves well in a dynamically growing database environment, even when the database size deviates from the estimated size when the signature parameter were chosen.

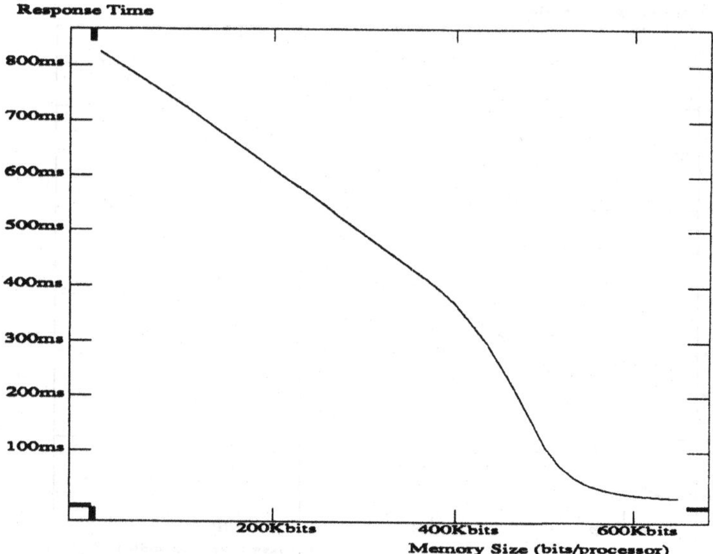

Fig. 5. Response time vs. memory size (P = 64K processors, $N = 10^7$ documents, $c = 1$ terms per query, PF policy); the design parameters are optimized for the given memory size

These values in general depend on the database size, but for large databases all methods favor large signature lengths, therefore they set F = 4Kbits, with $m = 10$ bits set per term. When the optimal signature length is used, a database of size 1GB enables the entire signature file to reside in main memory, and a database of size 1000GB permits only 0.4% of the signature file to be memory resident. The diagram shows that interactive response times (up to 2sec) are derived in such a system for databases of size up to 128GB (32 million documents). For larger databases, each processor is assigned more documents and fewer signature slices are kept resident. Even as the proportion of resident slices decreases, the algorithm keeps the number of slices to be fetched low. Nevertheless the increased size of each slice makes slice I/O more expensive. Most of the cost observed is slice I/O, and to a lesser extent false drop elimination.

5.3 Effect of Memory Size

Figure 5 shows the effect of the memory size on the response time of the algorithm for single-word queries ($c = 1$). The number of processors was set to 64K and the database to 10^7 documents. The memory size ranges from M = 8Kbits per processor, which gives a memory capacity of 64MB (1.25% the size of the signature file) to M = 640Kbits per processor, which makes a total memory size that exceeds the size of the signature file. The signature length F was optimized for each given memory size.

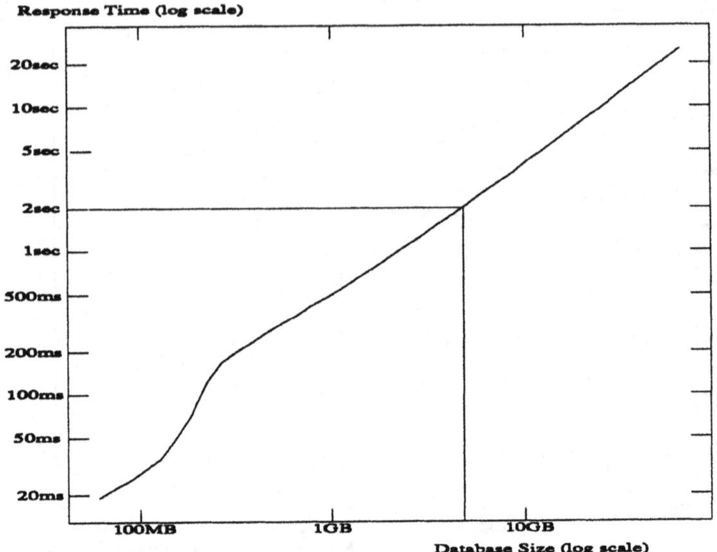

Fig. 6. Response time vs. database size on a uniprocessor machine ($P = 1$ processor, $M = 16$MB main memory, PF policy) in log-log scale

For small capacity memories most of the cost is signature slice I/O. The drop in the retrieval time on the left side of the curve savings are due to the fewer slice faults. When the memory size increases to more than $M = 400$Kbits per processor, the optimal signature length F becomes smaller and therefore the slice fault rate drops dramatically and the total retrieval cost decreases, until no more slices are fetched into memory. For large memories which make the database signature resident, the increase in memory does not offer significant savings in response time and tends to stabilize to the CPU cost.

5.4 Performance of a Uniprocessor Machine

The partial fetch/partial match idea and the analysis can be easily applied to a uniprocessor ($P = 1$) system. Our method can exploit the large main memories that are commercially available to improve performance. Figure 6 shows the time cost of the retrieval algorithm on a serial architecture with 16MB of main memory, for single-word queries ($c = 1$). The transfer rate was adjusted to 10Mbits/sec and the t_{op} was adjusted for a 20 MIPS machine like a Sparcstation. The database size ranges from 64MB (16,000 documents) to 64GB (16 million documents). The signature design parameters were optimized for each database size. The results show that a Sparc-class machine with 16MB of main memory devoted to the application can achieve a 2sec response time for a 5GB database. For such a configuration, the design was optimized for signature length $F = 4096$ bits and $m = 6$ bits set per term. Such light-weight signatures keep the false drop probability low. In the serial machine case, the most significant factor in the cost formula is the CPU cost for signature matching.

6 Conclusions

In this paper we have studied the application of a full text retrieval method based on Bit-Sliced Signature Files on a SIMD machine architecture with limited main memory. The contributions of the paper are the following:

- We have proposed a Parallel BSSF (PBSSF) method which uses *partial fetch* slice swapping for full text retrieval on large text databases.
- We have derived a formula (equation (2)) for the optimal number of signature slices to be fetched.
- We have provided an analytic performance evaluation of the proposed retrieval algorithm for various system and database parameters.

The results demonstrate that a SIMD architecture is well suited to a full-text database retrieval application. In particular, we derived the following conclusions:

- The retrieval method described exhibits satisfactory interactive performance (less than 2sec) for databases of size up to 128GB (32 million documents) on a system with 64K processors with 64K bits memory each, assuming no more than 12.5% storage overhead for the signature file and timing characteristics similar to a Connection Machine CM-2 system (figure 4).
- The method behaves well in a growing database environment, causing graceful performance degradation when the database size increases, even if the database grows much beyond the initial expectations of the designer.
- Long and light-weight document signatures (i.e. large F) are in general beneficial for the Parallel Bit-Sliced Signature File method, especially for large databases. This allows the false drop probability to be very low.
- Consequently, the signature slice I/O is normally the dominating factor in the total cost, compared with the false drop elimination and CPU costs. Therefore a partial fetch policy greatly improves the performance of the retrieval method compared with the total fetch policy (figure 3).

Moreover, the partial fetch method is also useful for a uniprocessor system. This policy helps a serial processor benefit from existing large main memories, which is the trend in commercial workstations. A response time of 2sec can be expected from a Sparc-like architecture with a main memory buffer of 16MB, operating on a 5GB database (figure 6).

Future research could examine (a) the effects of skewness in the frequencies of query terms (e.g. Zipf distribution [Zip49]), (b) the parallelization of vertical [LF92] and horizontal [SD83, LL89] partitioning signature methods, and (c) the parallelization of hybrid methods that combine signature retrieval with inverted indices [FJ91].

References

[CF84] Stavros Christodoulakis and Christos Faloutsos. Design Considerations for a Message File Server. *IEEE Transactions on Software Engineering*, 10(2):201–210, March 1984.

[Fal90] Christos Faloutsos. Signature-Based Text Retrieval Methods: A Survey. *IEEE Data Engineering*, pages 25–32, March 1990.

[FC87] Christos Faloutsos and Stavros Christodoulakis. Description and Performance Analysis of Signature File Methods for Office Filing. *ACM Transactions on Office Information Systems*, 5(3):237–257, July 1987.

[FC88] Christos Faloutsos and Raphael Chan. Fast Text Access Methods for Optical Disks: Designs and Performance Comparison. In *Proceedings of the 14th International Conference on Very Large Databases*, pages 280–293, Long Beach, California, August 1988.

[FJ91] Christos Faloutsos and H. V. Jagadish. Hybrid Index Organizations for Text Databases. Technical Report UMIACS-TR-91-33 and CS-TR-2621, Department of Computer Science, University of Maryland, March 1991.

[Has81] R. Haskin. Special-Purpose Processors for Text Retrieval. *Database Engineering*, 4(1):16–29, September 1981.

[LF92] Zheng Lin and Christos Faloutsos. Frame Sliced Signature Files. *IEEE Transactions on Knowledge and Data Engineering*, 4(3):158–180, June 1992. Also available as UMD CS-TR-2146 and UMIACS-TR-88-88.

[Lin92] Zheng Lin. CAT: An Execution Model for Concurrent Full Text Search. In *PDIS*, 1992.

[LL89] D. L. Lee and C. W. Leng. Partitioned Signature File: Designs and Performance Evaluation. *ACM Transactions on Office Information Systems*, 7(2):158–180, April 1989.

[Pan92] George Panagopoulos. Bit-Sliced Signature Files for Very Large Databases on a Parallel Machine Architecture. Technical Report CSC-809, Department of Computer Science, University of Maryland, April 1992.

[SD83] Ron Sacks-Davis. Two Level Superimposed Coding Scheme for Partial Match Retrieval. *Information Systems*, 8(4):273–280, 1983.

[SM83] G. Salton and M. J. McGill. *Introduction to Modern Information Retrieval*. McGraw–Hill, 1983.

[Sta88] Craig Stanfill. Parallel Computing for Information Retrieval: Recent Developments. Technical Report DR88-1, Thinking Machines Corporation, Cambridge, Mass., January 1988.

[Sti60] Simon Stiassny. Mathematical Analysis of Various Superimposed Coding Methods. *American Documentation*, 11(2):155–169, February 1960.

[Sto87] Harold S. Stone. Parallel Querying of Large Databases: A Case Study. *IEEE Computer*, 20(10):11–21, October 1987.

[TC83] D. Tsichritzis and S. Christodoulakis. Message Files. *ACM Transactions on Office Information Systems*, 1(1):88–98, January 1983.

[Thi89] Thinking Machines Corporation, Cambridge, Mass. *Parallel Instruction Set, Version 5.2*, October 1989.

[Zip49] G. K. Zipf. *Human Behavior and Principle of Least Effort: An Introduction to Human Ecology*. Addison–Wesley, Cambridge, MA, 1949.

Schemas for Telling Stories in Medical Records

Carole Goble and Peter Crowther

Medical Informatics Group, Department of Computer Science, University of Manchester, Oxford Road, Manchester, M13 9PL, UK
tel: +44 61 275 6195, fax: +44 61 275 6236, email: carole@cs.man.ac.uk

Abstract. To accurately support a patient's medical record, at least four interrelated models are required: a simple static one-level schema is inadequate. The models must support the medical record as a coherent story reconstructed from the sequence of recorded events within the medical record. We propose one representation which unifies all four models by a three space approach, each space acting as a schema for the space below. The three spaces assist atemporal summarisation of a patient's medical record and illustrate the difficulties of recording retrospective or contradictory observations. The approach uses a generative, descriptive subsumption-based classification formalism with a sophisticated system of semantic constraints controlling the generation of implied intensional concepts. We report our experiences in its use in a prototype clinical workstation. We believe that this model can be used for complex applications where contradictory and incomplete information is captured over time and a complex semantic constraint model is required.

1 Introduction

Medicine needs databases, but the information is so large, variable and complex as to render simple intensional models ineffective. A schema which relies on static pre-defined entities and domain values and simple semantic constraints is unsatisfactory. In medicine incomplete, inconsistent, contradictory, uncertain, speculative and possibly irrelevant data must be collected in case it becomes useful. Prescriptive models of medicine have led to over-simplification, inappropriate compartmentalisation, and the inability to handle the required levels of accuracy, varying levels of granularity and flexibility [1]. In traditional paper-based notes a problem might be described in one line or two pages, and this flexibility must be reflected in any electronic medical note system. The current approach of encoding and classifying each and every possible clinical condition supports standardisation and data interchange but is either combinatorially explosive, or requires additional semantic control mechanisms [14,4].

Medical care is administered by many professionals during one episode of illness, let alone throughout a patient's lifetime. Hence the medical record has to support a wide range of users with different viewpoints.

An accurate reflection of an individual's medical record is that of a story of observations that may well be temporally independent of the real state of the patient. Hence the model of the medical record requires fine-grained temporal attribution, but should also reflect the atemporal persistence of some clinical conditions—e.g. diabetes is a disease for life. It is essential to support not only the clinician's history-taking task but also the reconstruction task needed to reveal the patient's story as against the order it was told in, and to support retrospective enhancement of observations separate from the original.

The problem is to tame complexity, both computationally, and cognitively to avoid swamping the clinician with masses of data. To achieve this we use four interrelated models, described in section 2. As demonstrated in section 4, these are unified by a three space approach which we present in section 3. These four models are not conventional data models, because conventional data models do not handle the required expressiveness, complexity and constraints demanded by medical applications. The models lie at the fusion of concepts drawn from artificial intelligence, object oriented and database domains, synthesised for this application area by the Medical Informatics Group at the University of Manchester. Section 5 deals with related work and we conclude with a discussion in section 6.

2 The Intensional Requirements of a Medical Record

In order to accurately support the medical record at least four interrelated models are required: a system of medical concepts, the tasks, the actors (e.g clinicians and patients) and the medical record structure itself. The four models are shown diagrammatically in figure 1.

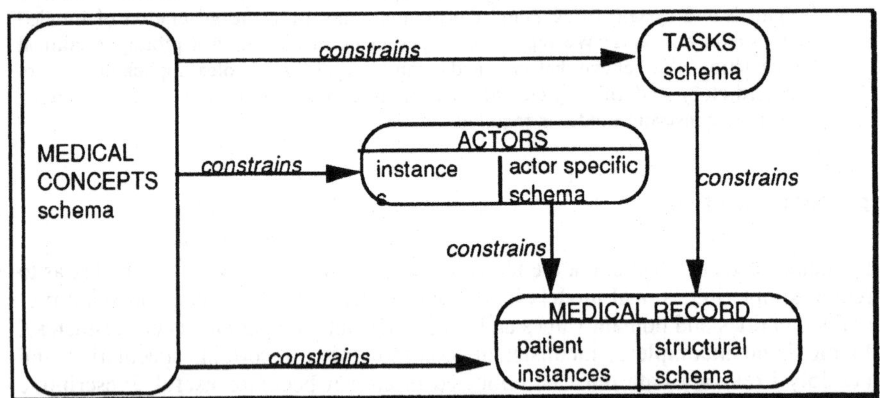

Figure 1. The four models of a patient's medical record

The CONCEPTS model describes the clinical terminology and information model of the medical record and decision-making tasks. This is equivalent to Brachman's T-box, but certain assertions are included as the classic T-box is too restrictive [4].

The TASKS model represents the process of care—implicit and explicit goals, alternative ways of achieving these, activity models, pre-defined protocols, plans and criteria for making choices. How repeated measurements are entered into the physical record is part of the task of recording information; that patients ought to have their blood pressure taken repeatedly is part of a model of the process of care. This is similar to software system specifications.

The ACTORS model represents non-observational information such as preferences and the ways in which the actors interact with each other and with other models. This moel is related to the adaptive user models in knowledge engineering systems, where autonomous agents actively maintain a user profile. Here the actor model does more by further restricting the intension of the medical record extension to make it actor-specific.

Finally the MEDICAL RECORD model represents the structure of a patient's record, e.g sessions, encounters and complaints. The information model for the medical record, which describes the structural intension of the collection of instances making up the patient's extension, is separate from the model of the concepts it uses [15].

The CONCEPTS model constrains what the other models may represent and conversely the other models have requirements for the system of concepts. It can be divided into static and dynamic ontologies [17]. The static ontology includes statements such as 'arthritis is a disease'. In addition the system must be semantically restricted, both statically (eyes cannot fracture) and dynamically (a disease can be a diagnosis or a problem needing treatment). This restriction must be achieved without having to enumerate every clinical concept with all possible modifiers, as the number of such concepts is certainly large and possibly infinite, depending on the precise model. In section 3 we present a generative descriptive model of medicine which is suited to the scale and complexity, based on controlling of base concepts and relationships [1,4,14] to *generate* a schema for the medical record. In this sense the concepts model is a semantic constraint model controlling the possible domain values for the medical record.

The ACTORS model represents instances of specific actors (Dr Smith and Mrs Jones) as well as schema information restricting the medical record structure and content specific to those actors, defining the assertional applicability of CONCEPTS, TASKS and MEDICAL RECORD models to the individual—an amputee cannot have an ingrowing toenail in the amputated limb. The CONCEPTS model states that only women can have children, but it is the ACTORS model that indicates that the patient instance is a man which will restrict the medical intensional schema making the model concerning pregnancy inapplicable. The medical model can be viewed as a large attribute-value model where the values of instances control the applicability of the medical intension.

Similarly, the medical record model represents both instances of observations of patients by clinicians and schema information such as that a patient can have repeated measurements of blood pressure but only a single blood pressure at any one time. The information model of the medical record must allow an authentic account of clinicians' understanding and not force clinicians to premature commitment. This permits statements that can be conflicting, uncertain (clinicians need to record their doubt about symptoms, diagnoses, etc.), negative observations such as excluded diagnoses, and arbitrary levels of detail. These allows the clinician to record the patient's story, in the order of its telling and with all its contradictions.

2.1 Every Patient Tells a Story

The patient record is a story told through observations made by an agent (a doctor, a nurse, a piece of monitoring equipment) without retrospective tampering in an attempt to model what actually happened to the patient. Every observation must be attributable to an agent at a particular place and time; this is vital for security and data protection in electronic medical records. An observation must be unalterable, even if subsequent events lead to contradictory statements.

Let us take the example of *hypothyroidism* (too little thyroid hormone). Its onset is slow, with the patient presenting a series of symptoms which in themselves could be unrelated: a slowing down, tiredness, weight gain. The changes between each encounter between doctor and patient will register as a slight deterioration. It is only when all the symptoms are put together and viewed non-incrementally that the true condition is recognised.

Mrs Jones visits Dr. Smith—her first visit. Dr. Smith records that Mrs Jones had been fatigued for about 1 year. Mrs Jones' medical record will not start one year in the past, but now, with a dated observation that Dr. Smith recorded that Mrs Jones reported she has been fatigued for about a year. Mrs Jones has come complaining of breathlessness which started 3 days before. A few days later Mrs Jones returns, still complaining of breathlessness, and adds that she has had constipation for around six months. A blood test taken at this second visit shows anaemia and she is admitted to hospital with hypothyroidism, which was the cause of her complaints. The story is recorded in the order it is told, *not* the order in which it happened (see figure 2). We cannot add retrospectively that Mrs Jones had hypothyroidism in her consultations because that was not observed at the time. Neither *was* her fatigue considered a clinically significant problem, but it is *now*.

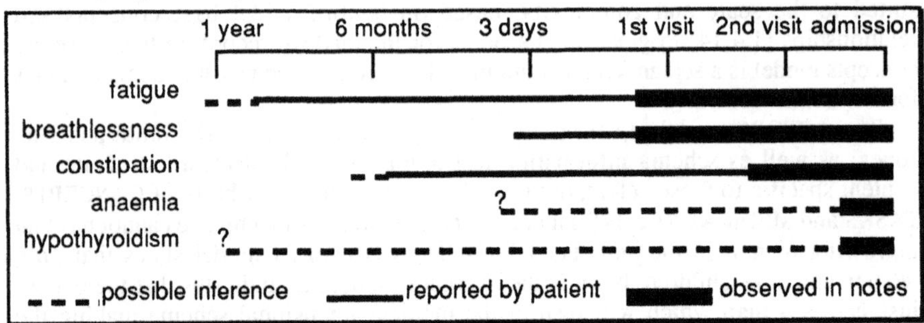

Figure 2. The story of a medical record told by observations

Once made an observation cannot be retracted, only modified by another observation. The medical record holds temporal and atemporally persistent knowledge about an individual patient *inferable* from recorded observations. The statements in the medical record correspond not to facts about the patient, but to what clinicians have said that they have heard, seen, thought and done. What actually occurred to the patient is, strictly speaking, unknowable and is a matter for inference based on the observations in the record. For example, we can infer that Mrs Jones was fatigued a year before her first visit because Dr. Smith has recorded that Mrs Jones said she was—this is only inferable, because it may not be true or accurate. On a different level we can also infer that it is plausible that Mrs Jones had hypothyroidism since that time, but this is only recorded from the time of her admission.

These requirements appear similar to those of bitemporal historic databases [19]. Transaction time and observation time seem equivalent. However, there are a number of points that distinguish such databases from the story telling of medical records: (i) the interplay between transaction time and valid time is important and they are not independent; (ii) the uncertainty, inaccuracy and complexity of valid time; (iii) the contradictions in the story at different times or at the same time by different observers and (iv) histories are not histories of data changes because the data cannot change, only be enhanced or interpretated.

This leaves us with the requirement for atemporal and temporal abstractions orientated around a patient or any other object (e.g. a disease or clinician) and implies that the model of the medical record has two parts: a series of *direct observations* and *meta-observations* about those direct observations[18].

3 A Unified Model

Structured Meta Knowledge (SMK), developed in Manchester by the Medical Informatics Group since 1988, is a generative representation with subsumption and multiple inheritance based on semantic networks. It integrates medical concepts, a medical record model, patient instances, actors and tasks into a single formalism, with the knowledge base of medical terminology providing the semantic control over the patients' medical records.

SMK is generative, defining complex entities in terms of composite descriptions made up of a limited set of elementary concepts and assembled according to explicit rules. In contrast to some representations certain constructs are excluded (notably existential quantification) and others restricted, in particular universal quantification, disjunction and negation [14,1,4]. Certain types of defeasible descriptions and default statements are included but tightly controlled.

The function of SMK is to represent statements that allow the expression and validation of all and only semantically correct descriptions. Briefly, and somewhat simplified, SMK describes a subsumption network consisting of simple, elementary entities, defined by explicitly asserting their positions in a subsumption or *'isa'* hierarchy; bi-directional binary relationships linking concepts; and particularizations [10] which are new composite concepts implied by the descriptive relationship. Particularizations are placed in the subsumption hierarchy by a classifier and are a form of implied subtype of their base supertype, inheriting the properties of their supertype. The relationships have cardinalities and qualifiers and provide a system of semantic sanctioning constraints that control and restrict the creation of self-consistent and non-redundant particularizations [1,4,5,14,15].

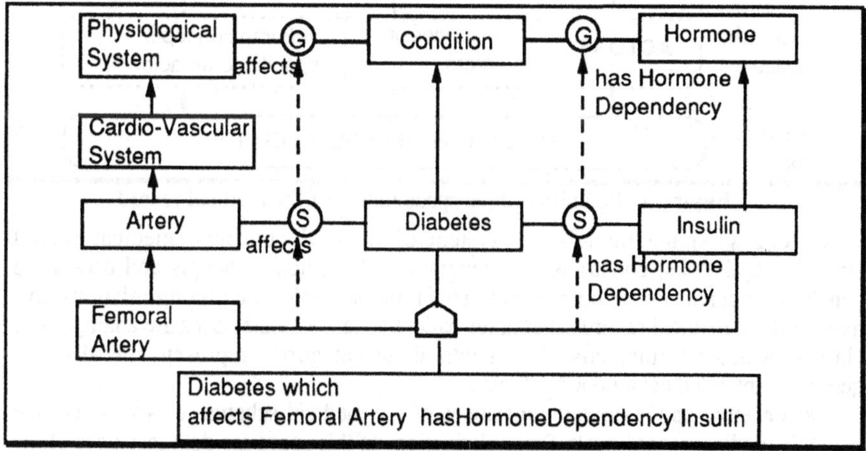

Figure 3. An example of a particularization.

An example of a particularization is shown in figure 3. The ⌂ symbol represents the particularization operator. *Diabetes which affects FemoralArtery hasHormoneDependency Insulin* is a subtype (not an instance) of the elementary concept *Diabetes*. It is semantically sensible for Diabetes to affect Arteries (the *FemoralArtery* is a subtype), shown by the (S)ensible relationship. This in turn was sanctioned (indicated by the dotted arrows) by the syntactic (G)rammatical relationship between *Condition* and *PhysiologicalSystem*.

Figure 3 represents two levels of schema. The first is that of elementary medical concepts such as *Artery*, *Insulin* and *Diabetes*, together with relationships between those entities such as components, causality, locality and dependency. This higher level schema implies and controls the existence of composite and more specialised schema concepts, which can in turn have instances in the medical record of a patient. Particularizations are inferred (automatically) by the intensional schema of medical concepts and hence represent an expansion of what is already there rather than adding to it. Consequently a patient may have an instance of the concept *Diabetes which affects Femoral Artery hasHormoneDependency Insulin*. The model has a deductive quality in the sense that the elementary concepts and relationships form an intensional 'object factory' or metaschema for more specialised concepts generated on demand and usually 'virtual'. The whole is an intension for instances of the medical record.

Our intention is to use SMK to unify the representation of all four of the models outlined in section 2 using particularizations and sanctioned relationships to hold schema and patient instance data. The model's entities and particularizations partition into three spaces, as illustrated in figure 4. The medical record model has been split into its two constituents of schema and instance.

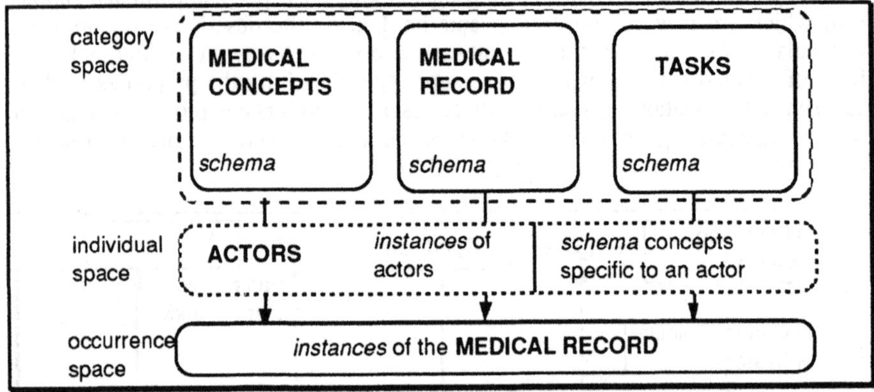

Figure 4. the unified three space model of the medical record

Category space models the system of medical concepts, medical record structure, and tasks, constrains the generation of medical concepts and drives the constraint mechanism. It holds grammatical and sensible sanctioning relationships, making it the medical record schema for patient instances. Categories are analogous to classes in other formalisms. Statements about categories represent the abstract, general or intended behaviour of objects.

Occurrence space contains instances of the medical schema 'classes'—i.e. the patient's medical record itself. Particularizations in this space are data instances of the MEDICAL RECORD called 'occurrences'. This space models the 'authentic' historical part of the medical record as described in section 2.1.

Individual space represents concepts that are neither part of the full medical record schema (category-space) nor observations (occurrence-space). In most object-oriented systems there are two levels of abstraction—usually called 'classes' and 'instances'. However, because the medical record is made up of observations localised at a particular point in time and space, SMK requires an additional level of abstraction. The *individual space* represents:

(i) instances of actors such as 'Mrs Jones' and 'Dr. Smith'. These are instances of ACTORS concepts such as Patient and Doctor.

(ii) concrete instances of categories which persist in time and space about the individual patient's medical record such as Mrs Jones's diabetes or Dr. Smith's treatment preferences. These instances are individual particularizations and form part of the ACTORS *schema* for those actor's instances (occurrence particularizations). They may include atemporal and aspatial assertions about the patient.

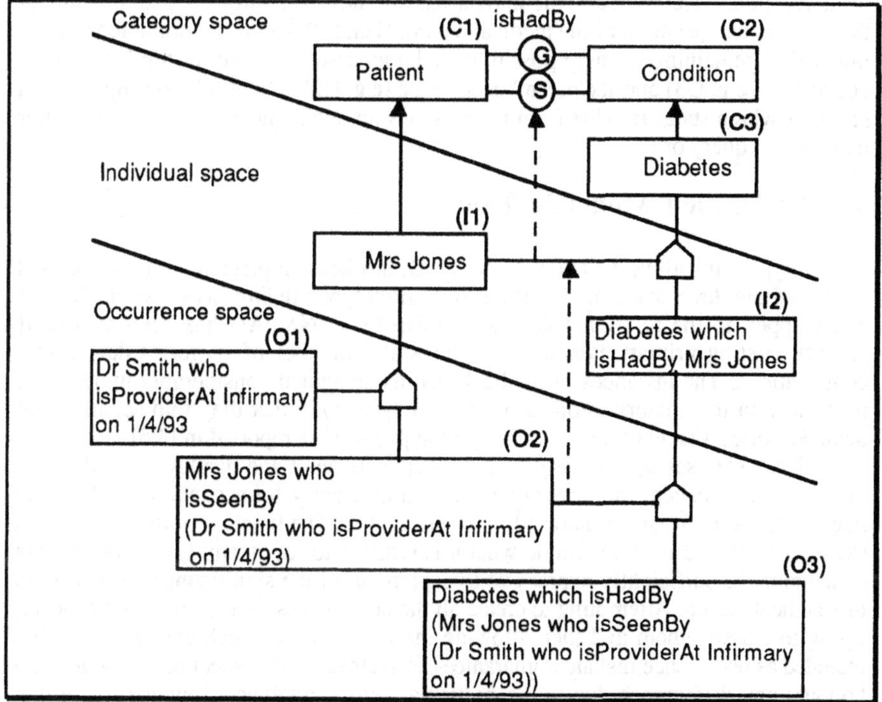

Figure 5. An example of the three spaces

Figure 5 illustrates the three spaces. I1 is an individual instance of a category concept (C1): Patient is part of the MEDICAL RECORD schema and Mrs Jones is an instance of an actor in the ACTORS model. The individual particularization (I2) is an instance of its base type (C3): Diabetes which isHadBy Mrs Jones is an instance of Diabetes, not a type of Diabetes. In individual and occurrence space particularizations are instances of their base entity, not subtypes of the base entity as in category space. (I2) is both an instance of the CONCEPTS schema and part of the ACTORS schema. The occurrence particularization (O3) is a MEDICAL RECORD instance of Mrs Jones' diabetes (I2), not an instance of the concept diabetes (C3). By attaching further constraining relationships to individual (I2) we can represent actor-specific schema concepts, for example cancelling a relationship which, though true of diabetes, is not appropriate for Mrs Jones. All occurrences of Mrs Jones' diabetes will be instances of (I2), so (I2) can serve as an index into the occurrence space, or an abstraction of occurrence space.

The occurrence instances of clinical concepts are always grounded to a date, place, agent and observed individual. (O1) represents the concept of a *clinical session* - an agent at a place on a date - and (O2) adds an observed individual and represents a *clinical encounter*. (O1) and (O2) are instances of the MEDICAL RECORD model.

Occurrences are fine-grained and once asserted cannot be deleted, only modified by another occurrence particularization. This, and the use of occurrence particularizations as instances of individual particularizations, cause problems which are discussed in section 4.

The presence of a particularization in category space merely implies the possibility of its creation. Occurrence particularizations are, however, stronger than this in that they are factual instances of the medical record. Hence they must be promoted to data, rather than remaining as mere possibilities, by an assertion relationship between an occurrence (e.g. O3) and its 'parent' occurrence (e.g. O2). These relationships carry a *qualifier* which states in what form the relationship holds; the values of this qualifier may be yes, query or no.

4 The Unified Model in Use

A prototype clinical workstation, PEN&PAD, has been implemented, based around SMK and the three space model. It has been prototyped in Objectworks\Smalltalk™ and mapped to the relational database Sybase™. PEN&PAD has been evaluated against existing primary healthcare systems at a number of surgeries during real consultations. The instances of medical records contained considerably more detail than those in the doctors' more conventional systems in that they told accurate and detailed stories. Our experiences of the prototype itself are reported in [3,6].

PEN&PAD uses *predictive data entry* [5] as its input and display method. For a given clinical concept the system generates a data entry form containing all of the likely options for modifiers and additional statements. The function of the ACTOR and CONCEPT schema is to determine what it is sensible to say in any given context and hence must be sufficiently expressive to capture all of the significant information in the medical record. Attempting to create all the occurrences of any requested concept, trying to classify them and then allowing the user to pick which entities should be included as occurrence instances guarantees correctness with respect to the model, and honours any differences due to the particular actors involved. However, there is a danger of naively generating several hundred occurrences, many of which may be unwanted.

The process of predictive data entry may be thought of as the clinician asserting or refuting belief in potential statements thrown up by the CONCEPT model and modified by the patient's ACTOR model. The TASKS model is principally of the user interface and was completely configurable for each doctor evaluating the prototype. The operation of the interface and the choice of data presented is tailored to be actor-specific by assertions in individual space.

SMK category space proved to be an effective approach to the generative modelling of medical concepts. Issues concerning assertional statements as part of the medical terminology, transitive constraining relationships, cancellation of relationships and the modelling of values and dimensions are reported elsewhere [15] and in future papers. Our interest in this paper lies with issues encountered in the individual and occurrence spaces.

4.1. The Semantics of Individuals

Individual space, and individuals, arose as (i) a distillation of unattributed, atemporal data about actors and (ii) a way of representing actor-specific constraints on the more general category space. As first presented in section 2.1, the patient record is a story told through unalterable observations and subsequent events lead to contradictory statements. As observations are made, so are subsuming, constraining yet unattributable individuals. However, in order to be useful in sanctioning occurrence space statements individual space needs to be set up first in order to 'set the scene' for the story. This seems to imply that individual space is playing too many roles.

Individuals as indices and abstraction summaries.
Individual space can serve as an index into occurrence space. A particularization in individual space such as *Hypothyroidism which isHadBy-mrsJones* subsumes all observations of it in occurrence space. Likewise an individual actor instance such as Mrs Jones subsumes all occurrence encounters concerning that actor.

However, there is a danger of treating the individual space 'index' as existential—that is as summarising data instances about the subsumed occurrences of the actors. An individual exists because some occurrence observation has been recorded concerning it, and that observation may not have been positive. For example, the only observation recorded about Mrs Jones' hypothyroidism may be that, in Dr Foster's opinion, she did *not* have hypothyroidism. This is because the occurrences have assertion relationships which can carry 'no' or 'query' qualifiers. Consequently, if we tried to use the individual particularizations for aggregation purposes, counting hypothyroid patients by counting their indexing individuals would give an incorrect result in this case.

This could be countered by ensuring the consistency of the negation qualifiers; if the observation is *not X*, the individual is also *not X'* (where 'not' isn't strictly part of the network). However, this poses a further problem, as the medical record is viewed as observations, and the observers may record conflicting observations about a patient. For example, Dr Foster observes *not X*, implying a *not X'* individual, meanwhile Dr Smith observes *X* giving an *X'* individual. *X'* and *not X'* in the same individual space (which is aspatial, atemporal and unattributable) is a contradiction. General attribution could be introduced into individual space, such as the concept of 'Mrs Jones' diabetes as observed by any clinician'. If a particular clinician disagrees, the more specific individual 'Mrs Jones' diabetes as observed by Dr. Smith' could be created and the disagreement asserted there. Observations made by a clinician would be subsumed by the individuals attributed to that clinician, so observations made by Dr. Smith would use Dr. Smith's viewpoint. This would make the ACTORS model more sophisticated.

Conflicting observations raises the issue of what to use as an encompassing index for different observations. Consider two observations of the same clinical condition: one, by Dr. Smith, that the patient is complaining of depression; another, by Dr. Foster two weeks later, that the patient has hypothyroidism. Relating these concepts by subsuming them under the same individual is difficult, as the only property common to hypothyroidism and depression is that they are both conditions. Grouping both under *Condition which isHadBy-mrsJones* is neither informative nor effective.

These difficulties arise because individual space is at a best discursive or conceptual index, but not an existential one. As it stands individual space is good for 'scene setting' the occurrence space 'story' (by placing observations in context) but bad for reconstruction because of its lack of temporal or actor attribution.

Individuals as actor-specific schema.

Individual particularizations can restrict the TASKS, CONCEPTS and MEDICAL RECORD models represented in category space by ACTOR-specific constraints. However, as suggested in section 2.1, a patient's record is recorded in the order it is told, not the order in which it happened. Observations about a patient restrict what may be said in future encounters causing difficulties when making retrospective statements.

For example, Mrs Jones's leg has been amputated at the knee. 'Mrs Jones' lower leg' (I1) is created as an individual particularization with statements asserted in individual space to cancel the statements in the category space. The statements asserted around I1 promote this individual to be a permanent part of Mrs Jones' medical record rather than an implied, virtual concept as particularizations usually are. These statements form part of the schema specific to Mrs Jones, restricting the creation of occurrences concerning her lower leg and banning any references to it. However should we wish to make a retrospective reference to a past observation about her leg before its amputation we are forbidden to do so as individual space is atemporal. Any references to Mrs Jones' leg in her past medical record have also become incoherent.

Since patient's circumstances do change we need to introduce a limited notion of time into individual space. Observations happen at discrete points in time, whereas individuals persist over intervals of time. If Mrs Jones had her lower leg amputated at time t, we could create the concept of 'Mrs Jones' lower leg after t' (I2). This would be a temporally attributable subtype of I1. I2 would automatically subsume all new observations of the lower leg after t, and retrospective observations of the pre-amputated leg would be subsumed by I1. Old observations would be coherent as they would not be subsumed by the new individual. Such a scheme would require the use of individuals as subtypes and extends the semantics of individual space from being atemporal to having some temporal representation. A full interval and event calculus would be overkill in most clinical systems, though it could be useful in epidemiological systems.

Meta-observations.

The individual space's difficulty with retrospective occurrences also extends to disagreements between clinicians and the uncertainty of observations. Meta-observations solve the problem of grouping a number of related observations together. For example, Dr Smith could state that hypothyroidism is a *clinical problem* for Mrs Jones by creating an individual *ClinicalProblem which isProblemFor mrsJones*, and recording in an occurrence that it is defined by *Hypothroidism which isHadBy mrsJones*. This is a meta-observation about her hypothyroidism. It resides in occurrence space and is attributable. Dr Smith could then go onto observe that Mrs Jones' fatigue, breathlessness, constipation and anaemia were all pertinent to this same problem. Once these meta-observations have been introduced, it is no longer necessary to try to group related observations using the subsumption hierarchy.

4.2. The Semantics of Occurrences

Occurrences are particularizations representing instances of the MEDICAL RECORD model. In the unified model they are treated in the same way as category and individual particularizations, however they turn out to have quite different semantics. To ensure that contradictions are easily dealt with there can never be two entities in occurrence space which are identical. All observations made by a particular observer, at a particular time and place are bound into one occurrence particularization. In this way the same classification process as used for the other spaces is used. However, this has the effect that occurrence particularizations are strictly *instances* of categories and individuals and cannot subsume one another.

Particularizations in category space are implied by the schema in that they are virtual and may be created automatically. They do not add to the schema. Particularizations in individual space are implied unless they are being used as actor-specific schema in which case they are extending the schema and so must be asserted. Particularizations in occurrence space, however, are used to hold the data for medical records and so must be asserted as data rather than implied concepts. Requesting an occurrence particularization from the classifier merely to test its legality or its properties has the danger of unintentionally creating new data. Thus the creation splits into two parts: the occurrence particularization itself and an assertion to make it permanent data.

5 Related work

SMK shares some of the properties of systems in the KL-ONE [16] tradition and, as such, has many features in common with its relatives such as BACK [13] and Krypton [8]. Perhaps the closest of the relatives is Classic [2]. As with Classic, SMK can be used to define schema, is a compositional and generative system and can be used to represent incomplete information about individuals. SMK has more limited cardinality constraints than Classic's *atleast* and *atmost* constraints; it has a form of *atmost* that is limited to taking *none*, *one* or *many* as values. The adoption of a limited form of *atleast* would allow the modeller to enforce presence of data, such as attribution in individual space, however we suspect that it might make the restriction operations far more computationally expensive or intractable. It is also possible in CLASSIC to declare a relationship 'closed' for an individual, that is that there are no more fillers for that relationship and hence the closed-world assumption applies to it. SMK does not yet perform inferences that require this, as it is designed for use in medical systems that record observations rather than maintain a notion of 'truth'.

Classic appears to have no equivalent of SMK's individuals such as 'Mrs Jones' diabetes'. Individuals in Classic are instances and are therefore much closer to SMK's occurrences; SMK's occurrence space could be created using Classic individuals with appropriate constraints. However SMK takes advantage of occurrences being subsumed by individuals in order to find the occurrences quickly and use them as actor-specific schema concepts. In addition SMK's use of sanctioning relationships as constraint mechanisms controlling the automatic generation of concepts extends the role of the classification process and ensures that particularizations (generated concepts) are well-formed.

Like Classic and CANDIDE [11] SMK uses the classification process as a querying process, and also uses the schema in order to generative predictive data entry interfaces.

In addition SMK can be used to express contradictions about individuals. The major addition in SMK is the split between an atemporal, unattributable individual space and an occurrence space where observations are fixed in time and space and may conflict with each other. Although representations such as Classic have the notion of individuals and could form an equivalent of each space, SMK has additional constraints in these two spaces that have proved useful in modelling patient records. We need to unravel two things: the telling of a patient's story through observations made by an agent without retrospective tampering, and what actually happened to the patient in absolute and relative time. This adds extra complication to the actor-specific schema generation and instance representation. We have found the standard temporal modelling approaches to be too simplistic. The semantic data models [12] resemble SMK in the sense that they exploit subclass hierarchies and have an object-oriented view. However, such systems have a static view of the structure of classes and do not support the controlled generative creation of new compositional concepts with the attendent support of complex constraints.

6 Discussion

SMK provides a set of constructs which are specific and practical and are a considerable advance over current approaches to representing medical records. SMK is not a complete system for representing medical knowledge. It covers terminological knowledge and those aspects of assertional knowledge which can be expressed without the need for shared variables or existential quantifiers. It is deliberately restricted in order to avoid the computational intractability of any formalism which is equivalent to first order logic [9]. It does, however, provide a highly structured formalism within which to represent and validate the static facts for use by complete logic based or rule based systems.

Medicine and the medical record are difficult to model in a way that will capture the stories of patients' ill-health. The requirement to allow for contradictory information to be held in a patient's record has led to the development of a novel architecture, the distinguishing features of which are separate individual and occurrence spaces.

Modelling all four schemas—the system of CONCEPTS, TASKS, ACTORS and the MEDICAL RECORD—using a single formalism has allowed a tight integration of the four; it has proved possible to impose constraints from one schema on any other. This has led to a powerful, tailorable clinical workstation. This integration has led to greater complexity in the models and tools for visualising and manipulating these connected schemas and they are correspondingly more difficult to specify and implement. As a result large models have been slow and difficult to construct. However, there is the potential for tools that make direct use of the semantic content of the models and this is the subject of current work.

The clear distinction between observations and individuals, and between what is observed and what is true, has come as a direct result of building a medical record to be used by many different healthcare workers. The three levels of categories, individuals and observations are more appropriate to medical applications than the traditional two levels of classes and instances. Representing the medical record as separate spaces for individuals and observations is a powerful idea and allows us to succesfully restrict the CONCEPTS, TASKS and MEDICAL RECORD schema to be actor-specific. However, there are problems in relating new constraints on individuals to observations of older data. It is possible that these constraints, currently modelled as meta-observations, should not be represented as a part of the data model, but should instead be represented as rules within a higher part of the system.

Future work includes a formal specification of SMK and the support of data aggregation across patient records. Aggregation requires work on the temporal and constraint modelling, more assertional knowledge and the enrichment of individual space. A large scale demonstration of a multi-lingual knowledge base is part of the GALEN project under the EC initiative on Advanced Informatics in Medicine (AIM).

Acknowledgements

The authors would like to acknowledge the other members of the Medical Informatics Group who have contributed to the work discussed in this paper, notably Anthony Nowlan and Alan Rector. Special thanks to Andrzej Glowinski for his medical examples, comments and support. Steve Kay originally coined the story-telling metaphor. This research is supported in part by the United Kingdom Medical Research Council grant number SPG 8800091, the Department of Health, and the European Community under the Advanced Informatics in Medicine (AIM) GALEN project 2012.

References

[1] Goble CA, Glowinski AJ, Nowlan WA, Rector AL (1992) ''A Descriptive Semantic Formalism for Medicine'' in: Proceedings of the Ninth International Conference on Data Engineering, IEEE Computer Society Press, pp. 624-632

[2] Borgida A, Brachman RJ, McGuinness DL and Resnick LA (1989) "CLASSIC: A structural data model for objects" in: SIGMOD Record **18**(2), pp. 58-67

[3] Rector AL, Goble CA, Horan B, Howkins TJ, Kay S, Nowlan WA and Wilson A (1990)."Shedding Light on Patient's Problems: Integrating Knowledge Based Systems into Medical Practice", in: L Aiello (ed), Proceedings of the Ninth European Conference on Artificial Intelligence, ECAI 90, Pitman Publishing, pp 531-534

[4] Rector AL, Nowlan WA and Kay S (1992) "Conceptual Knowledge: The Core of Medical Information Systems" in: Lun KC, Degoulet P, Pierre TE, Rienhoff (eds) MEDINFO 92, Proceedings of the Seventh World Congress on Medical Informatics, Geneva, North-Holland pp.1420-1426

[5] Nowlan WA and Rector AL. (1991) "Medical Knowledge Representation and Predictive Data Entry". in: Stefanelli M, Hasman A, Fieschi M, Talmon J, (eds). Proceedings of AIME 91, Lecture notes in Medical Informatics **44** Berlin: Springer-Verlag, pp.105-116

[6] Rector AL, Horan B, Fitter M, Kay S, Newton PD, Nowlan WA, Robinson D and Wilson A (1991) "User Centred Design Development of a General Practice Medical Workstation: The PEN&PAD Experience" in: Bauersfeld P, Bennett J, Lynch G (eds) Proceedings of Computer Human Interaction CHI '92, ACM, Monterey, Addison Wesley pp.447-453

[7] Brachman RJ and Levesque HJ (1985) "A fundamental tradeoff in knowledge representation (revised version)" *in* Brachman RJ, Levesque HJ (eds) Readings in knowledge representation, Morgan Kaufmann, California pp. 41-70

[8] Brachman RJ, Fikes RE and Levesque HJ (1983) "KRYPTON: A functional approach to knowledge representation" in: IEEE Computer **16**(10) pp. 73-76

[9] Brachman RJ and Levesque HJ (1984). "The tractability of subsumption in frame-based description languages" in: AAAI-84 pp. 34-37

[10] Doyle J and Patil RS (1989) "Two dogmas of knowledge representation: language restrictions, taxonomic classification and the utility of representation servers". in: MIT internal report MIT.LCS/TM-387.b

[11] Beck HW, Gala SK and Navathe SB (1989) "Classification as a query processing technique in the CANDIDE data model" in: Proceedings Fifth International Conference on Data Engineering, pp. 572-581.

[12] Hull R and King R (1987) "Semantic database modelling: survey, applications and research issues" *in* ACM Computing Surveys **19**(3) pp. 210-260

[13] Nebel B, (1988) "Computational complexity of terminological reasoning in BACK" in: Artificial Intelligence, **34**(3) pp. 371-383

[14] Goble CA, Glowinski AJ , Jeffrey KG (1993). ''Semantic Constraints in a Medical Information System'' in: (Eds) Worboys M, Grundy F, Proceedings of BNCOD11, Lecture Notes in Computer Science 696 Advances in Databases, Springer-Verlag, pp. 40-57

[15] Rector AL, Nowlan WA, Glowinski AJ, Matthews G (1993) ''The Master Notation, Version 1''. AIM project 2012 (GALEN), Deliverable 6

[16] Brachman RJ and Schmoize JG (1985) ''An overview of the KL-ONE knowledge representation system'' in: Cognitive Science **9**, pp. 171-216

[17] Alexander JH, Freiling MJ, Shulman SJ, Staley JL, Rehfuss S and Messick SL (1986) ''Knowledge level engineering: ontological analysis'' in: AAAI-86 pp. 963-968

[18] Rector AL, Nowlan WA, Kay S, Goble CA, Howkins TJ (1993) "A Framework for Modelling the Electronic Medical Record" in: Methods of Information in Medicine **32**(2) pp. 109-119

[19] Snodgrass R (1990) "Temporal Databases: Status and Research Directions" in SIGMOD Record **19**(4) pp. 83-89.

Lecture Notes in Computer Science

For information about Vols. 1–704
please contact your bookseller or Springer-Verlag

Vol. 705: H. Grünbacher, R. W. Hartenstein (Eds.), Field-Programmable Gate Arrays. Proceedings, 1992. VIII, 218 pages. 1993.

Vol. 706: H. D. Rombach, V. R. Basili, R. W. Selby (Eds.), Experimental Software Engineering Issues. Proceedings, 1992. XVIII, 261 pages. 1993.

Vol. 707: O. M. Nierstrasz (Ed.), ECOOP '93 – Object-Oriented Programming. Proceedings, 1993. XI, 531 pages. 1993.

Vol. 708: C. Laugier (Ed.), Geometric Reasoning for Perception and Action. Proceedings, 1991. VIII, 281 pages. 1993.

Vol. 709: F. Dehne, J.-R. Sack, N. Santoro, S. Whitesides (Eds.), Algorithms and Data Structures. Proceedings, 1993. XII, 634 pages. 1993.

Vol. 710: Z. Ésik (Ed.), Fundamentals of Computation Theory. Proceedings, 1993. IX, 471 pages. 1993.

Vol. 711: A. M. Borzyszkowski, S. Sokołowski (Eds.), Mathematical Foundations of Computer Science 1993. Proceedings, 1993. XIII, 782 pages. 1993.

Vol. 712: P. V. Rangan (Ed.), Network and Operating System Support for Digital Audio and Video. Proceedings, 1992. X, 416 pages. 1993.

Vol. 713: G. Gottlob, A. Leitsch, D. Mundici (Eds.), Computational Logic and Proof Theory. Proceedings, 1993. XI, 348 pages. 1993.

Vol. 714: M. Bruynooghe, J. Penjam (Eds.), Programming Language Implementation and Logic Programming. Proceedings, 1993. XI, 421 pages. 1993.

Vol. 715: E. Best (Ed.), CONCUR'93. Proceedings, 1993. IX, 541 pages. 1993.

Vol. 716: A. U. Frank, I. Campari (Eds.), Spatial Information Theory. Proceedings, 1993. XI, 478 pages. 1993.

Vol. 717: I. Sommerville, M. Paul (Eds.), Software Engineering – ESEC '93. Proceedings, 1993. XII, 516 pages. 1993.

Vol. 718: J. Seberry, Y. Zheng (Eds.), Advances in Cryptology – AUSCRYPT '92. Proceedings, 1992. XIII, 543 pages. 1993.

Vol. 719: D. Chetverikov, W.G. Kropatsch (Eds.), Computer Analysis of Images and Patterns. Proceedings, 1993. XVI, 857 pages. 1993.

Vol. 720: V.Mařík, J. Lažanský, R.R. Wagner (Eds.), Database and Expert Systems Applications. Proceedings, 1993. XV, 768 pages. 1993.

Vol. 721: J. Fitch (Ed.), Design and Implementation of Symbolic Computation Systems. Proceedings, 1992. VIII, 215 pages. 1993.

Vol. 722: A. Miola (Ed.), Design and Implementation of Symbolic Computation Systems. Proceedings, 1993. XII, 384 pages. 1993.

Vol. 723: N. Aussenac, G. Boy, B. Gaines, M. Linster, J.-G. Ganascia, Y. Kodratoff (Eds.), Knowledge Acquisition for Knowledge-Based Systems. Proceedings, 1993. XIII, 446 pages. 1993. (Subseries LNAI).

Vol. 724: P. Cousot, M. Falaschi, G. Filè, A. Rauzy (Eds.), Static Analysis. Proceedings, 1993. IX, 283 pages. 1993.

Vol. 725: A. Schiper (Ed.), Distributed Algorithms. Proceedings, 1993. VIII, 325 pages. 1993.

Vol. 726: T. Lengauer (Ed.), Algorithms – ESA '93. Proceedings, 1993. IX, 419 pages. 1993

Vol. 727: M. Filgueiras, L. Damas (Eds.), Progress in Artificial Intelligence. Proceedings, 1993. X, 362 pages. 1993. (Subseries LNAI).

Vol. 728: P. Torasso (Ed.), Advances in Artificial Intelligence. Proceedings, 1993. XI, 336 pages. 1993. (Subseries LNAI).

Vol. 729: L. Donatiello, R. Nelson (Eds.), Performance Evaluation of Computer and Communication Systems. Proceedings, 1993. VIII, 675 pages. 1993.

Vol. 730: D. B. Lomet (Ed.), Foundations of Data Organization and Algorithms. Proceedings, 1993. XII, 412 pages. 1993.

Vol. 731: A. Schill (Ed.), DCE – The OSF Distributed Computing Environment. Proceedings, 1993. VIII, 285 pages. 1993.

Vol. 732: A. Bode, M. Dal Cin (Eds.), Parallel Computer Architectures. IX, 311 pages. 1993.

Vol. 733: Th. Grechenig, M. Tscheligi (Eds.), Human Computer Interaction. Proceedings, 1993. XIV, 450 pages. 1993.

Vol. 734: J. Volkert (Ed.), Parallel Computation. Proceedings, 1993. VIII, 248 pages. 1993.

Vol. 735: D. Bjørner, M. Broy, I. V. Pottosin (Eds.), Formal Methods in Programming and Their Applications. Proceedings, 1993. IX, 434 pages. 1993.

Vol. 736: R. L. Grossman, A. Nerode, A. P. Ravn, H. Rischel (Eds.), Hybrid Systems. VIII, 474 pages. 1993.

Vol. 737: J. Calmet, J. A. Campbell (Eds.), Artificial Intelligence and Symbolic Mathematical Computing. Proceedings, 1992. VIII, 305 pages. 1993.

Vol. 738: M. Weber, M. Simons, Ch. Lafontaine, The Generic Development Language Deva. XI, 246 pages. 1993.

Vol. 739: H. Imai, R. L. Rivest, T. Matsumoto (Eds.), Advances in Cryptology – ASIACRYPT '91. X, 499 pages. 1993.

Vol. 740: E. F. Brickell (Ed.), Advances in Cryptology – CRYPTO '92. Proceedings, 1992. X, 593 pages. 1993.

Vol. 741: B. Preneel, R. Govaerts, J. Vandewalle (Eds.), Computer Security and Industrial Cryptography. Proceedings, 1991. VIII, 275 pages. 1993.

Vol. 742: S. Nishio, A. Yonezawa (Eds.), Object Technologies for Advanced Software. Proceedings, 1993. X, 543 pages. 1993.

Vol. 743: S. Doshita, K. Furukawa, K. P. Jantke, T. Nishida (Eds.), Algorithmic Learning Theory. Proceedings, 1992. X, 260 pages. 1993. (Subseries LNAI)

Vol. 744: K. P. Jantke, T. Yokomori, S. Kobayashi, E. Tomita (Eds.), Algorithmic Learning Theory. Proceedings, 1993. XI, 423 pages. 1993. (Subseries LNAI)

Vol. 745: V. Roberto (Ed.), Intelligent Perceptual Systems. VIII, 378 pages. 1993. (Subseries LNAI)

Vol. 746: A. S. Tanguiane, Artificial Perception and Music Recognition. XV, 210 pages. 1993. (Subseries LNAI).

Vol. 747: M. Clarke, R. Kruse, S. Moral (Eds.), Symbolic and Quantitative Approaches to Reasoning and Uncertainty. Proceedings, 1993. X, 390 pages. 1993.

Vol. 748: R. H. Halstead Jr., T. Ito (Eds.), Parallel Symbolic Computing: Languages, Systems, and Applications. Proceedings, 1992. X, 419 pages. 1993.

Vol. 749: P. A. Fritzson (Ed.), Automated and Algorithmic Debugging. Proceedings, 1993. VIII, 369 pages. 1993.

Vol. 750: J. L. Díaz-Herrera (Ed.), Software Engineering Education. Proceedings, 1994. XII, 601 pages. 1994.

Vol. 751: B. Jähne, Spatio-Temporal Image Processing. XII, 208 pages. 1993.

Vol. 752: T. W. Finin, C. K. Nicholas, Y. Yesha (Eds.), Information and Knowledge Management. Proceedings, 1992. VII, 142 pages. 1993.

Vol. 753: L. J. Bass, J. Gornostaev, C. Unger (Eds.), Human-Computer Interaction. Proceedings, 1993. X, 388 pages. 1993.

Vol. 754: H. D. Pfeiffer, T. E. Nagle (Eds.), Conceptual Structures: Theory and Implementation. Proceedings, 1992. IX, 327 pages. 1993. (Subseries LNAI).

Vol. 755: B. Möller, H. Partsch, S. Schuman (Eds.), Formal Program Development. Proceedings. VII, 371 pages. 1993.

Vol. 756: J. Pieprzyk, B. Sadeghiyan, Design of Hashing Algorithms. XV, 194 pages. 1993.

Vol. 757: U. Banerjee, D. Gelernter, A. Nicolau, D. Padua (Eds.), Languages and Compilers for Parallel Computing. Proceedings, 1992. X, 576 pages. 1993.

Vol. 758: M. Teillaud, Towards Dynamic Randomized Algorithms in Computational Geometry. IX, 157 pages. 1993.

Vol. 759: N. R. Adam, B. K. Bhargava (Eds.), Advanced Database Systems. XV, 451 pages. 1993.

Vol. 760: S. Ceri, K. Tanaka, S. Tsur (Eds.), Deductive and Object-Oriented Databases. Proceedings, 1993. XII, 488 pages. 1993.

Vol. 761: R. K. Shyamasundar (Ed.), Foundations of Software Technology and Theoretical Computer Science. Proceedings, 1993. XIV, 456 pages. 1993.

Vol. 762: K. W. Ng, P. Raghavan, N. V. Balasubramanian, F. Y. L. Chin (Eds.), Algorithms and Computation. Proceedings, 1993. XIII, 542 pages. 1993.

Vol. 763: F. Pichler, R. Moreno Díaz (Eds.), Computer Aided Systems Theory – EUROCAST '93. Proceedings, 1993. IX, 451 pages. 1994.

Vol. 764: G. Wagner, Vivid Logic. XII, 148 pages. 1994. (Subseries LNAI).

Vol. 765: T. Helleseth (Ed.), Advances in Cryptology – EUROCRYPT '93. Proceedings, 1993. X, 467 pages. 1994.

Vol. 766: P. R. Van Loocke, The Dynamics of Concepts. XI, 340 pages. 1994. (Subseries LNAI).

Vol. 767: M. Gogolla, An Extended Entity-Relationship Model. X, 136 pages. 1994.

Vol. 768: U. Banerjee, D. Gelernter, A. Nicolau, D. Padua (Eds.), Languages and Compilers for Parallel Computing. Proceedings, 1993. XI, 655 pages. 1994.

Vol. 769: J. L. Nazareth, The Newton-Cauchy Framework. XII, 101 pages. 1994.

Vol. 770: P. Haddawy (Representing Plans Under Uncertainty. X, 129 pages. 1994. (Subseries LNAI).

Vol. 771: G. Tomas, C. W. Ueberhuber, Visualization of Scientific Parallel Programs. XI, 310 pages. 1994.

Vol. 772: B. C. Warboys (Ed.),Software Process Technology. Proceedings, 1994. IX, 275 pages. 1994.

Vol. 773: D. R. Stinson (Ed.), Advances in Cryptology – CRYPTO '93. Proceedings, 1993. X, 492 pages. 1994.

Vol. 774: M. Banâtre, P. A. Lee (Eds.), Hardware and Software Architectures for Fault Tolerance. XIII, 311 pages. 1994.

Vol. 775: P. Enjalbert, E. W. Mayr, K. W. Wagner (Eds.), STACS 94. Proceedings, 1994. XIV, 782 pages. 1994.

Vol. 776: H. J. Schneider, H. Ehrig (Eds.), Graph Transformations in Computer Science. Proceedings, 1993. VIII, 395 pages. 1994.

Vol. 777: K. von Luck, H. Marburger (Eds.), Management and Processing of Complex Data Structures. Proceedings, 1994. VII, 220 pages. 1994.

Vol. 778: M. Bonuccelli, P. Crescenzi, R. Petreschi (Eds.), Algorithms and Complexity. Proceedings, 1994. VIII, 222 pages. 1994.

Vol. 779: M. Jarke, J. Bubenko, K. Jeffery (Eds.), Advances in Database Technology — EDBT '94. Proceedings, 1994. XII, 406 pages. 1994.

Vol. 780: J. J. Joyce, C.-J. H. Seger (Eds.), Higher Order Logic Theorem Proving and Its Applications. Proceedings, 1993. X, 518 pages. 1994.

Vol. 782: J. Gutknecht (Ed.), Programming Languages and System Architectures. Proceedings, 1994. X, 344 pages. 1994.

Vol. 783: C. G. Günther (Ed.), Mobile Communications. Proceedings, 1994. XVI, 564 pages. 1994.